PSYC 1100 and PSYC 1300

Learning Framework

COLLIN COLLEGE

12 13 14 15 SCI SCI 19 18 17

ISBN-13: 978-1-259-82730-3
ISBN-10: 1-259-82730-5

Solutions Program Manager: Joyce Berendes
Project Manager: Gina Schilling

Project: Atkinson.Choosing Success.341461

Module 1: Resources for College Success

First Steps to Choosing Success   3

Interacting with Your College Community   27

Making Choices about Today's Technology   55

Module 2: Motivation & Goal Setting

Choosing Goals for College and Life   119

Module 1
Resources for College Sucess

CHAPTER **ONE**

First Steps to Choosing Success

College opens many doors to your future. What are some of the doors you see college opening to you? What factors will you use to decide which to open and which to close?

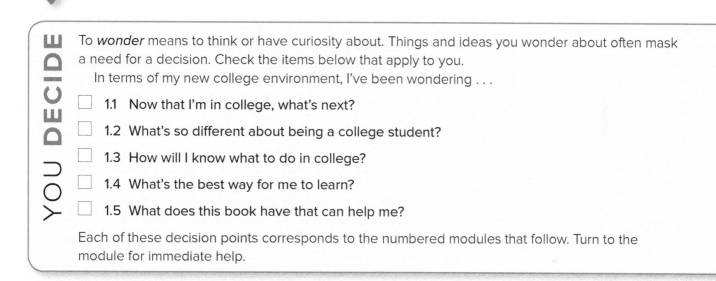

YOU DECIDE

To *wonder* means to think or have curiosity about. Things and ideas you wonder about often mask a need for a decision. Check the items below that apply to you.

In terms of my new college environment, I've been wondering . . .

☐ 1.1 Now that I'm in college, what's next?

☐ 1.2 What's so different about being a college student?

☐ 1.3 How will I know what to do in college?

☐ 1.4 What's the best way for me to learn?

☐ 1.5 What does this book have that can help me?

Each of these decision points corresponds to the numbered modules that follow. Turn to the module for immediate help.

Congratulations! You are a college student! You may find you have more choices and greater responsibility for the decisions you make. That's why this text is titled *Choosing Success*. It provides a way for you to recognize your options and make conscious choices to get the outcomes you want in college and in life.

COLLEGE SUCCESS BEGINS NOW ❯

The First Week of Class

I need a degree for my job–that's why I am here. . . . I did well in high school, but I can already tell that classes here will be different. . . . As a dual-credit student, I'm still in high school–but I want to fit in here. . . . I planned to go to work after high school. With so many new experiences available to me here, I don't know what to do first. After looking at the job market, I decided to come to college but I am undecided about a career. . . . I dropped out of high school and got a GED. Now I want a college degree. I need to do well here because I want to go to law school.

Retention
Keeping students in school until they meet their goals or finish a degree or program.

Notice anything in common in these statements? All reflect typical feelings and concerns of new students. All colleges are in the business of **retention.** They want students to stay in school until they meet their goals or finish a degree or program. Their goal is student success. Thus, your college provides resources like this course to help you and other students address college concerns and succeed. This text gives you strategies for thinking through decisions on topics from career decision making to wellness. Your course instructor will help you apply what you learn to your specific college.

College is a lot to take in at once. That's OK. Take a look at the table of contents of this book. Read through the twelve tips for week 1. Together they form the big picture of what you need to know. Thus, if you need information before it's covered in class, you'll know which chapter focuses on it. But you need to decide to be proactive. The twelve tips for week 1 help you get started.

❯ Twelve Tips for Week 1

Get oriented. You probably already know where your classes meet. If you are taking courses online, you need to know how to log into your coursework. It's also a good idea to know how to find your instructors outside of class. You need phone and office numbers as well as e-mail addresses for them. Instructors that are **adjunct** faculty often don't have offices of their own. But they probably have mailboxes in departmental offices where you can leave messages, and they have their own e-mail addresses.

adjunct
Part-time faculty.

- Make sure you know where to find basic campus services. Depending on what's available at your campus, this might include the student center, food services, recreation facilities, financial aid office, and library.

- Try to find out what other activities or services are on hand. You may want to find where to use a computer, obtain services if you have a disability, cash a check, print papers, or get tutoring if you need help.

- Your campus website serves as a good reference for general services. These include campus security and administrative offices like academic offices and student services. Call campus information if you need help finding a specific department.

- Finally, ask for help if you need it. Some students don't ask questions because they think they'll "sound dumb." Nothing could be further from the truth. Everyone at your college—student, faculty, or staff—was once new to the campus. Stop in offices and ask for directions. Ask students you meet for help.

- Still, know that your campus is like any other place. Some people will be patient, helpful, and kind. Others might not. Don't take it personally. The first few weeks of a term are demanding for both students and faculty. If the first person you talk to isn't helpful, talk to someone else. And keep in mind that you don't need to know everyone and everything at once.

Mix and mingle. Make a decision to meet new people. Choose to get to know the people in your classes right away. If you are taking online courses, use the discussion board or forum tool to introduce yourself to your classmates. If possible, upload a picture.

- Even though you may feel a little uncomfortable doing so, try to introduce yourself to at least one person in each class. If that feels too strange, start by nodding and smiling at the students around you.

- Plan to read campus newspapers or online newsletters regularly. Most newspapers have a calendar section that lists campus activities, meetings, or other events and campus websites. You might also look at what's on the bulletin boards in each building. They often give helpful information and insights into your college's culture. (*See Chapter 2 to find out more about your campus's community.*)

Open up. Make choices that open your mind to learning more about yourself. Figure out how you learn best. Become aware of your options and the way you make decisions. (*Chapter 13 shows you how your aptitudes and abilities, interests, values, and learning preferences can contribute to your academic success.*)

Get the big picture. Once you get a **syllabus** from each class, make a term planner. Your term planner will help you prioritize choices throughout the term.

- To make your term planner, get a cheap monthly print calendar or a digital calendar with large blocks for each day and then get your school's **academic calendar.** It is often found at your college website.

---

syllabus
Outline of course content for a term.

academic calendar
Calendar of the school year starting in August or September rather than in January; shows information such as registration and drop dates or exam periods.

If you record all important events and assignments for the term in a monthly planner, you will be less likely to miss a crucial deadline.

- Using the academic calendar, first record all holidays, school vacations, and academic due dates. Second, using your syllabus, record test dates and due dates for papers, exams or projects. Third, set up intermediate deadlines for completing phases of lengthy projects. For instance, for a major paper, you can set deadlines for completing the research, first draft, and last draft. Fourth, record important personal events. These would include fun and family activities, medical appointments, and so on.

- Now, remove or print all the pages for the term. Post where you can see all the months–the whole term–at the same time. Seeing your commitments all at once will help you make better decisions about time management. (*See Chapter 5 for more time management tips.*)

Network. As you meet new people, tell them about your interests, needs, and goals. Faculty, staff, and other students may know someone or something that can help you. This helps you create a network of support. (*Chapter 6 provides more information about ways to achieve your goals.*)

Prepare to think differently. College is about the process of thinking as well as the product of thinking. Although you will have much to learn, the focus is less on memorizing ideas and more on thinking critically about them when it comes to taking exams. (*You'll learn more about critical thinking as well as ways to prepare for and take tests in Chapter 14.*)

Go to class. Starting with the first day of class, decide to attend your classes each time they meet even if your instructors don't take attendance. If your class is online, log into the class on the first day of the term. Plan to check in every couple of days. You're the one going to college. You want to get the most from your classes.

- When possible, choose to sit at the front of the classroom. Studies show students who sit in the front do better than those who sit in the back.

- Be sure to take notes. As soon as you can after class, try to spend three to five minutes reviewing your notes.

- Attendance is just as important in an online class. Log into your online course daily to check e-mail and announcements.

Work for yourself as well as for grades. As a college student, you're working for yourself and your future. Learning is not a spectator sport. Just as regular workouts exercise your body, regular completion of assignments and readings exercises your mind and skills.

- Faculty assume students know to read the chapters listed on the syllabus. As a result, instructors may never actually assign them. They just expect you to read them. This is even more important in online courses where you have more autonomy for completing assignments.

- Choosing to read, or at least **preview,** the text before class helps you make sense of lectures. To "preview" is to read a chapter's introduction, headings, subheadings, boldfaced terms, and summary before a full reading. (*You'll learn more about reading and learning from textbooks and online materials in Chapter 15.*)

preview
Reading a chapter's introduction, headings, subheadings, boldfaced terms, and summary before a full reading of the content.

Get (tech) help. **Technology** is an integral part of learning in today's colleges. Some students, and you may be one of them, have concerns or fears about using it. That's OK. Whatever your technology skills, you'll need to know how technology is used on your campus.

- This means that there are aspects of technology that are new to everyone. College staff know this. They provide resources and assistance to help, but it's up to you to choose to use them. Know where to find these on your campus and when they are available. Most colleges provide quick links or references on their websites.

- If you cannot easily use a computer to find information, use e-mail, access campus information, or navigate a **course management system,** be sure to get help now. Look for workshops and orientation sessions to show you how to use your campus's online systems.

- Your instructors should explain how to use the technology required in their courses. Take notes for future use. Try using the course technology on your own or check with your campus help services. If you still have questions, ask other students in the class or make an appointment to see your instructor. (*Chapter 3 describes how to maximize your skills as a learner in the information age.*)

Don't worry yet. If you haven't chosen a career goal, don't worry. Most first term courses are basic classes that apply to most programs. Focus on getting to know your campus and maximizing your academic success. Make plans to visit your advisor or career-planning office to explore options.

Watch your money. Make a budget for the rest of the term. The first week of classes is generally the most costly. That's because you pay tuition and buy books and other supplies. Analyze your remaining funds. Then, divide the amount by the number of weeks in the term. Don't forget to plan for financial emergencies. Remember that everything you buy–from coffee to college supplies–represents a choice you make about how to spend your money.

Stay healthy. New academic experiences–and less time–may cause you to eat and worry more and sleep and exercise less. Pay attention to what you eat and the amount of rest and exercise you get. What you eat and do are choices you make each day. (*Chapter 16 gives information about ways to handle these and other wellness issues.*)

Top 10 Things to Do the First Week of School

Check each task as you complete it.

- [ ] 1. Find basic campus services both on campus and online. Save phone numbers on your phone and bookmark links to services. There is also a place to record this information on page ••• of this book.

- [ ] 2. Make a term planner.

- [ ] 3. Get names and phone numbers or e-mail addresses for one person in each class. Save this information in your cell phone or in your notebook for each class.

- [ ] 4. Get a college catalog and/or bookmark the catalog link from the college website on your computer.

- [ ] 5. Find two people you want to add to your network of support.

- [ ] 6. Sit at the front of room in each class and check into online classes daily.

- [ ] 7. Learn the features of any course management software used in your classes. Get a flash drive or a cloud account to save electronic information.

- [ ] 8. Buy a notebook or folder for each class and create class folders on your computer or flash drive. Get or download a syllabus for each class and put it with the corresponding notebook or folder.

- [ ] 9. Even though they are expensive, buy your books right away. They are your tools for the courses you take. Be sure you have the right books and materials for each course.

- [ ] 10. Decide to make the most of your college experience.

How College Is Different

If you're like most students, you'll find that higher education differs from high school and work experiences. Why?

First, you are an unknown. In terms of academics, your new instructors don't know if you graduated top in your class or dropped out of school. They don't know if you like, dislike, or fear their subjects.

Second, in high school, you had a year for most subjects. Now you must complete more work in less time than ever before. You have only yourself to oversee your workload. You may have hundreds of pages to read with only two or three exams during the term. There may be no assignments due one week, and something due each day the next. Also, you–not your instructors–hold the responsibility for learning. Instructors give you information and assignments, but you'll more often learn on your own rather than in class.

That's why most colleges consider 12 hours of credit a full-time load. It's not that they think 12 hours of time per week in class is a full-time job. Instead, they assume the work you must do outside class added to the time you're in class equals a full-time job.

Your college experience differs from work as well. For instance, at work, your boss supervises your workload and work. In college, you determine your workload. If you take too many classes, you alone are responsible for the results. And instructors may not see your work until you submit a completed assignment.

Where and when you learn differs from where and when you work. You rarely get to choose a worksite. Where you study, however, is your choice. A work day is a specific period of time, usually 8 hours. If you work overtime, you get paid extra for that time. Class time is hardly ever 8 hours straight. Study time, as well as most online classes, has no specific hours. Studying "overtime" may–or may not–pay benefits in better grades.

A key difference in any college experience involves choices and the decisions you make about them. Unlike high school in which most students took many of the same courses on a daily basis, college courses provide more options. You get to choose your major. Although there are requirements such as math, English, and science courses, you often get some choice (e.g., chemistry versus geology) depending on your major. You decide where and when to take courses (onsite, online, evening, weekend, daytime) and how many courses to take at one time.

You decide how you approach each course and how you will prove yourself each term. You can choose to be interested or bored. You can decide to give it all you've got or just give up. You also decide how to handle your workload. You can choose to attend classes or skip them. You can decide to plan ahead and work hard on assignments or do them at the last minute. You also make choices about if, when, and where to study as well as how and what to study. You choose which organizations to join, which opportunities to accept, and what campus resources to use.

You can also decide how to respond to the experiences, interests, and attitudes of people around you. So, if your peers, friends, family, co-workers, or former teachers/counselors value higher education and financially or emotionally support you, you can choose to rely on them in order to maximize your success. But if friends, family, or co-workers view college as a waste of time or if former teachers/counselors viewed you as "not college material," then you can decide to look elsewhere for support.

Some decisions are clear. In general, going to class is better than not going to class. However, what if an emergency arises—a friend needs a ride to work, a relative needs help, or sick children need your care? Your choice suddenly becomes more difficult as you weigh options.

Some choices have lasting or life-changing effects. Should you pursue a two-year certification program or go on for a four-year degree? Will you major in information technology or in nursing? Will you love one person or another? Should you take this job or that one?

Other decisions, like what to eat for lunch or what to wear, are less important because of their short-lived effects. Still, some people seem to give the same kind of attention to both types of decisions. Indeed, some students seem to spend more time choosing *when* to take a course than they spend in deciding *which* course to take. As a result, they often struggle with the minor decisions of life while failing to give important choices the consideration they deserve. Because the important choices are not thought out, they often don't work out.

The decisions you make now affect your future. For instance, some students decide to take the first semester easy. Their grades are average at best. Then, a course sparks their interest. They decide that this is what they want to major in. But they discover that this degree is a competitive program. It only takes the students with the highest **GPAs.** Even if students don't choose competitive programs, average grades still affect their futures. After they complete their programs or degrees, they will compete for jobs. Just having a degree or certification is no longer enough in today's job market. The best (and sometimes only) jobs go to students that show they can work well with others, write and communicate well, and act honestly. Some students don't see the long-term consequences of the choices they make on a day-to-day basis. The rest of this chapter helps you avoid this mistake. You already know how higher education differs from other situations. Next, you'll learn a strategy for making choices. You'll also learn how to manage the changes you face. Moreover, the rest of this text provides you with chances to think through the decision-making process in different situations.

GPA
Grade point average.

activity 2

What Do *You* Need to Know?
Ask the Experts!

Your instructor will provide an in-class panel of "experts" from your college either in person or on video. They may be students, other faculty, staff, and/or administrators.

PART 1:   The Experts

The experts will respond to the following questions and/or any other prompts your instructor creates. Your instructor may also ask you to create a list of questions you want answered. Take notes on what they say.

I feel the biggest challenge students face is . . .

The biggest decision I see students as having to make is . . .

The question I get asked most often is . . .

Students tell me they (and/or I) like . . . about college.

Students tell me they (and/or I) dislike . . . about college.

The thing that surprised me most about this college when I first arrived here was . . .

I think the biggest difference between college, work, and high school is . . .

My advice to new students would be . . .

PART 2:   Summarize Your Findings

_____

_____

_____

PART 3:   Your College Future

Now that you've heard from college "experts" and other new students, what do you need to learn or do in order to be successful at your college?

_____

_____

_____

GROUP APPLICATION: In small groups of 3–5 students, answer the following questions and compare answers.

1. What do you like best about this college?

2. What do you like least about this college?

3. What surprised you about this college when you first arrived here?

4. What do you think are the biggest differences between college, work, and high school?

5. What helped you get oriented here?

6. What piece of advice would you offer to someone new to this college?

7. What do you think contributes to a student's success on campus?

8. What do you think is the biggest cause of failure on campus?

5C Approach for Decision Making

How do *you* make decisions? The choices some people make seem to be little more than a roll of the dice. Decision making is the very core of this text. You'll learn to use a basic five-point process for making decisions. Each point begins with the letter **C.** You can recall the points by remembering the **5Cs**–Define the **C**hallenge; Identify the **C**hoices; Predict the **C**onsequences; **C**hoose an option; **C**heck your outcome. You can also visualize the points on a star. See Figure 1.1.

5Cs
Five-point decision-making process.

Each chapter helps you identify how to make decisions that will affect your success at your college . . . and in life. Your decisions then result from conscious choices rather than unconscious responses. You will use the 5Cs throughout this text to think critically through a variety of topics and issues. While you might not always think through every choice you make, knowing and using the 5Cs gives you a concrete strategy for making important decisions.

Define the Challenge

Solving a problem involves first clearly defining what the problem is. To do so, consider the context. What issues or actions surround the problem? What other people are involved and what part do they play? Second, determine the relevant importance of the problem and long-term effects of

Define the **C**hallenge

Check your Outcome

Identify the **C**hoices

Choose an Option

Predict the **C**onsequences

Figure 1.1 The 5C Model for Decision Making.

the decision. Will this still be important tomorrow, next week, next month, or next year? Third, talk to others about the situation. Different viewpoints help you become more objective. Finally, as clearly as possible state your problem, or challenge, verbally or in writing. If you can't clearly state it, you don't have enough information to make a decision.

For instance, choosing a major is a problem that many students face. Issues that affect the choice might include your prior high school experiences and grades, your aptitudes and abilities, the time you have to devote to classes, the amount of time and money needed to achieve that career goal, job opportunities, and potential salary. If you have a family, your decision affects their future as well as yours.

Choosing a career is an important decision with long-term effects. Perhaps you've discussed your situation with family and friends as well as college advisors. They've helped you assess your interests and needs. You describe your challenge as "a need to choose a major that will result in an interesting career that provides job security and matches my lifestyle needs."

Identify Choices

Unlike math problems that have a single right answer, many possible right answers exist when making decisions. Thus, the first step in making a decision is finding out what choices you face. At first, you might consider all options from the most logical to the most unlikely. Although each might have value, you'll probably find that some can be quickly discarded. Your goal might be to identify three to five choices that you want to explore further.

Next, you identify workable options–in the case of choosing a major, one that will lead to a career that will get you where you want to go. For instance, in thinking about majors, you might decide that, as a practical matter, your options consist of those programs available at your school. You visit the campus career center. You check course requirements in the college catalog. You search for information on the Web. The outcome is a list of your possible choices.

Predict Consequences

Once you make a short list of choices, your next task is to consider the consequences of each one. To do so, you think of the negative and positive results of each choice by reviewing your personal experiences and preferences and through research (e.g., talking to others, looking up additional information). This helps you make a kind of balance sheet.

A balance sheet gives you only your odds. For instance, suppose your choices are nursing, elementary education, and computer programming. You decide that completing an elementary education program will take too long–a minus. Your research tells you that there are few jobs for computer programmers in your community–another minus. The nursing program has two plusses. One, you could get a degree in a two-year program. Two, jobs are available in your community right away. These are items you'd put on a balance sheet to help you predict the consequences of your choice.

You may be able to add a lot more items to your balance sheet. In the end you may see that the logical choice would be to pursue a particular major. Perhaps employees in that field make a lot of money, or get their choice of jobs, or attain prestigious status. It might be something you do well. It might be something others urge you to do. Still, if you know you could never be happy in that field, that would go on your balance sheet, and it would never be your best choice. So, no matter the results of your balance sheet, the choice remains yours. You decide how much risk you're willing to take in your choice or the level of safety or comfort you need about this choice. As you make college decisions, you weigh your choices against the context of your institution and your values (*see Chapter 13*).

Your attitude toward the choices you must make also plays a part. For instance, some people are overwhelmed by their choices and get stuck in a situation. They think that maintaining their current status helps them avoid making a choice. Not so. Staying in the same situation is a choice whether you realize it or not. Or some people think of themselves as being in no-win situations. But you can just as easily think of your challenge as win-win.

In other words, each choice has benefits. Each presents opportunities. In deciding what major to pursue, you may be thinking about what you'll miss by choosing one curriculum over another. Instead, focus on the opportunities and remind yourself that, either way, you won't lose. Remember that separating a good choice from a bad one isn't usually difficult. The results are obvious. The difficult decision is when you have to choose between two or more good options.

Choose an Option

After you've considered your choices, it's time to choose one and put your decision into effect. How do you do that? First, *set a deadline for enacting your decision*. This gives you a target to reach.

Second, *think of your decision in positive instead of negative terms*. In other words, phrase your decision so that you anticipate opportunities for success rather than threats of failure. For instance, a decision to make the dean's list at the term's end is more motivating than the decision *not* to be placed on probation at the end of the term.

Third, *make the outcome of your choice dependent solely on you*. Forming a study group the week before the final exam seems like a good goal–unless the members of the group get sick or otherwise fail to show up. If you depend only on the group for success on the test, you may be disappointed with the results.

Fourth, *use others for support*. This seems like a contradiction of the previous tip. But, there is a big difference. Instead of making a decision contingent on others, you use others only for help and assistance. This kind of network provides information, advice, and friendship.

Fifth, *visualize success*. Most people tend to replay mentally their personal errors. They end up rehearsing them so well that the same mistakes happen again and again. You avoid some problems by visualizing and rehearsing the success of your decision instead of its failure.

Last, *become aware of self-sabotage*. Set yourself up for success. For instance, if your decision is to study for an exam rather than socialize with friends or family, avoid places (noisy student center, busy kitchen, etc.) in which you might be unable to focus. Instead, find a quiet place with few distractions.

Consider again the example of choosing a major. Suppose, after careful thought, you decide to start the nursing program. You arrange your work schedule to take lab courses. You take learning skills workshops to brush up on notetaking and test taking. You go to tutoring for help in math and science. You have good grades at the end of the first term. Things appear to be fine. What's next?

Check Your Outcome

Congratulations! You identified several choices. You looked at the consequences and selected what you thought was the best choice. But did experience prove you out? Checking your outcome helps you see if your decision is working. Luckily, most decisions can be rethought. Even major decisions often can be altered.

For instance, you chose to major in nursing because you thought it was a career in which you would always be able to find a job. But at the end of the first term, you find that majoring in nursing isn't working out. Maybe you found that you didn't like science as much as you thought. The sight of blood made you ill. You may still feel you must stick with your decision though. Why?

If you made a choice that didn't work out, what's better now–being unhappy or rethinking your decision and making another choice? Was it really the best choice, or did it only seem so based on the information available at the time?

How do you know, and when do you know, if the choice you made is a good one?

First, find out if you are satisfied with the outcome. At the very least, the situation you wanted to resolve should be improving. Next, check to see if your choice has had enough time to work. Look to see if there were any choices that you failed to consider, and if you successfully predicted the outcomes and/or risks of the choice you made.

activity 3

Applying the 5Cs to a Problem

You can use the 5C approach to help you make decisions about a variety of problems. Identify a problem in your life and respond to the following prompts. Use additional paper if needed.

PROBLEM: _____

Step	Action(s)	Your Response	
STEP 1: Define the **C**hallenge.	Describe the problem you face.		
STEP 2: Identify **C**hoices.	Make a list of options for consideration		
STEP 3: Predict **C**onsequences.	Identify the positive and negative outcomes for each option or for the best two or three options. Create a balance sheet that shows the plusses and minuses for the good and bad consequences of each option.	PLUSSES	MINUSES
STEP 4: **C**hoose an option.	Set a deadline for putting the choice into effect. Be sure that you described your choice in positive terms (what you will do instead of what you won't do). Identify what you need to do to implement the choice. Make a list of people who will support your choice. Imagine what life will be after your option has been put into effect. How do you like the picture you see? Think of any thoughts or behaviors that might sabotage your efforts and identify ways to control them.		
STEP 5: **C**heck your outcome.	Determine when and how you will know if your option proved to be successful.		

Learning as an Active Decision

As a college student, learning is your priority, and learning is not a spectator sport. It's an active practice. You get from learning what you put into it. The way you approach coursework–in class, online, and on your own–is an ongoing choice. Thus, you have a pressing need for effective learning strategies as well as chances to practice them regularly. The key is deciding to change your approach from a passive to an *active* one. Active learning is an ongoing process of thinking and doing that you purposefully control. Such new ways of thinking require new tools and strategies to help you absorb the process.

SQ3R is one of these strategies. SQ3R helps you read print materials more actively. It also helps you remember more about what you read. You'll learn other active learning strategies throughout this text.

SQ3R
An active reading strategy developed by Francis Robinson consisting of five steps: Survey, Question, Read, Recite and Review.

skim
Read quickly for key ideas.

SQ3R: A Plan for Active Learning from Print Materials

Survey. A survey is your preparation for learning. When you survey a chapter, you purposefully **skim** it. You can use the title to capture the main idea. Skimming the chapter introduction, outline, headings, and visual content adds details. This forms the "big picture" of what the chapter contains. It creates a framework for your next in-depth reading. You also think about what you already know about the topic and what information will be new to you. Thus, right away, you are making reading more active because you are making conscious decisions about content and your role in learning it.

Question. Once you gain a general sense of the content through your survey, you can be more purposeful about what you want to learn from

SURVEY

Before reading a chapter, prepare for learning. Purposefully skim the title, introduction, headings, and graphics. As you survey, decide what information you already know and what information is new to you.

QUESTION

Change each module section's heading into a question. This forms your learning goal for reading.

◀ **CHOOSING TO BE AN ACTIVE LEARNER**

it–your learning goals. As you read you can set learning goals about the content by asking questions about each section. You can do so by turning a heading into a question. For instance, in reading Module 1.4 of this text right now, as you are doing, you might rephrase the module's heading *Learning as an Active Decision* as the question: *How can learning be an active decision?* or *What can I do to make learning an active decision?* Ask questions about other aspects of the chapter text as well, as it strikes you to do so (e.g., key terms, photos or exhibits). Questions make learning more active because they create a need for finding their answers.

Read. Read each section of text to answer your questions and achieve your learning goals. Some people find that their attention wanders as they read. Before they realize it, they've marked (highlighted or underlined) an entire section or read to the end of the page without really paying attention to any of it. You can avoid this by adding purposeful action to the reading process. As you read the section, do not mark anything. After you've read the section, skim through it again and mark only key words and details. Avoid marking whole sentences.

> CHOOSING TO BE AN ACTIVE LEARNER ▶
>
> ### READ
> Read each module in the chapter without marking. Reread and mark key information that answers your questions.
>
> ### RECITE
> Stop after reading each module and make sure you understood the content. Organize or summarize content and make notes.

Recite. Check your understanding after each section before continuing. You should now be able to answer the question you asked at the start of the section. If you can't, review your marked content or reread the section. To make this step more active, organize or summarize ideas that answer your question and make notes. Deciding how to organize or summarize the content makes this step more active. Putting it in your own words in notes increases retention. And rather than rereading what you marked to recall its importance in future study sessions, your notes will serve as study cues.

Review. Most people close their books at the end of a chapter. Instead, spend five or ten minutes quickly thinking through the chapter from the beginning. Now that you have all the information, the "big picture" you created should have more detail. This review solidifies your understanding as you put all the pieces together. Make notes of sections you still have questions about or ideas that are still unclear to you.

> CHOOSING TO BE AN ACTIVE LEARNER ▶
>
> ### REVIEW
> Skim the notes you made throughout the chapter. How does the content fit together? What information is still unclear? Were your learning goals met? Can you answer the review questions and define terms?

The rest of the chapters in this text include prompts at their beginnings and ends to remind you of this process. At the start of each chapter, you will find the Survey, Question, Read, and Recite prompts. At the end of each chapter will be the Review prompt. This will help you practice the process. By the end of the text, SQ3R will be a natural part of your learning strategies.

1.5 module

What does this
book have that
can help me?

Maximizing Your Use of *Choosing Success*

Each chapter of this text helps you look at yourself and your college environment from a decision-making viewpoint. To this end, each chapter begins with a reminder to use the first four steps of the SQ3R process to approach your reading; this feature is called *Choosing to Be an Active Learner*.

You'll also find at the beginning of each chapter a list of *Learning Outcomes*, key concepts within the chapter. These fulfill two goals. One, by reading them, you learn about chapter content. Two, they tell you what you need to grasp from the chapter. You will also find a kind of self-assessment–called *You Decide*–at the start of each chapter. *You Decide* consists of questions that give you a chance to see what choices and decisions about the chapter topic are most important to you. Each question you check represents an aspect of your new learning environment. Each is tied to a module of the chapter, a self-contained unit on the specific issues it involves. You can turn to the numbered module for immediate help, or you can pay special attention when you get to that module as you read the chapter in its entirety.

Each module in each chapter contains useful information and practical tips for building your skills and most also include an *Activity* that allows you to practice what you've learned. Many of the activities also include

Group Applications, in which you will work with others to achieve results. *Key terms* in the chapter discussion are marked with boldfaced text; definitions for these terms appear in the margin.

At the end of each chapter you will find a *Chapter Review.* These review questions help you recall and apply what you have learned. You'll also have a chance to rethink your responses to *You Decide* at the start of the chapter in a revised form–*Did You Decide?* This time you will mark the areas in which you feel you've gained skills or strength since starting the chapter and record how you have done so. This will help you see where you've made progress and where you still need to do some work. If you save your answers from each chapter, you'll eventually have a portfolio of ideas and strategies that you can use in all of your courses.

One of the chapter ending features is a journal activity, *Reflecting on Decisions,* that asks you to think about decisions you have made or need to make in terms of the subject of that chapter. At the end of each chapter, *Perspectives* is written by people who work at or learn about colleges. Each *Perspectives* section is preceded by questions to consider as you read it, as well as another opportunity to think through the 5C process. You will also find a *Choosing to Serve* feature at the end of each chapter. It identifies ways in which you can decide to serve and learn while in college.

Finally, you will find another SQ3R prompt (*Choosing to Be an Active Learner*) to remind you to *review* the chapter in its entirety.

chapter review

Respond to the following on a separate sheet of paper or in your notebook.

1. Review the 12 tips for the first week of class in Module 1.1. Put a check by the ones you were already planning to use. Which of the other items were most surprising to you? Why?

2. Review the italicized statements at the very beginning of Module 1.1. List one that you identify with. Why?

3. How does it feel to be a new student at your college? List three feelings you've had since arriving on campus and the situation that caused them. What does your campus do or provide to orient students? Have you decided to take advantage of any orientation services or activities? Why or why not?

4. Which of the differences between your college and high school or your college and the work world have you already noticed? What effect is that having on your decision to attend college?

5. Describe a decision you made as the result of your adjustment to life as a college student. How did you make the decision? How satisfied are you with the outcome of that decision at this time?

6. Review your response to the previous question. How is the decision-making process you used like the 5C process? How is it different?

7. What text feature of this book do you think will be most useful to you? Why?

8. What changes do you think you face or will face as a college student? How do you plan to adjust to those changes? List three strategies that may help you make a smooth transition to your college.

did you decide?

Did you accomplish what you wanted to in this chapter? Check the items below that apply to you.

Review the *You Decide* statements that you identified at the beginning of the chapter, but look at them from a new direction. If you didn't check an item below, review that module until you feel you can confidently apply the strategies to your own situation. However, the best ideas are worthless unless they are put into effect. Decide what information you found helpful in the chapter and how you plan to use it. Record your comments after the statements below.

☐ 1.1 I know what it takes to be successful in college.

_____

☐ 1.2 I know where on campus to get help if I need it.

_____

☐ 1.3 While college is still new to me, I know and accept my role as a learner.

_____

☐ 1.4 I know that active learning is the best way to learn information.

_____

☐ 1.5 I understand how to use information in this textbook.

_____

perspectives

As a college student, you will encounter new people, places, and ideas as you navigate your new environment. The decisions you make about each one depend on how you view yourself and the world around you. In this passage, Mark David Milliron, president and CEO of the League for Innovation in the Community College, reflects on the backgrounds of learners who decide to attend colleges and what they face when they arrive. He also discusses the role of choices in college coursework and in life.

The questions you need to answer precede the passage. Why? As you now know from the SQ3R process, questions make reading a more active process. They provide clues to what is important. They provide reasons to read. In your own study, you will form questions to answer in your reading, as we discussed. Asking questions before reading and answering them afterward makes reading a more effective and efficient process.

Think about and answer the questions that follow.

1. What is your reaction/feeling to the passage?
2. What are some of the pressures YOU face?
3. How would you describe your personal or academic background?
4. What do you see as the main idea of the last three paragraphs?
5. What effect does this article have on you?
6. Choose ONE of the issues/problems described in the passage (e.g., finding child care, not knowing how to navigate the college environment, recent high school graduate, older adult student). Describe how the 5C decision-making process applies.

   A. What problem situation or **C**hallenge did the individual need to solve?

   B. What key **C**hoices might be open to the individual?

   C. What would be the major **C**onsequence(s) of each choice?

   D. What would you recommend that this individual **C**hoose?

   E. How might the individual **C**heck the outcome of the decision?

Your courage astounds us. We probably don't tell you this enough. You see, we too are pushed and pulled by classes, calendars, and the constant press of our work in education. But when we slow down, look around, and soak in all of your stories, we are humbled.

Many of you will be the first in your family to set foot on a college campus. At times it can feel as though there is no one who really understands how strange and awkward your first steps are. You fill out our forms, meet our advisors, take our placement tests, piece together a schedule, step into our classrooms—whether they're online or on campus—and enter a new world. Sometimes it's

hard for us to remember how overwhelming our rules and procedures seem to you. And we should remember. What you may not realize is that many of us started our higher education journey at a community or technical college. We've just been in this world so long that we sometimes lose touch with how we felt *our* first day. Be patient with us.

Some family and friends don't know much about the journey you're on. Their ideas about college are shaped by movies and TV. Nonetheless, they truly want you to succeed. Some of them have fought, struggled, begged, and borrowed to give you this opportunity. While you are so happy to have their support, you sometimes feel pressured by the weight of their expectations.

You may have different pressures. We've seen some of you suffer through unsupportive, angry, or abusive parents, spouses, or friends. This inner circle plays out their fears or insecurities by discouraging you at every turn, trying to convince you that you too will fail. Some are afraid that your success will take you away from them, so they subtly sabotage your journey. Many of you struggle with uncooperative supervisors or job schedules that make attending class difficult or impossible. Weekend or night courses are a must, even though you're mentally tired and physically worn out. Some of you have major family responsibilities. You search to find good child care and wrestle with the guilt of being away from your kids even though you're going to college to better *their* lives. Still, others must strive to care for parents, nieces, nephews, cousins, and grandchildren. We know that at times it feels as though a higher power is working to keep you from taking this new path. But have faith, because nothing could be further from the truth.

"Will there be people who look like me?" You worry you won't see familiar faces when you look at the students, teachers, and leaders on campus. Or you are differently labeled and wonder whether we'll understand your needs. While we may not be perfect, we work hard to serve and connect with you and your communities. More than almost anywhere in higher education, the diversity that strengthens us and inspires you will be there.

For many of you, beginning with us fresh out of high school makes perfect sense because of where we're located, our cost, our size, or a host of other reasons. You hit the ground running in our honors programs or jump into our student activities. Some of you share your strengths as peer tutors, student leaders, or community volunteers. You are models of service and learning for us all.

Many of you, however, come through our open doors later in life. You may have reached a turning point in your life—the kids are getting older, your job is getting colder, or your dreams are getting further away. It's time for a radical shift. But you wonder what to expect and what will be expected of you as you move into this new world. You're going from waiting tables to mastering computer networking, or from working in a factory to spending sleepless nights pursuing a nursing degree. Others are simply right sizing, training for a job closer to home or one that will allow you to slow down and enjoy life in a different way. More and more of you are coming back for short courses, certifications, or degrees after already achieving a bachelor's degree or higher. For you, it's about staying up to speed and giving yourself new options.

But no matter where you start, you can finish well. Some of you start with us in programs to learn to read and move on to complete a GED; you move through math, reading, and pre-college writing; you complete certifications and degrees on your way to jobs or a university. Along the way, you strive with each passing day, month, and year to get better. Remember, "better" is not about how you compare to others. Better is about how *you* compare to how *you* were yesterday.

Your persistence in getting better teaches us that the time it takes to complete a course or program isn't really the issue. That time will pass either way. What matters is whether you remain at a dead end or move to a place where new learning opens up different pathways for your career and life. With each passing day, you continue on, riding with the ebbs and flows. Obstacles of all sorts flood your way from semester to semester or quarter to quarter: births, deaths, marriages, divorces, getting jobs, losing jobs, and just about every other kind of life experience you can imagine. Some of you need to step out for a time to take care of these situations; but you dive back in, and we welcome you with open arms.

What do you do when it's all said and done? What happens after you move on to work or other education? Some of you go on to run multinational corporations, fly through space, star in movies, run statehouses, and map the human genome. Others target your talents closer to home: raising families, serving communities, creating new businesses, fighting fires, saving lives, or teaching children. In short, you throw yourself into the pool of humanity and the positive ripples cascade out.

And it all begins with a choice—an incredibly courageous choice. You choose to try, to walk through the open doors of our college and begin. You make this choice again and again as you take each step along the journey. You choose to stay, to engage, to give it your best. This choice can and will change your life forever. All because you have the courage to learn.

reflecting
on decisions

What have you learned about college and decision making that can help you decide which opportunities to pursue?

◀ CHOOSING TO SERVE

VOLUNTEERISM

Volunteerism is a way to learn more about yourself and career interests while helping others. Although Chapter 16 provides additional information on this topic, you can start volunteering now.

There is a quick and easy way to find volunteer experiences that can help you learn about possible majors or gain career experience. *Volunteermatch.org* lets you search by city or zip code for opportunities to serve. You can even find virtual opportunities (e.g., e-mail pen pals, grant writing, researching topics, writing thank-you notes) to serve. Use the 5Cs—Define the **C**hallenge; Identify the **C**hoices; Predict the **C**onsequences; **C**hoose an option; **C**heck your outcome—to select three local and two virtual opportunities that interest you and that meet your schedule demands.

CHAPTER **TWO**

LEARNING OUTCOMES

In this chapter you will learn

2.1 How to use your college catalog and website

2.2 How to access resources and services on your campus

2.3 Who is in your college community

2.4 How to identify which organizations at your college fit your needs

2.5 How to communicate effectively with your faculty

2.6 How to better communicate with others and resolve conflicts when they occur

CHOOSING TO BE AN ACTIVE LEARNER ▶

S U R V E Y

Before reading this chapter, prepare for learning. Purposefully skim the title, introduction, headings, and graphics. As you survey, decide what information you already know and what information is new to you.

Q U E S T I O N

Change each section's heading into a question. This forms your learning goal for reading.

R E A D

Read the section without marking. Reread and mark key information that answers your question.

R E C I T E

Stop after each section and make sure you understood the content. Organize or summarize content and make notes.

Interacting with Your College Community

A community is a social network of people who interact within a specific place. At your college, this network includes campus resources, faculty, students . . . and now, you. You not only need to know with whom to interact, but you also need to know how to interact with them to maximize your success. What campus resources and individuals have you already visited on your campus? What made you decide to go to them?

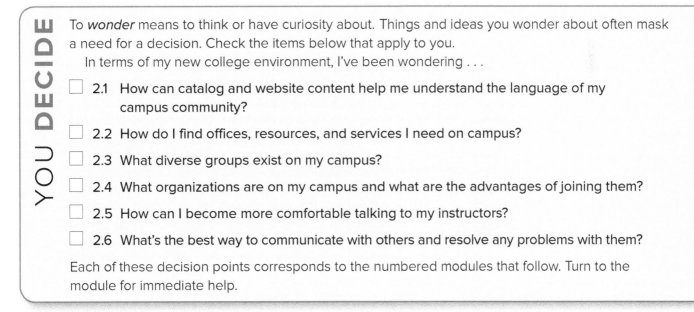

YOU DECIDE

To *wonder* means to think or have curiosity about. Things and ideas you wonder about often mask a need for a decision. Check the items below that apply to you.

In terms of my new college environment, I've been wondering . . .

- ☐ 2.1 How can catalog and website content help me understand the language of my campus community?

- ☐ 2.2 How do I find offices, resources, and services I need on campus?

- ☐ 2.3 What diverse groups exist on my campus?

- ☐ 2.4 What organizations are on my campus and what are the advantages of joining them?

- ☐ 2.5 How can I become more comfortable talking to my instructors?

- ☐ 2.6 What's the best way to communicate with others and resolve any problems with them?

Each of these decision points corresponds to the numbered modules that follow. Turn to the module for immediate help.

A community is more than a network of people. It also implies a sense of identity—the feelings and expectations related to it. How does your sense of community at this school compare with what you thought it would be?

Perhaps you expected to explore the mysteries of the universe as part of a group of interesting classmates led by fascinating professors. Instead, you've found yourself in the back of the classroom, reviewing what you already know. Maybe you imagined yourself effortlessly balancing work, family, and school only to find yourself overwhelmed and exhausted. In many ways, your expectations may have failed to match reality.

The best way to avoid such surprises is to learn, understand, and adjust. In order to interact effectively, you need to know the language of your school. Your campus catalog and website are good sources of information. You will also need to learn about campus services and resources, as well as faculty, organizations, and your fellow students. Finally, you need effective communication skills and conflict resolution strategies for times when communication fails.

Understanding the Language of Your School: Catalog and Website Content

Even when two groups of people speak the same language, differences exist among them. For instance, in Great Britain, *queue* refers to what we call *line*. Their *biscuits* are our *cookies*. A British *chemist* would be called a *pharmacist* in the U.S. Such language differences often result in misunderstandings. Thus, it's important to know the language of your college community. The two most important resources for doing so are your campus website and college catalog.

Your first introduction to your college may have been a virtual one if you explored its website before ever visiting the campus. Most colleges have specific links for prospective or future students that give them information before they are admitted. But now you are a member of the college community. Your needs have changed. You need specific and current information about interacting with your campus community on a day-to-day basis.

Key Parts of Your Campus Website

Information Management System. Collegewide system for e-mail and other announcements. Faculty, staff, and campus office use this to inform or contact you. Get into the habit of logging in and checking it daily.

Academic Calendars. Schedules of deadlines and events. The most important calendar is the academic calendar which identifies exam schedules, enrollment, withdrawal, and other key deadlines.

QuickLinks. Short list of the most important links on the site. These often include the library, computer services, degrees/departments, catalogs, class schedules, directories of phone numbers and e-mail addresses, and financial aid.

Academics. Information about specific departments in terms of their degree and certification programs, course descriptions, and faculty. Advising, tutoring, and learning assistance resources may be listed here as well.

Student Services/Campus Life. Information about nonacademic resources and services. These include campus activities and organizations, career services and internships, student government, and information for students with disabilities.

Key Parts of the College Catalog

The **college catalog** forms a key source for understanding the language of your college community. Revised each year, the catalog you use in the year you first enroll is your contract with the college. This means that if program requirements change in the future, you will still meet requirements as stated in your governing catalog. Thus, your college catalog is your first resource for identifying and understanding the language of your college community as well as the rules and policies that guide interactions within it.

> **college catalog**
> Book describing services, curricula, courses, faculty, and other information pertaining to a postsecondary institution.

- **Academic classification.** Describes how the number of completed credit hours translates into freshman, sophomore, or other status. Credit-hour value is approximately equal to the number of hours per week of in-class instruction (lab, studio, or performance courses often involve more hours of in-class instruction than are reflected in credit-hour value). Course-load requirements describe the maximum and minimum hours required to be at full-time status.

- **Academic policies and regulations.** Describes certification or degree requirements, academic standards, and registration regulations.

- **Academic standards.** Lists the rules governing student conduct, including disciplinary sanctions, academic disciplinary actions, and appeal procedures. These rules apply in cases of academic dishonesty (cheating or plagiarism) or other institutional infractions.

- **Admissions information.** Explains criteria for admission to the institution, regulations for the transfer of credits, and availability of special programs.

- **College degree requirements.** Outlines the required and elective courses needed for completion of a degree. These are often divided by semester/quarter or academic year.

- **Course descriptions.** Summarizes the content of each course, which is usually identified by a number and title.

- **Student services.** Identifies nonacademic activities and services available to students, including campus organizations, internships, career planning, and food service information.

- **Tuition and fees.** Lists in-state and out-of-state costs, including tuition, room and board, fee schedules, student health fees, parking fees, and lab fees. May also identify financial aid opportunities (scholarships, grants, loans, campus jobs).

- **Glossary.** Provides meanings of higher education terms as defined by your college.

activity 1

Using Your Campus Website and College Catalog

PART 1: Campus Website

Answer the following questions:

1. List three items you can find on the **campus homepage:**

    1. _____
    2. _____
    3. _____

2. Locate the following information from your **academic calendar** and record on the inside cover of this text for quick reference:

    1. When is the last day to withdraw from courses?

    2. What holidays occur this term?

    3. What is the last day of classes?

    4. Where do finals begin? end?

3. List three items you can find on **campus library** page:

    1. _____
    2. _____
    3. _____

    Does the library have an online catalog that you can use to see if a particular book is in the library?

    _____ YES   _____ NO

4. Find the list of degree or certification programs. List three that interest you.

    1. _____
    2. _____
    3. _____

5. Find the calendar of campus events. List one event that you would like to attend and its date/time.

    _____

6. Find the student handbook. List three topics within it.

    1. _____
    2. _____
    3. _____

7. Find a list of student organizations. List one that you would be interested in joining.

    _____

8. Find information on financial assistance. Identify one type of financial assistance on your campus.

    _____

9. What is the name of your campus information system? _____

10. Find information about any other campus office or service that interests you. List the office or service and describe why it interests you. _____

11. Search for and explore the ways your college incorporates social media (i.e., Facebook, Twitter, college apps, LinkedIn, YouTube, Podcasts, etc.) into its campus community. List the ones you find and identify the one(s) you would probably use most often.

12. Choose from items 1–11. Use the 5C approach to identify a challenge you might face on campus and identify how you would use information in the item to make a decision.

PART 2: College Catalog

Use your college print or online catalog to complete the following.

1. Find and record information about two scholarships/loans for which you might be eligible.

_____

_____

_____

2. Find the curriculum in which you plan to major.

    a. Compare/contrast courses suggested for your first term with those suggested for your final term. How do you account for similarities/differences?

    _____

    _____

    b. Examine the curriculum carefully. Locate two courses in your major area and read their descriptions. Which will you find more enjoyable? Why?

    _____

    _____

    c. Read the description for each of the courses in which you are now enrolled. How do the descriptions compare to the actual content of the course? What conclusion(s) might you draw about the courses and descriptions you identified in *b*?

    _____

    _____

3. Using your college catalog glossary or other campus resource, define each of the following terms in your own words:

    Academic calendar_____

    Drop_____

    Withdrawal_____

    Residency_____

    Elective_____

    Syllabus_____

    Transcript_____

    Prerequisites_____

    Transfer credit_____

    Credit hour_____

GROUP APPLICATION: Identify three to five additional words or phrases you've heard around campus but aren't sure you understand on a piece of paper. Don't sign your name to the paper. After all of the pages are collected, your instructor will randomly select several words or phrases for discussion by the group.

Campus Offices, Resources, and Services

Have you ever heard someone say, "It's not what you know, but who you know?" Although what you know is vitally important in college, who you know in your campus community can be just as worthwhile. You'll find the people you need to know in offices around campus. They can help you locate the resources and services you need.

While every campus is different, all college communities share some common offices and services. Knowing the location of each one and the services it offers helps you become better oriented to your new environment.

⟫ Key Places on Campus

- **Registrar's Office.** Also called Office of Records or Registration. Tracks courses you take and grades you get. Evaluates advanced, transfer, or correspondence work. Provides transcripts. May have the responsibility to determine if you meet graduation requirements.

- **Business Office.** Records student financial transactions, such as tuition, fees, fines, or other payments.

- **Financial Aid Office.** Also called Student Aid and Scholarship Office. Provides assistance in locating and distributing supplemental funds such as grants, loans, scholarships, and on-campus employment.

- **Advising Office.** May also be called Academic Advising or Academic Counseling. Provides information and assistance in life, career, and educational planning as well as help in preparing for university transfer or workforce development.

- **Dean's Office.** Academic "home" for courses and degree programs (e.g., Liberal Arts, Basic Sciences, Business, Technology, Allied Health).

- **Student Development.** Source for services and programs outside of academics. Includes student government, campus clubs and organizations, career counseling.

- **Library.** Contains online and print materials for reference and recreation, including books, magazines, newspapers, journals, DVDs, and reference books. May also contain computer lab, tutoring, and photocopying facilities. Workshops or classes may be available to familiarize you with library services and holdings.

- **Campus Bookstore.** Since you are reading this textbook, you've probably found the campus bookstore, but did you notice that the bookstore also sells notebooks, art supplies, and other materials? Many also carry over-the-counter drugs and toiletries, snack foods, and school-related clothing and gear.

- **Campus Security.** Also called Campus Police or Public Safety. Provides parking and traffic guidelines. Many campus security offices maintain an escort service to ensure the safety of students walking across campus late in the evening.

- **Learning Center.** Also called Learning Resource Center, Learning Assistance Center, and Learning Lab, among other names. Offers assistance in study skills or specific content areas through workshops or individualized lessons, tutoring, and/or taped, online, or computerized instruction.

- **Residential Life.** Supports your college's academic goals by providing opportunities for student engagement and academic success in campus living communities.

activity 2 | Identifying Campus Resources

PART 1: Campus Chart

Complete the chart of offices and contact information located on the inside back cover of this text.

PART 2: Campus Resources

What's on your campus? Go to each of the following locations on your campus and find out what it offers in order to answer the following questions:

1. College Bookstore. Other than textbooks, what does the bookstore sell?

   _____

2. Library. Other than books for checkout, what other materials and/or services are available at your library?

   _____

3. Student Center/Student Services. What's available at your student center? If your campus doesn't have a student center, go to the student services office and find out what it offers.

   _____

4. Career Services. What resources are available at your campus career services office?

   _____

5. Learning Center. What resources are available at your campus learning center?

   _____

Experiencing Campus Diversity

Diversity characterizes today's typical college campus. Students come from different academic backgrounds. People of every age, ethnic identity, and socioeconomic level have found a place on campus. Students with learning and other disabilities are attending college in greater numbers. International students and U.S. students from urban, suburban, and rural communities share classrooms and ideas. Faculty and staff are also members of diverse groups representing different academic backgrounds, viewpoints, geographic areas, and cultural backgrounds. Although many people think of individual aspects of diversity (e.g., race or gender), diversity is more a complex combination of factors that come together in each individual. Although these aspects may be used to identify people, no individual is–or should be–defined by a single aspect.

Diversity in theory is one thing. Diversity in terms of people sitting next to you or teaching you might be quite a different experience. You–or they–may hold preconceptions about people whose race, gender, culture, religion, political views, age, clothes, sexual orientation, or other factor differs from your own. You–or they–may harbor thoughts and feelings of dismay, distrust, and even discrimination. Awareness of such thoughts and feelings is a first step toward change. Maybe you realize that the person that sits next to you in math makes you feel uncomfortable because of the clothes she wears. Recognition of stereotypical characteristics rather than individual ones is a second step. Now you think about why clothes–rather than the individual–could make you feel uncomfortable. Choosing to have an open mind is a third step. You decide to talk to the student and find that both of you are majoring in the same thing. This leads to a conversation about your shared interest in the field. Being more open-minded and ready to interact with others, then, allows you to learn more about who people are as individuals rather than who you perceive them to be as members of a specific group. Part of the college experience is to provide you with information and courses from which you can better understand and appreciate the world around you. Diversity in the classroom allows you to move beyond theory to firsthand experience . . . if you decide to do so.

> **diversity**
> Variety in the academic environment as the result of individual differences.

activity 3

Finding Commonalities in Our Differences

PART 1:   True or False?

For this activity create a list of four statements about yourself that you wouldn't mind sharing. Three of the statements should be true and one should be false. The statements should reflect some aspect of the diversity that describes you but that is not clearly obvious from looking at you (e.g., age, home state/country, interests/hobbies, background, political view, academic or personal accomplishment, jobs, degree/career interests and so on) rather than a superficial aspect of yourself (current address, favorite color, name of pet).

Example Statements: I am 25 years old. I am from Texas. I worked as the Mickey Mouse character at Disneyland for a summer. I enjoy playing guitar.

PART 2:   True or False?

Divide into small groups. After a person shares his/her statements, the other members of the group should guess which one is false and, as appropriate, discuss any stereotypes that might be involved (e.g., all Texans are cowboys/girls and you don't look like a cowboy/girl).

The person reveals which statement is false. Members of the group that share one of the aspects or a similar aspect should provide that information (e.g., I am also from Texas/I visited Texas on a vacation; I'm also majoring in a health field).

PART 3:   "Who Are You?"

Form groups of three. Student 1 will ask the question, "Who are you?" Student 2 will answer the question with one or more descriptive sentences. Student 3 will observe the interaction. However, after Student 2 responds, Student 1 repeats the question, "Who are you?" and Student 2 must provide additional information. Student 3 continues to observe. In total, Student 1 will ask and Student 2 will respond to the same question five times, with each response being a different answer. Each member of the group takes turns as the person who asks, responds, and observes. At the end of the three rounds of questions, the group should discuss the following: What was difficult about answering the questions? What did you observe about the person asking the questions? What did you observe about the person answering the questions? How did the answers change? What did you learn about the other two students? What did you learn about yourself?

Getting Involved: Joining Campus Groups

What organizations are on my campus and what are the advantages of joining them?

All work and no play can be almost as bad as all play and no work. Academics is clearly your main goal. Your classes should, and do, take much of your time. But friendships and campus life are important, too. They foster important interpersonal and leadership skills. Even if you are a full-time student who works and has family responsibilities, check with your student services office to see what options might be available to you. Online groups and campus pages on social networking sites can provide you with similar opportunities to network and contribute.

Students who actively participate in an extracurricular or community group or who have other campus interests tend to remain in school longer than those who have no such ties. This is because they don't just go to college; they are part of college life. In addition, job recruiters and employers like candidates who are well-rounded with a variety of interests. In today's job market, everyone they see has a degree. They want to see students who set themselves apart. They are looking for people that can handle a diverse range of activities while remaining academically successful.

What group(s) should you join? Your needs, values, and interests determine which groups suit you best. For instance, if you like outdoor activities, you might join a club that schedules hiking and camping trips. In general, it really doesn't matter which group you choose, as long as you become involved in campus life. There's really no substitute.

Name of Group	Eligible Members	Purpose of Membership	Advantages of Membership
Intramural sports	Students who are not part of school-sponsored athletic teams	To organize teams and play various athletic games against others	Encourages teamwork, fair play, leadership, health, and fun
Special interest groups	Any student	To meet and share ideas about a topic or mutual interest	Provides opportunities to meet others with similar interests or to develop new interests
Service organizations	Any student	To volunteer time for the benefit of others or to gain experience in a particular field	Provides various opportunities to work for the common good of your institution or community
Fraternities and sororities (also known as Greek Life)	Any student	To have fun and make friends	Affords greater assimilation into the institution
Campus employment	Any student	To get involved in campus life while getting paid	Offers the opportunity to work within area of study and chances to meet and know students, faculty, and staff
Noncredit or leisure classes	Any student	To learn more about an interest or gain practice or expertise without the cost or stress of grades in credit courses	Provides ways to gain information (e.g., conversational version of a foreign language) or practice skills (choral groups; exercise classes)
Residence life associations	Any student who lives on campus	To get involved in campus life	Offers opportunities to interact with the people with whom you live
Student government associations	Any student	To represent and give a voice to college students through an elected body	Provides leadership and management opportunities and experience with government

Students participating in Habitat for Humanity.

How Do You Want to Grow?

Under the first heading below, list the personal characteristics you feel you need to develop—this is your *Challenge*. For example, perhaps speaking in front of groups, working with others, improved health, and stress management might be areas you feel you need to develop. Then under the next heading (to the right), identify and list several *Choices* on your campus that might help you develop these characteristics. What would be the *Consequences* of participating in each group (e.g., time, cost, effort)? List these next. Which do you think you would *Choose*? What plan do you have to *Check* the outcome? Briefly describe.

Challenge: *Characteristics Needing Development*	Choice: *Organization/Activities to Support These Characteristics*	Consequences: *How Will You Check?*

GROUP APPLICATION: After completing the activity, share individual answers with your group. What similarities and differences do you discover among your group's answers? What factors might contribute to these similarities and differences?

Working with Faculty

A popular urban legend tells of an instructor whose students changed his behavior. Whenever he walked to the left side of the room, they seemed to lose interest in what he said. They yawned, wrote notes, whispered, and paid little or no attention. When he moved to the right, they sat up straight. They listened carefully, took notes, and asked questions. The instructor soon began to lecture only from the right side of the class. Is it true? According to urban legend website www.Snopes.com, maybe not. What is true, however, is that you *can* influence the behavior of your instructors. Instructors try to be fair and impartial, but they are people, too.

Think about the people you meet. Some act in ways that make you want to know them better. Others do not. Instructors feel the same way about students. When they meet a new group of students, they react to and with each one. Whether in class or out of class, your behavior determines if their reactions to you are positive or negative. You control whether or not you are a student worth knowing better.

Classroom Behavior

To obtain and keep an instructor's goodwill, you need to be polite and respectful. Arriving on time and dressing appropriately make a good first impression. Prompt and consistent attendance proves your commitment to the course. Avoiding the inappropriate use of technology (e.g., texting or talking on your cell phone) during class shows respect and commitment. The quality of your work also reveals your regard for the instructor and the course. Your work is, after all, an extension of you. Only work of the highest quality in content, form, and appearance should be submitted.

Sitting near the front of the room in about the same seat for each class gives the instructor a visual fix on you. Although the instructor may not keep attendance records, he or she will subconsciously look for you and know you are there. Sitting near the front of the room also helps you maintain eye contact with the instructor. This too registers positively on an instructor.

Nonverbal cues tell your instructors how you are reacting to their presentations.

Your apparent interest in the lecture is often reflected in your *actions*. **Body language,** such as sitting straight, facing the instructor, arms uncrossed, shows your openness and desire to learn. Body language includes facial expressions, like smiling, and movements, nodding your head, raising your eyebrows in recognition. The opposite of this is also true. Nonverbal responses of skepticism or boredom clearly show through body language (yawning, reading the newspaper, texting on your cell phone, sighing, looking out the window, rolling your eyes, frowning).

body language
Nonverbal communication.

Body language is especially important when you read your instructor's comments on returned assignments in class. Constructive criticism is part of the academic process and should be a learning experience. An instructor's critical comments are not a personal attack. Your body language should reflect your ability to accept those comments in the spirit in which they are given.

Inappropriate use of technology is a recent form of nonverbal communication. If you can see your instructor, your instructor can see you. Your instructor can see who is paying attention and who is sending text messages on cell phones. Your instructor can also see who is taking notes on a computer and who is playing games, checking e-mail or Facebook, or simply surfing the net. Although you may be able to multitask while listening to a lecture, your instructor may perceive it as a lack of interest or rudeness.

Some students fear speaking aloud in class. Often they think their questions will sound "dumb" to either the instructor or other students. Still others feel too shy to speak up in class. Maybe they've had embarrassing experiences in the past and speaking in class frightens them. Generally, however, if something in the lecture confused you, it confused other students, too. Others are often waiting for someone else to make the first move. That person can be you.

Speaking in class is less stressful if you know how to phrase your questions or comments. Be relevant and respectful. Nothing frustrates an instructor more than rude questions, long, unrelated stories, or questions whose answers were just discussed. Preceding your question with what you *do* understand helps the instructor clarify what confuses you. By briefly stating what you think was just said, you aid the instructor in finding gaps in your knowledge. Be sure to be precise about the information you need. For example, in a math class, instead of saying, "I don't get it," you would say, "I understand the first two steps of the problem, but I don't know how to get to the next step."

Active participation in class discussions proves your interest. If you ask questions or make comments about the lecture topic, you show your attention. But if you feel you simply cannot ask a question in class, then see your instructor before or after class or make an appointment.

If you have to be late for class, enter as discreetly as you can. After class, wait for your instructor and apologize. If you are often late, make an appointment to see your instructor to explain your tardiness. If your instructor is sympathetic and accepts your excuse, thank him or her. If your instructor indicates that your continued lateness will negatively impact your grade, you have three choices: get to class on time, accept the penalty, or drop the class.

Out-of-Class Behavior

Getting to know an instructor personally involves special effort. Smiling and saying hello when you see an instructor outside of class is a friendly opening gesture. Positive, sincere feedback about course content, exams, and so on often opens lines of communication. Visiting an instructor's office often and for long time periods also affects how an instructor feels about you but, unfortunately, in a negative way. Instructors maintain office hours so students with valid problems can reach them. They also use that time to grade papers, prepare lectures, complete paperwork, and conduct research. Thus, many instructors resent students who–without reason–constantly visit them. This does not mean that instructors do not like to talk to you and other students. They do. Talking to you helps them understand your problems and learning needs. It gives them an opportunity to interest you in their content areas.

Today's faculty are also available via e-mail, and many of the same rules apply. Don't overload your instructor's e-mail box with forwarded information (e.g., good luck chain letters or jokes). When you do write your instructor, include your full name in the body of the e-mail as well as the class and section in which you are enrolled. This helps a busy instructor respond more efficiently and effectively. When you ask questions, be specific. Rather than writing, "I'm having a problem in your course," you could write, "I'm unsure of what you mean in assignment 3 in terms of the content of the essay." Also, asking for assistance well before a due date makes a better impression than last-minute pleas. Asking for clarification of a grade is another good reason to contact your instructor. However, you should convey a sincere interest in improving future papers rather than pleading for a change on the grade you received. Your tone should be inquisitive rather than accusing.

Although faculty appreciate student friendliness, address your instructor in the same manner that you would in class. Mr./Mrs./Ms./Dr. are the safest choices. Refrain from calling your instructor by first name unless he or she specifically asks you to do so. Do not address your professor informally–leave Dude, Lady, Man, Buddy, Bro, and Girlfriend for your friends. Use standard formats, spelling, and punctuation.

Your best bet is to e-mail your instructors only when you have a serious issue–filling their inboxes with e-mails with many questions and comments is not a good idea. Also, while it may seem easier to e-mail and ask questions and favors, instructors tend to look less favorably upon these long-distance requests. Rather, visit an instructor's office and make it personal.

What do you do if you think a grade was unfairly or incorrectly assigned? First, you should contact your instructor for clarification, especially if your concern is about a final grade. If, after discussing a grade with an instructor, you feel you have been unfairly treated, you have the right to an appeal. This appeal involves, first, meeting with the professor and attempting to resolve your problem. During the second step of the appeal process, you write a letter to the head of the department in which the course is taught asking for a meeting with that person and your instructor. If you are not satisfied with the results of this hearing or if your instructor is the department chair, you may appeal to the dean of the department in which the course was taught. If you are firmly convinced that you are in the right, your final appeal is made to the head of academic affairs at your institution.

It is possible to influence instructors favorably. You can do it by treating them as you want them to treat you.

tips

TIPS FOR GETTING ALONG WITH YOUR INSTRUCTOR

1. Never miss class.

2. Never be inattentive or impolite.

3. Use standard written and spoken English in communicating with your instructor.

4. Never, ever, say or e-mail, "I missed class today. Did we do anything important?" (Instructors never feel that they are teaching unimportant information.)

Online Behavior

In today's online environments, instructors and students often interact through e-mail, online chats, and posts to discussions in course management systems. Some courses are **hybrids,** that is, a combination of face-to-face and online content. Some are fully online. Even instructors in face-to-face classes use the course management system to e-mail students, post content, and make other class assignments.

Even if an instructor never meets a student face-to-face, that instructor can form impressions–good or bad–from interactions with them. Communication today (e.g., text messages, e-mail) is often informal. But the kinds of casual comments between friends (Cn u help me? 'S up?) are not appropriate when contacting online faculty. Faculty expect you to use correct spelling and grammar in your e-mails and other work.

Failure to check into online classes regularly is just as problematic as failure to show up for onsite classes. Course management systems have tools that allow faculty to "see" how many times you access the course and what aspects of the course you have–or have not–used.

More than in onsite classes, instructors expect you to read course materials, follow directions, and promptly contact them when you have questions.

hybrids
Courses that are a combination of face-to-face and online content.

Pleas for extra time to complete work due to procrastination on your part will not be granted.

Finally, online courses often have group work in which students interact virtually to create a response or project. Shirking your group work often results in negative impressions by peers as well as the instructor.

activity 5

Classroom Behavior: What Are They Saying?

Next time you are in a face-to-face class, spend some time observing the students around you, but look at them from your instructor's viewpoint. What do you think the students are communicating through their body language and nonverbal behavior? Which students do you think would be enjoyable to teach if you were the instructor? Why? Which ones would be more difficult to teach? Why? What do you want your instructor's perspective of you to be? How can you achieve that goal?

Communication and Conflict Resolution

Interactions with others characterize human life. You communicate daily with others at home, in workplaces, and, now, in college. Some of these interactions are face-to-face. Others are in writing both online and on paper. Learning to communicate more effectively and to handle any problems that arise are skills that you will use throughout life.

Communication Skills

Communication involves understanding and being understood. Communication can be verbal or nonverbal. Thus, face-to-face communication involves how something is said (gestures, facial expressions, body language) as well as what is said. Communication can also be spoken or written. Conversations, lectures, discussions, text chapters, e-mails, Web pages all involve communication.

Communication depends on context. What and how you communicate informally to a close friend probably differs from what and how you communicate with a stranger. What and how you communicate with your peers should differ from what and how you communicate with college faculty and staff. For instance, the kind of shorthand used in text messages (*cn u c me 2day?*) is not appropriate for corresponding with college faculty and staff.

Communication also depends on an almost infinite number of factors within the speaker/writer and listener/reader. Emotions, interests, relationships, skills, and background are just some of the factors. These can affect what is said or written as well as how it is understood. For instance, a student who has had a bad day (unexpected bill in the mail, missed bus, forgot assignment) might react more strongly to a professor's comments. Or, a student with numerous responsibilities (family, work, academic) may be less patient with a group member who fails to show up for meetings. A student who has been taught to agree with authority figures may not know how to respond to an advisor's questions about career choices. Awareness of the dimensions of communication as well as the communication strengths and weaknesses in yourself and others is the first step in communication success.

Luckily, communication skills are learned. Good communication skills pay off in benefits for all kinds of relationships–personal, academic, and career. The following tips and suggestions help improve communication skills.

Developing Effective Communication Skills

1. **Think before speaking or writing.** Choose your words carefully. Consider how they will be heard or read.

2. **Listen actively.** Consider the viewpoint of the speaker or writer. In face-to-face communication, pay attention to how and what information is communicated. In writing, pay attention to the words the writer uses.

3. **Ask questions.** In face-to-face communications, ask the speaker for more information or explanations.

4. **Use *I* rather than *you*.** Use of *you* (e.g., *you* aren't being clear) can sound accusatory. Using *I* takes the pressure off others (*I* don't understand what you mean).

5. **Observe and learn from communication interactions between other people.** Become a student of communication. Look for interactions that model the kinds of communications you want for yourself. Similarly, pay attention to interactions that don't go well so you can learn what to avoid in communication.

6. **Take a speech course.** No matter who you are or what career you choose to pursue, you will be communicating with others. A speech course gives you the skills you need for a variety of communications situations.

Conflict Resolution

As you interact with others on your campus, conflicts may arise. Psychologists list several reasons why problems occur between people. First, defensiveness or excuses for inappropriate behavior instead of accepting responsibility for it often cause conflict. Second, always complaining and never complimenting build friction. Third, making countercharges for every charge instead of seeing that some accusations might be valid causes disunity. Last, being stubborn, uncompromising, belligerent, and rude quickly dooms any relationship.

Conflict resolution occurs in one of three ways. One, you give the person with whom you have conflict the gift of agreement. To do so, you make a conscious choice to give in. This gift needs to be offered with a willing spirit, free of complaint, or it is not a gift at all. Second, you and your opponent compromise. This does not make one of you the winner and the other the loser. Rather, the goal is to reach an outcome that is fair for both of you. Finally, you and your adversary need to see differences between you as positives, not negatives. Learning to accept people who are unlike you might be the greatest lesson you learn in college.

Techniques for Resolving Conflicts

1. **Can we talk?** Ask if the two of you can talk. Then ask permission to discuss a specific problem. For example, say, "Something's been worrying me, and I'd like to discuss it with you. Do you have a minute so

we could talk?" If the other person indicates that this is not a good time, then ask when you can talk.

2. **Practice, practice, practice.** Think about what you want to say. Role-play both yourself and the other person. This way you can anticipate points of disagreement and be prepared for them.

3. **Choose your battles.** Determine if the situation is really a conflict situation worthy of the effort. If you belabor small points, you lose the value of large ones.

4. **Fault lines.** Don't assess blame. Neither of you is likely to think the fault lies with you. Remember that since conflict causes problems for both of you, both of you must work on its solution.

5. **Open communication.** Avoid questions with *Yes* or *No* responses. That is, ask *How do you feel about this? not Do you like this?*

6. **Give and take.** Give information to the other person. Don't judge or interpret the other person's behavior. Then, give the other person a chance to speak. Really listen to what he or she is saying.

7. **Avoid airing your dirty laundry.** This is a problem between you and the other person. Don't discuss it with or in front of others.

8. **Winners never quit.** Once the subject has been broached (the hardest part), keep the discussion going until a mutual agreement has been reached.

9. **Stick like glue.** When an agreement has been reached, honor it. The only way to build trust is to respect the commitments and decisions the two of you make.

10. **Leave the scene.** Suppose you and another person have a huge argument in a group meeting. To resolve it, you might need to leave the scene of the conflict. Going to lunch, meeting outside the classroom, and so on help alleviate stress and encourages positive results.

11. **If at first . . .** If your initial efforts fail, try another approach. For instance, try e-mail or leaving a voice mail if face-to-face efforts fail.

Winning at Conflict

activity 6

Apply the 5C process to a conflict challenge you recently faced. The conflict could be one that occurred on campus, at work, in a store, or with friends or family. What *Choices* did you have in the situation? What were the *Consequences* of each choice? What did you *Choose* to do? How did you *Check out* the results of your choice?

chapter review

Respond to the following on a separate sheet of paper or in your notebook.

1. Identify the three campus offices or resources you feel every entering student should know. Why did you choose these offices?

2. Which campus offices or resources have you found to be most helpful to you? Are these the same as those listed in your answer to question 1? Why or why not?

3. Identify two groups on your campus that you are eligible to join. Use the 5C process to decide which of the two groups you should join. What is the *Challenge?* What are your *Choices?* What do you think are the *Consequences* of each choice? Which would you *Choose* to join? How could you *Check out* the results of your choice?

4. How is interacting with faculty the same as or different from interacting with your boss at work, your family, or your friends?

5. Consider the suggestions for interacting with faculty in class. Create a list of suggestions to help you make a good impression on classmates.

6. Have you ever been in conflict with someone? How would the information about conflict resolution have helped or hindered you in the outcome of this situation?

did you decide?

Did you accomplish what you wanted to in this chapter? Check the items below that apply to you.

Review the *You Decide* questions that you identified at the beginning of the chapter, but look at them from a new direction. If you didn't check an item below, review that module until you feel you can confidently apply the strategies to your own situation. However, the best ideas are worthless unless they are put into effect. Decide what information you found helpful in the chapter and how you plan to use it. Record your comments after the statements below.

☐ **2.1** I can use catalog and website content to help me understand the language of my campus community.

_____

_____

☐ **2.2** I know where to find offices, resources, and services I need on campus.

_____

_____

☐ **2.3** I recognize the diverse groups that exist on my campus.

_____

_____

☐ **2.4** I know what organizations are on my campus and the advantages of joining them.

_____

_____

☐ **2.5** I can use ideas from this book to talk comfortably with my instructors.

_____

_____

☐ **2.6** I know ways to communicate with others and resolve any problems with them.

_____

_____

perspectives

Communication skills (listening, speaking, and writing) are keys for college and life success. As a college student, you have numerous opportunities to observe and learn these skills both in and out of classes. The following article, "The Maxed-Out Tech Student's Guide to Mastering Communication Skills" by Patrick Amaral, explains how you can use your college experiences to improve communication skills.

Think about and answer the questions that follow.

1. What communication skills can you gain from observing your faculty and peers?
2. In addition to what you learn from the content of a lecture, what can you learn from the ways in which information is presented?
3. How can you use your ability to ask questions in class or contribute to class discussions as the foundation for other verbal communication skills?
4. How can your notetaking skills contribute to your writing skills?
5. How does an in-depth conversation contribute to communication skills?
6. Think of a communication skill that you want to develop. Describe how the 5C decision-making process applies.
   A. What is the **C**hallenge, the communication skill you want to develop?
   B. What key **C**hoices for developing the skill are open to you?
   C. What would be the major **C**onsequence(s) of each choice?
   D. What do you plan to **C**hoose?
   E. How might you **C**heck the outcome of the decision?

You've already heard about the importance of communication skills—that catch-all phrase that encompasses everything from speaking to a crowd, writing memos, working in teams, conducting meetings, talking on the phone, conversing over a business lunch, introducing your boss to a business associate and most importantly, listening. So we won't go there. Rather, a more pertinent question is: How do you gain these communication skills when your curriculum allows one, maybe two, electives per semester and you have little time?

One of the best ways to build communication skills is to use them. Simply take advantage of any opportunity to practice communicating, especially outside of your discipline's setting. Taking part in some painless, perhaps even enjoyable, activities will build communication skills.

THE NO-PAIN WAY TO BUILD COMMUNICATION SKILLS Read newspapers and magazines to learn how to have well-informed conversations.

Staying current on the latest news and topics of general interest gives you the ability to converse intelligently with others.

Go to a movie or play with someone and then discuss it to learn how to persuade people to your point of view. Debating the merits and content of a movie or play with others allows you to explore some of the more abstract aspects of a topic. Without realizing it, you are learning about persuasive speaking.

Start or join a book club to learn how to connect your thoughts and opinions to someone else's ideas. What's good about this suggestion is that (1) you pick the book; and (2) you decide what you want to discuss. Regardless of the books or subjects, you practice connecting your thoughts and opinions to someone else's work.

Volunteer for campus or community organizations to learn how to empathize with your audience. The more variety of people you have contact with, the better your communication skills become. If you are tutoring a fifth grader, you have to learn to communicate complex ideas in a simple way. If you are working in a homeless shelter, you must empathize with the homeless. Such situations make you a better communicator because you master the art of understanding the people you want to reach.

Attend presentations by speakers, musicians, artists or authors, etc., to identify what good public speaking is. You don't have to be familiar with the topic in order to listen to what they are saying and how they are saying it. Figure out why they are effective communicators.

Challenge yourself to attend a presentation on a topic you know nothing about. Attend a debate to learn how to present material effectively and persuasively. As you listen, question why debaters present their arguments in a certain order. Look at how they get their points across and use inflection. Ask yourself what makes a good debate?

Talk to people in industry to learn how to organize your thoughts. By speaking with people in industry, you find out how they use language, how they organize their thoughts, and how they communicate information about fields they know well.

Read, read, read to learn basic speaking and writing skills. It doesn't matter what you read: novels, magazines, newspapers, reports, technical papers. The more you read, the more you know, and the more effectively you will speak and write.

Give presentations in class to practice public speaking. Take advantage of every opportunity to give oral presentations in class, any class. This is a great exercise, and you will never get fired from college if your presentation isn't perfect.

Join student organizations to learn how to interact effectively with others. Officers of clubs and organizations are responsible for scheduling, planning and conducting meetings, filing reports, submitting requests and interacting with people in various functions. Team members must communicate with each other to achieve the team's goals. Whatever your role, you are building communication skills.

Contribute articles to school or department publications to learn concise writing. One great way to master how to communicate is to write about something you believe in and make it comply with guidelines set by an editor. You also learn to accept criticism by having your document edited.

Get to know people outside of your major to observe how they communicate their ideas to you. Knowing a diverse group of people exposes you to new experiences and ways of thinking. Just talking with people who have different interests and backgrounds broadens your ability to communicate. Listening to others allows you to better understand different points of view.

Attend classes to take advantage of all the information out there about how to communicate. Take as many courses as you can. There is a wealth of knowledge that they offer. But don't rely solely on the classes. Communicating is something you can do every day. Socialize to learn how to listen, organize your thoughts, respect others' opinions and present your ideas. This may sound a little too obvious, but think back to the last time you had a substantial conversation with someone and talked about a topic that was really important to both of you. Having an in-depth conversation forces you to listen, organize your thoughts, respect the other person's opinion, and present your ideas clearly.

reflecting on decisions

Now that you've gotten the big picture about your college community, what insights have you gained about the way your interactions within the college community might affect your academic progress and the outcomes of your life?

GET **ACTIVE**

Many campuses and campus organizations include service as a vital part of their mission. Joining an organization that does so allows you to become a citizen of your campus and community at one time—what a great time management win! You learn about these groups by visiting your campus office of Student Services. There organizations often list their charters or mission statements. You can also find out about them by announcements on your campus website, newspaper, or bulletin boards. Even if you don't want to join the organization, you can generally still participate in service activities such as a race/walk to raise funds for cancer research, food or clothing drive, or campus recycling initiative. Use the 5Cs—Define the **C**hallenge; Identify the **C**hoices; Predict the **C**onsequences; **C**hoose an option; **C**heck your outcome—to determine which organization you would choose to join to meet your service goals.

◄ **CHOOSING TO SERVE**

R E V I E W

Skim the notes you made throughout the chapter. How does the content fit together? What information is still unclear? Were your learning goals met? Can you answer the review questions and define terms?

◄ **CHOOSING TO BE AN ACTIVE LEARNER**

CHAPTER **THREE**

Making Choices about Today's Technology

With the arrival of the Internet, the World Wide Web, e-mail, and cell phones, access to education now occurs almost anytime or anyplace. As a result, education is available to more people more of the time. Just about any information you might need is literally at your fingertips 24/7. But you can't use all of it. This chapter shows you how to make informed choices about using technology to maximize your college experience.

YOU DECIDE

To *wonder* means to think or have curiosity about. Things and ideas you wonder about often mask a need for a decision. Check the items below that apply to you.

In terms of technology, I've been wondering . . .

- [ ] **3.1** How much computer experience do I need to be successful in college?
- [ ] **3.2** How can I use the Web to help me succeed?
- [ ] **3.3** How do I decide if what I find on the Web is worthwhile?
- [ ] **3.4** In what ways will I use electronic course content, e-mail, and campus portals?
- [ ] **3.5** What rights and responsibilities come with using technology?
- [ ] **3.6** Are distance learning courses right for me?

Each of these decision points corresponds to the numbered modules that follow. Turn to the module for immediate help.

CHOOSING TO BE AN ACTIVE LEARNER

SURVEY

Before reading this chapter, prepare for learning. Purposefully skim the title, introduction, headings, and graphics. As you survey, decide what information you already know and what information is new to you.

QUESTION

Change each section's heading into a question. This forms your learning goal for reading.

READ

Read the section without marking. Reread and mark key information that answers your question.

RECITE

Stop after each section and make sure you understood the content. Organize or summarize content and make notes.

Learning in the Digital Age

When were you born? In 1991, the Bureau of Transportation reported that approximately 120 million Americans had cell phones. A decade later almost 300 million (91 percent of the U.S. population) owned a cell phone. Google started as one of many search engines in 1998 with 9,800 average searches per day. By 2006, *google* was added to the Oxford English Dictionary as a word meaning "to use the Google search engine to obtain information on the Internet. Over 6 billion google searches are now made daily." Facebook started in 2004 and had 400 million subscribers six years later. The first video was uploaded to YouTube in 2005. Today 100 hours of video are uploaded every minute, and 6 billiion hours are watched each month on YouTube. Twitter, created in 2006, had only about 500 thousand tweets per quarter in 2007. Now 58 million tweets are made on average per day. Instagram was launched in October of 2010 and sold for approximately $1 billion in cash and stocks eighteen months later. Video-sharing service Vine launched in January 2013 and became the most used video sharing applications in less than three months.

How does life in the digital age affect the choices *you* make? The world has changed in your lifetime. You not only access information; you create it. College websites . . . campus portals . . . course management systems . . . e-mail . . . online library catalogs. . . . Today's colleges rely on technology to deliver information. They depend on you to know how to access and use it. Just as college students have varying levels of knowledge and skills in academic subjects, they have varying degrees of computer expertise.

If you already feel confident about your technology skills, look for ways to apply your expertise to learning. If, however, you feel less than confident, you're not alone. Many people starting college–or returning to it after years away from school–have not had extensive experience with computers. Every campus offers a range of computer courses, help desks, workshops, and computer labs for users. Each of these is expressly designed to help you in different ways. Ask your instructors, advisor, or other students to help you find the one(s) that best meet your needs.

Assessing Your Computer Skills and Attitudes

PART 1: Your Computer Knowledgability

Respond to each of the following using the following scale:

0. This does not describe me.

1. I've done this a couple of times, but I'm not confident about my ability to do so again.

2. I think my knowledge or ability to do this is OK.

3. This describes me very well.

COMPUTER USAGE

_____ **1.** When I have a minor problem with my computer, I know how to fix it.

_____ **2.** I know how to use basic editing functions (e.g., copy, paste, delete).

_____ **3.** I own a computer or have regular access to one.

_____ **4.** I know where I can use a computer on campus.

_____ **5.** When my instructor gives assignments that involve computer applications (e.g., word processing, spreadsheet), I know what to do.

_____ **6.** I easily understand computer terms and know how to use these functions (e.g., start, document, file, folder, save).

Now add up your total responses and divide by the number of questions:

TOTAL POINTS: ___ /6 = _____

INTERNET/WEB USE

_____ **1.** I use the Web almost every day.

_____ **2.** I know what a URL is and how to use it to find a specific website.

_____ **3.** I know how to follow links from one Web page to another.

_____ **4.** I know how to navigate backward and forward among many Web pages.

_____ **5.** I know how to download a document.

_____ **6.** I know how to create favorites of sites I visited.

TOTAL POINTS: ___ /6 = _____

FINDING AND EVALUATING INFORMATION

_____ **1.** I know what kinds of information are available on the Internet.

_____ **2.** I know how to use a search engine to locate information.

_____ **3.** I know how to use a subject directory to locate information.

_____ **4.** I know how to evaluate a website to determine if it is credible and valid.

TOTAL POINTS: ___ /4 = _____

ELECTRONIC ACCESS AND COMMUNICATION

_____ **1.** I have accessed and used my college's website.

_____ **2.** I know how to use the campus library electronic catalog and databases.

_____ **3.** I have used a course information system (e.g., Blackboard, WebCT, Moodle, Angel) to access information about one of my classes.

_____ **4.** I have an e-mail account.

_____ **5.** I send and receive e-mail almost every day.

_____ **6.** I know how to attach a document to send to someone via e-mail.

TOTAL POINTS: ____ /6 = _____

USE OF TECHNOLOGY FOR LEARNING

_____ **1.** I study without getting distracted by games or social networking sites.

_____ **2.** I know how to use a tablet or mobile device in class to take notes or access digital content.

_____ **3.** Using a table or mobile device in class does not detract from my attention to course content.

_____ **4.** I do not check e-mail or send text messages during class unless it is an emergency.

_____ **5.** I would get the instructor's permission to record course content in class.

_____ **6.** I know how to find and use Web 2.0 tools for maximizing learning.

TOTAL POINTS: ____ /6 = _____

ONLINE AND HYBRID COURSES

_____ **1.** I know how to use my college course management system.

_____ **2.** know how to locate my grades and returned assignments in the course management system.

_____ **3.** I know how to contact my college tech support by phone or e-mail.

_____ **4.** I have a personal Plan B (e.g., going to campus computer lab) for times when my personal computer or other devices might be unavailable.

_____ **5.** I check into my online course daily.

_____ **6.** I have a plan for keeping track of online assignments, exams, and discussions.

_____ **7.** I know that online classes may take more time than face-to-face classes.

TOTAL POINTS: ____ /7 = _____

ETHICAL USE OF DIGITAL CONTENT

_____ **1.** I know how to identify copyright information on the Web.

_____ **2.** I can cite information from a website correctly.

_____ **3.** I use, but do not abuse, technology.

_____ **4.** I know the basics of "netiquette."

TOTAL POINTS: ____ /4 = _____

SCORING

If your total score is less than 2 for any part, you need to look for resources and ways to increase your knowledge, skills, and confidence in that area.

If your total score is 2 for any part, you probably have average or satisfactory knowledge and skills in that area.

If your total score is greater than 2 for any part, your knowledge and skills are strengths for you.

PART 2: Where Do You Go from Here?

Choose the section in the quiz above in which you had the lowest scores. Apply the 5C process—Define the **C**hallenge; Identify the **C**hoices; Predict the **C**onsequences; **C**hoose an option; **C**heck your outcome—in order to improve your score. What do you need to learn about computers and the Internet and how will you do so?

GROUP APPLICATION: Compare answers with others in your class. What contributed to similarities and differences in challenges? What other options did your classmates identify? Find someone in your class who has a high score in an area that poses a challenge for you. What tips or suggestions does that person have for increasing your skill level?

How can I use
the Web to help
me succeed?

Choices for Successful Use of the Internet and the Web

websites

Sites (locations) on the Web owned by a person, company, or organization that have a home page, the first document users see when they enter the site, and often additional documents and files.

web pages

Specially formatted documents that support links to other documents, as well as graphics, audio, and video files.

hyperlink

A piece of text or a graphic that serves as a cross-reference between parts of a document or between files or websites.

browse

Follow links in a Web page, or explore without specific direction, as the spirit moves you, until you find what you want.

The Internet does for information what the U.S. interstate highway system did for people and products. That is, it increases access and the speed with which information travels. When you use the Internet, you access a worldwide network of millions of educational, government, commercial, and personal computers. As a student, you'll use the Internet to locate information for your courses, complete assignments, and communicate with your faculty and fellow students.

The World Wide Web, also called the Web, is composed of **websites** owned by a person, company, or organization containing collections of documents called **web pages** that can include information in graphic, audio, video, animated, or other formats.

Through the Web you can access resources that were once available only in library or museum holdings or through traditional classroom instruction. In addition, Web pages use special links called **hyperlinks** between parts of a document or between files. These let you automatically access more information at another location–either within the document or in a different document or site.

Have you ever heard someone say that looking for something was like looking for a needle in a haystack? Finding information on the Internet is a little like that. There are billions of websites with no system of organization. There are, however, several ways to find what you need.

Often your course textbook or instructor can suggest a good starting point. From there, you can **browse,** or follow links in a Web page, or explore without specific direction as the spirit of what you see or read moves you, until you find what you want. This strategy, however, can be less productive because you are depending on luck to find exactly what you want. It is better to use a search strategy.

Search strategies are more productive because they allow you to target your needs more specifically. Dr. Bernie Dodge at San Diego State University

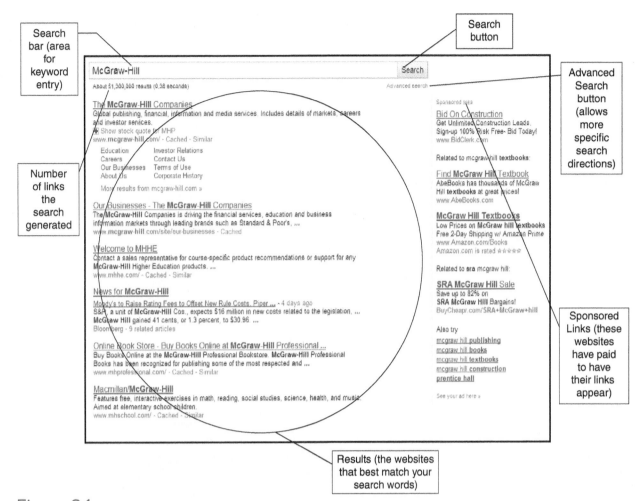

Figure 3.1 Diagram of a Search Engine.

recommends a *Step Zero* to precede your search. In this *Step Zero,* Dodge suggests that you start by identifying the specific question you're trying to answer and generating a list (e.g., people, terms, organizations, places, objects) that might be in a response.

Next, Dr. Dodge says you create a 3M list of MUSTS (words that you think would definitely appear in Web content on the topic), MIGHTS (words that are relevant or synonyms that could appear in Web content), and MUSTN'TS (words that use some of the words you want but that are incorrect in terms of context). When you enter the terms in your **search engine,** put a + in front of MUST terms and a − in front MUSTN'T terms. You don't need to mark MIGHT terms in any special way.

As you search, Dr. Dodge recommends use of a second search strategy abbreviated as NETS. First, use the 3M plan to **N**arrow your search and specify **E**xact terms. Once you get to a site, **T**rim the URL by deleting part of the address bit by bit to see other pages at the site. (For example, http://www.finaid.org/loans/parentloan.phtml could be trimmed to http://www.finaid.org/loans/parentloan; http://www.finaid.org/loans; or http://www.finaid.org.) Finally, click on the **S**imilar pages link for hits you find particularly interesting.

search engine
An Internet program that searches documents for specified keywords and returns a list of the documents where the keywords were found.

Some of the most commonly used search engines are http://www.google.com, http://www.search.aol.com, http://www.bing.com/, http://www.altavista.com, http://www.excite.com, http://www.hotbot.com, http://www.lycos.com, http://www.northernlight.com, and http://www.msn.com.

A **subject directory,** or a set of topical terms that can be browsed or searched by using keywords, is another specialized Internet tool. Unlike search engines that use electronic robots to identify information, subject directories use humans—often experts in their fields—who look for the best and most relevant sites for each category. In some cases, the information may also be more up to date because human researchers often update topics of special interest (e.g., new information about different sports during the Olympics).

To use a subject directory, you identify the broad category from a list or enter a search term. You continue browsing in subcategories or searching until you find the information you need. Common directories include http://www.yahoo.com/, http://search.looksmart.com, http://www.academicinfo.net, and http://about.com/.

Once you find what you want, you can read it on your computer screen, print a hard copy, **bookmark** it for future reference, or, in some cases, **download** it.

subject directory
A set of topical terms that can be browsed or searched by using keywords.

bookmark
To mark a document or a specific address (URL) of a Web page so that you can easily revisit the page at a later time.

download
To copy data (usually an entire file) from their main source to your own computer or disk.

Applying 5Cs to Internet and Database Searching

Using a textbook chapter from one of the classes in which you are now enrolled, identify a topic that you want to know more about. This is your **C**hallenge.

PART 1: The 5Cs on the Internet

Use the rest of the 5Cs—Identify the **C**hoices; Predict the **C**onsequences; **C**hoose an option; **C**heck your outcome—to find what you need on the Internet.

PART 2:

Again, using the rest of the 5Cs—Identify the **C**hoices; Predict the **C**onsequences; **C**hoose an option; **C**heck your outcome—search for the same information on your library database or at WorldCat.org and determine if there are libraries near you that have what you want.

GROUP APPLICATION: Compare your results with others in your group. Which search (Internet versus WorldCat databases) provided better results? In what way were they better?

Evaluating Worth

There's no one place where the Internet exists. It's really just a connected collection of computers around the world. Thus, no one owns or manages the Internet. As a result, no one checks the accuracy of what's on it. What you find could be truly worthy or just worthless. It may be legitimate news or just advertising. It may be obsolete or even obscene. Even sites sponsored by reputable institutions may contain inaccurate or flawed information. Thus, you have to evaluate every site you find. To do so, seek answers to some basic questions.

First, examine the source. Real people with real information generally don't mind putting their names or the names of their sponsors on their work. The site should also tell you how to reach the author or sponsor (physical address, phone number, or e-mail address). Credible sites often provide information that supports or verifies the information they contain. This might include a list of references or the professional experience or educational background of the author. If that information is unavailable, look at the sponsor's credentials.

For instance, perhaps you find information written by J. Doe as part of the NASA government website. Although you might not know who J. Doe is, you know that NASA is a credible source of information. If you don't recognize the author's name, try using it as the term on a search engine or search the Library of Congress Online Catalog (http://lcweb.loc.gov/catalog) or an online bookstore such as Amazon.com. A credible author often has several articles or books on the topic.

Next, determine the site's apparent purpose and target audience. Does it seem to be informational or commercial? Is it written in easily understandable language or technical jargon? Analyze the tone, or attitude, of the site. Is it serious (includes specific facts and data), humorous (provides outrageous details and ideas; spoof or hoax), or emotional (creates fear, anger, or sorrow)? Purpose also involves deciding if the site's content is nonacademic or academic. Nonacademic information is more general. Online encyclopedias (e.g., Britannica, Wikipedia) provide informational overviews, but are too general to use as resources at the college level. Academic resources are subject area journals and materials written by experts in the field. Your campus librarian can help you identify academic sources appropriate for the kind of research you need.

Third, note when the information was published. The importance of this factor depends on your purpose. Is what you need well-known and stable information (e.g., list of works by Mark Twain, names of state capitals), or do you need the latest news or research? Credible sites often include a *last date page updated* notation to show how current the information is. Also look at the links within the site. If you find several links that are no longer functioning (called "dead links"), then the site is not regularly maintained.

Fourth, assess the accuracy of the information. Consider how what you find in one site compares with information in other sites or in print materials. Determine if it includes facts and data or generalizations and suppositions. Check to see if the content has been reviewed or edited by others.

Finally, examine the content for evidence of bias. Ask what the author or sponsor wants you to do or believe and why. Look for ways in which the author or sponsor could profit from your actions or beliefs. If you have questions or concerns, e-mail the site's author/sponsor. You can also consult a librarian at your institution's library or ask your instructor for assistance.

Evaluating Websites

Go to the following websites, and evaluate each in terms of validity of the source, purpose of the site, recency of information, accuracy of information, and evidence of bias. Identify the spoofs and tell how you knew they were spoofs. *HINT: Two of the sites are spoofs intended to fool the reader.*

George Bush Presidential Library   http://www.bushlibrary.tamu.edu

National Rifle Association   http://www.nra.org

The Onion   http://www.theonion.com

The Green Party of the United States   http://www.gp.org

Dihydrogen Monoxide Research Division   http://www.DHMO.org

Choices in Electronic Access

course management system
An electronic message center that serves groups with similar interests.

Most colleges now have websites for the general public. However, colleges also have other online services such as grades, scheduling, or course-specific information that are only for enrolled students. Sometimes websites with campus-only information are called "portals."

Portals give you, the student, access to a vast array of information from current campus events to schedules of final exams. You access these from a computer terminal by using a log-on identification number (log-on ID) and a password. If you don't have these or have questions about using them, ask your instructors or advisor to refer you to the appropriate campus service.

Some faculty use **course management systems** such as Blackboard, Canvas or Moodle as integral parts of their course delivery. These are also accessed by a log-on ID and password. The management system looks like a kind of website and is used to facilitate course-specific communication and interactions. The instructor places assignments, resources, review questions, lecture notes, and other course materials there for student use. Students can also post comments and questions to the site. Other students can access comments and questions from other students and respond. The instructor adds to the discussion, clarifies questions or comments, and posts other messages for the entire class such as "Don't forget Friday's test," or "Class canceled on Wednesday." The instructor may require that students place electronic copies of completed assignments on the site. Exams can be taken online and scored as soon as the test is completed. The instructor can even ask students to meet online and discuss a topic together in a special chat area. If your instructor utilizes a course management system, it's important to know how to access and use it well before the time when an assignment is due or an exam is available. If you have problems, ask your instructor for help.

A library's holdings are the collection of books and other reading materials. They are available through a catalog either from computer terminals within the library or online from another site. You can search for documents or books by author, subject, or title. If you can't find what you need, you can contact your library's staff for help. Some libraries also provide links to instant message chats with librarians for immediate assistance.

In addition, libraries often subscribe to online database services that provide access to other science, social science, and humanities materials. You can have more confidence in the credibility of what you find because libraries specifically choose materials for their content and scholarly value. Because each library differs in the way its catalog is used and the other electronic services it provides, brief library orientation programs are often available. Library staff members are always on hand to answer questions and help you find what you need. Experts in the contents and use of your campus's library, library staff also know about materials and services of other libraries and can help you secure materials through an interlibrary loan. You can generally reach your campus librarian by e-mail or instant message as well as onsite.

Information Access Scavenger Hunt

Access your campus portal to answer the following questions:

1. What is the name of your campus portal?

_____

2. List three kinds of information available on it.

_____

_____

_____

If you use a course management system in one or more of your classes, answer questions 3–6. Otherwise, skip to question 7.

3. What communication tools are available?

_____

4. How do you submit assignments?

_____

5. How do you access your grades?

_____

6. What other tools are available?

_____

Access your campus library Web page to answer the following:

7. What are the library's hours?

_____

8. What is the policy on overdue books?

_____

9. Other than books, what materials can be checked out of the library?

_____

10. List three materials available on the library's electronic catalog.

_____; _____; _____

Rights and Responsibilities of Digital Citizenship

Digital citizenship involves the rights and responsibilities of technology use. The decisions you make about the use–or abuse–of technology or digital content define the kind of digital citizen you are. Ethical behavior regarding content on the Web and communication with others ultimately affects yourself.

❯ Choices in Using and Citing Content

Once you find information that is relevant and credible, what do you do with it? Some students use the computer's edit tools to copy and paste information until they have all the information they need. In practically no time, their papers are complete . . . aren't they?

Copying and pasting is fine as you collect information. But all Internet information is copyrighted at the moment of its creation whether it contains a specific copyright symbol or not. The content (everything from websites to e-mail communications) belongs to the person who developed or wrote it. "Borrowing" information by cutting and pasting it into your own document or electronic format without **citing** it is no different than using print information without referencing it. You must summarize what you find and cite electronic materials just as carefully as you would print materials.

citing
Telling the source of information.

Summarizing is much like recording the main ideas in your notes during a lecture (see Chapter 14). Both require you to record main points but there is a key difference. In lecture notes, you record all the main points. In summarizing, you record only what's important to your topic. Thus, you decide what to include. What you choose depends on its **relevance** or importance to your topic.

relevance
Importance to your topic.

You do not, of course, need to reference ideas that are your own. You also need not reference information that is commonly known (such as the dates of the American Revolution, a math formula, or symbols for chemical elements). When in doubt, your best bet is to cite the information you use. The same websites you used to find ways to cite online information can be used to get guidelines for citing print materials.

Just as there are ways to cite different kinds of print materials, there are ways to cite different kinds of electronic ones. The format you use depends on style manuals (e.g., APA Style, www.apa.org; MLA Style, www.mla.org; Columbia Guide to Online Style, www.columbia.edu/cu/cup/cgos/idx_basic.html). Ask your instructor to identify the one you should use. No matter which format you use, include the author (if known), the page's title, any publication information available (e.g., sponsor/publisher, date), URL, and the date you accessed the material. If the name of the author or the owner is not readily found, you can delete ending information from the URL to find the site's homepage. Usually, this means that you delete everything after the first slash (/) in the address.

There are rules about how much you can borrow from a source without citing it. Become familiar with those guidelines so that you don't plagiarize someone else's work.

To make sure that you do choose to act ethically by citing resources, many faculty require students to submit papers to online sites such as TurnItIn.com. This is used to reveal **plagiarism.** Plagiarism can be either unintentional or intentional. Unintentional, or accidental, plagiarism occurs through inaccurate notetaking, by incorrect citing of references, and/or from poor writing ability. Intentional plagiarism is deliberate, premeditated theft of another person's work or published information. Intentional plagiarism includes getting a paper from a friend or from a term paper service or copying information from a website and using it as your own. It results from poor time management, fear of not doing well, and pure laziness. While the motive for unintentional and intentional plagiarism differs, the punishment is the same.

> **plagiarism**
> Stealing another person's work and presenting it as your own.

Netiquette

Just as etiquette applies to proper rules of social behavior, **netiquette** describes expectations for proper behavior online. How you use the Internet to communicate and interact makes a difference to others and to yourself.

In terms of the format of an e-mail, include your full name and section identification (e.g., 2:30 T/TH class or online class 43897) in the body or subject line of your e-mails when corresponding with your instructor or classmates. They may not know you by your user name (e.g., JSmith34), or they may have more than one JSmith in their classes. Use the subject line to label the contents of your correspondence. This helps the recipients to whom you are writing gauge the response that will be required to your message without having to open your note. These subject labels are not as important when you are sending an e-mail within your course management system. Such e-mails are often part of an **intranet** which includes only those individuals in your course section.

> **netiquette**
> Abbreviation for Internet etiquette.

> **intranet**
> Internal network.

Beware of sending out jokes or personal notices to lots of recipients at once. Such "spam" is annoying to many people. Make sure that anyone you send this kind of information to really wants to receive it. Finally, don't mark e-mail as "urgent" or "priority" unless it really is.

The tone of your e-mails can be as important as what you write about. It's always a good idea to write, think, and revise before you send. Don't write anything that you wouldn't say in person. If you write in anger or frustration, reread your message *before* sending. Better yet, save your message and reread when you feel calmer.

Don't assume e-mail communications are private. Most electronic communications are stored somewhere on your computer and can be accessed at later times. Don't write anything you would not want everyone to see. Avoid using all-caps–it's perceived as yelling. Overuse of emoticons such as :) or :(can be annoying to some readers.

Because much of today's communications take place solely online, you can't always assume that people are who they say they are. Tabloids and TV news are filled with stories of people who formed relationships online only to find that their online "friends" took their money, love, identity, or even their lives. Unless you know someone in person, you should be wary. Beware of anyone or any company that asks for personal information or money or that seems "too good to be true."

In some ways, proper use of the Internet and other technologies also applies to yourself. Spending too much time online, missing work or school due to online activities, obsessive checking of e-mails and social networking sites, constant text messaging can affect relationships with others as well as your performance and productivity. Although it may seem like you're multitasking, you may actually be addicted to technology use. If you have a problem, awareness of it is the first step toward regaining the balance between your actual and virtual lives.

activity 5: Defining Plagiarism

For each of the following situations, circle Y (yes) if you think it is cheating or plagiarism, N (no) if you think it is NOT cheating, or D (depends) if there are specific circumstances under which the situation might or might not be considered as a form of cheating or plagiarism.

1. You are typing a paper for a friend who doesn't have time to finish the paper due to a work shift. As you type, you realize that the paper has a lot of misspelled words and quite a few grammatical mistakes. In addition, you think the paper lacks a good conclusion. As a helpful friend, you make the changes and add a couple of concluding paragraphs.   **Y   N   D**

2. You are taking a history course with Dr. Smith. Your roommate had Dr. Smith last semester and kept copies of Dr. Smith's exams. You use them to study for your tests.   **Y   N   D**

3. You are writing a term paper. You find many resources on the Internet. You copy sections from government websites because you know they are owned by the public and don't need to be cited. You paste them into your document and add a few transitional sentences of your own.   **Y   N   D**

4. Your instructor uses a personal website to provide your class with information. Prior to each class, the instructor posts a file which contains PowerPoint slides of key points in the lecture. You download the file to your own computer and print a copy.   **Y   N   D**

5. Your instructor does not have an attendance policy. You skip class because you prefer to sleep late. You get a copy of the notes from your roommate who never misses a class.   **Y   N   D**

GROUP APPLICATION: Compare your answers with other students in your group. Are your responses the same? Why or why not? What surprised you about the results? What did you learn?

Deciding to Become a Distance Learner

Distance learning sounds like a dream come true. You can log on to the class when you want. You can wear what you want. Bad weather and heavy traffic are no longer problems. What could be easier?

Although online classes do offer convenience, most distance learners report that they are actually harder than face-to face ones. Rather than a free-flowing course that you can complete on your own time, most online classes feature weekly content with scheduled tests, assignments, and assessments. The complexities of the course information systems sometimes result in technological glitches. Posted websites and content are not always available. Content that seemed clear in a lecture sometimes seems less organized in technological forms. You have to be vigilant in keeping up with due dates for responding to discussions, taking tests, or submitting assignments. Questions and comments have to be delayed until the instructor or other student responds to an e-mail. In addition, there's always something else at home or at work that needs to be done. Family and friends don't always see your online time as in-class time.

Many colleges offer courses in **hybrid** formats that blend face-to-face and distance learning. The distance learning component can consist of online, media (video or audio), print, or another source. Depending on how your college defines hybrid, the alternative format provides one-fourth to one-half of the content **synchronously** (at the same time) or **asynchronously** (not at the same time). Hybrid classes can form a good transition to fully online courses. They provide some classroom support while allowing opportunities to complete other activities independently.

Just as there is no one-size-fits-all online, there is no universal online experience. Just as faculty vary in the ways in which they organize face-to-face classes (few versus many tests, assignments, or other work), faculty differ in the ways in which they organize online classes. Factors in your own life change from term to term and can impact your online academic success either positively or negatively, too. The following chart identifies

hybrid courses
Blend of distance learning and face-to-face formats.

synchronously
Hybrid course content delivered at the same time.

asynchronously
Hybrid course content delivered not at the same time.

factors to consider as you decide about online courses: why these factors are important, how to analyze them, and their effect on your overall course success. No list, however, can cover every situation. There may be other factors that are unique to your situation. The factors that are problems in one semester may have no effect in another semester. Your success depends on how clearly you understand the challenge of your decision in terms of the present context, that is, all factors in the present situation that could impact your grades.

Consider the following decision factors each semester:

Factors	Why Important	How to Think About Them	Online Course Impact
Total number of credits in which you enroll	The more credits in which you are enrolled, the more course tasks you need to juggle.	At the end of a term, reflect on what went well and what needs to be changed. Consider relative difficulty of the courses you plan to take as well as other demands on your time and energy.	Online courses require you to be more self-motivated to maintain deadlines. If you have too many courses, you may find it difficult to keep up.
Relative difficulty of each course	More difficult courses require more time and effort.	Analyze each course you plan to take. Some faculty post copies of the course syllabus prior to the start of a class. You can also e-mail professors and see if they can send you a copy of the syllabus. Look at each syllabus to see what it demands in terms of time and energy. What are the reading demands? How many exams and what kind of exams are given? What kinds of course activities are assigned (e.g., group work, labs, online work, internships)? If possible, look at the course text in your college bookstore to get an idea of your current level of knowledge. The less you know about a topic, the more effort you will need to expend. Estimate how much time you will need on a weekly basis. Try to balance a demanding course with one or two less difficult courses. You should rate no more than half your courses as "difficult" for you.	When possible, choose hybrid or traditional classroom options for more difficult courses because they provide more structure and face-to-face assistance from faculty. Less difficult courses can be managed more easily in online formats. If you must take a more difficult course in an online format, create a calendar of due dates and reminders. Look for and use any supplemental forms of learning (e.g., tutoring centers; online tutoring services; academic success centers). Consider forming a virtual or face-to-face study group to review course content. Don't hesitate to contact your instructor when you have questions or concerns.

Factors	Why Important	How to Think About Them	Online Course Impact
Life changes	Work, family, other life demands impact time and energy.	Change is really the only constant in life, but changes come and go. For example, you may play a sport (e.g., baseball) that has more demands in the spring than in the summer or fall terms. Children's school or vacation schedules could affect the time you have available to study.	As well as possible, predict the changes that might impact the time you have for online learning. There are times when online classes are the only way to remain in school and keep up with new work schedules or other life demands. On the other hand, jobs and life can also prevent you from having enough time online to achieve academic success.
Technology	New and/or fewer technology options impact success.	Getting new hardware or software or learning a new management system often involves a learning curve as you acclimate to the new system. Or, you may lose access to technology through a move, relationship change, or other cause.	Online courses require you to have consistent and ongoing access to course content. Although you may be able to use a cell phone for many tasks, you shouldn't rely on it for your only form of access. If you don't have access at home, your campus will have computers available in either labs, the library, or other location. Most public libraries also provide computers. If you have a computer/tablet but no regular Internet provider, look for wifi access on campus or at a local hotspot.
Tech support	The complexities of technology often cause problems.	Course management systems are complex. Often a change to one part of the system has an impact on another part. And, sometimes, there are "known problems" that haven't yet been solved. Find out if there is help available, that is, if there is good tech support for you.	Most course management systems have tutorials to help you maximize your use of their components. Completing these tutorials at the beginning of a class will maximize your success in the course. Know how to reach tech support on your campus in case other problems occur.

Becoming a distance learner can be the best–or the worst–decision you make. Taking a traditional face-to-face class that also uses the course management system to deliver some content can provide you with experience, and experience is one way to learn more about the format. Talking to your advisor or other students can provide other insights about distance learning at your college.

At the end of an online course, evaluate your performance so that you can either repeat successful efforts or improve them in the future.

	Yes/Always	Sometimes	Rarely	No/Never
I made the grade I intended to make in the course.				
I never missed a course deadline.				
I contacted my instructor whenever I had a question.				
I participated in online discussions.				
I was able to manage my time effectively to complete coursework.				
I had consistent access to online content.				
I checked into the course management system daily.				
I felt I was part of a learning community.				
I never missed any assignments or points because I didn't know how to use one of the course management components.				

Are You Ready to Be a Distance Learner?

Are online courses for me? Take this quick questionnaire to find out.

1. My need to take this course now is:

   a. High. I need it immediately for degree, job, or other important reason

   b. Moderate. I could take it on campus later or substitute another course

   c. Low. It's a personal interest that could be postponed

2. Feeling that I am part of a class is:

   a. Not particularly necessary for me

   b. Somewhat important to me

   c. Very important to me

3. I would characterize myself as someone who:

   a. Often gets things done ahead of time

   b. Needs reminding to get things done on time

   c. Puts things off until the last minute

4. Classroom discussion is:

   a. Not necessary for me to understand what I have read

   b. Sometimes helpful to me

   c. Almost always helpful to me

5. When an instructor hands out directions for an assignment, I prefer:

   a. Figuring out the instructions myself

   b. Trying to follow the instructions on my own, then asking for help if I need it

   c. Having the instructions explained to me

6. I need instructor comments on my assignments:

   a. Within a few days, so I can review what I did

   b. Within a few hours, or I forget what I did

   c. Right away, or I get frustrated

7. Considering my job and personal schedule, the amount of time I have to work on an online class is:

   a. More than enough for a campus class or a distance learning class

   b. The same as for a class on campus

   c. Less than for a class on campus

8. When I am asked to use computers, voice mail, or other technologies that are new to me:

   a. I look forward to learning new skills

   b. I feel apprehensive, but try anyway

   c. I put it off or try to avoid it

9. As a reader, I would classify myself as:

   a. Good. I usually understand the text and other written materials without help

   b. Average. I sometimes need help to understand the text or other written materials

   c. Needing help to understand the text or other written materials

10. As a writer I would classify myself as:

    a. A strong writer. I am comfortable with writing and have strong organizational, grammar, punctuation and spelling skills

    b. An average writer. I am moderately comfortable with writing and occasionally need help with organization, grammar, punctuation and spelling

    c. Needing help with my writing, especially with organization, grammar, punctuation, and spelling

11. I have dropped a college class after the term has started:

    a. Never

    b. Once

    c. More than once

Scoring: Add 3 points for each "a" that you selected, 2 for each "b," and 1 for each "c." If you scored:

28 and over: You may be a self-motivated independent learner, and online courses are a real possibility for you.

15–27: Online courses may work for you, but you may need to make a few adjustments in your schedule and study habits in order to succeed. Online courses take at least as much time and effort and in some cases more than traditional face-to-face classes.

14 or less: Online courses may not be currently the best alternative for you. Online courses take at least as much time and effort and in some cases more than traditional face-to-face classes.

chapter review

Respond to the following on a separate sheet of paper or in your notebook.

1. How do you feel the concept of college access relate to learning in the digital age?

2. What did you learn about yourself as a learner in the digital age?

3. Is evaluation often a more important skill for Internet information than for print information? Why do you believe this?

4. What should you include when citing an Internet source?

5. Describe the process for using your college's library catalog.

6. Does your college use course management systems to deliver some of its courses? How could you find out?

7. Describe the Dodge search processes of 3M and NETS. How would they enable you to search more effectively?

8. What is your college's plagiarism policy?

9. What technology do you use most often? How can you adapt this for use in studying?

did you decide?

Did you accomplish what you wanted to in this chapter? Check the items below that apply to you.

Review the *You Decide* questions that you identified at the beginning of the chapter, but look at them from a new direction. If you didn't check an item below, review that module until you feel you can confidently apply the strategies to your own situations. However, the best ideas are worthless unless they are put into effect. Use the 5Cs to help you decide what information you found most helpful in the chapter and how you plan to use it. Record your comments after the statements below.

☐ 3.1 I know the computer skills I need to improve to be successful in college.

_____

☐ 3.2 I know how to search the Web to help me succeed.

_____

☐ 3.3 I understand how to assess the value of what I find on the Web.

_____

☐ 3.4 I am able to use electronic course content, e-mail, and campus portals.

_____

☐ 3.5 I grasp the rights and responsibilities that come with using technology.

_____

☐ 3.6 I know whether distance learning courses fit my needs.

_____

perspectives

As a college student, you will probably use the Internet and other electronic formats to learn and communicate. The following article from a college newspaper by Richard Okagbue discusses how the internet can befriend you or not.

Think about and answer the questions that follow.

1. Do you see the Internet as "good" or "bad" for society? For students? Why?
2. What kind of "friend" is the Internet to you?
3. Where does the writer put the blame for the "bad" things on the Internet? Do you agree? Why?
4. This article was written in 2002. How has the role of the Internet changed in the last decade?
5. Imagine that you have a friend who is concerned about Internet security. Use the 5C process to convince your friend that this concern is unfounded.

   A. What's your **C**hallenge?
   B. What **C**hoices does a person have in terms of using the Internet (both safely and unsafely)?
   C. What's the major **C**onsequence(s) of each choice?
   D. What would be the best **C**hoice?
   E. How could the outcome of the decision be **C**hecked to address security concerns?

Imagine the Internet as a human being, with all the features of humans including the ability to experience different emotions and to speak out to protect itself. Then, take about 30 minutes each morning to browse various news websites and read all the bad stuff that is being said about the Internet. Next, get back to your imagination that the Internet is a human being.—What do you think its response is to all that is said about it?

My opinion is that the Internet is crying out, "I am a friend, please stop making me look bad," or a variation of that because so much is blamed on the Internet every day. Once in a while, the Internet receives some praise for the good it has delivered to our lives. Nevertheless, when compared to how much it is criticized and made to look bad, I wouldn't consider any of the positive comments regarding the Internet as any form of praise.

It seems everything bad is blamed on the Internet lately, including children accessing pornography, children going to chat rooms and newsgroups and learning all sorts of bad stuff

there, people having their credit cards accessed by strangers who use complex computer skills to steal their credit card numbers, extramarital affairs resulting from Internet chats, etc. The list goes on forever and may never end.

Like I already said, the Internet is our friend, and a very welcome one at that. A friend that delivers all that it promises and much more. A friend that never really wants anything from us but is always willing to give us nearly anything we want. I don't think there are any friends like that in this world. The Internet is one of a kind.

Let's face it, the Internet is perhaps the very best thing that has happened to the computer industry during the 90s. In fact some people deeply involved in the computer industry have such high regard for the Internet that they named it the best thing to ever happen in the history of computing. And since the involvement of computing in our lives has increased immeasurably during the 90s, one wouldn't be so wrong in saying that the Internet is also one of the best things to ever happen to our lives.

Then, why do we have this hostile treatment towards it? Is it some unknown problem with us humans that makes us unable to appreciate such a good thing as the Internet? I don't know and I suppose nobody knows, but any form of explanation would be greatly appreciated.

We can't blame *anything* bad on the Internet! Are your kids now able to view pornography on the Internet? Well, if your answer to the above question is yes, then you better supervise their Web activities. Various software packages are available which can monitor all the websites visited on a computer. If you tell your kids to stop viewing pornography and they don't, *get rid of the Internet from your home computer*. It won't kill them, or you. Before we unleash any complaints on the Internet, we should remember one important thing: nobody is forcing us to use it.

We use it by our own choice and as a result we bear all the risks associated with its usage. If some Web hackers are able to obtain someone's credit card number and use it for their own personal gain, then as much as that is unfortunate to that person, it is a risk he or she takes once they use their credit card online. It's just like our daily activities.

When someone uses his or her credit card in a supermarket and it gets stolen, then it is pretty much the same story. But rarely do we blame the supermarket for the loss of our cards because we know that no one forced us to shop there with them instead of using cash or check. Additionally, we know that truly the loss of our credit cards is not the supermarket's fault.

However, chances are that if a Web hacker uses one's credit card number he/she will complain about it and blame it on the Internet. Why does the Internet have to get the bad treatment? Well, for one thing, it can't speak out to defend itself, it can't sue us for our bad, unfair comments against it, and generally speaking, it can't do anything about the way we treat it. In other words we just keep blaming all sorts of bad things on the Internet because it can't react back, it is helpless.

The Internet was created by human beings and is also used by human beings. Since this is so, we should expect all the risks we face in our daily lives to exist on the Internet. In fact the risks are greater on the Internet because it is such a great medium that it allows everyone to do whatever they want to do to the best of their abilities.

This means that hackers get to do great hacking and people who just intend to improve their lives by using the Internet also get to improve their lives a great deal. It's a two-way deal: if you want the good things online then you have to risk the bad things along the way.

Another thing we can expect and do experience on the Internet is its lack of perfection. When you really get to think about it, you will realize that the Internet isn't perfect because it was created by human beings and is used by human beings. Since we ourselves aren't even close to perfection, the Internet will remain imperfect. We are the ones who create all the bad websites that are unhealthy for our children. We are also responsible for the creation and distribution of all those viruses.

We shouldn't blame anything on our dear friend the Internet. We should be blaming everything on ourselves.

reflecting on decisions

Now that you have learned about using the Internet for class, what kinds of decisions will you be making about information on the Web?

DONATING BY
SEARCHING

Search engines help you find the information you need on the Internet. To finance their work, most search engines use advertisements. Some socially conscious search engines donate a part of their advertisement revenues to charity. These search engines work just like Google or Yahoo in terms of what you see. So using one of these search engines is a no-cost way you can support a favorite cause. Visit the sites, choose a search engine, and begin donating.

- CatchTommorow (http://catchtomorrow.com/) Supports public education in your state

- Clicks4Cancer (http://www.clicks4cancer.com/) Supports cancer research and charity

- GoodSearch (http://www.goodsearch.com/) Supports a school or charity of your choice

- GoodTree (http://goodtree.com/) Supports a variety of causes of which you choose a selection

- Ripple (http://www.ripple.org/) Supports one of four social issues in third world countries

◀ CHOOSING TO SERVE

REVIEW

Skim the notes you made throughout the chapter. How does the content fit together? What information is still unclear? Were your learning goals met? Can you answer the review questions and define terms?

◀ CHOOSING TO BE AN ACTIVE LEARNER

Module 2
Motivation & Goal Setting

Expand Your Emotional Intelligence

LEARNING OUTCOMES

In this chapter, you will learn to

4.1 Describe emotional intelligence and the key personal qualities

4.2 Explain the importance of good character, including integrity, civility, and ethics

4.3 Demonstrate responsibility, self-management, and self-control

4.4 Define self-esteem and confidence

4.5 Incorporate a positive attitude and motivation

4.6 List the benefits of a higher education

SELF-MANAGEMENT

" On my commute to class, a car cut me off. I was furious and yelled at the driver. I was fuming and distracted during classes, and later I blew up at a co-worker. This just ruined my entire day. How can I handle my angry feelings in a more constructive way? "

Have you ever had a similar experience? Are you easily offended by what others do or say? Have you said things in anger that have caused a rift in a relationship? In this chapter, you will learn how to control your emotions and create a positive and resourceful state of mind.

JOURNAL ENTRY In **Worksheet 4.1** on page 112, describe a time when you were angry and lost control of your emotions. How did you feel? How did others react to your outburst? What would you do differently? Visualize yourself calm and in control, and realize you have a choice in how you interpret events.

There is a tendency to define intelligence as a score on an IQ test or the SAT or as school grades. Educators trying to predict who will succeed in college have found that high school grades, achievement test scores, and ability are only part of the picture. Emotional intelligence and maturity have more effect on school and job success than traditional scholastic measures. In fact, research has indicated that persistence and perseverance are major predictors of college success. A landmark study by the American College Test (ACT) indicated that the primary reasons for first-year students' dropping out of college were not academic but, rather, emotional difficulties, such as feelings of inadequacy, depression, loneliness, and a lack of motivation or purpose.

Employers list a positive attitude, motivation, honesty, the ability to get along with others, and the willingness to learn as more important to job success than a college degree or specific skills. SCANS identifies many personal qualities as important competencies for success in the workplace. These qualities and competencies are also essential for building and maintaining strong, healthy relationships throughout life. Essential personal qualities should be viewed as a foundation on which to build skills, experience, and knowledge.

In this chapter, you will learn the importance of emotional intelligence and why character is so important for school and job success. You will also develop personal strategies for maintaining a positive attitude and becoming self-motivated. You may realize that you are smarter than you think. You are smarter than your test scores or grades. Success in your personal life, school, and career depends more on a positive attitude, motivation, responsibility, self-control, and effort than on inborn abilities or a high IQ. Peak performers use the whole of their intelligence.

Emotional Intelligence and Maturity

Emotional intelligence is the ability to understand and manage yourself and relate effectively to others. **Maturity** is the ability to control your impulses, think beyond the moment, and consider how your words and actions affect yourself and others before you act. People who have developed a set of traits that adds to their maturity level increase their sense of well-being, get along better with others, and enhance their school, job, and life success.

Emotional maturity contributes to competent behavior, problem-solving ability, socially appropriate behavior, and good communication. Being unaware of or unable to control emotions often accompanies restlessness, a short attention span, negativism, impatience, impulsiveness, and distractibility. Clearly, having emotional intelligence distinguishes peak performers from mediocre ones. Becoming more emotionally mature involves three stages:

1. Self-awareness—tuning in to yourself
2. Empathy—tuning in to others
3. Change—tuning in to results

You explored strategies to increase your self-awareness and tune in to yourself. You assessed your skills and personal qualities in the Peak Performance Self-Assessment Test. By learning personality types, you also began to tune in to others as well. The central theme of this book is that you can use self-management to begin changing your thoughts, images, and behaviors to produce the results you want in every aspect of your life. Enhancing your emotional intelligence and focusing on positive personal qualities are key to achieving those results.

Character First: Integrity, Civility, and Ethics

Good **character** is an essential personal quality for true success. A person of good character has a core set of principles that most of us accept as constant and relatively noncontroversial. These principles include fairness, honesty, respect, responsibility, caring, trustworthiness, and citizenship. Surveys of business leaders indicate that dishonesty, lying, and lack of respect are top reasons for on-the-job difficulties. If an employer believes an employee lacks integrity, all of that person's positive qualities—from skill and experience to productivity and intelligence—are meaningless. Employers usually list honesty or good character as an essential personal quality, followed by the ability to relate to and get along with others.

Following The Golden Rule (treating others as we want to be treated) is a simple way to weave integrity and civility into our everyday lives. The word **integrity** comes from the Latin word *integre,* meaning "wholeness." Integrity is the integration of your principles and actions. In a sense, people who have integrity "walk the talk" by consistently living up to their highest principles. Integrity is not adherence to a rigid code but, rather, an ongoing commitment to being consistent, caring, and true to doing what is right—and the courage to do it even when it is difficult.

Civility is a set of tools for treating others with respect, kindness, and good manners, or etiquette. It also includes the sacrifices we make each day so that we live together peacefully. Civility (like integrity) requires **empathy**—understanding of and compassion for others. You can practice civility in your classes by being on time, turning off your cell phone, staying for the entire class, and listening to the instructor and other students when they speak.

Ethics are the principles of conduct that govern a group or society. Because a company's reputation is its most important asset, most organizations have a written code of ethics that describes how people are expected to behave. It is your responsibility to know and understand the code of ethics at your place of employment and at school. Look on your school's website for statements regarding academic integrity, honesty, cheating, and plagiarism. **Cheating** is using or providing unauthorized help in test taking or on projects. One form of cheating is **plagiarism**, which means presenting someone else's ideas as if they were your own. The consequences of unethical behavior could result in an *F* grade, suspension, expulsion, or firing from a job. You always have the choice of telling the truth and being responsible for your own work.

WORDS TO SUCCEED

> **"**Character is like a tree and reputation like its shadow. The shadow is what we think of it; the tree is the real thing.**"**
>
> ABRAHAM LINCOLN
> *U.S. president*

● **Be a "Class Act"**
These may seem like harmless acts, but they are clear examples of disrespect—for your instructor, your classmates, and your education. *How would an employer respond to this behavior on the job?*

Incivility in the Classroom

- Walking in late
- Ringing cell phones
- Falling asleep
- Texting
- Blurting out questions
- Interrupting classmates
- Talking during lecture
- Leaving early

Devon's midterm exam will determine 50 percent of his final grade. He's been so busy at home and his part-time job that he skipped class and study group all last week. He's afraid of bombing the exam, and someone he met in the cafeteria tells him he can buy a copy of the test.

- If he buys it, what are the repercussions if he gets caught?
- What are potential repercussions if he *doesn't* get caught?
- What would you do to prepare for the exam?

THINK FAST

"The measure of a man's character is what he would do if he knew he never would be found out."

THOMAS MACAULAY
British writer and politician

Every day, you run into situations that test your character. **Personal Evaluation Notebook 4.1** includes questions and situations to get you thinking about your experiences. While completing this exercise, consider the personal qualities that make you smarter than you think you are, such as positive attitude, motivation, dependability, and honesty—for example, "I was raised on a farm in Michigan. What personal quality makes me smarter than my IQ or test scores?" If you answer "hard work," you're right. That one personal quality—putting in extra effort—has helped many people be more successful in life.

Personal qualities, especially honesty, are very important when you are think of hiring someone to work for a business you own. A candidate sends in an outstanding resumè. She has a college degree, experience, and a great personality, and she is positive and motivated, but you find out she stole from her last employer. No matter how bright or talented someone is, you don't want a dishonest person working for you. Complete **Personal Evaluation Notebook 4.2** on page 90 to see what qualities you would look for in a potential employee and which of those qualities you possess.

There is no universal code of ethics, and many questions about ethical issues do not have clear-cut answers. For example, taking money out of a cash drawer is clearly dishonest, but what about coming in late to work, padding your expense account, or using someone else's words without giving credit? You will be faced with situations in your personal, school, and business lives that will force you to make decisions that will be viewed as either ethical or unethical. Sometimes it is not easy. You will have to call on your own personal code of ethics. When defining your code and subsequent actions, you may find the following questions helpful:

- Is this action against the law?
- Is this action against company policy or code of behavior?
- How would this situation read if reported on the front page of the newspaper?
- How would you explain this to your mother? To your child?
- What might be the negative consequences?
- Are you causing unnecessary harm to someone?
- If unsure, have you asked a trusted associate outside of the situation?
- Are you treating others as you would want to be treated?

Remember, unethical behavior rarely goes unnoticed!

Responsibility

Peak performers take responsibility for their thoughts, state of mind, and behavior. They don't blame others for their problems but, rather, use their energy to solve them. They are persistent and patient and exert a consistently high effort to achieve their goals. When they say they are going to do something, they keep their commitment. People can depend on them.

Personal Evaluation Notebook

4.1

Character and Ethics

Integrity and honesty are essential qualities. It is important for you to assess and develop them as you would any skill. Use critical thinking to answer these questions.

1. What is the most difficult ethical dilemma you have faced in your life?

   _____

   _____

2. Do you have a code of ethics that helps guide you when making decisions? Explain.

   _____

   _____

3. Who have you known that is a role model for displaying integrity and honesty?

   _____

   _____

4. Do you have a code of ethics at your college? Where did you find it? (Hint: Check your school's website or ask the dean of students.)

   _____

   _____

Examples of being responsible include showing up on time and prepared for class, work, meetings, study teams, and so on. Responsible people own up to their mistakes and do what they can to correct them. The model in **Figure 4.1** on page 90 illustrates many important, interrelated personal responsibilities. Other personal qualities related to responsibility include perseverance, punctuality, concentration, attention to details, follow-through, high standards, and respect for others.

Peak performers realize they are responsible for their attitudes and actions and know they have the power to change. They have an **internal locus of control**, meaning they believe that they have control over their lives and that their rewards or failures are a result of their behavior, choices, or character. People with an **external locus of control** credit outside influences, such as fate, luck, or other people, with their success or failure. They are impulsive about immediate pleasures and easily swayed by the influences of others, and they often have a negative attitude and an inability to cope effectively with change, conflict, and frustration.

Learning to adjust to frustration and discouragement can take many forms. Some people withdraw or become critical, cynical, shy, sarcastic, or unmotivated. Blame, excuses, justification, and criticism of others are devices for those who cannot accept personal responsibility. Acknowledge your feelings and attitudes. Decide if they support your goals; if they do not, adopt a state of mind and actions that do.

Personal Evaluation Notebook

Skills and Personal Qualities

1. Jot down the skills, personal qualities, and habits you are learning and demonstrating in each of your classes.

Skills	Personal Qualities	Habits
_____	_____	_____
_____	_____	_____
_____	_____	_____

2. Pretend you own a business. List the skills and personal qualities you would want in your employees. *Which answers also appear in your lists above?*

Type of business: _____

Employees' Skills	Employees' Personal Qualities
_____	_____
_____	_____
_____	_____

Figure 4.1
Personal Responsibilities

What you do or don't do in one area of life can affect other areas of your life and other people. *What one area of personal responsibility would you improve?*

Being responsible creates a sense of integrity and a feeling of self-worth. For example, if you owe someone money or have a student loan, take responsibility for repaying the debt on schedule or make new arrangements with the lender. Not repaying can result in years of guilt and embarrassment, as well as a poor credit rating. It is important to your self-worth to know you are a person who keeps commitments and assumes responsibility.

Self-Control

If anger were a disease, there would be an epidemic in this country. Road rage, spousal and child abuse, and a lack of civility are just a few examples. Emotionally mature people know how to control their thoughts and behaviors and how to resolve conflict. Conflict is an inevitable part of school and work, but it can be resolved in a positive way. Try these tips for redirecting and transforming your anger:

1. **Calm down.** Step back from the situation and take a deep breath. Take the drama out of the situation and observe what is happening, what behavior is triggering angry emotions, and what options you have in responding appropriately and positively. If you lash out verbally, you may cause serious harm to your relationship. You cannot take back words once they are spoken. Resist the urge to overreact.

2. **Clarify and define.** Determine exactly with whom or what you are angry and why. What specific behavior in the other person is causing your anger or frustration? Determine whose problem it is. For example, your instructor may have an annoying tone and style of lecturing. If a behavior annoys only you, perhaps it is something you alone need to address.

3. **Listen with empathy and respect.** Empathy includes the ability to listen, understand, and respond to the feelings and needs of others. Take the tension out of the conflict by really listening and understanding the other person's point of view. Communicate that you have heard and understood by restating the other person's position.

4. **Use "I" statements.** Take ownership of your feelings. Using "I" statements—direct messages you deliver in a calm tone with supportive body language—can diffuse anger. Instead of blaming another person, express how a situation affects you. For example, you can say, "Carlos, when I hear you clicking your pen and tapping it on the desk, I'm distracted from studying." This is usually received better than saying, "Carlos, you're so rude and inconsiderate. You're driving me nuts with that pen!"

5. **Focus on one problem.** Don't rattle off every annoying behavior you can think of. Let's continue with the previous example: "In addition to clicking your pen, Carlos, I don't like how you leave your dishes in the sink, drop your towels in the bathroom, and make that annoying little sound when you eat." Work to resolve only one behavior or conflict at a time.

6. **Focus on win–win solutions.** How can you both win? Restate the problem and jot down as many different creative solutions as you can both agree on.

Don't let anger and conflict create more stress in your life and take a physical and emotional toll. You can learn to step back automatically from explosive situations

> **"Holding onto anger is like grasping a hot coal with the intent of throwing it at someone else; you are the one who gets burned."**
>
> BUDDHA

WORDS TO SUCCEED

and control them, rather than let your emotions control you. **Peak Progress 4.1** explores how you can use the Adult Learning Cycle to manage your emotions.

Self-Esteem and Confidence

Self-esteem is how you feel about yourself. People with positive self-esteem have the confidence that allows them to be more open to new experiences and accepting of different people. They tend to be more optimistic. They are more willing to share their feelings and ideas with others and are willing to tolerate differences in others. Because they have a sense of self-worth, they do not feel a need to put down or discriminate against others.

Confidence can develop from

- Focusing on your strengths and positive qualities and finding ways to bolster them. Be yourself and don't compare yourself with others.
- Learning to be resilient and bouncing back after disappointments and setbacks. Don't dwell on mistakes or limitations. Accept them, learn from them, and move on with your life.
- Using affirmations and visualizations to replace negative thoughts and images.
- Taking responsibility for your life instead of blaming others. You cannot control other people's behavior, but you have control over your own thoughts, emotions, words, and behavior.
- Learning skills that give you opportunities and confidence in your abilities. It is not enough to feel good about yourself; you must also be able to do what is

Peak Progress

Applying the Adult Learning Cycle to Self-Control

The Adult Learning Cycle can help you increase your emotional intelligence. For example, you may have felt the same anger and frustration mentioned in the Self-Management exercise on the first page of this chapter. Maybe it happened when you lost your keys, had three papers due, or felt so overwhelmed with responsibilities that you developed a negative attitude.

1. **RELATE. Why do I want to learn this?** What personal meaning and interest does controlling my anger have for me? Has it been a challenge? Has it hurt important relationships in my personal life or at school or work? How will controlling my anger help me in those situations?

2. **OBSERVE. How does this work?** I can learn a lot about anger management by watching, listening, and engaging in trial and error. Whom do I consider an emotionally mature person? Whom do I respect because of his or her patience, understanding, and

ability to deal with stressful events? When I observe the problems other people have, how do they exhibit their emotional maturity in general and anger specifically?

3. **REFLECT. What does this mean?** Test new ways of behaving, and break old patterns. Explore creative ways to solve problems instead of getting angry. Look into anger management strategies, and reflect on what works and doesn't work.

4. **DO. What can I do with this?** Learn by doing and finding practical applications for anger management. Practice the steps outlined on page 91. Apply the ABC Method of Self-Management to situations to determine positive outcomes.

5. **TEACH. Whom can I share this with?** Talk with others and share experiences. Model by example.

Now return to Stage 1 and realize your accomplishment in taking steps to control your anger better.

required to demonstrate that you are competent, honest, and responsible. The more skills and personal qualities you acquire, the more confident you will feel.

- Focusing on giving, not receiving, and make others feel valued and appreciated. You will increase your self-esteem when you make a contribution.

- Surrounding yourself with confident and kind people who feel good about themselves and make you feel good about yourself.

If you want to change your outer world and experiences for the better, you must begin by looking at your thoughts, feelings, and beliefs about yourself. Assess your self-esteem at the end of the chapter in **Worksheet 4.3** on page 114.

A Positive Attitude and Personal Motivation

There is an old story about three men working on a project in a large city in France. A curious tourist asks them, "What are you three working on?" The first man says, "I'm hauling rocks." The second man says, "I'm laying a wall." The third man says with pride, "I'm building a cathedral." The third man has a vision of the whole system. When college and work seem as tedious as hauling rocks, focus on the big picture.

Your attitude, possibly more than any other factor, influences the outcome of a task. **Motivation** is the inner drive that moves you to action. Even when you are discouraged or face setbacks, motivation can help you keep on track. You may have skills, experience, intelligence, and talent, but you will accomplish little if you are not motivated to direct your energies toward specific goals.

A positive attitude results in enthusiasm, vitality, optimism, and a zest for living. When you have a positive attitude, you are more likely to be on time, alert in meetings and class, and able to work well even on an unpleasant assignment. A negative attitude can drain you of enthusiasm and energy. It can result in absenteeism, tardiness, and impaired mental and physical health.

A Positive Attitude Encourages:

- Higher productivity
- An openness to learning at school and on the job
- School and job satisfaction
- Creativity in solving problems and finding solutions
- The ability to work with diverse groups of people
- Enthusiasm and a "can do" outlook
- Confidence and higher self-esteem
- The ability to channel stress and increase energy
- A sense of purpose and direction

A Negative Attitude Makes You:

- Feel like a victim and helpless to make a change
- Focus on the worst that can happen in a situation
- Blame external circumstances for your attitude
- Focus on the negative in people and situations
- Believe adversity will last forever
- Be angry and blame other people

Take 3 minutes right now and make a list of all the positives in your life:

- What opportunities do you have that your parents or grandparents didn't?
- Who is there to support you when you need help?
- Who or what on the list makes you the happiest?

What else can you do in 3 minutes?

- Write down anything negative that happened today, the outcome, and how it could be addressed the next time.
- Close your eyes, breathe deeply, and meditate to relieve the day's stressors.
- Make a list of commitments you must keep tomorrow.

Take 3

As discussed, peak performers display a positive attitude even when faced with adversity. Having a positive attitude is more than simply seeing the glass as half full—it's a way of life.

How Needs and Desires Influence Attitudes and Motivation

One of the deepest needs in life is to become all that you can be by using all of your intelligence and potential. Abraham Maslow, a well-known psychologist, developed the theory of a hierarchy of needs. According to his theory, there are five levels of universal needs. **Figure 4.2** illustrates these levels, moving from the lower-order needs—physiological and safety and security needs—to the higher-order needs—the needs for self-esteem and self-actualization. Your lower-order needs must be met first before you can satisfy your higher-order needs. For example, participating in hobbies that foster your self-respect is difficult if you don't have enough money for food and rent. For some people, the lower-order needs include a sense of order, power, or independence. The higher levels, which address social and self-esteem factors, include the need for companionship, respect, and a sense of belonging.

As your lower-order needs are satisfied and cease to motivate you, you begin to direct your attention to the higher-order needs for motivation. As you go up the

Figure 4.2

Maslow's Hierarchy of Needs

Maslow's theory states that most people need to satisfy the universal basic needs before considering the higher-order needs. *Which level of needs is motivating you right now?*

Level	Needs	Job-Related Satisfiers
Self-Actualization	Creativity, spontaneity, problem solving, morality, lack of prejudice, acceptance of facts	Strategic planning, freedom to make decisions, creative work, opportunities for growth and development
Self-Esteem	Positive self-image, confidence, achievement, respect of others, respect by others	Merit awards, challenging work, sharing in decisions, opportunity for advancement
Love/Belonging	Friendship, family, intimacy	Interaction with others, team spirit, collaborative co-workers
Safety and Security	Security of body, health, family, employment, property	Safe working conditions, seniority, fringe benefits, supervision, sound company policies, programs, and practices
Physiological Needs	Breathing, food, water, sleep	Pleasant working conditions, adequate wages, rest periods, efficient work methods

Source: "Hierarchy of Needs" from *Motivation and Personality*, 3rd ed., by Abraham H. Maslow. Revised by Robert Frager, James Fadiman, Cynthia McReynolds, and Ruth Cox. Copyright 1954, © 1987 by Harper & Row, Publishers, Inc. Copyright © 1970 by Abraham H. Maslow. Reprinted by permission of HarperCollins, Inc.

Personal Evaluation Notebook

4.3

Needs, Motivation, and Commitment

1. What needs motivate you at this time?

   _____

   _____

2. What do you think will motivate you in 20 years?

   _____

   _____

3. Complete this sentence in your own words: "For me to be more motivated, I need . . . "

   _____

   _____

4. Describe a time in your life when you were committed to something—such as a goal, a project, an event, or a relationship—that was important to you.

   _____

   _____

5. Regarding your answer to Question 4, what kept you motivated?

   _____

   _____

ladder of higher-order needs, you'll find that you're learning for the joy of new ideas and the confidence that comes from learning new skills. You have more energy and focus for defining and pursuing your dreams and goals. You want to discover and develop your full potential. You not only love learning new ideas but also value emotional maturity, character, and integrity. You are well on the path to self-actualization. According to Maslow, self-actualizing people embrace the realities of the world rather than deny or avoid them. They are creative problem solvers who make the most of their unique abilities to strive to be the best they can be. Complete **Personal Evaluation Notebook 4.3** to assess what motivates you.

The Motivation Cycle

The motivation cycle in **Figure 4.3** on page 96 amplifies what you learned about the power of visualization. It illustrates how your self-esteem influences what you say to yourself, which in turn influences your physical reactions—breathing, muscular tension, and posture. These physical reactions influence your behavior—both your verbal and your nonverbal responses. Your emotions, body, and mind are interrelated—if you change one part, you change the whole system.

Figure 4.3
The Motivation Cycle

Your emotions, body, and mind respond to what you say to yourself. *What positive message can you send to yourself?*

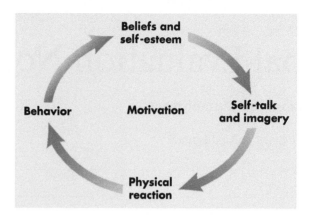

Motivational Strategies

Keeping yourself motivated isn't always easy when you're feeling pressures from school, work, and family. However, you can use these motivational strategies:

1. **Act as if you are motivated.** Your attitude influences your behavior, and behavior influences attitude. The key is to first make a personal commitment to remaining positive and motivated.

   For example, pretend you are performing in a movie. Your character is a positive, motivated student. How do you enter the room? Are you smiling? What are your breathing, posture, and muscle tension like? What kinds of gestures and facial expressions do you use to create this character? What kinds of friends does this person enjoy being with? If you develop positive study and work habits and do them consistently, even when you don't feel like it, you'll be successful, and this will create a positive state of mind.

2. **Use affirmations.** Any discussion of motivation must include your self-talk, what you say to yourself throughout the day. Once you start paying attention to your self-talk, you may be amazed at how much of it is negative. Countless thoughts, images, and phrases go through your brain daily almost unnoticed, but they have a tremendous influence on your mood and attitude. The first step, then, is to replace negative self-talk with affirmations (positive self-talk). For example, don't say, "I won't waste my time today." Instead, affirm, "I am setting goals and priorities and achieving the results I want. I have plenty of energy to accomplish all that I choose to do, and I feel good when I'm organized and centered." Complete **Personal Evaluation Notebook 4.4** to determine if your self-talk needs to become more positive.

3. **Use visualization.** If you imagine yourself behaving in certain ways, that behavior will become real. For example, businessman Calvin Payne knows the power of visualization. Before he graduated from college, he bought his graduation cap and gown and kept them in his room. He visualized himself crossing the stage in his gown to accept his diploma. This visual goal helped him when he suffered setbacks, frustration, and disappointments. He graduated with honors and now incorporates visualization techniques in his career.

Personal Evaluation Notebook

4.4

Self-Talk and Affirmations

Listen to your self-talk for a few days. Jot down the negative thoughts you say to yourself. For example, when you first wake up, do you say, "I don't want to go to class today"?

Do your thoughts and self-talk focus on lack of time, lack of money, or other problems? Observe when you are positive. How does this change your state of mind and your physical sense of well-being? List examples of your negative self-talk and positive affirmations:

Negative Self-Talk	Positive Affirmations
1. _____	1. _____
2. _____	2. _____
3. _____	3. _____

Most right-brain dominant people are visual and use imagery a great deal. They can see scenes in detail when they read or daydream. In fact, their imagery is like a movie of themselves, with scenes of how they will react in certain situations, or a replay of what has occurred in the past. These images are rich in detail, expansive, and ongoing. Left-brain dominant people tend to use imagery less, but using imagery is a technique that can be learned.

4. **Use goals as motivational tools.** Just as an athlete visualizes crossing the finish line, you can visualize your final goal. Working toward your goal can be a great motivator; however, you first must know what your goal is. **Peak Progress 4.2** on page 98 will help you distinguish desires from goals and long-term goals from short-term goals.

   Besides visualizing goals peak performers often write them down. Try keeping yours in your wallet, taping them on your bathroom mirror, or putting them on yellow sticky notes around your computer screen. Without a specific goal, it's not easy to find the motivation, effort, and focus required to go to classes and complete assignments. Make certain your goals are realistic. Achieving excellence doesn't mean attaining perfection or working compulsively toward impossible goals. Trying to be a perfectionist sets you up for frustration, which can decrease your motivation, lower productivity, increase stress, and lead to failure.

5. **Understand expectations.** You will be more motivated to succeed if you understand what is expected of you in each class. Most instructors hand out a syllabus on the first day. Read it carefully and keep a copy in your class notebook. Review the syllabus with a study partner and clarify expectations with your instructor. Meet with your academic advisor to review general college and graduation requirements. You will find that what is expected of

Setting Goals

As the Cheshire cat said to Alice: "If you don't know where you are going, any road will take you there." The key, then, is to figure out where you are going, and then you can determine the best way to get there. Goal setting will help you do that. But goals provide more than direction and a clear vision for the future. When appropriately understood and applied, they are very effective motivators.

It is helpful first to distinguish between goals and desires. Identifying what you want out of life (that is, creating your mission statement) is certainly an important step in developing effective goals, but the goals themselves are not mere desires; rather, they are specific, measurable prescriptions for action. For example, if you want to be financially secure, you should start by identifying the actions that will help you fulfill that desire. Knowing that financial security is tied to education, you might make college graduation your first long-term goal. However, be careful how you construct this goal. "My goal is to have a college degree" is passive and vague. "I will earn my Bachelor of Science degree in computer technology from State University by June 2017" prescribes a clear course of action that you can break down into sequences of short-term goals, which then can be broken down into manageable daily tasks.

Your long-term goal always comes first. Sometimes when people are uncomfortable with long-term commitment, they try to address short-term goals first. Do not fall into this trap. Short-term goals are merely steps toward achieving the long-term goal, so they cannot even exist by themselves. To understand this better, imagine driving to an unfamiliar city and then trying to use a road map without having first determined where you are going. It cannot be done. You must know where you are going before you can plan your route (as illustrated in the accompanying figure).

When defining your goals, remember:

- Desires and wishes are not goals.
- Goals prescribe action.
- Effective goals are specific.
- Goal setting always begins with a long-term goal.
- Short-term goals are the steps in achieving the long-term goal.
- Daily tasks are the many specific actions that fulfill short-term goals.

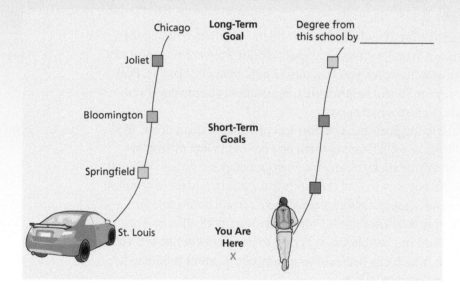

Goal Setting

Setting goals is like planning a trip—first you need to know your destination (long-term goal). Then you determine the best route to get there, including the milestones along the way (short-term goals). *If your long-term goal is to obtain your college degree, write in some of the short-term goals you need to accomplish (such as completing coursework, consulting with advisors and instructors, obtaining financial resources, and completing internships).*

Peak Progress

Differences between High School and College

Entering college brings a new level of responsibility and expectations as compared to your previous educational experiences, mimicking what is expected on the job as well as managing your personal life. For example, in college, you are expected to

- Have more responsibilities and budget your time and money
- Express your opinions logically, not just give facts
- Motivate yourself
- Handle more freedom and independence
- Attend larger classes that meet for longer periods but less often
- Be responsible for knowing procedures and graduation requirements

- Write and read more than you have before
- Think critically and logically
- Receive less feedback and be tested less often but more comprehensively
- Use several textbooks and supplemental readings
- Complete more work and turn in higher-quality work
- Interact with people of different values, cultures, interests, and religions
- Learn to be tolerant and respectful of diversity
- Encounter new ideas and critique those ideas in a thoughtful way
- Get involved in the community, school clubs, volunteer work, and internships related to your major

---

you in college—from personal responsibility to independent thinking—is likely to be much more intense than your previous educational experiences. (See **Peak Progress 4.3**.)

6. **Study in teams.** Success in the business world relies on teamwork—the sharing of skills, knowledge, confidence, and decision-making abilities. Teamwork aims for *synergy*, meaning the whole (the team's output) is greater than the sum of the parts (each member's abilities). Working as a team in school you can

   - Teach each other material and outline main points.
   - Read and edit each other's reports.
   - Develop sample quizzes and test each other.
   - Learn to get along with and value different people.

7. **Stay physically and mentally healthy.** It is difficult to motivate yourself if you don't feel well physically or emotionally. If you are ill, you will miss classes, fall behind in studying, or both. Falling behind can cause you to worry and feel stressed. Talk out your problems, eat well, get plenty of exercise and rest, and create a balance of work and play.

8. **Learn to reframe.** You don't have control over many situations or the actions of others, but you do have control over your responses. **Reframing** is choosing to see a situation in a new way. For example, to pay for school, Joan works at a fast-food restaurant. She could have chosen to see this negatively. Instead, she has reframed the situation to focus on learning essential job skills. She is learning to be positive, dependable, hardworking, service-oriented, flexible, and tolerant.

9. **Reward yourself.** The simplest tasks can become discouraging without rewards for progress and completion. Set up a system of appropriate rewards for finishing projects. For an easier task, the reward might be a snack or a

phone call to a friend. For a larger project, the reward might be going out to dinner or a movie. What rewards would motivate you?

10. **Make learning relevant.** Your coursework will be more motivating if you understand how the knowledge you gain and new skills you learn will relate to your career performance. You may be attending college just because you love to learn and meet new people. However, it's more likely that you are enrolled to acquire or enhance your knowledge and skills, increasing your marketability in the workforce.

The Benefits of Higher Education

As just mentioned, you will be more motivated in your schoolwork—and more likely to graduate and excel—if you understand how attending college benefits you today and in the future.

HIGHER EDUCATION ENCOURAGES CRITICAL THINKING

Many years ago, being an educated person meant having a liberal arts education. *Liberal* comes from the Latin root word *liber,* which means "to free." A broad education is designed to free people to think and understand themselves and the world around them. The liberal arts include such areas as the arts, humanities, social sciences, mathematics, and natural sciences. Classes in philosophy, history, language, art, and geography focus on how people think, behave, and express themselves. The liberal arts integrate many disciplines and provide a foundation for professional programs, such as criminal justice, journalism, computer systems, business, medicine, and law.

Technology is no longer a separate field of study from liberal arts but is an important tool for everyone. Employers want professionals who are creative problem solvers, have good critical thinking skills, can communicate and work well with others, can adapt to change, and understand our complex technical and social world. Liberal arts classes can help make a skilled professional a truly educated professional who integrates and understands history, culture, self, and the world.

HIGHER EDUCATION IS A SMART FINANCIAL INVESTMENT

As mentioned earlier, you will be more motivated to put in long hours of studying when you feel the goal is worth it. With rising costs everywhere—including higher education—and fluctuating job opportunities, some wonder if college is worth the investment. Statistics show it is. College graduates earn an average of well over $800,000 more in a lifetime than do high school graduates. (See **Figure 4.4.**) Although graduating from college or a career school won't guarantee you a job in your chosen field, it can pay off with more career opportunities, better salaries, more benefits, more job promotions, increased workplace flexibility, better workplace conditions, and greater job satisfaction. Many college career centers are committed to helping their students find employment.

Also, various reports from the U.S. Department of Labor indicate that people who attend at least 2 years of college tend to be more disciplined, have more self-confidence, make better decisions, and be more willing to adapt to change and learn new skills. They often have more hobbies and leisure activities, are more involved in their communities, and live longer, healthier lives.

"Education's purpose is to replace an empty mind with an open one."
MALCOLM FORBES
Publisher

Figure 4.4
Annual Earnings and Employment Opportunities Based on Education

Statistically, the level of your education is directly related to your potential employment and income. *What other advantages, besides a good job and income, do you think education offers?*

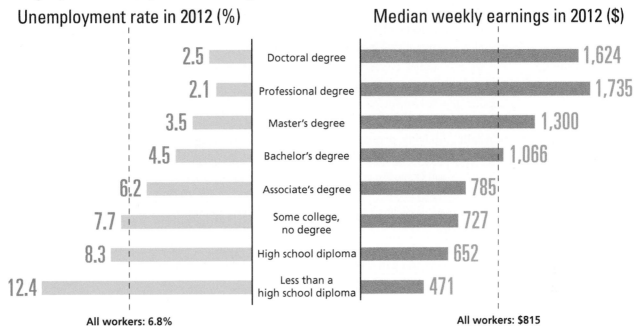

Unemployment rate in 2012 (%)		Median weekly earnings in 2012 ($)
2.5	Doctoral degree	1,624
2.1	Professional degree	1,735
3.5	Master's degree	1,300
4.5	Bachelor's degree	1,066
6.2	Associate's degree	785
7.7	Some college, no degree	727
8.3	High school diploma	652
12.4	Less than a high school diploma	471

All workers: 6.8% All workers: $815

Source: Bureau of Labor Statistics, Current Population Survey.

HIGHER EDUCATION PREPARES YOU FOR LIFE ON THE JOB

What you learn in school today correlates directly with finding and keeping a job, as well as succeeding in a chosen career. As you go through school, think about how the skills, personal qualities, and habits you are learning and demonstrating in class are related to job and life success. **Peak Progress 4.4** on page 102 lists skills and qualities you are learning, practicing, and enhancing in your coursework and indicates how you will use them on the job.

As you develop your time- and stress-management skills, which we will explore in more detail later in this text, your habits in school and on the job will improve. Time management helps you show up for class on time and be prepared every day, leading to better grades. Punctuality in school will carry over to punctuality for work. Stress management may help you get along better with your roommates, instructors, or co-workers. Learning how to succeed in the school or college system can serve as a model for working effectively in organizational systems. Do you think you are maximizing your strengths, skills, and personal qualities? See **Peak Progress 4.5** on page 103 to determine what kind of student/worker you are and what you need to do to improve.

Overcome Obstacles

Don't Get Discouraged

Even peak performers sometimes feel discouraged and need help climbing out of life's valleys. To create and maintain a positive state of mind and learn self-management, you cannot just read a book, attend a lecture, or use a few strategies for a day or two.

Peak Progress

Skills for School and Career

Skills	School Application	Career Application
Motivation	Attending class, being prepared and participating, submitting quality work on time	Performing exceptional work, striving to become proficient at necessary skills
Critical thinking	Solving case studies, equations, essays	Solving work problems, improving employee relations, responding to market changes
Creativity	Conducting experiments, developing term papers	Creating work solutions, developing products, launching sales campaigns
Time management	Scheduling studying, prepping for exams, completing papers and projects	Prioritizing workflow, hitting deadlines, product launches
Financial management	Paying fees and expenses, personal budgeting and saving, repaying student loans	Developing and managing departmental budgets, projecting growth and profits
Writing	Writing papers, speeches, essay exams, e-mails, blogs	Writing reports, e-mails, product descriptions, promotional material
Public speaking	Giving classroom speeches, presenting research, participating in class discussions	Delivering product presentations, leading and participating in meetings
Test taking	Taking quizzes and exams, applying for advanced degrees	Receiving performance reviews, certification and licensure exams
Research	Finding, evaluating, and citing information	Linking processes to results, testing new products
Learning	Learning new content to fulfill major, maximizing learning styles	Learning new job skills, adapting to changes in technology
Systems	Understanding college rules, procedures, deadlines, expectations, resources	Understanding company rules, policies, reporting procedures
Technology	Using technology for papers, team projects, research, testing, course management	Using technology for developing reports, communicating, managing systems

● **Being Strong**

We've seen numerous examples of resilience in the aftermath of events such as Hurricane Sandy, the Boston Marathon bombings, and devasting tornadoes. *What characteristics make people persevere through such tragic losses?*

Peak Progress

What Kind of Student/Worker Are You?

A peak performer or an *A* student

- Is alert, actively involved, and eager to learn
- Consistently does more than required
- Consistently shows initiative and enthusiasm
- Is positive and engaged
- Can solve problems and make sound decisions
- Is dependable, prompt, neat, accurate, and thorough
- Attends work/class every day and is on time and prepared

A good worker or a *B* student

- Frequently does more than is required
- Is usually attentive, positive, and enthusiastic
- Completes most work accurately, neatly, and thoroughly
- Often uses critical thinking to solve problems and make decisions
- Attends work/class almost every day and is usually on time and prepared

An average worker or a *C* student

- Completes the tasks that are required
- Shows a willingness to follow instructions and learn
- Is generally involved, dependable, enthusiastic, and positive
- Provides work that is mostly thorough, accurate, and prompt
- Misses some work/classes

A problem worker or a *D* student

- Usually does the minimum of what is required
- Has irregular attendance, is often late, or is distracted
- Lacks a positive attitude or the ability to work well with others
- Often misunderstands assignments and deadlines
- Lacks thoroughness
- Misses many days of work/classes

An unacceptable worker or an *F* student

- Does not do the work that is required
- Is inattentive, bored, negative, and uninvolved
- Is undependable and turns in work that is incorrect and incomplete
- Misses a significant amount of work/class time

It takes time and effort. Everyone gets off course now and then, but the key is to realize that setbacks are part of life. You have to become **resilient**—adapt to difficult or challenging life experiences and overcome adversity, bounce back, and thrive under pressure. Demonstrating **hardiness** (a combination of commitment, control, and challenge) will give you the courage and motivation to turn rough patches into opportunities for personal growth.

"I've missed more than 9,000 shots in my career. I've lost almost 300 games. 26 times, I've been trusted to take the game winning shot and missed. I've failed over and over and over again in my life. And that is why I succeed."

MICHAEL JORDAN
Professional basketball player

Figure 4.5 shows reasons students have given for dropping out of college. Many of these seem out of the student's control, but many may simply be excuses for not finding a way to persevere. For example, not all classes will be exhilarating and indeed may seem boring at times—but is that a reason to give up? If you think, "I'll be more motivated as soon as I graduate and get a real job," you may never develop the necessary qualities and skills to achieve that. Starting today, you should

- Commit to being motivated and positive.
- Focus on your successes and accomplishments.
- Surround yourself with positive, supportive, and encouraging friends.
- Tell yourself, "This is a setback, not a failure."
- Learn self-control and self-management strategies.
- Make certain you are physically renewed; get more rest, exercise more, and every day do something you love.
- Replace negative and limiting thoughts and self-talk with affirmations and positive visualization.
- Collect short stories about people who were discouraged, received negative messages, and bounced back.

Create Positive Mind Shifts

Your beliefs and expectations about yourself can either limit or expand your success. Other people's expectations of you may cause you to redefine who you think you are and what you think you can achieve. You may start to believe what you tell yourself or hear from others again and again, which may limit your thinking.

Figure 4.5
Reasons Students Do Not Graduate.

Juggling the demands of work and school is a major reason why students drop out of college. Besides the reasons cited in this survey, students also struggle with poor study habits, managing their social time, and taking responsibility for their education—including asking for help. *Which "reasons" in the survey are you facing and how are you coping in order to achieve your goals?*

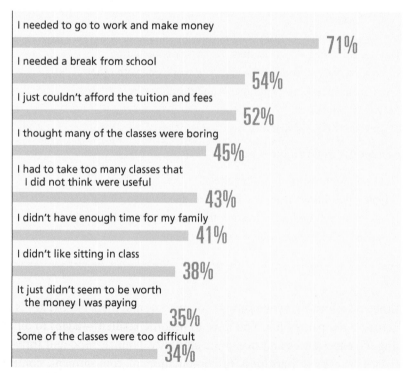

Reason	Percentage
I needed to go to work and make money	71%
I needed a break from school	54%
I just couldn't afford the tuition and fees	52%
I thought many of the classes were boring	45%
I had to take too many classes that I did not think were useful	43%
I didn't have enough time for my family	41%
I didn't like sitting in class	38%
It just didn't seem to be worth the money I was paying	35%
Some of the classes were too difficult	34%

Source: Jean Johnson and Jon Rochkind with Amber N. Ott and Samantha DuPont, "With Their Whole Lives Ahead of Them: Myths and Realities About Why So Many Students Fail to Finish College." A Public Agenda Report for The Bill & Melinda Gates Foundation, December 20, 2009. Reprinted with permission.

For example, Steve comes from a long line of lumber mill workers. Although they have lived for generations in a college town, his family has never had anything to do with the college. Steve was expected to go to work at the mill right after high school. He never thought about other options. However, during his senior year in high school, he attended Career Day. He met instructors and students from the local college who were friendly and encouraging. His world opened up, and he saw opportunities he had never considered. Steve experienced a major mind shift. Although he had to overcome a lack of support at home, he is now a successful college student with a bright future.

College is an ideal time to develop your natural creativity and explore new ways of thinking. Try the following:

1. **Create a support system.** Without support and role models, you may question whether you can succeed. First-generation college students, women in technical programs, and men in nursing programs may feel uncomfortable and question whether they belong. Cultural minorities, veterans, and physically challenged or returning students may feel out of place. Some students may be told that they are not college material. You can find encouragement with a support system of positive, accepting people. Join a variety of clubs. Make friends with diverse groups of students, instructors, and community leaders.

2. **Reprogram your mind.** Affirmations and visualization can create a self-fulfilling prophecy. If you think of yourself as a success and are willing to put in the effort, you will succeed. Focus on your successes and accomplishments, and overcome limitations. For example, if you need to take a remedial math class, take it and don't label yourself as "dumb" or "math-impaired." Instead, focus on how improved your math skills will be.

3. **Use critical thinking.** Question limiting labels and beliefs. Where did they come from, and are they accurate?

4. **Use creative thinking.** Ask yourself, "What if?" Explore creative ways of achieving your goals. Find out how you learn best, and adopt positive habits.

5. **Take responsibility.** You are responsible for your thoughts, beliefs, and actions. You can question, think, and explore. You can achieve almost anything you dream.

6. **Learn new skills.** Focus on your strengths, but be willing to learn new skills and competencies continually. Feeling competent is empowering.

7. **Use the whole of your intelligence.** You definitely are smarter than you think you are. Use all your experiences and personal qualities to achieve your goals. Develop responsibility, self-control, dependability, sociability, character, manners, and all the other qualities necessary for school, job, and life success.

TAKING CHARGE

Summary

In this chapter, I learned to

- **Use the whole of my intelligence.** Developing emotional maturity and strong personal qualities is just as, if not more, important to my future success as learning new skills and information. Essential personal qualities include character, responsibility, self-management and self-control, self-esteem, confidence, attitude, and motivation.

- **Focus on character first.** Strong leaders have an equally strong set of values. Having personal integrity gives me the courage to do the right thing, even when it is difficult. I display civility and empathy by interacting with family, friends, and colleagues with respect, kindness, good manners, empathy, and compassion. It's important for me to have a personal code of ethics that I follow in all facets of my life.

- **Take responsibility for my thoughts, actions, and behaviors.** I don't blame others for my setbacks, and I focus my energy on positive solutions. Others can depend on me to keep my commitments.

- **Manage and control my emotions, anger, and negative thoughts.** Conflict is an inevitable part of life, but it can be resolved in a positive way. Steps I can follow to redirect my negative thoughts and anger are (1) calm down; (2) clarify and define; (3) listen with empathy and respect; (4) use "I" statements; (5) focus on one problem; and (6) focus on win-win solutions.

- **Develop self-esteem and confidence.** Through self-assessment, I understand my strengths and will continue to learn new skills and competencies that will build my confidence.

- **Maintain a positive attitude and keep myself motivated.** A positive attitude is essential for achieving success; it influences the outcome of a task more than any other factor. Motivation is the inner drive that moves me to action. Working toward goals increases my motivation. Maslow's hierarchy of needs shows that I can fulfill my higher needs for self-esteem and self-actualization only when I have fulfilled my more basic needs first. The motivation cycle further demonstrates how affirmations, visualization, and self-talk affect my physical responses and behavior.

- **Realize the benefits of higher education.** Higher education has its roots in the liberal arts. Liberal arts classes can help make me a truly educated professional by providing an integration and understanding of history, culture, ourselves, and our world. My pursuit of a higher education should pay off with more career opportunities, a higher salary, more benefits, more job promotions, increased workplace flexibility, better workplace conditions, and greater job satisfaction. I will become more prepared for life on the job.

- **Overcome the barriers to staying positive and motivated.** Discouragement is the number one barrier to motivation. Setbacks will occur, but I am resilient by focusing on my successes and accomplishments, surrounding myself with supportive and encouraging people, keeping physically renewed, and replacing negative self-talk with positive affirmations and visualization.

- **Create positive mind shifts.** My beliefs and perceptions must be realistic. If they aren't, I must refocus my expectations in order to achieve my goals. I should not allow my beliefs to limit my potential, and I will use critical thinking techniques to expand my mind and comfort zone.

Performance Strategies

Following are the top 10 strategies for expanding your emotional intelligence and personal qualities:

- Cultivate character and integrity.
- Create a personal code of ethics.
- Take responsibility for your thoughts, actions, and behaviors.
- Practice self-control.
- Develop positive self-esteem and confidence.
- Determine personal motivators.
- Use goals as motivational tools.
- Reward yourself for making progress, and strive for excellence, not perfection.
- Become resilient to bounce back from setbacks.
- Create positive mind shifts.

Tech for Success

Take advantage of the text's web site at **www.mhhe.com/ferrett9e** for additional study aids, useful forms, and convenient and applicable resources.

- **Ethics information on the Web.** Search for articles on ethics, business etiquette, and codes of ethics. Check out different businesses, the military, government agencies, and colleges to find out if each has a code of ethics. Print some samples and bring them to class. What do the codes of ethics have in common?

- **Online discussion groups.** When you are interested in a topic or goal, it's very motivating to interact with others

who share your interests. Join a discussion group and share your knowledge, wisdom, and setbacks with others. You will learn their stories and strategies in return.

- **Goal-setting examples.** Although your goals should be personal, sometimes it helps to see how others have crafted theirs. This may inspire you to realize that setting goals isn't difficult—it just takes thinking critically about what you want out of life. A number of resources on the Web provide goal-setting ideas on everything from becoming more financially responsible to learning a second language.

Study Team Notes

Jacqui Williams
SALES REPRESENTATIVE

Related Majors: Business, Marketing, Public Relations

Positive Attitudes at Work

As a sales representative for a large medical company, Jacqui Williams sells equipment, such as X-ray and electrocardiograph (EKG) machines, to hospitals nationwide. Her job requires travel to prospective clients, where she meets with buyers to show her products and demonstrate their installation and use. Because Jacqui cannot take the large machines with her, she relies on printed materials and her iPad, from which she can point out new aspects of the machines she sells. The sales process usually takes several months and requires more than one trip to the prospective client.

Jacqui works on commission, being paid only when she makes a sale. Because she travels frequently, Jacqui must be able to work independently without a lot of supervision. For this reason, being personally motivated is a strong requirement for her position. Jacqui has found that what motivates her most is believing in the products she sells. Jacqui keeps up on the latest in her field by reading technical information and keeping track of the competition. She sets sales goals and then rewards herself with a short vacation.

Because personal relations with buyers are so important, Jacqui is careful about her appearance. While traveling, she keeps a positive mindset through affirmations, and she gets up early to eat a healthy breakfast and exercise in the hotel gym. She uses integrity by presenting accurate information and giving her best advice, even if it means not making a sale. Her clients describe Jacqui as positive and helpful, someone whom they look forward to seeing and whose advice they trust.

CRITICAL THINKING In what way does having integrity, good character, and a code of ethics enhance a sales representative's business?

Peak Performer

PROFILE

Christiane Amanpour

"Amanpour is coming. Is something bad going to happen to us?"* That's how CNN's Chief International Correspondent, Christiane Amanpour, says she's often greeted. Whether she appreciates the grim humor or not, Amanpour knows that her name and face have become linked in people's minds with war, famine, and death. But she has earned the respect of journalists and viewers around the world with her gutsy reporting from war-ravaged regions, such as Afghanistan, Iran, Israel, Pakistan, Somalia, Rwanda, and the Balkans.

Amanpour launched her career at CNN as an assistant on the international assignment desk in 1983, when some observers mockingly referred to the fledgling network as "Chicken Noodle News." "I arrived at CNN with a suitcase, my bicycle, and about 100 dollars,"* she recalls. Less than a decade later, Amanpour was covering Iraq's invasion of Kuwait, the U.S. combat operation in Somalia, and the breakup of the Soviet Union as these events unfolded.

Amanpour's globe trotting began early. Born in London, Amanpour soon moved with her family to Tehran, where her father was an Iranian airline executive. Her family fled the country and returned to England during the Islamic Revolution of 1979. After high school, Amanpour studied journalism at the University of Rhode Island. She took a job after college as an electronics graphic designer at a radio station in Providence. She worked at a second radio station as a reporter, an anchor, and a producer before joining CNN.[†]

"I thought that CNN would be my ticket to see the world and be at the center of history—on someone else's dime,"* she says, noting that she's logged more time at the front than most military units. Fear, she admits, is as much a part of her daily life as it is for the soldiers whose activities she chronicles: "I have spent almost every working day [since becoming a war correspondent] living in a state of repressed fear."*

Amanpour worries about the changes that have transformed the television news industry in recent years, as competition for ratings and profits has heated up.

But Amanpour remains optimistic. "If we the story-tellers give up, then the bad guys certainly will win," she says. "Remember the movie *Field of Dreams* when the voice said 'Build it and they will come'? Well, somehow that dumb statement has always stuck in my mind. And I always say, 'If you tell a compelling story, they will watch.'"*

PERFORMANCE THINKING Christiane Amanpour demonstrates courage, integrity, and commitment. In what ways do you speak out for freedom, justice, and equality?

CHECK IT OUT The Committee to Protect Journalists indicates that 70 journalists were killed in 2012 because of their work. Visit **www.cpj.org** to see what's being done to safeguard the lives of journalists in the world's hotspots. Use the search field to find the manual "Journalist Security Guide" to see what precautions journalists themselves must take in high-risk situations.

*AIDA International, 2000 Murrow Awards Ceremony Speech, September 13, 2000. **www.aidainternational.nl**.
[†]CNN Anchors and Reporters: Christiane Amanpour. **www.cnn.com/CNN/anchors_reporters/amanpour.Christiane.html**.

Starting Today

At least one strategy I learned in this chapter that I plan to try right away is

_____

_____

_____

What changes must I make in order for this strategy to be most effective?

_____

_____

_____

Review Questions

Based on what you have learned in this chapter, write your answers to the following questions:

1. What personal qualities are essential to success in school and work?

_____

_____

2. Give an example of a short-term goal versus a long-term goal.

_____

_____

3. List at least five motivational strategies.

_____

_____

4. Explain how affirmations and visualization affect the motivational cycle.

_____

_____

5. Explain what a mind shift is.

_____

_____

To test your understanding of the chapter's concepts, complete the chapter quiz at **www.mhhe.com/ferrett9e**.

Getting Motivated

In the Classroom

Carol Rubino is a drafting and design major at a community college. To pay her expenses, she needs to work several hours a week. She is very organized and responsible with her school and work obligations. Most of her peers would describe Carol as motivated because she attends every class, is punctual, and works hard in school and at work. Throughout high school, Carol participated in extracurricular activities but never really enjoyed them. She likes college but questions if she'll be able to find a job in her field when she graduates. As a result, Carol sometimes feels as if she is just wasting time and money.

1. What strategies in this chapter can help Carol find a strong sense of purpose and motivation?

   _____

   _____

2. What would you recommend to Carol for creating a more resourceful and positive attitude?

   _____

   _____

In the Workplace

Carol is now a draftsperson for a small industrial equipment company. She has been with the company for 10 years. Carol is a valuable employee because she is competent and well liked. Carol has a supportive family, is healthy, and travels frequently. Although she enjoys her job, Carol feels bored with the mundane routine. She wants to feel more motivated and excited on the job, as well as in her personal life.

3. What strategies in this chapter can help Carol become more enthusiastic about work or find new interest in her personal life?

   _____

   _____

4. What would you suggest to Carol to help her get motivated?

   _____

   _____

Applying the ABC Method of Self-Management

In the Journal Entry on page 85, you were asked to describe a time when you were angry and lost control of your emotions. Describe that event here and indicate how others reacted to your actions.

_____

_____

_____

_____

_____

Now apply the ABC method to the situation and visualize a situation under control:

A = Actual event:

_____

_____

B = Beliefs:

_____

_____

C = Challenge:

_____

_____

While completing this exercise, were you surprised by the amount of time you spend on negative thoughts?

PRACTICE SELF-MANAGEMENT

For more examples of learning how to manage difficult situations, see the "Self-Management Workbook" section of the Online Learning Center website at **www.mhhe.com/ferrett9e.**

My Reinforcement Contract

Use this example as a guide; then fill in the following contract for one or all of the courses you are taking this term.

Name *Sara Jones*

Course *General Accounting*   Date *September 2014*

If I *study for 6 hours each week in this class and attend all lectures and labs*

Then I will *be better prepared for the midterm and final exams.*

I agree to *learn new skills, choose positive thoughts and attitudes, and try out new behaviors.*

I most want to accomplish *an "A" in this course to qualify for advanced accounting courses.*

The barriers to overcome are *my poor math skills.*

The resources I can use are *my study group and the Tutoring Center.*

I will reward myself for meeting my goals by *going out to dinner with some friends.*

The consequences for not achieving the results I want will be *to reevaluate my major.*

REINFORCEMENT CONTRACT

Name _____

Course _____ Date _____

If I _____

Then I will _____

I agree to _____

_____

I most want to accomplish _____

The barriers to overcome are _____

The resources I can use are _____

I will reward myself for meeting my goals by _____

The consequences for not achieving the results I want will be _____

Self-Esteem Inventory

Do this simple inventory to assess your self-esteem. Circle the number of points that reflects your true feelings.

4 = all the time

3 = most of the time

2 = some of the time

1 = none of the time

1.	I like myself and I am a worthwhile person.	4	3	2	1
2.	I have many positive qualities.	4	3	2	1
3.	Other people generally like me and I have a sense of belonging.	4	3	2	1
4.	I feel confident and know I can handle most situations.	4	3	2	1
5.	I am competent and good at many things.	4	3	2	1
6.	I have emotional control and I am respectful of others.	4	3	2	1
7.	I am a person of integrity and character.	4	3	2	1
8.	I respect the kind of person I am.	4	3	2	1
9.	I am capable and willing to learn new skills.	4	3	2	1
10.	Although I want to improve and grow, I am happy with myself.	4	3	2	1
11.	I take responsibility for my thoughts, beliefs, and behavior.	4	3	2	1
12.	I am empathetic and interested in others and the world around me.	4	3	2	1
	Total points	____	____	____	____

Add up your points. A high score (36 and above) indicates high self-esteem. If you have a high sense of self-esteem, you see yourself in a positive light. If your self-esteem is low (below 24), you may have less confidence to deal with problems in college or on the job. If you scored at the lower end, list some strategies you can implement that may help boost your self-esteem:

Learning Styles and Motivation

You will feel more motivated and positive when you align your efforts with your learning and personality styles. Review your preference and style and think of the factors that help motivate you.

For example, *auditory learners* may be more motivated when they listen to their favorite inspirational music and say affirmations. *Visual learners* may be more motivated when they surround themselves with pictures and practice visualizing themselves as motivated and positive. *Kinesthetic learners* may be more motivated when they work on activities, dance, hike, jog, and work with others.

Analyzers may be more motivated when they think, reflect, and organize information into sequential steps. *Supporters* may be more motivated when they work in a group and make information meaningful. *Creators* may be more motivated when they observe, make active experiments, and build models. *Directors* may be more motivated when they clearly define procedures and make practical applications.

List the ways you can motivate yourself that are compatible with your learning style and personality type:

1. _____

_____

_____

2. _____

_____

_____

3. _____

_____

_____

4. _____

_____

_____

5. _____

_____

_____

6. _____

_____

_____

Assessment of Personal Qualities

Category	Assessment	Y/N	Example
Emotional intelligence	Do I value and practice essential personal qualities?		
Character	Do I value and practice being a person of character and integrity?		
Civility	Do I treat others with respect and courtesy?		
Ethics	Do I have a code of ethics?		
Responsibility	Do I take responsibility for my thoughts and behavior?		
Self-control	Do I have self-control and know how to manage anger?		
Self-esteem	Do I have a realistic and positive sense of myself?		
Positive attitude	Do I strive to be positive and upbeat?		
Motivation	Do I create the inner drive and determination to achieve my goals?		
Self-actualization	Am I committed to growing and realizing my full potential?		
Visualization	Do I use visualization as a powerful tool for change and growth?		
Affirmation	Do I dispute and replace negative self-talk with affirmations?		
Critical thinking	Do I use critical thinking to challenge my beliefs and see new possibilities?		

The area I most want to improve is:

Strategies I will use to improve are:

CHAPTER **FIVE**

Choosing Goals for College and Life

Goal setting includes facing the past . . . and anticipating the future. How do you think the goals you've decided to pursue will affect your future?

YOU DECIDE

To *wonder* means to think or have curiosity about. Things and ideas you wonder about often mask a need for a decision. Check the items below that apply to you.
   In terms of setting goals, I've been wondering . . .

☐ 5.1   What are my goals?

☐ 5.2   Do I have a realistic plan for achieving my goals?

☐ 5.3   What contributes to my success or failure?

☐ 5.4   Am I working toward my goals?

☐ 5.5   How does GPA contribute to the achievement of my goals?

Each of these decision points corresponds to the numbered modules that follow. Turn to the module for immediate help.

Most people would not purchase a cell phone without knowing the coverage details that come with it. They'd want to know what areas of the country the plan covers. They'd want to know how many text messages come free with it each month. They'd want to know if Internet usage was part of the plan. Oddly enough, few people put the same kind of thought into their daily lives. This chapter gives you the tools to help you make decisions about and plan your life course.

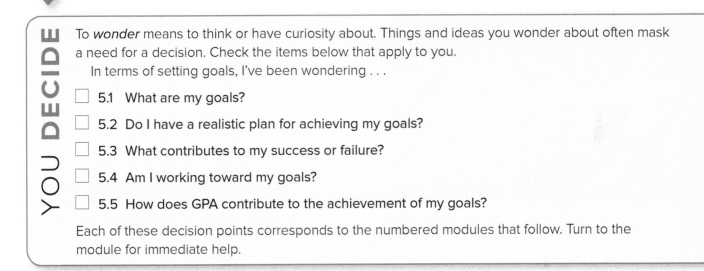

CHOOSING TO BE AN ACTIVE LEARNER

SURVEY

Before reading this chapter, prepare for learning. Purposefully skim the title, introduction, headings, and graphics. As you survey, decide what information you already know and what information is new to you.

QUESTION

Change each section's heading into a question. This forms your learning goal for reading.

READ

Read the section without marking. Reread and mark key information that answers your question.

RECITE

Stop after each section and make sure you understood the content. Organize or summarize content and make notes.

Identifying Goals

Short-term goals can lead to long-term happiness.

short-term goals
Goals that can be achieved in a relatively short amount of time.

mid-range goals
Goals that serve as a checkpoint on the way to achieving long-term goals.

long-range goals
Goals that take a long time, even a lifetime, to accomplish.

Goals form the compass by which you organize and manage your life. Just as a compass shows direction, your goals shape the path you take. The decisions you make either take you closer—or farther—from the goals you set. One way goals vary is in the length of time it takes to achieve them.

You set **short-term goals** all the time. By their very definition, short-term goals don't relate to any specific length of time. They can be met in a day, week, month, year, etc. Their length depends on the context in which the goal is set. Short-term goals could include developing a new skill, gaining work experience, or getting married.

Each goal you set in life should contribute to the achievement of larger goals. Your current goals are probably short-term goals. Current goals might include ending the semester with a 3.5 grade average, running for office in a campus group, volunteering time at a neighborhood school, or becoming more fit.

Mid-range goals are short-term goals with a longer payout. They act as checkpoints for success, as you complete them within the next three to five years. Mid-range goals might include completing a degree, having a successful career, buying a house, raising a family, or owning a business. By reaching a mid-range goal, you know that you are closer to your anticipated outcome. They ultimately lead to your lifetime goals.

Lifetime or **long-range goals** are those ambitions you hope to attain in life. Few worthy goals are achieved overnight. Most require years of effort. Goals like happiness, health, and success will take a lifetime. You will work on them until you die.

Goals affect all aspects of your life. *Personal goals* are those that relate only to you. They focus on you as a person. For instance, getting more exercise is a personal goal. As a college student, it's easy to forget personal goals. You can become so fixated on your responsibilities to your family, friends, and work that you forget yourself. That's a mistake. Flight attendants include the following in their preflight instructions—in case of emergency, put your oxygen mask on before helping anyone else. At first, that seems kind of self-centered. But if you can't keep yourself healthy and productive, how can you help others? Take time to set and meet some personal goals.

Social goals are those goals that focus on you and your relationships with others. Wanting to spend time with friends and family is a social goal. Similar to personal goals, social goals can get lost while you are in school. Work and school pressures can force you to ignore relationships. Not a good idea. Find a way to involve family and friends in your new school community. Perhaps they would be interested in attending campus activities and events with you.

An academic goal relates to you as a college student. An academic goal might be to make certain grades. This is probably one of your goals, whether you were an "A" or "C" student in the past. In other words, having been successful in high school doesn't guarantee that college will be a breeze. Having had past academic difficulties doesn't mean college is going to blow you away. In college and beyond, you'll find that your academic history is just that: history. Although it may–or may not–have prepared you for college-level work, you're here. What you do now is what counts. If you had a successful academic history, congratulations, but don't rely on past efforts. Set some high academic goals and get started. If your academic history was less than perfect, set goals to use the resources you need for a second chance at academic success.

Write Your Goals

Brainstorm as many academic, career, or personal goals as you can in the chart below.

PERSONAL GOALS	ACADEMIC GOALS	CAREER GOALS

Do I have a
realistic plan for
achieving my
goals?

Setting S.M.A.R.T.E.R. Goals

S.M.A.R.T.E.R.

Acronym for the necessary
parts of a goal: Specific,
Measurable, Achievable,
Relevant, Time-Sensitive,
Evident, and Recorded.

Reaching goals depends on the decisions and choices you make along the way. You need a plan with goals that are **S.M.A.R.T.E.R.** This acronym stands for the necessary parts of a goal: **S**pecific, **M**easurable, **A**chievable, **R**elevant, **T**ime-Sensitive, **E**vident, and **R**ecorded. S.M.A.R.T.E.R. changes a goal from a general idea to one that is action-oriented.

For instance, perhaps your goal is to finish school while you work. A S.M.A.R.T.E.R. goal would be to complete an AA degree in business in three years with a 3.0 GPA. It's *specific* because you have a clear idea of what you want to achieve. It's *measurable* in two ways: the degree itself and the GPA you want to have when you graduate. Your choice to complete a two-year degree in three years makes it *achievable*. This gives you time to study and work. It is *relevant* to your particular situation and your long-range goal of success. It is also *time-sensitive* because it includes a deadline for completion. If your goal is written (*recorded*) and put somewhere (e.g., a bathroom mirror, refrigerator) that you will see often (*evident*), you won't forget what you were trying to achieve.

Additionally, goals should be stated in positive form–what you want to achieve, rather than what you want to avoid. For instance, one of your goals might be to complete your degree. Stated positively, your goal is to stay in college until you graduate. Stated negatively, the goal is to avoid dropping out of college before completing a degree. The positive one is more inspiring.

No matter what goals you set, each involves gaining knowledge and using strategies. For instance, to enroll in college, you had to learn new terms (e.g., transcript, registrar, catalog) and new skills (e.g., how to apply for admission; locate campus resources). Part of your responsibility in achieving your goals is to decide exactly what you need to know and what you need to do. Unfortunately, that's not always clear early in the process. Sometimes you have only a vague sense of what you want. It's only after you learn more and try different things that you refine and continue–or discontinue–a goal.

The 5C approach–Define the **C**hallenge; Identify **C**hoices; Predict **C**onsequences; **C**hoose an option; **C**heck your outcome–can be particularly useful in goal setting. For instance, as you learn more about your college's resources and services, you'll be more able to identify choices available to you and the consequences of each choice. As you narrow your options and make a choice, you use your new knowledge and skills to determine if the choice was right for you. Then you either pursue the goal or make the decision to go in a different direction.

Backward planning involves setting goals by starting with an end goal in mind and working backward. This is a method of goal setting that helps you deal with the unknowns that might cause you to give up on your plan. The interim goals have an organic connection to the end that helps you visualize it. The idea is to start with your end goal and then work backward by setting milestones you need to reach along the way. A backward plan doesn't look much different from any other set of goals. The difference is in the way you think about your goal. To create a backward plan, you think from a new perspective.

The Backward Planning Process

1. Write down your final S.M.A.R.T.E.R. goal. What do you want to achieve, and by what date?

2. Ask yourself what milestone immediately precedes your goal. What do you have to do, and by when, so that you're in a position to reach your final objective?

3. Continue to work backward. What do you need to do to make sure each previous goal is reached?

4. Continue this process until you identify the very first milestone that you need to complete.

Visualization is a tool you can use to work through goal setting as you consider and keep or eliminate options. Some people think visualization is the same as daydreaming, but it is quite different. To visualize, you actively picture yourself working through the steps until your goal is realized. Keep in mind that visualization is not a substitute for the actions required to achieve the goal. For instance, perhaps your goal is to make an A on your next math test. Without the practice and study required to learn the math, visualizing an A on your returned paper is not likely to achieve the goal. Instead, as you study, you visualize yourself successfully recalling formulas and using them to solve problems. You visualize yourself taking the test with competence and confidence.

S.M.A.R.T.E.R.: Parts of a Goal

- Specific: Is the goal clearly described?

- Measurable: Is your goal quantifiable?

- Achievable: Is the goal possible given your current resources?

- Relevant: Does the goal contribute to the achievement of a larger goal?

- Time-Sensitive: Does the goal have a deadline for completion?

- Evident: Is your goal in a place where you will see it often?

- Recorded: Did you put your goal in writing?

What's Your Plan?

Complete Figure 5.1. Write your birth date to the right of point A. Write today's date to the right of point X. You don't have to put a date for the Z point. Go back and examine your answers to Activity 1. Now write what you hope to *do*, the qualities and experiences you hope to *have*, the things you want to *be*, and the things or services you want to *give* by the end of your life. Consider what you need to do in order to accomplish the goals you set at the Z point. Identify at least three mid-range goals that will take you closer to the achievement of your lifetime goals. Now identify at least three short-term goals that will take you closer to the achievement of your mid-range goals. What can you do today to take you closer to your short-term, mid-range, and lifetime goals? Make sure all of your goals are S.M.A.R.T.E.R.

Figure 5.1 Your Life Plan.

GROUP APPLICATION: Compare your timeline with others in your class. Then discuss these questions together: What can you learn from the way they identify and specify goals? What do you think they can learn from you? What did you like about completing this activity? What was difficult for you? What challenges or obstacles might keep you from obtaining a goal? How could you overcome those?

TIPS FOR MAKING YOUR GOALS REALITY

1. **Make a plan.** Research shows it's essential to think ahead about what you'll do and when, says John C. Norcross, PhD, a psychologist at the University of Scranton. Consider what you want to accomplish, what you need to do to meet your goal, and what could stop you from reaching it.

2. **Be realistic.** Remember the saying "Rome wasn't built in a day." Don't set goals that are unachievable.

3. **Be positive.** Consider other goals you've met. Talk with others who have similar goals as yours and get advice for succeeding.

4. **Believe in yourself.** The belief that you will succeed keeps you trying when the going gets tough. Start with quick, short-term goals first and then move on to bigger ones.

5. **Have a support system.** Having people who care about you helps in good times and bad. Plus their concern can be a big motivator.

6. **Keep your goal in mind.** Think about why you want to meet this goal and the rewards you'll receive for doing so.

7. **Keep a record of your success.** Knowing what you've already accomplished toward your goal helps you stay motivated.

8. **Change your perspective.** Changing viewpoints can change your interpretation. Observing yourself as a third person—looking at yourself from an outside observer's perspective—can help accentuate the changes you've made, says Thomas Gilovich, professor of psychology at Cornell.

9. **Reward yourself.** Set short-term goals and reward yourself when you meet them. This encourages you to set and meet other goals.

10. **Keep trying.** If you falter, pick yourself back up. Remember that mistakes are learning opportunities.

Locus of Control

locus of control
A person's expectations about who or what causes events to occur.

Who or what do you see as responsible for your failures or achievements? In the 1950s, psychologist Julian Rotter suggested that behavior can be explained by whether a person has an internal or external **locus of control.** Locus means "place" in Latin. Locus of control is a person's expectations about whether their behavior is controlled by external or internal factors. People with an internal locus of control are more optimistic. They attribute their decisions to themselves. They take personal responsibility for the outcomes– good or bad. As a result, they feel confident and have high self-esteem.

People with an external locus of control tend to be more negative. They see events that happen as the result of luck, destiny, or other people and outside influences. They don't take credit for the successes they achieve. Their perceived lack of success and control often creates feelings of low self-esteem.

How does your locus of control affect you? The control you perceive you have over your life affects your decisions. If your locus of control is strongly external, then you may feel that you have little control over your life. As a result, you may not see how seeking out resources and finding solutions can ever help. And you won't recognize that studying–or lack of studying– might affect test performance and grades. Rather, you'll continue to view life as something that happens to you rather than something that you make happen. You may think "Why bother? It doesn't matter what I do anyway." You'll tend to see success as something that results from chance or from the intervention of others. You'll also tend to see failure as something that results from nothing you do or are responsible for. If, however, your locus of control is internal, then you see yourself as having the personal power for making decisions that affect the outcome of your life. Thus, you'll see success–and failure–as outcomes that you affect and control.

What if your locus of control is external, and you want it to be more internal? Changing your locus of control is much easier said than done. In fact, some people spend years trying to do so.

Awareness is the first step in altering your locus of control. A second step might be keeping a written record of your successes and failures. The record should answer the following questions: (1) If the result was successful, who or what deserves the credit? (2) If the result was not successful, who or what deserves the blame? (3) How would someone else view this success or failure? (4) If someone else had the same success or failure, how would you view it? (5) If the result was successful, what did you do that affected the success? (6) If the result was not successful, what could you realistically have done to avoid the failure?

In addition to reviewing your own decisions and sources of control, talk to others about how they make decisions and view the results. For instance, after an exam, talk to other students about what they did to prepare for the test and how that affected their grades. Specifically, see if you can find out how successful students justify their grades. Do they think they were just lucky? Do they think the instructor just gives them good grades? Do they think their high school or other academic background prepared them for the course? Do they think they studied hard to get the grades they got?

Being aware that *you* are in control of your future is an important step in getting the future you want. Once you recognize that *you* are the creator of your fate, you become more conscious of the decisions you make and how they'll affect your future.

Who Controls Your Grades?

PART 1: Locus of Control

Directions: Answer Y if you agree with the statement and N if you do not.

_____ **1.** My grades reflect the amount of effort I put into classes.

_____ **2.** I came to college because someone told me it would be a good idea.

_____ **3.** I decided for myself what I would have as a career.

_____ **4.** Some people are good in math, but some people will never understand it.

_____ **5.** I look for easy classes.

_____ **6.** Some instructors either like or dislike me and there's not much I can do about it.

_____ **7.** There are some subjects in which I will never make good grades.

_____ **8.** Some students get by easy in college classes.

_____ **9.** There's nothing I can do to change the way I study.

_____ **10.** I am in control of my life.

_____ **11.** School is more important than partying.

_____ **12.** Friends, family, and work are all more important than getting good grades.

_____ **13.** I study almost every day.

_____ **14.** It's not important to go to class all the time.

_____ **15.** I am and will be successful.

_____ **16.** I am a good writer.

_____ **17.** I hate being late and missing deadlines.

_____ **18.** I am here to take the courses I'm told to take—the courses I want to take have nothing to do with it.

_____ **19.** I like to think through a situation and make decisions for myself.

_____ **20.** I get distracted easily.

_____ **21.** I can always find something to do rather than study.

_____ **22.** It depresses me to know there is no way I can get done all I know I should be doing.

_____ **23.** If things can go wrong, they will.

_____ **24.** I cannot decide what to do with my life.

_____ **25.** I can change the world, even if it is a small change.

_____ **26.** Friends, family, and work have interfered with my study needs.

_____ **27.** I may get my degree but there are more important things in my life.

_____ **28.** Once I make a plan, I stick to it.

Scoring: Circle the answers that match your own answers. Add up the number of matches.

1. N   2. Y   3. N   4. Y   5. Y   6. Y   7. Y   8. Y   9. Y   10. N   11. N   12. Y   13. N   14. Y   15. N
16. N   17. Y   18. N   19. Y   20. Y   21. Y   22. Y   23. Y   24. Y   25. N   26. Y   27. Y   28. N

Total = _____

Interpretation of score:

If your score is between 0 and 13, your locus of control is INTERNAL.
If your score is between 14 and 28, your locus of control is EXTERNAL.

PART 2:   Whose Goals Are They?

Take another look at the goals you set in Activity 1. Then think of the source of these goals: Does the goal come from you or is it something someone else wants from you? Which goals are easier for you to achieve—lifetime, mid-range, short-term, or current goals? How does the source of the goals affect their importance and ease in achieving?

PART 3:   Use the 5Cs

Use the 5C approach to identify one area in your life where your locus of control is external and identify a method for moving that locus of control to within you.

Myths and Realities of Achieving Goals

According to Nike, you "just do it" and your goals are achieved . . . unless of course, you're just not doing much of anything. The answer may lie in what you *think* is true–and what *is* true–about achieving the goals you set.

For instance, some people think that there's a right time to work on goals and, in some respects, that may be true. Time, money, resources, and responsibilities affect what you can and can't do. But in other respects, delaying a goal for an arbitrary date is a myth that works against you. You've already decided that the time is right for you to pursue your college goals. What other goals need your attention today?

Maybe you think you should work on only one goal at a time. Then, when you achieve it, you can move on to the next goal. But the reality of life is that it is more about balance than about single-mindedness. College may be your newest goal but don't forget to maintain goals that involve your health, family, friends, work, and so on.

Although you may think that maintaining your status quo is not an acceptable goal, that's a myth. As a new college student, you're literally juggling a number of roles–student, friend, parent, employee, volunteer, and so on. You're also juggling many responsibilities–household, work, study, financial, and health. You really don't have to set new and higher goals in every area of life. Balance in your life is a goal within itself, even if it means maintenance rather than progress.

As a new college student, you–and others–may have certain expectations. You may think that you have to be a "perfect" student with an A+ in every class. You may feel pressure from family members to be perfect. But your reason for attending college (e.g., a 2-year degree, transfer to a 4-year program, certifications, personal fulfillment) affects the kinds of grades you make, and perfection is rarely necessary. For instance, if you want to transfer into a 4-year program that is competitive, you need to focus more on good grades than if you are attending college to complete a certification program. If your goal is to become certified, then your completion of coursework may be more important than perfect grades.

Some people think that setting and achieving goals is too much work. That's also a myth. Certainly, most things worth doing require effort. That's a reality. Goals are no different. But goals should also be something that you *want* to do. Personal goals do require effort, but you should enjoy

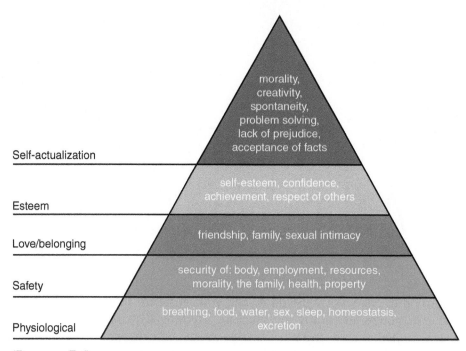

Figure 5.2 Maslow's Hierarchy of Needs.

pursuing them. Why? Because goals aren't just occasional milestones in your life–they *are* your life.

Goals result from needs as well as wants. This statement is true–it is no myth. Twentieth-century psychologist Abraham Maslow wanted to examine the relationship between human needs and motivation. He theorized that there was a hierarchy of needs (see Figure 5.2). As lower-level needs were achieved, humans were motivated to pursue needs in the next level. For example, the most basic needs involve physical well-being and security. If you have those (e.g., a safe place to live, food), you are more motivated to pursue your higher need to form relationships with others. How does all this affect achievement of goals? If you are struggling to satisfy a lower-level need, you will find it difficult to focus on a higher-level need. In the short run, if you are hungry or tired (basic needs), you might find it harder to focus in class because you are thinking about eating or sleeping. The question is: What sort of need does college fulfill for you? If you see college as the way to satisfy basic needs and achieve personal/family security, you will be motivated to succeed. If you are in college to make friends and form relationships, that need might take precedence over studying. If you are satisfied with your friendship/relationship status, then your focus could be esteem, and getting a college degree would be a way to boost that. Once that need is attained, whatever you see as personally fulfilling–career, family, other–will be the need that motivates you. As life changes, your needs may also change. Perhaps you lose your job and find it difficult to pay bills, afford rent, and buy groceries–basic physical and safety needs. You will then be motivated to do what it takes to secure these again, which may put you back on the road to achieving educational or other goals.

It may seem that when you achieve a goal, you should acknowledge it only modestly, if at all. This is completely untrue. While you don't need to brag about achieving your goals, you should definitely acknowledge what you did to achieve them. For instance, your goal might be to make an A in a particular class. And at the end of the term, you achieve that goal. When a friend congratulates you on your success, you respond, "It was no big deal." Rather, what you want to appreciate and savor is the new knowledge and strategies you used to make that A—regular class attendance, active participation in class, and efforts on tests and projects that resulted in the grade you wanted. The reality is that you need to celebrate your successes.

Finally, you may think that you should remain committed to your goal no matter what. The truth is you can change your mind and abandon a goal that is no longer important to you. For instance, maybe you're attending college because you want to become a nurse. But you've already realized that you don't like science and the sight of blood makes you faint. If so, then you need to re-evaluate that goal and work on a different one.

Achieving *S.M.A.R.T.E.R.* Academic Goals

Complete the following on a separate sheet of paper.

1. List the courses you are taking, the grades you wish to make, and the biggest challenge you face in each course.

2. What study habits do you need to improve to overcome these obstacles and reach your academic goals?

3. Create a chart that identifies a S.M.A.R.T.E.R. goal for each course you are taking.

Course	Specific	Measureable	Attainable	Realistic	Timely	Evident	Recorded

4. Identify five people who can help you reach your goals.

Grade Point Average

The main goal in attending college is to get an education. The learning you acquire will remain with you the rest of your life. While it may then seem hypocritical to emphasize grades, grades are how the college system measures learning. Your GPA (grade point average) is also a way that employers judge how hard you worked and how much you learned in college. What then is GPA and how is it calculated?

Traditional grading systems consist of the letter grades A, B, C, D, and F. Other marks include NC (no credit), P (pass), W (withdraw), W-grade (withdraw with a grade), and I (incomplete). NC, P, W, and I grades are not used to compute GPA. Policies about W-grades vary. Some colleges use the W-grade in computing GPA while others do not. Check your college's rules to be sure.

quality points
Numerical value assigned to each letter grade from A to F when given as the final grade in a course; used to calculate grade point average.

Computation of GPA is a ratio of **quality points,** or the numerical value assigned to each letter grade from A to F, earned to course hours attempted. Quality points use the following scale: A = 4, B = 3, C = 2, D = 1, and F = 0. Because courses vary in credit hours, you cannot always assume that the average of an A, a B, and a C equals a 3.0 GPA. (See Table 5.1.)

All colleges set requirements for obtaining a degree. One of the most important requirements is that you maintain a minimum grade point average (GPA). A college usually places students on academic probation whenever their grade point average is 10 or more quality points below a 2.0 or C

Table 5.1 GPA Computation

Course	Grade	Credit Hours	×	Point Equivalent	=	Total Quality Points
English 101	C	3		(C) 2		6
Math 104	D	4		(D) 1		4
Speech 130	B	3		(B) 3		9
Music 106	A	1		(A) 4		4
Biology 103	W	3				0
TOTALS		**11**				**23**

23 QUALITY POINTS/SEMESTER HOURS ATTEMPTED = **23/11 = 2.09** GPA

average. If you are ever placed on probation, you stay there until your grade point average reaches 2.0 or higher.

At the end of the first and each succeeding term, the school requires that you make a 2.0. If you do not, you may stay on probation for a period of time before being academically suspended. The first **suspension** is usually for one regular term (summers often don't count). A second suspension often spans an entire calendar year. Suspensions for colleges other than the one you are currently attending often count in computing this formula. Any additional suspensions will also be for a whole year.

Clearly, you can't take coursework from the suspending college during the time you are suspended. And coursework you take from another school during your suspension most likely will not count toward your degree at your present college. Most colleges will not even admit students who are currently suspended from another school. Once your suspension ends, you must reapply for admission to your institution. Readmission is not guaranteed.

GPA can also affect your eligibility for grants or loans. Federal programs specify what GPA is needed and how many credits must be passed in order to be considered as satisfactory academic progress. College scholarships also have specific GPA requirements to apply for or keep them. Once you've lost a scholarship, it is usually lost forever, no matter how high your GPA climbs.

Once you let your GPA drop, it takes more time than you might imagine to improve it. If it can be done at all and how long it will take depend on your current GPA, your future grades, and the number of credit hours you have left. For instance, perhaps your goal is to transfer to a 4-year college to complete a degree. You now have 45 hours with a GPA of 2.0. You need 83 hours to graduate (including the 15 you are taking this term) and wish to graduate with a 3.3 GPA. To reach your goal, you'll need to maintain a 4.0 for each remaining term you are in school.

If you are considering transferring to a different school, you need to understand that the school may have GPA requirements of its own. It's a good idea for you to know those now before you move very far along your academic plan. These guidelines can usually be found online or by contacting the school and asking they be sent to you.

suspension
Prohibition from enrolling in coursework.

activity 5

Determining Effects of GPA on Your Future

Grades affect your future. But what grades do you need for the future you want? You may not know exactly what you want to do in the future; but what you want to do may depend on the grades you get. For instance, you may want to transfer to a 4-year school; to do so you will need to be in good standing (2.0 GPA) at your future university. But some programs within the 4-year school may require a higher GPA. First, you need to know what you have now. Then, you need to know what you will need to have in the future.

PART 1: The GPA You Want

1. Identify the number of quality points your institution gives for an A, B, C, D, or F. Then determine how your institution treats the W and W-grade.

2. List the courses you are currently taking, the number of credits each course is worth, and the grade you currently have in each course. Then compute the grade point average these grades would give you.

3. List the courses you are currently taking, the number of credits each course is worth, and the grade you wish to make in each course. Then compute the grade point average.

PART 2: Calculating GPA

Raising a GPA is harder than maintaining a GPA. Go to the *GPA Calculator* on this textbook's website (or visit http://appl015.lsu.edu/slas/cas.nsf/$Content/Study+Strategies+Helpful+Links/$FILE/gpa.htm). *Now answer the following:*

1. You have 30 hours of credit and a 2.5 GPA. What GPA do you need if you want to have a 3.5 GPA at 60 hours of credit?

2. You have 45 hours of credit with a 2.8 GPA. You need a 3.2 GPA to transfer to the college you want. Will you be able to do so with 60 hours of credit? Why or why not?

3. You had a good time in your first semester of college but your GPA is now a 1.5 for the 15 hours you took. You want to finish your AA degree (60 hours) with a 3.0. What grades do you need?

What have you learned about your future GPA needs? How will you use that information to set academic goals for this term?

chapter review

Respond to the following on a separate sheet of paper or in your notebook.

1. What's the difference between identifying and specifying goals?

2. Why do you think goals should be stated in positive, rather than negative, form?

3. Which tip for making goals into realities was most surprising to you? Why? Which tip do you think is easiest for you to accomplish? Why?

Which tip do you think is most difficult for you to apply to your life? Why?

4. Did Activity 2 experiences cause you to view your life experiences differently? If so, how?

5. Based on your academic history, what would you predict your chances for success at college would be? Do you think those predictions will be accurate? Why or why not?

6. Identify what you perceive to be your current level of basic, technical, and other skills and your current GPA? How might these affect your ability to achieve—or fail to achieve—your goals?

7. What is backward goal setting?

8. Do you think your locus of control is internal or external? If it is external, what can you do to alter it?

9. List myths of goal setting. Identify the realities of each.

10. Explain how GPA is computed.

did you decide?

Did you accomplish what you wanted to in this chapter? Check the items below that apply to you.

Review the *You Decide* questions that you identified at the beginning of the chapter, but look at them from a new direction. If you didn't check an item below, review that module until you feel you can confidently apply the strategies to your own situation. However, the best ideas are worthless unless they are put into effect. Use the 5Cs to help you decide what information you found most helpful in the chapter and how you plan to use it. Record your comments after the statements below.

☐ 5.1 I know what my goals are.

_____

_____

☐ 5.2 I have a realistic plan for achieving my goals.

_____

_____

☐ 5.3 I can identify what contributes to my success or failure.

_____

_____

☐ 5.4 I am working toward my goals.

_____

_____

☐ 5.5 I understand how GPA contributes to the achievement of my goals.

_____

_____

perspectives

How can your college experience help you achieve your goals? In the following passage, Philip Berry describes how he used his college experiences as a launching pad for his goals.

Think about and answer the questions that follow.

1. Berry discusses how he used community college as a stepping stone to a 4-year degree. What is your reason for attending?

2. Explain the phrase "short-term pain for long-term gain." How does this relate to your goal setting? Provide some examples from your own life.

3. Explain the saying, "When life gives you lemons, make lemonade." How did Berry accomplish this? How can or have you?

4. What do you see as the main idea of the last three paragraphs?

5. Berry has two graduate degrees. Identify each one, and explain how you think this combination might contribute to Berry's success in his current position at Colgate-Palmolive.

6. Working nights while going to college was a decision Berry describes in the passage. Explain how he might have used the 5C process to make this choice.

   A. What was Berry's **C**hallenge?

   B. What key **C**hoices might have been open to Berry?

   C. What would have been the major **C**onsequence(s) of each choice?

   D. What do you think made Berry **C**hoose to work at night?

   E. In what way(s) might Berry have **C**hecked the outcome of the decision?

Since graduating from BMCC (Borough of Manhattan Community College) in 1971, Philip Berry has become vice president of global workplace initiatives at Colgate-Palmolive; he is one of the "100 Most Powerful Minority Leaders in New York City," according to Crain's New York Business *magazine, and vice chairperson of the CUNY (City University of New York) Board of Trustees.*

"BMCC had an excellent marketing curriculum and a good reputation," he said. "I got a very sound foundation in that area, and they also gave me perspectives on the whole business world—not just marketing, but accounting, economics and finance." While there, Berry took courses that would be a foundation for his goals in life, from his move to CUNY's Queens College for his Bachelor's degree, to his career when school was over. "That was how I used BMCC," said Berry, who went on to get his Master's from Columbia University's School of Social Work, and an M.B.A. from Xavier University. "It was a great launching pad for me. It really helped me to transition."

But he didn't have it easy, as is the story for most BMCC students. To pay for his education, Berry worked 11 p.m. to 7 a.m., then came to classes at 8 a.m. "It was difficult, but that was what I needed to do to pay for my education. I always kept in mind that this was only for a short period of time," he said. "That kind of context helps you feel a lot more comfortable about what you're doing. It helps you to understand that this is short-term pain for long-term gain."

Berry said those leaving BMCC this spring should always maintain focus—whether it's while searching for a job, when settled into one, or even as a student elsewhere. "Stay focused on what it is you want to do, and be able to define that very clearly," he said. "Understand what your strengths are, and your development needs, and set some goals for yourself, and then a mission for yourself, so that you can understand exactly how to realize those goals and objectives within an organization. You have to be very strategic, and you have to be willing to work hard."

One way of doing this successfully is to keep a three-year plan, Berry said. "Your one-year horizon should be in the context of a three-year plan," he said. "I have had a rolling three-year plan in my mind ever since I was at BMCC, and I update it every three years."

Finally, Berry said that while remaining focused, graduates should remain flexible as well. "All of the jobs and opportunities don't happen to be in New York City," he said. "When you look at BMCC, it's an extremely diverse college. You have students from all kinds of other countries, and they uproot themselves from their country and they come here to the United States looking for opportunity. People here ought to have that same degree of flexibility to go wherever they have to in order to get the job or opportunity. As old adage goes, 'When life gives you lemons, make lemonade.'"

reflecting
on decisions

Now that you've learned about setting goals, what can you do this week that will
contribute to the achievement of one of your future goals?

MAKE A DIFFERENCE **DAY**

Make A Difference Day is a national day with the goal of
helping others. Created by *USA Weekend* Magazine and
supported by its 600 carrier newspapers, Make A Difference
Day is an annual event that takes place on the fourth Saturday
of every October. In addition to the good done on this day,
some projects done on Make A Difference Day are selected
for honors, headlines and charitable donations. For example,
Paul Newman and the Newman's Own Foundation provide
$10,000 donations to the charities of each of 10 national
honorees. These honorees, plus others, are highlighted in an
April edition of *USA Weekend* Magazine. Projects can be big
or small and done in conjunction with another group or alone.
Use the 5Cs—Define the **C**hallenge; Identify the **C**hoices;
Predict the **C**onsequences; **C**hoose an option; **C**heck your
outcome—to identify a project that you could do to make a
difference.

◀ CHOOSING TO SERVE

R E V I E W

Skim the notes you made throughout the chapter.
How does the content fit together? What information
is still unclear? Were your learning goals met? Can
you answer the review questions and define terms?

◀ CHOOSING TO BE AN ACTIVE LEARNER

CHAPTER **SIX**

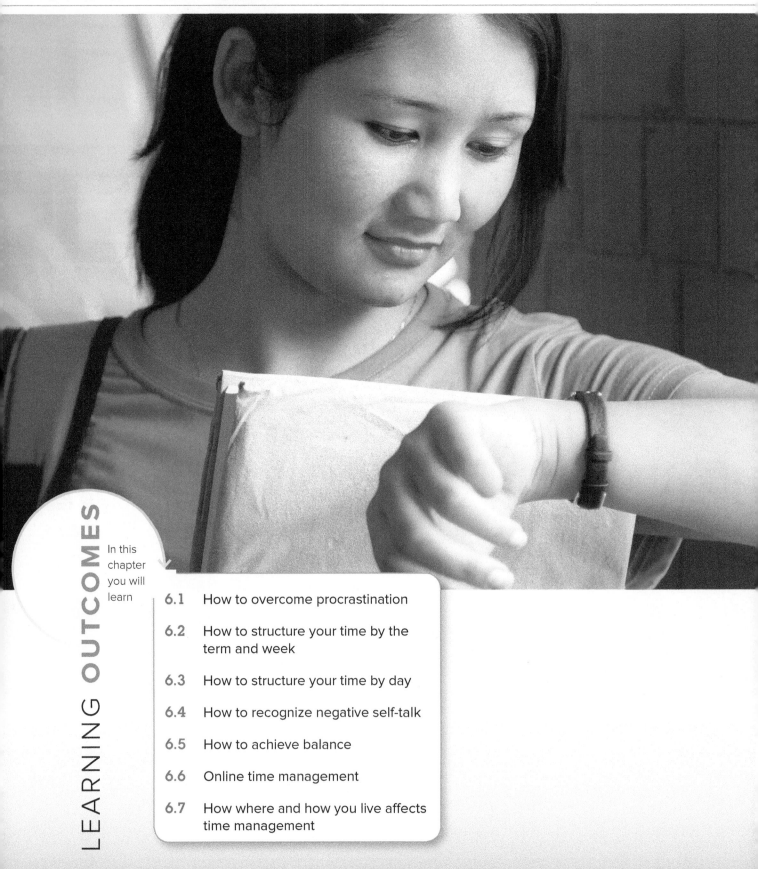

LEARNING OUTCOMES

In this chapter you will learn

6.1 How to overcome procrastination

6.2 How to structure your time by the term and week

6.3 How to structure your time by day

6.4 How to recognize negative self-talk

6.5 How to achieve balance

6.6 Online time management

6.7 How where and how you live affects time management

Decisions for Managing Time

Time management is life management. Explain how the way you manage your time reflects the way you manage your life.

CHOOSING TO BE AN ACTIVE LEARNER ➤

SURVEY

Before reading this chapter, prepare for learning. Purposefully skim the title, introduction, headings, and graphics. As you survey, decide what information you already know and what information is new to you.

QUESTION

Change each section's heading into a question. This forms your learning goal for reading.

READ

Read the section without marking. Reread and mark key information that answers your question.

RECITE

Stop after each section and make sure you understood the content. Organize or summarize content and make notes.

Congratulations! You have just received $86,400 from a rich aunt! Unfortunately, your aunt is a little bit odd. To get the $86,400, you must agree to the following:

1. You must spend all of the money in the next 24 hours.
2. Stores will be closed part of this time. But that's not a problem. You'll need to get some sleep.
3. You must attend all your classes today. Your professor accepts no excuses, and your rich aunt believes in education.
4. If you wish, your family and friends, as well as the other people you meet today, can help you spend the $86,400.

Take just a moment and decide what you will choose to buy. Jot your choices in the space below.

With my $86,400, I choose . . .

Now imagine that someone stole some of your $86,400 or that you carelessly lost part of it. How would you feel? What items on your list would you have to give up?

Having $86,400 would, indeed, be wonderful. But unless you really do have a rich aunt, that's unlikely to happen today. What you do have, however, is 86,400 seconds each day to spend as you choose. What you do and how you spend your time can take you closer—or farther—from the goals you set.

Time management problems often come from an inability to organize time and from ineffective self-talk. Like other challenges you face, you can change your behaviors based on the decisions you make. This chapter gives you tools to help manage time more effectively and shows you how to use the 5C process (Define the **C**hallenge; Identify **C**hoices; Predict **C**onsequences; **C**hoose an option; **C**heck your outcome) to achieve your goals.

Overcoming Procrastination

People put things off and fail to complete goals for many reasons. One of the most common misconceptions about **procrastination** is that it results from laziness. Another is that people just don't care enough about the work to do it. Generally, if you've had enough drive and ambition to get into a college, laziness is not your problem. Lack of **closure,** unfinished business, and **burnout** are far more common reasons for procrastination.

Closure results when you divide a task into manageable goals, list them, and check them off as you complete them. Closure helps you avoid procrastination. For instance, suppose your history professor assigns three chapters of reading. If your goal is to read all three chapters, you may feel overwhelmed. This feeling will most likely cause you to put the assignment off.

A more effective way to complete the assignment involves dividing the assignment into smaller goals. Think of each chapter as a separate goal. You could even subdivide the chapters into sections. You experience success by completing each section or chapter. Even if you fail to complete all three chapters in one sitting, your progress results in feelings of success.

Without closure, changing tasks too often wastes time. Each time you switch, you lose momentum. You may be unable to change gears fast enough or find yourself out of the studying mood. In addition, when you return to the first task, you lose time. This happens because you have to review where you were and what steps remain. Often you solve this problem by determining how much time you have to work. If the time available is short (that is, an hour or less), focus on one task. Alternate tasks when you have more time. Completing one task or a large portion of a task contributes to the feeling of closure.

Sometimes, when working on a long-term assignment (e.g., writing a paper, completing a project), other unrelated tasks (e.g., a more pressing assignment, going to work, carpool) often take priority. If this occurs, take time to write a few notes before moving to the new task. The clarity of your thinking or the status of your progress may seem fresh at the time. It's always possible, though, that you'll forget what you were doing after a while. Your notes could include the goal of the task, where you are toward its completion, and a list of questions or next steps. You need to store materials and notes for the project together either in hard copy or electronic form. This provides important organization when you return to your work.

procrastination
Delaying or putting off assignments or other activities.

closure
The positive feeling that occurs when you complete a task.

burnout
Physical or emotional exhaustion.

TIPS FOR AVOIDING PROCRASTINATION

- Focus on how completion of tasks or assignments leads to achievement of goals.
- Divide work into small, manageable chunks.
- Set deadlines and share them with others. You're more likely to finish if you know someone may ask about your commitment.
- After you complete one task, plan the next one. This helps you achieve closure and saves time when you prepare to begin again.
- Reward yourself for completing a task, especially one that is difficult or unpleasant.
- Never stop when the going gets tough. Stopping then makes it more likely you will have a hard time starting again.
- If you get stuck, don't be afraid to ask for help. Friends, family, and faculty are available resources.
- Establish a routine. Having a set study time makes it harder for you to procrastinate.
- Create a study environment. Like having a routine, having a place to study makes it more likely that you *will* study when you get there.
- Let technology work for, not against, you. Make conscious choices about how and when you will use technology to lighten, instead of add to, your workload.

Burnout also contributes to procrastination. It often results when you work without breaks. Burnout is odd in that its causes are the same as its symptoms. Fatigue, boredom, and stress are both signs and causes of burnout. Tough course loads and cramming add to burnout. Balancing work, family, and academic schedules can overburden you. And while it may be fun, an overloaded social or family calendar often results in burnout. Burnout commonly occurs around exam times such as midterms and finals, in December as the result of the long, unbroken stretch between Labor Day and Thanksgiving holidays, and at the end of the academic year.

Balancing break time and worktime helps you avoid burnout. Thus, you need to plan for breaks as well as study time. A break does not have to be recreational to be effective. It simply might be a change from one task to another, such as switching from working math problems to responding to an online discussion question. Although you sometimes lose momentum by switching tasks, doing so is better than burning out. Another way to avoid burnout is to leave flexibility in your schedule. If you schedule commitments too tightly, you won't complete your goals and achieve closure. This defeats you psychologically because you fail to do what you planned. This defeat may lead you to procrastinate the next time a commitment appears.

Not long ago, technology was hailed as a time-saver. Computers would shorten work days. Instead of going to the library, you could find what you needed online. But in many cases, technology extends, rather than shortens, worktime. Instead of only getting mail once a day, e-mail arrives continuously. Instead of getting news once a day in the newspaper or on television, news is updated 24/7. Rather than working on a paper only when the library is open, online research can continue all night. As a new college student, you're probably adding a new layer of technology to what you already use. Students are advised to check college e-mail accounts and online coursework daily. Pay attention to when and how long you use technology as well as how you use it. Although you may feel productive, you may be using technology to keep you from doing other tasks.

Procrastination can also be affected by your learning style. For instance, if you have global preferences, you may be a spontaneous multitasker. You might look at the big picture more than the details. But too many spontaneous choices and too many tasks may overwhelm you. You may be putting off tasks because you don't have enough time or energy. You may forget about the details. This will appear as procrastination even if you consciously don't realize it is.

Why Do You Choose to Procrastinate?

Think of the last time you procrastinated on a task. What do you think contributed to your procrastination? Then identify your next major assignment. Use the 5C process (Define the **C**hallenge; Identify **C**hoices; Predict **C**onsequences; **C**hoose an option; **C**heck your outcome) and what you have learned about closure, unfinished business, technology overuse, burnout, and learning style to create a schedule, in the space below, for completing this assignment while avoiding your usual procrastination problems.

How does what
I have to
accomplish this
term affect my
weekly
schedule?

Managing Your Term and Week

Most people think of time as being divided into parts–days, weeks, months, terms, or years. The concept of *day* or *week* is just a way of dividing what really occurs in a continuous form. Managing a term involves relating the time available and information you need to learn into one big picture. This helps you prioritize and plan more effectively in order to get your work done and achieve your goals.

Many students organize time by carrying small planners or by using the calendars on their cell phones. They record everything they need to do; but

A weekly calendar helps you recognize and set priorities.

they can only look at one week or month of the planner's calendar at a time or they can only see the activities for a specific day on their cell phones. So, in looking at the current week, they might see few assignments due and no tests scheduled. They breathe a sigh of relief and relax . . . until the next week when they turn the page or get an event alarm on their cell phones. They find that three major tests and an important paper are due in the next few days. This forces them into a frantic, cramming mode. You want to avoid this.

A term calendar lets you see a whole term's requirements at one time. This helps you become proactive in planning ahead during weeks with few assignments, rather than reactive by panicking at the last minute. Of course, the best time to create a term planner is at the beginning of a term. But it's never too late to organize for the rest of the term. The twelve tips we gave you for your first week in college (take a look at them again in Chapter 1) provide you with the steps you need. Just start with the current month and continue through the end of the term.

Looking at your term calendar, you may feel overwhelmed by the number and difficulty of the tasks before you. Luckily, not all assignments are due at the same time. You can get work done bit by bit, week by week. A weekly schedule helps you identify fixed commitments and free time. Reviewing your term calendar activities on a weekly basis helps you begin to set **priorities** and schedule them into your weekly plan.

priorities
The people or items that you feel are most important to you.

Steps in Planning Your Week

1. **List fixed commitments first.** These include classes, meals, work, family responsibilities, sleep, travel time to class, and so on. Allow a realistic amount of time for each activity. For instance, commuting times differ by time of day, amount of traffic, and route taken. You may spend more time getting to campus at rush hour than at other times of the day.

2. **Plan to review.** Just as you tend to forget the name of someone you meet only once, you tend to forget information you see or hear only once. Set aside a few minutes before each class to review your notes. You can often do this in the time you have between getting to class and waiting for it to start. This review jogs your memory. Then preview that day's topic to begin building a memory. Leave a few minutes following each class to review, correct, and add to your notes. This provides an additional review and helps you fill in any gaps in understanding you might have while lecture information is still fresh in your mind. If you are taking online classes, you can start your online session in much the same way. Complete a quick review of what you last learned. Preview that session's content. When the session ends, take a few moments to review what you did and learned.

3. **Estimate your time needs.** By the third or fourth week in the term, you probably can estimate how long it takes to do certain tasks without interruption. For instance, you may be able to read a chapter in an hour. You may be able to work 10 math problems in a half-hour. Be aware, however, that work and/or family commitments affect your ability to schedule as much study time as your course load may require.

4. **Identify and maximize your use of remaining free time.** As you schedule time to study, complete projects, or refine skills, look for ways to group activities. For example, if you have to buy supplies for a project, try to use that time to get other items you need rather than making two trips.

5. **Plan ahead.** Schedule completion dates prior to the due date to allow for unexpected delays.

6. **Schedule recreational breaks.** This helps you avoid burnout.

activity 2

Making a Weekly Schedule

Use your term calendar to develop a weekly plan for next week using the Steps in Planning Your Week list in Module 6.2.

GROUP APPLICATION: Bring your weekly plan to class and compare it with those of other students. How do your priorities and commitments differ from theirs?

Daily To-Do Lists

Once you set your weekly priorities, you need to create a daily to-do list–an agenda of items to complete that day. While many people make such lists, few people use them well. The secret lies in prioritizing your activities. Without setting priorities, most people tend to do those items that are most fun or finished most quickly. The dreadful or difficult tasks–those you really need to complete–get left until later. Sometimes later never arrives because you don't get around to getting started. Prioritizing your list and scheduling a specific time (from blocks of free time on your weekly schedule) to work on each item help you make decisions get the work done.

To create a to-do list, you list (1) that day's commitments transferred from your weekly calendar and (2) any items left over from the previous day. You add other items as you think of them. Your next step is to rank the items in the order of their importance. Next, you look for free blocks of time in your day and schedule tasks for specific times.

Chances are you may not complete your to-do list by the end of the day. But if you ranked your commitments, you will have finished the most important items. Keep in mind that what is a priority today may not be a priority tomorrow. Buying gas for the car today may be a top priority if the gauge has been on empty for three days. Buying gas for the car when you still have a half-tank left is less important.

What's the best way to set learning priorities? You might think you should save the best for last. But in time management, you need to use the best time you have available to work on your most important, most difficult, or least interesting courses. These require your greatest concentration and effort. You'll always have enough energy to do easy or interesting tasks later. Most people–even night owls–tend to think more clearly during daylight hours. Specifically, more efficient mental processing (such as solving difficult problems or synthesizing ideas for a paper) and short-term memory learning (for example, memorizing a speech) occur in morning hours. If you work, consider scheduling study time before work or during lunch. If you have family responsibilities, consider getting up earlier than the rest of the family and studying while they are occupied during the day.

On the other hand, you often can get the best results from long-term memory activities (such as learning concepts) and tasks requiring physical activity (for example, lab classes and course projects) during afternoon hours. Unless you work or have other afternoon commitments, it's a good idea to protect those time periods (from friends, activities, technology, or yourself) and use them for the academic or technical activities. It also helps to save the last hours of the day for routine, physical and/or recreational activities.

You also need to think about how you use waiting time. At the beginning of this chapter, you learned that you have 86,400 seconds each day. One way to cut down on wasted time is to rearrange your schedule so that you do things at off times. If you can commute at a later time, you'll miss the early-morning rush hour. If you can eat an early or late lunch, your wait in line or for service will be shortened. If you can go to the post office or bank in the middle of the morning or afternoon, you'll miss the people who take care of business before work or at lunch. You can use a laptop's built-in microphone to create your own MP3 study files and play those as you exercise or drive. If you review flash cards as you wait or listen to podcasts of lectures as you commute, you'll have more time to do the things you want or need to do.

You need to design your to-do lists to foster feelings of closure and achievement. For instance, as you divide a lengthy project (e.g., a research paper) into manageable tasks (e.g., select a topic, do the research, write rough draft, etc.), you estimate how long you need to complete each step. You schedule these intermediate points on your term planner and weekly schedule (select topic Wednesday, research topic Thursday, complete rough draft Sunday). Then, you add these as appropriate to your daily to-do list. These interim deadlines ensure that you will finish without rushing at the last minute. Checking them off your daily to-do list gives you a feeling of progress toward your goal.

If you create your weekly schedule at the end of the previous week and tomorrow's daily to-do list at the end of the day, you will find that you manage time more effectively. At the end of the week or day, what

Table 6.1 To-Do Lists or Not-To-Do Lists?

Common Reasons People Don't Use To-Do Lists	The Reality
Takes too much time to make the list.	It's only the first list that takes time. Once you start, you remove things from the list that are completed. You add new items.
Can't find the list when I need it.	Keep your list in the same place. If you use a computer, consider keeping a list as a digital document. Then, you can copy and e-mail it to yourself for reference at school.
I don't need it. I can keep track of everything.	College life adds a new layer of complexity to what you're doing. Your brain has a limited memory capacity. Keep what you need to do on a list and save your memory for other, more important information.
I'm not sure what to put on the list.	Start with information on your weekly calendar. Add other priorities. As you develop your list-making skills, you'll get a better idea of what you need to include.
Lists are too confining.	A list is just a starting point. Changing priorities can change the list.
When I look at everything on the list, I just get discouraged.	Don't put everything on your daily to do list . . . just those things that need to be—and can be—done that day. If you have too many items, you need to rethink your priorities and commitments.
I made a list, but never looked at it.	Place your list in a place where you will see it (e.g., refrigerator door, kitchen table, mirror).

you still have to do is fresh in your mind. If you wait until the start of the next week or day, you'll have to re-create where you were on each project or assignment. If your list is already prepared, you'll be ready to go.

You might feel confined by having a list of tasks, but that's not the point. While you want to stick to your schedule, you also need to remain flexible. Your time management plan is designed to help you structure your time and achieve your goals. Its purpose is not to bind you to an inflexible schedule. If you get started on a project and want to work on it longer than you planned rather than moving to another task, you can choose to do so without guilt. Even if you decide you need a break rather than work more math, you can choose to do so. The key is knowing you are making choices and that you will return to your schedule.

Finally, you should regularly review and revise your time management procedures. You want to know where your time management problems start and end. If you're not happy with your progress, you need to analyze how you spend your time and what keeps you from spending your time effectively. From time to time, you should ask yourself, "Is what I'm doing now the best use of my time? If not, why not?" Or, at the end of the day, you need to compare your scheduled to-do list with what you actually did. What or who altered your schedule and why?

Making a To-Do List

Create a prioritized to-do list for tomorrow. Follow it. At the end of the day, review your to-do list. Evaluate its effectiveness and accuracy. What better ways can you plan and manage your time? Create a prioritized to-do list for the next day. Use the space below to draft your to-do list.

How does what I think affect my time management?

Choices about Self-Talk

self-talk
The internal communication that you have with yourself; can be positive or negative; affects time management and self-confidence.

child
The part of you that wants to have *fun* and have it *now*.

critic
Role that suggests that you are unworthy or incapable.

adult
One of the three inner dialogue voices, the part of you that thinks analytically and solves problems rationally.

Do you talk to yourself? Of course you do. You constantly carry on a mental conversation with yourself. This mental conversation–your thoughts–or **self-talk**–directs and shapes your behavior. Some self-talk is informational. It might consist of mental rehearsal of what you are learning (e.g., a math formula) or an ongoing commentary about your daily life (e.g., it looks like rain). But other kinds of self-talk can affect your use of time. Worrying, procrastination, overcommitment, unfinished business, lack of self-discipline, and indecision often result in self-sabotage occurring from your **child** (the part of you that wants to have *fun* and have it *now*) or **critic** (voice that suggests that you are unworthy or incapable) roles and their self-talk. Both negatively affect your ability to achieve your goals.

Recognizing these roles and the kind of self-talk each uses is the first step to controlling them and regaining your ability to think in the role of the **adult** (the part of you that thinks analytically and solves problems rationally). The role in which you function affects the way you work and the way in which you perceive problems.

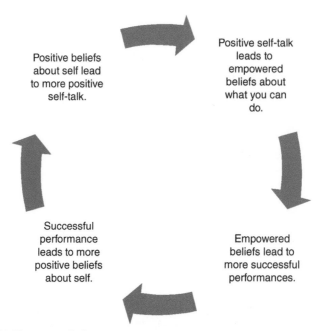

Positive self-talk leads to empowered beliefs about what you can do.

Empowered beliefs lead to more successful performances.

Successful performance leads to more positive beliefs about self.

Positive beliefs about self lead to more positive self-talk.

Figure 6.1 The Positive Self-Talk Cycle.

Who Says What: Self-Talk of the Child, Critic, and Adult Roles

CHILD COMMENTS

I'm too hungry/tired/thirsty to work on this now.

I don't feel well.

I don't want to do this.

I wish I hadn't taken this course.

This is boring.

I think I'll skip this next class. The professor is dull.

I don't see how this assignment will help me when I graduate.

CRITIC COMMENTS

This is too much for me to do. I feel so overwhelmed.

I don't know where to start on a project like this.

I should be able to handle a job, family responsibilities, and going to school full-time.

This is too hard for me. Everyone said I wouldn't make it.

I studied last time and I failed. No matter how hard I try, I'll fail again.

Everyone in my family is bad at math.

I've always been an A student. What's the matter with me?

Maybe I am just not cut out for college.

ADULT COMMENTS

This is difficult, but I have a plan.

I didn't do well on the last test, but I know what to do now.

I can do this, one step at a time.

Other people have learned this, and I can too.

This isn't very interesting, but I know I still need to do it.

These problems are hard, but I've learned hard things before.

Child Behaviors

The child is the fun-loving part of you that lives in the present without worrying about the future. When the child within you gains control, you avoid those tasks that seem dull, boring, or too difficult. Talking with friends, partying, and other leisure activities prevent the child from ever getting to work.

The child often responds to logic and rewards. If you find that you fail to start some activities because they're boring or unappealing, remind yourself that every career and job involves some tasks that just aren't fun. Learning to cope with such tasks in college will benefit you on future jobs. But you may find that the future is so far in the distance that you just can't see the benefit. In that case, create a reward system (e.g., a short break to do something fun for small tasks; larger rewards for more complex tasks).

Critic Comments

The role of the critic causes you to doubt your abilities, goals, and self. The critic predicts failure at every turn. It says that a task is too hard for you or that you don't have the right background or skills to get the job done. With such encouragement, why even try?

Worry is the critic's chief activity. By definition, worry has no productive outcome. Thus, instead of studying, the critic worries about studying. Instead of logically and calmly taking a test for which you have prepared, the critic insists that you're not ready and you're doomed to fail. When worry causes you to avoid a task or freeze from fear, you find it hard to do the task well. This results in poor performance that supports the critic's claim. When you find yourself worrying, ask, "Am I worrying or am I solving?" It's OK to have worries, but you need to recognize them for what they are and move on to a solution. The 5C process helps you do so.

Worrying also results in overcommitment that stems from a desire for approval. If you don't agree to go places with your friends, the critic worries that you may not be invited again. If you don't agree to do everything anyone asks you to do (e.g., at school, work or home), you fear people might think you can't cope. The critic suggests that you should be able to do more and more, if only you managed your time well. But the truth is that overcommitment results in a list of tasks that all the superheroes in the world couldn't complete on a good day. If that's the case, why should you be able to do so?

You can control overcommitment by the way you use your calendar. When someone asks you to do something, your first response should be, "Let me check my calendar." As you do so, you think, "Is this something I really want to do or have time to do?" As you analyze your other commitments, you also should also ask yourself, "Would agreeing take me closer to my goals?" If the answer to your questions is yes, then add it to your list. If not, graciously refuse. If you feel guilty or pressured, remember that your "no" allows someone else to say "yes."

Perfectionism is a by-product of the critic and worry as well. The critic says that if you are to do something, it must be done perfectly. You must be the perfect friend, student, roommate, relative, worker, and on and on. Like overcommitment, it's hard to do everything and do it perfectly every time.

Perfectionism leads to procrastination and burnout. If you get a late start, you can logically say that a low grade resulted from a lack of time rather than to what the critic says was a lack of ability. Or, you may find yourself overcome with indecision. If you can't decide, you can't get started. If you can't get started, you can't be expected to meet the critic's standards of perfection. As a result, you fall behind and don't finish the job. You can avoid perfectionism by deciding what must be done well and what does not need to be completed to those standards. For instance, writing a paper needs to be done well. Handwriting on your notes does not.

The critic is a difficult role to control because it strongly influences your thoughts and behavior. The self-talk it generates often has been internalized as a belief system. Thus, when you refute the critic's worries through logic, your heart often fails to go along. The solution is to replace those worries with other thoughts.

What's the difference? You really can't *not* think about something once you identify what that concept is. For example, if you try to *not* think about elephants, it's too late; you've already thought about them. Instead, you replace the thought. So, don't think "I'm not going to worry that I will get nervous and forget all I know." Instead, think, "I know this. I will do the best I can. I will be calm and careful. I'll take it a question at a time."

Replacing thoughts sounds deceptively easy. But if you have a strong critic voice within you, controlling it will be one of the most difficult–and rewarding–goals you achieve.

Adult Actions

The adult in you provides the voice of reason and logic. The adult knows that some tasks are no fun but must be finished anyway. The adult then musters the internal motivation to begin dull and distasteful tasks and see them through. To do so, the adult must outtalk the critic, stop worrying, and start solving.

The 5C process is particularly applicable to study problems. When it's time to study, the adult in you identifies the challenge and thinks about your choices. "What do I have to learn? What would be the best way to learn this?" Then you consider the consequences in terms of which study methods best match the materials you have to learn and the amount of time you have available. Once you make a choice of study methods, you begin studying. From time to time, you stop and check the outcome of your choice: how well your study process is working.

As an adult, you can also use procrastination to an advantage. Suppose you have a problem and decide to postpone its solution. What seems to be simple procrastination is actually a good choice. The difference is in why you procrastinated. For instance, you may be wondering if you should drop a course after the first month of class. You've regularly attended class. Your grades are good. However, your financial status shows that you need to increase your work hours. Logically, you decide you cannot do well in the course and work more hours. What looks like procrastination (e.g., taking the class next term) is actually a logical decision based on the reality of the situation.

How to Motivate Yourself to Get Things Done

1. You can do almost anything for 10 minutes, and you can choose to work on a task for only that amount of time. At the end of the time, you may find that the task was not as dreadful as you thought. You can choose to work for another 10 minutes. Or, you can quit and schedule another 10 minutes for another day or study session.

2. Forming or joining a study group motivates you because if you know others are depending on you to prepare and meet, you may be psychologically more inclined to do so. (See Chapter 15 for more on study groups.)

3. Varying your tasks and active study prevents the child in you from getting bored and losing interest.

4. Use visualizations to your advantage. When you sense yourself losing focus, stop and visualize the content of the information you're studying. How could you picture or sketch an algebra problem? How would you visualize the process of mitosis? Can you sense the imagery in a poem?

5. Monitor your concentration. Select a short time period (e.g., 30 minutes) and write a check mark each time you become distracted. The goal of the game is to decrease the number of check marks within the specified time period (and increase your attention span).

activity

What Are You Saying to Yourself?

1. Identify a time management situation that causes you problems. What child statements do you make to yourself that perpetuate the problem? What critic statements?

2. Draw a line down the center of the sheet of paper. In the left column, list all of the child and critic self-talk statements you have used in this particular time management situation. In the right-hand column, list examples of adult self-talk you can substitute in that situation.

3. Create a circle graph that shows your amounts of self-talk for critic, child, and adult roles.

4. Create a second circle graph to show how you would prefer to allocate your self-talk among child, critic, and adult roles.

5. Use the 5C process to analyze and resolve your situation so that the two graphs are more alike. What **C**hallenge do you face? What **C**hoices are available? What are the **C**onsequences of each choice? What do you think you will **C**hoose to do? How could you **C**heck the outcome, or the results, of your choices?

GROUP APPLICATION: Compare answers with others in your class. What similarities and differences did you notice? What do you think caused those similarities and differences?

Achieving Balance

You're doing it all: full-time student, part-time employee, team player in intramural sports, scholarship student, Web designer for a campus organization, and member of the debate team. How do you do it all?

You're doing it all, too: full-time student, full-time parent, part-time employee, member of the National Guard, scholarship student, Spanish Club treasurer, and member of a student government committee. How do you manage everything?

So, how are you doing? Most students feel overwhelmed by the number of roles they hold. The truth is, you may not be able to do it all and do it well. At some point, you must reassess your priorities. Your goal is to achieve balance, not lose your balance!

Unrealistic expectations may add to your situation. Perhaps you plan to complete your associate's degree and transfer to a four-year college. Your goal is to finish your coursework in four years and graduate with a 4.0 average. If you are a traditional freshman student who begins college at age 17 or 18, this means that you will finish at age 21 or 22. And then what? You get to work for the rest of your life! If you work until you're 65, this means you will work for the next 43 or 44 years. It may be better to take an extra semester and do well in your classes.

If you are a nontraditional student, you may feel compelled to complete your courses quickly in order to make up for lost time in your next career. You may feel that you need to take the maximum number of hours. Perhaps you see the suggested course loads in your college catalog as written in stone. For instance, suppose you are working toward an associate's degree in nursing. The catalog suggests that you take 17–18 course hours each term. But catalog suggestions are merely that–suggestions. Students who are financially independent and who have no responsibilities beyond academic ones might consider such heavy course loads. In truth, few students take more than 15 hours per semester. That's because there is more to getting an education than just taking courses. You owe it to yourself to take full advantage of the college experience.

Adding college to an already busy life can be overwhelming.

Keep in mind, too, that some academic goals (for instance, transferring to a four-year college, admission to programs with limited enrollments, and so on) require a show of academic excellence. If you schedule too many classes, you cannot make the grades you need to accomplish your longer-term goals. While grades are important, many employers prefer to see a prospective employee that can handle a variety of tasks in addition to academic pursuits.

Values also play a key role in achieving balance. If what you do as a student conflicts with what you believe is important in life, you will not feel fulfilled no matter how well you do academically. For instance, you might value academic achievement and family. But doing well as a full-time student takes too much time from your role as a parent. Taking fewer courses at a time might take you longer to graduate but allow you to both raise a family and complete a degree in a way that is a better fit with your values. Or perhaps you like to be involved in campus or civic organizations. You value what you learn as a result but find that your grades are suffering. Again you could choose to take fewer classes in order to serve in organizations and make the grades you want. In both cases, your choice might take you another year or so to complete your degree. If you are a traditionally aged student, an extra year means you still get to work for the next 40 or so years instead of the next 41 or 42 years. Seen from that perspective, the trade-off is worth achieving the balance you want. If you are a nontraditionally aged student, the trade-off is a decision you will need to make with your life goals in mind.

Thus, whatever your academic goals, view them in terms of your life goals (see Chapter 5) and values (see Chapter 2). Choose to take the time you need to get the experiences and education that will take you closer to the goals you set while maintaining the life you want to lead.

How Am I Doing with Time Management?

For each of the following statements, put an X by the one word (agree, disagree, unsure) that best describes your general experience and actions.

	Agree	Disagree	Unsure
1. I have difficulty thinking about the future and setting long-range goals.			
2. My long-range goals are too far in the future to predict a time frame for completion.			
3. I file things for future reference but often forget to refer to them later on.			
4. I grab odd, spare bits of time in order to chip away at relatively complex tasks.			
5. I handle a glut of information by categorizing things and then going back to deal with them when I have a chance.			
6. I put decisions and problems on "hold" until I have a block of time to give to them.			
7. My intentions—my plans and goals—are my own business. I rarely announce them to others.			
8. I know where I want to be in 5 years; deciding how to get there is the hard part.			
9. I do what I have to do at the time; it's confusing to think about tomorrow or next week.			
10. Making daily or weekly lists makes me feel overwhelmed.			
11. I'm too busy to plan each week's schedule.			
12. I always have to alter my schedule, so I often don't bother to create one.			
13. Making a "to-do" list is a waste of time.			
14. Writing a "to-do" list down is a waste of paper; I keep a "to-do" list in my head.			
15. I can make a list, but I find it difficult to decide in what order to do things.			

	Agree	Disagree	Unsure
16. When I have many tasks to complete, I plunge into any one in order to get started.			
17. I like to work my way into difficult or boring tasks by doing the easier ones first.			
18. I don't think about my peak energy time; I have to perform well all of the time.			
19. Things often take longer than I plan, so I seem to be in a perpetual state of "catch-up."			
20. I tend to procrastinate since I work better under pressure.			
21. I make plans and set aside time for projects but don't usually use that time as planned; other things seem to get in the way.			
22. I usually run to answer the telephone when it rings.			
23. Most major household/office responsibilities seem to fall on my shoulders.			
24. Piles of paper in my house/office are getting out of control.			
25. I usually say "yes" when I'm asked to be on a committee, bake a cake, do some optional overtime, etc.			
26. Others don't do things as I like them done, so I do them myself.			
27. I often solve other people's problems.			
28. Each time I start something, I seem to be interrupted by family, friends, co-workers.			
29. People and situations to whom I am responsible (small children, spouse, elderly parents, work) really do make demands on my time.			
30. I seem to add to instead of eliminate activities.			
31. I will not lower my standards just to save a bit of time.			
TOTALS OF EACH COLUMN			

RESULTS

Look at the totals in the "Agree" columns. Agreement with more than 4 for questions 1–8 indicates problems in Area 1: goals or setting them. Agreement with more than 6 for questions 9–20 indicates problems in Area 2: prioritizing or short-term goals. Agreement with more than 6 for questions 21–31 indicates problems in Area 3: controlling your environment.

Use the 5C process and your results above to respond to the following:

1. Based on your results, what area is most problematic for you? Within that area, how do you define the most important **C**hallenge?

2. What **C**hoices do you have for managing time and achieving balance?

3. Identify **C**onsequences by describing what would logically happen as the result of each option.

4. What will you **C**hoose to do to meet this challenge?

5. Identify how you will **C**heck the outcome of your choice.

GROUP APPLICATION: Share individual answers with your group. What similarities and differences do you discover among your group's answers? What factors might contribute to these similarities?

Using Digital Time Management Tools

Are you online more than you're offline? Do you have a cell phone? Do you have problems keeping up with your to-do list? Online and cell phone time management tools may be the solutions you need. (To find these and others, see the text website for links or search for the name of the tool online.)

Google Calendar is a free online shareable calendar service. Using Google Calendar, you can add events, share with friends and family (or keep things to yourself), and search across the Web for public calendars, including television and sports events as well other scheduled events. You can share your calendar with family and friends and view theirs as well. Google Calendar is available in a number of languages. It allows you to view a day, a 4-day period, a week, or a month at a time. One special feature lets you get reminders on your cell phone.

Although you can easily create paper and pencil to-do lists, there are several websites such as *Rememberthemilk.com* that allow you to create electronic to-do lists. *Toodledo* is a to-do list creator that also includes tools to analyze your dates, priorities, and time estimates to create a schedule that helps you get everything done on time. If you tend to procrastinate or forget, try *HassleMe* which nags you via e-mail or *BitBomb* which sends reminder text messages to your cell phone. The Apple App store also contains programs that can help you manage time. *Things* seems like a traditional to-do list. You can create and add items to a list. You can add due dates and assign categories and projects. The app lets you manage time over a day, a week, or longer. *To Do!* is another app that helps you manage time. It contains a "to-do list" as well as call/e-mail reminders. The app lets you set due dates and prioritize items. Android apps that can help you manage time include *2DO* and *TODOIST*. Both are check/task list applications.

Work often expands to fill the time you have. For instance, if you have a whole day to write a one-page paper, that's probably how long it will take. But if you only have an hour and a half in which to write it, you'll be more focused and complete it in the time you have. One way to monitor your time is to install a digital timer on your computer desktop. Set a time for reasonable completion of a task to help you complete it. You can download free shareware for digital clocks and timers at *Brothersoft*. Another tool for monitoring time online is at Rescuetime.com. *It tracks time spent in different applications online and sends you a report based on your activity. You might be surprised how long you spend on Facebook, Pinterest, or other social media.*

Digital Time Management Tools

activity 6

Choose one of the time management tools and create a week's calendar, showing academic, personal, and work-related events as well as a to-do list for one day.

GROUP APPLICATION: Compare tools with others in your class in terms of ease of use and features.

Living Arrangements and Time Management

College changes the way you live, and the way you live affects your time management. You may be on your own for the first time living in a residence hall or apartment in a different city. Or you may be commuting to campus from home or work. How you decide to arrange your life is a choice you make on a daily–and sometimes hourly–basis. Reread Module 1.2 *How College Is Different* in Chapter One. Now that you've been in college a few weeks, you can probably see more clearly the ways in which your college experience differs from what you experienced in high school.

Life on Your Own

If you are living on your own for the first time in a residence hall or apartment, you may have already discovered some major differences. Freedom has its advantages–and disadvantages. You may find yourself doing anything and everything except schoolwork. You may let roommates and new acquaintances talk you into going out/staying in rather than going to class. You let others make time management decisions for you or you may not be making any decisions at all.

If you are overwhelmed by the college experience and homesick, you may be staying in your room, playing music or games, and sleeping rather than going to class. The key in managing freedom is remembering that you are the boss . . . of your time. You are now working for yourself and your future. As a worker, you need some structure. As the boss, you get to choose what that structure will be. College is your workplace so you need to go to class even if no one takes attendance. The strategies for setting goals, managing your day and week, and creating to-do lists provide the structure you need.

You also have to figure out what is and isn't working for you. Your residence hall or apartment may be noisy. If so, you need to find another place to study or study with earphones or earplugs. If you are studying at a coffee shop or other business and spending more money on food and drinks than you can afford, you need to find a place to study where you don't feel compelled to buy something. If you are missing classes, identify the reason and look for solutions.

Maybe you aren't used to having people around all the time. You can look for quiet study carrels or other areas in the library or other buildings on campus. You thought you would love your major and classes, but find you are bored and not interested. Or you have discovered a different field of study that you think is better for you. Depending on when you come to this conclusion, you may need to stick it out in the courses or drop them. This will affect the time it takes for you to graduate and may affect financial aid. Thus it is a decision that requires the advice of an expert. Talk to your advisor, RA, faculty and other college staff first.

Coping with Commuting

In the 1930s, the *rat race* was a jazz dance. Then the business world changed it to mean *struggling to stay ahead of the competition.* Today, *rat race* refers to any undertaking in which you feel that time moves faster than you do. If you've ever seen a hamster playing on an exercise wheel, you understand the term. If you commute, you live it

As a commuter, no matter how short or long your commute, you face unique problems: courses that meet at inconvenient times; schedule conflicts that cause you to miss the learning experiences that enrich academic life; traffic jams and constant search for the elusive "good" parking space; or mass transit schedules that don't match your needs. As a commuting student, you are part of a group often called suitcase students. With no room or office to serve as a base, you often find that the materials you need are at home, in your car, or at your job. Traveling back and forth limits your contact with both your family and people on campus. Creative planning is the secret to being a successful commuter student.

Solving scheduling problems involves effective time management. Each minute you stay on campus needs to be stretched to two. You can stretch time through careful organization and planning.

The biggest problem that commuters face is often limited involvement in campus life. You can avoid feeling separated from others on campus by consciously trying to make yourself a part of campus life. Reading the campus newspaper, talking with others before and after class, and exchanging phone numbers and e-mail addresses with classmates help decrease your feelings of alienation. You can look for or add campus friends to your social networking site. Campus activities organizers plan events that meet the interests—and schedules—of the students they serve. You may find breakfast meetings, lunch study groups, or afternoon club meetings. You will probably find that many cultural events—concerts, plays, art exhibits, science demonstrations and so on—will interest family members and give you a chance to participate in campus life. If not, be sure to reserve family time on weekends or evenings. And don't forget to build some time in for exercise and relaxation—even just by parking a bit

Commuters have opportunities to study or meet other students in transit.

farther away from the classroom building so that you get in a brisk walk before class.

As a commuter, you get to choose how you spend the time while you commute. You can choose for that to be "your" time and listen to music or just relax. But if you'd rather spend "your" time doing something else, you need to choose to use that time more productively.

Commuting Time

- If you drive to campus, find other commuters and car pool. If you and your fellow commuters are in the same classes, you can discuss course content in the car. On days you don't drive, you can study. As a driver, although some technologies (e.g., books on tape, audio notes) can be used, you should never text message or use technology in a way that distracts you from driving.

- Listen to notes or review questions. Obtain lecture podcasts or create your own. Commuting time then becomes study time.

- If you use public transportation, use commuting time as study time. You can read course materials, make note cards, listen to review tapes and podcasts, or review for exams.

- If you are not driving, you can return cell calls or text messages. This will free time.

Time on Campus

- To avoid misplacing important materials, get organized and be prepared. Organize your backpack each night so that you are ready for the next day. Keep a box in your car that contains your textbooks, notebooks, and other supplies.

- Most students have some time between classes. Use that time to study while the information is still fresh from lectures.

- Think of your time on campus like worktime. Plan to study as much as you can in the library or another quiet place before you leave campus. This gives you uninterrupted study time and allows your home time to be home time.

Study Time

- If an emergency prevents you from going to a class, use your neighborhood library, notes from other students, information from the Web, lecture podcasts, and course websites to supplement what you missed.

- Be flexible. Leave time in your schedule for unplanned events, and schedule extra time between appointments or activities in case of traffic or other emergencies. If an emergency arises, you will still have time to study or do other things.

What Took You So Long?

activity 7

If you commute, describe what you do to make the most of your commuting time. If you are not a commuter, create a list of three activities that commuters could safely do to maximize their time.

chapter review

Respond to the following on a separate sheet of paper or in your notebook.

1. What is procrastination? Do you procrastinate? Try to identify some of the reasons you procrastinate. If not, explain how you avoid procrastination.

2. Observe the kinds of self-talk you employ in the courses in which you are enrolled. How would you categorize these according to the three modes of self-talk?

3. What do you see as your greatest obstacles to making and/or using a term calendar? Why?

4. What do you see as your greatest obstacles to constructing, maintaining, and/or following a weekly calendar and to-do list? Why?

5. How do you prioritize family vs. work vs. school? List your priorities in terms of each.

6. Which of the digital time management tools most appeals to you? Why?

7. How do your living arrangements affect your time for study? Should improvements be made? Why or Why not?

did you decide?

Did you accomplish what you wanted to in this chapter? Check the items below that apply to you.

Review the *You Decide* questions that you identified at the beginning of the chapter, but look at them from a new direction. If you didn't check an item below, review that module until you feel you can confidently apply the strategies to your own situation. However, the best ideas are worthless unless they are put into effect. Use the 5Cs to help you decide what information you found most helpful in the chapter and how you plan to use it. Record your comments after the statements below.

☐ 6.1   I know to what extent I put assignments off until the last minute.

_____

☐ 6.2   I recognize that what I have to accomplish this term affects my weekly schedule.

_____

☐ 6.3   I am able to get my more important tasks done each day.

_____

☐ 6.4   I know how my thinking affects my time management.

_____

☐ 6.5   I can devise strategies to avoid feeling overextended.

_____

☐ 6.6   I know some digital time management tools that might help me organize.

_____

☐ 6.7   I know how my living arrangements affect time management.

_____

perspectives

You may have a job, a family, or a hobby that makes time management difficult for you. Volleyball players at Penn State are busy with a full academic course load and a tough practice and game schedule. Here are some ways they manage time. Maybe they'll help you as well.

Think about and answer the questions that follow.

1. Explain the phrase "the offseason blurs together." How does this relate to your goal setting? Provide some examples from your own life.

2. Consider what the athletes do in the off-season. Identify the on- or off-seasons in your life. When would this be? What could you do to maximize your off-season?

3. What is the main idea of this reading?

4. The volleyball team also supports other Penn State teams. Explain how they might have used the 5C process to make this choice.

   A. What is their **C**hallenge?

   B. What key **C**hoices might they have to make?

   C. What would have been the major **C**onsequence(s) of each choice?

   D. Beyond what the article states, why do you think they give valuable time to this?

   E. In what way(s) might they **C**heck the outcome of the decision to support other teams?

They miss football games. They miss class. They miss their friends. They miss summer. They miss sleep. Sometimes they even miss meals.

To churn out the last four national championships like the Penn State women's volleyball team has, everything starts with volleyball. Well, at least for the fall. But sophomore libero Ali Longo said even the offseason blurs together with August through December.

"In the offseason, we have more time to go through personal things," she said. "During the season, it's more team focused. You do have a little more free time [in the offseason], but it's not that big of a difference, I think."

Student-athletes choose to forego many parts of a typical college experience when they commit to play varsity sports, and that includes the volleyball players. However, most of them have already dedicated rigorous hours toward their club or high school teams before Penn State, so the time commitment doesn't come as a surprise.

Technically, the volleyball team does have an offseason when it's not competing in matches, but the players never stop practicing except for the very occasional week off during breaks.

Teammates create bonds off the court through this constant amount of time they spend in the gym. The lone seniors on the team, Megan Shifflett and Katie Kabbes, are roommates to this day. Freshmen Lacey Fuller and Micha Hancock, also roommates, said they go to Five Guys together on the weekends. On the road, they spawn fun out of long nights staying in their hotel or traveling on their charter plane. In Rec Hall, they've bonded with athletes on other Penn State teams who also train there.

The volleyball players like to spend some of their free time supporting other Penn State teams. They have been spotted at wrestling meets, soccer games, and basketball games this year. Basketball players, soccer players and wrestlers have been spotted at volleyball matches, as well.

"They're always at our game, so we want to give back to them and support them too," Kabbes said.

Volleyball is especially close with the wrestlers, having Sunday night dinners with them every week, Kabbes added.

It can be tedious prioritizing what other free time they're afforded, but Longo said it's something they're used to. Personally, the Penn State libero likes to eat, study and hang out when she's not diving for balls in the back row.

But that's not always as easy as it sounds, especially when the Nittany Lions are traveling. They don't have to wait around at airports because of their charter airline, but that also means there's no grace period between away matches. If they finish up at 10 p.m., they could be in the air en route to State College by midnight.

"It can get hectic depending on how your school schedule is," Longo said. "You have to be really good with talking to your professors."

Kabbes writes everything she has to do and when it's due on a calendar to mitigate any stress. She looks at it every Sunday and tries to get stuff done as early possible. She doesn't procrastinate because she doesn't have that kind of time. Her organization may have actually made Kabbes' academic life easier. She said that it's something she's never struggled with because it's a top priority.

When they have open space on their schedule, it's just the simple stuff. "Besides normal computer stuff like Facebook," Kabbes said, "I like to catch up with old friends I don't see all the time, shopping, and just hanging out."

reflecting on decisions

Based on what you learned about time management in this chapter, what insights have you gained about the way your decisions about time affect the outcomes of your life?

CURING ILLNESS WITH
COMPUTER DOWNTIME

How would you like to help cure an incurable disease in your spare time? If you have a computer, you can . . .

To understand how you can help cure illness with your computer's downtime, you need to know about distributed computing. Distributed computing uses different computers in different places to perform an application that is connected to a network. Professor Vijay Pande of Stanford University came up with the idea of distributed computing in 1991. That's when he needed calculations that would take about a million days on a fast computer. So he thought that if he and his students wanted to get the work done in 10 days, they needed access to 100,000 processors. Using distributed computing, they ran pieces of the simulation through networked computers to speed up the results. It worked!

Their current project, folding@home, has the goal of studying proteins. Before proteins work in the body, they assemble themselves, or "fold." When proteins misfold, there can be serious consequences such as Alzheimer's, ALS, Parkinson's disease, and cancer. The folding@home project asks people throughout the world to run software during the downtime of their home computers. It's safe and takes no more of your time than downloading a program. Ready to help find a cure? Visit **https://folding.stanford.edu/home/**.

◀ **CHOOSING TO SERVE**

R E V I E W

Skim the notes you made throughout the chapter. How does the content fit together? What information is still unclear? Were your learning goals met? Can you answer the review questions and define terms?

◀ **CHOOSING TO BE AN ACTIVE LEARNER**

Module 3
Critical Thinking

7

CRITICAL THINKING
WHY IT'S IMPORTANT

Nazi war criminal Adolf Eichmann was tried in Israel in 1960 for crimes against humanity. Despite his claim that he was just following the orders of his superiors when he ordered the deaths of millions of Jews, the court found him guilty and sentenced him to death. Was Eichmann an inhuman monster? Or was he, as his defense lawyer claimed, just doing what many of us would do— following orders from our superiors?

To address this question, social psychologist Stanley Milgram of Yale University conducted, between 1960 and 1963, what has become a classic experiment. Milgram placed an advertisement in a newspaper asking for men to take part in a scientific study of memory and learning.[1] Those chosen to participate were told that the purpose of the experiment was to study the effects of punishment on learning—and that their job was to give electric shocks as punishment when the learner gave a wrong answer. The participants were instructed that

In what ways does sharing ideas with others and listening to their feedback help develop our critical thinking skills?

173

THiNK
FIRST

- What are the characteristics of a skilled critical thinker?
- What are the three levels of thinking?
- What are some of the barriers to critical thinking?

>> the shocks would be given at the direction of the experimenter and would range in intensity from 15 volts to 450 volts. In fact, no shocks were actually being given, but the participants didn't know this.

As the intensity of the shocks "increased," the learner (actually an actor) responded with increased anguish, screaming in pain and pleading with the participant delivering the shocks to stop. Despite the repeated pleas, all the participants gave shocks of up to 300 volts before refusing to go on. In addition, 65 percent continued to deliver shocks of 450 volts simply because an authority figure (a scientist in a white lab coat) told the participants to continue. Most who continued were clearly disturbed by what they were doing. However, unlike the participants who refused to continue, they were unable to provide logical counterarguments to the scientist's insistence that "the experiment requires that you must continue."

How could this happen? Were the results of Milgram's study some sort of aberration? As it turns out, they were not.

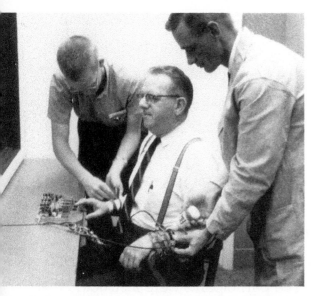

Milgram Experiment *Scene from the Milgram experiment on obedience. The "learner" is being hooked up to the machine that will deliver bogus electric shocks each time he gives a wrong answer.*

Several years later, in 1971, the U.S. Navy funded a study of the reaction of humans to situations in which there are huge differences in authority and power—as in a prison. The study was administered under the direction of psychologist Philip Zimbardo, who selected student volunteers judged to be psychologically stable and healthy.[2] The volunteers were randomly assigned to play the role of either "guard" or "prisoner" in a two-week prison simulation in the basement of the Stanford University building in which the psychology department was located. To make the situation more realistic, guards were given wooden batons and wore khaki, military-style uniforms and mirrored sunglasses that minimized eye contact. The prisoners were given ill-fitting smocks without underwear and rubber thongs for their feet. Each prisoner was also assigned a number to be used instead of a name. The guards were not given any formal instructions; they were simply told that it was their responsibility to run the prison.

The experiment quickly got out of control. Prisoners were subjected to abusive and humiliating treatment, both physical and emotional, by the guards. One-third of the guards became increasingly cruel, especially at night when they thought the cameras had been turned off. Prisoners were forced to clean toilets with their bare hands, to sleep on concrete floors, and to endure solitary confinement and hunger. They were also subjected to forced nudity and sexual abuse—much like what would happen many years later in 2003–2004 at Abu Ghraib prison in Iraq. (see Analyzing Images: Abuse at Abu Ghraib prison, Iraq, page 188). After only six days, the Stanford prison experiment had to be called off.

These experiments suggest that many, if not most, Americans will uncritically follow the commands of those in authority. Like the Milgram study, the Stanford prison experiment demonstrated that ordinary people will commit atrocities in situations where there is social and institutional support for behavior that they would not do on their own and if they could put the blame on others. Milgram wrote:

> Ordinary people, simply doing their jobs and without any particular hostility on their part, can become agents in a terrible destructive process. Moreover, even when the destructive effects of their work become patently clear, and they are asked to carry out actions incompatible with fundamental standards of the majority, relatively few people have the resources needed to resist authority.[3]

What are these resources that people need to resist authority? Good critical-thinking skills are certainly one. Those who refused to continue in the Milgram study were able to give good reasons for why they should stop: for example, "it is wrong to cause harm to another person." In contrast, those who continued, even though they knew what they were doing was wrong, simply deferred to the authority figure even though he was making unreasonable demands of them.[4]

Although most of us may never be in a situation in which our actions have such grim consequences, a lack of critical-thinking skills can still have negative consequences in our everyday decisions. When it comes making to personal, educational, and career choices, we may defer to our parents or cave in to pressure from friends rather than think through the reasons for our decisions. When major life decisions are not carefully thought out, there can be long-lasting consequences, such as dropping out of school or choosing a career in which we are ultimately unhappy. In addition, because critical-thinking skills are transferable across disciplines, improving these skills can have a positive impact on our success in college. In this chapter we'll be looking at some of the components of critical thinking as well as the benefits of developing good critical-thinking skills. We'll conclude by examining some of the barriers to critical thinking. Specifically, we will:

- Define *critical thinking* and *logic*
- Learn about the characteristics of a good critical thinker
- Distinguish between giving an opinion and engaging in critical thinking
- Explain the benefits of good critical thinking
- Relate critical thinking to personal development and our role as citizens in a democracy
- Identify people who exemplify critical thinking in action
- Identify barriers to critical thinking, including types of resistance and narrow-mindedness

At the end of the chapter, we will apply our critical-thinking skills to a specific issue by discussing and analyzing different perspectives on affirmative action in college admissions.

> These experiments suggest that many, if not most, Americans will uncritically follow the commands of those in authority.

WHAT IS CRITICAL THINKING?

Critical thinking is a collection of skills we use every day that are necessary for our full intellectual and personal development. The word *critical* is derived from the Greek word *kritikos,* which means "discernment," "the ability to judge," or "decision making." Critical thinking requires learning *how* to think rather than simply *what* to think.

Critical thinking, like logic, requires good analytical skills. **Logic** is part of critical thinking and is defined as "the study of the methods and principles used in distinguishing correct (good) arguments from incorrect (bad) arguments."[5] Critical thinking involves the application of the rules of logic as well as gathering evidence, evaluating it, and coming up with a plan of action.

critical thinking A collection of skills we use every day that are necessary for our full intellectual and personal development.

logic The study of the methods and principles used to distinguish correct or good arguments from poor arguments.

opinion A belief based solely on personal feelings rather than on reason or facts.

Critical Thinking in Everyday Life

Critical thinking provides us with the tools to identify and resolve issues in our lives. Critical thinking is not simply a matter of asserting our opinions on issues. **Opinions** are based on personal feelings or beliefs, rather than on reason and evidence. We are all certainly entitled to our own opinions. Opinions, however, are not necessarily reasonable. While some may happen to turn out to be correct, opinions, no matter how deeply and sincerely held, may also be mistaken. As a critical thinker you need to be willing to provide logical support for your beliefs.

Uninformed opinions can lead you to make poor decisions in your life and act in ways that you may later come to regret. Sometimes uninformed opinions can negatively impact society. For example, even though antibiotics kill bacteria and have no effect on cold viruses, many people try to persuade their doctors into prescribing them for cold symptoms. Despite doctors telling patients that antibiotics have no effect on viral infections, studies show that about half of doctors give in to patient pressure for antibiotics for viral infections.[6] Such overuse of antibiotics makes bacteria more drug resistant and has led to a decline in the effectiveness of treatment in diseases where they are really needed.[7] This phenomenon

SELF-EVALUATION QUESTIONNAIRE

Rate yourself on the following scale from 1 (strongly disagree) to 5 (strongly agree).

1 2 3 4 5   There are right and wrong answers. Authorities are those who have the right answers.

1 2 3 4 5   There are no right or wrong answers. Everyone has a right to his or her own opinion.

1 2 3 4 5   Even though the world is uncertain, we need to make decisions on what is right or wrong.

1 2 3 4 5   I tend to stick to my position on an issue even when others try to change my mind.

1 2 3 4 5   I have good communication skills.

1 2 3 4 5   I have high self-esteem.

1 2 3 4 5   I would refuse to comply if an authority figure ordered me to do something that might cause me to hurt someone else.

1 2 3 4 5   I don't like it when other people challenge my deeply held beliefs.

1 2 3 4 5   I get along better with people than do most people.

1 2 3 4 5   People don't change.

1 2 3 4 5   I have trouble coping with problems of life such as relationship problems, depression, and rage.

1 2 3 4 5   I tend to sacrifice my needs for those of others.

1 2 3 4 5   Men and women tend to have different communication styles.

1 2 3 4 5   The most credible evidence is that based on direct experience, such as eyewitness reports.

Keep track of your results. As you read this book and gain a better understanding of critical thinking, you'll find out what your responses to each of these statements mean. A brief summary of the meaning of each rating can also be found at the back of the book.

"All or Nothing" Thinking

DISCUSSION QUESTIONS

1. Discuss Calvin's claim that seeing the complexities of knowledge is "paralyzing."

2. Think back to a time when you felt, as does Calvin in the cartoon, that life is easier if you can think in dualist terms of black and white rather than "seeing the complexities and shades of gray." Referring back to this and other similar experiences, what are some of the drawbacks of making decisions or taking action on the basis of all-or-nothing thinking? Be specific.

has been linked to the emergence of new, more virulent strains of drug-resistant tuberculosis. In addition, the incidence of some sexually transmitted diseases such as syphilis, which was once treatable by penicillin, is once again on the rise.[8]

The ability to think critically and to make effective life decisions is shaped by many factors, including our stage of cognitive development, the possession of good analytical communication, and research skills and such characteristics as open-mindedness, flexibility, and creativity.

Cognitive Development in College Students

Becoming a critical thinker is a lifelong process. Education researcher William Perry, Jr. (1913–1998) was one of the first to study college students' cognitive development.[9] **Cognitive development** is the process by which each of us "becomes an intelligent person, acquiring intelligence and increasingly advanced thought and problem-solving ability from infancy to adulthood."[10] Perry's work has gained wide acceptance among educators. Although Perry identified nine developmental positions, later researchers have simplified his schemata into three stages: dualism, relativism, and commitment. These three stages are represented by the first three questions

in the Self-Evaluation Questionnaire in the Think Tank feature on page 176.

cognitive development The process of acquiring advanced thinking and problem-solving skills from infancy through adulthood.

Stage 1: Dualism.

Younger students such as freshmen and many sophomores tend to take in knowledge and life experiences in a simplistic, "dualistic" way, viewing something as either right or wrong. They see knowledge as existing outside themselves and look to authority figures for the answers.

This dualistic stage is most obvious when these students confront a conflict. Although they may be able to apply critical-thinking skills in a structured classroom environment, they often lack the ability to apply these skills in real-life conflicts. When confronted with a situation such as occurred in the Milgram study of obedience,[11] they are more likely to follow an authority figure even if they feel uncomfortable doing so. In addition, a controversial issue such as affirmative action, where there is little agreement among authorities and no clear-cut right or wrong answers, can leave students at this stage struggling to make sense of it. We'll be studying some perspectives on affirmative action at the end of this chapter.

Connections

How do you determine if the statistics found in the results of a scientific experiment are credible?

When researching an issue, students at the dualistic stage may engage in **confirmation bias**, seeking out only evidence that supports their views and dismissing as unreliable statistics that contradict them.[12] The fact that their "research" confirms their views serves to reinforce their simplistic, black-and-white view of the world.

> **confirmation bias** At the dualistic stage of research, seeking out only evidence that supports your view and dismissing evidence that contradicts it.

HIGHLIGHTS

COGNITIVE DEVELOPMENT IN COLLEGE STUDENTS

Stage 1: Dualism There are right and wrong answers. Authorities know the right answers.

Transition to Stage 2 There are some uncertainties and different opinions, but these are temporary.

Stage 2: Relativism When the authorities don't have the right answers, everyone has a right to his or her own opinion; there are no right or wrong answers.

Transition to Stage 3 All thinking is contextual and relative but not equally valid.

Stage 3: Commitment I should not just blindly follow or oppose authority. I need to orient myself in an uncertain world and make a decision or commitment.

➤ *APPLICATION: Identify an example of thinking at each of three stages in the text.*

Adapted from Ron Sheese and Helen Radovanovic, "W. G. Perry's Model of Intellectual and Ethical Development: Implications of Recent Research for the Education and Counseling of Young Adults," paper presented at the annual meeting of the Canadian Psychological Association (Ottawa, Ontario, June 1984).

In one study, 48 undergraduates, who either supported or opposed capital punishment, were given two fictitious studies to read.[13] One study presented "evidence" contradicting beliefs about the deterrent effect of capital punishment. The other study presented "evidence" confirming the effectiveness of capital punishment as a deterrent. The results showed that students uncritically accepted the evidence that confirmed their preexisting views, while being skeptical about opposing evidence. In other words, despite the fact that both groups read the same studies, rather than modifying their position, the students used the confirming study to support their existing opinion on capital punishment and dismissed the opposing evidence.

Students at this stage may also be unable to recognize ambiguity, conflicting values, or motives in real-life situations. In light of this, it is not surprising that young people are most likely to fall victim to con artists, financial fraud, and identity theft, despite the stereotype that the elderly are more vulnerable to scam artists.[14]

Students are most likely to make the transition to a higher stage of cognitive development when their current way of thinking is challenged or proves inadequate. During the transition they come to recognize that there is uncertainty in the world and that authorities can have different positions. Some educators called this period of disorientation and doubting all answers "sophomoritis."[15]

Stage 2: Relativism. Rather than accepting that ambiguity and uncertainty may be unavoidable and that they need to make decisions despite this, students at the relativist stage go to the opposite extreme. They reject a dualistic worldview and instead believe that all truth is relative or just a matter of opinion. People at this stage believe that stating your opinion is the proper mode of expression, and they look down on challenging others' opinions as "judgmental" and even disrespectful. However, despite their purported belief in relativism, most students at this stage still expect their professor to support his or her opinion.

Having their ideas challenged, grappling with controversial issues, encountering role models who are at a higher stage of cognitive development, and learning about their limits and the contradictions in their thinking can all help students move on to the next stage of cognitive development.

Stage 3: Commitment. As students mature, they come to realize that not all thinking is equally valid. Not only can authorities be mistaken but also in some circumstances uncertainty and ambiguity are unavoidable. When students at this stage experience uncertainty, they are now able to make decisions and commit to particular positions on the basis of reason and the best evidence available. At the same time, as independent thinkers, they are open to challenge, able to remain flexible, and willing to change their position should new evidence come to light.

> As students mature,
> they come to realize that not
> all thinking is equally valid.

As we mature and acquire better critical-thinking skills, our way of conceptualizing and understanding the world becomes increasingly complex. This is particularly true of older students who return to college after spending time out in the "real world." Unlike people at the first stage who look to authority for answers, people at the third stage accept responsibility for their interactions with their environment and are more open to challenges and more accepting of ambiguity.

STOP AND ASSESS YOURSELF

I. Imagine that you are a participant in Milgram's study of obedience. What would you have done if you protested and the experimenter in charge answered, "The experiment requires that you continue"? Discuss your answer in light of the stages of cognitive development. Discuss also what you might do to make it less likely that you would obey an authority figure in a situation such as the Milgram study.

2. College professor Stephen Satris maintains that the relativism of the second stage of development is not a genuine philosophical position but a means of avoiding having one's ideas challenged. Student relativism, he writes, "is primarily a method of protection, a suit of armor, which can be applied to one's own opinions, whatever they may be—but not necessarily to the opinion of others. . . . It is an expression of the idea that no one step forward and judge (and possibly criticize) one's own opinion."[16] What is your "suit of armor"? Discuss strategies you might take to break out of this "suit of armor." Relate your answer to your own stage of cognitive development.

3. Most college students do not make the transition to the third, or commitment, stage of cognitive development. Why do you think this is so? Discuss ways in which the curriculum and college life in general might be restructured to encourage cognitive growth in students.

4. Today, more people are returning to college after having children and/or having worked for several years. This phenomenon is especially prevalent in community colleges, where the average age is 28.[17] Discuss whether there are differences in how students of different ages in your class think about the world, and how interaction among students at different stages might enrich our thinking.

5. The first three questions of the "Self-Evaluation Questionnaire" in the Think Tank feature represent the three stages of cognitive development. Which stage, or transition between stages, best describes your approach to understanding the world? What are the shortcomings and strengths of your current stage of cognitive development? Develop a plan to improve your skills as a critical thinker. Put the plan into action. Report on the results of your action plan.

CHARACTERISTICS OF A GOOD CRITICAL THINKER

Critical thinking is a collection of skills that enhance and reinforce each other. In this section we'll be discussing some of the more important skills for effective critical thinking.

Analytical Skills

As a critical thinker, you need to be able to analyze and provide logical support for your beliefs rather than simply rely on your opinions. Analytical skills are also important in recognizing and evaluating other people's arguments so that you are not taken in by faulty reasoning.

Effective Communication

In addition to analytical skills, critical thinking requires communication and reading skills.[18] Communication skills include listening, speaking, and writing skills. Being aware of your own communication style, as well as of cultural variations and differences in the communication styles of men and women, can also go a long way toward improving communication in a relationship.

Research and Inquiry Skills

Understanding and resolving issues requires research and inquiry skills such as competence in gathering, evaluating, and pulling together supporting evidence. For example, in researching and gathering information on what would be the best major or career path for you, you need to identity your interests and talents first and then evaluate possible majors and careers in light of these interests and talents. Research skills are also important in understanding and moving toward a resolution of a complex issue such as affirmative action in college admissions.

Inquiry and gaining greater insight requires asking the right questions, as Milgram did in designing his study of obedience. While most people were asking what sort of twisted monsters the Nazis were or why the German people allowed Hitler to have so much power, Milgram asked the more basic question: How far would ordinary citizens go in obeying an authority figure? Despite the fact that experiments such as Milgram's were declared unethical by the American Psychological Association in 1973 because of long-term psychological distress suffered by many of the participants, his scientific experiments still stand as classics in the field.

As critical thinkers we need to avoid confirmation bias and the tendency to selectively see and interpret data to fit into our own world-views, as happened in the study on student's views of capital punishment (see page 178). This is a practice that often leads to stalemates and conflict in personal as well as in political relations. Our research should also be accurate and based on credible evidence. We'll be learning more about researching and evaluating evidence in Chapter 8.

René Descartes (1596–1650) proposed the method of doubt, in which we never accept anything as true without evidence and reason to support our conclusion.

Flexibility and Tolerance for Ambiguity

Too many people defer to others or fail to take a position on a controversial issue simply because they are unable to evaluate conflicting views. As we mature, we become better at making decisions in the face of uncertainty and ambiguity. Effective decision making includes setting clear short-term and long-term goals in our lives and developing a realistic strategy for achieving these goals. Critical thinkers also build flexibility into their life plans so that they can adapt to changes, especially since most of us haven't had sufficient experience to finalize our life plan during our first few years of college. We'll be discussing the process of developing a life plan in more depth later in this chapter.

Connections

How do scientists identify a problem and develop a hypothesis for studying a problem?

Open-Minded Skepticism

Critical thinkers are willing to work toward overcoming personal prejudices and biases. They begin with an open mind and an attitude of reflective skepticism. The point is not simply to take a stand on an issue—such as What career is best for me? Is abortion immoral? Does God exist? What should be the role of women in the family?—but rather to critically examine the evidence and assumptions put forth in support of different positions on the issue before coming to a final conclusion. In doing so, effective critical thinkers are able to balance belief and doubt.

First put forward by French philosopher and mathematician René Descartes (1596–1650), the **method of doubt** suspends belief. This method of critical analysis,

which has traditionally been preferred in fields such as science and philosophy, begins from a position of skepticism in which we put aside our preconceived ideas. Descartes wrote regarding the rules for using the method of doubt:

> The first of these [rules] was never to accept anything as true if I did not have evident knowledge of its truth: that is to say, carefully to avoid precipitate conclusions and preconceptions, and to include nothing more in my judgments than what presented itself to my mind so clearly and distinctly that I had no occasion to doubt it.[19]

It is especially important that you be willing to adopt a position of doubt or skepticism when critically examining your own cherished beliefs and the claims of authority figures. Albert Einstein (1879–1955), in developing his theory of relativity, used the method of doubt regarding the generally accepted belief that time is "absolute"—that is, fixed and unchanging.

The **method of belief**, in contrast, suspends doubt. Becoming immersed in a good book, movie, or play often involves what English poet Samuel Taylor Coleridge (1772–1834) called the "willing suspension of disbelief." This approach is also productive when we are discussing issues on which we hold strong views and are not as open as we should be to opposing viewpoints. In dialogues between people who are pro-choice and pro-life, for example, a pro-choice critical thinker, in order to compensate for his or her biases, should be genuinely open to believing what the pro-life person is saying, rather than start from the traditional position of doubt. This task requires empathy, active listening skills, and intellectual curiosity.

Creative Problem Solving

Creative thinkers can view problems from multiple perspectives and come up with original solutions to complex problems. They use their imagination to envision possibilities, including potential future problems, and to develop contingency plans to effectively deal with these scenarios.

When staff members of the U.S. Department of Homeland Security put together a handbook of possible disaster scenarios, they failed to foresee the possibility of civil unrest and social breakdown following a disaster. Because of lack of preparedness for such occurrences as Hurricane Katrina, which struck the Gulf Coast in 2005, hundreds of people died who might have been saved and thousands of others were left homeless and living in chaotic and squalid conditions for weeks and months. Practice in problem-solving for disasters enabled the United States to respond quicker and more effectively when the East Coast was struck by Superstorm Sandy in 2012.

The Tokyo Electric Power Company, operator of the Fukushima Daiichi nuclear power plant, failed to take measures to prevent disasters, like the one that followed an earthquake and tsunami off the coast of Japan in 2011. Rather than taking on the challenge of making the plant secure from such events, they ignored the possibility that there could be such a large tsunami. Consequently, they failed to install adequate backup generators and cooling systems and as a result the power plants experienced a nuclear meltdown spewing toxic radiation into the surrounding area.

Creativity also involves "a willingness to take risks, to cope with the unexpected, to welcome challenge and even failure as a part of the process to arrive at a new and deeper understanding."[20] Instead of giving up when

method of doubt A method of critical analysis in which we put aside our preconceived ideas and beliefs and begin from a position of skepticism.

method of belief A method of critical analysis in which we suspend our doubts and biases and remain genuinely open to what people with opposing views are saying.

About 20,000 people died as a result of the tsunami that struck Japan in 2011. The tsunami also caused extensive damage to the nuclear power plants on the coast.

times are difficult or resources are lacking, creative critical thinkers are able to make creative use of available resources. In 1976, when he was only 21, Steve Jobs built the first Apple personal computer in his family's garage. His innovative idea of user-friendly software changed the way people perceived computers and heralded the age of personal computing. He later went on to introduce the iPod, which revolutionized portable music players.

Creative thinking is a much sought-after skill in the business world.[21] Because young people are usually less invested in traditional ideas and ways of doing things than are people who have been working in a field for years, they tend to be more open to new ideas. Being able to recognize creative solutions to a problem and to generate and communicate new ideas requires not just creative thinking but also being open-minded, confident, intellectually curious, and an effective communicator.

Attention, Mindfulness, and Curiosity

Critical thinkers are intellectually curious. They are attentive and mindful to what's going on around them and to their own thoughts and feelings. The Buddhist concept of the "beginner's mind" is closely related to the Western concept of the critically open mind, or mindfulness. Zen master Shunryu Suzuki defined the beginner's mind as "wisdom which is seeking for wisdom." He wrote:

> The practice of Zen mind is beginner's mind. The innocence of first inquiry—what am I? . . . The mind of the beginner is empty, free of the habits of the expert, ready to accept, to doubt, and open to all possibilities. . . . If your mind is empty, it is always ready for anything; it is open to everything. In the beginner's mind there are many possibilities. . . .[22]

Like the beginner's mind, good critical thinkers do not reject, without sound reasons, views that conflict with their own. Instead, they are willing to consider multiple perspectives. One of the recent breakthroughs in neuroscience is the discovery that the brains of Buddhist monks who meditate regularly—a practice that involves being mindful, open, and attentive to what is going on in the present moment—are neurally much more active and more resilient in neuroplasticity than are the brains of

people who do not meditate.[23] Many large corporations, including some Fortune 500 companies, are encouraging their executives to take meditation breaks on the job, since it has been found to improve their performance.[24]

Collaborative Learning

Critical thinking occurs in a real-life context. We are not isolated individuals—we are interconnected beings. As critical thinkers we need to move beyond the traditional, detached approach to thinking and develop a more collaborative approach that is grounded in shared dialogue and community.

The failure to take into account context and relationships can lead to faulty decisions that we may later regret. An example of this type of faulty reasoning is the tendency of many individuals to neglect both feedback and complexity. Because of this, they tend not to fully and accurately consider the other side's response. In a relationship we may do something in an attempt to get our partner to pay more attention to us—for example, threatening to leave a partner if he or she doesn't stop spending so much time with friends—only to see this backfire, losing the relationship altogether because we failed to consider how the other person might react.[25]

To use another example, military planners in developing strategies sometimes fail to consider what the enemy might do in return to minimize the effectiveness of these strategies. During the War of 1812, a group of politicians in Washington, D.C., decided the time had come to add Canada to the United States. Their military strategy failed primarily because they did not adequately assess the Canadian response to the U.S. mission to annex Canada. Instead of greeting the American invaders as liberators from British rule, Canadians regarded the war as an unprovoked attack on their homes and lives. Rather than uniting Canada and

Did You Know

The ancient Greek thinker Socrates (469–399 BCE) spent much of his time in the marketplace of Athens surrounded by his young followers. He used this public venue to seek out people in order to challenge their traditional beliefs and practices. He did this by engaging people in a type of critical thinking, now referred to as the Socratic method, in which his probing questions provoked them into realizing their lack of rational understanding and their inconsistencies in thought.

the United States, the War of 1812 gave rise to the first stirring of Canadian nationalism (and even provoked a movement in New England to secede from the United States).[26]

HIGHLIGHTS

CHARACTERISTICS OF A SKILLED CRITICAL THINKER

As a skilled critical thinker, you should

- Have good **analytical skills**
- Possess effective **communication skills**
- Be **well informed** and possess good **research skills**
- Be **flexible** and able to **tolerate ambiguity** and uncertainty
- Adopt a position of **open-minded skepticism**
- Be a creative **problem solver**
- Be **attentive, mindful, and intellectually curious**
- Engage in **collaborative learning**

➤*APPLICATION: Identify an example of each of the characteristics in the text.*

Good critical thinkers adopt a collaborative rather than an adversarial stance, in which they listen to and take others' views into account. Let's go back to the relationship example. Rather than accusing our partner of not spending enough time with us, a good critical thinker would express his or her feelings and thoughts and then listen to the other person's side. Critical thinkers carefully consider all perspectives and are open to revising their views in light of their broader understanding. Using our critical-thinking skills, we might come to realize that

---

Good critical thinkers adopt a collaborative rather than an adversarial stance.

---

our partner's friends are very important to him or her. Perhaps we are being insecure and need to spend more time with our own friends, giving our partner more space. Maybe we can find a solution that meets both our needs. For example, the sports lovers can bring their partners or another friend along once or twice a month to watch the games with them.

STOP AND ASSESS YOURSELF

EXERCISE 7-2

1. Watch the Milgram film *Obedience*. Discuss ways in which the participants in the film demonstrated, or failed to demonstrate, good critical-thinking skills.

2. Identifying good role models in your life can help you come up with a picture of the person you would like to be. Think of a person, real or fictional, who exemplifies good critical-thinking skills. Make a list of some of the qualities of this person. Discuss how these qualities help the person in his or her everyday life.

3. Adopt the stance of the Buddhist "beginner's mind." Be attentive only to what is happening in the now. After one minute, write down everything you observed going on around you as well as inside of you (your feelings, body language, and the like). Did you notice more than you might have otherwise? Share your observations with the class. Discuss ways in which this practice of being more attentive to what is going on might enhance your effectiveness as a critical thinker.

4. Working in groups of four to six students, select an issue about which the group is evenly divided into positions for or against it. Each side should adopt a stance of belief and open-mindedness when listening to the other side's position. After the pro side presents its views for two minutes, the anti side takes one minute to repeat back the pro's views without interjecting their own doubts. Repeat the process with the anti side presenting their views. Discuss as a class how this exercise helped you to suspend your biases and to actively listen to views that diverge from your own.

5. Referring to the Self-Evaluation Questionnaire on page 176, share your strengths and weaknesses as well as your plans for improving your critical-thinking skills with others, whether it be friends, family, or in class. Discuss steps you might take or have already taken to work toward or overcome some of your weaknesses.

CRITICAL THINKING AND SELF-DEVELOPMENT

Critical thinking is not just about abstract thought. It is also about self-improvement and your whole development as a person. Working on your self requires that you be honest with yourself and others about your biases, your expectations, your strengths, and your limitations. Are your expectations realistic? Do you have a well thought out plan and goals for your life? People who are inflexible in their thinking may be unable to adapt to changing or new or unusual circumstances and may instead get caught up in rules and inflexible ways of thinking that are inadequate to resolve the situation.

Living the Self-Examined Life

"The unexamined life is not worth living," Socrates said. Often we flounder in college because we have not taken the time to learn about ourselves or develop a plan for our future. The lives of too many people are controlled more by circumstances than by their own choices. Good critical thinkers, in contrast, take charge of their lives and choices rather than opting for the security of fitting into the crowd or simply blindly following an authority figure as happened in the Milgram study at the beginning of this chapter. In addition to being rational thinkers, they are in touch with their emotions and feelings.

Some psychologists and psychiatrists believe that irrational beliefs and poor critical-thinking skills contribute to many of the "problems of life," such as depression, rage, and low self-esteem.[27, 28] While depression often has a biochemical component that needs to be treated, poor critical-thinking skills can aggravate or even be a major factor in some types of situational depression where a student feels overwhelmed and unable to cope or make a decision in a particular set of circumstances. In a 2011 survey by the American College Health Association, about 30 percent of college students reported that at least once during the past year they felt "so depressed, it was difficult to function." Since people tend to become better at problem-solving as they get older, it is not surprising that depression rates start to drop beginning at age 30. Compared to people over the age of 60, 18–29 year-olds are 70 percent more likely to experience depression.[29]

Although by no means a cure-all, improving critical-thinking skills has been shown to help people deal more effectively with their problems.[30] Rather than view the problems in our lives as being out of our control, we should—as cognitive psychologists in particular counsel us—develop strategies for taking charge of our lives, develop realistic expectations, and commit ourselves to acknowledging and developing the skills to resolve our problems.

Developing a Rational Life Plan

American philosopher John Rawls (1921–2002) wrote that in order to get the most out of life, everyone needs to develop a "rational life plan"—that is, a plan that would be chosen "with full deliberative rationality, that is, with full awareness of the relevant facts and after a careful consideration of the consequences. . . . Someone is happy, when his plans are going well and his more important aspirations are being fulfilled."[31]

In drawing up our life plan, we make a hierarchy, with our most important plans or goals at the top, followed by a list of subplans. Organize your goals according to a schedule when they are to be carried out, although the more distant a goal is, the less specific the plan will be. Of course, we can't predict everything that will happen in life, and there will be times when circumstances hinder us from achieving our goals. Think of a life plan as being like a flight plan. Airplanes are off course about 90 percent of the time because of such factors as weather, wind patterns, and other aircraft. The pilot must constantly correct for these conditions to get the plane back on course. Without a flight plan, the pilots and their planes would be at the mercy of winds and weather, blown hither and thither, and never reaching their destination.

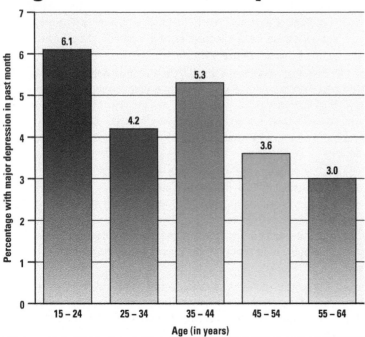

Age Differences in Depression

Source: Santrock (2009) *Life-Span Development,* McGraw-Hill, p. 404.

Begin putting together your life plan by making a list of your values, interests, skills, and talents. Values are what are important to you in life and include things such as financial security, love, family, career, independence, spirituality, health and fitness, education, contributions to society, friends, sense of integrity, and fun. Your goals in life should be rational as well as consistent with your values. According to the 2013 American Freshman Survey, "raising a family," the most important goal for several years, has now taken a back seat to being "able to get a good job," with 87.9 percent of freshman listing this as their top goal, the highest since 1966.[32] Take time to deliberate about your hierarchy of values. It is possible that after careful consideration of the implications of a particular value, such as "being well off financially," you may want to place it lower on your hierarchy of values.

If you are unsure of your skills and talents, go to the career office at your college and take some of the aptitude and personality tests available there, such as the Myers-Briggs Indicator.[33] These tests are useful in helping you to

maintain a 3.0 average, or get more exercise. These goals should be consistent with your interests, talents, and the type of person you want to be. Also come up with a plan of action to achieve these short-term goals.

Next, list your long-term goals. Ideally your long-term and short-term goals should augment each other. Your plans for achieving the long-term goals should be realistic and compatible with your short-term goals and interests. Think creatively about how certain goals can fit together.

People who are skilled critical thinkers not only have reasonable, well thought out goals and strategies to achieve them but also act from a sense of integrity or personal authenticity and respect for the integrity and aspirations of others in their lives. We are not isolated individuals but social beings whose decisions affect the lives of all those around us.

Facing Challenges

Sometimes traditional practices and cultural beliefs get in the way of our achieving our life plan. In these cases we may need to develop subgoals that involve challenging the

---

HIGHLIGHTS

MY LIFE PLAN

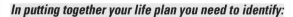

In putting together your life plan you need to identify:

1. **Your most important values**

2. **Your strengths (interests, skills, talents, and assets)**

3. **Your weaknesses (for example, lack of financial resources or skill)**

4. **Your goals**

   a. **Short term**

   b. **Long term**

5. **A plan of action to achieve short-term goals**

6. **A plan of action to achieve long-term goals**

➤ *APPLICATION: Identify an example of each of the six steps in the text.*

---

determine which career or careers might be most fulfilling for you. The Web site www.collegeboard.org also provides helpful information on choosing a major and a career.

But don't just list your strengths, assets, and competencies; take note of your weaknesses too. Weaknesses are something we do poorly or something we lack, such as financial resources, information, or technical expertise.

Once you've written down your values, interests, talents, skills, and weaknesses, list your goals. Goals are important in helping you organize your day-to-day life and in giving your life direction. Start out by listing short-term goals, or those that you want to accomplish by the time you graduate from college; for example, choose a major,

A life plan is like a flight plan; it helps keep us on course.

Martin Luther King's willingness to go to jail, rather than back down on his goal of equality for all people, made him one of the most effective civil rights leaders in American history.

obstructing beliefs rather than give up our life plan. Openly questioning traditional belief systems and effectively addressing challenges to deeply held beliefs requires courage and self-confidence. The abolitionists and early feminists and civil rights advocates were often ridiculed and even imprisoned because they challenged traditions they believed were unjust. See "Thinking Outside the Box: Elizabeth Cady Stanton, Women's Rights Leader."

When Martin Luther King Jr. was thrown in jail for his role in organizing the 1955 bus boycott in Montgomery, Alabama, he refused to back down despite the beseeching of his fellow clergy. Fortunately, King had the courage to stand by his convictions. In his "Letter from Birmingham Jail," King wrote:

> My Dear Fellow Clergy,
>
> I am in Birmingham because injustice is here. . . .
> We know through painful experience that freedom is never voluntarily given by the oppressor; it must be demanded by the oppressed.
>
> You express a great deal of anxiety over our willingness to break laws. . . . This is a legitimate concern . . . an unjust law is a code that is out of harmony with the moral law. . . . Any law that degrades human personality is unjust. . . . I submit that an individual who breaks a law that conscience tells him is unjust, and willingly accepts the penalty by staying in jail to arouse the conscience of the community over its injustice, is in reality expressing the very highest respect for law.

Critical thinking, as we noted earlier, requires being in touch with our emotions, such as indignation or anger,

elicited by unjust treatment, as in the case of King, or by a shocking image such as the photo showing the abuse at Abu Ghraib prison (see page 188).

In addition to being able to effectively challenge social injustices, as critical thinkers we need to be able to respond thoughtfully to challenges to our own belief systems rather than engaging in resistance. This requires good critical-thinking skills as well as self-confidence.

The Importance of Self-Esteem

Effective critical-thinking skills appear to be positively correlated to healthy self-esteem. Healthy self-esteem emerges from effectiveness in problem solving and success in achieving our life goals. The task of sorting out genuine self-worth from a false sense of self-esteem requires critical thinking. Healthy self-esteem is not the same as arrogant pride or always putting one's own interests first. Nor are people with proper self-esteem habitually self-sacrificing, subverting their interests and judgment to those of others.

People with low self-esteem are more vulnerable to manipulation by others. They experience more "depression, irritability, anxiety, fatigue, nightmares . . . withdrawal from others, nervous laughter, body aches and emotional tension."[34] Some of these traits, such as anxiety and nervous laughter, were seen in the Milgram study participants who complied with the request of the authority figure. Indeed, many of these men later came to regret their compliance and even required psychotherapy.

Good critical-thinking skills are essential in exercising your autonomy. Critical thinkers are proactive. They are aware of the influences on their lives, including family, culture, television, and friends; they can build on the positive influences and overcome the negative ones, rather than be passively carried through life and blaming others if their decisions turn out poorly.

An autonomous person is both rational and self-directing and therefore less likely to be taken in by poor reasoning or contradictions in his own or other's reasoning. Being self-directing entails making decisions on the basis of what is reasonable instead of getting swept up in groupthink or blindly obeying an authority figure. To achieve this end, autonomous critical thinkers seek out different perspectives and actively participate in critical dialogues to gain new insights and expand their own thinking.

Did You Know

Studies show that young people who have positive self-esteem "have more friends, are more apt to resist harmful peer pressure, are less sensitive to criticism or to what people think, have higher IQs, and are better informed."[35]

ELIZABETH CADY STANTON, *Women's Rights Leader*

Elizabeth Cady Stanton (1815–1902) was a social activist and leader in the early women's rights movement. In 1840, when she was a young newlywed, Stanton attended the World Anti-Slavery Society convention in London, which her husband was attending as a delegate. It was there that Stanton met Lucretia Mott (1793–1880). At the convention the women delegates from the United States were denied seats after some of the male U.S. delegates vehemently objected. Mott, in response, demanded that she be treated with the same respect accorded any man—white or black. During these heated discussions, Stanton marveled at the way Mott, a woman of 47, held her own in the argument, "skillfully parried all their attacks . . . turning the laugh on them, and then by her earnestness and dignity silencing their ridicule and jeers."*

Following the Civil War, Stanton refused to support passage of the Fifteenth Amendment, which gave voting rights to black men but not to women. She argued that the amendment essentially was based on the fallacy of false dilemma—either black men get the vote (but not women) or only white men can vote. Instead she pointed out that there was a third option: both men and women should have the right to vote. Unfortunately, her line of argument and her challenges to traditional beliefs about the role of women were ridiculed. Although black men received the vote in 1870 with passage of the Fifteenth Amendment, it would be another 50 years before women were finally given the right to vote in the United States. Nevertheless, Stanton's persistence and refusal to back down in her fight for equal opportunity for women paved the way for the final passage of this amendment so that other women could achieve their life plans of equal participation in the political life of the country.

DISCUSSION QUESTIONS

1. Elizabeth Cady Stanton had close friends such as Lucretia Mott and Susan B. Anthony in her fight for women's rights. Discuss ways in which having a support network of people who are skilled critical thinkers can enhance your ability not to use or fall for faulty reasoning. Discuss ways in which you do, or could, serve as a critical-thinking mentor to others.

2. Think of a time when your ability to pursue your goals was compromised by ridicule. Explain, using specific examples. Discuss steps you might take to make yourself less likely to give into faulty reasoning or to give up on an aspect of your life plan under such circumstances.

*Lloyd Hare, *The Greatest American Women: Lucretia Mott* (New York: American Historical Society, 1937), p. 193.

Abuse at Abu Ghraib Prison, Iraq
Being an autonomous thinker makes it less likely that you will uncritically follow orders or conform to peer pressure. The abuse and humiliation of Iraqi prisoners by U.S. soldiers at Abu Ghraib prison in Iraq in 2003–2004 provides a real-life illustration of what happened in the Milgram and Stanford prison experiments. In 2005, Army reservist and prison guard Charles Graner was convicted and sentenced to 10 years in prison for his role as ringleader in the abuse and humiliation of Iraqi detainees. In his defense he said that he was simply following orders. His defense lawyers also pointed out that the U.S. Army's intelligence units were poorly trained and badly managed, factors that contributed to the reservists' poor judgment. Graner's defense was rejected by the court. Graner was released from prison in 2011 after serving six years of his term.

DISCUSSION QUESTIONS

1. *Was Graner's reason for his treatment of the Iraqi prisoners justified? Should he be held responsible for his actions? Discuss what you might have done had you been a low-ranking guard at Abu Ghraib and had witnessed your fellow soldiers mistreating Iraqi prisoners.*

2. *What was your initial emotional reaction to this image? Discuss how learning to be aware of and critically analyzing your reaction to this or other upsetting images might make you more likely to question authority or rethink some of your world views. Support your response in light of what you know about autonomous thinkers.*

3. *Similar situations have occurred during fraternity and sorority initiation hazings. If you know of, or have been witness to, any situations where this happened, discuss why it most likely happened and what might have been done to prevent it.*

Critical Thinking in a Democracy

Critical-thinking skills are essential in a democracy. **Democracy** literally means rule by the people; it is a form of government in which the highest power in the state is invested in the people and exercised directly by them or, as is generally the case in modern democracies, by their elected officials. As citizens of a democracy, we have an obligation to be well informed about policies and issues so that we can effectively participate in critical discussions and decisions.

Thomas Jefferson wrote, "In a republican nation, whose citizens are to be led by reason and persuasion and not by force, the art of reasoning becomes of the first importance."[36] The purpose of democracy is not to achieve consensus through polling or majority vote but to facilitate open-ended discussion and debates by those with diverse views. Truth, argued British philosopher John Stuart Mill (1806–1873), often is found neither in the opinion of those who favor the status quo nor in the opinion of the noncon-formist but in a combination of viewpoints. Therefore, freedom of speech and listening to opposing views, no matter how offensive they may be, are essential for critical thinking in a democracy.

Corrupt politicians have been elected or appointed to public office and high-ranking positions in their parties because the

> **democracy** A form of government in which the highest power in the state is invested in the people and exercised directly by them or, as is generally the case in modern democracies, by their elected officials.

ANALYZING **IMAGES**

Student Protestor in Front of Tanks at Tiananmen Square,

China On June 3rd and 4th, 1989, hundreds, possibly thousands, of unarmed demonstrators protesting the legitimacy of China's communist government were shot dead in a brutal military operation to crush a democratic uprising in Beijing's Tiananmen Square. The demonstrators, who were mostly university students, had occupied the square for several weeks, refusing to leave until their demands for democratic reform were met. A photographer captured the above picture of a lone, unnamed demonstrator standing in front of the tanks, bringing to a halt the row of advancing tanks. To this day, no one knows who the demonstrator was or what his fate was.

DISCUSSION QUESTIONS

1. *What do you think the student in the photo is thinking and feeling? What do you think led up to his decision to take this action? Does his action show good critical thinking? Discuss ways in which the student's action demonstrates, or does not demonstrate, good critical-thinking skills. Relate your answer to the actions of reformers such as Stanton and King.*

2. *Imagine yourself in a similar situation. Discuss how you would most likely react and how your reaction is a reflection of your current self-development. What steps could you take in your life to make yourself more likely to engage in civil disobedience, particularly in a case where your life was not at stake?*

What critical-thinking skills do you need to participate in campaigns and elections, influence public policy, and understand the legal system?

Connections

people failed to educate themselves about their activities and ideals. Indeed, in a 1938 poll of Princeton freshmen, Adolf Hitler was ranked first as the "greatest living person"![37] And in New York City in the mid-nineteenth century, politician William Marcy "Boss" Tweed (1823–1878) conned citizens out of millions of dollars. He also managed to get his corrupt associates, known as the Tweed Ring, appointed and elected to high offices.

Unlike totalitarian societies, modern democracies encourage diversity and open discussion of different ideas. Research on the effects of race, ethnicity, class, and diversity on college students reveals "important links between experiences with diversity and increased commitment to civic engagement, democratic outcomes and community participation."[38] Exposure to diversity on campus and in the classroom broadens students' perspectives and improves critical thinking and problem-solving skills.[39]

In his book *The Assault on Reason* (2007), Al Gore argues that there has been a decline in participation by ordinary citizens in the democratic process since television overtook the printed word as the dominant source of information. Television as a one-way source of information appeals mainly to our uncritical emotions rather than requiring critical reflective thought, thus rendering viewers passive consumers of prepackaged information and ideologies. Political engagement tends to rise during a presidential election year and drop off following the election. For example, 39.5 percent of college freshmen in 2008 stated that "keeping up to date with political affairs" was an essential or very important objective for them. However, this figure had dropped to 36 percent one year after the election of Barack Obama.[40]

People who are skilled at critical thinking are less likely to be taken in by faulty arguments and rhetoric. They are also more likely, like the pro-democracy Chinese students in Tiananmen Square, to demand the same clarity and reasonableness of thinking in their leaders that they require in themselves rather than remain passive in the face of government abuses of power. Thus, critical thinking contributes to your own well-being as well as to the well-being of society as a whole, by teaching you how to stand up to authority and irrational thinking.

STOP AND ASSESS YOURSELF

1. According to German philosopher Immanuel Kant (1724–1804), one of our primary moral duties is self-respect and the development of proper self-esteem.[41] To truly respect others and their perspectives, we must first respect ourselves. Discuss and relate your answer to how proper self-respect might enhance your critical thinking skills. Use specific examples to support your answer.

2. Choose one of your short-term or long-term goals. Working in small groups, brainstorm about ways each of you might best achieve your goals. Also discuss the role good critical-thinking skills play (or played) in helping you achieve your goals.

3. In small groups, discuss a time when you deferred to the view of someone else and did (or failed to do) something you later came to regret because you were unable to give good reasons at the time for why you should not accept that person's view. Brainstorm with your group about ways in which you might make yourself less prone to this behavior.

4. A June 2004 article in *Altermedia Scotland* states: "America as a nation is now dominated by an alien system of beliefs, attitudes, and values that has become known as 'political correctness.' It seeks to impose a uniformity in thought and behaviour among all Americans and is therefore totalitarian in nature."[42] Do you agree that political correctness imposes "a uniformity of thought and behavior"? Come up with examples of political correctness on college campuses to illlustrate your answer. Discuss what role, if any, political correctness might play in increasing respect for diversity and enhancing the democratic process.

5. What is diversity? What are the educational benefits of diversity? Discuss ways in which your college, including your classes, addresses and facilitates diversity.

6. The student pro-democracy movement in Tiananmen Square was unsuccessful in terms of bringing democracy and a more open society to China. Does this failure mean that the movement and the lives that were lost were a waste? Support your answer.

7. Al Gore argues that the "mental muscles of democracy have begun to atrophy."[43] Discuss his claim. Relate your answer to the exercise of your "mental muscles" and those of other college students in political dialogue.

8. When the *Brown Daily Herald,* the student newspaper at Brown University, ran an ad from conservative activist David Horowitz entitled "Ten Reasons Why Reparation for Slavery Is a Bad Idea—and Racist Too," a coalition of Brown students stole and destroyed nearly 4,000 newspapers at campus distribution points. Defendants of the action argued that the ad was "an attempt to inject blatantly revisionist and, yes, racist arguments into a legitimate debate about black reparations . . . ."[44] Is it ever appropriate to censor views? Did the students have a legitimate right, on the basis of their freedom of speech, to destroy the newspapers? To what extent, if any, do we have an obligation in a democracy to listen attentively to and consider views that we find offensive? What would you have done had your school newspaper decided to publish the ad by Horowitz?

9. What are your strengths and talents? If you are not sure of your talents, go to the career office at your college and ask if you can take some of the personality and aptitude tests available there. These tests are also useful in helping you to determine which career or careers might be most fulfilling for you. Be creative; don't limit or underrate yourself.

BARRIERS TO CRITICAL THINKING

By sharpening your critical-thinking skills, you can become more independent and less susceptible to worldviews that foster narrow-mindedness. In this section we'll be looking at some of the barriers to critical thinking that keep us from analyzing our experiences or worldviews, as well as the experiences and worldviews of others.

The Three-Tier Model of Thinking

The processes used in critical thinking can be broken down into three tiers or levels: experience, interpretation, and analysis. Keep in mind that this division is artificial and merely helps to highlight the critical-thinking process. Although analysis is at the pinnacle of the process, the three-tier model is also recursive and dynamic, with analysis returning to experience for confirmation and interpretation being modified in light of the analysis of the new information. People never have pure experience or engage in pure analysis.

Experience, the first level, includes firsthand experience as well as information or empirical facts that we receive from other sources. Experience is the foundation of critical thinking and argumentation. It provides the material for interpretation and analysis. At this level of thinking we merely describe our experiences rather than try to understand them. For example:

1. I was turned down for the job I interviewed for.

2. Mark held the door open for me when I was leaving class.

3. Human cloning is illegal in the United States.

4. Although blacks represent only 12.8 percent of the U.S. population, they make up 37 percent of the prison inmates.[45]

Interpretation, the second level, involves trying to make sense of our experiences. This level of thinking includes individual interpretations of experiences as well as collective and cultural worldviews. Some of our interpretations may be well informed; others may be based merely on our opinions or personal feelings and prejudices.

Connections

How has the Internet enhanced your ability to participate in political life? In what ways is the news media biased? How can we as citizens participate in the law-making process?

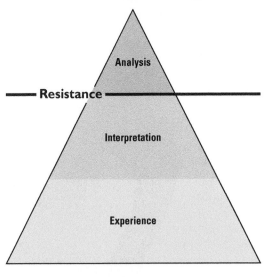

The Three Levels of Thinking

Analysis

Resistance

Interpretation

Experience

Some possible interpretations of the experiences previously listed are

1. I didn't get the job because I didn't have the right connections.
2. Mark is a chauvinist pig who thinks women are too weak to open their own doors.
3. If human cloning is illegal, it must be immoral.
4. Black men make up such a large percentage of the prison population because black men are innately more violent than white men.

Connections

How can you use the three-tier model of thinking to analyze media messages? What model of thinking do scientists use?

Analysis, the third level, requires that we raise our level of thinking and critically examine our interpretations of an experience, as well as those of others, refusing to accept either narrow interpretations of an experience or interpretations that are too broad. Analysis is most productive when it is done collectively because we each bring different experiences and interpretations, as well as skills in analysis, to the table. Analysis often begins by asking a question. The following are examples of questions we might ask in order to begin our analysis of the interpretations:

1. Was it my lack of connections or my poor interviewing skills or lack of job qualifications that caused me not to get the job?
2. What was Mark's intention in holding the door open for me?
3. Why is human cloning illegal? Are there circumstances in which human cloning might be acceptable?
4. Is there evidence that black men are innately more violent, or is it possible that black men are simply discriminated against more than white men? Or are other factors at work to account for their overrepresentation in the prison population?

The three-tier model of thinking provides a dynamic model of critical thinking in which analysis is always returning to experience for confirmation. As critical thinkers, it is not only our reasoning process that is important but also that our reasoning is connected to reality.

Resistance

Because most of us hate to be proven wrong, we may create barriers to keep our cherished worldviews from being challenged. Resistance, defined as "the use of immature defense mechanisms that are rigid, impulsive, maladaptive, and nonanalytical," can act as a barrier to critical thinking.

Almost all of us use defense mechanisms when we feel overwhelmed. Resistance, however, becomes a problem when it is used as a habitual way of responding to issues. Such habitual use interferes with our self-development, since it involves avoiding novel experiences and ideas that challenge our world-views. People who hold views that are backed by public opinion or the law may be particularly likely to resist when these views are challenged: They don't want to see the status quo upset.

> People who hold views that are backed by public opinion or the law may be particularly likely to resist when these views are challenged: They don't want to see the status quo upset.

In addition, resistance can create anxiety, since it puts us in a defensive mode and can shield us from the ideas and viewpoints of others, thus preventing us from working collaboratively and coming up with a well thought out plan of action.

Types of Resistance

There are several types of resistance, including avoidance, anger, clichés, denial, ignorance, conformity, struggling, and distractions.

Avoidance. Rather than seeking out different points of view, we may avoid certain people and situations. Some people who hold strong opinions but are insecure in their ability to defend these positions hang out only with people who agree with them or read literature and watch television news shows that support their worldview. I attended a church service during which the minister in her sermon lambasted Mel Gibson's movie *The Passion of the Christ* (2004) as a violent and inaccurate depiction of the betrayal and death of Jesus. I asked her after the service if she had seen the movie, and she said no. When I told her that I liked the movie, she frowned and quickly moved on to talk to someone else. As a form of resistance, avoidance can lead to a serious lack of communication and even hostility among people who hold opposing points of view.

Anger. We cannot always avoid people who disagree with us. Rather than using critical thinking when confronted with an opposing viewpoint, some people respond with anger. People with physical and/or social power are more likely than those without it to use anger to silence those who disagree with them. Anger may be expressed overtly by glares, threats, physical violence, gang activity, or even war.

Not all anger is resistance. We may feel anger or moral indignation when we hear that one of our favorite professors was denied tenure because he is Arab. This anger may motivate us to correct this injustice by writing a letter of protest to the local newspaper.

Clichés. Resorting to clichés—often-repeated statements such as "Don't force your views on me," "It's all relative," "To each his own," "Things always work out for the best," and "I have a right to my own opinion"—can keep us from thinking critically about issues. Advertisers and politicians often use clichés as a means of sidetracking us from considering the quality of the product or the issue at hand.

Resistance to analyzing one's position is seen in the abortion debate where each side has become entrenched in the clichés pro-choice or pro-life, with the pro-choice side focused on having few or no legal restrictions and the pro-life side wanting abortion to be illegal, at least in most cases. To overcome this divisive thinking, the term "reproductive justice" was coined by a group of black feminists to address the concerns of African-American women, whose abortion rate is three and one-half times that of white women. Loretta Ross, cofounder of the group Sister-Song Women of Color Reproductive Justice Collective, maintains that we need to think differently about the abortion debate. "Those of us in the reproductive justice movement, would say, 'Let's ask why there is such a high rate of unintended pregnancies in our community: What are the factors driving it?'"[46]

Used sparingly, clichés can be helpful to illustrate a point. However, the habitual use of clichés acts as a barrier to critical thinking.

Denial. According to the U.S. National Center for Injury Prevention and Control, alcohol-related motor vehicle accidents kill someone every 30 minutes and account for 41 percent of all traffic-related deaths.[47] Despite these startling statistics, people who drink and drive often deny that they are drunk. They may refuse to let someone else drive, claiming that they are quite capable of doing so.

Many Americans are also in denial about the possibility that world oil reserves may soon run out. Despite improved exploration technology, discovery of new oil reserves peaked in 1962 and has been dropping ever since. According to some predictions, active oil reserves may run out by anywhere from 2020 to 2030.[48] Yet, faced with declining fossil-fuel sources, many Americans continue to drive large vehicles and to live in large homes that cost more and more to heat.

Ignorance. Confucius taught that "Ignorance is the night of the mind." The modern Hindu yogi Swami Prabhavananda wrote, "Ignorance creates all the other obstacles." People are more likely to think critically about

Connections

How can our critical-thinking skills help us recognize misleading advertisements?

ANALYZING IMAGES

Is Ignorance Bliss?

DISCUSSION QUESTIONS

1. *Has there even been a time when, like the man in the picture above, you've preferred ignorance to being informed? Why? Support your answer with specific examples.*

2. *Some people accuse college students of taking the attitude that "ignorance is bliss" when it comes to participation in public life. Analyze this claim using research findings as well as examples to support your answer.*

issues about which they have knowledge in depth. In certain situations, we are ignorant about an issue simply because the information about it is not available to us. However, sometimes we just don't want to know.

Ignorance is a type of resistance when we intentionally avoid learning about a particular issue, about which information is readily available, in order to get out of having to think or talk about it. Ignorance is often used as an excuse for inaction. For example, Joe told his colleagues that he wanted to make a donation to help the Haitians following the 2010 earthquake but he didn't because "you just can't tell which charities are ripping you off and keeping most of the money for themselves." In fact, there are websites such as www.charitynavigator.org that inform potential donors exactly how much money each major charitable organization uses directly for charity and how much goes to administrative and fundraising costs. Some people believe that being ignorant excuses them from having to think critically about or take action on an issue. As a result, the issue is not resolved or even becomes worse.

How does the news media influence and reinforce narrow-minded worldviews?

Connections

Conformity. Many people fear that they will not be accepted by their peers if they disagree with them. Even though they may actually disagree, they go along with the group rather than risk rejection. We've probably all been in a situation where someone at work or a party makes a racist or sexist joke or an offensive comment about gays or women. Rather than speaking up, many people keep quiet or even laugh, thus tolerating and perpetuating bigotry and negative stereotypes.

Other people conform because they don't have a point of view of their own on an issue. Saying "I can see both sides of the issue" often masks a reluctance to think critically about it. Martin Luther King Jr. once pointed out, "Many people fear nothing more terribly than to take a position which stands out sharply and clearly from prevailing opinion. The tendency of most is to adopt a view that is so ambiguous that it will include everything, and so popular that it will include everyone."

Struggling. During the Nazi occupation of France in World War II, the people of the village of Le Chambonsur-Lignon provided refuge for Jews who were fleeing the Nazis. When Pierre Sauvage, director of *Weapons of the Spirit*—a documentary about the people and resistance movement of Le Chambon—was asked by PBS television's Bill Moyers years later why they did this when other people were still struggling about what to do, Sauvage replied, "Those who agonize don't act; those who act don't agonize."[49]

It is appropriate to struggle with or agonize over difficult issues before coming to a tentative stand. However, some people get so caught up in the minute details and "what ifs" of an issue—a situation sometimes referred to as "analysis paralysis"—that nothing gets accomplished. Procrastinators are most likely to use this type of resistance. Although struggling with an issue as part of the analytical process of coming up with a resolution and plan for action is an important component of critical thinking, when the struggle becomes an end-in-itself, we are engaging in resistance, not critical thinking.

Distractions. Some people hate silence and being left alone with their own thoughts. Many of us use television, loud music, partying, work, drugs, alcohol, or shopping to prevent our minds from critically thinking about troublesome issues in our lives. People may overeat instead of examining the causes of their cravings or unhappiness. Mental hindrances like distractions, according to Buddhist teaching, keep us from clear understanding. Instead, Buddhist philosophy values stillness and contemplation as means of achieving wisdom and understanding.

Narrow-Mindedness

Like resistance, narrow-mindedness and rigid beliefs, such as absolutism, egocentrism, and ethnocentrism can become barriers to critical thinking.

Absolutism. As we noted earlier, we may find ourselves acting contrary to our deeply held moral beliefs—as happened to most of the subjects in the Milgram study—simply because we do not have the critical-thinking skills necessary for standing up to unreasonable authority. In particular, college students at the first stage of cognitive development, where they regard information as either right or wrong, have an "expectation that authorities provide them with absolutely correct knowledge."[50]

When confronted with a situation like the one faced by those who administered electric shocks in Milgram's study, such students lack the critical-thinking skills to counter the authority's reasoning.

THINKING Outside the Box

STEPHEN HAWKING, *Physicist*

Stephen Hawking (b. 1942) is perhaps the most famous physicist alive. Shortly after graduating from college, he learned that he had ALS (Lou Gehrig's disease), a devastating and incurable neurological disease. About half of the people with it die within three years. After enduring depression and waiting to die, Hawking pulled himself together and decided to live his life to his fullest rather than give up. He enrolled in graduate school, married, and had three children. He writes: "ALS has not prevented me from having a very attractive family and being successful in my work. I have been lucky that my condition has progressed more slowly than is often the case. But it shows that one need not lose hope."

In 2004, Hawking publicly recanted a position he had held for the past 30 years that the gravity of black holes is so powerful that nothing can escape it, not even light.* In doing so, he conceded, with some regret, that CalTech astrophysicist John Preskill had been right all along about black holes. Preskill theorized that information about objects swallowed by black holes is able to leak from the black holes, a phenomenon known as the "black hole information paradox." Hawking paid Preskill off with an agreed-upon prize—an encyclopedia of baseball.

DISCUSSION QUESTIONS

1. Discuss what characteristics of a good critical thinker, listed in the text, are demonstrated by Hawking's response to adversity and uncertainty.

2. Think of a position that you held (or still hold) against all evidence. Compare and contrast Hawking's action with how you respond when someone challenges your views or position. Discuss what extent resistance and/or narrow-mindedness is responsible for your reluctance to change or modify your position.

*See Mark Peplow, "Hawking Changes His Mind about Black Holes," http://www.nature.com/news/2004/040712/full/news040712-12.html.

Fear of Challenge. We may also fail to stand up to others because we fear that others will challenge our beliefs. Some people believe that is it a sign of weakness to change their position on an issue. Good critical thinkers, however, are willing to openly change their position in light of conflicting evidence. Unlike physicist Stephen Hawking, who is described in "Thinking Outside the Box: Stephen Hawking, Physicist," many people—especially those with low self-esteem or an egocentric personality—resist information and evidence that are at odds with what they believe. They may view the expression of opposing views or evidence as a personal attack.

Egocentrism. Believing that you are the center of all things is called **egocentrism**. Egocentric, or self-centered, people have little regard for others' interests and thoughts. Studies of cognitive development in college students suggest that as students develop cognitively and become better at critical thinking, they are less likely to view themselves egocentrically.[51] Although we all tend to fall for compliments and be skeptical of criticism, this tendency is especially true of egocentric people. Flattery impedes our ability to make sound judgments and increases our chances of being persuaded by the flatterer. Advertisers and con artists are well aware of this human tendency and thus use flattery to try to get us to go along with them or to buy products that we wouldn't otherwise buy.

> **egocentrism** The belief that the self or individual is the center of all things.
>
> **ethnocentrism** The belief in the inherent superiority of one's own group and culture.
>
> **anthropocentrism** The belief that humans are the central or most significant entities of the universe.

Ethnocentrism. An uncritical or unjustified belief in the inherent superiority of one's own group and culture is called **ethnocentrism**. It is characterized by suspicion of and a lack of knowledge of foreign countries and cultures.[52] Ethnocentric people often make decisions about other groups, cultures, and countries on the basis of stereotypes and opinions rather than on factual information. In addition, we tend to remember evidence that supports our worldview or stereotypes and forget or downplay that which doesn't. (See page 225 for more on self-serving biases in our thinking.)

Since the September 11, 2001 terrorist attacks on New York City and the Pentagon, Arab Americans have been subjected to hate crimes as well as to racial profiling by police and federal officials, despite official policies against this practice.

According to the U.S. Department of Justice, anti-Muslim crimes soared in 2010 to the highest level since 2001. This increase was due in part as a response to the "Ground Zero Mosque" (which was in fact a community center, not a mosque) in New York City and because of the incendiary rhetoric of groups such as "Stop Islamization of America." Hundreds of Muslims and Americans of Arab descent have been detained without charges and imprisoned under the USA Patriot Act, which was extended by President Obama in 2011. These types of hasty reactions can lead to misunderstandings and even increased hostility.

Uncritical nationalism—a form of ethnocentrism—can blind us to flaws and deteriorating conditions in our own culture. Americans who engage in this type of narrow-mindedness, for example, may bristle at the mere suggestion that the United States may not be the greatest and freest nation ever. Yet according to the Worldwide Governance Indicators 2011 report, which ranks governments by the amount of freedom citizens have to voice opinions and select their government, the United States, ranks lower than Canada, Australia, and most European nations.[53] This represents a drop from 2005, in part because of increased restrictions on freedom of the press.

Anthropocentrism. A belief that humans are the central or most significant entities of the universe, called **anthropocentrism**, can blind people to the capabilities of other animals. In his theory of evolution, Charles Darwin postulated that differences in cognitive function between humans and other animals were simply a matter of degree or quantity, rather than human cognitive function being of a qualitatively different "higher" type. However, the anthropocentric view of humans as unique among all other creatures or as beings created in the image of God and therefore above and separate from nature still dominates. This is found in the use of the term *animal,* even in scientific journals and books, as excluding humans, even though we are an animal species. Under the anthropocentric view, other animals and nature exist not in their own right but as resources for humans. Anthropocentrism can hinder us from critically thinking about our relationship with the rest of nature and can thereby threaten not only the survival of other species and the environment, as is happening with global warming, but our own survival as well.

Connections

How does the government exert influence on what gets reported in the media? What is our responsibility as citizens living in a democracy?

HIGHLIGHTS

TYPES OF RESISTANCE AND NARROW-MINDEDNESS

Resistance: The habitual use of immature defense mechanisms when our worldviews are challenged.

Avoidance	Denial	Struggle
Anger	Ignorance	Rationalization
Clichés	Conformity	Distractions

Narrow-mindedness: Rigid beliefs that interfere with critical analysis of our worldviews.

Absolutism	Egocentrism
Anthropocentrism	Fear of challenge
Ethnocentrism	

➤ *APPLICATION: Identify an example in the text of each of the types of resistance and narrow-mindedness.*

Sunando Sen, of Queens, New York, was pushed to his death in front of a train in December 2012 by a woman who told police she had pushed him off the subway platform because she has hated Muslims ever since September 11th. Sen was from India.

The belief that artificial intelligence, in which a computer, robot, or other device is programmed to learn and make decisions, will never match human intelligence is also a product of anthropocentrism.

Rationalization and Doublethink

While sometimes the best alternative is clear, it's often the case that competing claims require our analysis before we can come to a decision. When presented with conflicting alternatives, some people make a decision quickly because of their bias in favor of one of the alternatives. In doing so, they justify or rationalize their choice on the basis of personal preferences or opinion, rather than on a critical analysis of the competing claims. In an experiment on making choices, psychologist A. H. Martin found that with rationalization the decision is often accompanied by a "rush" of satisfaction, thus convincing the person that his or her preference was correct.[54]

We may also use rationalization in an attempt to justify past actions that are inconsistent with our image of ourselves as a decent, rational person. Child molesters may see themselves as affectionate and loving people whom children enjoy being with. A person may cheat on a sweetheart and then, when confronted, lie about the affair, justifying the lie on the grounds that he or she is a caring person who is looking out for the best interests of the sweetheart by not saying something that will hurt his or her feelings.

Because rationalization involves ignoring competing claims, people who engage in it often get caught up in doublethink. **Doublethink** involves holding two contradictory views, or "double standards," at the same time and believing both to be true. This is particularly prevalent in response to highly charged issues. Rather than analyze the arguments surrounding these issues, people may unwittingly engage in doublethink.

For example, when asked, most college students state that they believe in equality of men and women. However, when it comes to lifestyle and career, the same students who claim to believe in equality and freedom of choice also say that women should be the primary caretakers of children. Most teachers, even the most ardent feminists, treat their female students differently from their male students, calling on boys and praising their accomplishments more often, and having more tolerance of boys' disruptive behavior.[55] When shown videotapes of their classes, many of these teachers are horrified at the extent to which they ignore the girls and downplay their contributions and achievements.

Similarly, the majority of white Americans champion equality as a principle when it comes to race but may harbor unconscious prejudice. Unexamined prejudices can distort our perception of the world. In a study, people were asked to match negative and positive words with names associated with Americans of both European and African descent. The more implicitly prejudiced the subjects were, the more likely they were to match the negative words with African Americans and the positive words with European Americans.[56]

Doublethink can have an impact on our real-life decisions. According to the U.S. Bureau of Labor Statistics, women, including those who work full time outside the home, still perform the great majority of housework and child care.[57] At work, women and minorities suffer from job discrimination and earn significantly less than white men earn. The wage disparity between men and women increases with age. Yet, in spite of the evidence to the contrary, many college students, when asked, maintain that sex-based and race-based discrimination in the work-place are things of the past.

> **doublethink** Holding two contradictory views at the same time and believing both to be true.
>
> **cognitive dissonance** A sense of disorientation that occurs in situations where new ideas directly conflict with a person's worldview.
>
> **social dissonance** A sense of disorientation that occurs when the social behavior and norms of others conflict with a person's worldview.

Connections

To what extent is anthropocentrism implicit in the scientific worldview? How does the news media influence and reinforce narrow-minded worldviews?

Cognitive and Social Dissonance

We are most likely to critically analyze or modify our views when we encounter **cognitive dissonance** and **social dissonance**, situations where new ideas or social behavior directly

U.S. Median Income by Race, Ethnicity, and Gender, 2011

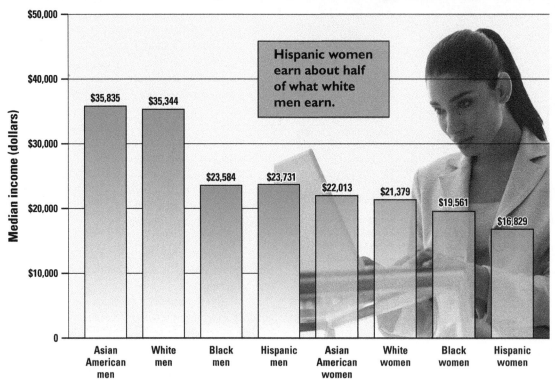

Median income (dollars)

Asian American men	White men	Black men	Hispanic men	Asian American women	White women	Black women	Hispanic women
$35,835	$35,344	$23,584	$23,731	$22,013	$21,379	$19,561	$16,829

Hispanic women earn about half of what white men earn.

The average income, except for Hispanic females, who made a slight gain, is lower than it was in 2008 for all groups. The most significant drop in income was among white males, whose average income dropped by $2,065 over the three-year period.

Source: U.S. Census Bureau, 2011.

conflict with our worldviews. People who are forced to live or work in an integrated community, be it a dorm, college classroom, or a public housing project, often encounter occasions and behavior that conflict with their ethnocentric attitudes. Evidence indicates that once a person's behavior is changed—that is, after they share a meal or discuss issues in class with people of other races or ethnicities—a change in belief is likely to follow.[58] Exposing yourself to role models who are skilled in critical thinking can also strengthen your motivation to think clearly rather than engage in resistance.

Stress as a Barrier

While some stress can be good in motivating us, when we experience excessive stress our brain—and our ability to think critically—slows down. Researchers have found that when people get caught up in disasters, such as an airplane crash, hurricane, flood, or fire, the vast majority freeze up. According to Mac McLean of the FAA and Civil Aerospace Medical Institute, instead of taking action to remove themselves from the danger, most people are "stunned and bewildered."[59] (See Thinking Outside the Box: Captain Chesley "Sully" Sullenberger.)

We can counteract the effect of stress by mentally rehearsing our responses to different stressful scenarios.[60]

People, such as Captain Sullenberger, who have mentally rehearsed the best route for evacuating their building repeatedly are far more likely than those who haven't rehearsed to take action and escape in cases of emergencies, such as a fire or a terrorist attack. More importantly, mental rehearsal can enhance our performance on familiar tasks. For example, basketball players who engaged in fifteen minutes of mental rehearsal on most days and fifteen minutes of actual practice on the other days actually performed better after twenty days than players who only engaged in physical practice each day.[61]

Did You Know

In a study, college students were shown a picture of a black man in a business suit standing on a subway next to a white man who is holding a razor. When asked later what they had seen, the majority reported seeing a black man with a razor standing next to a white man in a business suit.

CAPTAIN CHESLEY "SULLY" SULLENBERGER, *Pilot*

On January 9, 2009, shortly after takeoff from LaGuardia Airport, US Air flight 1549 struck a large flock of geese, disabling both engines. After quickly determining that neither returning to LaGuardia nor continuing on to the next closest airport was feasible, Captain Chesley "Sully" Sullenberger made the decision to attempt to land the plane in the Hudson River. With the help of his co-pilot, he successfully landed the disabled plane in the river. While some passengers and crew sustained injuries, there was no loss of life. Sullenberger remained aboard until he was sure everyone had been safely evacuated before disembarking himself.

Three years later, in January 2012, the cruise ship *Costa Concordia* navigated too close to the coast of Italy. The ship struck a rock, tearing a huge gash in the side of the ship, causing it to capsize onto its side. Unlike Sullenberger's, Captain Francesco Schettino's reaction intensified the disaster. Schettino failed to order passengers to evacuate the ship until over an hour after the accident. He also abandoned the ship before all passengers were evacuated. Thirty-two passengers died in the accident. When later questioned about his actions, Schettino blamed his helmsman for the incident. As for his abandoning the ship, he claims he accidently fell into one of the lifeboats. Rather than accepting Schettino's excuses, the Costa cruise company places the blame squarely on Captain Schettino for taking the ship off course and for the aftermath.

Why did Captain Schettino so mishandle the *Costa Concordia* incident, whereas Captain Sullenberger remained calm and in control? Sullenberger credits his years of experience and practice as an aviation safety expert and accident investigator. In a February 8, 2009 news interview, Sullenberger told Katie Couric, "One way of looking at this might be that for 42 years, I've been making small regular deposits in this bank of experience, education, and training. And on January 15 the balance was sufficient so that I could make a very large withdrawal."

DISCUSSION QUESTIONS

1. Compare and contrast the responses of Captains Sullenberger and Schettino. Relate your answer to the types of resistance. Discuss how the development of your critical thinking skills might make you less prone to using resistance in a stressful situation.

2. What deposits are you making in your "bank of experience, education, and training" that will help you respond effectively to stressful situations or a crisis? Be specific. Discuss how these "deposits" will help you achieve this objective.

STOP AND ASSESS YOURSELF

1. Reread the interpretation examples on page 192. Come up with an additional interpretation for each item. Which interpretations are most reasonable? Support your answer using the two other levels of thinking, experience, and analysis.

2. Using the three-tiered model of thinking, discuss the experiences listed below. The interpretations that you list for each experience do not have to be ones that you personally accept. Share your interpretations with others in the class. Discuss how your past experiences have been shaped by your interpretations and how applying critical-thinking skills to analyze this issue might affect your future actions.

a. Affirmative action in college admissions discriminates against white males.

b. When I invited Chris to go to the movies with me last weekend, Chris said, "No thanks."

c. College tuition is rising faster than the cost of living in the United States.

d. According to CNN, more than half of the agricultural workers in the United States are illegal aliens.

e. Marijuana use has been decriminalized in Canada.

f. In 2012, 53 percent of college graduates under the age of 25 were unemployed or underemployed.

g. The college graduate rate for female student athletes is significantly higher than the rate for male student athletes.

h. In a recent survey, 45 percent of Americans stated that they feel that their pet listens to them better than their spouse does.

i. More and more men are going into nursing as a profession.

j. People who cohabitate before marriage are more likely to get divorced than those who do not.

3. According to the International Energy Commission, North Americans use more energy per person than any other people in the world. As a class, discuss ways in which we use rationalization or other types of resistance to justify our high energy-consumption lifestyle.

4. At the opposite end of the spectrum from egocentric people are those who sacrifice their needs and dreams for others. Harvard professor of education Carol Gilligan maintains that women in particular tend to be self-sacrificing—putting others' needs before their own. How does the tendency to be self-sacrificing interfere with effective critical thinking? Use examples from your own experience to illustrate your answer.

5. Douglas Adams (1952–2001), author of *The Hitchhiker's Guide to the Galaxy*, compared humans to a puddle of water as a way of illustrating anthropocentric thinking, or what he called "the vain conceit" of humans. He wrote:

> Imagine a puddle waking up one morning and thinking, "This is an interesting world I find myself in, an interesting hole I find myself in. It fits me rather neatly, doesn't it. In fact, it fits me staggeringly well. It must have been made to have me in it." Even as the sun comes out and the puddle gets smaller, it still frantically hangs on to the idea that everything is going to be all right; that the world was made for it since it is so well suited to it.[62]

Are humans, in fact, a lot like the puddle in Adams's analogy? Support your answer, using examples from your own experience. Discuss how this type of anthropocentric thinking shapes or distorts our interpretation of the world.

6. Working in small groups, expand on the list of barriers to critical thinking presented in the text. Come up with examples of each barrier and explain how they get in the way of critical thinking.

7. Think of a stressful situation—such as a job interview, breaking bad news, asking someone for a date, or giving a presentation in front of a class—that you will be facing in the next few weeks. Write down the task at the top of a page. Spend 15 minutes a day over the next week mentally rehearsing the task. Note the dates and times you spent mentally rehearsing the task. After you have performed the actual task, write a short essay on how well you did. Were you satisfied with the outcome? Discuss the extent to which mental rehearsal helped you perform this task, compared with similar tasks you performed in the past.

8. Write down three experiences relating to yourself and your life goals. For example, "I am good at science," "I am shy," "I haven't chosen a major yet," or "I want a job in which I can make a lot of money." Now write down at least three interpretations of each of these experiences. Analyze your interpretations. Are the interpretations reasonable? Share your interpretations with others in the class or with friends or family. Do they agree with your interpretations? If not, why not?

9. Working in small groups, discuss the types of resistance or narrow-mindedness that you are most likely to engage in when your views are challenged and steps you might take to overcome your resistance and narrow-mindedness.

10. Compare and contrast the reaction of Captain Sullenberger to a potential disastrous situation to that of Captain Schettino. Discuss how improving your critical thinking skills might improve your response to stressful situations and what deposits you are putting in your "bank of experience, education, and training," to use Sullenberger's words, to help you when you encounter situations beyond your control.

THiNK AGAIN

1. What are the characteristics of a skilled critical thinker?
   - A skilled critical thinker is well informed, open-minded, attentive, and creative, and has effective analytical, research, communication, and problem-solving skills.

2. What are the three levels of thinking?
   - The three levels are experience, which includes first-hand knowledge and information from other sources; interpretation, which involves trying to make sense out of our experiences; and analysis, which requires that we critically examine our interpretations.

3. What are some of the barriers to critical thinking?
   - Barriers include narrow-mindedness, such as absolutism, egocentrism, anthropocentrism, and ethnocentrism, as well as the habitual use of resistance, such as avoidance, anger, clichés, denial, ignorance, conformity, rationalization, and distractions.

Perspectives on Affirmative Action in College Admissions

Affirmative action involves taking positive steps in job hiring and college admissions to correct certain past injustices against groups such as minorities and women. In 1954, the Supreme Court ruled in *Brown v. Board of Education* that school segregation was unconstitutional and that black children have a right to equal education opportunities. The first affirmative action legislation was proposed by Vice President Richard Nixon in 1959. Affirmative action programs and legislation were expanded during the civil rights era in the 1960s.

In 1978, Allan Bakke, a white man, sued the University of California at Davis Medical School because his application was rejected while minority students with lower test scores were admitted. The Supreme Court agreed with Bakke, ruling that reverse discrimination was unconstitutional. In 1996, with the passage of Proposition 209, California became the first state to ban affirmative action in the public sector, including admission to state colleges. Washington, Texas, and other states have also passed referenda banning affirmative action in state college admissions.

In June 2003, in *Grutter v. Bollinger,* the Supreme Court found that the admissions policy of the University of Michigan Law School, which awarded points to applicants based on race, was flawed. However, in its final ruling the court permitted race to be considered as one among many factors when considering individual applications. On June 24, 2013, the Supreme Court ruled on *Fisher v. University of Texas,* which was brought in response to *Grutter v. Bollinger* and requested overturn of the use of affirmative action in college admissions. It sent the case back to the lower court and ordered it to review the university's admission policy.

According to a 2012 Rasmussen Report, the majority of Americans aged 18 to 25 years (55 percent) oppose college affirmative action programs that give preference in admissions to blacks and other minorities, arguing that it constitutes reverse discrimination and, as such, is unjust. In contrast, in 2012 the Obama administration weighed in with briefs in support of affirmative action at the University of Texas, arguing that race should be one of many factors considered in admission. Proponents of affirmative action note that a ban on affirmative action in college admissions will cause a 2 percent drop in admissions of minorities at American colleges, including a 10 percent drop at the most elite colleges, and that this is unacceptable.[63]

Affirmative Action and Higher Education

BEFORE AND AFTER THE SUPREME COURT RULINGS

ON THE MICHIGAN CASES   NANCY CANTOR

Nancy Cantor is chancellor of Syracuse University. She was provost of the University of Michigan when the affirmative action cases were filed with the U.S. Supreme Court. In this article, published in the *Chicago Tribune* on January 28, 2003, she presents an argument for affirmative action in college admissions.

Integration takes hard work, especially when we have little other than collective fear, stereotypes and sins upon which to build. It is time America sees affirmative action on college campuses for what it is: a way to enrich the educational and intellectual lives of white students as well as students of color. We must not abandon race as a consideration in admissions.

The debate now before the U.S. Supreme Court over admissions at the University of Michigan is about the relative advantages people are getting, and it is a debate that misses the point. College admission has always been about relative advantage because a college education is a scarce resource, and the stakes are high.

In this era of emphasis on standardized tests, it may be easy to forget that colleges and universities have always taken into account many other aspects of students' experiences, including the geographic region from which they come, their families' relationship to the institution and their leadership experiences.

It is appropriate, and indeed critical, for the best institutions in the world to create the broadest possible mix of life experiences. Race is a fundamental feature of life in America, and it has an enormous impact on what a person has to contribute on campus. College admissions should be race-conscious to take the cultural and historical experiences of all students—Native American, African-American, Hispanic, Asian-American and white—and build on these in an educational setting. President Bush was wrong when he labeled the affirmative-action programs at the University of Michigan "quota systems.". . .

. . . There are no quotas at Michigan. All students compete for all seats. Race is used as a plus factor, along with other life experiences and talents, just as the president has suggested should happen. The percentages of students of color at Michigan vary annually.

Bush says he believes college admissions should be "race neutral," and he says he supports the principles of *Regents of the University of California vs. Bakke.* He cannot have it both ways. Race is not neutral in the Bakke decision; it is front and center, just as it was nearly 50 years ago in *Brown vs. Board of Education.* In both cases, the Supreme Court urged our nation to boldly and straightforwardly take on the issue of race. . . .

The decision by Justice Lewis F. Powell in *Bakke* brought more than students of color to the table. It brought race in America to the table, urging educators to join hands in creating a truly integrated society of learners.

How are we to fulfill the dream of Brown and Bakke, to build a positive story of race in America, if we are told to ignore race—to concoct systems constructed around proxies for race such as class rank in racially segregated public school districts or euphemisms such as "cultural traditions" that both avoid our past and fail to value the possibility that race can play a constructive role in our nation's future?

. . . We want to include, not exclude. We want to use race as a positive category, as one of many aspects of a life we consider when we sit down to decide which students to invite to our table.

REVIEW QUESTIONS

1. According to Cantor, how does affirmative action benefit both white students and students of color?

2. What does Cantor mean which she says that "college admissions should be race-conscious"?

3. What is President Bush's stand on affirmative action, and why does Cantor disagree with him?

4. How does Cantor use the Supreme Court's rulings to bolster her argument for affirmative action in college admissions?

Achieving Diversity on Campus

U.S. SUPREME COURT JUSTICE SANDRA DAY O'CONNOR

In the following excerpt U.S. Supreme Court Justice Sandra Day O'Connor delivers the majority opinion in the landmark Supreme Court case *Grutter v. Bollinger*, in which it was argued that the use of affirmative action in college admissions is constitutional if race is treated as one factor among many and if the purpose is to achieve diversity on campus.

The University of Michigan Law School (Law School), one of the Nation's top law schools, follows an official admissions policy that seeks to achieve student body diversity through compliance with *Regents of Univ. of Cal. v. Bakke*, . . . Focusing on students' academic ability coupled with a flexible assessment of their talents, experiences, and potential, the policy requires admissions officials to evaluate each applicant based on all the information available in the file, including a personal statement, letters of recommendation, an essay describing how the applicant will contribute to Law School life and diversity, and the applicant's undergraduate grade point average (GPA) and Law School Admissions Test (LSAT) score. Additionally, officials must look beyond grades and scores to so-called "soft variables," such as recommenders' enthusiasm, the quality of the undergraduate institution and the applicant's essay, and the areas and difficulty of undergraduate course selection. The policy does not define diversity solely in terms of racial and ethnic status and does not restrict the types of diversity contributions eligible for "substantial weight," but it does reaffirm the Law School's commitment to diversity with special reference to the inclusion of African-American, Hispanic, and Native-American students, who otherwise might not be represented in the student body in meaningful numbers. By enrolling a "critical mass" of underrepresented minority students, the policy seeks to ensure their ability to contribute to the Law School's character and to the legal profession.

When the Law School denied admission to petitioner Grutter, a white Michigan resident with a 3.8 GPA and 161 LSAT score, she filed this suit, alleging that respondents had discriminated against her on the basis of race in violation of the Fourteenth Amendment, Title VI of the Civil Rights Act of 1964, and 42 U.S.C. § 1981; that she was rejected because the Law School uses race as a "predominant" factor, giving applicants belonging to certain minority groups a significantly greater chance of admission than students with similar credentials from disfavored racial groups; and that respondents had no compelling interest to justify that use of race. The District Court found the Law School's use of race as an admissions factor unlawful. The Sixth Circuit reversed, holding that Justice Powell's opinion in *Bakke* was binding precedent establishing diversity as a compelling state interest, and that the Law School's use of race was narrowly tailored because race was merely a "potential 'plus' factor" and because the Law School's program was virtually identical to the Harvard admissions program described approvingly by Justice Powell and appended to his *Bakke* opinion.

Held: The Law School's narrowly tailored use of race in admissions decisions to further a compelling interest in obtaining the educational benefits that flow from a diverse student body is not prohibited by the Equal Protection Clause, Title VI, or §1981.

In the landmark *Bakke* case, this Court reviewed a medical school's racial set-aside program that reserved 16 out of 100 seats for members of certain minority groups. . . . expressed his view that attaining a diverse student body was the only interest asserted by the university that survived scrutiny. . . . Grounding his analysis in the academic freedom that "long has been viewed as a special concern of the First Amendment," . . . Justice Powell emphasized that the "'nation's future depends upon leaders trained through wide exposure' to the ideas and mores of students as diverse as this Nation.". . . However, he also emphasized that "[i]t is not an interest in simple ethnic diversity, in which a specified percentage of the student body is in effect guaranteed to be members of selected ethnic groups," that can justify using race. . . . Rather, "[t]he diversity that furthers a compelling state interest encompasses a far broader array of qualifications and characteristics of which racial or ethnic origin is but a single though important element." Since *Bakke,* Justice Powell's opinion has been the touchstone for constitutional analysis of race-conscious admissions policies. Public and private universities across the Nation have modeled their own admissions programs on Justice Powell's views. . .

The Court endorses Justice Powell's view that student body diversity is a compelling state interest that can justify using race in university admissions. The Court defers to the Law School's educational judgment that diversity is essential to its educational mission. . . . Attaining a diverse student body is at the heart of the Law School's proper institutional mission, and its "good faith" is "presumed" absent "a showing to the contrary.". . . Enrolling a "critical mass" of minority students simply to assure some specified percentage of a particular group merely because of its race or ethnic origin would be patently unconstitutional. . . . But the Law School defines its critical mass concept by reference to the substantial, important, and laudable educational benefits that diversity is designed to produce, including cross-racial understanding and the breaking down of racial stereotypes. The Law School's claim is further bolstered by numerous expert studies and reports showing that such diversity promotes learning outcomes and better prepares students for an increasingly diverse workforce, for society, and for the legal profession. Major American businesses have made clear that the skills needed in today's increasingly global marketplace can only be developed through exposure to widely diverse people, cultures, ideas, and viewpoints. High-ranking retired officers and civilian military leaders assert that a highly qualified, racially diverse officer corps is essential to national security. Moreover, because universities, and in particular, law schools, represent the training ground for a large number of the Nation's leaders . . . the path to leadership must be visibly open to talented and qualified individuals of every race and ethnicity. Thus, the Law School has a compelling interest in attaining a diverse student body. . . . (d) The Law School's admissions program bears the hallmarks of a narrowly tailored plan. To be narrowly tailored, a race-conscious admissions program cannot "insulat[e] each category of applicants with certain desired qualifications from competition with all other applicants." . . . Instead, it may consider race or ethnicity only as a "'plus' in a particular applicant's file"; *i.e.,* it must be "flexible enough to consider all pertinent elements of diversity in light of the particular qualifications of each applicant, and to place them on the same footing for consideration, although not necessarily according them the same weight," . . . It follows that universities cannot establish quotas for members of certain racial or ethnic groups or put them on separate admissions tracks. . . . The Law School's admissions program, like the Harvard plan approved by Justice Powell, satisfies these requirements. Moreover, the program is flexible enough to ensure that each applicant is evaluated as an individual and not in a way that makes race or ethnicity the defining feature of the application. See *Bakke, supra,* at 317 (opinion of Powell, J.). The Law School engages in a highly individualized, holistic review of each applicant's file, giving serious consideration to all the ways an applicant might contribute to a diverse educational environment. . . . Also, the program adequately ensures that all factors that may contribute to diversity are meaningfully considered alongside race. Moreover, the Law School

frequently accepts nonminority applicants with grades and test scores lower than underrepresented minority applicants (and other nonminority applicants) who are rejected. . . . The Court is satisfied that the Law School adequately considered the available alternatives. The Court is also satisfied that, in the context of individualized consideration of the possible diversity contributions of each applicant, the Law School's race-conscious admissions program does not unduly harm nonminority applicants. . . . The Court takes the Law School at its word that it would like nothing better than to find a race-neutral admissions formula and will terminate its use of racial preferences as soon as practicable. The Court expects that 25 years from now, the use of racial preferences will no longer be necessary to further the interest approved today.

REVIEW QUESTIONS

1. Why did Grutter maintain that she had been treated unfairly by the University of Michigan Law School?

2. Why is Justice Powells's opinion in the *Bakke* case considered a landmark decision regarding college admissions?

3. On what grounds did the Supreme Court argument argue that attaining a diverse student body is part of an important part of institution's mission?

4. What conditions and limitations did the court place on using race in college admissions?

THiNK AND DISCUSS

PERSPECTIVES ON AFFIRMATIVE ACTION

1. Agreeing on a definition is one of the first steps in debating an issue. How are the Supreme Court justices and Nancy Cantor each using the term *affirmative action?*

2. Discuss whether affirmative action has a place in a democracy that is built on equal rights for all citizens, or if it is a violation of the fundamental principle of fairness.

3. Compare and contrast the arguments used by Nancy Cantor and U.S. Supreme Court justice Sandra Day O'Connor regarding the use of affirmative action in college admissions. Which person makes the best argument? Support your answer.

4. Some people argue that instead of race, we should use an economic or class-based criterion for affirmative action. How would you support that premise?

5. Research the policy at your college regarding affirmative action in admission. To what extent has this policy had an impact on diversity in the student body and the quality of your education? Support your answer using specific examples.

6. What criteria (for example, experiences, talents, alumni status of parents) do you think should be used in college admissions? Working in small groups, develop a list of relevant criteria and assign each criterion a point value (for example, 10 or 20) out of a total of 100 points based on how important each criterion is to the admissions decision.

8

KNOWLEDGE, EVIDENCE, & ERRORS IN THINKING

In what became one of the most publicized cases of medical error, in 1995 a surgeon at University Community Hospital in Tampa, Florida, mistakenly amputated the wrong leg of 52-year-old Willie King. More recently, a surgeon at Milford Regional Medical Center in Massachusetts removed a woman's right kidney instead of her gallbladder as planned. In a high-profile case, actor Dennis Quaid's newborn twins nearly died from a dose of the blood-thinner heparin that was 1,000 times the prescribed dose. Each of these unfortunate incidents was the culmination of a chain of errors, many of them avoidable. Indeed, Healthgrades, an independent health care rating company, estimates that almost 3 percent of hospital patients in the United States are victims of potentially preventable medical errors.[1]

How can this happen? Cognitive errors, such as those we will be studying in this chapter, are the leading contributing

Our eyes want to join the picture of the White House on this $20 bill with the actual building, but our minds tell us that the continuation is an illusion.

207

■ What are some of the sources of knowledge?

■ In what ways might experience be misleading?

■ What are some of the types of cognitive and social errors in our thinking?

>> factor in medical mistakes, many of which result in death and long-term disability.[2] It is estimated that diagnostic errors alone result in 40,000 to 80,000 hospital deaths per year in the United States.[3]

Following the 1995 incident with Willie King, hospitals have started taking extra precautions, including double back-up identification systems, computerized error-tracking systems, and the use of patient safety officers to monitor and educate medical professionals. Many medical schools are also teaching their students about cognitive biases and training them to think about how they are thinking (meta-analysis) as well as how to better communicate with and get feedback from other staff.

The prevalence of medical mistakes illustrates how cognitive errors can lead otherwise highly trained professionals to make erroneous decisions.

Good critical-thinking skills require that we evaluate evidence thoroughly and be aware of social and cognitive errors in our thinking to effectively evaluate any given situation and avoid jumping to a conclusion or acting hastily based on preconceived ideas. In Chapter 8 we will:

Actor Dennis Quaid's newborn twins were given a dose of blood thinner that was ten times that prescribed.

- Learn about the nature and limitations of human knowledge
- Distinguish between rationalism and empiricism
- Learn about different types of evidence
- Set guidelines for evaluating evidence
- Look at sources for researching claims and evidence
- Study different types of cognitive/perceptual errors, including self-serving biases
- Learn how social expectations and group pressure can lead to erroneous thinking

Finally, we will examine the evidence and arguments regarding unidentified flying objects (UFOs) and what type of proof would be necessary to establish their existence.

HUMAN KNOWLEDGE AND ITS LIMITATIONS

Knowledge is information or experience that we believe to be true and for which we have justification or evidence. Understanding how we acquire knowledge as well as having an awareness of the limitations of human understanding are essential in logical reasoning.

Rationalism and Empiricism

Our views of ourselves and the world around us are shaped by our understanding of the nature of truth and the ultimate sources of knowledge. **Rationalists** claim that most human knowledge comes through reason. Greek philosopher Plato (427–347 BCE) believed that there is an unchanging truth we can know through reason and that most of us confuse truth with worldly appearance.

The empiricists reject the rationalists' claim that it is through reason that we discern truth. **Empiricists** instead claim that we discover truth primarily through our physical senses. Science is based primarily on empiricism. The scientific method involves making direct observations of the world, and then coming up with a hypothesis to explain these observations.

Structure of the Mind

German philosopher Immanuel Kant (1724–1804) argued that how we experience reality is not simply a matter of pure reason (rationalism) or of using physical senses (empiricism) but depends on the structure of our minds. Like computers—which are designed to accept and process particular kinds of inputs from the outside world—our brains must have the correct "hardware" to accept and make sense of incoming data.

Most neurologists believe, as did Kant, that we do not see "reality" directly as it is but that instead our mind or brain provides structure and rules for processing incoming information. In other words, as we noted in Chapter 7, we *interpret* our experiences rather than directly perceiving the world "out there."

> **knowledge** Information which we believe to be true and for which we have justification or evidence.
>
> **rationalist** One who claims that most human knowledge comes through reason.
>
> **empiricist** One who believes that we discover truth primarily through our physical senses.

Connections

How is the assumption of empiricism reflected in the scientific method?

SELF-EVALUATION QUESTIONNAIRE*

THiNK Tank

Rate yourself on the following scale from 1 (strongly disagree) to 5 (strongly agree)

1 2 3 4 5   Knowledge comes primarily through reason rather than the senses.

1 2 3 4 5   I have a tendency to look only for evidence that confirms my assumptions or cherished worldviews.

1 2 3 4 5   The most credible evidence is that based on direct experience, such as eyewitness reports.

1 2 3 4 5   When I look at a random shape such as a cloud or craters on the moon, I tend to see meaning or an image in it.

1 2 3 4 5   The probability that there are two students in a class of twenty-four who have a birthday on the same day and month is about 50 percent.

1 2 3 4 5   When I buy a lottery ticket, I use my lucky number.

1 2 3 4 5   I can truly enjoy life only if I have perfect control over it.

1 2 3 4 5   I am better than most at getting along with other people.

1 2 3 4 5   Americans are more trustworthy than other people, especially people from non-Western cultures.

* Keep track of your results. As you read this book and gain a better understanding of critical thinking, you'll find out what your responses to each of these statements mean. A brief summary of the meaning of each rating can also be found at the back of the book.

While our brain helps us make sense of the world, it also limits us. For example, according to the new string theory in physics, there are at least nine spatial dimensions.[4] However, our brains are structured to perceive a three-dimensional world. Consequently, it is difficult, if not impossible, for us to imagine a nine-dimensional world. Because of the structure of our brains, we are also prone to certain perceptual and cognitive errors. We'll be studying some of these errors later in this chapter.

Effective critical thinking requires that we be aware of our strengths and limitations and that we strive to improve our style of inquiry and our understanding of the world. Because complete certainty is almost always an impossible goal, we need to learn how to assess evidence and to remain open to multiple perspectives.

are addressed in greater detail in subsequent chapters, we first need to make sure the evidence on which we base our analysis is accurate and complete. Evidence can come from many different sources, some more reliable than others.

Evidence can be based on information from other sources or on firsthand experience. It is reasonable to use our experience as credible evidence for a claim, *if* it is not contradicted by other evidence. Likewise, if a claim conflicts with our experience, then we have good reason to be suspicious of that claim. Learning how to evaluate the credibility and accuracy of evidence is a key skill in critical thinking and logic.

Direct Experience and False Memories

Effective critical thinking requires that we be willing to check the accuracy of our experience. As we noted earlier, our brains interpret rather than directly record sensory experience. Consequently, direct sensory experience is not infallible. Even though we may remember major events "as

EVALUATING EVIDENCE

Evidence is something that tends to prove or disprove a particular view. In arguments, evidence is used as the grounds or premises for our belief in a particular conclusion. While analytical skills are essential in evaluating an argument and

False memories can significantly alter how witnesses "remember" an event, as happened in the case of the Challenger explosion.

though they were yesterday," these memories are not as stable as scientists once thought. A study done four years after the 1986 *Challenger* explosion found that many of the witnesses had dramatically altered their memories of the shuttle disaster, even to the point of "seeing" things that had never happened.[5]

Language can also alter memories. This is particularly problematic when police inadvertently use leading questions that can bias a person's testimony or even alter the person's memories of an incident.

The power of words to shape our reality is poignantly illustrated by how leading questions can alter eyewitnesses' perception of a particular event. In a study, participants were shown a film of a car accident.[6] They were then asked one of the following questions about the speed of the cars. Their averaged responses are given in parentheses after each question:

James Calvin Tillman was released from prison in July 2006, with the help of the Innocence Project, after serving 16 years for a rape he did not commit. His conviction was based on a false eyewitness report.

How fast were the cars going when they smashed each other? (41 mph)

How fast were the cars going when they collided? (40 mph)

How fast were the cars going when they bumped each other? (38 mph)

How fast were the cars going when they hit each other? (35 mph)

How fast were the cars going when they contacted each other? (32 mph)

Despite the fact that they had all seen the same film, participants responded with higher speeds based on the intensity of the verb. Those who were told the cars smashed or collided reported significantly higher speed estimates than those who were told that the cars merely contacted each other.

Inaccurate or false memories can be as compelling and believable as real memories. In police work, eyewitness identifications are incorrect up to 50 percent of the time. Mistaken eyewitness identifications of a suspect are the greatest single cause of wrongful convictions. Although jurors regard eyewitness identification as trustworthy, scientists have found that eyewitness reports are notoriously unreliable. According to The Innocence Project, an organization dedicated to exonerating wrongfully convicted individuals through DNA testing, misidentification by eyewitnesses is the most common cause of wrongful convictions in the U.S. It is estimated that even under the best conditions, eyewitness are incorrect about half the time.[7]

Indeed, we are so suggestible that we may go beyond inadvertently altering memories to vividly recalling events that never happened, a phenomenon known as **false memory syndrome**. Psychologists have found that after only three sessions in which there are repeated suggestions about a nonexistent childhood event, such as being lost in a mall at age 5 or spilling grape juice on a guest at a wedding, about 25 percent of the subjects will "recall" the event, and many will provide details. What's more, there is little connection between their confidence in their memory and the truth of their memory.[8]

Why are some people more prone than others to memory distortions? Elizabeth Loftus, one of the foremost researchers in the field, suggests that false memory is most likely to occur in people who don't engage in critical thinking about their memories but just accept them as reported.[9] The use of memorization strategies, such as those discussed in "Critical Thinking in Action: Memorization Strategies," can help us in accurately remembering new information. By being more attentive and analyzing events as they happen and by being alert to inconsistencies in our "memories," we are less likely to be taken in by false or distorted memories.

false memory syndrome The recalling of events that never happened.

Critical THiNKing in Action

Memorization Strategies

In a study of why some people are better at accurately memorizing new information, magnetic resonance brain imaging was used to determine which brain regions are correlated with specific memorization strategies.* Researchers found that most people use one or a combination of the following four strategies for remembering the picture to the right.

1. **Visualization inspection.** Participants carefully study the visual appearance of an object. Some people are much better at this strategy and are able to commit pictures as well as pages of books to visual memory.

2. **Verbal elaboration.** Individuals construct sentences about the objects or material they are trying to memorize. For example, they may say to themselves, "The pig is key to this image."

3. **Mental imagery.** Individuals form interactive mental images, much like an animated cartoon. For example, they may imagine the pig jumping into a pool off the end of a diving board shaped like a key.

4. **Memory retrieval.** People reflect and come up with a meaning for the object or association of the object with personal memories.

Participants who use one or a combination of these different strategies performed better at learning new material than those who used these strategies only rarely or not at all. In addition, it was found that each of these strategies used different parts of the brain and that people seem to have different learning styles that work best for them.

DISCUSSION QUESTIONS

1. What strategy, if any, do you use for learning new information? For example, what strategy might you use for remembering the picture below? Evaluate the effectiveness of the strategy or strategies in helping you be a better critical thinker and in your performance in classes.

2. Think of a time when you later discovered that a memory you had was inaccurate or false. Discuss how the use of these strategies might make you less prone to memory distortions. Be specific.

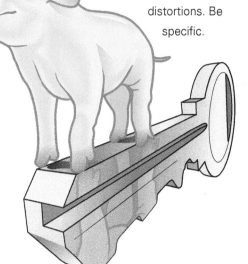

The Unreliability of Hearsay and Anecdotal Evidence

We should be skeptical of what others tell us, especially if it's hearsay evidence or comments taken out of context. **Hearsay,** evidence that is heard by one person and then repeated to another person and so on until you hear it, is notoriously unreliable. As children, we've probably all played the game of "telephone," in which we whisper something to one person and she whispers the message to the next person and so on down the line until the last person says what he has heard. It is almost always different, often amusingly so, from the original message.

Anecdotal evidence, which is based on personal testimonies, is also unreliable because of the problem of inaccurate memory as well as the human tendency to exaggerate or distort what we experience to fit our expectations. For example, many people have reported seeing UFOs and, in some cases, being abducted by aliens. However, despite the apparent sincerity of their beliefs, anecdotal evidence in the absence of any physical evidence cannot be used as proof that UFOs and aliens exist. We'll be looking at

hearsay Evidence that is heard by one person and then repeated to another.

anecdotal evidence Evidence based on personal testimonies.

different perspectives on the credibility of the evidence for UFOs in the readings at the end of this chapter.

Experts and Credibility

One of the most credible sources of information is that of experts. When turning to an expert, it is important that we find someone who is knowledgeable in the particular field under question. When we use the testimony of a person who is an expert in a different field, we are committing the fallacy of *appeal to inappropriate authority.*

For example, many students believe, on the basis of the testimony of their friends, that marijuana use is harmless and that it is perfectly safe to drive after smoking a joint. In fact, research by medical experts shows that, although marijuana does not impair driving as much as alcohol, reaction time is reduced by 41 percent after smoking one joint and 63 percent after smoking two joints.[10] Despite evidence from experts, most people will still base their judgments on smoking marijuana on information from their peers until they develop stronger critical-thinking skills.

In seeking out experts, we should look at their credentials, including:

1. *Education* or training from a reputable institute
2. *Experience* in making judgments in the field
3. *Reputation* among peers as an expert in the field
4. *Accomplishments* in the field such as academic papers and awards

Unfortunately, expert testimony is not foolproof. Experts may disagree, in which case we will have to reserve judgment or look to others in the field. Furthermore, sometimes experts are biased, particularly those who are being paid by special-interest groups or corporations who stand to gain financially from supporting a particular position.

Connections

How can you determine whether a science news story is well done and accurate?

How do scientists design experiments to avoid bias?

How can you recognize and avoid being taken in by misleading advertisements?

For example, it has long been assumed that milk and dairy products help maintain strong bones in adults. However, this claim has not been supported by scientific research. Instead this claim has been mainly promoted by groups that financially depend on the sale of dairy products. While the National Dairy Council extols the benefits of milk for people of all ages, many medical experts, including researchers at the Harvard School of Public Health[11] and the Physicians Committee for Responsible Medicine, argue, based on research, that milk may actually accelerate the process of bone loss in adults. In light of these findings, the Federal Trade Commission, a government agency charged with protecting consumers and eliminating unfair and deceptive marketplace practices, ordered the National Dairy Council to withdraw its ads that claimed drinking milk can prevent bone loss in adults.

Preconceived ideas can also influence how experts interpret evidence. Brandon Mayfield, an Oregon lawyer and a Muslim convert, was taken into custody in Portland, Oregon, after the March 2004 train bombing in Madrid, Spain, when what appeared to be his fingerprint mysteriously turned up on a plastic bag used by the bombers. Although Spanish law-enforcement agencies expressed doubt that the fingerprint was Mayfield's, U.S. officials insisted that it was an "absolutely incontrovertible match."[12] As it later turned out, the fingerprint belonged to an Algerian living in Spain. The U.S. officials succumbed to preconceived notions in making a false arrest of Mayfield.

The game "telephone" is an amusing example of how hearsay can result in misinterpretation.

got milk?

Liquid Gold.

9 essential nutrients to make big waves.

Inadequate research can lead to misrepresentation of a product—advertisers, for example, claimed that milk built strong bones in adults, a claim that was later proven false. The above ad also contains the fallacy of appeal to inappropriate authority, since Olympic swimmer Michael Phelps is not an expert on the health benefits of milk.

While experts are usually a good source of credible evidence, even experts can be biased and can misinterpret data, as we noted in the opening scenario on medical errors. Because of this, it is important that we be able to evaluate claims, especially those that may be slanted or that conflict with other experts' analysis.

Evaluating Evidence for a Claim

Our analysis of the evidence for a claim should be accurate, unbiased, and as complete as possible. Credible evidence is consistent with other relevant evidence. In addition, the more evidence there is to support a claim, the more reasonable it is to accept that claim. In critical thinking, there is no virtue in rigid adherence to a position that is not supported by evidence (see "Thinking Outside the Box: Rachel Carson, Biologist and Author")

Sometimes we don't have access to credible evidence. In cases like these, we should look for contradictory evidence. For example, some atheists reject the belief that there is a God because, they argue, it is contradicted by the presence of so much evil in the world. When there is evidence that contradicts a claim, we have good reason to doubt the claim. However, if there is no contradictory evidence, we should remain open to the possibility that a position may be true.

In evaluating a claim, we need to watch out for **confirmation bias**, the tendency to look only for evidence that confirms our assumptions and to resist evidence that contradicts them. This inclination is so strong that we may disregard or reinterpret evidence that runs contrary to our cherished beliefs.[13] In research about people who were opposed to and those who supported capital punishment, both sides interpreted the findings of a study on whether capital punishment deterred crime to fit their prior views. If the evidence did not fit, they focused on the flaws in the research and dismissed its validity or, in some cases, actually distorted the evidence to support their position.[14] Politicians may also cherry-pick the evidence, reading only reports and listening to evidence that supports their previous beliefs. This happened in 2002 when the Bush administration claimed there was conclusive proof that Iraq had weapons of mass destruction. Newscasters and journalists who have strong beliefs about particular issues may also engage in confirmation bias.

Sources that are usually reliable can inadvertently pass on incorrect information. A friend of mine told me that women in their 20s now earn more than men. My friend went on to tell me that he had read this in an opinion piece by a *New York Times* columnist.[15] When I checked out the information in the article, I found that, according to the National Labor Statistics, women in their 20s, despite the fact that they are better educated, earn only about 92 percent of what men earn. While my friend would normally have checked out the sources of the columnist's claims, confirmation bias kept him from doing so. He believed, prior to reading the article, that boys are getting a raw deal in school, since the majority of teachers are women, and that we are entering an age of reverse sexism. The "fact," albeit incorrect, that women in their 20s are now earning more than men are "confirmed" his views.

Confirmation bias may also take the form of more rigorously scrutinizing contrary evidence than that which supports our position. Peter Jennings, of ABC's *World News Tonight*, presented a study that "disproved" therapeutic touch, a healing method used extensively in India that involves a therapist's using the "energy" in his or her hands to help correct the "energy field" of a sick person.[16] The study, which was previously quoted in a prestigious medical journal, had been carried out by a fourth grader, Emily Rosa, as a project for her science class. On the basis of this single fourth grader's project, the editor of

THINKING Outside the Box

RACHEL CARSON, *Biologist and Author*

After graduating with a master's degree in Zoology from Johns Hopkins University, Rachel Carson (1907–1964) was hired as a writer by the U.S. Fish and Wildlife Service. The success of her 1951 book, *The Sea Around Us*, allowed her to leave her job and concentrate on her life goal of becoming a writer.

As early as 1945 she had become concerned about the overuse of chemical pesticides, such as DDT. Although others before her had tried to warn the public about the dangers of these powerful pesticides, it was her reputation as a complete and meticulous researcher, along with her intellectual curiosity, that contributed to her success. She began by examining the existing research on the effect of pesticides. Her reputation also allowed her to enlist the expertise and support of scientists in the field.

When *Silent Spring* was published in 1962, it created an immediate uproar and backlash. A huge counterattack was launched by the big chemical companies, including Monsanto and Velsicol, which denounced her as a "hysterical woman" unqualified to write on the topic. Despite threats of lawsuits, Carson didn't back down. Because her research was informed and accurate, her opponents were unable to find holes in her argument. *Silent Spring* changed the course of American history and launched a new environmental movement.

DISCUSSION QUESTIONS

1. Think of a time when you argued for a position that was supported by credible evidence even though doing so angered or alienated a family member, teacher, or employer. What was the outcome? Evaluate your response. In particular, discuss how you used (or didn't use) your critical thinking skills in responding to criticism of your position.

2. Rachel Carson is an example of how one person can make a huge difference. Looking into your future, think of ways in which you might be able to use your talents and critical-thinking skills to make the world a better place.

---

the journal had declared that therapeutic touch was bogus. Because the editor had a bias against nontraditional therapies, he held "studies" that suggested therapeutic touch might be ineffective to a lower standard of proof.

Even scientists sometimes look for evidence that supports their theories rather than evidence that challenges their thinking. Models used for testing hypotheses may promote confirmation bias and questionable interpretation of data. Science writer Matt Ridley, in his article "How Bias Heats up the [Global] Warming Debate," writes regarding the controversy over global warming:

The late novelist Michael Crichton, in his prescient 2003 lecture criticizing climate research, said: "To an outsider, the most significant innovation in the global-warming controversy is the overt reliance that is being placed on models. . . . No longer are models judged by how well they reproduce data from the real world—increasingly, models provide the data. As if they were themselves a reality."

It isn't just models, but the interpretation of

Connections

How do scientists use evidence to test a hypothesis?

How do we as consumers reinforce confirmation bias in the news media?

real data, too. The rise and fall in both temperature and carbon dioxide, evident in Antarctic ice cores, was at first thought to be evidence of carbon dioxide driving climate change. Then it emerged that the temperature had begun rising centuries earlier than carbon dioxide. Rather than abandon the theory, scientists fell back on the notion that the data jibed with the possibility that rising carbon dioxide levels were reinforcing the warming trend in what's called a positive feedback loop. Maybe—but there's still no empirical evidence that this was a significant effect compared with a continuation of whatever first caused the warming.[17]

Brain imaging studies have found that when we come to a conclusion that confirms our prior bias, the decision is associated with a pleasure response and a feeling of emotional comfort, even though our conclusion is erroneous.[18] When theories are disproved, it is generally by other scientists rather than by the scientists who proposed the theories (see "Thinking Outside the Box: Stephen Hawking, Physicist" in Chapter 7).

Because of the human propensity to engage in confirmation bias, many scholarly scientific journals require that researchers report disconfirmatory evidence as well as contradictory interpretations of their data. As critical thinkers,

Connections

How do scientists gather evidence to test their hypotheses?

What are the "rules of evidence" in a court of law?

How reliable is the news media as a source of information?

Hot or Not?

Do you tend to distort evidence to fit with your beliefs?

we need to develop strategies that compel us to examine evidence, especially that which confirms our prior views, and to be more open-minded about evidence that contradicts our views.

In evaluating evidence, the degree of credibility required depends on the circumstances. The greater the impact our actions might have, the greater the degree of credibility and certainty we should demand. Courts of law require a high degree of credibility for evidence of guilt because of the dire consequences of declaring an innocent person guilty.

We live in an age where information is proliferating at an astounding rate. We are inundated on a daily basis with information from newspapers, television, the Internet, and other media sources. When using evidence from the media—especially the mass media—we need to consider the sources and their slant, if any.

In addition, some writing, such as novels, poetry, movie scripts, and even some editorials, is not intended to be taken as factual. For example, the film *Zero Dark Thirty*, which recounted the search for and assassination of Osama bin Laden, drew considerable criticism from some people for portraying the CIA as using water boarding techniques on terrorist suspects in Guantanamo Bay. However, the movie was never intended as a documentary. Instead it was a dramatization, and as such a fusion of fact and fiction.[19]

Assessing claims, including distinguishing between fact and fiction, requires good research skills and competence in gathering, evaluating, and synthesizing supporting evidence. Like scientists, good critical thinkers spend a lot of time researching claims and collecting information before drawing a conclusion. Apply the criteria listed in the CRAAP test (which stands for currency, relevance, authority, accuracy, and purpose) to evaluate the reliability of information you find.

As you begin your research, try to set up an interview with someone who is an expert in the field under investigation, such as a faculty member or an

*The film **Zero Dark Thirty**, about the search for Osama bin Laden, was a blend of fact and fictional dramatization.*

outside expert. An expert can provide you with information as well as point you to reputable publications. When interviewing the expert, don't rely on your memory. Take accurate notes; repeat what you think you heard if you are unsure. Librarians are also a valuable source of information. In addition to their wealth of knowledge regarding resources, some college librarians have Ph.D.s in specialized fields.

Dictionaries and *encyclopedias* are another good place for you to start your research. Specialized reference books often contain extensive bibliographies of good source material. They may be accessed online or used in the reference section of your library. If you are doing time-sensitive research, make sure the reference sources are up-to-date. Make sure you use reputable encyclopedias. While sites such as Wikipedia might be a good starting point, Wikipedia entries, because they are not necessarily written by experts in their fields, cannot be used as references in research.

Library catalogues—most of which are online—are invaluable in research. Use key words to find your subject in the catalogue. In selecting resources, check the date of publication. If your library doesn't have a particular book or journal, you can usually get it through interlibrary loan.

Scholarly journals, also known as peer-reviewed journals, contain articles that have been reviewed by fellow experts in the field. Most scholarly journals are indexed on specialized databases that you can access through your library Internet home page. In some cases, the full journal articles are available on the Internet. For more general information, the Expanded Academic Index is a good place to start.

Government documents are also reputable sources of information about such things as employment statistics and demographics. You can access many of the government documents through Internet databases. Go to http://www.usa.gov/ to search for topics of interest.

Internet Web sites contain a wealth of information. Millions of new pages are added every week to the Internet. There are also specialized Web sites, such as Academic Search Complete, which are not available through search engines such as Google, Bing, and Yahoo, but that can generally be accessed through your college or university library's Web site. Many Web sites are sponsored by reputable organizations and individuals. The top-level domain at the end of a Web site's address (URL, or uniform resource locator) can help you in evaluating its reliability. All URLs for U.S. government sites end with the top-level domain *.gov*. URLs for sites ending with the top-level domain *.edu* indicate that the source of the information is a U.S. educational institution. Both of these types of sites can generally be counted on to provide reliable and accurate information. The global top-level domain *.org* indicates that the site belongs to a private or nonprofit organization such as Amnesty International or possibly a religious group. The information on these sites may or may not be reliable, depending on the reputability of the organization sponsoring

the Web site. The global top-level domain *.com* indicates that the site is sponsored by a commercial organization such as a corporation or private business, at least in the United States. In these cases you must try to determine the companies' motives in providing the information—for example, is it for advertising purposes? Generally, blogs should not be used as references. Blogs are notoriously unreliable and often based on opinion rather than facts. If you have any doubts about a site's credibility, it is best to ask a reference librarian or expert in the field about the most reliable sites to look at for information on an issue.

While doing your research, no matter what resource you are using, take accurate notes or make copies of articles. Keep full citation information for your sources so that you can refer to them later and cite them if necessary. If, in

Connections

How do scientists go about gathering information and evidence?

How does the Internet affect our lives?

presenting your research, you use material word for word, always put it in quotation marks and acknowledge the source. You should also cite the source of paraphrased information that is not widely known. In addition, remember to cite sources for any surveys, statistics, and graphics.

Researching a claim or issue requires that we be able to sort through and analyze the relevant data. Good research skills also help us make better decisions in our lives by providing us with the tools for evaluating different claims and available courses of action we might take.

STOP AND ASSESS YOURSELF

1. What evidence might be sufficient for you to conclude that an intelligent computer or android is conscious and has free will? Would this same evidence be sufficient to prove to you that another human you met was conscious and had free will? Explain using the criteria for evaluating evidence discussed in the chapter.

2. Think of a time when you saw something and were convinced that your interpretation of the event was true, but you later came to have doubts about your interpretation. Discuss the factors that contributed to your doubts.

3. Working in small groups, evaluate the following list of claims. If there are any ambiguous terms, define them as well as possible. Next, make a list of types of evidence you would need to support or reject each claim. State how you would go about doing the research.

a. Genetically modified food is dangerous.

b. Men are more aggressive by nature than are women.

c. Prayers are answered.

d. Toast is more likely to fall butter-side down.

e. Asian Americans are better at math than European Americans are.

f. Living together before marriage is associated with a lower divorce rate.

g. Human life begins at conception.

h. A flying saucer crashed over Roswell, New Mexico, in 1947.

i. Canadians, on average, live longer than Americans do.

j. God exists.

k. The sea level has risen almost a foot over the past century as a result of global warming.

l. Yawning is contagious.

m. Capital punishment deters crime.

n. Debbie was born under the sign Aquarius. Therefore, she must love water.

4. Select one of the following topics and research it.

a. The impact of global warming on your city or state

b. The average age of marriage for men and women now and when your parents got married

c. The number of members in the U.S. House of Representatives

d. The percentage of American college athletes who become professional athletes

e. The changes over the past 30 years in majors of college students

Make a list of the resources, including experts, books, journals, search engines, databases, and Web sites you used in your research. Rate each of the sources you used in terms of which generated the most credible and unbiased evidence. Compare your results with those of others in your class. To what extent did the topic chosen determine which research resources, including the Internet, were most useful?

5. Choose one of the claims from exercise 3 or a recent news story and research the evidence. Write a short essay or present your results to the class for evaluation.

6. Imagine that you are backing out of a parking spot on campus. Your view is somewhat obscured by an SUV parked beside you. As you back out, you hit another car that was driving through the parking lot. Write a paragraph describing the event for the police report.

Now imagine that you are the other person whose car was hit. Write a paragraph describing the event for the police report. Compare and contrast the two reports. Analyze how the words you chose in each report were selected to influence the perception of the police officer regarding what happened.

COGNITIVE AND PERCEPTUAL ERRORS IN THINKING

On the evening of October 30, 1938, a play based on H. G. Wells's novel *War of the Worlds* about a Martian invasion was broadcast to the nation on radio. Many of the people who listened to the show believed that the invasion was real. Some people even "smelled" the poisonous Martian gas and "felt" the heat rays being described on the radio. Others claimed to have seen the giant machines landing in New Jersey and the flames from the battle. One panicked person told police he had heard the president's voice on the radio ordering them to evacuate.

Our perceptions of the world around us are easily skewed by social influences. Most people underestimate the critical role that cognitive and social factors play in our perception and interpretation of sense data. Although emotion has traditionally been regarded as the culprit when reason goes astray, studies suggest that many of the errors in our thinking are neurological in nature.[20] In this

section, we'll be looking at some of these cognitive and perceptual errors.

Perceptual Errors

Our minds are not like blank sheets of paper or recording devices, such as cameras or video recorders, as the empiricists claimed. Instead, our brains construct a picture of the world much as an artist does. Our brains filter our perceptions and fill in missing information based in part on our expectations, as occurred in the broadcast of *War of the Worlds*.

Some skeptics believe that UFO sightings are based on perceptual errors, including optical illusions (see "Analyzing Images: The St. Louis Arch"). In 1969, an Air National Guard pilot spotted what he thought was a squadron of UFOs within several hundred feet of his plane.

Connections

As a consumer, how can you avoid being taken in by cognitive and perceptual errors used by marketers?

When the radio show based on the novel **The War of the Worlds** *was broadcast, many of the listeners believed that the invasion was real.*

The St. Louis Arch   Designed by architect Eero Saarinen, the St. Louis Arch in St. Louis, Missouri, was completed in 1965 on a site overlooking the Mississippi River. Although the height of the arch and its width at the base are both 630 feet, the graceful catenary creates the illusion that the arch is taller than it is wide. Even if we are told that its height and width are the same, we still have great difficulty making the cognitive adjustment to correct what is known as the vertical/horizontal illusion. Because of this optical illusion we also tend to overestimate the height of trees and tall buildings.

DISCUSSION QUESTIONS

1. *What was your first reaction when you were told that the height and width of the arch were the same? Did they look the same after you were told the dimensions of the arch? Share with the class other optical illusions that you have encountered in architecture or elsewhere.*

2. *Working in small groups, discuss why we might experience optical illusions such as the vertical/horizontal illusion. Discuss what resources you could use in developing your hypothesis (a hypothesis is an educated guess based on evidence and experimentation). Share your hypothesis with the class for analysis.*

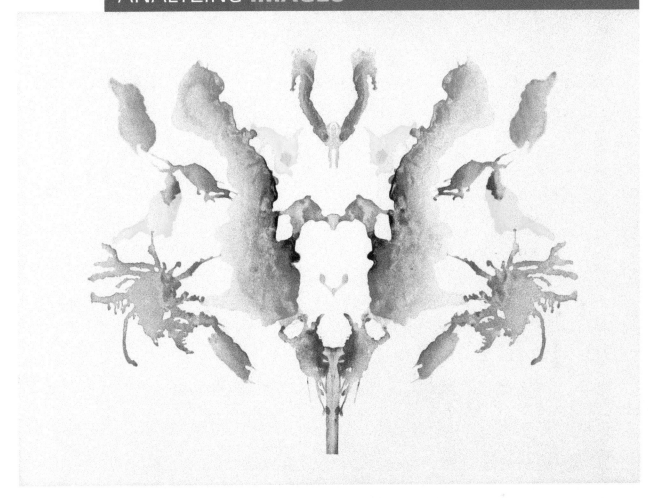

Inkblots In an inkblot test such as in the one above, a psychologist asks a person to describe what he or she sees. The psychologist uses the descriptions to learn more about a person's motivations and unconscious drives.

DISCUSSION QUESTIONS

1. *What do you see when you look at the above inkblot? Why do you think you saw what you did?*

2. *Discuss how the inkblot test illustrates our tendency to impose order on random data. Think of a time when you fell for this error in your everyday life. Come up with two or three critical-thinking strategies you might use to make yourself less prone to being taken in by our tendency to impose meaning on random data.*

He later described the UFOs as the color of "burnished aluminum" and "shaped like a hydroplane." As it turned out, the "squadron of UFOs" was most likely a meteor fireball that had broken up in the vicinity of the plane.[21] However, while being able to provide alternative explanations for most UFO sightings makes their existence less probable, we cannot conclude with certainty that *all* sightings are a result of perceptual errors. We'll be looking at the issue of the existence of UFOs in the "Critical Thinking Issue: Perspectives on Evaluating Evidence for the Existence of Unidentified Flying Objects" section at the end of this chapter.

Our minds may also distort objects we perceive. A straight stick, when inserted in water, appears to bend. A full moon appears to be much larger when it is near the

Connections

What tools and strategies do scientists use to minimize perceptual errors?

Radar photo of 2005 Hurricane Katrina that had an object that looked like a "fetus facing to the left in the womb" to some, leading some anti-abortion advocates to draw the conclusion that the hurricane was punishment for the presence of abortion clinics in the city.

horizon, a phenomenon that NASA refers to as the "moon illusion."

Misperception of Random Data

Because our brains loathe absence of meaning, we may "see" order or meaningful patterns where there are none. For example, when we look at clouds or see unexplained lights in the sky, our brains impose meaning on the random shapes we see. When we look at the moon, we see a "face," popularly known as the man in the moon. In 2004, a piece of toast with cheese, allegedly bearing the image of the Virgin Mary, sold on eBay for $28,000.

One of the most famous examples of this type of error is the "Martian Canals," first reported as channels by Italian astronomer Giovanni Schiaparelli in 1877. Many astronomers continued to believe in the existence of these canals up until 1965, when the spacecraft *Mariner 4* flew close to Mars and took photos of the planet's surface. No canals showed up in the photos. It turned out that the "canals" were a combination of an optical illusion, the expectation that there were canals, and the brain's tendency to impose order on random data. Because of our brain's inclination to impose meaning on random data, we should maintain a stance of skepticism about what we see.

The combination of the error of misperceiving random data with confirmation bias—interpreting data in a way that confirms our cherished views—is illustrated by the next example. After the devastation of New Orleans by Hurricane Katrina in 2005, a group known as the Columbia Christians for Life announced that God's purpose in sending the hurricane was to destroy the five abortion clinics in the city. Their proof was a radar photograph taken of the hurricane in which they claimed to have seen what looked like "a fetus facing to the left (west) in the womb, in the early weeks of gestation."[22]

Stress as well as preconceptions about the world can affect our perception. How many of us, walking alone at night, have seen a person or dog standing in a shadow, only to discover it was a bush or other object?

Critical THiNKing in Action

Food for Thought: Perception and Supersized Food Portions

Obesity is becoming an epidemic in the U.S. More than one-third of Americans adults are obese—more than double the rate in 1980, according to the U.S. Centers for Disease Control and Prevention. Supersized portions of junk food, such as potato chips, hamburgers, and sodas, have been blamed, in part, for this trend.* Do supersized portions lead to supersized people, or is this just all hype so that we can place the blame for our weight problems on Lay's potato chips and McDonald's burgers? In fact, studies show that downsizing our food portions does work to keep our weight down because it takes advantage of a perceptual error. Appetite is not a matter of just the physiological state of hunger but also a matter of perception—what we see in front of us. Most of us eat more when the table or our plates are loaded with food.

Humans are not the only species who make this error. When a researcher places a pile of 100 grams of wheat in front of a hen, she will eat 50 grams and leave 50. However, if we put 200 grams of wheat in front of a hen in a similar hunger condition, she will eat far more—83 to 108 grams of wheat or, once again, about half of what is in front of her.** Furthermore, if the food is presented as whole grains of rice, rather than cracked rice, where the grains are one quarter the size of whole rice grains, the hen will eat two to three times as much as she would otherwise.

In other words, by cutting down your portion sizes and cutting your food into smaller pieces, your brain will think you're full on less food.

DISCUSSION QUESTIONS

1. Many students put on weight in their first year of college, a phenomenon known as the "freshman 15." Critically evaluate your college environment and ways in which it promotes or hinders good eating habits. Make a list of suggestions for improving the environment so students are not so vulnerable to perceptual errors and overeact as a result. Carry out one of the suggestions or pass it on to someone who is in a position to make the change.

2. Examine your own eating habits. Evaluate ways in which being more aware of your thinking process, including inbuilt perceptual errors, can help you to maintain healthier eating habits.

*Nancy Hellmich, "How to Downsize the Student Body," *USA Today*, November 15, 2004.
**George W. Hartmann, *Gestalt Psychology* (New York: Ronald Press, 1935), pp. 87–88.

Memorable-Events Error

The **memorable-events error** involves our ability to vividly remember outstanding events. Scientists have discovered channels in our brains that actually hinder most long-term memories by screening out the mundane incidents in our everyday life.[23] However, these memory-impairing channels appear to close down during outstanding events. For example, most Americans recall exactly where they were and what they were doing on the morning of September 11, 2001. However, if you ask someone what they were doing on an ordinary weekday two months ago, most

> **memorable-events error** A cognitive error that involves our ability to vividly remember outstanding events.

Why do news stories lend themselves to memorable-events errors?

What methods and techniques do scientists use to minimize personal and social bias?

people would be unable to remember or would remember only if they could think of something special that happened on that day.

To use another example, airplane crashes and fatalities are reported in the national media, whereas automobile fatalities generally are not. However, per mile traveled, airplane travel is far safer. We're sixteen times more likely to be killed in an automobile accident than in an airplane accident. In fact, traffic accidents are one of the leading causes of death and disability of people between the ages of 15 and 44.[24] However, the memorable-events error exerts such control over our thinking that even after being informed of these statistics, many of us still continue to be more nervous about flying than about driving.

The memorable-events error is sometimes tied in with confirmation bias, in which we tend to remember events that confirm our beliefs and forget those that are contrary to our beliefs. A popular belief in the United States is that "death takes a holiday" and that terminally ill patients can postpone their death until after an important holiday or birthday. In fact, this belief is based purely on wishful thinking and anecdotal evidence. In an analysis of the death certificates of more than a million people who died from cancer, biostatisticians Donn Young

probability error Misunderstanding the probability or chances of an event by a huge margin.

gambler's error The belief that a previous event affects the probability in a random event.

and Erinn Hade found no evidence that there is a reduction in death rates prior to a holiday or important event.[25] Personal and social beliefs are remarkably strong even in the face of empirical evidence that logically should be devastating. When their results were published, Young and Hade received several angry e-mails criticizing them for taking away people's hope.

Probability Errors

What is the probability that two people in your class have a birthday on the same month and day? Most people guess that the probability is pretty low. In fact, in a class of 23, the probability is about 50 percent. In larger classes, the probability is even higher. When we misestimate the probably of an event by a huge margin, we are committing **probability error**.

Humans are notoriously poor at determining probability. We are inclined to believe that coincidences must have paranormal causes when actually they are consistent with

According to the Association for Psychological Science, 1.2 percent of the adult population are pathological gamblers and at least another 2.8 percent are problem gamblers.

probability. For example, you are thinking of a friend whom you haven't seen for a year when the phone rings and it's your friend on the other line. Are you psychic? Or is it just a coincidence? You've probably thought of your friend hundreds or even thousands of times over the course of the past year without receiving any phone calls, but we tend to forget such times because nothing memorable occurred.

One of the most insidious forms of probability error is **gambler's error**—the erroneous belief that previous events affect the probability in a random event. Research suggests that gambling addiction is based on gambler's error. In a study participants were invited to think aloud while gambling. Of the verbalized perceptions, 70 percent were based on erroneous thinking such as "The machine is due; I need to continue," "Here is my lucky dealer," "Today I feel great; it is my lucky day," "It's my turn to win." These statements reveal a failure to understand the random nature of probability.

When questioned about their verbalizations, nonproblem gamblers realized that their beliefs were wrong. They were able to use accumulated evidence to critically evaluate and modify their perceptions. Problem gamblers, in contrast, processed

Statistically, there is a far greater chance per mile traveled of being killed in a car accident than in an airplane crash, yet most people have a greater fear of flying.

the evidence much differently. They believed what they had said and interpreted their occasional random wins as confirming their belief that the outcome of a game can be predicted and controlled. The solution? Work to improve problem gamblers' critical-thinking skills. By making gamblers aware of their erroneous perceptions and the reasons why they continue to cling to these beliefs, clinicians work to help gamblers overcome their addiction.[26]

Self-Serving Biases

There are several types of self-serving biases or errors that impede our thinking and pursuit of truth, including:

- The misperception that we are in control

- The tendency to overestimate ourselves in comparison to others

- The tendency to exaggerate our strengths and minimize our weaknesses

We are predisposed to believe that we are in control of events that are outside our control. "I knew it would rain today," you groan. "I didn't bring my umbrella." Recently, the Powerball lottery jackpot reached over $100 million. I was standing in line at a mini-mart when I overheard the following conversation between the people in front of me, who were waiting to buy lottery tickets.

> **Person 1**: "What are you going to do? Are you going to pick your own numbers or let the computer do it for you?"
> **Person 2:** "Pick my own. It gives me a better chance of winning."

People who are poor critical thinkers may fall prey to more than one error in thinking in the same situation. In this case the control error was compounded by the probability error, which we discussed earlier. Although logically we know that lottery numbers are selected randomly, many of us also believe that choosing our own numbers— especially using our "lucky" numbers—increases our chances of

Gambler's error and an addiction to gambling is based on a misunderstanding of the random nature of probability.

winning. In fact, 80 percent of winning lottery tickets have numbers randomly generated by the computer, not so-called lucky numbers picked by the winners.[27]

The misperception that we are in control of random events also plays out in superstitious behavior such as wearing our lucky shirt during a big game or bringing a

Following the disastrous April 2010 oil rig explosion in the Gulf of Mexico, British Petroleum (BP) engaged in self-serving bias by grossly underestimating the amount of crude oil that flowed from the disabled well into the Gulf. BP also overestimated its control of the situation and its ability to stop the oil flow and clean up the oil spill without outside help.

good-luck charm to an exam. Before a game, most college and professional athletes engage in ritualistic superstitious behavior such as using a particular color shoelace or tape. Some baseball players sleep with their bats to break out of a hitting slump or to keep up their batting average. To some extent, the belief that we are in control can boost our confidence in achieving our goals. In fact, ritualistic behaviors have been found to have a calming effect on athletes before a game.

However, if we carry the belief that we are in control too far, it can distort our thinking and lead to poor decisions in our lives. The self-serving bias, and misjudgment about our ability to handle a challenge, can work against our rational self-interests. For example in the case of the British Petroleum oil leak, BP lost billions of dollars as well as the public confidence because of their erroneous belief in the beginning that they were in control of the situation and didn't need outside help. Thousands of people have died in wildfires and in hurricanes, despite repeated warnings to evacuate, because they thought they were in control of the situation and could ride out the storm.

This error is also expressed in the often-heard cliché "You can do anything you want if you put your mind to it," the implication being that if only we wanted to enough, we would have perfect control. Self-help gurus have become wealthy catering to this self-serving error. In her book *The Secret* (2006), Rhonda Byrne claims to have found the secret to happiness in what she calls "the law of attraction." According to Byrne, each of us has complete control over what happens to us in our lives. If we think positive thoughts, then like a magnet, we will attract whatever we want—whether it be a parking spot, a million dollars, a sexy figure, or a cure for cancer. The downside is that if we are not successful in getting what we want, then we have only ourselves and our negative thinking to blame.

The belief that we are in control of situations where we actually have little or no control can contribute to irrational guilt or posttraumatic stress syndrome.[28] A survivor of a traumatic event may believe that he or she should have been able to predict and do something to prevent an event such as sexual abuse, domestic violence, or the death of a loved one, especially an accidental or suicidal death.

Although genetic, physical, and environmental factors play a role in the onset of depression, the belief that we should be in control of our lives can also contribute to depression (see "Critical Thinking in Action: Irrational Beliefs and Depression"). People who are depressed may cling to the irrational belief that the only alternative to not having perfect control is having no control. Because they feel they lack any control over their lives, they tend to attribute their misfortune or sadness to other people's actions. A side effect of this negative behavior is that their behavior often alienates other people, thereby confirming a second irrational belief common to depressed people that they are worthless and unlikable. Thus, their distorted expectations lead to a self-fulfilling prophecy, a cognitive error we'll be studying in the next section.

A second self-serving bias is the tendency to overestimate ourselves in comparison to others. Most people rate themselves as above average when it comes to getting along with other people. Although it obviously can't be true that the majority of people are above average—except, perhaps, in the fictional town of Lake Wobegon in Garrison Keillor's *Prairie Home Companion* on Minnesota Public Radio—this self-serving bias can bolster our self-esteem and confidence. However, if we are unaware of the bias, it can become a problem and cause us not to take responsibility for our shortcomings. A Pew Research Center survey found that while 70 percent of Americans are overweight and that nine in ten agree that most of their fellow Americans are overweight, only 39 percent of Americans consider themselves to be overweight.[29] Clearly there seems to be a disconnect between being overweight and people's estimation of their own weight.

Another example of the self-serving bias

Critical THiNKing in Action

Irrational Beliefs and Depression

Albert Ellis (b. 1913), founder of rational emotive behavioral therapy, maintains that irrational ideas are the primary source of depression, rage, feelings of inadequacy, and self-hatred. Some of these irrational beliefs are:

- "I must be outstandingly competent, or I am worthless."
- "Others must treat me considerately, or they are absolutely rotten."
- "The world should always give me happiness, or I will die."
- "I must have perfect control over things, or I won't be able to enjoy life."
- "Because something once strongly affected my life, it will indefinitely affect my life."

According to Ellis, a depressed person feels sad because he (or she) erroneously thinks he is inadequate and abandoned, even though depressed people have the capacity to perform as well as nondepressed people. The purpose of therapy is to dispute these irrational beliefs and replace them with positive rational beliefs. To achieve this, the therapist asks questions such as:

- Is there evidence for this belief?
- What is the evidence against this belief?
- What is the worst that can happen if you give up this belief?
- And what is the best that can happen?

To assist the clients in changing their irrational beliefs, the therapist also uses other techniques such as empathy training, assertiveness training, and encouraging the development of self-management strategies.

DISCUSSION QUESTIONS

1. Discuss how cognitive errors contribute to irrational beliefs. Make a list of other irrational beliefs people hold that are based on cognitive errors.

2. Do you have any irrational beliefs that interfere with your achieving your life goals? If so, what are they? Discuss how you might use your critical-thinking skills to work toward overcoming these beliefs. Be specific.

See Albert Ellis, *The Essence of Rational Emotive Behavior Therapy.* Ph.D. dissertation, revised, May 1994.

is that most people take personal credit for their successes and blame outside forces for their failures. College students often attribute their "A" grades to something about themselves—their intelligence, quick grasp of the material, or good study skills. In contrast, they usually attribute their poor grades to something outside their control such as having an unfair teacher or having a touch of the flu on the day of the exam.[30] Similarly, when it comes to being overweight, many people blame a slow metabolism as the main reason why they can't lose weight, rather than their lifestyle or factors under their control. However, when overweight people do lose weight, they rarely attribute their success to a peppy metabolism but instead credit their willpower and good choices.

This type of self-serving bias can be found in the workplace. When office employees were asked in a survey "if they ever experienced backstabbing, rudeness, or incivility in the workplace," 89 percent said "yes." However, in the same survey 99 percent said that "they were never rude or the cause of the conflict."[31] In other words, most of us are quick to complain about other's irritating behaviors but give little thought to how our behavior might be the cause of workplace conflict.

According to Carol Tavris and Elliot Aronson, social psychologists and authors of *Mistakes Were Made (But Not By Me): Why We Justify Foolish Beliefs, Bad Decisions and Hurtful Acts*, being made aware of the gap between our self-image and our actual behavior creates cognitive dissonance and discomfort. To minimize this discomfort and maintain our good opinion of ourselves, we instinctively minimize the discrepancy through denial or by blaming someone else for our shortcomings. This sort of rationalization can prevent us from realizing that we're clinging to a mistaken belief.[32] As critical thinkers, we need to deal constructively with the discomfort that comes from cognitive dissonance and to work toward overcoming our mistaken beliefs about ourselves.

A third related self-serving bias is our inclination to exaggerate or place a greater value on our strengths and underestimate or downplay our weaknesses. In a study of intellectually gifted boys who thought they hadn't done well in class, the boys downplayed the importance of academics and instead emphasized the importance of other pursuits such as sports.[33] Seeing ourselves as having those traits and abilities that are important in life increases our sense of worth and helps us to achieve our life goals. This tendency, however, can also contribute to overconfidence and failure to seek or acknowledge other people's skills.

As we noted in the introduction to this chapter, overconfidence in physicians and jumping to a conclusion has been identified as one of the key factors in diagnostic errors. Unless we are willing, as critical thinkers, to make an honest

What is cognitive dissonance and when are people most likely to engage in it? *See Chapter 7, p 197.*

Connections

According to the Institute of Medicine of the National Academy of Sciences, medical errors are responsible for an estimated 44,000 to 98,000 deaths a year in the United States.

evaluation of ourselves, it is unlikely that we are going to take steps toward overcoming our shortcomings.

Self-Fulfilling Prophecy

A self-fulfilling prophecy occurs when our exaggerated or distorted expectations reinforce actions that actually bring about the expected event. Expectations can have a profound influence on our behavior. Rumors of impending bank failures during the Great Depression in the early 1930s led to mass panic in which people rushed to take their money out of banks before the banks crashed. As a result, lots of banks went bankrupt. Since banks invest some of the deposits rather than keeping all the money in the vault, the frenzy caused the collapse of the banks—the very thing the customers feared.

To use another example of a self-fulfilling prophecy, let's say a literature professor has a star football player in her class. On the basis of her (mistaken) expectations about college athletes, she assumes that he is not academically inclined but is taking the course only because it is reputed to be easy. Because of this she calls on him less and doesn't encourage him or make an effort to include him in class discussions. She justifies this behavior on her part as not wanting to embarrass him.

To preserve our expectations, we may interpret ambiguous data in ways that meet our expectations. For example, our football star may be particularly quiet and introspective during one class. The professor assumes that he is preoccupied with thinking about the upcoming game, when instead he is deep in thought about the poem that is being discussed in class. Our football player, who initially was very interested in the class and in literature and

Panicked citizens gather to withdraw their money from a federal bank during the Great Depression. This type of thinking also contributed to a plunge in the stock market in 2008, when people pulled their money from the stock market because of fears it would crash.

had even written several poems for his high school newspaper, soon begins to lose interest in the class and ends up getting only a mediocre grade. Thus, we have a self-fulfilling prophecy in which the professor's distorted expectation comes true. Clearly, preserving our expectations can come at a cost to others.

Humans are prone to several inborn cognitive and perceptual errors, including optical illusions, misperception of random data, memorable-events errors, probability errors, self-serving biases, and self-fulfilling prophecies. Because these errors are part of the way our brain interprets the world, we may fail to notice the influence they exert over our thinking. Developing our critical-thinking skills

> Rumors of impending bank failures during the Great Depression in the early 1930s led to mass panic in which people rushed to take their money out of banks before the banks crashed.

can help us be more aware of these tendencies and adjust for them when appropriate.

4. Given that humans are prone to cognitive errors, should we use computers rather than physicians for medical diagnoses? Support your answer.

5. Think of a time when you studied hard for a test but ended up with a low grade. To what did you attribute your poor performance? Now think of a time when you studied hard and did very well on a test. To what did you attribute your good performance? Discuss how self-serving biases may have contributed to the difference in your reaction in each of the two situations.

6. Do you tend to overestimate the amount of control you have over your life? Give specific examples. Discuss how a distorted sense of control has had an impact on your ability to achieve your life goals. Come up with at least two critical-thinking strategies you could use to correct for this cognitive error.

7. Which cognitive error are you most like to commit? Give a specific example of your using this error. If you are willing, share your strategies for overcoming these ideas with the class.

SOCIAL ERRORS AND BIASES

Humans are highly social animals. Because of this trait, social norms and cultural expectations exert a strong influence on how we perceive the world—so much so that we tend to perceive the world differently in groups from the way we do in isolation. Groups can systematically distort both the gathering and the interpretation of evidence.[34]

As we noted in Chapter 7, ethnocentrism—the unjustified belief that our group or culture is superior to that of others—can also bias our thinking and act as a barrier to critical thinking.

"One of Us/One of Them" Error

Our brains seem to be programmed to classify people as either "one of us" or "one of them." We tend to treat people who are similar to us with respect and those who are different from us—whether in regard to race, sex, religion, political party, age, or nationality—with suspicion or worse. Although most of us claim to believe in human equality, in our culture the use of qualifiers such as *gay judge*, *female doctor*, *Hispanic senator*, and *Down syndrome child* betray our tacit belief that any deviation from the norm needs to be specified. We rarely hear terms such as *straight judge*, *male doctor*, *European American senator*, or *able-bodied child*!

Prejudices may operate without any conscious realization on our part. In a Harvard study, subjects were asked to quickly associate positive or negative words with black or white faces. Seven out of ten white people, despite their claims that they had no racial prejudice, showed "an automatic preference for white over black."[35]

It is all too easy for people to fall into the "us versus them" mind-set, especially when they feel threatened. In 1994, the Hutu government in Rwanda stirred up Hutus' hatred and fear of the Tutsi, inciting them to carry out a brutal three-month slaughter of the Tutsi. Neighbors killed neighbors, students killed their fellow students, and doctors killed doctors. Even priests helped with the massacre of the Tutsi in their congregations, simply

Victims of the bombing of a Catholic church in Nigeria by Islamic militants in 2012.

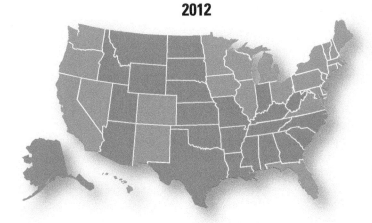

2012

Red States vs Blue States

because the Tutsi were the "other." When it was over, a million people were dead.

This error also contributes to our tendency to polarize issues into two camps. "They," whether it be "right-wing conservatives" or "far-left liberals," are irrational; there is no point in even arguing a point with them. Our group, on the other hand, holds a monopoly on Truth. There is no middle ground. During presidential elections, Americans are quick to divide up the country into two opposing camps: the red states (Republicans) and the blue states (Democrats) and to classify people in their group as "good" and "right" and those in the other group as "bad" and "mistaken."

If we are to overcome this social error we need to be aware of it in our thinking and to build in protective measures.[36] As critical thinkers, we can work toward minimizing this error in our thinking by first critically evaluating the situation and then consciously reprogramming our brains to come up with new, more reasonable definitions of who it is that we view as "us" by seeking a more immediate and inclusive basis for a connection, such as we all attend the same college, we all are Americans, we all are human beings. We also need to make a conscious effort to be open to multiple perspectives, even those we are initially convinced must be mistaken.

Societal Expectations

The late nineteenth and early twentieth centuries were times of extraordinary technological advancement, setting in motion the expectation of ever new and revolutionary technology. On December 13, 1909, six years after the Wright brothers' epic flight, the *Boston Herald* reported the invention of an airship by a local businessman, Wallace Tillinghast.[37] Over the next several weeks, hundreds of witnesses from the New England–New York area, including police officers, judges, and businesspeople, reported sightings of the airship sailing through the skies.[38] The reported sightings led to a massive search for the airship by reporters. The search was finally called off when it was revealed that the story was a hoax perpetuated by Tillinghast.

Connections

When you serve as a juror, how can cognitive and social errors distort your analysis of the evidence?

Social expectations can be so powerful that they may lead to collective delusions. Sometimes these social errors may even become institutionalized.[39] Acting on social expectations without subjecting them to critical analysis can have dire consequences. The Salem witch trials in colonial Massachusetts, in which over 200 people, predominantly young women, were accused of witchcraft, were rooted in the social expectations of the seventeenth century. Those of us living in the twenty-first century may regard the witch-hunters as crazed fanatics. However, they were simply behaving in a manner that was consistent with the prevailing worldview and social expectations of their time in which certain unfortunate circumstances, such as crop failures, disease, and untimely deaths, were interpreted as being brought about by the Devil and his worldly agents—witches.

The Salem witch hunts, which took place in Massachusetts in the late 17th century, targeted those mistakenly believed to be responsible for society's ills.

The social expectations of the police who interrogated Peter Reilly, a teenager who was accused in 1973 of killing his mother, also played a role in their use of leading questions to get a "confession" out of him. Reilly's mother had been an emotionally abusive woman. In our society we expect victims of parental abuse to be violent and vengeful, even though studies suggest that it is children who witness domestic violence, rather than those who are direct victims of it, who are at highest risk, since they come to accept violence as normal.[40] In addition, it is often a family member who commits this type of violent murder. Therefore, the police jumped to the conclusion, on the basis of their expectations, that Reilly must have committed the murder.

Stereotyping is another type of social bias based on socially generated group labels. In the study mentioned in Chapter 7, page 198, in which researchers showed students a picture of a black man on a subway next to a white man who was holding an open razor, when students were later asked to recall what they had seen, half of them reported that the black man was holding the razor.

ANALYZING IMAGES

Asch Experiment

In Asch's experiment, the naive subject (left) shows puzzlement when the other subjects give what is obviously a wrong answer.

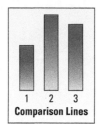

Standard Line   Comparison Lines

DISCUSSION QUESTIONS

1. *What do you think the naive subject in the picture above is thinking?*

2. *Think back to a time when you were in a similar situation where you thought you were correct, but everyone else with you thought something else. How did you respond to the discrepancy between your belief and theirs?*

Group Pressure and Conformity

Group pressure can influence individual members to take positions that they would never support by themselves, as happened in the Stanford prison experiment described in Chapter 7. Some religious cults exploit this tendency by separating their members from the dissenting views of family and friends. In many cults, people live together, eat together, and may even be assigned a buddy.

Group pressure is so powerful in shaping how we see the world that it can lead people to deny contrary evidence that is right before their eyes. In the 1950s, social psychologist Solomon Asch carried out a series of experiments in which he showed study subjects a screen containing a standard line on the left and three comparison lines on the right. (see "Analyzing Images: Asch Experiment"). One of the comparison lines was the same length as the standard line and the other two were of significantly different lengths.[41] In each case, an unsuspecting study subject was introduced into a group with six confederates, who had been told by the experimenter to give the wrong answer. The group was then shown the lines. The experimenter asked one of the confederates which of the three lines on the right they thought was the same length as the standard line. The confederate, without hesitation, gave a wrong answer. The next few confederates gave the same answer. By now, the naive subject was showing puzzlement and even dismay. How can six people be wrong?

After hearing six "wrong" answers, 75 percent of the naive study subjects, rather than trust the evidence of their senses, succumbed to group pressure and gave the same wrong answer. Even more surprising is the fact that when questioned afterward, some of these study subjects had actually come to believe the wrong answer was correct.

The desire for agreement is normal. However, this desire, when combined with our innate tendency to divide the world into "one of us" and "one of them," can lead to the exclusion of those who disagree with the majority, since people tend to prefer being around people who agree with them. In the corporate world, disagreement is often tacitly discouraged. "Outliers" or nonconformists who do not agree with group members may be excluded by committee chairs from further discussions or even fired.[42]

Because of our inborn tendency to conform to what others think, we cannot assume that agreement leads to truth without knowledge about the manner and conditions under which the agreement was arrived. Indeed, the current emphasis on seeking group consensus in decision making may be unreliable. In consensus seeking, the majority in a group is often able to sway the whole group to its view.

As with other errors in our thinking, we need to develop strategies to recognize and compensate for our human inclination to conform to groupthink, the tendency of members of a group to yield to the consensus of the group. When a group comes to a decision, we need to mentally step back from the group and carefully evaluate the evidence for a particular position rather than assume that the majority must be correct. In competitive ice skating and diving, because of the danger of a judge's scoring being contaminated by what other judges say, scoring is done individually, rather than as a group decision.

Diffusion of Responsibility

Diffusion of responsibility is a social phenomenon that occurs in groups of people above a critical size. If responsibility is not explicitly assigned to us, we tend to regard it as not our problem but as belonging to someone else. We are much more likely to come to someone's aid if we are alone than if we are in a crowd.

> **diffusion of responsibility** The tendency, when in a large group, to regard a problem as belonging to someone else.

This phenomenon is also known as *bystander apathy* or the *Kitty Genovese syndrome.* In 1964, 28-year-old Kitty Genovese was murdered outside her New York City apartment building. In the half hour that lapsed during the attack, none of Genovese's many neighbors,

5/30/2008 5:49:42 PM

The phenomenon of "diffusion of responsibility" was regrettably illustrated when no one came to the aid of a seriously injured man lying in a busy street in Hartford, Connecticut, after being struck by a hit-and-run driver in May 2008. The victim, Angel Torres, later died from the injuries he sustained.

who had heard her repeated cries for help, called the police. More recently, in June 2008, an elderly man was struck by a hit-and-run driver on a busy street in Hartford, Connecticut. The man lay in the street paralyzed and bleeding from his head while bystanders gawked at or

---

We are much more likely to come
to someone's aid if we are alone
than if we are in a crowd.

---

ignored him. Motorists drove around his body without stopping. No one offered any assistance until an ambulance finally turned up. Diffusion of responsibility can

also occur in group hazing at fraternities where no one comes to the rescue of a pledge who is clearly in distress.

As social beings, we are vulnerable to the "one of us/one of them" error, social expectations, and group conformity. When in groups, we also tend to regard something as not our problem unless responsibility is assigned to us. Although these traits may promote group cohesiveness, they can interfere with effective critical thinking. As good critical thinkers we need to be aware of these tendencies, and to cultivate the ability to think independently while still taking into consideration others' perspectives. Errors in our thinking also make us more vulnerable to falling for or using fallacies in arguments. We'll be studying some of these fallacies in the following chapter.

EXERCISE 8-4

STOP AND ASSESS YOURSELF

1. Whom do you define as "us" and whom do you put in the category of "them"? Discuss how you might go about widening the "us" category to include more people who are now in your "them" category.

2. Humans seem to have inborn biases toward particular types of people. According to a University of Florida study, when it comes to hiring, employers have a more favorable view of tall people. When it comes to earnings, every extra inch of height above the norm is worth almost $1,000 a year. In fact, nine of ten top executives are taller than the typical employee.[43] Given this cognitive error and its impact on hiring practices, discuss whether or not affirmative action policies should apply to very short people. Relate your answer to the discussion in the text of the effect of this cognitive error on our thinking.

3. Think of a time when your social expectations led you to misjudge a person or a situation. Discuss strategies for improving your critical-thinking skills so that this is less likely to happen.

4. Think of a time when the public got caught up in a "witch hunt." Identify the worldviews and social expectations that supported this "witch hunt." Which critical-thinking skills would make you less likely to go along with a "witch hunt"? Discuss what actions you could take to develop or strengthen these skills.

5. Polls before elections can influence how people vote by swaying undecided voters to vote for the candidate who is in the lead. Analyze whether election polls should be forbidden prior to the election itself.

6. The democratic process depends on social consensus. Given people's tendency to conform to social expectations and what others think, is democracy the best form of government? If so, what policies might be put in place to lessen the effect of social biases? Be specific.

7. Think of a time when you failed to speak out against an injustice or failed to come to someone's aid simply because you were in a large group and felt it wasn't your responsibility. Discuss ways in which improving your critical-thinking skills may make you less susceptible to the diffusion of social responsibility error.

8. Computers (AI) programmed with an inductive logic program can, after sufficient experience working with the ups and downs of the financial market, predict the market with greater accuracy than most experienced financial planners. Given that these computers are not as prone to cognitive errors as are humans, critically evaluate whether we should rely more on AI to make decisions about such issues as college admissions, medical diagnoses, matchmaking, and piloting an airplane.

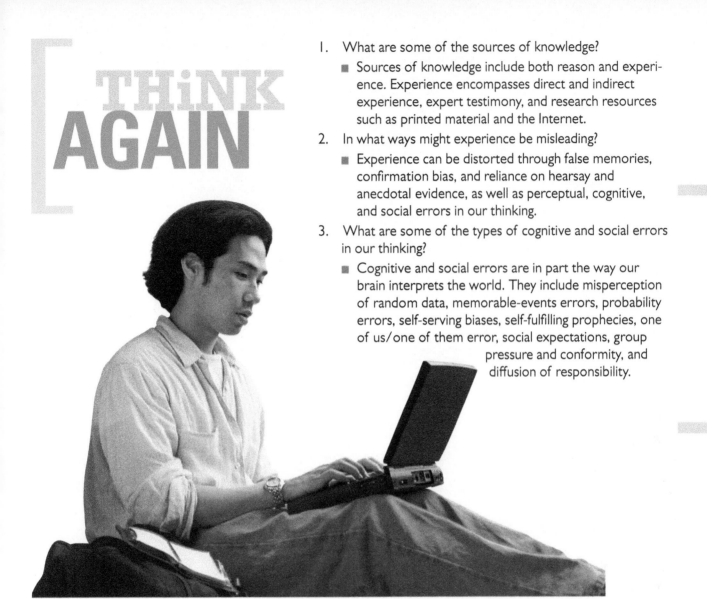

1. What are some of the sources of knowledge?
   - Sources of knowledge include both reason and experience. Experience encompasses direct and indirect experience, expert testimony, and research resources such as printed material and the Internet.

2. In what ways might experience be misleading?
   - Experience can be distorted through false memories, confirmation bias, and reliance on hearsay and anecdotal evidence, as well as perceptual, cognitive, and social errors in our thinking.

3. What are some of the types of cognitive and social errors in our thinking?
   - Cognitive and social errors are in part the way our brain interprets the world. They include misperception of random data, memorable-events errors, probability errors, self-serving biases, self-fulfilling prophecies, one of us/one of them error, social expectations, group pressure and conformity, and diffusion of responsibility.

Perspectives on Evaluating Evidence for the Existence of Unidentified Flying Objects (UFOs)

Sightings of unexplained phenomena in the sky have been reported since ancient times. However, it was not until the late 1940s, following the famous "flying saucer crash" incident in Roswell, New Mexico, that UFO reports began to proliferate. There is little doubt that sensationalist media coverage stimulated reports of more UFO sightings, just as the 1909 story in the *Boston Herald* of the invention of an airship was followed by hundreds of sightings of the bogus ship.

In 1948, the U.S. Air Force began to keep a file of UFO sightings as part of Project Blue Book. By 1969, the project had recorded 12,618 UFO sightings. Ninety percent of these UFO sightings have been identified with astronomical and weather phenomena, aircraft, balloons, searchlights, hot gases, and other natural events. Ten percent remain unexplained. In 1968, the U.S. Air Force commissioned a study under the direction of University of Colorado professor Edward Condon.[44] The study concluded that there was no evidence for UFOs and that scientific study of the phenomenon should be discontinued. As a result of the study, Project Blue Book was suspended.

Despite official consensus that UFOs do not exist, a 2012 National Geographic Society poll found that slightly more than one-third of Americans believe that UFOs exist.[45] In addition, 10 percent claim to have actually seen a UFO. The survey also found that 79 percent of Americans think that the government is hiding information from them about the existence of UFOs and alien life forms.

Following are readings from the U.S Air Force Blue Book Project and by Royston Paynter. Many if not most scientists believe that UFOs do not exist. These scientists argue that there are natural explanations for UFO phenomena, including meteorites, balloons, hallucinations, and perceptual and social error in our thinking. While Blue Book Project is more dismissive of UFOs, both readings leave open the possibility that UFOs may be real.

Project Blue Book: Analysis of Reports of Unidentified Aerial Objects

UNITED STATES AIR FORCE

Project Blue Book summarizes a series of studies of unidentified flying objects (UFOs) conducted by the U.S. Air Force beginning in 1952. The following selection is from the summary and conclusion of the report. To read the entire report, go to http://www.ufocasebook.com/pdf/specialreport14.pdf.

It is not possible to derive a verified model of a "flying saucer" from the data that have been gathered to date. This point is important enough to emphasize. Out of about 4,000 people who said they saw a "flying saucer," sufficiently detailed descriptions were given in only 12 cases. Having culled the cream of the crop, it is still impossible to develop a picture of what a "flying saucer" is. . . .

On the basis of this evidence, therefore, there is a low probability that any of the UNKNOWNS represent observations of a class of "flying saucers." It may be that some reports represent observations of not one but several classes of objects that might have been "flying saucers"; however, the lack of evidence to confirm even one class would seem to make this possibility remote. It is pointed out that some of the cases of KNOWNS, before identification, appeared fully as bizarre as any of the 12 cases of good UNKNOWNS, and, in fact, would have been placed in the class of good UNKNOWNS had it not been possible to establish their identity.

This is, of course, contrary to the bulk of the publicity that has been given to this problem. . . . It is unfortunate that practically all of the articles, books, and news stories dealing with the phenomenon of the "flying saucer" were written by men . . . had read only a few selected reports. This is accentuated by the fact that, as a rule, only the more lurid-sounding reports are cited in these publications. Were it not for this common psychological tendency to be captivated by the mysterious, it is possible that no problem of this nature would exist.

The reaction, mentioned above, that after reading a few reports, the reader is convinced that "flying saucers" are real and are some form of sinister contrivance, is very misleading. As more and more of the reports are read, the feeling that "saucers" are real fades, and is replaced by a feeling of skepticism regarding their existence. The reader eventually reaches a point of saturation, after which the reports contain no new information at all and are no longer of any interest. This feeling of surfeit was universal among the personnel who worked on this project, and continually necessitated a conscious effort on their part to remain objective.

CONCLUSIONS

It can never be absolutely proven that "flying saucers" do not exist. This would be true if the data obtained were to include complete scientific measurements of the attributes of each sighting, as well as complete and detailed descriptions of the objects sighted. It might be possible to demonstrate the existence of "flying saucers" with data of this type, IF they were to exist.

Although the reports considered in this study usually did not contain scientific measurements of the attributes of each sighting, it was possible to establish certain valid conclusions by the application of statistical methods in the treatment of the data. Scientifically evaluated and arranged, the data as such did not show any marked patterns or trends. The inaccuracies inherent in this type of data, in addition to the incompleteness of a large proportion, of the reports, may have obscured any patterns or trends that otherwise would have been evident. This absence of indicative relationships necessitated an exhaustive study of selected facets of the data in order to draw any valid conclusions.

A critical examination of the distributions of the important characteristics of sightings, plus an intensive study of the sightings evaluated as UNKNOWN, led to the conclusion that a combination of factors, principally the reported maneuvers of the objects and the unavailability of supplemental data such as aircraft flight plans or balloon-launching records, resulted in the failure to identify as KNOWNS most of the reports of objects classified as UNKNOWNS.

An intensive study, aimed at finding a verified example of a "flying saucer" or at deriving a verified model or models of "flying saucers", led to the conclusion that neither goal could be attained using the present data.

It is emphasized that there was a complete lack of any valid evidence consisting of physical matter in any case of a reported unidentified aerial object. Thus, the probability that any of the UNKNOWNS considered in this study are "flying saucers" is concluded to be extremely small, since the most complete and reliable reports from the present data, when isolated and studied, conclusively failed to reveal even a rough model, and since the data as a whole failed to reveal any marked patterns or trends. Therefore, on the basis of this evaluation of the information, it is considered to be highly improbable that any of the reports of unidentified aerial objects examined in this study represent observations of technological developments outside the range of present-day scientific knowledge.

Review Questions

1. How does *Project Blue Book* distinguish between KNOWNS and UNKNOWNS in assessing reports of UFO sightings?

2. How do the authors account for the fact that so many people believe in UFOs?

3. What conclusion do the authors of *Project Blue Book* draw regarding the existence of UFOs and why?

Physical Evidence and Unidentified Flying Objects   ROYSTON PAYNTER

Royston Paynter has a Ph.D. in materials science from the University of Surrey in the United Kingdom and is currently a professor at the Institut National de la Recherche Scientifique in Quebec, Canada. In this article, Dr. Paynter writes that claims about the existence of UFOs and alien abductions should be conducted "according to the highest standards of scientific inquiry."[47] Without any physical evidence, he argues, we should remain skeptical about these claims.

Skeptics are sometimes criticized for demanding physical evidence of alien visitations. It is an unreasonable demand, believers say, because aliens are intelligent and cunning, and one cannot expect them to leave physical evidence of their presence on Earth.

Well, such an argument may make sense to somebody who is prepared to believe in alien visitations as an act of faith, in the same way that some people believe in angels. But the undeniable fact of the matter is that there is **no** probative physical evidence that compels us to conclude that aliens are visiting the Earth.

There simply is no alien space ship on display in a museum somewhere, in fact, there is no object in existence on Earth of which we can say "this must have been made by aliens." Of course it is possible to *believe* in alien visitations nonetheless, as an act of faith, but the great majority of scientists do not believe it, because it has not been proven in a rigorous scientific manner.

Those believers that reject the more extreme claims of popular UFOlogy, such as cattle mutilations, crop circles and even perhaps alien abductions, tend to fall back upon government and military reports obtained under the Freedom of Information Act. A well-known example is the US Air Force's own Project Sign "Estimate of the Situation," issued in 1948, that concluded that flying saucers were real and that they came from outer space.

To what extent is such a report authoritative? A scientifically trained individual looking at such a statement would ask "is this conclusion justified by the data presented?" That is to say, is such a conclusion forced upon us as the most economical way to explain that data, or is it the result of sloppy analysis and/or wishful thinking? In the case of the Project Sign "estimate,"

General Hoyt S. Vandenberg did not believe that the report's evidence was sufficient to support its conclusions, and he rejected it.

For those among us that are not prepared to believe in alien visitations simply as an act of faith, **physical evidence** is the key to everything. We **will** believe, if some artifact can be found on Earth that is demonstrably **alien**. Let us note here that "unidentified" and "demonstrably alien" are not synonymous. Just because a given UFO sighting cannot be explained it does not follow that it has been proved to be an alien space ship.

Short of a flying saucer landing on the White House lawn, where lie the best chances to obtain a demonstrably alien artifact? If we are to believe the stories told (or "remembered" under hypnosis) by those claiming to have been abducted by aliens, it seems that we should direct our attention first to those "alien implants" recovered from these people.

The stakes here are extremely high. If these "implants" can be shown to have been manufactured by aliens, then people really are being abducted by aliens. If, on the other hand, it cannot be shown that the "implants" are alien, then we must ask serious questions of the "researchers" who have elicited the testimony from the "abductees."

With the stakes so high, it is essential, in our opinion, that these analyses be conducted in accordance with the highest standards of scientific inquiry. Most importantly, we must demand that the UFOlogists prove *what they claim*. They are claiming that the "implants" have an alien origin. It is therefore not enough to show that they are "*100% pure*" or that they have an "unusual composition" or that they *contain chemical elements* also found in radio transmitters. They have to show that *aliens made them*.

One simple test would be enough to prove such a claim to the satisfaction of most scientists—an isotopic analysis of the material from which the implant is composed. We can reasonably expect that a device made by aliens from materials obtained in another solar system will exhibit isotope ratios different than those found on Earth. Such a test goes straight to the heart of the claim being made for the "implant" and would avoid all the obfuscation and hyperbole about "100% purity" and the like.

We urge the UFOlogical community to adopt properly scientific standards of investigation and proof in their work. They have to support their conclusions with probative evidence and rigorous reasoning and to confront the skeptics with the evidence they so dearly seek—a demonstrably alien artifact.

REVIEW QUESTIONS

1. Why do some believers maintain that the demand for physical evidence of alien visitations is unreasonable? How does Paynter respond to their objection?
2. What type of evidence does a scientist such as Paynter argue is necessary to establish the claim that UFOs exist?
3. What type of evidence does Paynter argue is necessary to prove the claim that people have been abducted by aliens?

THiNK AND DISCUSS

PERSPECTIVES ON THE EXISTENCE OF UNIDENTIFIED FLYING OBJECTS

1. What conclusion do both readings draw regarding the existence of UFOs? Compare and contrast the arguments used by the authors of Project Blue Book and by Paynter to support their conclusion(s). Evaluate the evidence each uses. Which reading presents the best argument? Explain.
2. Discuss the role of cognitive and perceptual errors, as well as social errors, in the debate over the existence of UFOs. Be specific.
3. Both the authors of Project Blue Book and Paynter concede that neither the lack of actual physical evidence of UFOs nor the ability to explain UFO "sightings" as sightings of familiar objects is not sufficient prove that UFOs do not exist. Discuss what proof or evidence, if any, would be sufficient to convince a logical person that UFOs existed.
4. Do you believe in the existence of UFOs? Write down the evidence and premises you use to support your conclusion. Working in small groups, critically analyze each other's arguments.

9

RECOGNIZING, ANALYZING, & CONSTRUCTING ARGUMENTS

Abraham Lincoln and the incumbent Illinois senator, Stephen A. Douglas, held a series of seven political debates during the 1858 senatorial race. The debates addressed the hottest political issues of the day: whether slavery should be allowed to expand into western territories, whether states should have the authority to allow or ban slavery within their borders, and the wisdom of the U.S. Supreme Court's 1857 *Dred Scott* decision, which had ruled that a slave is "property in the strictest sense of the term" and had declared it unconstitutional for Congress to ban slavery in the western territories. Douglas argued for "popular sovereignty," claiming that the people of states and territories had the right to determine their own laws and policies on slavery. Lincoln opposed the expansion of slavery into the territories, arguing that slavery was "a moral, social and a political wrong."

How do politicians use logical arguments and rhetoric in political debates? How can developing skill in logical argumentation make us more effective in presenting and defending our positions?

THiNK FIRST

- What is an argument?
- What is the purpose of breaking down and diagramming arguments?
- What are some of the factors to take into consideration in evaluating an argument?

>> Although Lincoln lost the senatorial election, he emerged from the debates as a nationally renowned orator and critical thinker. Lincoln went on, as president of the United States, to issue the Emancipation Proclamation, which declared that all those enslaved in Confederate states were to be free. His skill in argumentation and debate, and his refusal to back down in the face of weak counterarguments, culminated in the passage in 1865 of the 13th Amendment, which abolished slavery in the United States.

The ability to recognize, construct, and analyze arguments is one of the most basic skills in critical thinking. To many of us, the word *argument* brings to mind images of quarreling and shouting. However, in logic and in critical thinking, argument refers to the use of reason and evidence to support a claim or conclusion. Arguments are a form of inquiry that provides us with reasons to accept or reject a particular position, so that we can make up our own minds about an issue.

In this information age we are constantly bombarded with arguments on issues from the Internet, television, newspapers, advertisers, politicians, and other sources. As citizens in a democracy, we need to develop the skills to critically analyze arguments and to make informed decisions that are based on our evaluations.

Skill in argumentation can help us make better decisions in our personal choices as well as in our public lives.

In Chapter 9 we will learn how to recognize, analyze, and construct arguments. Specifically, we will:

- Learn how to identify an issue
- Learn how to recognize the parts of an argument, including the premise, the conclusion, and premise and conclusion indicators
- Distinguish among an argument, an explanation, and a conditional statement
- Break down an argument into its premises and conclusion

- Diagram arguments
- Construct our own arguments
- Explore the basics of evaluating arguments

Finally, we will read about the issue of same-sex marriage and analyze arguments that approach that controversial question from different perspectives.

More than 50 years after the Brown v. Board of Education decision that declared segregation unconstitutional, many feel that African Americans still don't have the same opportunities for quality education as whites. This young woman is one of the "Little Rock Nine," of the first nine blacks to attend Central High in Little Rock, Arkansas, despite threats, scare tactics, and the necessary presence of the National Guard for protection.

WHAT IS AN ISSUE?

Arguments help us to analyze issues and to determine whether a particular position on an issue is reasonable. An **issue** is an ill-defined complex of problems involving a controversy or uncertainty.

One problem that many college students have in writing an essay or preparing a presentation on an issue is failing to define the issue clearly. An unfocused discussion about smoking, for example, may jump from health risks of secondhand smoking to the problem of addiction to corporate responsibility to subsidies for tobacco farmers. As a result, the discussion is shallow, and deeper insights into any one of these smoking-related issues are overlooked. Because of this, it is important that we first decide what issue we want to focus on.

Identifying an Issue

Identifying an issue requires clear thinking as well as good communication skills. We've probably all had the experience of finding ourselves arguing at cross-purposes with someone we care about. One person is upset because he or she feels the other isn't showing enough affection, while the other person perceives the issue as an attack on his or her ability as a provider. Because it is not clear what the real issue is, the argument goes nowhere and both people end up feeling frustrated and misunderstood.

Sometimes we don't have the opportunity to clarify an issue by talking to another person. This is often the case with written material, such as magazine or newspaper articles. In these cases, you may be able to determine the writer's focus by examining the title or the introductory paragraph. For example, Sohail H. Hashmi begins his article "Interpreting the Islamic Ethics of War and Peace" thus:

> Muslim writers of many intellectual persuasions have long argued that Westerners hold an inaccurate, even deliberately distorted, conception of *jihad*. In fact, however, the idea of *jihad* (and the ethics of war and peace generally) has been the subject of an intense and multifaceted debate among Muslims themselves.[1]

From this, you can presume that the issue Hashmi is addressing is something like "What is the best and most accurate interpretation of the Islamic concept of *jihad* and of war and peace in general?"

Asking the Right Questions

How we word our questions about an issue will influence how we go about seeking a resolution to it. During his debates with Senator (or, as he called him, "Judge") Douglas, Lincoln changed the national controversy about slavery by reframing the issue so that it was not simply a controversy over state sovereignty but a burning question that affected the very

issue An ill-defined complex of problems involving a controversy or uncertainty.

existence of the nation. In the final debate, Lincoln summed up the issue with these words:

> I have said and I repeat it here, that if there be a man amongst us who does not think that the institution of slavery is wrong in any one of the aspects of which I have spoken, he is misplaced and ought not to be with us. Has anything threatened the existence of the Union save and except this very institution of slavery? That is the real issue. That is the issue that will continue in this country when these poor tongues of Judge Douglas and myself shall be silent.[2]

In an article written 50 years after school segregation was declared unconstitutional by the Supreme Court in *Brown v. Board of Education* (1954), journalist Ellis Cose writes about the current lack of good schools for African American children: "When it comes to children of color, we ask the wrong question. We ask, 'Why are you such a problem?' when we should ask, 'What have we not given you that we routinely give to upper-middle-class white students?' What do they have that you don't?"[3]

To use another example, suppose you come back to your dorm room after class and find that your wallet is missing. You think that you left it on your dresser, but it isn't there. What is the issue? When asked, many students answer that that the issue is "Who stole my wallet?"[4] However, this question is a loaded question based on an as-yet-unfounded assumption—that someone stole your wallet. Maybe you misplaced your wallet or you lost it on your way to class or it got knocked behind the dresser. For now, all you know is that the wallet is missing. Therefore, rather than making assumptions you can't support, it would be better to state the issue as "What happened to my wallet?" rather than "Who stole my wallet?" Remember, one of the traits of a good critical thinker—and of great detectives—is open-mindedness.

THiNKing Outside the Box

ABRAHAM LINCOLN, *U.S. President*

Abraham Lincoln (1809–1865) was the sixteenth president of the United States. Self-educated, Lincoln had a knack for asking the right questions about important issues, such as slavery and war, and then examining all sides of the arguments before coming to a conclusion.

Lincoln's election as president in 1860 led to the secession in 1861 of southern slave-owning states (the Confederacy) and to a 4-year civil war that cost 600,000 American lives, North and South. Although Lincoln had long agreed that slavery should be permitted in states where it was already legal, in the course of the Civil War he concluded that if slavery is immoral, then it should not be legal at all in the United States. Lincoln also realized that taking a position on issues was not simply an intellectual exercise but should have real-life consequences. A man of action as well as strong principles, he issued the Emancipation Proclamation in 1863, freeing slaves in the Confederate states.

Lincoln's struggle to end slavery is depicted in the *movie Lincoln* (2012).

DISCUSSION QUESTIONS

1. Was Lincoln's decision to stand by his conclusion that slavery should be illegal a wise one, given that it escalated the hostilities in the Civil War? Are there times when it is best, from the point of view of critical thinking, to back down on an argument rather than risk conflict? Explain using specific examples.

2. Has there ever been a time when you stood your ground on an issue despite the risk of losing your friends or even a job? Discuss how your critical-thinking skills helped you to stand firm?

STOP AND ASSESS YOURSELF

I. Identify two or three issues that might arise out of the following broad topics or choose your own issue. Word the issue(s) in the form of question(s).

   a. Freedom of speech on college campuses

   b. Genetic engineering of food

   c. Cohabitation among college students

   d. Downloading music from the Internet

   e. Global warming

   f. Decriminalizing marijuana

   g. Prayer in public schools

   h. The preponderance of male science and engineering faculty at elite colleges

   i. Illegal immigration

2. Identify the issues in the following passages. Word all issues in the form of short questions.

   a. "The price of college education in Minnesota is going up again this fall. The University of Minnesota and the state's two- and four-year colleges are raising tuition by double digits. . . . Higher education officials say while most students are coming up with the extra cash for college the trend toward higher tuition is not sustainable in the long run."[5]

   b. There is a law pending in the Uganda legislature that would allow homosexuality to be punished with imprisonment and in certain circumstances even execution.

   c. More than 700,000 Americans die each year from heart disease. Fifty percent of people given cholesterol-lowering drugs don't use them as prescribed, and the more they have to pay, the more they stop taking them. It seems obvious that probably tens of thousands of Americans are dying today because they can't afford drugs.

   d. "By next June, over a million [college students] will graduate, many lost forever to the world of inertia and learned habits. While the debate rages about how the vegetarian movement can tailor its message to reach resistant adults, open-minded college students who care about animals are being neglected at an astounding rate. Our [animal rights] movement has not yet made a massive, organized effort to reach our best audience. We could be making tremendous progress among this group of people using animal-related literature that has been shown to work."[6]

   e. President Obama's educational reform agenda calls for longer school days and extending the school year in order to meet the challenges of the 21st century.

   f. It is now possible to track a person's location by using their cell phone.

   g. "Tibet is backward. It's a big land, rich in natural resources, but we lack the technology or expertise [to exploit them]. So if we remain within China, we might get a greater benefit, provided it respects our culture and environment and gives us some kind of guarantee."[7]

3. Working in small groups, select one of the following issues. Take a few minutes to write down different concerns that arise from the issue. To what extent does your list reflect your preconceptions on the issue? Compare your list with those of others in your group. Discuss how collaborative sharing can give you a wider perspective on the issue.

   a. Should we be eating meat?

   b. Should college students who are working full time be allowed to take a full-time course load?

   c. Is it a desirable goal for western nations to spread democracy throughout the world?

   d. What should we be doing in our own lives about global warming?

   e. What criteria should colleges use in admitting students?

   f. Should the United States bring back the military draft?

4. Looking back at your list of life goals in Chapter 8, identify any issues involved in achieving your life goals.

RECOGNIZING AN ARGUMENT

When we start with a position statement, rather than with an open-ended question that invites us to explore and analyze a particular issue, we are using rhetoric. Many people mistake rhetoric for logical arguments. Thus it is important to first understand the difference between the two.

Distinguishing Between Argumentation and Rhetoric

rhetoric The defense of a particular position usually without adequate consideration of opposing evidence in order to win people over to one's position.

argument Reasoning that is made up of two or more propositions, one of which is supported by the others.

deductive argument An argument that claims its conclusion necessarily follows from the premises.

inductive argument An argument that only claims that its conclusion probably follows from the premise.

proposition A statement that expresses a complete thought and can be either true or false.

Rhetoric, also known as *the art of persuasion*, is used to promote a particular position or worldview. In English classes, the term refers more narrowly to the art of persuasive writing or speaking. Rhetoric has its place and can help us learn more about a particular position on an issue and how to clarify that position. The art of persuasion can be useful once you have thoroughly researched all sides of an issue, have come to a reasoned conclusion, and are now trying to convince others of this conclusion, as Lincoln did in his debates with Douglas.

Rhetoric becomes a problem when it is *substituted* for unbiased research and logical argumentation. When using rhetoric this way, people present only those claims that support their own position. Because it does not require that a student first thoroughly research a topic and remain open-minded, rhetoric may deteriorate into heated and overly emotional fights in which each person resorts to resistance and fallacies rather than reason in order to "win."

Whereas the purpose of rhetoric is to *persuade* people of what you consider to be the truth, the purpose of argumentation is to *discover* the truth. The goal in rhetoric is to "win"—to convince others of the correctness of our position—rather than to analyze a position critically. The purpose of an argument, in contrast, is to present good reasons for a particular position or course of action and to offer a forum for evaluating the soundness of these reasons.

Good arguments also invite feedback and analysis of an issue in light of the feedback. You are more likely to move toward truth (if necessary, through revising your arguments and views) when all sides of an issue are presented and heard.

Types of Arguments

An **argument** is made up of two or more propositions, one of which, the conclusion, is supported by the other(s), the premise(s). In a valid **deductive argument**, the conclusion necessarily follows from the premises. In an **inductive argument**, the premises provide support but not necessarily proof for the conclusion.

Propositions

An argument is made up of statements known as propositions. A **proposition** is a statement that expresses a complete thought. It can be either true or false. If you're not sure whether a statement is a proposition, try putting the phrase *It is true that* or *It is false that* at the beginning of the statement. The following are examples of propositions:

> The earth revolves around the sun.
>
> God exists.
>
> Chris doesn't show me enough affection.
>
> Cheating on exams is wrong.
>
> Toronto is the capital of Canada.

The first of these propositions is true. Today it is a generally accepted fact that the Earth revolves around the sun. The truth or falsehood of the second and third propositions is less clear. We need more information as well as clarification of the word *God* in the second proposition and clarification of the term *affection* in the third proposition. The fourth proposition is less controversial: Most people, even those who cheat on exams, agree that it is true that "cheating on exams is wrong." Finally, the last proposition is false; Toronto is *not* the capital of Canada (Ottawa is).

A sentence may contain more than one proposition, as this example illustrates:

> Marcos is taking four courses this semester and working in his parents' store 20 hours a week.

This sentence contains two propositions:

1. Marcos is taking four courses this semester.

2. Marcos is working in his parents' store 20 hours a week.

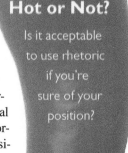

Hot or Not?

Is it acceptable to use rhetoric if you're sure of your position?

Rhetorical Standoff Anti-abortion and pro-abortion rights demonstrators debating each other at the Supreme Court on January 23, 2012, the anniversary of the Supreme Court's *Roe v. Wade* decision, which established a women's right to an abortion.

DISCUSSION QUESTIONS

1. *The use of rhetoric, without first researching and analyzing all perspectives on an issue, can lead to deepening polarization of an issue rather than a resolution. What do you think the two people in this photo might be saying to each other? Do you think they are engaging in rhetoric or argumentation? Working in small groups, role-play what you might say to them if you were on the scene in the capacity of resident critical thinker.*

2. *Have you ever been at a rally where people were deeply divided? If so, discuss how you responded to taunts or fallacies from those on the "other side" of the issue.*

Here is another sentence with more than one proposition:

Karen is smart but not very motivated to do well in school or to try to find a job that uses her talents.

It contains three propositions:

1. Karen is smart.
2. Karen is not very motivated to do well in school.
3. Karen is not very motivated to try to find a job that uses her talents.

Not all sentences are propositions. A sentence may be directive ("Let's go out and celebrate the end of final exams"), expressive ("Wow!"), or even a request for information ("What is the capital of Canada?"). In none of these sentences is any claim being made that something is true or false. Propositions, in contrast, make claims that are either true or false.

"The Earth revolves around the sun" is an example of a proposition.

Premises and Conclusions

The **conclusion** of an argument is the proposition that is supported or denied on the basis of other propositions or reasons. The conclusion is what the argument is trying to prove. Conclusions may also be called claims or positions. The conclusion can appear anywhere in an argument.

conclusion The proposition in an argument that is supported on the basis of other propositions.

premise A proposition in an argument that supports the conclusion.

descriptive premise A premise that is based on empirical facts.

A **premise** is a proposition that supports or gives reasons for accepting the conclusion. Reasoning goes from the premises to the conclusion.

Premise(s) ——————→ Conclusion

Good premises are based on fact and experience, not opinion and assumptions. The more credible the premises are, the better the argument is likely to be. We considered some of the ways in which to evaluate evidence in Chapter 8. The conclusion should be supported by or follow from the premises, as in the following argument:

> *Premise*: Canada has only one capital.
>
> *Premise*: Ottawa is the capital of Canada.
>
> *Conclusion*: Therefore, Toronto is not the capital of Canada.

There are several types of premises. **Descriptive premises** are based on **empirical facts**—scientific observation and/or the evidence of our five senses. "Ottawa is the capital of Canada" and "Lisa loves Antonio" are descriptive premises.

Prescriptive premises, in contrast, contain value statements, such as "We should strive for diversity on college campuses" or "It is wrong to cheat on exams."

An **analogical premise** takes the form of an analogy in which a comparison is made between two similar events or things. The ancient Greek philosopher Plato drew an analogy between a charioteer and reason. Just as the charioteer is in charge of the horses, said Plato, so too should our reason be in charge of our emotions and passions.

Finally, a **definitional premise** contains a definition of a key term. This is particularly important when the key term is ambiguous and has different definitions, such as *right* and *diversity*, or if the key term needs a precising definition. For example, *affirmative action* is defined in a dictionary as "a policy to increase opportunities for women and minorities, [especially] in employment."[8] However, this may not be precise enough for your argument, since it is unclear about the type of policy. To clarify this, you may want to make the definition more precise in your premise. "Affirmative action is a policy of giving preference in hiring and college admissions to qualified minorities and women over a qualified white male, to increase opportunities for women and minorities."

Nonarguments: Explanations and Conditional Statements

We sometimes confuse explanations and conditional statements with arguments. An **explanation** is a statement about why or how something is the case. With an explanation, we know that something has occurred—as in the following examples:

> The cat yowled because I stepped on her tail.
>
> I'm upset because you promised you would meet me at the student union right after class and you never turned up.

In both examples, we are not trying to *prove* or *convince* someone through supporting evidence that the cat yowled or that we're upset; instead, we are trying to *explain* why the cat yowled and why we are upset.

We can also use explanations to describe the purpose of something, as in "iPods are useful for storing large quantities of music." In

addition, we can use explanations as a means of trying to make sense of something, as in: "When Jane smiled at me, I think she was telling me that she liked me."

Good premises are based on fact and experience, not opinion and assumptions. The more credible the premises are, the better the argument is likely to be.

As with arguments, not all explanations are equally convincing. Explanations such as "I don't have my essay with me today because the dog ate it" usually raise at least a few skeptical eyebrows. Also, what might have seemed a reasonable explanation centuries or even a few decades ago may no longer be reasonable in light of new evidence. The explanation, presented to me by one of my elementary school teachers, that there have been very few famous female artists because women fulfill their creativity through having babies, is no longer considered a sound explanation.

Conditional statements may also be mistaken for arguments. A **conditional statement** is an "if . . . then . . ." statement.

> If Françoise comes from Montreal, then she understands French.

> If 18-year-olds are emotionally mature enough to go to war, then they should be allowed to drink alcohol.

A conditional statement by itself is not an argument, because no claim or conclusion follows from it. In the preceding examples, we are not drawing a conclusion that Françoise understands French or that 18-year-olds should be allowed to drink. However, conditional statements may appear as premises in an argument.

> *Premise*: If Françoise comes from Montreal, then she understands French.

> *Premise*: Françoise comes from Montreal.

> *Conclusion*: Françoise understands French.

> *Premise*: If 18-year-olds are emotionally mature enough to go to war, [then] they should be allowed to drink alcohol.

> *Premise*: Eighteen-year-olds are not emotionally mature enough to go to war.

> *Conclusion*: Eighteen-year-olds should not be allowed to drink alcohol.

To summarize: arguments are made up of two types of propositions—the conclusion and the premise(s). A conclusion is supported by the premise(s). The different types of premises include descriptive and prescriptive premises, analogies, and definitions. Unlike explanations and conditional statements, an argument tries to prove that something is true.

empirical fact A fact based on scientific observation and the evidence of our five senses.

prescriptive premise A premise in an argument containing a value statement.

analogical premise A premise containing an analogy or comparison between similar events or things.

definitional premise A premise containing the definition of a key term.

explanation A statement about why or how something is the case.

conditional statement An "If . . . then . . ." statement.

EXERCISE 9-2

STOP AND ASSESS YOURSELF

1. Working in small groups, select a controversial issue. After clearly defining the issue, debate it by first using rhetoric. After three minutes, stop and write a paragraph about what happened during the role-play. Now discuss the issue using argumentation instead. After three minutes, stop and write a paragraph about what happened during this role-play. Which approach worked better in terms of learning more about different perspectives on the issue? Explain.

2. It is easier to resolve a problem from a familiar context than one that is unfamiliar. Write down a problem that you encountered recently in a familiar context (for example, a social setting with friends or a class in your major). Now write down a similar problem that you encountered recently in an unfamiliar context (for example, a job interview or meeting new people). Which problem was easiest to resolve and why? How did familiarity with the context make it easier for you to resolve a problem? Write about what steps you could take to make yourself a better problem-solver and critical thinker in different contexts.

3. Which of the following statements is a proposition? Explain why or why not.
   a. Golly!
   b. I love you.
   c. The Solomon Islands were struck by an 8.0-magnitude earthquake in 2013.
   d. Most college students gain several pounds in their freshman year.
   e. Close the window.
   f. The average college student pays most of his or her own college tuition.

g. Please keep an eye on my place while I'm away on spring break.

h. It is irresponsible to drink and drive.

i. Iran possesses nuclear weapons.

j. Only humans are capable of language.

k. An atheist is a person who believes there is no God.

l. Excuse me.

m. Smoking in public buildings is illegal in many states.

4. For each of the following propositions, identify which type of premise it is (descriptive, prescriptive, definitional, or analogical).

a. Terrorism is the unlawful use or threat of violence by individuals or groups against civilians or property to achieve an ideological or political goal through intimidating government or society.

b. At least five of the al-Qaeda hijackers from September 11, 2001, came from Asir province in Saudi Arabia.

c. We should constantly strive to become better critical thinkers.

d. The universe is like a watch created by an intelligent designer or watchmaker.

e. The University of Toronto is the top-rated university in Canada.

f. It's wrong to download music from the Internet without paying.

g. Going to Las Vegas for spring break is like going to a weeklong fraternity party.

h. Living together before marriage for a trial period is like taking a car for a test drive.

i. Only humans are capable of language.

j. Language is a type of communication that involves a set of arbitrary symbols, whether spoken, written, or nonverbal.

5. Look back at the arguments on affirmative action at the end of Chapter 7 and identify the premises and conclusion in both Nancy Cantor's and Ward Connerly's arguments.

6. Identify each of the following as an argument, an explanation, or a conditional statement.

a. Jasmine really likes Daniel, but because she's planning on going to Guatemala for a semester to study Spanish, she isn't interested in getting involved with him right now.

b. The death toll in Chile following the 2010 earthquakes was not nearly as high as that in Haiti in part because the buildings in Chile were built to withstand earthquakes while those in Haiti were not.

c. If there is a snowstorm, class will be cancelled.

d. If there is a snowstorm, class will be cancelled. It is snowing heavily right now, so our class will probably be cancelled.

e. You should consider taking a trip abroad this summer while airfares are still low.

f. In the past few decades the Catholic Church has been training more priests and bishops to perform exorcisms, in part because the pope believes that Satan is a real force in our everyday lives.

g. If the bay freezes over, we can go ice skating on it.

h. It must have been colder than 28°F last week, because the ice froze in the bay last week and salt water freezes at 28°F or −2°C.

i. Herman failed the quiz because he didn't know there was going to be one today and hadn't read the material.

j. If you aren't a good boy or girl, Santa won't bring you any presents this Christmas.

k. "People react so viscerally to the decapitation executions because they identify strongly with the helpless victims, see the executioners as cruel foreigners, and are horrified by the grisly method of death."[9]

l. Same-sex marriage should be legalized, since the U.S. Constitution guarantees citizens equal rights under the law.

m. If you go to the movies with me tonight, I'll help you review for your chemistry exam.

7. Write down five examples of explanations. At least one should be from your own personal experience, one from a textbook, one from a newspaper or magazine, and one from the Internet. Briefly state why each is an explanation rather than an argument.

BREAKING DOWN AND DIAGRAMMING ARGUMENTS

Knowing how to identify the parts of and diagram an argument allows us to follow the line of thought in an argument more easily. Breaking down an argument and then using a diagram to represent the different parts of the argument lets us visualize the entire argument, its propositions, and the relationship between the premise(s) and the conclusion.

HIGHLIGHTS

HOW TO BREAK DOWN AN ARGUMENT

- **The entire argument may appear in one sentence or in several sentences.**

- **Put brackets around each proposition in the argument.**

- **Identify the conclusion.** Ask yourself: "What is this person trying to prove?" The conclusion is often, though not always, preceded by a word or phrase known as a conclusion indicator, such as

therefore	*which shows that*
thus	*for these reasons*
hence	*consequently*
so	*it follows that*

- **Identify the premises.** The premises are often, though not always, preceded by a word or phrase known as a premise indicator, such as

because	*may be inferred from*
since	*the reason is that*
for	*as shown by*
given that	*in view of*

- **Draw a double line under the conclusion and a single line under the premise(s). Circle any conclusion or premise indicators.**

➤*APPLICATION: Identify in the text an example of (1) a conclusion indicator followed by a conclusion, and (2) a premise indicator followed by a premise.*

Breaking Down an Argument into Propositions

Before you can diagram an argument, you must first break down the argument into its propositions. Here are the steps for diagramming an argument:

1. **Bracket the Propositions.** In breaking down an argument, start by putting brackets around each proposition so that you know where each begins and ends. Remember, an entire argument can be contained in one sentence, as in the first of the following examples. Or it can contain several sentences and propositions, as in the second example.

   [I think], therefore [I am].

   [Students who sit in the front of a classroom generally earn higher grades.] Therefore [you should move up to the front of the class], since [I know you want to improve your grade point average].

2. **Identify the conclusion.** The next step is to identify which proposition is the conclusion. Some, but not all, arguments contain terms known as *conclusion indicators* that help you identify which of the propositions is a conclusion. For instance, words such as *therefore* and *thus* often serve as conclusion indicators. If there is a conclusion indicator in the argument, circle it and, if you want, put the letters *CI* above it. In the two arguments above, the word *therefore* indicates that a conclusion follows.

   When there are no conclusion indicators, ask yourself: "What is this person trying to prove or convince me of?" If you are still unsure which proposition is the conclusion, try putting *therefore* in

We can improve our arguments by testing them out on others and then modifying them in light of the feedback we receive.

front of the proposition you think may be the conclusion. If the meaning of the argument remains the same, you have located the conclusion. Once you have identified the conclusion, draw a double line under it.

> CI *(Conclusion)*
> [I think], therefore [I am].

> [Students who sit in the front of a classroom generally earn higher grades.] Therefore, CI *(Conclusion)* [you should move up to the front of the class], since [I know you want to improve your grade point average].

3. **Identify the Premises.** The final step in breaking down an argument is to identify the premise(s). In the first argument, which is the famous cogito argument of French philosopher René Descartes (1596–1650), Descartes supports his conclusion ("I am") with the premise "I think." In other words, if he is thinking, it follows that he must exist, since someone must be doing the thinking. Draw a single line under the premise.

> CI *(Conclusion)*
> [I think], therefore [I am].

Some arguments contain *premise indicators*—words or phrases that signal a premise. *Because* and *since* are common premise indicators. If there is a premise indicator, circle it and put *PI* above it. In the argument about where to sit in the classroom, the word *since* indicates that the last part of this sentence is a premise. The first sentence in the argument is also a premise because it is offering evidence to support the conclusion "you should move up to the front of the class." Draw a single line under each premise.

> *(Premise)*
> [Students who sit in the front of a classroom generally earn higher grades.] CI Therefore, *(Conclusion)* [you should move up to PI *(Premise)* the front of the class], since [I know you want to improve your grade point average].

Identifying the Premise(s) and Conclusion in Complex Arguments

Not all arguments are as straightforward as the ones we have looked at so far. Some passages that contain arguments also include extra material, such as background and introductory information. In the following letter to the editor, the first sentence is the conclusion of the argument. The first part of the second sentence—"Although stories of overzealous parents sometimes grab the headlines"—is not part of the actual argument; rather, it is introductory material. This introduction is followed in the same sentence by the phrase *the truth is*, which serves as a premise indicator for the first premise. The

second premise doesn't appear until the third sentence in the passage.

> *(Conclusion)*
> [Sports at the high-school level are one of the last bastions of innocence in this century.] Although stories of overzealous parents sometimes grab the PI *Premise* headlines, the truth is, [most young people play for the love of their sport and nothing more.] [Many of the *Premise* values that help me every day in the business world (teamwork, unity, hard work, and tolerance) were taught by my football and baseball coaches.][10]

Words such as *because*, *since*, *therefore*, and *so*, which sometimes serve as premise and conclusion indicators in argument, do not always play this role. *Because* and *therefore* also appear in explanations, as in this example:

> Because the demographics and immigration pattern of the United States is changing, the workforce of today's college graduates will be much different from that of their parents.

In addition, the word *since* may indicate the passage of time rather than a premise.

> Since the September 11, 2001, attacks on the World Trade Center and Pentagon, the nature of intercultural relationships radically changed for most Americans.

Knowing how to break down an argument into its conclusion and premise(s) makes it easier for us to analyze arguments. Although words such as *therefore* and *because* can help us in this process, it is important to remember that they do not always serve as conclusion and premise indicators.

Diagramming an Argument

Once you have mastered the basics of breaking down an argument, you are ready to diagram arguments. Sometimes arguments fail simply because the other person does not follow our line of reasoning. Diagramming an argument clarifies the relationship between the premise(s) and the conclusion, as well as the relationship between premises, so we know to present these particular premises together.

Arguments with One Premise. Begin by breaking down the argument into its propositions and drawing two lines under the conclusion and one under the premise(s). Number each proposition in the order in which it appears in the argument. Put a circle around each number.

> (1) [I think], therefore (2) [I am].

The Debate Over Marijuana

DISCUSSION QUESTIONS

1. *Identify the conclusion and premises in the argument in this advertisement. Evaluate the argument.*

2. *What is the objective of this ad? Is the ad effective in meeting its objective? Discuss the strategies, including rhetorical devices and fallacies, if any, that the creators of the ad used to try to convince the reader to accept their conclusion.*

You are now ready to diagram the argument. Begin by writing down the number of the conclusion at the bottom of a space on the page. The premise(s) go above the conclusion. When there is only one premise, place the number of the premise directly above the number of the conclusion and draw an arrow from the premise number to the conclusion number.

(**1**) (Premise)

↓

(**2**) (Conclusion)

In this section, the parts of the diagram are identified (for example, premise, conclusion, dependent premises) purely for educational purposes. However, in the actual diagrams, only the numbers, lines, and arrows are used.

Arguments with Independent Premises. The next argument we'll be diagramming has more than one premise. Begin by breaking down the argument into its conclusion and premises, numbering each proposition in the order it appears in the argument.

(**1**) [Every physician should cultivate lying as a fine art]. . . . (**2**) [Many experiences show that patients do not want the truth about their maladies], and that (**3**) [it is prejudicial to their well-being to know it].[11]

In this argument, the conclusion is the first proposition—"Every physician should cultivate lying as a fine art." Write ① at the bottom of the space below. Now examine the two premises, the second and third propositions. In this argument below, each premise supports the conclusion on its own. A premise that can support the conclusion without the other premise is known as an **independent premise**.

> **independent premise** A premise that can support a conclusion on its own.
>
> **dependent premise** A premise that supports a conclusion only when it is used together with another premise.
>
> **subconclusion** A proposition that acts as a conclusion for initial premises and as a premise for the final conclusion.

You diagram an independent premise by drawing an arrow directly from each one to the conclusion.

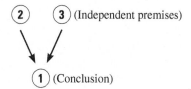

Arguments with Dependent Premises. When two or more of the premises support a conclusion only when they are used together, they are known as **dependent premises**. If you are unsure whether two premises are dependent or independent, try omitting one of them and see if the remaining premise still supports the conclusion on its own. If it does not, then it is a dependent premise.

In the argument below on Harry Potter, premises ①, ③, and ④ are all dependent on each other. Taken alone, they do not support the conclusion.

> ① [The Bible states in Leviticus 20:26, "You should not practice augury or witchcraft."] Therefore, ② [the Harry Potter books are not suitable reading for children,] since ③ [Harry Potter is a wizard] and ④ [wizards practice augury].

In diagramming dependent premises, you first draw a line between the premises and then draw a line from the center of this connecting line to the conclusion.

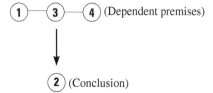

In the above argument, depending on your audience, you may not need ④, which is a definitional premise.

Some arguments have both dependent and independent premises. Consider the following argument:

> ① [Turkey should not be granted full membership in the European Union.] For one thing, ② [the majority of the country is located in Asia, not Europe.]

③ [Turkey also has a poor human rights record.] Finally, ④ [it is a poor country with high unemployment]. ⑤ [Allowing it to be a full member in the European Union might spark a mass migration of people to European countries with better economies.]

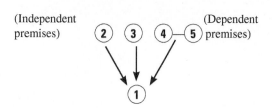

Arguments with a Subconclusion. Sometimes a premise acts as a conclusion for the final conclusion. This type of premise is known as a **subconclusion**.

> ① [My granddaughter Sarah is a college freshman.]
>
> ② [Sarah probably wouldn't be interested in hearing an AARP talk on Social Security reform.] So ③ [there's probably no point in asking her to come along with me.]

In the above argument, premise ① offers support for proposition ②: "My granddaughter Sarah is a college freshman. [Therefore] Sarah probably wouldn't be interested in hearing an AARP talk on Social Security." However, proposition ②, in addition to being a conclusion for premise ①, also serves as a premise for proposition ③. In diagramming an argument with a subconclusion (such as proposition ②), you put the subconclusion between the premise(s) that supports it and the final conclusion.

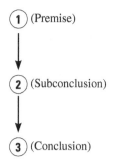

The following argument on capital punishment has a subconclusion as well as two independent premises.

> ① [The death penalty does not deter criminals] because ② [at the time the crime is done they do not expect to be arrested.] Also, since ③ [many offenders are mentally unbalanced,] ④ [they do not consider the rational consequences of their irrational actions.][12]

Here, proposition ② is an independent premise that supports the conclusion (proposition ①) on its own. If this were all there was to the argument, you would diagram it by placing the ② above the ① and drawing an arrow directly from the ② to the conclusion.

However, the argument goes on to present additional evidence (propositions ③ and ④) for the conclusion (proposition ①)) in the form of a separate supporting argument. Therefore, you'll need to adjust the diagram to allow room for this. In this case, proposition ④ is the subconclusion and proposition ③ the premise of the supporting argument. The complete argument can be diagrammed as follows:

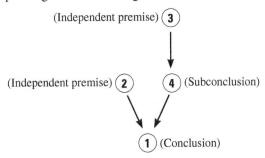

(Independent premise) ③

(Independent premise) ②　④ (Subconclusion)

① (Conclusion)

Arguments with Unstated Conclusions.

In some arguments the conclusion is unstated, allowing readers to draw their own conclusions. The following argument, for example, has two premises but no conclusion:

① [Laws that permit public colleges to discriminate against applicants on the basis of race or sex are unconstitutional.] ② [The University of Michigan's affirmative action policy that awards extra points on the basis of a person's race and sex discriminates against white males.]

In determining what is the unstated conclusion, ask yourself: What is the speaker trying to prove or to convince us of? In this example, it is that the University of Michigan's affirmative action policy is unconstitutional. When a conclusion is unstated, write it in at the end of the argument and number it; in this case, since it is the third proposition, put a ③ in front of it. The broken circle indicates that the proposition is unstated. You can also add a conclusion indicator if you like.

① [Laws that permit public colleges to discriminate against applicants on the basis of race or gender are unconstitutional.] ② [The University of Michigan's affirmative action policy that awards extra points based on a person's race and sex discriminates against white males.] Therefore, ③ [the University of Michigan's affirmative action policy is unconstitutional.]

Diagramming this argument makes it apparent that neither premise can support the conclusion on its own

These people are burning Harry Potter books based on their conclusion that Harry is a wizard and witchcraft should not be practiced.

without the other premise. In other words, they are dependent premises. When diagramming an argument with an unstated conclusion, put a broken circle around the number in front of the conclusion to indicate that it was not included in the original wording of the argument. Once again, the parts of the diagram (dependent premises and unstated conclusion) are identified for clarification purposes only. They are not part of the actual diagram.

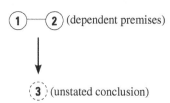

When you are arguing or discussing an issue, you usually do not have time to step back and diagram it. However, practice at breaking down and diagramming arguments will make it easier for you to recognize the conclusion and see the connections among the conclusion and premises in real-life arguments, the topic of the next section.

College students are divided regarding the morality and constitutionality of affirmative action in college admissions, a topic that is considered in the Critical Thinking Issue of Chapter 7.

STOP AND ASSESS YOURSELF

1. Break down the following arguments. Fill in any unstated possibilities.

   a. "Be an optimist. There is not much use being anything else."[13]

   b. Computers may soon fade into the background, since most people prefer portable handheld devices as well as ones that turn on instantly.

   c. "The right to vote is the very core of democracy. We cannot allow public apathy and political manipulation to undermine it."[14]

   d. Drinking alcohol is stupid. Alcohol has no taste at all; it's just a burning sensation. You don't drink to have a good time—you drink to forget a bad time.

   e. We should not be using military drones. Drone strikes can kill innocent civilians. They are also a violation of international law.

   f. Lack of experience, excessive speed, and tailgating are three of the most frequent causes of automobile accidents. For these reasons we should raise the driving age to 18, since older drivers might be more experienced and have better judgment.

   g. India should adopt a one-child policy like China. India's population has tripled in the last thirty years and it won't be long before food production will not be able to keep up with population growth.

   h. All college students should routinely be tested for HIV, the virus that causes AIDS. Half of the people who carry the virus don't know that they have it. The HIV virus is transmitted primarily through sexual contact. Not only are most college students sexually active but they also have multiple partners.

   i. You shouldn't date Matt. You don't want to end up with a black eye or worse.

   j. The great horned owls have just started calling to each other in the woods behind our house so it's probably the beginning of their courting season.

2. Break down and diagram the following arguments.

   a. "It is impossible to exaggerate the impact that Islam has on Saudi culture, since religion is the dominant thread that permeates every level of society."[15]

   b. God does not exist. There is much evil and suffering in the world. A good and loving God would not permit so much evil.

   c. I just read that Singapore is the only country in Asia where English is the first language. I know that English is also spoken throughout much of India but I guess this must mean that English is not India's first language.

   d. We should not buy a new car for Jack for his graduation. Jack is irresponsible because he doesn't care for the things he already owns. Also, we don't have enough money to buy him a new car.

   e. Prostitution should be legal. Women should have the right to use their bodies as they wish. Outlawing prostitution deprives women who want to be prostitutes of their right to choose how to use their body.

   f. It's unlikely that you'll find a job in manufacturing since we're in the middle of recession. You should consider going back to college to finish your degree in nursing since nursing is one of the fields where jobs are currently in demand.

   g. "An unbalanced diet can depress serotonin levels—and bingo, you're a grouch. Alcohol gives serotonin a temporary bump but then dramatically lowers it, so it pays to go easy on the sauce."[16]

   h. Freedom to decide what we do in our lives, as long as we're not harming others, is a basic right in the United States. Therefore, motorcyclists should not be required by law to wear helmets, because those who don't are not harming anyone else.

   i. Everything is going digital nowadays. Soon we will no longer need libraries since most journals and news sources are available online. In addition, books are being made available in electronic format.

   j. "There's a need for more part-time or job-sharing work. Most mothers of young children who choose to leave full-time careers and stay home with their children find enormous delights in being at home with their children, not to mention the enormous relief of no longer worrying about shortchanging their kids. On the other hand, women who step out of their careers can find the loss of identity even tougher than the loss of income."[17]

k. "The toughest part of buying life insurance is determining how much you need, since everyone's financial circumstances and goals are different. The best way to determine your life insurance needs is to have a State Farm Insurance professional conduct what's called a Financial Needs Analysis." (from an ad for State Farm Insurance)

l. You should learn how to speak Mandarin Chinese since you're going into international business as a career. Roughly one in five people in the world speak Mandarin. Also, learning a new language is supposed to be good for your brain.

m. "In schools, we should give equal time with Darwinism to theories of intelligent design or creationism. Darwin's theory of evolution is a theory, not a fact. The origin of life, the diversity of species and even the structure of organs like the eye are so bewilderingly complex that they can only be the handiwork of a higher intelligence."[18]

n. The new compact fluorescent light bulbs cut down on global warming since they use 75 percent less energy than the old light bulbs. For this reason you should switch to the new bulbs. And you'll save money on your electric bill too.

o. The creation of new jobs will put the American economy back on a solid footing. Therefore, the government should launch another major stimulus program because the stimulus money will benefit the community by creating more jobs.

p. You shouldn't bother trying out for that internship, because you won't get it. The company wants only students who are business majors. Besides, the company isn't on a bus line, and you don't own a car.

q. I saw Bob coming out of Mark's dorm room at 2 AM. Mark reported his cell phone stolen the next morning. Bob was caught stealing from a student's room once before. I think the evidence speaks for itself.

EVALUATING ARGUMENTS

Knowing how to break down and diagram arguments makes it easier for you to evaluate them. In this section we will briefly touch on some of the main criteria for evaluating arguments: clarity, credibility, relevance, completeness, and soundness.

Hot or Not?

Does knowing how to break down and diagram arguments serve any practical purpose in your life?

Clarity: Is the Argument Clear and Unambiguous?

The first step in evaluating an argument is to make sure that you understand it correctly. Examine each premise and conclusion. Are they stated in terms that are clear and understandable? If any part of the argument is unclear, or if the meaning of a key term is ambiguous, ask for clarification.

For example, at a party someone told me, "Immigration is ruining this country!" When I asked him for clarification—"Do you mean all immigrants?" and "What do you mean by *ruin*?"—he explained that he meant that Hispanic immigrants were a financial burden on the United States.

Credibility: Are the Premises Supported by Evidence?

As we noted earlier, arguments are made up of propositions that each make a claim that can be true or false. In a good argument, the premises are credible and backed by evidence. In other words, it is reasonable for us to accept them as true. In evaluating an argument, examine each premise individually. Watch for assumptions that are being passed off as facts, especially assumptions that are widely accepted in a culture or those that are being put forth by someone who is not an authority in the field.

When my daughter was in kindergarten, the teacher asked each student what he or she wanted to be when they grew up. My daughter said that she wanted to be a doctor. The teacher shook her head and replied, "Boys become doctors; girls become nurses." Breaking down and diagramming her teacher's argument, we have

(1) [You are a girl].

(2) [Boys become doctors; girls become nurses.]

Therefore, (3) [you cannot become a doctor].

(1) —— (2)
   ↓
  (3)

A few weeks later I asked my daughter why she no longer was playing with her doctor kit. She told me what her teacher had said. Fortunately, we were able to reveal the teacher's assumption about which medical professions men and women go into and expose it as false, since today many doctors are women and many men become nurses. Because the two premises are dependent, both premises are needed to support the conclusion. And because one of the premises is false, the premises do not support the conclusion.

Often assumptions are unspoken, as in the above argument. Because of this, we tend not to be aware of them. Although some assumptions are obviously false, in most cases we may have to do some research before making a determination. Returning to the immigration example, when the speaker was asked why he felt the way he did about immigrants from Hispanic countries, he replied: "Hispanics are lazy freeloaders who burden our public welfare system, especially in states like California." Is his premise true? What were his sources of evidence? Were they credible sources?

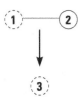

My research turned up an academic study using statistics from the state of California. According to these statistics, Hispanic immigrants living under the poverty level are less than half as likely as American-born citizens to be collecting welfare. In addition, the study found that one of the characteristics of Hispanic immigrants was that they were generally harder working than American-born citizens and preferred to take whatever jobs were available to get by rather than collect welfare.[19] If I hadn't bothered to research his premise, which as it turns out was unfounded, I might have found myself being persuaded by his "argument" and accepting his assumption as "fact."

Relevance: Are the Premises Relevant to the Conclusion?

In addition to being true, the premises should provide relevant evidence in support of the conclusion. In other words, the premises should provide good reasons for accepting the conclusion. The statistical study cited above about Hispanic immigrants is relevant—not to the conclusion that "immigration is ruining this country" but to the opposite conclusion that "Hispanic immigrants tend to be hardworking."

A premise can be relevant without providing sufficient grounds for accepting the conclusion. The fact that when my daughter was young, most doctors were men and most nurses were women did not provide sufficient support for the teacher's conclusion that my daughter should give up her dream to become a doctor. Today, about half of all students in medical school are women.

Completeness: Are There Any Unstated Premises and Conclusions?

In evaluating an argument, ask yourself: "Are there unstated premises?" Premises may be omitted for several reasons. We may simply be unaware of a particular bit of key information related to the issue. In addition, confirmation bias may cause us to overlook important information or reject premises that do not support our worldview. In the argument about Hispanic immigrants that we've just examined, the speaker failed to include premises with actual statistics supporting his claim. In a good argument, the list of relevant premises should be complete—and backed by credible sources.

That being said, sometimes premises are obvious and don't have to be stated. Consider this argument:

> Federal funding for education should be allocated on the basis of the size of a state. Therefore, Texas should get a larger share of federal money than Rhode Island.

In this argument the unstated premise is that "Texas is larger than Rhode Island," an uncontroversial fact known by most people in the United States. However, if we were presenting the argument to someone from another country, we might want to include the premise.

Leaving out a relevant premise can be problematic, especially when the premise is controversial or is based on an unfounded assumption—as in the immigration argument.

Connections

How can we recognize the use of faulty arguments in advertisements?

Hispanic Housekeeper

Hispanic immigrants tend to be hardworking and prefer to take low-paying jobs over collecting public assistance. In the United States they make up a significant portion of the labor force in jobs such as agricultural work, construction, and housekeeping.

DISCUSSION QUESTIONS

1. *Hispanic immigrants tend to be hardworking and prefer to take low-paying jobs, such as agricultural worker or housekeeper, rather than collect public assistance. Despite their work ethic Hispanic workers in the United States earn on the average only about two-thirds of what white workers earn. Is this fair? Create a list of premises this issue. Draw a conclusion based on your premises.*

2. *Refer to the argument you developed in the previous question and, working in small groups, evaluate your argument using the criteria listed in this section.*

Excluding relevant premises might lead us to a mistaken conclusion that is based on incomplete information.

In some cases, a premise is left out because it *is* controversial and stating it would weaken the position of the person who is making the argument. Consider:

> Abortion should remain legal. No woman should be forced to raise an unwanted child.

Breaking down and diagramming this argument, we have:

① [Abortion should remain legal.] **②** [No woman should be forced to raise an unwanted child.]

②

↓

①

At first glance it might look like the conclusion follows from the premise, since most people would accept this premise as reasonable. However, there is an unstated dependent premise in this argument: namely, that "a woman who gives birth to a child should also raise that child." Unlike the first premise, this one is certainly a questionable one, since adoption is an option.

Once you have identified a missing relevant premise, add it to the argument. Then go back and reevaluate the argument.

① [Abortion should remain legal.] **②** [No woman should be forced to raise an unwanted child.] **③** [A woman who gives birth to a child should also raise that child.]

In this case the unstated premise **③** weakens the argument, since many people do not accept it as true.

Soundness: Are the Premises True and Do They Support the Conclusion?

Finally, the reasoning process in an argument should be sound. A sound argument is one in which the premises are true and they support the conclusion. In the argument on page 259, the premise that "Hispanics are lazy freeloaders who burden our public welfare system" is false; therefore the argument is unsound. The connection between the premise(s) and conclusion should be based on reason rather than on fallacious appeals.

On the other hand, do not assume that a conclusion is false simply because it is not supported by the premises. When this happens, the most you can say is that you don't know whether the conclusion is true or false. Some issues, such as the existence of God or of consciousness in other people (or machines), probably cannot be proved or disproved through logical argumentation.

One of my most philosophically traumatic experiences as a child occurred when I was about 10 or 11 years old and realized that I could not prove the existence of anyone or anything else in the world except myself. For about a week, I wandered around in a miserable, solipsistic (the belief that I was the only being in the world) fog, estranging my concerned playmates in the process. Eventually, though, I decided that it was more practical and more conducive to my happiness just to accept on faith the existence of the world outside me. This experience also taught me that just because we can't prove something through the use of argumentation doesn't mean that it isn't true. To claim otherwise is to commit the fallacy of ignorance.

HIGHLIGHTS

GUIDELINES FOR EVALUATING AN ARGUMENT

Clarity: Is the argument clear and unambiguous?

Credibility: Are the premises supported by evidence?

Relevance: Are the premises relevant to the conclusion?

Completeness: Are there any unstated premises and conclusions?

Soundness: Are the premises true and do they support the conclusion?

➤ *APPLICATION: Find examples in the text of the application of each of these guidelines.*

STOP AND ASSESS YOURSELF

EXERCISE 9-4

I. Discuss whether the following are strong arguments. If you consider them weak, explain why.

  a. We need to protect American jobs. Therefore, we need stricter laws to keep illegal aliens from crossing the United States–Mexico border.

  b. Even though the stock market crashed in 2008, stocks are still a great long-term investment. After all, the Dow Jones stock index has increased over the past 100 years.

  c. People need to pass a driving test to get a license to drive a car. People should also have to take a parenting test and get a license before they can have a child. After all, parenting is a greater responsibility and requires more skill than driving.

  d. We should allow fraternities on our campus. After all, they provide volunteers to do a lot of charitable work.

  e. My dog Rex growls only at people who are untrustworthy. Rex growled at Bob when he brought me home after our date. Therefore, I should not trust Bob.

  f. If you're going to buy a new car, you should buy a Toyota Camry. They're one of the safest cars on the road, according to *Consumer Reports*.

  g. Abdul is a freshman at state community college. All freshmen at state community college are residents of Texas. Therefore, Abdul is a resident of Texas.

  h. Marijuana use should be legal in the United States. After all, our own president, George W. Bush, as much as admitted that he had used marijuana.

i. God is all powerful. God is all good. Terrible things happen to people through no fault of their own. Therefore, God does not exist.

j. You should stay away from Gloria because she's a troublemaker.

2. Identify the unstated premise(s) in each of the following arguments. Evaluate each of the arguments. Does leaving out the premise weaken or change the argument?

a. Maria is a single mother. We should reject her application to the pre-med program.

b. Buck's father is a successful doctor and a graduate of State University. Buck should do well in the pre-med program.

c. If you want to save money, buy your textbooks on Amazon.com instead of the college bookstore.

d. Cats don't bark. Therefore, Friskie doesn't bark.

e. If you're traveling in Europe you should buy a rail pass instead of renting a car.

f. I hear you'd like to do a semester in an African country. Given that the only languages you speak are Portuguese and German, you should consider doing an internship in Angola or Mozambique.

g. I wouldn't trust Ben around children. I hear he was abused as a child.

3. Select three of the arguments from the exercises above. After identifying the missing premises, use the Internet or other resources to research the credibility of each of the missing premises. If necessary, rewrite the arguments to take into account the information you uncovered in your research.

CONSTRUCTING AN ARGUMENT

Now that you know how to recognize, break down, and evaluate arguments, you are ready to construct your own arguments. Here is a list of steps to help you in this process:

Steps for Constructing an Argument

There are eight steps to follow when you construct an argument: (1) state the issue, (2) develop a list of premises, (3) eliminate weak or irrelevant premises, (4) establish a conclusion, (5) organize your argument, (6) try out your argument on others, (7) revise your argument, and, if appropriate, (8) put your solution or conclusion into action.

1. State the Issue. What question or issue are you going to address? Clearly identifying the issue first can help you stay on track. Word the issue in neutral terms. For example, "Should the United States have stricter gun-control laws?" and not "Should the government be doing more to keep guns out of the hands of hardened criminals?"

2. Develop a List of Premises. In coming up with possible premises, put your personal opinions aside. Avoid the trap of seeing the issue as having two sides in which rhetoric is used to settle issues, with one side winning and the other losing.

In developing a list of premises, remain objective and open-minded. Rather than select only those premises that support your particular worldview, try to explore all sides of the issue. Brainstorming with others—letting your ideas flow freely and creatively—is helpful in widening your perspective. Keep track of the premises by writing each of them down as you go along. Include references when appropriate in case you need to go back and check them.

Your premises should be relatively uncontroversial. Watch out for unsupported interpretations or assumptions. Adopt the skeptic's attitude. If you are at all unsure whether a particular premise is true, check it out. In doing your research, make sure you use only reliable sources and continue to consider all sides of the issue.

Sometimes a particular cultural world-view becomes so ingrained that we assume it is true and don't bother to question it. Dr. Joseph Collins's premise, written in 1927, that "every physician should cultivate lying as a fine art," was accepted for many years by the medical profession. The assumption that knowing the truth would harm the patient was not questioned, because it was widely accepted as true. It wasn't until 1961 that someone actually put the premise to the test and found that, in fact, the majority of cancer patients actually do better if they know the truth about their illness.[20]

Once you have established your preliminary list of premises, go back and check them. Each premise should be clearly stated, credible, and complete. Also, make sure you know the issue inside and out. You don't want to be taken by surprise by someone's question or counterargument when you present your argument. Did you leave out any important premises? For example, if your issue is whether

Before coming to a conclusion about an controversial legal issue such as allowing smoking in public places, we first need make sure our premises are based on facts.

smoking should be allowed in college dormitories, check your state's laws. Are there already laws against smoking in public buildings, and if so, is your dormitory (especially if you attend a state college) considered a public building?

If you find that your premises are heavily weighed in favor of the view you held before beginning this exercise, go back and spend more time looking at premises that support different perspectives on the issue.

3. Eliminate Weak or Irrelevant Premises.
After coming up with your list of premises, review them once again. Eliminate any premises that are weak or irrelevant to the issue. As in the proverbial chain, one weak link (premise) can destroy your whole argument. At the same time, resist the temptation to eliminate premises that don't mesh with your particular opinion regarding the issue.

Your final list of premises should be relevant to the issue. If your issue is "Should marijuana be legalized?" then you should avoid getting sidetracked by going on about how some of the legislators who oppose its legalization are hypocrites because they used marijuana when they were in college. Stick to the topic of marijuana and legalization. Also, eliminate any redundant premises—those

that say essentially the same thing as another premise but in different words.

Next, form groups of closely related premises. For example, the premise "Marijuana use has been shown to decrease reaction time" should be grouped with the premise "Studies have shown that long-term use of marijuana does not have any ill effects on brain functioning"; it does not belong with the premise "The use of marijuana has been deemed immoral by the Lutheran Church." Although the first two premises take different positions on the issue, they are both similar in that they represent scientific research and not moral judgments. Ask yourself if any of the premises in your list are dependent on each other. A premise may initially appear to be weak simply because it needs to be paired with another (dependent) premise.

If your list of premises is still very long, consider your audience in deciding which premises to eliminate and which to keep. If you are doing an essay for class, the audience will be your professor. If you are doing the argument as a class presentation, the class is your audience. Your audience may also be a friend, a partner, a relative, or the readers of a newspaper or Web site.

Don't leave out a relevant premise unless it is too obvious to your audience to be stated. If in doubt, it is better to include the premise rather than assume that your audience will know about it. On the other hand, if you have only a limited amount of time to present your argument, you should include only the strongest premises. Do, however, have your other premises ready in case you are asked to expand on or clarify your argument.

Next, check the wording of your remaining premises. The wording of each premise should be clear, with no

Hot or Not?
Does the two-party system in the United States discourage the use of logical argumentation in resolving issues?

Working collaboratively with others to identify and eliminate weak or biased premises can help make your argument stronger.

Finally, your conclusion must be supported by your premises. It should not go beyond what the premises say, as in the following example:

> Most freshman on our campus own cars. The parking garage at our college does not have enough parking spots to accommodate all of their cars. Therefore, we should build another parking garage.

The conclusion that another parking garage should be built on campus does not follow from these premises. For one thing, we have no information about how many freshmen use their cars to commute to college or keep their cars on campus. And there are alternative options in dealing with a parking shortage, including mass transit, carpooling, or shuttle service from off-campus parking lots.

vague or confusing terms or emotionally loaded language. Define any ambiguous key terms in the premises and use these terms consistently throughout your argument.

4. Establish a Conclusion.
Only after you are satisfied with your list of premises should you draw a conclusion. In developing a conclusion ask yourself "What conclusion follows from these premises?" Remember to avoid looking at your issue as a contest between two sides. Look at *all* the premises in your final list and consider how the conclusion can take into account as many of the premises as possible.

For example, physician-assisted suicide is often presented as a polarized—black-and-white—issue. However, some people who are opposed to a law permitting it nevertheless think that physician-assisted suicide is justified under certain limited circumstances. Instead of splitting the issue into two sides, ask yourself how you might come up with a policy or law on the issue that takes into account the premises shared by all parties.

Be careful not to draw your conclusion too soon. This is most likely to happen if you bring a preconceived view into the argument and wear the blinders of resistance when analyzing the evidence for your conclusion. Carefully analyze your premises and make sure you've looked at all the different perspectives on the issue before drawing a conclusion. Also, make sure the connection between your conclusion and premises is reasonable, rather than based on an emotional appeal or informal fallacy.

Connections

What are the similarities between the scientific method and the use of logical argumentation in papers?

5. Organize Your Argument.
There are many ways of organizing an argument. For example, you can first list or diagram your premises and conclusion, or you can present your argument in written or oral form. If you are presenting your argument in essay form, you should clearly

---

> Ask yourself "What conclusion follows from these premises?" Remember to avoid looking at your issue as a contest between two sides.

---

state the issue in the first paragraph of your essay or in your opening sentence. This will allow your audience to easily identify exactly what issue you are addressing. (See Critical Thinking in Action: Writing a Paper Based on Logical Argumentation, on page 265.).

The conclusion usually appears in the first paragraph or at the beginning of your presentation. In essays, this is sometimes called the *thesis statement*. If possible, limit your thesis statement to one sentence. Your opening paragraph can also let the reader know how you plan to defend your conclusion and organize your argument, as well as include a sentence or two to grab the reader's attention about the issue's importance.

The following excerpt from James Rachels's argument in his book *Active and Passive Euthanasia* is a good example of an opening paragraph:

> The distinction between active and passive euthanasia is thought to be crucial for medical ethics. The idea is that it is permissible, at least in some cases, to withhold treatment and allow a patient to die, but it is never permissible to take any direct action designed to kill the patient. This doctrine seems to be accepted by most

Critical THINKing in Action

Writing a Paper Based on Logical Argumentation

Many courses require students to write an essay or thesis paper using logical argumentation. These papers are usually organized as follows:

1. **Identify the issue.** Include a brief explanation of the issue in the introductory paragraph along with definitions of key terms. The conclusion of your argument may also be stated in the first paragraph.

2. **Present premises.** This section will make up the major part of your paper. Lay out and explain the premises supporting your conclusion. Premises used should be complete, clearly stated, backed by credible evidence, fallacy-free, and logically compelling.

3. **Present and address counterarguments.** Present and respond to each of the most compelling counterarguments against your position.

4. **Conclusion and summary.** In the final paragraph, restate the issue and briefly summarize your arguments and conclusion.

5. **References.** Include a list of references for the facts and evidence used in your argument.

DISCUSSION QUESTIONS

1. Select an issue. Write a two-page draft or outline of a paper on this issue using logical argumentation. Share your draft or outline with other members of the class for feedback on how well you presented your argument. Modify your draft in light of the feedback you receive.

2. Find an article presenting an argument in a journal or newspaper. Locate in the article each of the five steps listed. Evaluate the strength of the argument. Discuss how you might improve the argument as well as its presentation.

---

doctors. . . . However, a strong case can be made against this doctrine. In what follows I will set out some of the relevant arguments, and urge doctors to reconsider their views on this matter.[21]

If you have several premises, you might want to devote a separate paragraph to each independent premise. You can discuss dependent premises in the same paragraph. In any case, let the reader know that you are introducing a new premise by using some sort of premise indicator such as *because* or *a second reason*. If appropriate, use an example to illustrate your premise. Rachels's second paragraph begins with an example of a patient who is "dying of incurable cancer of the throat [and] is in terrible pain, which can no longer be satisfactorily alleviated." He uses this example to illustrate his first premise:

> Part of my point is that the process of being "allowed to die" can be relatively slow and painful, whereas being given a lethal injection is relatively quick and painless.

Your essay or presentation should also address counterarguments. Discuss each counterargument and explain why the premises you have used are stronger. You can discuss them in the same paragraph with your supporting premises. Address the counterarguments after you present the premises that support your conclusion. For example, after presenting his premises, Rachels

summarizes his argument and then addresses the counterarguments:

> I have argued that killing is not in itself any worse than letting die; if my contention is right, it follows that active euthanasia is not any worse than passive euthanasia. What arguments can be given on the other side? The most common, I believe is the following: The important difference between active and passive euthanasia is that, in passive euthanasia the doctor does not do anything to bring about the patient death. . . . In active euthanasia, however, the doctor does something to bring about the patient's death: he kills him.

The last part of your essay may also include action that people can take to implement your conclusion or resolution to the issue. Rachels concludes his argument with this advice:

> So, whereas doctors may have to discriminate between active and passive euthanasia to satisfy the law, they should not do any more than that. In particular, they should not give the distinction any added authority and weight by writing it into official statements of medical ethics.

6. Try Out Your Argument on Others. Once you have come up with what you think is a strong argument, you are ready to try it out on someone else. In doing this, keep in mind that as critical thinkers we need to be both

The Dangers of Jumping to a Conclusion

Jumping to a conclusion too soon can have far-reaching consequences. In the middle of my freshman year in high school, my family moved to a new school district. My first assignment in the new English class was to write an epic poem in the style of the classic epic poems. Wanting to make a good first impression, and having been writing my own "books" since I was 9, I threw myself wholeheartedly into the task. When I finished, I read my poem to my mother, who had always encouraged my passion for writing.

Full of enthusiasm, I handed in my poem. The following day my teacher, a young woman fresh out of college, stood up in front of the room and read my poem. When she had finished, she glared accusingly at me and began asking in rapid succession questions about how I'd written the poem without giving me a chance to answer. She then declared that the poem was much too good for a student to have written, accused me of cheating, and ripped up my poem. She also made me sit in the back of the classroom for the rest of the year and gave me an F as a final grade. As a result, I was put in a remedial English class. It wasn't until my senior year that I was allowed to petition to be in the college-track English class. I was so traumatized by this experience that I never told my mother or anyone else what had happened. For many years after, I stopped doing any kind of creative writing and in college avoided any English or creative-writing classes.

Rather than analyzing her interpretation of my work (this was a well-written poem) and considering alternative interpretations, my teacher had jumped to the conclusion that I must have copied the epic poem from somewhere, an assumption that breached both good critical-thinking and argumentation skills.

1. Imagine that you were a staff member at this school and found out from another student what had happened. Construct an argument to present to the teacher, encouraging her to reconsider her hasty generalization and come to a better-reasoned conclusion. Pair up and role play this scenario. Stop after two to three minutes and evaluate the effectiveness of your argument and your communication skills.

2. Think back on a time when a teacher or other authority figure hastily jumped to a conclusion about you or something you did. How did this event influence your life goals and decisions? Discuss ways in which your critical-thinking skills might help you to put this event in perspective.

open-minded and good listeners and not engage in resistence or resort to fallacies if others disagree with our argument. If you find that your argument is weak or that the particular conclusion you have drawn does not follow from the premises, go back and revise your argument.

7. Revise Your Argument. Revise your argument, if necessary, in light of the feedback you receive. If the other person's counterargument is more compelling, it would be irrational for you not to revise your own position in light of it. For example, a student in one of my ethics classes participated in a group presentation on capital punishment. At the end of the presentation, he was asked about his position on the issue by another student. He responded, "After doing this project I realize that capital punishment serves no purpose and that there are no good arguments for it. But," he added, "I still support capital punishment." That was poor critical thinking on his part. Stubbornly adhering to a position when there is contrary evidence is not a desirable quality.

8. Put Your Solution or Conclusion into Action.
If appropriate, put your solution or conclusion into action. Good critical thinking has a behavioral component. It involves taking critical action. For instance, if you are writing to your state senator about a need to increase community drug awareness in your hometown, you might want to suggest a realistic solution to the problem and offer to help with its implementation.

Knowing how to construct and present an argument are important skills for a critical thinker. It not only makes you more effective in presenting an argument on an issue but can also help you in resolving issues in your own life.

HIGHLIGHTS

STEPS FOR CONSTRUCTING AN ARGUMENT

1. **Clearly state the issue in the form of a question.**

2. **Develop a list of premises that address the issue.**

3. **Eliminate weak or irrelevant premises.**

4. **Establish a conclusion.**

5. **Organize your argument.**

6. **Try out your argument on others.**

7. **Revise your argument, if necessary.**

8. **If appropriate, put your solution or conclusion into action.**

►**APPLICATION: Identify in the text an example of each step being applied to an argument.**

Using Arguments in Making Real-Life Decisions

Arguments are useful tools for making real-life decisions, especially in situations that involve a conflict between what seem to be equally compelling alternatives. People who are poor at critical thinking not only are less likely to recognize a conflict until it gets out of control but are unable to evaluate competing alternatives to come up with an effective resolution to the problem.

Skilled critical thinkers, in contrast, are more likely to recognize a conflict. Instead of jumping to conclusions, good critical thinkers look at an issue from multiple perspectives, assigning weight when necessary to competing reasons, before reaching their final decision.

Consider this example:

> Amy was struggling with the decision of whether to go to China with her family over the summer or instead to go to summer school so that she could finish college in four years. She had been promised a job with a computer software company, following graduation in June. Unfortunately, the summer course schedule conflicted with her travel plans. What should she do?

The first thing you should do in a case like this is to come up with a list of all possible premises or reasons that are relevant to your final decision. In making her decision, Amy began by making this list:

- My grandparents, who live in China, are getting on in years, and this may be the last chance I have to see them.

- My parents are paying my fare, so the trip will not be a financial burden for me.

- I need to take a summer course to graduate next year.

- I have been promised a job with a computer software company after graduation in June.

- The summer course schedule at my college conflicts with my travel schedule.

In developing your list of premises, ask other people for ideas as well. Also, do your research and make sure that you have all the facts correct. In Amy's case, one of her friends suggested that she go to the registrar's office to see whether there was a way she could take a course that would not conflict with the trip dates. As it turned out, she could do an internship on contemporary Chinese business culture for the credits she needed to graduate. She added this option or premise to her list:

- I could do an internship for college credit while I'm in China.

After completing your list, go back and review the premises. Highlight those that are most relevant and delete those that are not. Review your final list before drawing a conclusion. Have you left anything out? Often, just by doing your research and listing various options, you may find that what first seemed to be a conflict is not a conflict at all, as happened in Amy's case.

Finally, put your decision or conclusion into action. As it turned out, Amy was able to go to China with her family *and* complete college in four years.

Arguments provide a powerful tool for analyzing issues and making decisions in our lives. As critical thinkers, we should take a stand or make an important decision only *after* we have examined the different perspectives and options. In addition, we should remain open to hearing new evidence and, in light of that evidence, to modifying our position. By trying to learn why someone holds a position different from our own, we can move closer to understanding and perhaps resolving a conflict.

STOP AND ASSESS YOURSELF

I. Select an issue that is currently being discussed on your campus. After following the eight steps outlined in this chapter, write a two to three page essay or a letter to the editor of the student newspaper presenting your argument for a resolution to the issue.

2. The growing number of child pornography sites on the Internet has led to a corresponding proliferation of cyberspace sleuths—adults who pose as children and attempt to expose cyber-pedophiles. Critics of these self-appointed citizen-sleuths point out that their techniques, because they involve deception, border on entrapment. Critics also argue that it is wrong for private citizens to take the law into their own hands. Others applaud the success of these citizen-sleuths in catching sex offenders and closing down child pornography sites. Working in small groups, construct an argument on the issue of using citizen-sleuths to catch pedophiles. Share your conclusion with the rest of the class. Reevaluate your conclusion, if necessary, in light of feedback from the class.

3. Working in small groups, select a situation with which one of the students in the group is currently struggling. Using the eight-step method outlined in this chapter, generate a suggested resolution or decision.

4. Select one of the goals from your life plan that you are having difficulty achieving. Construct an argument that will enable you to achieve this goal. Put your decision or conclusion into action.

THiNK AGAIN

1. What is an argument?
   - An argument is made up of two or more propositions, including the conclusion, which is supported by the other propositions, known as premises. An argument tries to prove or convince us that the conclusion is true, whereas an explanation is a statement about why something is the case.

2. What is the purpose of breaking down and diagramming arguments?
   - Breaking down arguments helps us to recognize the different premises and the conclusion so we can identify and analyze the issue under discussion, as well as examine the premises to determine if they support the conclusion.

3. What are some of the factors to take into consideration in evaluating an argument?
   - Some of the factors in evaluating an argument are clarity, credibility, relevance, completeness, and soundness of the argument.

Perspectives on Same-Sex Marriage

The issue of legalizing same-sex marriage has divided the United States for some time. Support for same-sex marriage is increasing, with 58 percent of Americans polled in 2013 agreeing that it should be legal. Women and young people are the most likely to support same-sex marriage.[22] The change in public opinion and laws has been rapid. Indeed, until 2003, when the U.S. Supreme Court's ruling in *Lawrence v. Texas* declared antisodomy laws unconstitutional, some states had laws on the books that punished sexual intercourse between two people of the same sex with up to 25 years in prison.

Supporters of same-sex marriage argue that marriage is a basic human right that should not be denied to a person simply because of his or her sexual orientation. Same-sex marriage has been legalized in Canada, Belgium, the Netherlands, Spain, and South Africa. In addition, same-sex couples have full legal rights in many other European countries. In the United States, 13 states including California, Massachusetts, Connecticut, Iowa, Maine, Maryland, New Hampshire, New York, Washington, Minnesota, Delaware, Rhode Island, and Vermont, as well as Washington, D.C. are the only states where same-sex marriage is legal—and those marriages are not recognized by the federal government or, in most cases, by other states. However, several states, including New Jersey, Illinois, and Hawaii, have civil-union legislation for same-sex couples, and still others recognize domestic partnerships.

In 1996, during the administration of Bill Clinton, Congress passed the Defense of Marriage Act (DOMA). The act states that "the word 'marriage' means only a legal union between one man and one woman as husband and wife," thereby prohibiting the federal government from recognizing same-sex marriages. In 2004, a proposal was submitted to Congress to add a Marriage Protection Amendment to the U.S. Constitution, which would define marriage as only between a man and a woman and would also prevent state laws and courts from recognizing same-sex marriages. The amendment failed to pass. On June 26, 2013, the U.S. Supreme Court ruled that Section 3 of DOMA is unconstitutional and that same-sex married couples are entitled to federal benefits.

In the first reading Chief Justice Marshall, in *Goodridge v. Department of Public Health* (2003), argues that same-sex couples have a constitutional right to marry. In the second reading, Matthew Spalding argues that redefining marriage to a form of contract fundamentally alters the nature and purpose of marriage.

Goodridge v. Department of Public Health (2003)

CHIEF JUSTICE MARGARET H. MARSHALL, MAJORITY OPINION

Goodridge v. Department of Public Health was a landmark state appellate court case that legalized same-sex marriage in Massachusetts, the first state to do so. In the following reading former Chief Justice Margaret H. Marshall presents the majority opinion in support of the ruling.

Marriage is a vital social institution. The exclusive commitment of two individuals to each other nurtures love and mutual support; it brings stability to our society. For those who choose to marry, and for their children, marriage provides an abundance of legal, financial, and social benefits. In return it imposes weighty legal, financial, and social obligations. The question before us is whether, consistent with the Massachusetts Constitution, the Commonwealth may deny the protections, benefits, and obligations conferred by civil marriage to two individuals of the same sex who wish to marry. We conclude that it may not. The Massachusetts Constitution affirms the dignity and equality of all individuals. It forbids the creation of second class citizens. In reaching our conclusion we have given full deference to the arguments made by the Commonwealth. But it has failed to identify any constitutionally adequate reason for denying civil marriage to same-sex couples.

The Court affirmed that the core concept of common human dignity protected by the Fourteenth Amendment to the United States Constitution precludes government intrusion into the deeply personal realms of consensual adult expressions of intimacy and one's choice of an intimate partner. The Court also reaffirmed the central role that decisions whether to marry or have children bear in shaping one's identity.

Barred access to the protections, benefits, and obligations of civil marriage, a person who enters into an intimate, exclusive union with another of the same sex is arbitrarily deprived of membership in one of our community's most rewarding and cherished institutions. That exclusion is incompatible with the constitutional principles of respect for individual autonomy and equality under law.

Without question, civil marriage enhances the "welfare of the community." It is a "social institution of the highest importance."Civil marriage anchors an ordered society by encouraging stable relationships over transient ones. It is central to the way the Commonwealth identifies individuals, provides for the orderly distribution of property, ensures that children and adults are cared for and supported whenever possible from private rather than public funds, and tracks important epidemiological and demographic data.

Marriage also bestows enormous private and social advantages on those who choose to marry. Civil marriage is at once a deeply personal commitment to another human being and a highly public celebration of the ideals of mutuality, companionship, intimacy, fidelity, and family. Because it fulfils yearnings for security, safe haven, and connection that express our common humanity, civil marriage is an esteemed institution, and the decision whether and whom to marry is among life's momentous acts of self-definition.

The benefits accessible only by way of a marriage license are enormous, touching nearly every aspect of life and death. The department states that "hundreds of statutes" are related to marriage and to marital benefits. Exclusive marital benefits that are not directly tied to property rights include the presumptions of legitimacy and parentage of children born to a married couple and evidentiary rights, such as the prohibition against spouses testifying against one another about their private conversations, applicable in both civil and criminal cases Other statutory benefits of a personal nature available only to married individuals include qualification for bereavement or medical leave to care for individuals related by blood or marriage an automatic "family member" preference to make medical decisions for an incompetent or disabled spouse who does not have a contrary health care proxy, the application of predictable rules of child custody, visitation, support, and removal out-of-State when married parents divorce.

Notwithstanding the Commonwealth's strong public policy to abolish legal distinctions between marital and nonmarital children in providing for the support and care of minors, the fact remains that marital children reap a measure of family stability and economic security based on their parents' legally privileged status that is largely inaccessible, or not as readily accessible, to nonmarital children. Some of these benefits are social, such as the enhanced approval that still attends the status of being a marital child. Others are material, such as the greater ease of access to family-based State and Federal benefits that attend the presumptions of one's parentage.

It is undoubtedly for these concrete reasons, as well as for its intimately personal significance, that civil marriage has long been termed a "civil right." See, e.g., Loving v. Virginia, The United States Supreme Court has described the right to marry as "of fundamental importance for all individuals" and as "part of the fundamental 'right of privacy' implicit in the Fourteenth Amendment's Due Process Clause."

Without the right to marry—or more properly, the right to choose to marry—one is excluded from the full range of human experience and denied full protection of the laws for one's "avowed commitment to an intimate and lasting human relationship.". . . Because civil marriage is central to the lives of individuals and the welfare of the community, our laws assiduously protect the individual's right to marry against undue government incursion. Laws may not "interfere directly and substantially with the right to marry.". . .

For decades, indeed centuries, in much of this country (including Massachusetts) no lawful marriage was possible between white and black Americans. That long history availed not when the Supreme Court of California held in 1948 that a legislative prohibition against interracial marriage violated the due process and equality guarantees of the Fourteenth Amendment.

The individual liberty and equality safeguards of the Massachusetts Constitution protect both "freedom from" unwarranted government intrusion into protected spheres of life and "freedom to" partake in benefits created by the State for the common good. . . . Both freedoms are involved here. Whether and whom to marry, how to express sexual intimacy, and whether and how to establish a family—these are among the most basic of every individual's liberty and due process rights. . . . And central to personal freedom and security is the assurance that the laws will apply equally to persons in similar situations. "Absolute equality before the law is a fundamental principle of our own Constitution." . . .

REVIEW QUESTIONS

1. Why is denying same-sex couples the right to marriage incompatible with the principles of respect for autonomy and equality under the law?

2. What does Marshall mean when she says that the laws of civil marriage do not privilege procreative heterosexual intercourse between married people?

3. How is denying the right to marry between whites and blacks similar to denying the right to marry between same-sex couples?

4. How does Marshall respond to the claim that legalizing same-sex marriage will undermine the institution of marriage?

A Defining Moment for Marriage and Self-Government   MATTHEW SPALDING

Matthew Spalding is vice president of American Studies and Director of the B. Kenneth Simon Center for Principles and Politics at the Heritage Foundation in Washington, D.C. In his reading, Spaulding presents arguments for why legalizing same-sex marriage will weaken traditional marriage and family.

What was once an important debate over the legal status of marriage has emerged as a critical national issue, the resolution of which will shape the future of our society and the course of constitutional government in the United States.

Family is and will always remain the building block of civil society, and marriage is at the heart of the family. Redefining marriage down to a mere form of contract fundamentally alters its nature and purpose and will usher in new threats to the liberty of individuals and organizations that uphold marriage and have moral or religious objections to its redefinition.

What Is at Stake For thousands of years, based on experience, tradition, and legal precedent, every society and every major religion have upheld marriage as the unique relationship by which a man and a woman are joined together for the primary purpose of forming and maintaining a family. This overwhelming consensus results from the fact that the union of man and woman is manifest in the most basic and evident truths of human nature. Marriage is the formal recognition of this relationship by society and its laws. While individual marriages are recognized by government, the institution of marriage pre-exists and is antecedent to the institution of government.

Society's interest in uniquely elevating the status of marriage is that marriage is the necessary foundation of the family, and thus necessary for societal existence and well-being. Family is the primary institution through which children are raised, nurtured, and educated, and developed into adults. Marriage is the cornerstone of the family: It produces children, provides them with mothers and fathers, and is the framework through which relationships among mothers, fathers, and children are established and maintained.

Moreover, because of the shared obligations and generational relationships that accrue with marriage, the institution brings significant stability, continuity, and meaning to human relationships and plays an important role in transferring basic cultural knowledge and civilization to future generations.

Redefining Marriage Redefining marriage does not simply extend benefits or rights to a larger class, but substantively changes the essence of the institution. It does not expand marriage; it alters its core meaning such that it is no longer intrinsically related to the relationship between fathers, mothers, and children. Expanding marriage supposedly to make it more inclusive, no matter what we call the new arrangement, necessarily ends marriage as we now know it by remaking the institution into something different: a mere contract between any two individuals.

Changing the definition of marriage—or even remaining neutral as to that definition—denies the very nature and purpose that gives marriage its unique and preferable status in society. If marriage becomes just one form of commitment in a spectrum of sexual relationships rather than a preferred monogamous relationship for the sake of children, the line separating sexual relations within and outside marriage becomes blurred, and so does the public policy argument against out-of-wedlock births or in favor of abstinence.

Based on current evidence and settled reasoning, it would be a terrible folly to weaken marriage either by elevating non-marital unions to the same position or by lowering the institution of marriage to the status of merely one form of household.

A Defining Moment Americans are a greatly tolerant and reasonable people. That continuing character depends on the strength of the American framework of constitutional government and the core principles of self-government—first among those the idea of religious liberty—that allow and encourage that character and our ability to govern ourselves despite our differences. Citizens and their elected representatives must be able to engage in free discussion and deliberation on the importance of the institution of marriage for civil society and popular self-government. Activist judges must not strip them of that freedom.

We should work to rebuild and restore marriage and not allow redefinition to further weaken the institution; break its fundamental connections between husband and wife, parents and child; and thereby sever our primary link to the formation of future generations. We must act in accord with our basic principles and deepest convictions to preserve constitutional government and the foundational structure of civilization by upholding the permanent institution of marriage.

Review Questions

1. Why does Spalding regard redefining marriage to include same-sex marriage as a threat to liberty?

2. According to Spalding, what is the source of the institution of marriage?

3. Why is heterosexual marriage a necessary foundation of family?

4. According to Spalding, how would redefining marriage to include same-sex couples weaken the institution of marriage?

THiNK AND DISCUSS

PERSPECTIVES ON SAME-SEX MARRIAGE

1. Identify the key premises in *Goodridge v. Department of Public Health* (2006) and by Spalding in their arguments regarding the legalization of same-sex marriage. Identify which type of premise each is. Diagram and evaluate both of the arguments. Should the definition of marriage be limited to a man and a woman or should the definition change to take into account changing views of marriage and family? Present an argument supporting your position, referring back to the role of definitions discussed in Chapter 8 on page 230.

2. Some people oppose legalizing same-sex marriage on a federal level but support civil unions and equal rights for same-sex couples. Evaluate whether this position is consistent with a belief in equal rights and opportunities for all people, regardless of their sexual orientation. Discuss also how both Spalding and the Supreme Court in *Goodridge v. Department of Public Health* (2006) might respond to legalizing civil unions, but not marriage, for same-sex couples. Which position do you support and why?

3. Looking back at your life goals, is marriage one of your goals? If so, why? Discuss how you would respond, and why, if you were legally denied the right to marry because of your sexual orientation.

4. Cheshire Calhoun, professor of philosophy at Arizona State University, has argued that lesbians should not buy into the traditional model of marriage and family that she says is inherently oppressive to women because women take a subordinate role to men in marriage, and women are expected to do the majority of housework and childrearing, which limits their career options. Discuss her concerns. Should the institution of marriage itself be dismantled? If so, what should replace marriage as the family unit and best means for raising children? Develop arguments to support your answers.

Module 4
Learning and Cognition

CHAPTER 10

COGNITIVE AND LANGUAGE DEVELOPMENT

Ah! What would the world be to us
If the children were no more?
We should dread the desert behind us
Worse than the dark before.

—Henry Wadsworth Longfellow
American Poet, 19th Century

Learning **Goals**

1 Discuss the development of the brain and compare the cognitive developmental theories of Jean Piaget and Lev Vygotsky.

Teaching **Stories**   Donene Polson

In this chapter you will study Lev Vygotsky's sociocultural cognitive theory of development. Donene Polson's classroom reflects Vygotsky's emphasis on the importance of collaboration among a community of learners. Donene teaches at Washington Elementary School in Salt Lake City, an innovative school that emphasizes the importance of people learning together (Rogoff, Turkanis, & Bartlett, 2001). Children as well as adults plan learning activities. Throughout the day at school, students work in small groups.

Donene loves working in a school where students, teachers, and parents work as a community to help children learn (Polson, 2001). Before the school year begins, she meets with parents at each family's home to prepare for the upcoming year, getting acquainted and establishing schedules to determine when parents can contribute to classroom instruction. At monthly teacher-parent meetings, Donene and the parents plan the curriculum and discuss children's progress. They brainstorm about community resources that can be used to promote children's learning.

Many students come back to tell Donene that experiences in her classroom made important contributions to their development and learning. For example, Luisa Magarian reflected on how her experience in Donene's classroom helped her work with others in high school:

> From having responsibility in groups, kids learn how to deal with problems and listen to each other or try to understand different points of view. They learn how to help a group work smoothly and how to keep people interested in what they are doing. . . . As coeditor of the student news magazine at my high school, I have to balance my eagerness to get things done with patience to work with other students. (Rogoff, Turkanis, & Bartlett, 2001, pp. 84–85)

As Donene Polson's story shows, theories of cognitive development can form the basis of innovative instructional programs.

Preview

Examining the shape of children's development allows us to understand it better. This chapter—the first of two on development—focuses on children's cognitive and language development. Before we delve into these topics, though, we need to explore some basic ideas about development.

1 **COGNITIVE DEVELOPMENT**

| The Brain | Piaget's Theory | Vygotsky's Theory |

Twentieth-century American poet Marianne Moore said that the mind is "an enchanting thing." How this enchanting thing develops has intrigued many psychologists. First, we explore increasing interest in the development of the brain and then turn to two major cognitive theories—Piaget's and Vygotsky's.

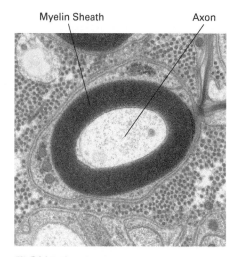

FIGURE **10.1** MYELINATED NERVE

Fiber. The myelin sheath, shown in brown, encases the axon (white). This image was produced by an electron microscope that magnified the nerve fiber 12,000 times. *What role does myelination play in the brain's development?*

DEVELOPMENT

myelination The process of encasing many cells in the brain with a myelin sheath that increases the speed at which information travels through the nervous system.

THE BRAIN

Until recently little was known about how the brain changes as children develop. Not long ago scientists thought that genes determine how children's brains are "wired." Whatever brain heredity dealt them, children were essentially stuck with it. This view, however, turned out to be wrong. Instead, the brain has considerable *plasticity,* or the ability to change, and its development depends on experience (Nelson, 2011; Toga & Mazziotta, 2011). In other words, what children do can change the development of their brain.

Development of Neurons and Brain Regions The number and size of the brain's nerve endings continue to grow at least into adolescence. Some of the brain's increase in size also is due to **myelination,** the process of encasing many cells in the brain with a myelin sheath (see Figure 10.1). This process increases the speed at which information travels through the nervous system (Schnaar & Lopez, 2009). Myelination in brain areas important in focusing attention is not complete until about 10 years of age. The implications for teaching are that children will have difficulty focusing their attention and maintaining it for very long in early childhood, but their attention will improve as they move through the elementary school years. The most extensive increase in myelination, which occurs in the brain's frontal lobes, where reasoning and thinking occur, takes place during adolescence (Giedd & others, 2009).

Another important aspect of the brain's development at the cellular level is the dramatic increase in connections between neurons (nerve cells) (Turrigiano, 2010). *Synapses* are tiny gaps between neurons where connections between neurons are made. Researchers have discovered an interesting aspect of synaptic connections. Nearly twice as many of these connections are made than ever will be used (Huttenlocher & Dabholkar, 1997). The connections that are used become strengthened and will survive, whereas the unused ones will be replaced by other pathways or disappear. That is, in the language of neuroscience, these connections will be "pruned." Figure 10.2 vividly shows the dramatic growth and later pruning of synapses in the visual, auditory, and prefrontal cortex areas of the brain. These areas are critical for higher-order cognitive functioning such as learning, memory, and reasoning.

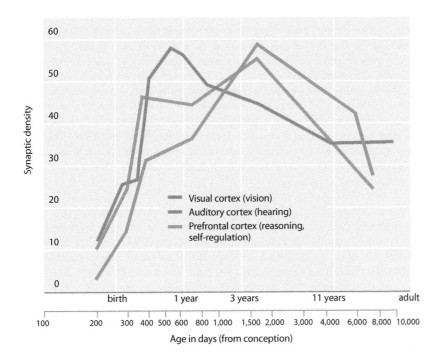

FIGURE **10.2** SYNAPTIC DENSITY IN HUMAN BRAIN FROM INFANCY TO ADULTHOOD

The graph shows the dramatic increase and then pruning of synaptic density for three regions of the brain: visual cortex, auditory cortex, and prefrontal cortex. Synaptic density is believed to be an important indication of the extent of connectivity between neurons.

Notice that in the prefrontal cortex (discussed further later on), where higher-level thinking and self-regulation take place, it is not until middle to late adolescence that the adult density of the synapses is achieved.

Figure 10.3 shows the location of the brain's four lobes. As just indicated, growth in the prefrontal cortex (the highest region of the frontal lobes) continues through adolescence. Rapid growth in the temporal lobes (language processing) and parietal lobes (spatial location) occurs from age 6 through puberty.

Brain Development in Middle and Late Childhood   Total brain volume stabilizes by the end of middle and late childhood, but significant changes in various structures and regions of the brain continue to occur (Gogtay & Thompson, 2010). In particular, the brain pathways and circuitry involving the prefrontal cortex continue to increase in middle and late childhood (Durston & Casey, 2006). These advances in the prefrontal cortex are linked to children's improved attention, reasoning, and cognitive control (Diamond, Casey, & Munakata, 2011).

Developmental neuroscientist Mark Johnson and his colleagues (2009) recently proposed that the prefrontal cortex likely orchestrates the functions of many other brain regions during development. As part of this neural leadership, organizational role, the prefrontal cortex may provide an advantage to neural connections and networks that include the prefrontal cortex. In their view, the prefrontal cortex likely coordinates the best neural connections for solving a problem.

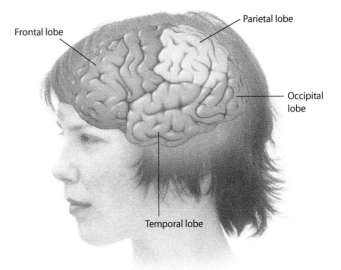

FIGURE **10.3** THE BRAIN'S FOUR LOBES

Shown here are the locations of the brain's four lobes: frontal, occipital, temporal, and parietal.

Thinking Back/Thinking Forward

A surge of interest has occurred in discovering the aspects of the brain that are involved in intelligence.

Links between the changing brain and children's cognitive development involve activation of some brain areas so that they increase in activity while others decrease (Goswami, 2011; Nelson, 2011). One shift in activation that occurs as children develop in middle and late childhood is from diffuse, larger areas to more focal, smaller areas. This shift is characterized by the synaptic pruning mentioned earlier, in which areas of the brain not being used lose synaptic connections and those being used show an increase in connections. The increased focal activation is linked to improved cognitive performance, especially in *cognitive control,* which involves flexible and effective control in a number of areas (Durston & others, 2006). These areas include controlling attention, reducing interfering thoughts, inhibiting motor actions, and being flexible in switching between competing choices (Diamond, Casey, & Munakata, 2011).

Brain Development in Adolescence   Along with the rest of the body, the brain is changing during adolescence. Earlier we indicated that connections between neurons become "pruned" as children and adolescents develop. What results from this pruning is that by the end of adolescence individuals have "fewer, more selective, more effective connections between neurons than they did as children" (Kuhn, 2009, p. 153). And this pruning indicates that the activities adolescents choose to engage in and not to engage in influence which neural connections will be strengthened and which will disappear.

Scientists have recently discovered that adolescents' brains undergo significant structural changes (Giedd & others, 2009; Jackson-Newsom & Shelton, 2010). The **corpus callosum,** where fibers connect the brain's left and right hemispheres, thickens in adolescence, and this improves adolescents' ability to process information. We described advances in the development of the **prefrontal cortex**—the highest level of the frontal lobes involved in reasoning, decision making, and self-control—earlier in this section. However, the prefrontal cortex doesn't finish maturing until the emerging adult years, approximately 18 to 25 years of age, or later, but the **amygdala**—the seat of emotions such as anger—matures earlier than the prefrontal cortex. Figure 10.4 shows the locations of the corpus callosum, prefrontal cortex, and amygdala.

corpus callosum Where fibers connect the brain's left and right hemispheres.

prefrontal cortex The highest level in the frontal lobes; involved in reasoning, decision making, and self-control.

amygdala The seat of emotions in the brain.

Leading researcher Charles Nelson (2011) points out that although adolescents are capable of very strong emotions, their prefrontal cortex hasn't adequately developed to the point at which they can control these passions. This means that the brain region for putting the brakes on risky, impulsive behavior is still under construction during adolescence (Giedd & others, 2009). Or consider this interpretation of the development of emotion and cognition in adolescence: "early activation of strong 'turbo-charged' feelings with a relatively unskilled set of 'driving skills' or cognitive abilities to modulate strong emotions and motivation" (Dahl, 2004, p. 18). This developmental disjunction may account for increased risk taking and other problems in adolescence (Steinberg, 2009). "Some things just take time to develop and mature judgment is probably one of them" (Steinberg, 2004, p. 56).

Lateralization   The cerebral cortex (the highest level of the brain) is divided into two halves, or hemispheres (see Figure 10.5). **Lateralization** is the specialization of functions in each hemisphere of the brain (van Ettinger-Veenstra & others, 2010). In individuals with an intact brain, there is a specialization of function in some areas.

The most extensive research on the brain's two hemispheres involves language. In most individuals, speech and grammar are localized to the left hemisphere (Carota & others, 2010; Gazzaniga, 2010). However, not all language processing is carried out in the brain's left hemisphere (Phan & Vicario, 2010). For example, understanding such aspects of language as appropriate use of language in different contexts, evaluation of the emotional expressiveness of language, and much of humor involves the right hemisphere (Kensinger & Choi, 2009). Also, when children lose much of their left hemisphere because of an accident, surgery for epilepsy, or other reasons, the right hemisphere in many cases can reconfigure itself for increased language processing (Staudt, 2010).

Because of the differences in functioning of the brain's two hemispheres, people commonly use the phrases "left-brained" and "right-brained" to say which hemisphere is dominant. Unfortunately, much of this talk is seriously exaggerated. For example, laypeople and the media commonly exaggerate hemispheric specialization by claiming that the left brain is logical and the right brain is creative. However, most complex functioning—such as logical and creative thinking—in normal people involves communication between both sides of the brain (Baars & Gage, 2010). Scientists who study the brain are typically very cautious with terms such as *left-brained* and *right-brained* because the brain is more complex than those terms suggest.

Plasticity   As we have seen, the brain has *plasticity* (Nelson, 2011; Toga & Mazziotta, 2011). What children do can change the development of their brain. By engaging students in optimal learning environments, you can stimulate the development of their brain (Goswami, 2010).

The remarkable case of Michael Rehbein illustrates the brain's plasticity. When Michael was 4½, he began to experience uncontrollable seizures—as many as 400 a day. Doctors said that the only solution was to remove the left hemisphere of his brain, where the seizures were occurring. Michael had his first major surgery at age 7 and another at age 10. Although recovery was slow, his right hemisphere began to reorganize and eventually took over functions such as speech that normally occur in

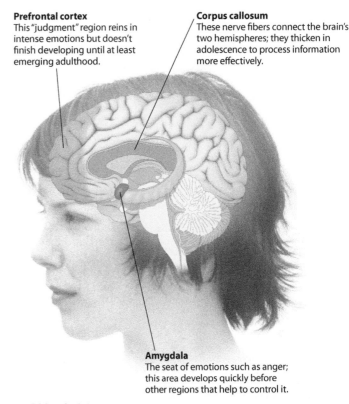

Prefrontal cortex
This "judgment" region reins in intense emotions but doesn't finish developing until at least emerging adulthood.

Corpus callosum
These nerve fibers connect the brain's two hemispheres; they thicken in adolescence to process information more effectively.

Amygdala
The seat of emotions such as anger; this area develops quickly before other regions that help to control it.

FIGURE **10.4**   CHANGES IN ADOLESCENT BRAIN

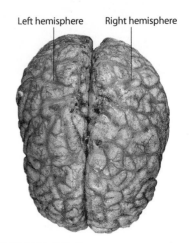

Left hemisphere   Right hemisphere

FIGURE **10.5**   HUMAN BRAIN'S HEMISPHERES

The two halves (hemispheres) of the human brain are clearly seen in this photograph.

lateralization The specialization of functions in each hemisphere of the brain.

(a)

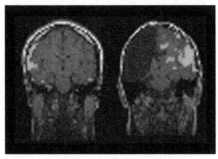

(b)

FIGURE **10.6** PLASTICITY IN BRAIN'S HEMISPHERES

(a) Michael Rehbein at 14 years of age. (b) Michael's right hemisphere (*right*) has reorganized to take over the language functions normally carried out by corresponding areas in the left hemisphere of an intact brain (*left*). However, the right hemisphere is not as efficient as the left, and more areas of the brain are recruited to process speech.

the brain's left hemisphere (see Figure 10.6). Individuals like Michael are living proof of the growing brain's remarkable plasticity and ability to adapt and recover from a loss of brain tissue.

The Brain and Children's Education Unfortunately, too often statements about the implications of brain science for children's education have been speculative at best and often far removed from what neuroscientists know about the brain (Geake, 2010). We don't have to look any further than the hype about "left-brained" individuals being more logical and "right-brained" individuals being more creative to see that links between neuroscience and brain education are incorrectly made (Sousa, 1995).

Another commonly promoted link between neuroscience and brain education is that there is a critical, or sensitive, period—a biological window of opportunity—when learning is easier, more effective, and more easily retained than later in development. However, some experts on the development of the brain and learning conclude that the critical-period view is exaggerated (Blakemore & Choudhury, 2006). One leading neuroscientist even told educators that although children's brains acquire a great deal of information during the early years, most learning likely takes place after synaptic formation stabilizes, which is after the age of 10 (Goldman-Rakic, 1996).

A major issue involving the development of the brain is which comes first, biological changes in the brain or experiences that stimulate these changes (Lerner, Boyd, & Du, 2008)? Consider a recent study in which the prefrontal cortex thickened and more brain connections formed when adolescents resisted peer pressure (Paus & others, 2008). Scientists have yet to determine whether the brain changes come first or whether the brain changes are the result of experiences with peers, parents, and others. Once again, we encounter the nature-nurture issue that is so prominent in examining children's and adolescents' development.

Given all of the hype and hyperbole about brain education in the media, what can we conclude from the current state of knowledge in applying the rapidly increasing research on the brain's development to education?

- *Both early and later experiences, including educational experiences, are very important in the brain's development.* Significant changes occur at the cellular and structural level in the brain through adolescence (Paus, 2009).

- *Synaptic connections between neurons can change dramatically as a consequence of the learning experiences of children and adolescents* (Nelson, 2011). Connections between neurons that are used when children focus their attention, remember, and think as they are reading, writing, and doing math are strengthened; those that aren't used are replaced by other pathways or disappear.

- *Development at the highest level of the brain—the prefrontal cortex, where such important cognitive processes as thinking, reasoning, and decision making primarily occur—continues at least through the adolescent years* (Steinberg, 2009). This development in the prefrontal cortex moves from being more diffuse to more focal and involves increased efficiency of processing information (Diamond, Casey, & Munakata, 2011). As activation in the prefrontal cortex becomes more focused, cognitive control increases. This is exemplified in children being able to focus their attention more effectively and ignore distractions while they are learning as they become older.

- *Despite the increased focal activation of the prefrontal cortex as children grow older, changes in the brain during adolescence present a challenge to increased cognitive control.* In adolescence, the earlier maturation of the amygdala, which is involved in processing of emotions, and the more drawn-out development of the prefrontal cortex, provides an explanation of the difficulty adolescents have in controlling their emotions and their tendency to engage in risk taking (Steinberg, 2009).

- *Brain functioning occurs along specific pathways and involves integration of function.* According to leading experts Kurt Fischer and Mary Helen Immordino-Yang (2008),

  > One of the lessons of educational neuroscience, even at this early point in its development, is that children learn along specific pathways, but they do not act or think in compartments. . . . On the one hand, they develop their learning along specific pathways defined by particular content, such as mathematics or history, but on the other hand they make connections between those pathways.

Reading is an excellent example of how brain functioning occurs along specific pathways and is integrated (Goswami, 2011). Consider a child who is asked by a teacher to read aloud to the class. Input from the child's eyes is transmitted to the child's brain, then passed through many brain systems, which translate the patterns of black and white into codes for letters, words, and associations. The output occurs in the form of messages to the child's lips and tongue. The child's own gift of speech is possible because brain systems are organized in ways that permit language processing.

These conclusions suggest that education throughout the childhood and adolescent years can benefit children's and adolescents' learning and cognitive development (Howard-Jones, 2010; Nelson, 2011). Where appropriate throughout the rest of the book, we will describe research on the development of the brain and children's education.

PIAGET'S THEORY

Poet Noah Perry once asked, "Who knows the thoughts of a child?" More than anyone, the famous Swiss psychologist Jean Piaget (1896–1980) knew.

Cognitive Processes   What processes do children use as they construct their knowledge of the world? Piaget stressed that these processes are especially important in this regard: schemas, assimilation and accommodation, organization, and equilibration.

Schemas   Piaget (1954) said that as the child seeks to construct an understanding of the world, the developing brain creates **schemas.** These are actions or mental representations that organize knowledge. In Piaget's theory, *behavioral schemas* (physical activities) characterize infancy, and *mental schemas* (cognitive activities) develop in childhood. A baby's schemas are structured by simple actions that can be performed on objects, such as sucking, looking, and grasping. Older children have schemas that include strategies and plans for solving problems. For example, a 6-year-old might have a schema that involves the strategy of classifying objects by size, shape, or color. By the time we have reached adulthood, we have constructed an enormous number of diverse schemas, ranging from how to drive a car, to how to balance a budget, to the concept of fairness.

Assimilation and Accommodation   To explain how children use and adapt their schemas, Piaget offered two concepts: assimilation and accommodation.

schemas In Piaget's theory, actions or mental representations that organize knowledge.

What are some applications of research on the brain's development to children's and adolescents' education?

Assimilation occurs when people incorporate new information into their existing schematic knowledge. *How might this 8-year-old girl first attempt to use the hammer and nail, based on her preexisting schematic knowledge about these objects?*

Accommodation occurs when people adjust their knowledge schemas to new information. *How might the girl adjust her schemas regarding hammers and nails during her successful effort to hang the picture?*

FIGURE 10.7 ASSIMILATION AND ACCOMMODATION

assimilation Piagetian concept of the incorporation of new information into existing knowledge (schemas).

accommodation Piagetian concept of adjusting schemas to fit new information and experiences.

organization Piaget's concept of grouping isolated behaviors into a higher-order, more smoothly functioning cognitive system; the grouping or arranging of items into categories.

equilibration A mechanism that Piaget proposed to explain how children shift from one stage of thought to the next. The shift occurs as children experience cognitive conflict, or disequilibrium, in trying to understand the world. Eventually, they resolve the conflict and reach a balance, or equilibrium, of thought.

Assimilation occurs when children incorporate new information into their existing schemas. **Accommodation** occurs when children adjust their schemas to fit new information and experiences.

Consider an 8-year-old girl who is given a hammer and nail to hang a picture on the wall. She has never used a hammer, but from observing others do this she realizes that a hammer is an object to be held, that it is swung by the handle to hit the nail, and that it usually is swung a number of times. Recognizing each of these things, she fits her behavior into this schema she already has (assimilation). But the hammer is heavy, so she holds it near the top. She swings too hard and the nail bends, so she adjusts the pressure of her strikes. These adjustments reflect her ability to slightly alter her conception of the world (accommodation). Just as both assimilation and accommodation are required in this example, so are they required in many of the child's thinking challenges (see Figure 10.7).

Organization To make sense out of their world, said Piaget, children cognitively organize their experiences. **Organization** in Piaget's theory is the grouping of isolated behaviors and thoughts into a higher-order system. Continual refinement of this organization is an inherent part of development. A boy with only a vague idea about how to use a hammer also may have a vague idea about how to use other tools. After learning how to use each one, he relates these uses, organizing his knowledge.

Equilibration and Stages of Development **Equilibration** is a mechanism that Piaget proposed to explain how children shift from one stage of thought to the next. The shift occurs as children experience cognitive conflict, or *disequilibrium*, in trying to understand the world. Eventually, they resolve the conflict and reach a balance, or *equilibrium*, of thought. Piaget pointed out that there is considerable movement between states of cognitive equilibrium and disequilibrium as assimilation and accommodation work in concert to produce cognitive change. For example, if a child believes that the amount of a liquid changes simply because the liquid is poured into a container with a different shape—for instance, from a container that is short and wide into a container that is tall and narrow—she might be puzzled by such issues as where the "extra" liquid came from and whether there is actually more liquid to drink. The child will eventually resolve these puzzles as her thought becomes more advanced. In the everyday world, the child is constantly faced with such counterexamples and inconsistencies.

Assimilation and accommodation always take the child to a higher ground. For Piaget, the motivation for change is an internal search for equilibrium. As old schemas are adjusted and new schemas are developed, the child organizes and reorganizes the old and new schemas. Eventually, the organization is fundamentally different from the old organization; it is a new way of thinking.

Thus, the result of these processes, according to Piaget, is that individuals go through four stages of development. A different way of understanding the world makes one stage more advanced than another. Cognition is *qualitatively* different in one stage compared with another. In other words, the way children reason at one stage is different from the way they reason at another stage.

Piagetian Stages Each of Piaget's stages is age-related and consists of distinct ways of thinking. Piaget proposed four stages of cognitive development: sensorimotor, preoperational, concrete operational, and formal operational (see Figure 10.8).

Sensorimotor Stage	**Preoperational Stage**	**Concrete Operational Stage**	**Formal Operational Stage**
The infant constructs an understanding of the world by coordinating sensory experiences with physical actions. An infant progresses from reflexive, instinctual action at birth to the beginning of symbolic thought toward the end of the stage.	The child begins to represent the world with words and images. These words and images reflect increased symbolic thinking and go beyond the connection of sensory information and physical action.	The child can now reason logically about concrete events and classify objects into different sets.	The adolescent reasons in more abstract, idealistic, and logical ways.
Birth to 2 Years of Age	**2 to 7 Years of Age**	**7 to 11 Years of Age**	**11 Years of Age Through Adulthood**

FIGURE **10.8** PIAGET'S FOUR STAGES OF COGNITIVE DEVELOPMENT

The Sensorimotor Stage   The **sensorimotor stage,** which lasts from birth to about 2 years of age, is the first Piagetian stage. In this stage, infants construct an understanding of the world by coordinating their sensory experiences (such as seeing and hearing) with their motor actions (reaching, touching)—hence the term sensorimotor. At the beginning of this stage, infants show little more than reflexive patterns to adapt to the world. By the end of the stage, they display far more complex sensorimotor patterns.

DEVELOPMENT

The Preoperational Stage   The **preoperational stage** is the second Piagetian stage. Lasting approximately from about 2 to 7 years of age, it is more symbolic than sensorimotor thought but does not involve operational thought. However, it is egocentric and intuitive rather than logical.

Preoperational thought can be subdivided into two substages: symbolic function and intuitive thought. The **symbolic function substage** occurs roughly between 2 and 4 years of age. In this substage, the young child gains the ability to represent mentally an object that is not present. This stretches the child's mental world to new dimensions. Expanded use of language and the emergence of pretend play are other examples of an increase in symbolic thought during this early childhood substage. Young children begin to use scribbled designs to represent people, houses, cars, clouds, and many other aspects of the world. Possibly because young children are not very concerned about reality, their drawings are fanciful and inventive (Winner, 1986). One 3½ year-old looked at the scribble he had just drawn and described it as a pelican kissing a seal (see Figure 10.9a). In the elementary school years, children's drawings become more realistic, neat, and precise (see Figure 10.9b).

Even though young children make distinctive progress in this substage, their preoperational thought still has an important limitation: egocentrism. *Egocentrism* is the inability to distinguish between one's own perspective and someone else's

sensorimotor stage The first Piagetian stage, lasting from birth to about 2 years of age, in which infants construct an understanding of the world by coordinating sensory experiences with motor actions.

preoperational stage The second Piagetian stage, lasting from about 2 to 7 years of age, symbolic thought increases, but operational thought is not yet present.

symbolic function substage The first substage of preoperational thought, occurring between about 2 to 4 years of age; the ability to represent an object not present develops and symbolic thinking increases; egocentrism is present.

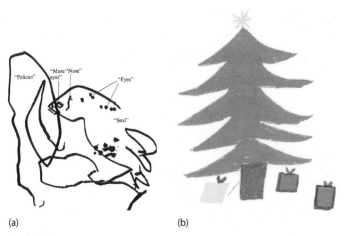

FIGURE 10.9 DEVELOPMENTAL CHANGES IN CHILDREN'S DRAWINGS

(*a*) A 3½-year-old's symbolic drawing. Halfway into this drawing, the 3½-year-old artist said it was "a pelican kissing a seal." (*b*) This 11-year-old's drawing is neater and more realistic but also less inventive.

"I still don't have all the answers, but I'm beginning to ask the right questions."

© Lee Lorenz/The New Yorker Collection/ www.cartoonbank.com

perspective. Piaget and Barbel Inhelder (1969) initially studied young children's egocentrism by devising the three-mountains task (see Figure 10.10). The child walks around the model of the mountains and becomes familiar with what the mountains look like from different perspectives. The child also can see that there are different objects on the mountains. The child then is seated on one side of the table on which the mountains are placed. The experimenter moves a doll to different locations around the table. At each location, the child is asked to select from a series of photos the one that most accurately reflects the view the doll is seeing. Children in the preoperational stage often pick the view that reflects where they are sitting rather than the doll's view.

What further cognitive changes take place in the preoperational stage? The **intuitive thought substage** is the second substage of preoperational thought, starting at about 4 years of age and lasting until about 7 years of age. At this substage, children begin to use primitive reasoning and want to know the answers to all sorts of questions. Piaget called this substage *intuitive* because the children seem so sure about their knowledge and understanding yet are unaware of how they know what they know. That is, they say they know something but know it without the use of rational thinking.

An example of young children's limitation in reasoning ability is the difficulty they have putting things into correct categories. Look at the collection of objects in Figure 10.11a. You would probably respond to the direction "Put the things together that you believe belong together" by grouping the objects by size and shape. Your sorting might look something like that shown in Figure 10.11b. Faced with a similar collection of objects that can be sorted on the basis of two or more properties, preoperational children seldom are capable of using these properties consistently to sort the objects into appropriate groupings.

Many of these preoperational examples show a characteristic of thought called **centration,** which involves focusing (or centering) attention on one characteristic to the exclusion of all others. Centration is most clearly present in preoperational children's lack of **conservation,** the idea that some characteristic of an object stays the same even though the object might change in appearance. For example, to adults it is obvious that a certain amount of liquid stays the same regardless of a container's

Model of Mountains

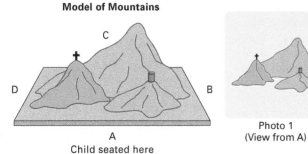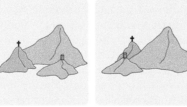

Photo 1 (View from A) Photo 2 (View from B) Photo 3 (View from C) Photo 4 (View from D)

FIGURE 10.10 THE THREE-MOUNTAINS TASK

The mountain model on the far left shows the child's perspective from view A, where he or she is sitting. The four squares represent photos showing the mountains from four different viewpoints of the model—A, B, C, and D. The experimenter asks the child to identify the photo in which the mountains look as they would from position B. To identify the photo correctly, the child has to take the perspective of a person sitting at spot B. Invariably, a child who thinks in a preoperational way cannot perform this task. When asked what a view of the mountains looks like from position B, the child selects Photo 1, taken from location A (the child's own view at the time) instead of Photo 2, the correct view.

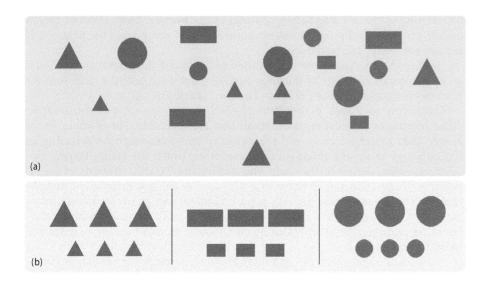

FIGURE **10.11** ARRAYS

(*a*) A random array of objects. (*b*) An ordered array of objects.

intuitive thought substage The second substage of preoperational thought, lasting from about 4 to 7 years of age. Children begin to use primitive reasoning and want to know the answer to all sorts of questions. They seem so sure about their knowledge in this substage but are unaware of how they know what they know.

centration Focusing, or centering, attention on one characteristic to the exclusion of all others; characteristic of preoperational thinking.

conservation The idea that some characteristic of an object stays the same even though the object might change in appearance; a cognitive ability that develops in the concrete operational stage, according to Piaget.

shape. But this is not obvious at all to young children. Rather, they are struck by the height of the liquid in the container. In this type of conservation task (Piaget's most famous), a child is presented with two identical beakers, each filled to the same level with liquid (see Figure 10.12). The child is asked if the beakers have the same amount of liquid. The child usually says yes. Then the liquid from one beaker is poured into a third beaker, which is taller and thinner. The child now is asked if the amount of liquid in the tall, thin beaker is equal to the liquid that remains in the second original beaker. Children younger than 7 or 8 usually say no. They justify their answer

FIGURE **10.12** PIAGET'S CONSERVATION TASK

The beaker test is a well-known Piagetian test to determine whether a child can think operationally—that is, can mentally reverse actions and show conservation of the substance. (*a*) Two identical beakers are presented to the child. Then, the experimenter pours the liquid from B into C, which is taller and thinner than A or B. (*b*) The child is asked if these beakers (A and C) have the same amount of liquid. The preoperational child says "no." When asked to point to the beaker that has more liquid, the preoperational child points to the tall, thin beaker.

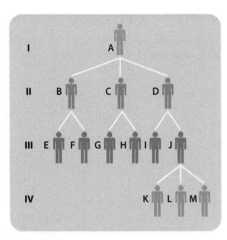

FIGURE **10.13** CLASSIFICATION: AN IMPORTANT ABILITY IN CONCRETE OPERATIONAL THOUGHT

A family tree of four generations (*I to IV*): The preoperational child has trouble classifying the members of the four generations; the concrete operational child can classify the members vertically, horizontally, and obliquely (up and down and across). For example, the concrete operational child understands that a family member can be a son, a brother, and a father, all at the same time.

concrete operational stage Piaget's third cognitive developmental stage, occurring between about 7 to 11 years of age. At this stage, the child thinks operationally, and logical reasoning replaces intuitive thought but only in concrete situations; classification skills are present, but abstract problems present difficulties.

by referring to the differing height or width of the beakers. Older children usually answer yes. They justify their answers appropriately: If you poured the liquid back, the amount would still be the same.

In Piaget's view, failing the conservation of liquid task indicates that the child is at the preoperational stage of thinking. Passing the test suggests the child is at the *concrete operational stage* of thinking (discussed later on).

According to Piaget, preoperational children also cannot perform what he called *operations*—mental representations that are reversible. For example, in the beaker task, preschool children have difficulty understanding that reversing an action brings about the original conditions from which the action began. Two other examples should further help you understand Piaget's concepts of operations. A young child might know that $4 + 2 = 6$ but not understand that the reverse, $6 - 2 = 4$, is true. Or let's say a preschooler walks to his friend's house each day but always gets a ride home. If asked to walk home from his friend's house, he probably would reply that he didn't know the way because he never had walked home before.

Some developmentalists do not believe Piaget was entirely correct in his estimate of when conservation skills emerge. For example, Rochel Gelman (1969) trained preschool children to attend to relevant aspects of the conservation task. This improved their conservation skills.

Further, children show considerable variation in attaining conservation skills. Researchers have found that 50 percent of children develop conservation of mass at 6 to 9 years of age, 50 percent demonstrate conservation of length at 4 to 9 years of age, 50 percent show conservation of area at 7 to 9 years of age, and 50 percent of children don't attain conservation of weight until 8 to 10 years of age (Horowitz & others, 2005; Sroufe & others, 1992).

Yet another characteristic of preoperational children is that they ask a lot of questions. The barrage begins around age 3. By about 5, they have just about exhausted the adults around them with "Why?" "Why" questions signal the emergence of the child's interest in figuring out why things are the way they are. Following is a sampling of 4- to 6-year-olds' questions (Elkind, 1976):

"What makes you grow up?"
"Who was the mother when everybody was a baby?"
"Why do leaves fall?"
"Why does the sun shine?"

The Concrete Operational Stage The **concrete operational stage,** the third Piagetian stage of cognitive development, lasts from about 7 to about 11 years of age. Concrete operational thought involves using operations. Logical reasoning replaces intuitive reasoning, but only in concrete situations. Classification skills are present, but abstract problems go unsolved.

A concrete operation is a reversible mental action pertaining to real, concrete objects. Concrete operations allow the child to coordinate several characteristics rather than focus on a single property of an object. At the concrete operational level, children can do mentally what they previously could do only physically, and they can reverse concrete operations.

An important concrete operation is classifying or dividing things into different sets or subsets and considering their interrelationships. Reasoning about a family tree of four generations, for example, reveals a child's concrete operational skills (Furth & Wachs, 1975). The family tree shown in Figure 10.13 suggests that the grandfather (A) has three children (B, C, and D), each of whom has two children (E through J), and one of these children (J) has three children (K, L, and M). Concrete operational thinkers understand the classification. For example, they can reason that person J can at the same time be father, brother, and grandson. A preoperational thinker cannot.

TEACHING CONNECTIONS: Best Practices
Strategies for Working with Preoperational Thinkers

As you have just read, young children think on a different plane than older children. Following are some effective strategies for advancing young children's thinking.

1. *Allow children to experiment freely with materials.* For example, give children various sizes of cups and a sandbox or water table. As they pour the sand or water back and forth between the cups, they will begin to understand the concepts of reversibility and conservation. If children are allowed to "play" with materials at a science table, they are likely to begin classifying objects.

2. *Ask children to make comparisons.* These might involve such concepts as bigger, taller, wider, heavier, and longer.

3. *Give children experience in ordering operations.* For example, have children line up in rows from tall to short and vice versa. Bring in various examples of animal and plant life cycles, such as several photographs of butterfly development or the sprouting of beans or kernels of corn.

4. *Have children draw scenes with perspective.* Encourage them to make the objects in their drawings appear to be at the same location as in the scene they are viewing. For example, if they see a horse at the end of a field, they should place the horse in the same location in the drawing.

5. *Construct an inclined plane or a hill.* Let children roll marbles of various sizes down the plane. Ask them to compare how quickly the different-size marbles reach the bottom. This should help them understand the concept of speed.

6. *Ask children to justify their answers when they draw conclusions.* For example, when they say that pouring a liquid from a short, wide container into a tall, thin container makes the liquid change in volume, ask, "Why do you think so?" or "How could you prove this to one of your friends?" This will help them to think more logically.

Some Piagetian tasks require children to reason about relations between classes. One such task is **seriation,** the concrete operation that involves ordering stimuli along some quantitative dimension (such as length). To see if students can serialize, a teacher might place eight sticks of different lengths in a haphazard way on a table. The teacher then asks the student to order the sticks by length. Many young children end up with two or three small groups of "big" sticks or "little" sticks rather than a correct ordering of all eight sticks. Another mistaken strategy they use is to evenly line up the tops of the sticks but ignore the bottoms. The concrete operational thinker simultaneously understands that each stick must be longer than the one that precedes it and shorter than the one that follows it.

Transitivity involves the ability to reason about and logically combine relationships. If a relation holds between a first object and a second object, and also holds between the second object and a third object, then it also holds between the first and third objects. For example, consider three sticks (A, B, and C) of differing lengths. A is the longest, B is intermediate in length, and C is the shortest. Does the child understand that if A is longer than B, and B is longer than C, then A is longer than C? In Piaget's theory, concrete operational thinkers do; preoperational thinkers do not.

The Formal Operational Stage The **formal operational stage,** which emerges at about 11 to 15 years of age, is Piaget's fourth and final cognitive stage. At this stage, individuals move beyond reasoning only about concrete experiences and think in more abstract, idealistic, and logical ways.

The abstract quality of formal operational thinking is evident in verbal problem solving. The concrete operational thinker needs to see the concrete elements A, B, and C to make the logical inference that if A = B and B = C, then A = C. In contrast, the formal operational thinker can solve this problem when it is verbally presented.

Accompanying the abstract nature of formal operational thought are the abilities to idealize and imagine possibilities. At this stage, adolescents engage in extended

seriation A concrete operation that involves ordering stimuli along some quantitative dimension.

transitivity The ability to reason and logically combine relationships.

formal operational stage Piaget's fourth cognitive developmental stage, which emerges between about 11 and 15 years of age; thought is more abstract, idealistic, and logical in this stage.

TEACHING CONNECTIONS: Best Practices
Strategies for Working with Concrete Operational Thinkers

As you have just learned, for most of elementary school, children think at a concrete operational level, which is a different level than young children and adolescents. Following are some effective strategies for advancing children's thinking at the concrete operational level.

1. *Encourage students to discover concepts and principles.* Ask relevant questions about what is being studied to help them focus on some aspect of their learning. Refrain from telling students the answers to their questions outright. Try to get them to reach the answers through their own thinking.

2. *Involve children in operational tasks.* These include adding, subtracting, multiplying, dividing, ordering, seriating, and reversing. Make the reversibility of these operations explicit for the children. For instance, show them that subtracting is the reverse of adding. Use concrete materi-

als (i.e. manipulatives) for these tasks, possibly introducing math symbols later.

3. *Plan activities in which students practice the concept of ascending and descending classification hierarchies.* Have students list the following in order of size (such as largest to smallest): city of Atlanta, state of Georgia, country of United States, western hemisphere, and planet Earth.

4. *Include activities that require conservation of area, weight, and displaced volume.* Realize that there is considerable variation in children's attainment of conservation across different domains.

5. *Continue to ask students to justify their answers when they solve problems.* Help them to check the validity and accuracy of their conclusions.

speculation about the ideal qualities they desire in themselves and others. These idealistic thoughts can merge into fantasy. Many adolescents become impatient with their newfound ideals and the problems of how to live them out.

At the same time that adolescents are thinking more abstractly and idealistically, they also are beginning to think more logically. As formal operational thinkers, they think more like scientists. They devise plans to solve problems and systematically test

Might adolescents' ability to reason hypothetically and to evaluate what is ideal versus what is real lead them to engage in demonstrations, such as this protest related to better ethnic relations? What other causes might be attractive to adolescents' newfound cognitive abilities of hypothetical-deductive reasoning and idealistic thinking?

solutions. Piaget's term **hypothetical-deductive reasoning** embodies the concept that adolescents can develop hypotheses (best hunches) about ways to solve problems and systematically reach a conclusion. Formal operational thinkers test their hypotheses with judiciously chosen questions and tests. In contrast, concrete operational thinkers often fail to understand the relation between a hypothesis and a well-chosen test of it, stubbornly clinging to ideas that already have been discounted.

A form of egocentrism also emerges in adolescence (Elkind, 1978). *Adolescent egocentrism* is the heightened self-consciousness reflected in adolescents' beliefs that others are as interested in them as they themselves are. Adolescent egocentrism also includes a sense of personal uniqueness. It involves the desire to be noticed, visible, and "on stage."

Egocentrism is a normal adolescent occurrence, more common in the middle school than in high school years. However, for some individuals, adolescent egocentrism can contribute to reckless behavior, including suicidal thoughts, drug use, and failure to use contraceptives during sexual intercourse. Egocentricity may lead some adolescents to think that they are invulnerable.

However, reason to question the accuracy of the invulnerability aspect of the personal fable is provided by research that reveals many adolescents don't consider themselves invulnerable (Reyna & Rivers, 2008). Indeed, recent research suggests that rather than perceiving themselves to be invulnerable, most adolescents tend to portray themselves as vulnerable to experiencing a premature death (Fischoff & others, 2010).

I recently asked teachers to describe how they apply Piaget's cognitive stages to their classroom. Following are their comments:

What characterizes adolescent egocentrism?

EARLY CHILDHOOD   When I teach songs to preschool students who are in the preoperational stage, I use PowerPoint slides projected on the board. The

 slides have either all the words of the song included, or just key words. I also include corresponding clip art and pictures on the page borders.

RESEARCH

—**Connie Christy,** *Aynor Elementary School (Preschool Program)*

ELEMENTARY SCHOOL: GRADES K–5   In my second-grade science class, I use the following method to help students move from concrete thinking to more abstract

 thinking: Children are given tasks and asked to discuss what happened (for example, the object sank or floated; when something is added to a system, the outcome changes). Then a theory or idea is developed from the actual observations. When children observe an occurrence and explain what was seen, they can more easily move from the concrete to the more abstract. Although these methods and others like it work well with my students, I need to repeat them often.

—**Janine Guida Poutre,** *Clinton Elementary School*

MIDDLE SCHOOL: GRADES 6–8   I challenge my seventh-grade students to share examples of how they've applied our classroom lessons to the real world. They can earn extra credit for doing so, but seem to care less about the points than they do about the opportunity to share their accomplishments. For example, after completing a unit on Progressivism, a student shared how he had gone online on his home computer and donated money to help Darfur refugees. He had previously planned to use this

hypothetical-deductive reasoning Piaget's formal operational concept that adolescents can develop hypotheses to solve problems and systematically reach (deduce) a conclusion.

TEACHING CONNECTIONS: Best Practices
Strategies for Working with Formal Operational Thinkers

As you have just learned, adolescents think on a different plane than children. Following are some effective strategies for working with adolescents who are formal operational thinkers.

1. *Realize that most adolescents are not full-fledged formal operational thinkers.* Thus, many of the teaching strategies discussed earlier regarding the education of concrete operational thinkers still apply to many young adolescents. As discussed in Through the Eyes of Teachers, Jerri Hall, a math teacher at Miller Magnet High School in Georgia, emphasizes that when a curriculum is too formal and too abstract, it will go over students' heads.

THROUGH THE EYES OF TEACHERS
Piaget as a Guide

I use Piaget's developmental theory as a guide in helping children learn math. In the sixth, seventh, and eighth grades, children are moving from the concrete to the abstract stage in their cognitive processes; therefore, when I teach, I try to use different methods to aid my students to understand a concept. For example, I use fraction circles to help students understand how to add, subtract, multiply, and divide fractions, and the students are allowed to use these until they become proficient with the algorithms. I try to incorporate hands-on experiences in which students discover the rules themselves, rather than just teaching the methods and having the students

practice them with drill. It is extremely important for students to understand the why behind a mathematical rule so they can better understand the concept.

2. *Propose a problem and invite students to form hypotheses about how to solve it.* For example, a teacher might say, "Imagine that a girl has no friends. What should she do?"

3. *Present a problem and suggest several ways it might be approached.* Then ask questions that stimulate students to evaluate the approaches. For example, describe several ways to investigate a robbery, and ask students to evaluate which way is best and why.

4. *Demonstrate how to conduct experiments that require the separation and control of variables. Later ask students to conduct their own experiments.* These might involve science concepts or simple student-generated research questions, such as "which chewing gum retains its flavor the longest?"

5. *Encourage students to create hierarchical outlines when you ask them to write papers.* Make sure they understand how to organize their writing in terms of general and specific points. The abstractness of formal operational thinking also means that teachers with students at this level can encourage them to use metaphors.

---

money to buy himself a new guitar. This student took the theory of social activism from the Progressive era 100 years ago and applied it to his life today. This student's actions clearly demonstrate Piaget's formal operational stage in action.

—**MARK FODNESS,** *Bemidji Middle School*

HIGH SCHOOL: GRADES 9–12 My high school art students take part in creativity competitions in which they build, create, explore, problem-solve, and perform solutions to challenges presented to them. The competition—Destination Imagination—has challenged my students to brainstorm ideas and solutions to seemingly impossible tasks. As a result of their participation in this event, they have won regional and state titles along with the world championship.

—**DENNIS PETERSON,** *Deer River High School*

TECHNOLOGY

Piaget, Constructivism, and Technology The basic idea of *constructivism* is that students learn best when they are actively constructing information and knowledge. Piaget's theory is a strong constructivist view. Early in the application of technology to children's learning, Seymour Papert (1980), who studied with Piaget for five years, created the Logo programming language for computers that was

Children at a Computer Clubhouse, one of 100 Computer Clubhouses worldwide, that provides students from low-income communities opportunities to creatively use technology to explore their ideas and develop their skills.

Source: www.computerclubhouse.org/

based on Piaget's constructivist view. A small robot labeled the "Logo Turtle" guided children in constructing solutions to problems. Today, all sorts of robotic kits are available, as well as Scratch (http://scratch.mit.edu/), an online programming and communication space for children, LifeLong Kindergarten (http://llk.media.mit.edu/projects.php), which has a number of creative projects for students of varying ages, and the Computer Clubhouse (www.computerclubhouse.org/), an international consortium of computer clubs linked over the Internet for 10–18-year-olds from low-income communities, providing a creative and safe out-of-school learning environment with adult mentors. Many others claim constructivism as their foundation and are used in schools worldwide.

Evaluating Piaget's Theory   What were Piaget's main contributions? Has his theory withstood the test of time?

Contributions   Piaget is a giant in the field of developmental psychology. We owe to him the present field of children's cognitive development. We also owe to him a long list of masterful concepts, including assimilation and accommodation, object permanence, egocentrism, conservation, and hypothetical-deductive reasoning. Along with William James and John Dewey, Piaget contributed to the current vision of children as active, constructive thinkers (Miller, 2011).

Piaget was a genius when it came to observing children. His careful observations showed us inventive ways to discover how children act on and adapt to their world. His work revealed some important things to look for in cognitive development, such as the shift from preoperational to concrete operational thinking, and showed us how children need to make their experiences fit their schemas (cognitive frameworks) while simultaneously adapting their schemas to experience.

Piaget is shown here with his family. Piaget's careful observations of his three children—Lucienne, Laurent, and Jacqueline—contributed to the development of his cognitive theory.

Having an outstanding teacher and gaining a good education in the logic of science and mathematics are important cultural experiences that promote the development of operational thought. *Might Piaget have underestimated the roles of culture and schooling in children's cognitive development?*

Criticisms Piaget's theory has not gone unchallenged. Questions have been raised in the following areas:

- *Estimates of children's competence.* Some cognitive abilities emerge earlier than Piaget thought, others later (Carpenter, 2011). Conservation of number has been demonstrated as early as age 3, although Piaget did not think it emerged until 7. Young children are not as uniformly "pre-" this and "pre-" that (precausal, preoperational) as Piaget thought (Flavell, Miller, & Miller, 2002). Other cognitive abilities can emerge later than Piaget thought. Many adolescents still think in concrete operational ways or are just beginning to master formal operations (Kuhn, 2009).

- *Stages.* Piaget conceived of stages as unitary structures of thought. Some concrete operational concepts, however, do not appear at the same time. For example, children do not learn to conserve at the same time as they learn to cross-classify.

- *Training children to reason at a higher level.* Some children who are at one cognitive stage (such as preoperational) can be trained to reason at a higher cognitive stage (such as concrete operational). However, Piaget argued that such training is only superficial and ineffective unless the child is at a maturational transition point between the stages (Gelman & Opfer, 2004).

- *Culture and education.* Culture and education exert stronger influences on children's development than Piaget envisioned. For example, the age at which children acquire conservation skills is related to the extent to which their culture provides relevant practice (Cole, 2006). An outstanding teacher can guide students' learning experiences that will help them move to a higher cognitive stage.

Despite the criticisms, some developmental psychologists conclude that we should not throw out Piaget altogether (Miller, 2011). These **neo-Piagetians** argue that Piaget got some things right although his theory needs considerable revision. In their revision of Piaget, neo-Piagetians emphasize how children process information through attention, memory, and strategies (Case, 2000). They especially stress that a more accurate vision of children's thinking requires more knowledge of strategies, how fast and how automatically children process information, the particular cognitive task involved, and the division of cognitive problems into smaller, more precise steps (Morra & others, 2008).

Despite such problems, Piaget's theory is a very useful one. As we see next, there are many ways to apply his ideas to educating children.

VYGOTSKY'S THEORY

In addition to Piaget's theory, another major developmental theory that focuses on children's cognition is Russian Lev Vygotsky's theory. In Vygotsky's theory children's cognitive development is shaped by the cultural context in which they live (Gauvain & Parke, 2010).

The Zone of Proximal Development Vygotsky's belief in the importance of social influences, especially instruction, on children's cognitive development is reflected in his concept of the zone of proximal development. **Zone of proximal development (ZPD)** is Vygotsky's term for the range of tasks that are too difficult for the child to master alone but that can be learned with guidance and assistance of adults or more-skilled children. Thus, the lower limit of the ZPD is the level of skill reached by the child working independently. The upper limit is the level of additional responsibility the child can accept with the assistance of an able instructor

---

Thinking Back/Thinking Forward

The information-processing approach emphasizes that children develop a gradually increasing capacity for processing information. Chapter 12, p. 344

DEVELOPMENT

neo-Piagetians Developmental psychologists who believe that Piaget got some things right but that his theory needs considerable revision; emphasize how to process information through attention, memory, and strategies.

zone of proximal development (ZPD) Vygotsky's term for the range of tasks that are too difficult for children to master alone but that can be mastered with guidance and assistance from adults or more-skilled children.

TEACHING CONNECTIONS: Best Practices
Strategies for Applying Piaget's Theory to Children's Education

Earlier in this chapter, you learned about applying Piaget's theory to teaching children at different stages of cognitive development. Following are five general strategies based on Piaget's theory for educating children.

1. *Take a constructivist approach.* In a constructivist approach, Piaget emphasized that children learn best when they are active and seek solutions for themselves. Piaget opposed teaching methods that treat children as passive receptacles. The educational implication of Piaget's view is that in all subjects students learn best by making discoveries, reflecting on them, and discussing them, rather than blindly imitating the teacher or doing things by rote.

2. *Facilitate rather than direct learning.* Effective teachers design situations that allow students to learn by doing. These situations promote students' thinking and discovery. Teachers listen, watch, and question students to help them gain better understanding. They ask relevant questions to stimulate students' thinking and ask them to explain their answers. As described in Through the Eyes of Teachers, Suzanne Ransleben creates imaginative classroom situations to facilitate students' learning.

THROUGH THE EYES OF TEACHERS
Stimulating Students' Thinking and Discovery

Suzanne Ransleben teaches ninth- and tenth-grade English in Corpus Christi, Texas. She designs classroom situations that stimulate students' reflective thinking and discovery.

Suzanne Ransleben, teaching English.

Suzanne created Grammar Football to make diagramming sentences more interesting for students and has students decipher song lyrics to help them better understand how to write poetry. When students first encounter Shakespeare, "they paint interpretations of their favorite line from *Romeo and Juliet*" (Source: Wong Briggs, 2004, p. 7D)

3. *Consider the child's knowledge and level of thinking.* Students do not come to class with empty heads. They have many ideas about the physical and natural world including concepts of space, time, quantity, and causality. These ideas differ from the ideas of adults. Teachers need to interpret what a student is saying and respond with discourse close to the student's level. Asking the children to do something for which they are not ready will not promote cognitive development. It will merely frustrate the children.

4. *Promote the student's intellectual health.* When Piaget came to lecture in the United States, he was asked, "What can I do to get my child to a higher cognitive stage sooner?" He was asked this question so often in the United States compared with other countries that he called it the American question. For Piaget, children's learning should occur naturally. Children should not be pushed and pressured into achieving too much too early in their development, before they are maturationally ready.

5. *Turn the classroom into a setting of exploration and discovery.* What do actual classrooms look like when the teachers adopt Piaget's views? Several first- and second-grade math classrooms provide some good examples (Kamii, 1985, 1989). The teachers emphasize students' own exploration and discovery. The classrooms are less structured than what we think of as a typical classroom. Workbooks and predetermined assignments are not used. Rather, the teachers observe the students' interests and natural participation in activities to determine what the course of learning will be. For example, a math lesson might be constructed around counting the day's lunch money or dividing supplies among students. Often games are prominently used in the classroom to stimulate mathematical thinking.

(see Figure 10.14). The ZPD captures the child's cognitive skills that are in the process of maturing and can be accomplished only with the assistance of a more-skilled person (Daniels, 2011).

Teaching in the ZPD reflects the concept of developmentally appropriate teaching we described earlier in the chapter. It involves being aware of "where students

Upper limit

Level of additional responsibility child can accept with assistance of an able instructor

Zone of proximal development (ZPD)

Lower limit

Level of problem solving reached on these tasks by child working alone

FIGURE **10.14** VYGOTSKY'S ZONE OF PROXIMAL DEVELOPMENT

Vygotsky's zone of proximal development has a lower limit and an upper limit. Tasks in the ZPD are too difficult for the child to perform alone. They require assistance from an adult or a more-skilled child. As children experience the verbal instruction or demonstration, they organize the information in their existing mental structures, so they can eventually perform the skill or task alone.

scaffolding A technique that involves changing the level of support for learning. A teacher or more-advanced peer adjusts the amount of guidance to fit the student's current performance.

are in the process of their development and taking advantage of their readiness. It is also about teaching to enable developmental readiness, not just waiting for students to be ready" (Horowitz & others, 2005, p. 105).

Scaffolding Closely linked to the idea of the ZPD is the concept of scaffolding. **Scaffolding** means changing the level of support. Over the course of a teaching session, a more-skilled person (a teacher or advanced peer) adjusts the amount of guidance to fit the child's current performance. When the student is learning a new task, the skilled person may use direct instruction. As the student's competence increases, less guidance is given. Scaffolding is often used to help students attain the upper limits of their ZPD.

Asking probing questions is an excellent way to scaffold students' learning and help them to develop more sophisticated thinking skills. A teacher might ask a student such questions as "What would an example of that be?" "Why do you think that is so?" "Now, what's the next thing you need to do?" and "How can you connect those?" Over time, students should begin internalizing these kinds of probes and improve monitoring their own work (Horowitz & others, 2005).

Many teachers who successfully use scaffolding circulate around the classroom, giving "just-in-time" assistance to individuals, or detecting a class-wide misconception and then leading a discussion to correct the problem. They also give "children time to grapple with problems" and guide them when they observe that the child can no longer make progress (Horowitz & others, 2005, pp. 106–107).

Language and Thought In Vygotksy's view, language plays an important role in a child's development (Gredler, 2009). According to Vygotsky, children use speech not only for social communication, but also to help them solve tasks. Vygotsky (1962) further argued that young children use language to plan, guide, and monitor their behavior. This use of language for self-regulation is called *private speech*. For example, young children talk aloud to themselves about such things as their toys and the tasks they are trying to complete. Thus, when working on a puzzle, a child might say, "This piece doesn't go; maybe I'll try that one." A few minutes later she utters, "This is hard." For Piaget private speech is egocentric and immature, but for Vygotsky it is an important tool of thought during the early childhood years (John-Steiner, 2007).

Vygotsky said that language and thought initially develop independently of each other and then merge. He emphasized that all mental functions have external, or social, origins. Children must use language to communicate with others before they can focus inward on their own thoughts. Children also must communicate externally and use language for a long period of time before they can make the transition from external to internal speech. This transition period occurs between 3 and 7 years of age and involves talking to oneself. After a while, the self-talk becomes second nature to children, and they can act without verbalizing. When this occurs, children have internalized their egocentric speech in the form of *inner speech,* which becomes their thoughts.

Vygotsky argued that children who use private speech are more socially competent than those who don't. He believed that private speech represents an early transition in becoming more socially communicative. For Vygotsky, when young children talk to themselves, they are using language to govern their behavior and guide themselves.

Piaget held that self-talk is egocentric and reflects immaturity. However, researchers have found support for Vygotsky's view that private speech plays a positive role in children's development (Winsler, Carlton, & Barry, 2000). Researchers have revealed that children use private speech more when tasks are difficult, after they make mistakes, and when they are not sure how to proceed (Berk, 1994). They also have found that children who use private speech are more attentive and improve their performance more than children who do not use private speech (Berk & Spuhl, 1995).

I recently asked teachers how they apply Vygotsky's theory to their classroom. After reading their responses about Vygotsky, you might want to compare these responses with teachers' responses about how they apply Piaget's theory in their classroom that were described earlier in the chapter.

EARLY CHILDHOOD   In teaching music to preschoolers, I use private speech to help children learn unfamiliar rhythms. When my young students are learning a new rhythm pattern on the African drums, for example, they don't count the eighth and quarter notes, because that is too difficult. Instead, I suggest certain words for them to repeat in rhythmic patterns to learn the beat, or they can come up with their own words to match the new rhythm. My guidance allows children to improve their understanding of musical rhythm.

—**CONNIE CHRISTY,** *Aynor Elementary School (Preschool Program)*

ELEMENTARY SCHOOL: GRADES K–5   One way to maximize students' zone of proximal development is by flexible grouping. In flexible grouping, groups change often based on need, interest, and so on. I use different group styles—for example, whole class, small group, homogenous groups, and heterogeneous groups. Variance in group members and group styles allows all students to be instructed within their zone of proximal development. This may be on grade level in one area, above grade level in another, and below grade level in still another. The point is that flexible grouping allows me to give students of varying levels the instruction necessary to learn.

—**SUSAN FROELICH,** *Clinton Elementary School*

MIDDLE SCHOOL: GRADES 6–8   When I teach my students a new skill, it is important that I stay close to them while they are working. This way if they need my assistance, I am there to help them master the new skill with some guidance. This practice works especially well when we are working on multistep projects.

—**CASEY MAASS,** *Edison Middle School*

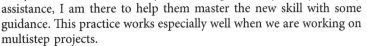

HIGH SCHOOL: GRADES 9–12   Advanced art students and independent-study students have always been an active part of my classroom, especially when it comes to helping other students maximize their zone of proximal development (and grow in their own skills as artists as well). In my ceramics class, for example, I have several advanced students—who have especially strong knowledge and skills on the ceramic wheel—help my first-year students, who are attempting to work on the wheel for the first time. This additional assistance from the advanced students allows me to help other students who need further instruction.

—**DENNIS PETERSON,** *Deer River High School*

We have discussed a number of ideas about both Piaget's and Vygotsky's theories and how the theories can be applied to children's education. To reflect on how you might apply their theories to your own classroom, complete Self-Assessment 10.1.

Evaluating Vygotsky's Theory   How does Vygotsky's theory compare with Piaget's? Although both theories are constructivist, Vygotsky's is a **social constructivist approach,** which emphasizes the social contexts of learning and the construction of knowledge through social interaction.

> **Thinking Back/Thinking Forward**
>
> Collaborative learning and cognitive apprenticeships reflect Vygotsky's social constructivist approach.

social constructivist approach Emphasizes the social contexts of learning and that knowledge is mutually built and constructed; Vygotsky's theory exemplifies this approach.

SELF-ASSESSMENT 10.1
Applying Piaget and Vygotsky in My Classroom

The grade level at which I plan to teach is _____

PIAGET

The Piagetian stage of the majority of children in my classroom will likely be _____

The Piagetian concepts that should help me the most in understanding and teaching children at this grade level are

Concept	Example

VYGOTSKY

The concepts in Vygotsky's theory that should help me the most in understanding and teaching children at this grade level are

Concept	Example

TEACHING CONNECTIONS: Best Practices
Strategies for Applying Vygotsky's Theory to Children's Education

Vygotsky's theory has been embraced by many teachers and has been successfully applied to education. Here are some ways Vygotsky's theory can be incorporated in classrooms:

1. *Assess the child's ZPD.* Like Piaget, Vygotsky did not think that formal, standardized tests are the best way to assess children's learning. Rather, Vygotsky argued that assessment should focus on determining the child's ZPD. The skilled helper presents the child with tasks of varying difficulty to determine the best level at which to begin instruction.

2. *Use the child's ZPD in teaching.* Teaching should begin toward the zone's upper limit, so that the child can reach the goal with help and move to a higher level of skill and knowledge. Offer just enough assistance. You might ask, "What can I do to help you?" Or simply observe the child's intentions and attempts and provide support when needed. When the child hesitates, offer encouragement. And encourage the child to practice the skill. You may

watch and appreciate the child's practice or offer support when the child forgets what to do. In Through the Eyes of Teachers, you can read about John Mahoney's teaching practices that reflect Vygotsky's emphasis on the importance of the ZPD. In contrast to in-class work, homework should be aimed at the zone's lower limit so that the child will be capable of completing it. Keeping instruction in the ZPD is likely to require differentiation as children's zones of proximal development are not uniform.

THROUGH THE EYES OF TEACHERS
Using Dialogue and Reframing Concepts to Find the Zone of Proximal Development

John Mahoney teaches mathematics at a high school in Washington, D.C. In Mahoney's view, guiding students' success in math is both collaborative and individual. He encourages dialogue about math during which he reframes concepts that help students subsequently solve problems on their own. Mahoney also never gives students the answers to math problems. As one student commented, "He's going to make you think." His tests always include a problem that students have not seen but have enough knowledge to figure out the problem's solution. (Source: Wong Briggs, 2005.)

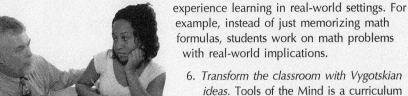

John Mahoney, teaching math.

3. *Use more-skilled peers as teachers.* Remember that it is not just adults that are important in helping children learn. Children also benefit from the support and guidance of more-skilled children (Gredler, 2009). For example, pair a child who is just beginning to read with one who is a more advanced reader. It is also desirable to use cross-age tutoring.

4. *Monitor and encourage children's use of private speech.* Be aware of the developmental change from externally talking to oneself when solving a problem during the preschool years to privately talking to oneself in the early elementary school years. In the elementary school years, encourage children to internalize and self-regulate their talk to themselves.

5. *Place instruction in a meaningful context.* Educators today are moving away from abstract presentations of material, instead providing students with opportunities to

experience learning in real-world settings. For example, instead of just memorizing math formulas, students work on math problems with real-world implications.

6. *Transform the classroom with Vygotskian ideas.* Tools of the Mind is a curriculum that is grounded in Vygotsky's (1962) theory with special attention given to cultural tools and developing self-regulation, the ZPD, scaffolding, private speech, shared activity, and play as important activity (Hyson, Copple, & Jones, 2006). Figure 10.15 illustrates how scaffolding was used in Tools of the Mind to improve a young child's writing skills. The Tools of the Mind curriculum was created by Elena Bodrova and Deborah Leong (2007) and has been implemented in more than 200 classrooms. Most of the children in the Tools of the Mind programs are at risk because of their living circumstances, which in many instances involve poverty and other difficult conditions such as being homeless and having parents with drug problems.

One study assessed the effects of the Tools of the Mind curriculum on at-risk preschool children (Diamond & others, 2007). The results indicated that the Tools of the Mind curriculum improved the self-regulatory and cognitive control skills (such as resisting distractions and temptations) of the at-risk children. Other research on the Tools of the Mind curriculum also has found that it improves young children's cognitive skills (Saifer, 2007).

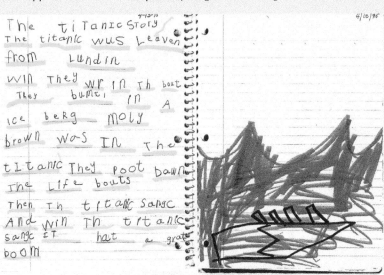

RESEARCH

(a) Five-year-old Aaron's independent journal writing prior to the scaffolded writing technique.

(b) Aaron's journal two months after using the scaffolded writing technique.

FIGURE 10.15 WRITING PROGRESS OF A 5-YEAR-OLD BOY OVER TWO MONTHS USING THE SCAFFOLDING WRITING PROCESS IN TOOLS OF THE MIND

	Vygotsky	Piaget
Sociocultural Context	Strong emphasis	Little emphasis
Constructivism	Social constructivist	Cognitive constructivist
Stages	No general stages of development proposed	Strong emphasis on stages (sensorimotor, preoperational, concrete operational, and formal operational)
Key Processes	Zone of proximal development, language, dialogue, tools of the culture	Schema, assimilation, accommodation, operations, conservation, classification
Role of Language	A major role; language plays a powerful role in shaping thought	Language has a minimal role; cognition primarily directs language
View on Education	Education plays a central role, helping children learn the tools of the culture	Education merely refines the child's cognitive skills that have already emerged
Teaching Implications	Teacher is a facilitator and guide, not a director; establish many opportunities for children to learn with the teacher and more-skilled peers	Also views teacher as a facilitator and guide, not a director; provide support for children to explore their world and discover knowledge

FIGURE 10.16 COMPARISON OF VYGOTSKY'S AND PIAGET'S THEORIES

In moving from Piaget to Vygotsky, the conceptual shift is from the individual to collaboration, social interaction, and sociocultural activity (Gauvain & Parke, 2010). The endpoint of cognitive development for Piaget is formal operational thought. For Vygotsky, the endpoint can differ, depending on which skills are considered to be the most important in a particular culture (Daniels, 2011). For Piaget, children construct knowledge by transforming, organizing, and reorganizing previous knowledge. For Vygotsky, children construct knowledge through social interaction. The implication of Piaget's theory for teaching is that children need support to explore their world and discover knowledge. The main implication of Vygotsky's theory for teaching is that students need many opportunities to learn with the teacher and more-skilled peers (Rogoff & others, 2007). In both Piaget's and Vygotsky's theories, teachers serve as facilitators and guides, rather than as directors and molders of learning. Figure 10.16 compares Vygotsky's and Piaget's theories.

Criticisms of Vygotsky's theory also have surfaced. Some critics point out that Vygotsky was not specific enough about age-related changes (Gauvain, 2008). Another criticism focuses on Vygotsky not adequately describing how changes in socioemotional capabilities contribute to cognitive development (Gauvain, 2008). Yet another charge is that he overemphasized the role of language in thinking. Also, his emphasis on collaboration and guidance has potential pitfalls. Might facilitators be too helpful in some cases, as when a parent becomes too overbearing and controlling? Further, some children might become lazy and expect help when they might have done something on their own.

In our coverage of cognitive development, we have focused on the views of two giants in the field: Piaget and Vygotsky. However, information processing also has emerged as an important perspective in understanding children's cognitive development (Martinez, 2010). It emphasizes how information

What are some contributions and criticisms of Vygotsky's theory?

enters the mind, how it is stored and transformed, and how it is retrieved to perform mental activities such as problem solving and reasoning. It also focuses on how automatically and quickly children process information. The subject of information processing is covered extensively in Chapter 12.

Review, Reflect, and Practice

1 Discuss the development of the brain and compare the cognitive developmental theories of Jean Piaget and Lev Vygotsky.

REVIEW

- How does the brain develop, and what implications does this development have for children's education?
- What four main ideas did Piaget use to describe cognitive processes? What stages did he identify in children's cognitive development? What are some criticisms of his view?
- What is the nature of Vygotsky's theory? How can Vygotsky's theory be applied to education and his theory compared to Piaget's? What is a criticism of Vygotsky's theory?

REFLECT

- Do you consider yourself to be a formal operational thinker? Do you still sometimes feel like a concrete operational thinker? Give examples.

PRAXIS™ PRACTICE

1. Sander is a 16-year-old boy who takes many risks, such as driving fast and drinking while driving. Recent research on the brain indicates that a likely reason for this risk-taking behavior is that Sander's
   a. hippocampus is damaged.
   b. prefrontal cortex is still developing.
   c. brain lateralization is incomplete.
   d. myelination is complete.

2. Mrs. Gonzales teaches first grade. Which of her following strategies would Piaget most likely endorse?
   a. demonstrating how to perform a math operation and having students imitate her
   b. creating flash cards to teach vocabulary
   c. using a standardized test to assess students' reading skills
   d. designing contexts that promote student's thinking and discovery

3. Mr. Gould's fourth-grade students are learning about the relations among percentages, decimals, and fractions. He distributes an assignment requiring students to convert fractions to decimals and then to percentages. Christopher can do this assignment without help from Mr. Gould or his classmates. What would Vygotsky say about this task for Christopher?
   a. This task is appropriate for Christopher because it is within his zone of proximal development.
   b. This task is inappropriate for Christopher because it is above his zone of proximal development.
   c. This task is inappropriate for Christopher because it is below his zone of proximal development.
   d. This task is inappropriate for Christopher because it is within his zone of proximal development.

Please see the answer key at the end of the book.

The Book Report

Mr. Johnson assigned his high school senior American government students to read two books during the semester that had "something, anything to do with government or political systems" and to write a brief report about each of their chosen books.

One student in the class, Cindy, chose to read *1984* and *Animal Farm*, both by George Orwell. Written well before the year 1984, the book *1984* is about what could happen in "the future," given certain earlier political decisions. In essence, the world turns into a terrible place in which "Big Brother" monitors all of one's actions via two-way television-like screens. Infractions of minor rules are punished severely. *Animal Farm* is a brief novel about political systems portrayed as various farm animals such as pigs and dogs. Cindy enjoyed both books and completed them both before midterm. Her reports were insightful, reflecting on the symbolism contained in the novels and the implications for present-day government.

Cindy's friend, Lucy, put off reading her first book until the last minute. She knew Cindy enjoyed reading about government and had finished her reports. Lucy asked Cindy if she knew of a "skinny book" she could read to fulfill the assignment. Cindy gladly shared her copy of *Animal Farm* with her friend, but as Lucy began reading the book she wondered why Cindy had given her this book. It didn't seem to fit the requirements of the assignment at all.

The day before the first reports were due, Mr. Johnson overheard the girls talking. Lucy complained to Cindy, "I don't get it. It's a story about pigs and dogs."

Cindy responded, "They aren't really supposed to be farm animals. It's a story about the promises of communism and what happened in the Soviet Union once the communists took over. It's a great story! Don't you see? The pigs symbolize the communist regime that overthrew the czars during the Russian Revolution. They made all kinds of promises about equality for everyone. The people went along with them because they were sick and tired of the rich and powerful running everything while they starved. Once the czars were eliminated, the communists established a new government but didn't keep any of their promises—they controlled everything. Remember in the book when the pigs moved into the house and started walking on two legs? That's supposed to be like when the communist leaders began acting just like the czars. They even created a secret police force—the dogs in the story. Remember how they bullied the other animals? Just like the secret police in the Soviet Union."

Lucy commented, "I still don't get it. How can a pig or a dog be a communist or a cop? They're just animals."

Cindy looked at her friend, dumbfounded. How could she *not* understand this book? It was so obvious.

1. Drawing on Piaget's theory, explain why Cindy understood the book.

2. Based on Piaget's theory, explain why Lucy didn't understand the book.

3. What could Mr. Johnson do to help Lucy understand?

4. How could Mr. Johnson have presented this assignment differently, so that Lucy did not need to rush through a book?

5. At which of Piaget's stages of cognitive development is Cindy operating?
   a. sensorimotor
   b. preoperational
   c. concrete operational
   d. formal operational
   [Explain your choice.]

6. At which of Piaget's stages of cognitive development is Lucy operating?
   a. sensorimotor
   b. preoperational
   c. concrete operational
   d. formal operational
   [Explain your choice.]

Cognitive and Language Development

① COGNITIVE DEVELOPMENT: Discuss the development of the brain and compare the cognitive developmental theories of Jean Piaget and Lev Vygotsky.

The Brain

An especially important part of growth is the development of the brain and nervous system. Myelination involving hand-eye coordination is not complete until about 4 years of age, and myelination involving focusing attention is not finished until about 10. Substantial synaptic pruning of the brain connections takes place, and the adult level of density of synaptic connections is not reached until some point in adolescence. Different regions of the brain grow at different rates. Changes in the brain in middle and late childhood included advances in functioning in the prefrontal cortex, which are reflected in improved attention, reasoning, and cognitive control. During middle and late childhood, less diffusion and more focal activation occurs in the prefrontal cortex, a change that is associated with an increase in cognitive control. Researchers have recently found a developmental disjunction between the early development of the amygdala, which is responsible for emotion, and the later development of the prefrontal cortex, which is responsible for reasoning and thinking. They argue that these changes in the brain may help to explain the risk-taking behavior and lack of mature judgment in adolescents. Changes in the brain during adolescence also involve the thickening of the corpus callosum. Lateralization in some verbal and nonverbal functions occurs, but in many instances functioning is linked to both hemispheres. There is considerable plasticity in the brain, and the quality of learning environments children experience influence the development of their brain. Too often links between neuroscience and education have been overstated. Based on recent research, what we do know indicates that educational experiences throughout childhood and adolescence can influence the brain's development.

Piaget's Theory

Jean Piaget proposed a major theory of children's cognitive development that involves these important processes: schemas, assimilation and accommodation, organization, and equilibration. In his theory, cognitive development unfolds in a sequence of four stages: sensorimotor (birth to about age 2), preoperational (from about ages 2 to 7), concrete operational (from about ages 7 to 11), and formal operational (from about ages 11 to 15). Each stage is a qualitative advance. In the sensorimotor stage, infants construct an understanding of the world by coordinating their sensory experiences with their motor actions. Thought is more symbolic at the preoperational stage, although the child has not yet mastered some important mental operations. Preoperational thought includes symbolic function and intuitive thought substages. Egocentrism and centration are constraints. At the concrete operational stage, children can perform operations, and logical thought replaces intuitive thought when reasoning can be applied to specific or concrete examples. Classification, seriation, and transitivity are important concrete operational skills. At the formal operational stage, thinking is more abstract, idealistic, and logical. Hypothetical-deductive reasoning becomes important. Adolescent egocentrism characterizes many young adolescents. We owe to Piaget a long list of masterful concepts as well as the current vision of the child as an active, constructivist thinker. Criticisms of his view focus on estimates of children's competence, stages, the training of children to reason at a higher cognitive level, and the neo-Piagetian criticism of not being precise enough about how children learn.

Vygotsky's Theory

Lev Vygotsky proposed another major theory of cognitive development. Vygotsky's view emphasizes that cognitive skills need to be interpreted developmentally, are mediated by language, and have their origins in social relations and culture. Zone of proximal development (ZPD) is Vygotsky's term for the range of tasks that are too difficult for children to master alone but that can be learned with the guidance and assistance of adults and more-skilled

(continued)

children. Scaffolding is an important concept in Vygotsky's theory. He also argued that language plays a key role in guiding cognition. Applications of Vygotsky's ideas to education include using the child's ZPD and scaffolding, using more-skilled peers as teachers, monitoring and encouraging children's use of private speech, and accurately assessing the ZPD. These practices can transform the classroom and establish a meaningful context for instruction. Like Piaget, Vygotsky emphasized that children actively construct their understanding of the world. Unlike Piaget, he did not propose stages of cognitive development, and he emphasized that children construct knowledge through social interaction. In Vygotsky's theory, children depend on tools provided by the culture, which determines which skills they will develop. Some critics say that Vygotsky overemphasized the role of language in thinking.

KEY TERMS

myelination 278
corpus callosum 280
prefrontal cortex 280
amygdala 280
lateralization 281
schemas 283
assimilation 284
accommodation 284

organization 284
equilibration 284
sensorimotor stage 285
preoperational stage 285
symbolic function
   substage 285
intuitive thought substage 287
centration 287

conservation 287
concrete operational
   stage 288
seriation 289
transitivity 289
formal operational stage 289
hypothetical-deductive
   reasoning 291

neo-Piagetians 294
zone of proximal development
   (ZPD) 294
scaffolding 296
social constructivist
   approach 297

PORTFOLIO ACTIVITIES

Now that you have a good understanding of this chapter, complete these exercises to expand your thinking.

Independent Reflection

1. Select the general age of the child you expect to teach one day. Make a list of that child's characteristic ways of thinking according to Piaget's theory of cognitive development. List other related characteristics of the child based on your own childhood. Then make a second list of your own current ways of thinking. Compare the lists. In what important cognitive ways do you and the child differ? What adjustments in thinking will you need to make when you set out to communicate with the child? Summarize your thoughts in a brief essay.

2. How might thinking in formal operational ways rather than concrete operational ways help students develop better study skills?

3. What is the most useful idea related to children's language development that you read about in this chapter? Write the idea down in your portfolio and explain how you will implement this idea in your classroom.

Research/Field Experience

4. Find an education article in a magazine or on the Internet that promotes "left-brained" and "right-brained" activities for learning. In a brief report, criticize the article based on what you read in this chapter about neuroscience and brain education.

Go to the Online Learning Center for downloadable portfolio templates.

STUDY, PRACTICE, AND SUCCEED

Visit www.mhhe.com/santrockep5e to review the chapter with self-grading quizzes and self-assessments, to apply the chapter material to two more Crack the Case studies, and for suggested activities to develop your teaching portfolio.

CHAPTER 11

BEHAVIORAL AND SOCIAL COGNITIVE APPROACHES

To learn is a natural pleasure.

—Aristotle
Greek Philosopher, 4th Century, B.C.

Learning **Goals**

1 Define learning and describe five approaches to studying it.

2 Compare classical conditioning and operant conditioning.

3 Apply behavior analysis to education.

4 Summarize social cognitive approaches to learning.

Teaching **Stories** Ruth Sidney Charney

Ruth Sidney Charney has been a teacher for more than 35 years. She is one of the developers of the Responsive Classroom® approach to teaching and learning, a method that emphasizes positive reinforcement of students' good behavior. Following are some of her thoughts about reinforcing students' learning (Charney, 2005, pp. 1–2):

> We reinforce children when we notice. We notice the personal detail our children bring to school and we notice their efforts to behave and learn. . . . We applaud the five correct answers on the math paper (when last week there were only two), the extra sentence in writing, the crisp adjectives, the ten minutes of fair play in a game. . . .
>
> We reinforce by noticing the positive attempts children make to follow the rules and meet class expectations. We reinforce when children are practicing new skills or when they demonstrate behaviors recently modeled. . . .
>
> Examples of noticing and reinforcing students include
>
> - "Today's the day, isn't it?" the teacher whispers to Hector. He smiles at her, and they share a quick high-five salute,

acknowledging Hector's impending solo performance in the church choir.

- "Snazzy new boots?" the teacher asks Leila as she struts into class. . . .
- "Thanks for helping Tessa with her spelling. I notice you gave her good hints so she could spell some of the words herself."
- "I noticed it took much less time today to get in line. What did you notice . . . ?"
- "I noticed you got your math done this morning with no interruption. That took lots of concentration. . . ."
- "Thank you for your very efficient clean-up today. I noticed caps back on markers, pencils with points down in cans, paper off the floor. . . ."
- "You really found an interesting way to solve the problem and complete the project together."

Preview

Virtually everyone agrees that helping students learn is an important function of schools. However, not everyone agrees on the best way to learn. We begin this chapter by examining just what learning involves, then turn to the main behavioral approaches to learning. Next we explore how behavioral principles are applied to educating students. In the final section we will discuss the social cognitive approaches to learning.

1 WHAT IS LEARNING?

What Learning Is and Is Not   Approaches to Learning

Learning is a central focus of educational psychology. When people are asked what schools are for, a common reply is, "To help children learn."

WHAT LEARNING IS AND IS NOT

When children learn how to use a computer, they might make some mistakes along the way, but at a certain point they will get the knack of the behaviors required to use the computer effectively. The children will change from being individuals who cannot operate a computer into being individuals who can. Once they have learned how, they don't lose those skills. It's like learning to drive a car. Once you have learned how, you don't have to learn all over again. Thus, **learning** can be defined as a relatively permanent influence on behavior, knowledge, and thinking skills that comes about through experience.

Not everything we know is learned. We inherit some capacities—they are inborn, or innate, not learned. For example, we don't have to be taught to swallow, to flinch at loud noises, or to blink when an object comes too close to our eyes. Most human behaviors, however, do not involve heredity alone. When children use a computer

learning A relatively permanent influence on behavior, knowledge, and thinking skills that comes about through experience.

in a new way, work harder at solving problems, ask better questions, explain an answer in a more logical way, or listen more attentively, the experience of learning is at work.

The scope of learning is broad (Domjan, 2010; Klein, 2009). It involves academic behaviors and nonacademic behaviors. It occurs in schools and everywhere else that children experience their world.

APPROACHES TO LEARNING

Approaches to learning can be categorized as behavioral or cognitive.

Behavioral Approach The learning approach that we discuss in the first part of this chapter is called *behavioral*. **Behaviorism** is the view that behavior should be explained by observable experiences, not by mental processes. For the behaviorist, behavior is everything that we do, both verbal and nonverbal, that can be directly seen or heard: a child creating a poster, a teacher explaining something to a child, one student picking on another student, and so on. **Mental processes** are defined by psychologists as the thoughts, feelings, and motives that each of us experiences but that cannot be observed by others. Although we cannot directly see thoughts, feelings, and motives, they are no less real. Mental processes include children thinking about ways to create the best poster, a teacher feeling good about children's efforts, and children's inner motivation to control their behavior.

For the behaviorist, these thoughts, feelings, and motives are not appropriate subject matter for a science of behavior because they cannot be directly observed (Shanks, 2009). *Classical conditioning* and *operant conditioning*, two behavioral views that we will discuss shortly, adopt this stance. Both of these views emphasize **associative learning,** which consists of learning that two events are connected or associated (Olson & Hergenhahn, 2009). For example, associative learning occurs when a student associates a pleasant event with learning something in school, such as the teacher smiling when the student asks a good question.

Cognitive Approaches *Cognition* means "thought," and psychology became more cognitive, or began focusing more on thought, in the last part of the twentieth century. The cognitive emphasis continues today and is the basis for numerous approaches to learning (Ashcraft & Radvansky, 2010; Martinez, 2010). We discuss four main cognitive approaches to learning in this book: social cognitive; information processing; cognitive constructivist; and social constructivist. The *social cognitive* approaches emphasize how behavior, environment, and person (cognitive) factors interact to influence learning (Bandura, 2009, 2010a). The *information-processing* approaches focus on how children process information through attention, memory, thinking, and other cognitive processes (Martinez, 2010). The *cognitive constructivist* approaches emphasize the child's cognitive construction of knowledge and understanding (Halford, 2008). The *social constructivist* approaches focus on collaboration with others to produce knowledge and understanding (Holzman, 2009).

Adding these four cognitive approaches to the behavioral approaches, we arrive at five main approaches to learning that we discuss in this book: behavioral, social cognitive, information processing, cognitive constructivist, and social constructivist. All contribute to our understanding of how children learn. A summary of the five approaches is presented in Figure 11.1.

As you read Chapters 11 and 12 on learning and cognition, keep in mind that students are more likely to learn in optimal ways in appropriate learning environments. Such learning environments should be tailored to specific learning goals, to the students' backgrounds and prior knowledge, and to the contexts in which learning will occur. Thus teachers not only need to understand the basic principles of learning but must also know how to use them to meet diverse learning goals in contexts where students' needs differ (Bransford & others, 2005, p. 78).

Thinking Back/Thinking Forward

Piaget's theory is a cognitive constructivist approach. Chapter 10, p. 283

Vygotksy's theory is a social constructivist approach. Chapter 10, p. 294

behaviorism The view that behavior should be explained by observable experiences, not by mental processes.

mental processes Thoughts, feelings, and motives that cannot be observed by others.

associative learning Learning that two events are connected (associated).

Behavioral	**Social Cognitive**	**Information-Processing**	**Cognitive Constructivist**	**Social Constructivist**
Emphasis on experiences, especially reinforcement and punishment as determinants of learning and behavior	Emphasis on interaction of behavior, environment, and person (cognitive) factors as determinants of learning	Emphasis on how children process information through attention, memory, thinking, and other cognitive processes	Emphasis on the child's cognitive construction of knowledge and understanding	Emphasis on collaboration with others to produce knowledge and understanding
First part of this chapter (11)	**Last part of this chapter (11)**	**Chapter 12**	**Chapter 10 (Piaget) and some parts of Chapter 12**	**Chapter 10 (Vygotsky)**

FIGURE **11.1** APPROACHES TO LEARNING

Review, Reflect, and Practice

1 Define learning and describe five approaches to studying it.

REVIEW

- What is learning? Are there any behaviors that don't reflect learning?
- What essentially is behaviorism? What are four main cognitive approaches to learning?

REFLECT

- How do you learn? Think of a behavior you engage in and describe how you learned it.

PRAXIS™ PRACTICE

1. According to the psychological definition of learning, all of the following are examples of learning *except*
   a. writing.
   b. sneezing.
   c. swimming.
   d. washing dishes.
2. Mr. Zeller does not believe his students have learned anything unless they demonstrate it to him. This demonstration could be through assignments they turn in to him, answering questions in class, or the way they behave. Which approach to learning is most consistent with Mr. Zeller's ideas?
   a. cognitive
   b. behavioral
   c. social cognitive
   d. conditioning

   Please see the answer key at the end of the book.

2 BEHAVIORAL APPROACH TO LEARNING

Classical Conditioning	Operant Conditioning

The behavioral approach emphasizes the importance of children making connections between experiences and behavior. It includes two views: classical conditioning and operant conditioning.

Before Conditioning

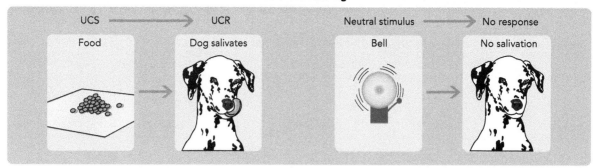

Conditioning

After Conditioning

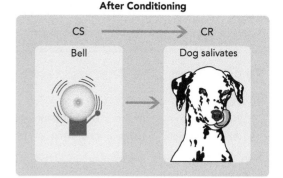

FIGURE **11.2** PAVLOV'S CLASSICAL CONDITIONING

In one experiment, Pavlov presented a neutral stimulus (bell) just before an unconditioned stimulus (food). The neutral stimulus became a conditioned stimulus by being paired with the unconditioned stimulus. Subsequently, the conditioned stimulus (bell) by itself was able to elicit the dog's salivation.

CLASSICAL CONDITIONING

Classical conditioning is a type of learning in which an organism learns to connect, or associate, stimuli so that a neutral stimulus (such as the sight of a person) becomes associated with a meaningful stimulus (such as food) and acquires the capacity to elicit a similar response. Classical conditioning was the brainchild of Ivan Pavlov (1927). To fully understand Pavlov's theory of classical conditioning, we need to understand two types of stimuli and two types of responses: unconditioned stimulus (UCS), unconditioned response (UCR), conditioned stimulus (CS), and conditioned response (CR).

Figure 11.2 summarizes the way classical conditioning works. An *unconditioned stimulus (UCS)* is a stimulus that automatically produces a response without any prior learning. Food was the UCS in Pavlov's experiments. An *unconditioned response (UCR)* is an unlearned response that is automatically elicited by the UCS. In Pavlov's experiments, the dog's salivation in response to food was the UCR. A *conditioned stimulus (CS)* is a previously neutral stimulus that eventually elicits a conditioned response after being associated with the UCS. Among the conditioned stimuli in Pavlov's experiments were various sights and sounds that occurred prior to the dog's actually eating the food, such as the sound of the door closing before the food was placed in the dog's dish. A *conditioned response (CR)* is a learned response to the conditioned stimulus that occurs after UCS-CS pairing.

Classical conditioning can be involved in both positive and negative experiences of children in the classroom. Among the things in the child's schooling that produce pleasure because they have become classically conditioned are a favorite song and feelings that the classroom is a safe and fun place to be. For example, a song could

classical conditioning A form of associative learning in which a neutral stimulus becomes associated with a meaningful stimulus and acquires the capacity to elicit a similar response.

be neutral for the child until he joins in with other classmates to sing it with accompanying positive feelings.

Children can develop fear of the classroom if they associate the classroom with criticism, so the criticism becomes a CS for fear. Classical conditioning also can be involved in test anxiety. For example, a child fails and is criticized, which produces anxiety; thereafter, she associates tests with anxiety, so they then can become a CS for anxiety (see Figure 11.3).

Some children's health problems also might involve classical conditioning (Chance, 2009). Certain physical complaints—asthma, headaches, and high blood pressure—might be partly due to classical conditioning. We usually say that such health problems can be caused by stress. Often what happens, though, is that certain stimuli, such as a parent's or teacher's heavy criticism, are conditioned stimuli for physiological responses. Over time, the frequency of the physiological responses can produce a health problem. A teacher's persistent criticism of a student can cause the student to develop headaches, muscle tension, and so on. Anything associated with the teacher, such as classroom learning exercises and homework, might trigger the student's stress and subsequently be linked with headaches or other physiological responses.

Generalization, Discrimination, and Extinction   In studying a dog's responses to various stimuli, Pavlov rang a bell before giving meat powder to the dog. By being paired with the UCS (meat), the bell became a CS and elicited the dog's salivation. After a time, Pavlov found that the dog also responded to other sounds, such as a whistle. The more bell-like the noise, the stronger was the dog's response. *Generalization* in classical conditioning involves the tendency of a new stimulus similar to the original conditioned stimulus to produce a similar response (Pearce & Hall, 2009). Let's consider a classroom example. A student is criticized for poor performance on a biology test. When the student begins to prepare for a chemistry test, she also becomes very nervous because these two subjects are closely related in the sciences. Thus, the student's anxiety generalizes from taking a test in one subject to taking a test in another.

Discrimination in classical conditioning occurs when the organism responds to certain stimuli but not others. To produce discrimination, Pavlov gave food to the dog only after ringing the bell, not after any other sounds. Subsequently, the dog responded only to the bell. In the case of the student taking tests in different classes, she doesn't become nearly as nervous about taking an English test or a history test because they are very different subject areas.

Extinction in classical conditioning involves the weakening of the conditioned response (CR) in the absence of the unconditioned stimulus (UCS). In one session, Pavlov rang the bell repeatedly but did not give the dog any food. Eventually the dog stopped salivating at the sound of the bell. Similarly, if a student who gets nervous while taking tests begins to do much better on tests, his anxiety will fade.

Systematic Desensitization   Sometimes the anxiety and stress associated with negative events can be eliminated by classical conditioning (Maier & Seligman, 2009). **Systematic desensitization** is a method based on classical conditioning that reduces anxiety by getting the individual to associate deep relaxation with successive visualizations of increasingly anxiety-producing situations. Imagine that you have a student in your class who is extremely nervous about talking in front of the class. The goal of systematic desensitization is to get the student to associate public speaking with relaxation, such as walking on a quiet beach, rather than anxiety. Using successive visualizations, the student might practice systematic desensitization two weeks before the talk, then a week before, four days before, two days before, the day before, the morning of the talk, on entering the room where the talk is to be given, on the way to the podium, and during the talk.

FIGURE **11.3** CLASSICAL CONDITIONING INVOLVED IN TEACHERS' CRITICISM OF CHILDREN AND TESTS

systematic desensitization A method based on classical conditioning that reduces anxiety by getting the individual to associate deep relaxation with successive visualizations of increasingly anxiety-provoking situations.

B. F. Skinner conducting an operant conditioning study in his behavioral laboratory. The rat being studied is in a Skinner box.

Desensitization involves a type of *counterconditioning*. The relaxing feelings that the student imagines (UCS) produce relaxation (UCR). The student then associates anxiety-producing cues (CS) with the relaxing feelings. Such relaxation is incompatible with anxiety. By initially pairing a weak anxiety-producing cue with relaxation and gradually working up the hierarchy (from two weeks before the talk to walking up to the podium to give the talk), all of the anxiety-producing cues should generate relaxation (CR).

Chances are you will have students who fear speaking in front of the class or have other anxieties, and there may be circumstances in your own life where you might benefit from replacing anxiety with relaxation. For example, it is not unusual for some teachers to feel comfortable when talking in front of their students but to get nervous if asked to give a presentation at a teaching conference. Counselors and mental health professionals have been successful at getting individuals to overcome their fear of public speaking using systematic desensitization. Should you be interested in adopting this strategy, do it with the help of a school psychologist rather than on your own.

Evaluating Classical Conditioning   Classical conditioning helps us understand some aspects of learning better than others (Domjan, 2010). It excels in explaining how neutral stimuli become associated with unlearned, involuntary responses (Rescorla, 2009). It is especially helpful in understanding students' anxieties and fears (Klein, 2009). However, it is not as effective in explaining voluntary behaviors, such as why a student studies hard for a test or likes history better than geography. For these areas, operant conditioning is more relevant.

OPERANT CONDITIONING

Operant conditioning (also called *instrumental conditioning*) is a form of learning in which the consequences of behavior produce changes in the probability that the behavior will occur. Operant conditioning is at the heart of B. F. Skinner's (1938) behavioral view. Consequences—rewards and punishments—are contingent on the organism's behavior.

Reinforcement and Punishment   A **reinforcement (reward)** is a consequence that increases the probability that a behavior will occur. In contrast, **punishment** is a consequence that decreases the probability a behavior will occur. For example, you might tell one of your students, "Congratulations. I'm really proud of the story that you wrote." If the student works harder and writes an even better story the next time, your positive comments are said to reinforce, or reward, the student's writing behavior. If you frown at a student for talking in class and the student's talking decreases, your frown is said to punish the student's talking.

To reinforce behavior means to strengthen the behavior (Domjan, 2010). Two forms of reinforcement are positive reinforcement and negative reinforcement. In **positive reinforcement,** the frequency of a response increases because it is followed by a rewarding stimulus, as in the example in which the teacher's positive comments increased the student's writing behavior. Similarly, complimenting parents on being at a parent-teacher conference might encourage them to come back again.

Conversely, in **negative reinforcement,** the frequency of a response increases because it is followed by the removal of an aversive (unpleasant) stimulus. For example, a father nags at his son to do his homework. He keeps nagging. Finally, the son gets tired of hearing the nagging and does his homework. The son's response (doing his homework) removed the unpleasant stimulus (nagging).

One way to remember the distinction between positive and negative reinforcement is that in positive reinforcement something is added. In negative reinforcement, something is subtracted, or removed. It is easy to confuse negative reinforcement and

operant conditioning Also called *instrumental conditioning,* this is a form of learning in which the consequences of behavior produce changes in the probability that the behavior will occur.

reinforcement (reward) A consequence that increases the probability that a behavior will occur.

punishment A consequence that decreases the probability that a behavior will occur.

positive reinforcement Reinforcement based on the principle that the frequency of a response increases because it is followed by a rewarding stimulus.

negative reinforcement Reinforcement based on the principle that the frequency of a response increases because an aversive (unpleasant) stimulus is removed.

Positive Reinforcement

Behavior:
Student asks a good question

Consequence:
Teacher praises student

Future behavior:
Student asks more good questions

Negative Reinforcement

Behavior:
Student turns homework in on time

Consequence:
Teacher stops criticizing student

Future behavior:
Student increasingly turns homework in on time

Punishment

Behavior:
Student interrupts teacher

Consequence:
Teacher verbally reprimands
student

Future behavior:
Student stops interrupting teacher

Remember that reinforcement comes in positive and negative forms. In both forms,
the consequences increase behavior. In punishment, behavior is decreased.

FIGURE **11.4** REINFORCEMENT AND PUNISHMENT

punishment. To keep these terms straight, remember that negative reinforcement *increases* the probability a response will occur, whereas punishment *decreases* the probability it will occur. Figure 11.4 summarizes and presents examples of the concepts of positive reinforcement, negative reinforcement, and punishment.

Generalization, Discrimination, and Extinction   In our coverage of classical conditioning, we discussed generalization, discrimination, and extinction. These processes also are important dimensions of operant conditioning (Chance, 2009). Remember that in classical conditioning, *generalization* is the tendency of a stimulus similar to the conditioned stimulus to produce a response similar to the conditioned response. Generalization in operant conditioning means giving the *same* response to similar stimuli. Especially of interest is the extent to which behavior generalizes from one situation to another. For example, if a teacher praises the student for asking good questions related to English, will this generalize to stimulating the student to do harder work in history, math, and other subjects?

Remember that in classical conditioning, *discrimination* means responding to certain stimuli but not others. Discrimination in operant conditioning involves differentiating among stimuli or environmental events. For example, a student knows that the tray on the teacher's desk labeled "Math" is where she is supposed to place today's math work, whereas another tray labeled "English" is where today's English assignments are to be put. This might sound overly simple, but it is important because students' worlds are filled with many such discriminative stimuli. Around school these discriminative stimuli might include signs that say "Stay Out," "Form a Line Here," and so on.

In operant conditioning, *extinction* occurs when a previously reinforced response is no longer reinforced and the response decreases. In the classroom, the most common use of extinction is for the teacher to withdraw attention from a behavior that the attention is maintaining. For example, in some cases a teacher's attention inadvertently reinforces a student's disruptive behavior, as when a student pinches another student and the teacher immediately talks with the perpetrator. If this happens on a regular basis, the student might learn that pinching other students is a good way to get the teacher's attention. If the teacher withdraws his attention, the pinching might be extinguished.

Review, Reflect, and Practice

 Compare classical conditioning and operant conditioning.

REVIEW

- What is classical conditioning? What are the UCS, UCR, CS, and CR? In the context of classical conditioning, what are generalization, discrimination, extinction, and systematic desensitization?
- What is operant conditioning? Explain the different types of reinforcement. Explain punishment. In the context of operant conditioning, what are generalization, discrimination, and extinction?

REFLECT

- Do you think that your emotions are the result of classical conditioning, operant conditioning, or both? Explain.

PRAXIS™ PRACTICE

1. Sylvia is participating in a class spelling bee. The teacher asks her to spell the word *mortgage.* "Don't forget the *t,* don't forget the *t,*" Sylvia says to herself. "M-O-R-T-A-G-E," says Sylvia. "I'm sorry, that's incorrect, Sylvia," says her teacher. One of the students in the back of the class snickers and comments, "Gee, about time Miss Smarty-pants got one wrong. See, she's not so smart." Some other students join in the laughter. Sylvia begins to cry and runs out of the room. After that, Sylvia becomes very anxious about spelling bees. According to classical conditioning theory, what is the conditioned stimulus in this scenario?
   a. the teacher telling her she is incorrect
   b. the other students' laughter
   c. the word *mortgage*
   d. spelling bees
2. Tyler is a fourth-grade student. He loves to crack jokes, often at his teacher's expense. One day he called his teacher, Ms. Bart, "Ms. Fart." Ms. Bart quickly admonished him for his behavior and told him that name-calling was unacceptable. She made him stay after school to discuss his behavior. The other students in the class thought Tyler's nickname for Ms. Bart was hilarious, laughing along with Tyler and later telling him what a good name that was for Ms. Bart. The next day, Tyler again called Ms. Bart by the insulting nickname. According to operant conditioning theory, Tyler continued to use this name in spite of having to stay after school the day before because
   a. the behavior had continued for a lengthy period of time.
   b. he was positively reinforced by his classmates for the behavior.
   c. he was negatively reinforced by his teacher for his behavior.
   d. he was punished by his teacher for his behavior.

Please see the answer key at the end of the book.

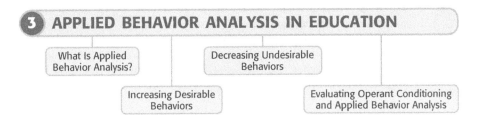

3 APPLIED BEHAVIOR ANALYSIS IN EDUCATION

- What Is Applied Behavior Analysis?
- Decreasing Undesirable Behaviors
- Increasing Desirable Behaviors
- Evaluating Operant Conditioning and Applied Behavior Analysis

Many applications of operant conditioning have been made outside research laboratories in the wider worlds of classrooms, homes, business settings, hospitals, and other real-world settings (Moore Parten & others, 2010; Scarlett, Ponte, & Singh, 2009). This section describes how teachers can use *applied behavior analysis* to improve students' behavior and learning.

WHAT IS APPLIED BEHAVIOR ANALYSIS?

Applied behavior analysis involves applying the principles of operant conditioning to change human behavior. Two uses of applied behavior analysis are especially important in education: increasing desirable behaviors and decreasing undesirable behaviors (Alberto & Troutman, 2009; Kraft, 2010). Applications of applied behavior analysis often use a series of steps (Reed & others, 2010). These typically begin with some general observations, then turn to determining the specific target behavior that needs to be changed, as well as observing its antecedent conditions. Next, behavioral goals are set, particular reinforcers or punishers selected, a behavior management program carried out, and the success or failure of the program evaluated (Dunlap & others, 2010).

INCREASING DESIRABLE BEHAVIORS

Six operant conditioning strategies can be used to increase a child's desirable behaviors: choose effective reinforcers, make reinforcers contingent and timely, select the best schedule of reinforcement, consider contracting, use negative reinforcement effectively, and use prompts and shaping.

Choose Effective Reinforcers   Not all reinforcers are the same for every child. Applied behavior analysts recommend that teachers find out what reinforcers work best with which children—that is, individualize the use of particular reinforcers (Scarlett, Ponte, & Singh, 2009). For one student it might be praise, for another it might be getting to spend more time participating in a favorite activity, for another it might involve being a hall monitor for a week, and for yet another it could be getting to surf the Internet. To find out the most effective reinforcers for a child, you can examine what has motivated the child in the past (reinforcement history), what the student wants but can't easily or frequently get, and the child's perception of the reinforcer's value. Some applied behavior analysts recommend asking children which reinforcers they like best. Another recommendation is to consider novel reinforcers to reduce the child's boredom. Natural reinforcers such as praise and privileges are generally recommended over material rewards such as candy, stars, and money.

Activities are some of the most common reinforcers that teachers use. Named after psychologist David Premack, the **Premack principle** states that a high-probability activity can serve as a reinforcer for a low-probability activity. The Premack principle

"Once it became clear to me that, by responding correctly to certain stimuli, I could get all the bananas I wanted, getting this job was a pushover."

© Jack Ziegler/The New Yorker Collection/www.cartoonbank.com

Thinking Back/Thinking Forward

Applied behavior analysis can be used as part of managing the classroom effectively.

---

applied behavior analysis Application of the principles of operant conditioning to change human behavior.

Premack principle The principle that a high-probability activity can serve as a reinforcer for a low-probability activity.

is at work when an elementary school teacher tells a child, "When you complete your writing assignment, you can play a game on the computer" (but only effective if playing games on a computer is more desirable for the student than writing). The Premack principle also can be used with the entire class. A teacher might tell the class, "If all of the class gets their homework done by Friday, we will take a field trip next week."

Make Reinforcers Contingent and Timely For a reinforcer to be effective, the teacher must give it only after the child performs the particular behavior. Applied behavior analysts often recommend that teachers make "If . . . then" statements to children—for example, "Tony, if you finish 10 math problems, then you can go out to play." This makes it clear to Tony what he has to do to get the reinforcer. It is important to make the reinforcer contingent on the child's behavior. That is, the child has to perform the behavior to get the reward. If Tony does not complete 10 math problems and the teacher still lets him go out to play, the contingency has not been established.

Reinforcers are more effective when they are given in a timely way, as soon as possible after the child performs the target behavior (Umbreit & others, 2007). This helps children see the contingency connection between the reward and their behavior. If the child completes the target behavior (such as doing 10 math problems by midmorning) and the teacher doesn't give the child playtime until late afternoon, he might have trouble making the contingency connection.

Select the Best Schedule of Reinforcement Most of the examples given so far assume continuous reinforcement—that is, the child is reinforced every time he or she makes a response. In continuous reinforcement, children learn very rapidly, but when the reinforcement stops (for example, the teacher stops praising), extinction also occurs rapidly. In the classroom, continuous reinforcement is rare. A teacher with a classroom of 25 or 30 students can't praise a child every time he or she makes an appropriate response.

Partial reinforcement involves reinforcing a response only part of the time. Skinner (1957) developed the concept of **schedules of reinforcement,** which are partial reinforcement timetables that determine when a response will be reinforced. The four main schedules of reinforcement are fixed-ratio, variable-ratio, fixed-interval, and variable-interval.

On a *fixed-ratio schedule,* a behavior is reinforced after a set number of responses. For example, a teacher might praise the child only after every fourth correct response, not after every response. On a *variable-ratio schedule,* a behavior is reinforced after an average number of times, but on an unpredictable basis. For example, a teacher's praise might average out to being given every fifth response but be given after the second correct response, after eight more correct responses, after the next seven correct responses, and after the next three correct responses.

Interval schedules are determined by the amount of time elapsed since the last behavior was reinforced. On a *fixed-interval schedule,* the first appropriate response after a fixed amount of time is reinforced. For example, a teacher might praise a child for the first good question the child asks after two minutes have elapsed or give a quiz every week. On a *variable-interval schedule,* a response is reinforced after a variable amount of time has elapsed. On this schedule, the teacher might praise the child's question-asking after three minutes have gone by, then after fifteen minutes have gone by, after seven minutes have gone by, and so on. Giving a pop quiz at uneven intervals is another example of a variable-interval schedule.

What is the effect of using these schedules of reinforcement with children? Initial learning is usually faster with continuous rather than partial reinforcement. In other words, when students are first learning a behavior, continuous reinforcement works better. However, partial reinforcement produces greater persistence and greater

schedules of reinforcement Partial reinforcement timetables that determine when a response will be reinforced.

resistance to extinction than continuous reinforcement does. Thus, once children master a response, partial reinforcement works better than continuous reinforcement.

Children on fixed schedules show less persistence and faster response extinction than children on variable schedules (Waller & Higbee, 2010). Children show the most persistence on a variable-interval schedule. This schedule produces slow, steady responding because children don't know when the reward will come (Borrero & others, 2010). As we mentioned earlier, giving pop quizzes at uneven intervals is a good example of the variable-interval schedule. If the teacher starts making the quizzes more predictable (for example, once a week on Fridays), children will begin to show the stop-start work pattern that characterizes the fixed-interval schedule. That is, they won't work hard for most of the week; then toward the end of the week they will start cramming for the quiz. Thus, if your goal as a teacher is to increase children's persistence after the behavior has been established, variable schedules work best, especially the variable-interval schedule. Figure 11.5 shows the different response patterns associated with the different schedules of reinforcement.

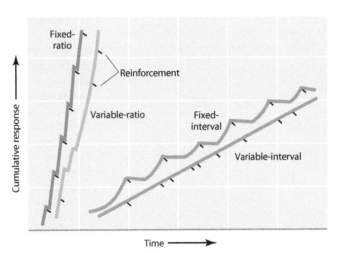

FIGURE 11.5 SCHEDULES OF REINFORCEMENT AND DIFFERENT PATTERNS OF RESPONDING

In this figure, each hash mark indicates the delivery of reinforcement. Notice that ratio schedules (reinforcement is linked with number of responses) produce higher rates of responding than interval schedules (reinforcement is linked with the amount of time elapsed). The predictability of a reward also is important in that a predictable (fixed) schedule produces a higher response rate than an unpredictable (variable) schedule.

Consider Contracting   In **contracting,** reinforcement contingencies are put in writing. If problems arise and children don't uphold their end of the bargain, the teacher can refer the children to the contract they agreed to. Applied behavior analysts suggest that a classroom contract should be the result of input from both the teacher and the student. Classroom contracts have "If . . . then" statements and are signed by the teacher and child, then dated. A teacher and child might agree on a contract that states that the child agrees to be a good citizen by doing _____, _____, and _____. As part of the contract, the teacher agrees to _____ if the student behaves in this manner. In some instances, the teacher asks another child to sign the contract as a witness to the agreement.

Use Negative Reinforcement Effectively   Remember that in *negative reinforcement,* the frequency of response increases because the response removes an aversive (unpleasant) stimulus (Alberto & Troutman, 2009). A teacher who says, "Thomas, you have to stay in your seat and finish writing your story before you join the other students in making a poster," is using negative reinforcement. The negative condition of being left in his seat while the other children are doing something enjoyable will be removed if Thomas finishes the story he should have completed earlier.

Using negative reinforcement has some drawbacks. Sometimes when teachers try to use this behavioral strategy, children throw a tantrum, run out of the room, or destroy materials. These negative outcomes happen most often when children don't have the skills or capabilities to do what the teacher asks of them.

Use Prompts and Shaping   Earlier in our discussion of operant conditioning, we indicated that discrimination involves differentiating among stimuli or environmental events. Students can learn to discriminate among stimuli or events through differential reinforcement. Two differential reinforcement strategies available to teachers are prompts and shaping (Alberto & Troutman, 2009).

Prompts   A **prompt** is an added stimulus or cue that is given just before a response that increases the likelihood that the response will occur. A reading teacher who holds up a card with the letters *w-e-r-e* and says, "Not was, but . . ." is using a verbal prompt. An art teacher who places the label "Watercolors" on one group of paints and "Oils" on another also is using prompts. Prompts help get behavior going. Once the students consistently show the correct responses, the prompts are no longer needed.

contracting Putting reinforcement contingencies into writing.

prompt An added stimulus or cue that is given just before a response, thus increasing the likelihood the response will recur.

Instructions can be used as prompts (Alberto & Troutman, 2009). For example, as the art period is drawing to a close, the teacher says, "Let's get started on reading." If the students keep doing art, the teacher adds the prompt, "Okay, put away your art materials and come with me over to the reading area." Some prompts come in the form of hints, as when the teacher tells students to line up "quietly." Bulletin boards are common locations for prompts, frequently displaying reminders of class rules, due dates for projects, the location of a meeting, and so on. Some prompts are presented visually, as when the teacher places her hand on her ear when a student is not speaking loudly enough.

Shaping When teachers use prompts, they assume that students can perform the desired behaviors. But sometimes students do not have the ability to perform them. In this case, shaping is required (Peterson, 2008). **Shaping** involves teaching new behaviors by reinforcing successive approximations to a specified target behavior. Initially, you reinforce any response that in some way resembles the target behavior. Subsequently, you reinforce a response that more closely resembles the target, and so on until the student performs the target behavior, and then you reinforce it (Wildman, 2008).

Suppose you have a student who has never completed even 50 percent of her math assignments. You set the target behavior at 100 percent, but you reinforce her for successive approximations to the target. You initially might provide a reinforcer (some type of privilege, for example) when she completes 60 percent, then the next time only when she completes 70 percent, then 80, then 90, and finally 100 percent.

Shaping can be an important tool for the classroom teacher because most students need reinforcement along the way to reaching a learning goal (Chance, 2009). Shaping can be especially helpful for learning tasks that require time and persistence to complete. However, when using shaping, remember to implement it only if the other types of positive reinforcement and prompts are not working. Also remember to be patient. Shaping can require the reinforcement of a number of small steps en route to a target behavior, and these might take place only over an extended period of time.

DECREASING UNDESIRABLE BEHAVIORS

When teachers want to decrease children's undesirable behaviors (such as teasing, hogging a class discussion, or smarting off to the teacher), what are their options? Applied behavior analysts Paul Alberto and Anne Troutman (2009) recommend using these steps in this order:

1. Use differential reinforcement.
2. Terminate reinforcement (extinction).
3. Remove desirable stimuli.
4. Present aversive stimuli (punishment).

Thus, the teacher's first option should be differential reinforcement. Punishment should be used only as a last resort and always in conjunction with providing the child information about appropriate behavior.

Use Differential Reinforcement In *differential reinforcement,* the teacher reinforces behavior that is more desired and different than what the child is doing (Pipkin, Vollmer, & Sloman, 2010). For example, the teacher might reinforce a child for doing learning activities on a computer rather than playing games with it, for being courteous rather than interrupting, for being seated rather than running around the classroom, or for doing homework on time rather than late.

shaping Teaching new behaviors by reinforcing successive approximations to a specified target behavior.

Terminate Reinforcement (Extinction) The strategy of terminating reinforcement involves withdrawing positive reinforcement from a child's inappropriate behavior.

Many inappropriate behaviors are inadvertently maintained by positive reinforcement, especially the teacher's attention. Applied behavior analysts point out that this can occur even when the teacher gives attention to an inappropriate behavior by criticizing, threatening, or yelling at the student.

Many teachers find it difficult to determine whether they are giving too much attention to inappropriate behavior. A good strategy is to get someone to observe your classroom on several occasions and chart the patterns of reinforcement you use with your students (Alberto & Troutman, 2009). If you become aware that you are giving too much attention to a student's inappropriate behavior, ignore that behavior and give attention to the student's appropriate behavior. Always combine taking attention away from inappropriate behavior with giving attention to appropriate behavior. For instance, when a student stops monopolizing the conversation in a group discussion after you withdraw your attention, compliment the student on the improved behavior.

TEACHING CONNECTIONS: Best Practices
Strategies for Using Time-Out

In using time-out, you have several options:

1. *Keep the student in the classroom, but deny the student access to positive reinforcement.* This strategy is most often used when the student misbehaves in some minor way. The teacher might ask the student to put his head down on the desk for a few minutes or might move the student to the periphery of an activity where he can still observe other students experiencing positive reinforcement. In Through the Eyes of Teachers, kindergarten teacher Rosemary Moore describes an innovative use of time-out.

THROUGH THE EYES OF TEACHERS
The Peace Place

Resolving conflicts is always difficult for children. When my kindergartners engaged in power struggles, they often turned to me to referee. I thought it would be much more beneficial if they could arrive at their own compromise. Ownership of the plan would make it more acceptable to all parties. To accomplish this, I put two small chairs in a corner of the room. Above the chairs was a sign that said, "Peace Place." Then when I heard a struggle begin, I would send the parties to this corner. There they sat facing each other with their knees almost touching. Their task was to negotiate a "peace plan." When the plan was agreed upon, they were to come to me. I would listen to their plan and either approve it or send them back for another try. Initially, this took some time, but as the children began to realize that the time they spent arguing was time away from the activity they were arguing about, they arrived at their plan much more quickly. It was a pleasure to watch them grow in their negotiating abilities.

2. *For time-out to be effective, the setting from which the student is removed has to be positively reinforcing, and the setting in which the student is placed has to lack positive reinforcement.* For example, if you seat a student in the hall outside your classroom and students from other classes come down the hall and talk with the student, the time-out is clearly not going to serve its intended purpose.

3. *Before using time-out, be sure to tell the student what behaviors are responsible for the time-out.* For example, say to the student, "You tore up Corey's paper, so go to time-out right now for five minutes." Don't get into an argument with the student or accept lame excuses as to why the student should not get a time-out. If necessary, take the student to the time-out location. If the misbehavior occurs again, identify the behavior once again and repeat the time-out. If the student starts yelling, knocking over furniture, and so on, add time to time-out. Be sure to let the student out of time-out when the designated time away from positive reinforcement is up. Don't comment on how well the student behaved during time-out; just return the student to the prior activity.

4. *Positively reinforce the student's positive behavior when he or she is not in time-out.* Reinforce positive behavior during regular class time. For example, if a student got time-out for disruptive behavior, the teacher can praise her for quietly working on an assignment during class.

5. *Keep records of each time-out session, especially if a time-out room is used.* This will help you monitor effective and ethical use of time-outs.

This second-grade student has been placed in "time-out" for misbehaving. *What is the nature of time-out?*

Remove Desirable Stimuli Suppose you have tried the first two options, and they haven't worked. A third option is to remove desirable stimuli from the student. Two strategies for accomplishing this are time-out and response cost.

Time-Out The most widely used strategy for removing desirable stimuli is **time-out,** in which the student is taken away from positive reinforcement (Kazdin, 2008).

Response Cost A second strategy for removing desirable stimuli involves **response cost,** which refers to taking a positive reinforcer away from a student, as when the student loses certain privileges. For example, after a student misbehaves, the teacher might take away 10 minutes of recess time or the privilege of being a class monitor. Response cost typically involves some type of penalty or fine. As with time-out, response cost should always be used in conjunction with strategies for increasing the student's positive behaviors.

I recently asked teachers how they use applied behavior analysis in their classroom. Following are their responses.

EARLY CHILDHOOD We use applied behavior analysis with our preschoolers by giving time-out to students who are misbehaving. For example, if a child throws a

toy across the room during free play, hits another student, or speaks disrespectfully, we explain why this behavior is inappropriate and give time-out. The child has to sit in a chair, away from other students, and misses five minutes of free-play time. As a result, the child learns that negative behavior will not be tolerated.

—MISSY DANGLER, *Suburban Hills School*

ELEMENTARY SCHOOL: GRADES K–5 For my second-grade students, tangible or implied (a smile from me or attention) rewards work best. I also find that a com-

bination of individual and group rewards work well in my classroom. For example, I give each student a "Compliment Sheet" at the beginning of the school year. When I see behavior that I want to encourage, I tell the student publicly that he or she may have a compliment. The student fills in one of the circles on the compliment page, and the others in the class—seeing that this student's particular behavior has been rewarded—imitate the student's behavior almost immediately. The rules are that no compliment may be removed and that a student may not ask for a compliment. When the Compliment Sheet is completed, a big deal is made of it, and the student can go to the prize box and choose a small token such as stickers. At first this is an external way of conditioning behavior, but the children seem to move rapidly from wanting the "thing" to wanting the compliment to wanting the positive attention to doing the right thing.

—JANINE GUIDA POUTRE, *Clinton Elementary School*

MIDDLE SCHOOL: GRADES 6–8 I'm not big on rewards for my sixth-grade students. I think students who act inappropriately in class need to learn how to cope

and deal with controlling their behavior without expecting to receive something in return. Instead of rewards, I give students who turn from negative behavior to positive behavior more responsibility in the classroom. For example, students who engage in good behavior are given classroom jobs—for example, handing out pencils and paper, checking my mailbox in the main office, and turning on/shutting off computers. Students love responsibility and are happy when I depend on them to perform important duties in the classroom.

—FELICIA PETERSON, *Pocantico Hills School*

time-out Removing an individual from positive reinforcement.

response cost Taking a positive reinforcer away from an individual.

HIGH SCHOOL: GRADES 9–12   I set clear expectations for my high school students. For example, it is a classroom expectation that students are in my classroom, ready to work, when the bell rings. Students soon learn that walking in late results in not knowing what is going on in class and may lower their grade if they cannot complete an activity. It is important to start class on time and not let the stragglers determine when class will start.

—**Sandy Swanson,** *Menomonee Falls High School*

What are some effective strategies for using reprimands?

Present Aversive Stimuli (Punishment)   Most people associate the presentation of aversive (unpleasant) stimuli with punishment, as when a teacher yells at a student or a parent spanks a child. However, in accordance with the definition of punishment given earlier in the chapter, an aversive stimulus is punishment only if it decreases the undesirable behavior. All too often, though, aversive stimuli are not effective punishments in that they do not decrease the unwanted behavior and indeed sometimes increase the unwanted behavior over time (Bordin & others, 2009). A history of harsh physical discipline is linked to adolescent depression and externalized problems, such as juvenile delinquency, and is also related to poor school performance (Alyahri & Goodman, 2008; Bender & others, 2007). A recent study found that experiencing harsh corporal punishment in childhood was related to prefrontal cortex volume in young adults (Tomoda & others, 2009). Recall from Chapter 10 that the prefrontal cortex—where thinking, reasoning, and decision making take place—is the brain's highest level.

The most common types of aversive stimuli that teachers use are verbal reprimands. These are more effectively used when the teacher is near the student rather than across the room and when used together with a nonverbal reprimand such as a frown or eye contact. Reprimands are more effective when they are given immediately after unwanted behavior and when they are short and to the point. Such reprimands do not have to involve yelling and shouting, which often just raise the noise level of the classroom and present the teacher as an uncontrolled model for students. Instead, a firmly stated "stop doing that" with eye contact is often sufficient to stop unwanted behavior. Another strategy is to take the student aside and reprimand him in private rather than in front of the entire class.

Many countries, such as Sweden, have banned the physical punishment of schoolchildren (which usually involves school paddling) by principals and teachers (Durrant, 2008). However, in 2003, 23 U.S. states still allowed it, with the greatest prevalence in southern states. A study of college students in 11 countries found that the United States and Canada have more favorable attitudes toward corporal punishment than many other countries (Curran & others, 2001; Hyman & others, 2001) (see Figure 11.6). Use of corporal punishment by parents is legal in every state in America, and it is estimated that 70 to 90 percent of American parents have spanked their children (Straus, 1991). A national survey of U.S. parents with 3- and 4-year-old children found that 26 percent of parents reported spanking their children frequently, and 67 percent of the parents reported yelling at their children frequently (Regaldo & others, 2004).

In U.S. schools, male minority students from low-income backgrounds are the most frequent recipients of physical punishment. Many psychologists and educators argue that physical punishment of students should not be used in any circumstance.

Numerous problems are associated with using aversive stimuli, physical or otherwise, as intended punishment (Durrant, 2008):

* Especially when you use intense punishment such as yelling or screaming, you are presenting students with an out-of-control model for handling stressful situations.

> **Thinking Back/Thinking Forward**
>
> Authoritarian parenting is restrictive and punitive and so is an authoritarian classroom management style. Both are less effective styles than authoritative (rather than authoritarian) parenting and an authoritative classroom management style.

Country	Mean score (5 point scale)	
Canada	3.14	
United States	3.13	
South Korea	3.00	
Malaysia	2.90	
Great Britain	2.68	
Finland	2.34	
Greece	2.26	
Germany	2.13	
Spain	2.05	
Argentina	1.96	
Sweden	1.35	

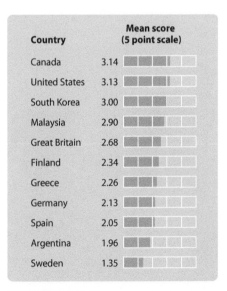

FIGURE **11.6** ATTITUDES ABOUT CORPORAL PUNISHMENT IN DIFFERENT COUNTRIES

A 5-point scale was used to assess attitudes toward corporal punishment, with scores closer to 1 indicating an attitude against its use and scores closer to 5 suggesting an attitude for its use.

- Punishment can instill fear, rage, or avoidance in students. Skinner's biggest concern was this: What punishment teaches is how to avoid something. For example, a student who experiences a punitive teacher might show a dislike for the teacher and not want to come to school.

- When students are punished, they might become so aroused and anxious that they can't concentrate clearly on their work for a long time after the punishment has been given.

- Punishment tells students what not to do rather than what to do. If you make a punishing statement, such as, "No, that's not right," always accompany it with positive feedback, such as, "but why don't you try this."

- What is intended as punishment can turn out to be reinforcing. A student might learn that misbehaving will not only get the teacher's attention but put the student in the limelight with classmates as well.

- Punishment can be abusive. When parents discipline their children, they might not intend to be abusive, but they might become so upset and angry when they are punishing the child that they become abusive. Teachers in all 50 states are legally required to report reasonable suspicions of child abuse to the police or local child protective services. Teachers should learn about their state's laws and their school district's policy regarding the reporting of child abuse (Brodkin, 2009).

A debate about punishment that is ongoing involves a distinction between mild punishment and more intense punishment (Grusec, 2011; Knox, 2010; Thompson, 2009d). A research review of 26 studies concluded that only severe or predominant use of spanking, not mild spanking, compared unfavorably with alternative discipline practices with children (Larzelere & Kuhn, 2005). Indeed, there are few longitudinal studies of punishment and few studies that distinguish adequately between moderate and heavy use of punishment. Thus, in the view of some experts, based on the research evidence available, it is still difficult to tell whether the effects of physical punishment are harmful to children's development—even though the idea that it might not be harmful is distasteful to some individuals (Grusec, 2009). One thing that is clear regarding research on punishment of children is that if physical punishment is used it needs to be mild, infrequent, age-appropriate, and used in the context of a positive parent-child relationship (Grusec, 2011). And also clear is that when physical punishment involves abuse, it can be very harmful to children's development (Cicchetti & Toth, 2011).

A final lesson related to using punishment less often is to spend more class time monitoring what students do right rather than what they do wrong. Too often disruptive behavior, not competent behavior, grabs a teacher's attention. Every day make it a point to scan your classroom for positive student behaviors that you ordinarily would not notice and give students attention for them.

EVALUATING OPERANT CONDITIONING AND APPLIED BEHAVIOR ANALYSIS

Operant conditioning and applied behavior analysis have made contributions to teaching practice (Kraft, 2010; Moore Parten & others, 2010). Reinforcing and punishing consequences are part of teachers' and students' lives. Teachers give grades, praise and reprimand, smile and frown. Learning about how such consequences affect students' behavior improves your capabilities as a teacher. Used effectively, behavioral techniques can help you manage your classroom. Reinforcing certain behaviors can improve some students' conduct and—used in conjunction with time-out—can increase desired behaviors in some incorrigible students.

When used effectively, what are ways that operant conditioning and applied behavior analysis can be used to help teachers manage the classroom? What are some criticisms that have been leveled at these approaches?

TEACHING CONNECTIONS: Best Practices
Strategies for Using Applied Behavior Analysis to Change Behavior

1. *Focus on what you want students to do, rather than on what you want them not to do.* This will help you in using differential reinforcement. If you reinforce desirable behaviors that are incompatible with undesirable behaviors (for instance, being on-task, which is incompatible with being off-task), students will know what it is you want from them. In addition, tell students what they are doing right.

2. *Remember that one size does not fit all when it comes to reinforcement.* It is only reinforcement if the behavior increases. What is reinforcing to one student may be punishing to another. Extra recess may be highly valued by many children, but not by the child whose peers have rejected him/her. There are developmental differences in what students find to be reinforcing. What is reinforcing to first-graders is not likely to be reinforcing to middle school students. A very popular reinforcer among young children is lunch with the teacher. This is often used as punishment at the middle school level.

3. *Teachers often inadvertently reinforce behavior we do not want to continue.* As discussed above, this may be in the form of attention. For some students any attention (even negative) is better than no attention. However, we do it in other ways as well. We might inadvertently negatively reinforce a student's disruptive behavior by sending him/her out of the classroom, and thereby removing what the student considers to be an aversive stimulus (some content area, a test, reading aloud . . .).

4. *When using the Premack principle, we give students information about what they should find enjoyable.* "If you finish your math problems, then you may use the computer." This statement tells young children that using the computer is preferable to completing math problems. Is this a message you want to send?

5. *Teachers are not the only sources of reinforcement and punishment in the classroom.* Classmates often reinforce behavior that we are trying to extinguish. For instance, the class clown is reinforced by laughter from peers. As children develop peers have greater influence, thus reinforcement from peers may become more important than reinforcement from teachers.

6. *Punishment is not punishment unless the behavior decreases.* Just as reinforcement is not one-size-fits-all, neither is punishment. We see similar individual and developmental differences in what children see as punishing.

7. *Taking away recess as punishment (response cost) is a bad idea.* Children need unstructured time to engage in physical activity, play, and socialize (e.g., Pellegrini, 2005). Breaks such as recess can increase young children's attention to academic tasks (Pellegrini, Huberty, & Jones, 1995; Pellegrini & Smith, 1998). Older children and adolescents benefit from recess in similar ways.

8. *Given the problems associated with punishment, it should be a last resort.* Try other ways of getting students to do what it is you want them to do before you resort to punishment.

Critics of operant conditioning and applied behavior analysis argue that the whole approach places too much emphasis on external control of students' behavior; they say a better strategy is to help students learn to control their own behavior and become internally motivated (Eisenberger, 2009). Some critics argue that it is not the reward or punishment that changes behavior but, rather, the belief or expectation that certain actions will be rewarded or punished (Schunk, 2011). In other words, the behavioral theories do not give adequate attention to cognitive processes involved in learning (Anderson, 2009). Critics also point to potential ethical problems when operant conditioning is used inappropriately, as when a teacher immediately resorts to punishing students instead of first considering reinforcement strategies, or punishes a student without also giving the student information about appropriate behavior. Another criticism is that when teachers spend a lot of time using applied behavior analysis, they might focus too much on student conduct and not enough on academic learning.

Thinking Back/Thinking Forward

The new trend in classroom management places more emphasis on guiding students toward self-discipline and less on externally controlling the student.

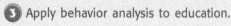

Review, Reflect, and Practice

3 Apply behavior analysis to education.

REVIEW

- What is applied behavior analysis?
- What are six ways to increase desirable behaviors?
- What are four ways to decrease undesirable behaviors?
- What are some effective and ineffective uses of operant conditioning and applied behavior analysis?

REFLECT

- Come up with your own example for each of the six ways to increase desirable behavior in an educational setting.

PRAXIS™ PRACTICE

1. The uses of applied behavior analysis in education include all of the following *except*
   a. asking a child to reflect about undesirable behavior.
   b. increasing desirable behavior.
   c. using prompts and shaping.
   d. decreasing undesirable behavior.

2. Ms. Sanders wants her students to be quiet and ready to learn as soon as possible after coming in from recess. Sometimes the children are so excited that they have difficulty quieting down. To help remind them that it is time to be quiet and listen, Ms. Sanders flicks the light switch on and off several times. The children immediately quiet and listen to her instructions. According to applied behavioral analysis, what is Ms. Sanders doing when she turns the lights on and off?
   a. prompting
   b. punishing
   c. coercing
   d. shaping

3. Sid is a real handful in class. He talks when he should be working quietly. He gets out of his seat without permission. He often disrupts class. His third-grade teacher, Ms. Marin, sends him out into the hall when he misbehaves as a form of time-out. However, Sid continues to misbehave. At one point, Ms. Marin checks on Sid in the hall and finds him quietly tossing a ball back and forth with a child from another class. Why has time-out been ineffective with Sid?
   a. Ms. Marin did not present an aversive enough stimulus to Sid.
   b. Ms. Marin did not use differential reinforcement effectively.
   c. Sid finds being in class to be reinforcing.
   d. Sid finds being in the hallway to be reinforcing.

4. Critics of applied behavior analysis techniques often point out that when these techniques are used in the classroom they
   a. lead to physical abuse of students.
   b. do not work effectively.
   c. take time away from academics.
   d. emphasize external control of behavior.

Please see the answer key at the end of the book.

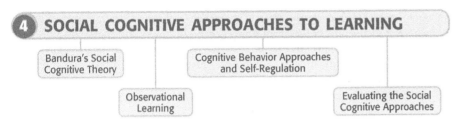

④ SOCIAL COGNITIVE APPROACHES TO LEARNING

- Bandura's Social Cognitive Theory
- Observational Learning
- Cognitive Behavior Approaches and Self-Regulation
- Evaluating the Social Cognitive Approaches

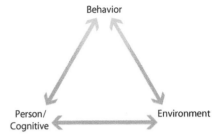

FIGURE 11.7 BANDURA'S SOCIAL COGNITIVE THEORY

Bandura's social cognitive theory emphasizes reciprocal influences of behavior, environment, and person/cognitive factors.

Because students' thoughts affect their behavior and learning, a number of cognitive approaches to learning have been proposed. In this section, we will explore several social cognitive approaches, beginning with social cognitive theory. This theory evolved out of behavioral theories but has become increasingly more cognitive (Spiegler & Guevremont, 2010).

BANDURA'S SOCIAL COGNITIVE THEORY

Social cognitive theory states that social and cognitive factors, as well as behavior, play important roles in learning. Cognitive factors might involve the student's expectations for success; social factors might include students' observing their parents' achievement behavior. Social cognitive theory is an increasingly important source of classroom applications (Schunk, 2011).

Albert Bandura (1986, 1997, 2001, 2009, 2010a,b,c) is the main architect of social cognitive theory. He says that when students learn, they can cognitively represent or transform their experiences. Recall that in operant conditioning, connections occur only between environmental experiences and behavior.

Bandura developed a *reciprocal determinism model* that consists of three main factors: behavior, person/cognitive, and environment. As shown in Figure 11.7, these factors can interact to influence learning: Environmental factors influence behavior, behavior affects the environment, person (cognitive) factors influence behavior, and so on. Bandura uses the term *person*, but I have modified it to *person/cognitive* because so many of the person factors he describes are cognitive. The person factors Bandura describes that do not have a cognitive bent are mainly personality traits and temperament. Cognitive factors include expectations, beliefs, attitudes, strategies, thinking, and intelligence.

Consider how Bandura's model might work in the case of the achievement behavior of a high school student we will call Sondra:

- *Cognition influences behavior.* Sondra develops cognitive strategies to think more deeply and logically about how to solve problems. The cognitive strategies improve her achievement behavior.
- *Behavior influences cognition.* Sondra's studying (behavior) has led her to achieve good grades, which in turn produce positive expectancies about her abilities and give her self-confidence (cognition).
- *Environment influences behavior.* The school Sondra attends recently developed a pilot study-skills program to help students learn how to take notes, manage their time, and take tests more effectively. The study-skills program improves Sondra's achievement behavior.
- *Behavior influences environment.* The study-skills program is successful in improving the achievement behavior of many students in Sondra's class. The students' improved achievement behavior stimulates the school to expand the program so that all students in the high school participate in it.
- *Cognition influences environment.* The expectations and planning of the school's principal and teachers made the study-skills program possible in the first place.

> **Thinking Back/Thinking Forward**
>
> The Big Five Personality Factors are openness, conscientiousness, extraversion, agreeableness, and neuroticism (emotional stability).

Albert Bandura, who developed social cognitive theory.

social cognitive theory Bandura's theory that social and cognitive factors, as well as behavior, play important roles in learning.

Thinking Back/Thinking Forward

Your self-efficacy as a teacher will have an important impact on the quality of learning your students' experience.

FIGURE 11.8 BANDURA'S MODEL OF OBSERVATIONAL LEARNING

In Bandura's model of observational learning, four processes need to be considered: attention, retention, production, and motivation. *How might these processes be involved in this classroom situation in which a teacher is demonstrating how to tell time?*

Thinking Back/Thinking Forward

Four types of attention are selective, divided, sustained, and executive. Chapter 12, p. 348

Thinking Back/Thinking Forward

For memory to work, students have to take information in (encoding), store it or represent it (storage), and retrieve it for some purpose later (retrieval). Chapter 12, p. 353

self-efficacy The belief that one can master a situation and produce positive outcomes.

observational learning Learning that involves acquiring skills, strategies, and beliefs by observing others.

• *Environment influences cognition.* The school establishes a resource center where students and parents can go to check out books and materials on improving study skills. The resource center also makes study-skills tutoring services available to students. Sondra and her parents take advantage of the center's resources and tutoring. These resources and services improve Sondra's thinking skills.

In Bandura's learning model, person/cognitive factors play important roles. The person/cognitive factor that Bandura (2009, 2010a) has emphasized the most in recent years is **self-efficacy,** the belief that one can master a situation and produce positive outcomes. Bandura (2009, 2010a) says that self-efficacy has a powerful influence over behavior. For example, a student who has low self-efficacy might not even try to study for a test because he doesn't believe it will do him any good.

Next we discuss the important learning process of observational learning, which is another of Bandura's main contributions. As you read about observational learning, note how person/cognitive factors are involved.

OBSERVATIONAL LEARNING

Observational learning is learning that involves acquiring skills, strategies, and beliefs by observing others. Observational learning involves imitation but is not limited to it. What is learned typically is not an exact copy of what is modeled but rather a general form or strategy that observers often apply in creative ways (Bandura, 2010b). The capacity to learn behavior patterns by observation eliminates tedious trial-and-error learning. In many instances, observational learning takes less time than operant conditioning.

Processes in Observational Learning Bandura (1986) describes four key processes in observational learning: attention, retention, production, and motivation (see Figure 11.8):

• *Attention.* Before students can produce a model's actions, they must attend to what the model is doing or saying. Attention to the model is influenced by a host of characteristics. For example, warm, powerful, atypical people command more attention than do cold, weak, typical people. Students are more likely to be attentive to high-status models than to low-status models. In most cases, teachers are high-status models for students.

• *Retention.* To reproduce a model's actions, students must code the information and keep it in memory so that they retrieve it. A simple verbal description or a vivid image of what the model did assists students' retention. For example, the teacher might say, "I'm showing the correct way to do this. You have to do this step first, this step second, and this step third," as she models how to solve a math problem. A video with a colorful character demonstrating the importance of considering other students' feelings might be remembered better than the teacher's instruction by itself. Such colorful characters are at the heart of the popularity of *Sesame Street* with children. Students' retention will be improved when teachers give vivid, logical, and clear demonstrations.

FIGURE 11.9 BANDURA'S CLASSIC BOBO DOLL STUDY: THE EFFECTS OF OBSERVATIONAL LEARNING ON CHILDREN'S AGGRESSION

(*Left*) an adult model aggressively attacks the Bobo doll. (*Right*) a kindergarten-age girl who has observed the model's aggressive actions follows suit. *In Bandura's experiment, under what conditions did the children reproduce the model's aggressive actions?*

- *Production.* Children might attend to a model and code in memory what they have seen, yet because of limitations in their motor ability, not be able to reproduce the model's behavior. A 13-year-old might watch basketball player Lebron James and golfer Michelle Wie execute their athletic skills to perfection, or observe a famous pianist or artist, but not be able to reproduce their motor actions. Teaching, coaching, and practice can help children improve their motor performances.
- *Motivation.* Often children attend to what a model says or does, retain the information in memory, and possess the motor skills to perform the action but are not motivated to perform the modeled behavior. This was demonstrated in Bandura's (1965) classic Bobo doll study when children who saw the model being punished did not reproduce the punished model's aggressive actions (see Figure 11.9). However, when they subsequently were given a reinforcement or incentive (stickers or fruit juice), they did imitate the model's behavior.

Bandura argues that reinforcement is not always necessary for observational learning to take place. But if the child does not reproduce the desired behaviors, four types of reinforcement can help do the trick: (1) reward the model; (2) reward the child; (3) instruct the child to make self-reinforcing statements such as, "Good, I did it!" or, "Okay, I've done a good job of getting most of this right; now if I keep trying I will get the rest"; or (4) show how the behavior leads to reinforcing outcomes.

Models in the Classroom   As you can see, you will be an important model in students' lives. Your students will be observing your behavior countless times every day of the school year (Bandura, 2010b). An intentional way that teachers can use observational learning is through *modeled demonstrations,* in which the teacher describes and shows students how to solve problems and successfully complete academic tasks. For example, a teacher might demonstrate how to create an outline for a paper or do a PowerPoint presentation. Also students can become more reflective and think more critically by observing models.

In addition to being a key model yourself for children to observe and learn from, students learn from observing many other models, including parents, mentors, and peers. Students especially are likely to attend to and attempt to learn the behaviors of individuals who are competent and have prestige (Schunk, 2011). For example, a teacher might invite a well-known professional athlete to come to her class and talk about how important reading and doing well in school is. Because of the athlete's prestige, the students are likely to attend to what the athlete says and be motivated to adopt the behaviors she recommends.

Peers also can be important models in the classroom (Schunk, 2011). By observing peers successfully do school tasks, especially peers that a student likes or admires, the student's self-efficacy for performing well in school likely increases.

DIVERSITY

RESEARCH

One concern about the models that children and adolescents observe and interact with in the classroom is the lack of ethnic and gender diversity. As students in U.S. schools have become more ethnically diverse in recent decades, their teachers are still overwhelmingly non-Latino White females. In 2004 approximately 15 percent of U.S. public school students were African American, but just over 7 percent of their teachers were African American (National Center for Education Statistics, 2007). Only a small percentage of the African American teachers were males. In the same year, Latinos made up more than 19 percent of U.S. public school students, but just over 6 percent of their teachers were Latino. A majority of U.S. public schools still do not have a single ethnic minority teacher.

Men comprise about 10 percent of elementary school teachers but comprise nearly half of middle and high school teachers (many of whom are lured by additional incentives for coaching athletic teams). The situation is likely to get worse. In a recent national survey of college students, only .05 percent of males said their probable career would be as an elementary school teacher or administrator, and only 1.8 percent indicated that a similar career in secondary education was likely to be in their future (Pryor & others, 2008).

Regardless of your ethnic background, look around the community for possible mentors for students, especially students who come from low-income backgrounds and who lack positive role models. For example, the aim of the *3-to-1 mentoring program* is to surround each ethnic minority male student with three positive ethnic minority role models. The program began when several African American men were challenged by a sermon delivered by Zach Holmes at the St. Luke's Methodist Church in Dallas. In the sermon, Reverend Holmes urged his congregation to become more involved with children, both their own and children in the community, who don't have good role models. The 3-to-1 mentoring program has signed up more than 200 men and 100 boys (ages 4 to 18). That's far short of the goal of three mentors for each boy, but the men are working on increasing the number of mentors in the program. Some of the men in the mentoring program have their own children, like Dr. Leonard Berry, a physician, who has two sons and a daughter. He heeded the minister's challenge and regularly participates in the mentoring program, which involves academic tutoring as well as outings to activities such as sporting and cultural events. The mentors also take the students to visit the Johnson Space Center in Houston. To evaluate the roles that models and mentors have played in your own life and can play in your students' lives, complete Self-Assessment 11.1.

I recently asked teachers how they use observational learning in the classroom. Following are their responses.

Dr. Leonard Berry is a mentor in the 3-to-1 program in Dallas. He is shown here with Brandon Scarbough, 13 (*front*), and his own son, Leonard, 12 (*back*). Brandon not only has benefited from Dr. Berry's mentoring but also has become friends with his son.

EARLY CHILDHOOD Preschool children spend a lot of time doing informal observation and may try to imitate what someone else has done to see if they can

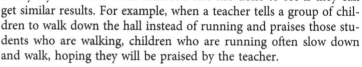

get similar results. For example, when a teacher tells a group of children to walk down the hall instead of running and praises those students who are walking, children who are running often slow down and walk, hoping they will be praised by the teacher.

—HEIDI KAUFMAN, *Metro West YMCA Child Care and Educational Program*

ELEMENTARY SCHOOL: GRADES K–5 My basic assumption with my elementary school students is that they learn appropriate behavior by observation and expe-

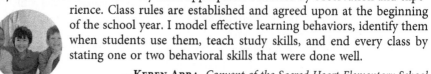

rience. Class rules are established and agreed upon at the beginning of the school year. I model effective learning behaviors, identify them when students use them, teach study skills, and end every class by stating one or two behavioral skills that were done well.

—KEREN ABRA, *Convent of the Sacred Heart Elementary School*

SELF-ASSESSMENT 11.1

Models and Mentors in My Life and My Students' Lives

Having positive role models and mentors can make an important difference in whether individuals develop optimally and reach their full potential. First, evaluate the role models and mentors who have played an important part in your life. Second, think about the type of role model you want to be for your students. Third, give some thought to how you will incorporate other models and mentors into your students' lives. Fourth, explore who your education mentor might be.

MY MODELS AND MENTORS

List the most important role models and mentors in your life. Then describe what their positive modeling and mentoring have meant to your development.

Role Models and Mentors   Their Contributions

1. _____ _____

2. _____ _____

3. _____ _____

4. _____ _____

5. _____ _____

The Type of Role Model I Want to Be for My Students

Describe which characteristics and behaviors you believe are the most important for you to model for your students.

1. _____

2. _____

3. _____

4. _____

5. _____

How Will I Incorporate Models and Mentors in My Classroom?

Describe a systematic plan for bringing models and mentors into your students' lives in one or more domain(s) you plan to teach, such as math, English, science, and music.

_____

_____

Who Will Be My Education Mentor? What Would My Ideal Education Mentor Be Like?

Do you have someone in mind who might serve as an education mentor when you become a teacher? If so, describe the person.

_____

What would your ideal education mentor be like?

_____

_____

MIDDLE SCHOOL: GRADES 6–8 I use observational learning with my sixth-grade students all the time. I make sure that they understand my expectations by not only discussing them but also showing them what I expect. For example, I create checklists for my students at the beginning of the year so they can assess their work and monitor their progress. We then go over the checklists one-on-one and as a group and discuss ways that they can improve their work or behavior in order to reach their desired goals.

—CASEY MAASS, *Edison Middle School*

HIGH SCHOOL: GRADES 9–12 As a high school art teacher, I am fortunate to work in an area that is visual, hands-on, and creative. Through one-on-one demonstrations, small-group and sometimes total class lectures/demonstrations, my students observe and learn artistic skills.

—DENNIS PETERSON, *Deer River High School*

TECHNOLOGY

DEVELOPMENT

What educational lessons can be learned from Sesame Street?

Thinking Back/Thinking Forward

Attention is a key aspect of processing information. Chapter 12, p. 344

Thinking Back/Thinking Forward

Gardner proposed that intelligence consists of eight different domains.

Models in the Media—the Example of Sesame Street Children also are exposed to an extensive number of models in the media, so it's especially important that those experiences be positive. The television show *Sesame Street* is a very effective educational program that includes many positive observational learning opportunities for young children, and is designed to teach both cognitive and social skills (Bryant, 2007). The program began in 1969 and is still going strong. A fundamental message of *Sesame Street* is that education and entertainment work well together (Lesser, 1972). On *Sesame Street*, learning is exciting and entertaining. One study found that preschool children who watched the program were more likely to positively resolve conflicts, make positive comments about others, and engage in less stereotyping than their counterparts who did not watch it (Cole & others, 2003).

Sesame Street also illustrates the point that teaching can be done in both direct and indirect ways. Using the direct way, a teacher tells children exactly what they are going to be taught and then actually teaches it to them. This method is often used on *Sesame Street* to teach cognitive skills. But social skills usually are communicated in indirect ways on the show. Thus, rather than telling children, "You should cooperate with people," a sequence of events is shown to help them figure out what it means to be cooperative and what the advantages are.

Some of the attentional techniques used on *Sesame Street* are worthwhile to consider in the classroom. These involve first *catching* the child's attention, then *directing* it, and finally *sustaining* it. Music and sound are very effective in eliciting children's attention. For example, in teaching children to discriminate sounds, an automobile horn might be sounded or a computer's keyboard repeatedly pressed. Music is especially useful because it leads children to become actively involved in what they are watching or listening to. It is not unusual for children watching *Sesame Street* to get up out of their seats and start dancing and singing along with the jingles. Once the child's attention has been captured, it should be directed to something. Surprise and novelty are especially helpful in this regard; children's attention is directed because they begin to anticipate what is going to happen next. Once attention is directed, it then needs to be sustained. *Sesame Street* especially uses humor to accomplish this. Humor is judiciously placed: Ernie outsmarts Bert; the Cookie Monster annoyingly interrupts a lecture given by Kermit the Frog. For young children, physical gags often are funnier than verbal ones, and much of the humor that is effective involves physical acts that are surprising and incongruous.

TEACHING CONNECTIONS: Best Practices
Strategies for Effectively Using Observational Learning

1. *Think about what type of model you will present to students.* Every day, hour after hour, students will watch and listen to what you say and do. Just by being around you, students will absorb a great deal of information. They will pick up your good or bad habits, your expectations for their high or low achievement, your enthusiastic or bored attitude, your controlled or uncontrolled manner of dealing with stress, your learning style, your gender attitudes, and many other aspects of your behavior. A good strategy, then, is that you behave as you want your students to behave.

2. *Demonstrate and teach new behaviors.* Demonstrating means that you, the teacher, are a model for your students' observational learning. Demonstrating how to do something, from solving a math problem, reading, writing, thinking, to controlling anger or performing physical skills, is a common task for teachers. For example, a teacher might model how to diagram a sentence, develop a strategy for solving algebraic equations, or shoot a basketball. When demonstrating how to do something, you need to call students' attention to the relevant details of the learning situation. Your demonstrations also should be clear and follow a logical sequence.

3. *Think about ways to use peers as effective models.* The teacher is not the only model in the classroom. Children can also pick up their peers' good and bad habits, high or low achievement orientations, and so on, through observational learning. Remember that students are often motivated to imitate high-status models. Older peers usually have higher status than same-age peers. Thus, a good strategy is to have older peers from a higher grade model how to engage in the behaviors you want your students to perform. As children develop, peers increase in importance and therefore their influence increases as well. Older children and adolescents are much more likely to look to their peers as models. For students with low abilities or who are not performing well, another low-achieving student who struggles but puts considerable effort into learning and ultimately performs the behaviors can be a good model.

4. *Think about ways that mentors can be used as models.* Students and teachers benefit from having a mentor—someone they look up to and respect, someone who serves as a competent model, someone who is willing to work with them and help them achieve their goals. Just spending a few hours a week with a mentor can make a difference in a student's life, especially if the student's parents have not been good role models. As a teacher, a potential mentor for you is a more experienced teacher, possibly someone who teaches down the hall and has had a number of years of experience in dealing with some of the same problems and issues you will have to cope with.

5. *Evaluate which classroom guests will provide good models for students.* To change the pace of classroom life for you and your students, invite guests who have something meaningful to talk about or demonstrate. Recall Gardner's theory of multiple intelligences: There likely are some domains (physical, musical, artistic, or other) in which you don't have the skills to serve as a competent model for your students. When you need to have such skills demonstrated to your students, spend some time locating competent models in the community. Invite them to come to your classroom to demonstrate and discuss their skills. If this can't be arranged, set up field trips in which you take students to see them where they are working or performing. In Through the Eyes of Teachers, fourth-grade teacher Marlene Wendler describes a positive role model her school brings to teachers' classrooms.

THROUGH THE EYES OF TEACHERS
Here Comes the Judge

Our local judge has taken a proactive role in trying to eliminate teen behavioral problems. With a half dozen adults from the community, he comes to the fourth-grade classrooms in our areas and puts on skits about bullying. They show the whole group picking on a student in a bus situation. Then they do the skit again with someone in the group stopping the bullying. The students then role-play bullying situations, learning what to do if they are bullied and how to help someone who is bullied. Having the judge come to our school has made a lasting impression on our students.

6. *Consider the models children observe on television, videos, and computers.* Students observe models when they watch television programs, videos, films, or computer screens in your classroom. The principles of observational learning we described earlier apply to these media. For example, the extent to which the students perceive the media models as high or low in status, intriguing or boring, and so on will influence the extent of their observational learning.

TECHNOLOGY

Poster 1
While listening

1. Does this make sense?
2. Am I getting this?
3. I need to ask a question before I forget.
4. Pay attention.
5. Can I do what the teacher is saying to do?

Poster 2
While planning

1. Do I have everything together?
2. Do I have my friends tuned out so I can get this done?
3. I need to get organized first.
4. What order can I do this in?
5. I know this stuff.

Poster 3
While working

1. Am I working fast enough?
2. Stop staring at my girlfriend (boyfriend) and get back to work.
3. How much time is left?
4. Do I need to stop and start all over?
5. This is hard for me but I can manage it.

Poster 4
While checking

1. Did I finish everything?
2. What do I need to recheck?
3. Am I proud of this work?
4. Did I write all of the words?
5. I think I'm finished. I organized myself. Did I daydream too much, though?

FIGURE 11.10 SOME POSTERS DEVELOPED BY A FIFTH-GRADE CLASS TO HELP THEM REMEMBER HOW TO EFFECTIVELY TALK TO THEMSELVES

From Brenda H. Manning and Beverly D. Payne, *Self-Talk for Teachers and Students,* "Four posters developed by a fifth grade class" p. 125, © 1996. Reproduced by permission of Pearson Education, Inc.

cognitive behavior approaches Changing behavior by getting individuals to monitor, manage, and regulate their own behavior rather than letting it be controlled by external factors.

self-instructional methods Cognitive behavior techniques aimed at teaching individuals to modify their own behavior.

COGNITIVE BEHAVIOR APPROACHES AND SELF-REGULATION

Operant conditioning spawned applications and other real-world settings, and the interest in cognitive behavior approaches has also produced such applications. In the fifth century B.C., the Chinese philosopher Confucius said, "If you give a man a fish, you feed him for a day. If you teach a man to fish, you feed him for a lifetime." As you read about the cognitive behavior approaches and self-regulation, you will discover that they reflect Confucius' simple expression.

Cognitive Behavior Approaches In the **cognitive behavior approaches,** the emphasis is on getting students to monitor, manage, and regulate their own behavior rather than letting it be controlled by external factors. In some circles, this has been called *cognitive behavior modification* (Rait, Monsen, & Squires, 2010; Ryum & others, 2010). Cognitive behavior approaches stem from both cognitive psychology, with its emphasis on the effects of thoughts on behavior, and behaviorism, with its emphasis on techniques for changing behavior. Cognitive behavior approaches try to change students' misconceptions, strengthen their coping skills, increase their self-control, and encourage constructive self-reflection (Spiegler & Guevremont, 2010).

Self-instructional methods are cognitive behavior techniques aimed at teaching individuals to modify their own behavior by talking to themselves in positive ways. Following are some self-talk strategies that students and teachers can use to cope more effectively with stressful situations such as preparing to take a test (Meichenbaum, Turk, & Burstein, 1975):

- *Prepare for anxiety or stress.* "What do I have to do?" "I'm going to develop a plan to deal with it." "I'll just think about what I have to do." "I won't worry. Worry doesn't help anything." "I have a lot of different strategies I can use."
- *Confront and handle the anxiety or stress.* "I can meet the challenge." "I'll keep on taking just one step at a time." "I can handle it. I'll just relax, breathe deeply, and use one of the strategies." "I won't think about my stress. I'll just think about what I have to do."
- *Cope with feelings at critical moments.* "What is it I have to do?" "I knew my anxiety might increase. I just have to keep myself in control." "When the anxiety comes, I'll just pause and keep focusing on what I have to do."
- *Use reinforcing self-statements.* "Good, I did it." "I handled it well." "I knew I could do it." "Wait until I tell other people how I did it!"

In many instances, the strategy is simply to replace negative self-statements with positive ones. For example, a student might say to herself, "I'll never get this work done by tomorrow." This can be replaced with positive self-statements such as these: "This is going to be tough, but I think I can do it." "I'm going to look at this as a challenge rather than a stressor." "If I work really hard, I might be able to get it done." Or in having to participate in a class discussion, a student might replace the negative thought of "Everyone else knows more than I do, so what's the use of saying anything" with positive self-statements such as these: "I have as much to say as anyone else." "My ideas may be different, but they are still good." "It's okay to be a little nervous; I'll relax and start talking." Figure 11.10 shows posters that students in one fifth-grade class developed to help them remember how to talk to themselves while listening, planning, working, and checking.

Talking positively to oneself can help teachers as well as students reach their full potential. Uncountered negative thinking has a way of becoming a self-fulfilling prophecy. You think you can't do it, and so you don't. If negative self-talk is a problem for you, at random times during the day ask yourself, "What am I saying to myself right now?" Moments that you expect will be potentially stressful are excellent times to examine your self-talk. Also monitor your students' self-talk. If you hear students saying, "I can't do this" or "I'm so slow I'll never get this done," spend some time getting them to replace their negative self-talk with positive self-talk.

Cognitive behaviorists recommend that students improve their performance by monitoring their own behavior (Schunk, 2011). Such monitoring can involve getting students to keep charts or records of their behavior. When I (your author) wrote this book, I had a chart on my wall with each of the chapters listed. I planned how long it would take me to do each of the chapters, and then as I completed each one I checked it off and wrote down the date of completion. Teachers can get students to do some similar monitoring of their own progress by getting them to keep records of how many assignments they have finished, how many books they have read, how many homework papers they have turned in on time, how many days in a row they have not interrupted the teacher, and so on. In some cases, teachers place these self-monitoring charts on the walls of the classroom. Alternatively, if the teacher thinks that negative social comparison with other students will be highly stressful for some students, then a better strategy might be to have students keep private records (in a notebook, for example) that are periodically checked by the teacher.

Self-monitoring is an excellent strategy for improving learning, and one that you can help students learn to do effectively. By completing Self-Assessment 11.2, you should get a sense of the benefits of self-monitoring for your students.

Self-Regulatory Learning   Educational psychologists increasingly advocate the importance of self-regulatory learning (Winne & Nisbett, 2010). **Self-regulatory learning** consists of the self-generation and self-monitoring of thoughts, feelings, and behaviors in order to reach a goal. These goals might be academic (improving comprehension while reading, becoming a more organized writer, learning how to do multiplication, asking relevant questions) or they might be socioemotional (controlling one's anger, getting along better with peers).

As children become older, their capacity for self-regulation increases (McClelland & others, 2011; Thompson & Goodman, 2009). The increased capacity in self-regulation is linked to developmental advances in the brain's prefrontal cortex, which was discussed in Chapter 10 (Nelson, 2011).

Self-regulatory learners do the following (Winne, 2001, 2005):

- Set goals for extending their knowledge and sustaining their motivation
- Are aware of their emotional makeup and have strategies for managing their emotions
- Periodically monitor their progress toward a goal
- Fine-tune or revise their strategies based on the progress they are making
- Evaluate obstacles that may arise and make the necessary adaptations.

Self-regulation is an important aspect of school readiness (Ponitz & others, 2009). In a recent study, children who could regulate their emotions effectively in early childhood had better math and literacy scores in the early elementary school years than their counterparts who had poor emotion regulation (Graziano & others, 2007).

RESEARCH

Researchers also have found that high-achieving students are often self-regulatory learners (Anderman & Anderman, 2010). For example, compared with low-achieving students, high-achieving students set more specific learning goals, use more strategies to learn, self-monitor their learning more, and more systematically evaluate their progress toward a goal. In one study of adolescents from low-income families, a higher level of self-regulation was linked to higher achievement and better grades (Buckner, Mezzacappa, & Beardslee, 2009).

Researchers have found that teaching students strategies as well as self-regulation skills is critical in many academic areas (Winne & Nesbitt, 2010). For example, most students with writing problems don't have adequate writing strategies to review and assess the quality of a story. Thus, to become better writers they not only need to

self-regulatory learning The self-generation and self-monitoring of thoughts, feelings, and behaviors in order to reach a goal.

SELF-ASSESSMENT 11.2
Self-Monitoring

Self-monitoring can benefit you as well as your students. Many successful learners regularly self-monitor their progress to see how they are doing in their effort to complete a project, develop a skill, or perform well on a test or other assessment. For the next month, self-monitor your study time for this course you are taking in educational psychology. To achieve high grades, most instructors recommend that students spend two or three hours out of class studying, doing homework, and working on projects for every hour they are in class in college (Santrock & Halonen, 2009). The experience of self-monitoring your own study time should give you a sense of how important such skills are for your students to develop. You might adapt this form for students' homework, for example. Remember from our discussion of Bandura's social cognitive theory that self-efficacy involves your belief that you can master a situation and produce positive outcomes. One way to evaluate self-efficacy is your expectancy for attaining a particular score on an upcoming quiz or test. Determine what score or grade you want to achieve on your next quiz or test. Then each day you study, rate your self-efficacy for achieving the score you desire on a 3-point scale: 1 = not very confident, 2 = moderately confident, and 3 = very confident.

FORM FOR SELF-MONITORING STUDY TIME

Date	Assignment	Time Started	Time Finished	STUDY CONTEXT			
				Where?	With Whom?	Distractions	Self-Efficacy

learn self-regulation skills but also need training in writing strategy instruction (Harris & others, 2008).

Teachers, tutors, mentors, counselors, and parents can help students become self-regulatory learners. Barry Zimmerman, Sebastian Bonner, and Robert Kovach (1996) developed a model for turning low-self-regulatory students into students who engage in these multistep strategies: (1) self-evaluation and monitoring, (2) goal setting and strategic planning, (3) putting a plan into action and monitoring it, and (4) monitoring outcomes and refining strategies (see Figure 11.11).

Zimmerman and colleagues describe a seventh-grade student who is doing poorly in history and apply their self-regulatory model to her situation. In step 1, she self-evaluates her studying and test preparation by keeping a detailed record of them. The teacher gives her some guidelines for keeping these records. After several weeks, the student turns the records in and traces her poor test performance to low comprehension of difficult reading material.

FIGURE **11.11** A MODEL OF SELF-REGULATORY LEARNING

In step 2, the student sets a goal, in this case of improving reading comprehension, and plans how to achieve the goal. The teacher assists her in breaking the goal into components, such as locating main ideas and setting specific goals for understanding a series of paragraphs in her textbook. The teacher also provides the student with strategies, such as focusing initially on the first sentence of each paragraph and then scanning the others as a means of identifying main ideas. Another support the teacher might offer the student if available is adult or peer tutoring in reading comprehension.

In step 3, the student puts the plan into action and begins to monitor her progress. Initially, she may need help from the teacher or tutor in identifying main ideas in the reading. This feedback can help her monitor her reading comprehension more effectively on her own.

In step 4, the student monitors her improvement in reading comprehension by evaluating whether it has had any impact on her learning outcomes. Most importantly, has her improvement in reading comprehension led to better performance on history tests?

Suppose that self-evaluations in this case reveal that the strategy of finding main ideas has only partly improved her comprehension, and only when the first sentence contains the paragraph's main idea. Consequently, the teacher recommends further strategies. Figure 11.12 describes how teachers can apply the self-regulatory model to homework.

The development of self-regulation is influenced by many factors, among them modeling and self-efficacy (Bandura, 2010a,b). Consider how modeling can be an effective strategy for building self-regulatory skills and self-efficacy in improving reading and writing in Zimmerman's four-phase model (Schunk & Zimmerman, 2006). Among the self-regulatory skills that models can engage in are planning and managing time effectively, attending to and concentrating, organizing and coding information strategically, establishing a productive work environment, and using social resources. For example, students might observe a teacher engage in an effective time management strategy and verbalize appropriate principles. By observing such models, students can come to believe that they also can plan and manage time effectively, which creates a sense of self-efficacy for academic self-regulation and motivates students to engage in those activities.

Self-efficacy can influence a student's choice of tasks, effort expended, persistence, and achievement (Bandura, 2010a). Compared with students who doubt their learning capabilities, those with high self-efficacy for acquiring a skill or performing a task participate more readily, work harder, persist longer in the face of difficulty, and achieve at a higher level. Yet self-efficacy is not the only influence on achievement.

FIGURE 11.12 APPLYING THE SELF-REGULATORY MODEL TO HOMEWORK

1. Self-evaluation and monitoring

- The teacher distributes forms so that students can monitor specific aspects of their studying.

- The teacher gives students daily assignments to develop their self-monitoring skills and a weekly quiz to assess how well they have learned the methods.

- After several days, the teacher begins to have students exchange their homework with their peers. The peers are asked to evaluate the accuracy of the homework and how effectively the student engaged in self-monitoring. Then the teacher collects the homework for grading and reviews the peers' suggestions.

2. Goal setting and strategic planning

- After a week of monitoring and the first graded exercise, the teacher asks students to give their perceptions of the strengths and weaknesses of their study strategies. The teacher emphasizes the link between learning strategies and learning outcomes.

- The teacher and peers recommend specific strategies that students might use to improve their learning. Students may use the recommendations or devise new ones. The teacher asks students to set specific goals at this point.

3. Putting a plan into action and monitoring it

- The students monitor the extent to which they actually enact the new strategies.

- The teacher's role is to make sure that the new learning strategies are openly discussed.

4. Monitoring outcomes and refining strategies

- The teacher continues to give students opportunities to gauge how effectively they are using their new strategies.

- The teacher helps students summarize their self-regulatory methods by reviewing each step of the self-regulatory learning cycle. She also discusses with students the hurdles the students had to overcome and the self-confidence they have achieved.

What are some contributions of the social cognitive approaches to educating children? What are some criticisms of these approaches?

High self-efficacy will not result in competent performance when requisite knowledge and skills are lacking.

Teachers who encourage students to be self-regulatory learners convey the message that students are responsible for their own behavior, for becoming educated, and for becoming contributing citizens to society. Another message conveyed by self-regulatory learning is that learning is a personal experience that requires active and dedicated participation by the student.

EVALUATING THE SOCIAL COGNITIVE APPROACHES

The social cognitive approaches have made important contributions to educating children (Spiegler & Guevremont, 2010). While keeping the behaviorists' scientific flavor and emphasis on careful observation, they significantly expanded the emphasis of learning to include social and cognitive factors. Considerable learning occurs through watching and listening to competent models and then imitating what they do. The emphasis in the cognitive behavior approach on self-instruction, self-talk, and self-regulatory learning provides an important shift from learning controlled by others to responsibility for one's own learning (Spiegler & Guevremont, 2010). These self-enacted strategies can significantly improve students' learning.

TEACHING CONNECTIONS: Best Practices
Strategies for Encouraging Students to Be Self-Regulated Learners

Following are some effective strategies for guiding students to engage in self-regulated learning:

1. *Gradually guide students to become self-regulated learners.* Helping students become self-regulated learners takes time and requires considerable monitoring, guidance, and encouragement on your part. High-achieving students are more likely to already be self-regulated learners than low-achieving students. All students can benefit from practicing their self-regulated learning skills, but recognize that low-achieving students will need more instruction and time to develop these skills. We should start this in very early elementary school and gradually increase the requirement and opportunity for self-regulation until in high school students are largely self-regulated. In early elementary years, we might do this by giving the children a week to complete all the learning center activities we have prepared, but allowing them to choose in what order they accomplish them. They would check them off as they complete them and we would monitor their progress throughout the week. Later, we might assign students to read a book and write a report about it. Students would determine how long they are going to allow for each piece of the assignment. Again, we would monitor their progress toward the goal of a completed book report, perhaps having interim due dates. Finally, at the high school level, students would be responsible for doing their own progress monitoring unless they request help.

2. *Make the classroom learning experience challenging and interesting for students.* When students are bored and uninterested in learning, they are less likely to become self-regulated learners. Instead of giving students one particular book to read, providing them with a choice from a variety of interesting books is likely to encourage their motivation to read. Giving students choices increases students' personal investment in their learning and increases their self-regulation (Blumenfeld, Kempler & Krajcik, 2006).

3. *Provide tips about thoughts and actions that will help students engage in self-regulation.* These might include specific guidelines, such as, "Planning for 30 minutes will help you . . ." and, "Every day stop and monitor where you are in what you want to accomplish." Other suggestions include encouraging students to reflect on their strengths and weaknesses in a learning situation and encouraging them to search for help and ways to use help effectively (All Kinds of Minds, 2009).

4. *Give students opportunities to experience the type of activities recommended by Zimmerman and his colleagues (1996).* That is, create projects for students in which they self-evaluate their current learning, set a goal to improve their learning and plan how to reach the goal, put the plan into action and monitor their progress toward the goal, and monitor the outcome and refine their strategies. Monitor students' progress through these steps and encourage their ability to engage in these learning activities independently. Provide scaffolding only as needed.

5. *Model self-regulated learning.* Verbalize effective self-regulation strategies for students, and tell them how you use self-regulation in your learning.

6. *Make sure that students don't just self-regulate but combine self-regulation with effective strategies for learning.* Students can self-regulate all they want, but if they don't have the "know-how," their self-regulation is unlikely to be beneficial.

Critics of the social cognitive approaches come from several camps. Some cognitive theorists point out that the approaches still focus too much on overt behavior and external factors and not enough on the details of how cognitive processes such as thinking, memory, and problem solving actually take place. Some developmentalists criticize them for being nondevelopmental, in the sense that they don't specify age-related, sequential changes in learning. It is true that social cognitive theory does not address development in great depth because it is mainly a theory of learning and social behavior. But labeling it as nondevelopmental is not accurate. Also, humanistic theorists fault social cognitive theorists for not placing enough attention on self-esteem and caring, supportive relationships. All of these criticisms also have been leveled at the behavioral approaches, such as Skinner's operant conditioning.

Review, Reflect, and Practice

 Summarize social cognitive approaches to learning.

REVIEW

- How does Figure 11.7 help to summarize Bandura's social cognitive theory? What does he mean by self-efficacy?
- What is Bandura's model of observational learning?
- What is the focus of self-instructional methods? What does self-regulatory learning involve?
- What are some contributions and criticisms of the social cognitive approaches?

REFLECT

- Give some examples of how you use self-instructional and self-regulatory methods in your personal life. How effective are these methods? Should you use them more than you do? Explain.

PRAXIS™ PRACTICE

1. Macy sits staring at her math homework. She has not attempted a single problem. "What's the use?" she says with a sigh. "I'll never get it right." According to Bandura's social cognitive theory, what is the most plausible explanation for Macy's response?
   a. Macy does not have the requisite language skills to do her homework.
   b. Macy has low self-efficacy.
   c. Macy has too much math anxiety.
   d. Macy's teacher has not provided enough negative feedback about her math homework.

2. Matt is the star of his high school's basketball team. The team is doing very well this year, in large part because of Matt's performance. This makes him a very popular student. About halfway through basketball season, Matt decides to shave his head. Soon other members of the basketball team shave their heads. Then the trend spreads to the rest of the school. By the end of February, 30 percent of the male students in the school have shaved heads. According to Bandura's social cognitive theory, what is the most plausible explanation for the students' behavior?
   a. Matt is a high-status role model.
   b. Matt was not punished.
   c. Matt was positively reinforced.
   d. Matt's self-efficacy was raised.

3. Marsha, a junior in high school, has debilitating test anxiety. She is particularly anxious about high-stakes tests, such as final exams. She often becomes so anxious that she "blanks out" and forgets everything that she has studied. What would a teacher using a cognitive behavior modification approach do to help her with her test anxiety?
   a. Help Marsha to develop anxiety management strategies and use self-instructions.
   b. Give her a study-skills book to read.
   c. Encourage her to think more about the consequences if she does do better on the tests.
   d. Tell Marsha to study until she has overlearned the material.

Review, Reflect, and Practice

PRAXIS™ PRACTICE (CONTINUED)

4. An important way in which social cognitive theory builds on behavioral theory is its emphasis on
   a. personality.
   b. self-efficacy.
   c. attitudes.
   d. careful observation.

Please see the answer key at the end of the book.

Connecting with the Classroom: Crack the Case

Consequences

Adam, a student in Mr. Potter's fourth-grade class, is disruptive from time to time although he is very bright. One day during language arts, Adam began talking loudly to other students in his area. He was also laughing and telling jokes. Mr. Potter chose to ignore Adam's behavior, hoping he would stop on his own. But Adam didn't stop. Instead, his behavior became more raucous. Still Mr. Potter ignored it. Soon Adam was making enough noise that Mr. Potter was afraid that students in the neighboring classrooms would be disturbed, so he verbally reprimanded Adam.

Adam was a bit quieter for the next few minutes. After that, however, he once again became loud and disruptive. Again Mr. Potter verbally reprimanded him. This time he also told Adam that if he continued with his disruptive behavior, he would have to go to the office. Adam's behavior became even more disruptive, so Mr. Potter sent him to the office. When Adam arrived at the office it was full of people—teachers getting their mail and making copies, volunteers signing in, students who were ill, students sent on errands, and other students who had been sent for disciplinary reasons. The school secretary told Adam to have a seat, which he did. He conversed with every person who entered the office as well as those who were there when he arrived. Half an hour after his arrival, he was sent back to class. He behaved quite well for the rest of the day, to Mr. Potter's relief.

The next day when students were assigned to write a paragraph, Adam once again became disruptive. He loudly told jokes to his classmates, laughed until tears were streaming down his face, and threw a paper airplane across the room. Mr. Potter reprimanded him and asked him to stop. When Adam didn't comply, Mr. Potter sent him to the office, which was once again bustling with activity.

Over the course of the next two weeks, Adam was sent to the office for disrupting class each day, always during a writing assignment. Mr. Potter was perplexed. Even more perplexing was that within three school days other children were becoming disruptive as well, requiring that they too be sent to the office.

1. What are the issues in this case?

   Answer the following questions using principles of behavioral learning theories and correct terminology:

2. Why did Adam continue to disrupt class despite the consequences?

3. What has Adam learned?

4. Why did the other students join Adam in his disruptive behavior?

5. What should Mr. Potter do now?

6. What was Mr. Potter most likely trying to do when he initially ignored Adam's disruptive behavior?
   a. He was trying to extinguish the behavior by not reinforcing it.
   b. He was trying to negatively reinforce the behavior.
   c. He was trying to positively reinforce the behavior.
   d. He was trying to punish the behavior.

7. If Adam's goal was to escape writing assignments, which of the following best explains the consequences in operant conditioning terms?
   a. Adam was negatively reinforced for his behavior. An aversive stimulus was removed.
   b. Adam was positively reinforced for his behavior. A pleasant stimulus was presented.
   c. Adam was punished for his behavior. A pleasant stimulus was removed.
   d. Adam was punished for his behavior. An aversive stimulus was presented.

Behavioral and Social Cognitive Approaches

① WHAT IS LEARNING? Define learning and describe five approaches to studying it.

What Learning Is
and Is Not

Learning is a relatively permanent change in behavior, knowledge, and thinking skills that occurs through experience. Learning is not involved in inborn, or innate, behaviors, such as blinking or swallowing.

Approaches to Learning

Behaviorism is the view that behavior should be explained by experiences that can be directly observed, not by mental processes. Classical conditioning and operant conditioning are behavioral views that emphasize associative learning. Psychology became more cognitive in the last part of the twentieth century, and the cognitive emphasis continues today. This is reflected in four cognitive approaches to learning we discuss in this book: social cognitive, information processing, cognitive constructivist, and social constructivist. Social cognitive approaches emphasize the interaction of behavior, environment, and person (cognition) in explaining learning. Information-processing approaches focus on how children process information through attention, memory, thinking, and other cognitive processes. Cognitive constructivist approaches emphasize the child's cognitive construction of knowledge and understanding. Social constructivist approaches focus on collaboration with others to produce knowledge and understanding.

② BEHAVIORAL APPROACH TO LEARNING: Compare classical conditioning and operant conditioning.

Classical Conditioning

In classical conditioning, the organism learns to connect, or associate, stimuli. A neutral stimulus (such as the sight of a person) becomes associated with a meaningful stimulus (such as food) and acquires the capacity to elicit a similar response. Classical conditioning involves these factors: unconditioned stimulus (UCS), conditioned stimulus (CS), unconditioned response (UCR), and conditioned response (CR). Classical conditioning also involves generalization, discrimination, and extinction. Generalization is the tendency of a new stimulus similar to the original conditioned stimulus to produce a similar response. Discrimination occurs when the organism responds to certain stimuli and not to others. Extinction involves the weakening of the CR in the absence of the UCS. Systematic desensitization is a method based on classical conditioning that reduces anxiety by getting the individual to associate deep relaxation with successive visualizations of increasingly anxiety-producing situations. Classical conditioning is better at explaining involuntary behavior than voluntary behavior.

Operant Conditioning

In operant conditioning (also called instrumental conditioning), the consequences of behavior produce changes in the probability that the behavior will occur. Operant conditioning's main architect was B. F. Skinner. Reinforcement (reward) is a consequence (either positive or negative) that increases the probability that a behavior will occur; punishment is a consequence that decreases the probability that a behavior will occur. In positive reinforcement, a behavior increases because it is followed by a rewarding stimulus (such as praise). In negative reinforcement, a behavior increases because the response removes an aversive (unpleasant) stimulus. Generalization, discrimination, and extinction also are involved in operant conditioning. Generalization means giving the same response to similar stimuli. Discrimination is differentiating among stimuli or environmental events. Extinction occurs when a previously reinforced response is no longer reinforced and the response decreases.

❸ APPLIED BEHAVIOR ANALYSIS IN EDUCATION: Apply behavior analysis to education.

What Is Applied Behavior Analysis?

Applied behavior analysis involves applying the principles of operant conditioning to change human behavior.

Increasing Desirable Behaviors

Strategies to increase desirable behaviors include choosing effective reinforcers, making reinforcers timely and contingent, selecting the best schedule of reinforcement, contracting, using negative reinforcement effectively, and using prompts and shaping. Find out which reinforcers work best with which students. The Premack principle states that a high-probability activity can be used to reinforce a low-probability activity. Applied behavior analysts recommend that a reinforcement be contingent—that is, be given in a timely manner and only if the student performs the behavior. "If . . . then" statements can be used to make it clear to students what they have to do to get a reward. Skinner described a number of schedules of reinforcement. Most reinforcement in the classroom is partial. Skinner described four schedules of partial reinforcement: fixed-ratio, variable-ratio, fixed-interval, and variable-interval. Contracting involves putting reinforcement contingencies in writing. Although negative reinforcement can increase some students' desirable behavior, exercise caution with students who don't have good self-regulatory skills. A prompt is an added stimulus or cue that increases the likelihood that a discriminative stimulus will produce a desired response. Shaping involves teaching new behaviors by reinforcing successive approximations to a specified target behavior.

Decreasing Undesirable Behaviors

Strategies for decreasing undesirable behaviors include using differential reinforcement, terminating reinforcement, removing desirable stimuli, and presenting aversive stimuli. In differential reinforcement, the teacher might reinforce behavior that is more appropriate or that is incompatible with what the student is doing. Terminating reinforcement (extinction) involves taking reinforcement away from a behavior. Many inappropriate behaviors are maintained by teacher attention, so taking away the attention can decrease the behavior. The most widely used strategy for removing desirable stimuli is time-out. A second strategy for removing desirable stimuli involves response cost, which occurs when a positive reinforcer, such as a privilege, is taken away from the student. An aversive stimulus becomes a punisher only when it decreases behavior. The most common forms of punisher in the classroom are verbal reprimands. Punishment should be used only as the last option and in conjunction with reinforcement of desired responses. Physical punishment should not be used in the classroom.

Evaluating Operant Conditioning and Applied Behavior Analysis

Used effectively, behavioral techniques can help you manage your classroom. Critics say that these approaches place too much emphasis on external control and not enough on internal control. They also argue that ignoring cognitive factors leaves out much of the richness of students' lives. Critics warn about potential ethical problems when operant conditioning is used inappropriately. And some critics say that teachers who focus too much on managing the classroom with operant techniques may place too much emphasis on conduct and not enough on academic learning.

❹ SOCIAL COGNITIVE APPROACHES TO LEARNING: Summarize social cognitive approaches to learning.

Bandura's Social Cognitive Theory

Albert Bandura is the main architect of social cognitive theory. His reciprocal determinism model of learning includes three main factors: person/cognition, behavior, and environment. The person (cognitive) factor given the most emphasis by Bandura in recent years is self-efficacy, the belief that one can master a situation and produce positive outcomes.

Observational Learning

Observational learning is learning that involves acquiring skills, strategies, and beliefs by observing others. Bandura describes four key processes in observational learning: attention, retention, production, and motivation. Observational learning is involved in many aspects of children's lives, including the classroom and the media.

Self-instructional methods are cognitive behavior techniques aimed at teaching individuals to modify their own behavior. In many cases, it is recommended that students replace negative self-statements with positive ones. Cognitive behaviorists argue that students can improve their performance by monitoring their behavior. Self-regulatory learning consists of the self-generation and self-monitoring of thoughts, feelings, and behaviors to reach a goal. High-achieving students are often self-regulatory learners. One model of self-regulatory learning involves these components: self-evaluation and monitoring, goal setting and strategic planning, putting a plan into action, and monitoring outcomes and refining strategies. Self-regulation is an important aspect of school readiness. An important aspect of self-regulatory learning is that it gives students responsibility for their learning.

The social cognitive approaches have significantly expanded the scope of learning to include cognitive and social factors in addition to behavior. A considerable amount of learning occurs by watching and listening to competent models and then imitating what they do. The cognitive behavior emphasis on self-instruction, self-talk, and self-regulatory learning provides an important shift from learning controlled by others to self-management of learning. Critics of the social cognitive approaches say that they still place too much emphasis on overt behavior and external factors and not enough on the details of how cognitive processes such as thinking occur. They also are criticized for being nondevelopmental (although social cognitive advocates argue this label is not justified) and not giving enough attention to self-esteem and warmth.

KEY TERMS

learning 307
behaviorism 308
mental processes 308
associative learning 308
classical conditioning 310
systematic desensitization 311
operant conditioning 312

reinforcement (reward) 312
punishment 312
positive reinforcement 312
negative reinforcement 312
applied behavior
    analysis 315
Premack principle 315

schedules of reinforcement 316
contracting 317
prompt 317
shaping 318
time-out 320
response cost 320
social cognitive theory 325

self-efficacy 326
observational learning 326
cognitive behavior
    approaches 332
self-instructional
    methods 332
self-regulatory learning 333

PORTFOLIO ACTIVITIES

Collaborative Work Decreasing Undesirable Behaviors. Together with three or four other students in your class, consider the following students' undesirable behaviors. You want to decrease the behaviors. What is the best strategy for each? Discuss and compare your strategies with the group. (1) Andrew, who likes to utter profanities every now and then; (2) Sandy, who tells you to quit bugging her when you ask her questions; (3) Matt, who likes to mess up other students' papers; and (4) Rebecca, who frequently talks with other students around her while you are explaining or demonstrating something. (INTASC: Principles 2, 5)

Independent Reflection Design a Self-Regulation Plan. Letitia is a high school student who doesn't have adequate self-regulatory skills,

and this lack is causing her to have serious academic problems. She doesn't plan or organize, has poor study strategies, and uses ineffective time management. Using Zimmerman's four-step strategy, design an effective self-regulation program for Letitia. (INTASC: Principle 5)

Research/Field Experience *Sesame Street* and Social Cognitive Learning. *Sesame Street* uses many effective techniques to increase children's attention and help them learn. Watch an episode. Analyze the show. How were these techniques used on the show you watched? Describe any additional techniques you observed that you might be able to use in your classroom. (INTASC: Principles 2, 7, 9)

STUDY, PRACTICE, AND SUCCEED

Visit www.mhhe.com/santrockep5e to review the chapter with self-grading quizzes and self-assessments, to apply the chapter material to

two more Crack the Case studies, and for suggested activities to develop your teaching portfolio.

CHAPTER 12

THE INFORMATION-PROCESSING APPROACH

The mind is an enchanting thing.

—Marianne Moore
American Poet, 20th Century

Chapter Outline

Learning Goals

1 Describe the information-processing approach.

2 Characterize attention and summarize how it changes during development.

3 Discuss memory in terms of encoding, storage, and retrieval.

4 Draw some lessons about learning from the way experts think.

5 Explain the concept of metacognition and identify some ways to improve children's metacognition.

Teaching **Stories**   Laura Bickford

Laura Bickford chairs the English Department at Nordoff High School in Ojai, California. She recently spoke about how she encourages students to think:

> I believe the call to teach is a call to teach students how to think. In encouraging critical thinking, literature itself does a good bit of work for us, but we still have to be guides. We have to ask good questions. We have to show students the value in asking their own questions, in having discussions and conversations. In addition to reading and discussing literature, the best way to move students to think critically is to have them write. We write all the time in a variety of modes: journals, formal essays, letters, factual reports, news articles, speeches, or other formal oral presentations. We have to show students where they merely scratch the surface in their thinking and writing. I call these moments "hits and runs." When I see this "hit and run" effort, I draw a window on the paper. I tell them it is a "window of opportunity" to go deeper, elaborate, and clarify. Many students don't do this kind of thinking until they are prodded to do so.
>
> I also use metacognitive strategies all the time—that is, helping students know about knowing. These include asking students to comment on their learning after we have finished particular pieces of projects and asking them to discuss in advance what we might be seeking to learn as we begin a new project or activity. I also ask them to keep reading logs so they can observe their own thinking as it happens. For example, they might copy a passage from a reading selection and comment on it. Studying a passage from J. D. Salinger's *The Catcher in the Rye,* a student might write, "I've never thought about life the way that Holden Caulfield does. Maybe I see the world differently than he does. He always is so depressed. I'm not depressed. Salinger is good at showing us someone who is usually depressed. How does he manage to do that?" In addition, I ask students to comment on their own learning by way of grading themselves. This year a student gave me one of the most insightful lines about her growth as a reader that I have ever seen from a student. She wrote, "I no longer think in a monotone when I'm reading." I don't know if she grasps the magnitude of that thought or how it came to be that she made that change. It is magic when students see themselves growing like this.

Preview

In the opening story, teacher Laura Bickford tells how she uses metacognitive strategies, one of the important aspects of cognitive learning and a major topic of this chapter. In addition to addressing metacognition, we'll explore what it means to take an information-processing approach in teaching, and we will examine three important aspects of cognition: attention, memory, and expertise.

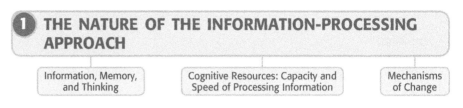

① THE NATURE OF THE INFORMATION-PROCESSING APPROACH

| Information, Memory, and Thinking | Cognitive Resources: Capacity and Speed of Processing Information | Mechanisms of Change |

How capable are children? Proponents of the information-processing approach to learning believe they are highly capable. Children attend to information being presented and tinker with it. They develop strategies for remembering. They form concepts. They reason and solve problems. These important skills are the topics of this section.

INFORMATION, MEMORY, AND THINKING

information-processing approach A cognitive approach in which people manipulate information, monitor it, and strategize about it. Central to this approach are the cognitive processes of memory and thinking.

The **information-processing approach** emphasizes that children manipulate information, monitor it, and strategize about it. Central to this approach are the processes of memory and thinking. According to the information-processing approach, children develop a gradually increasing capacity for processing information, which allows them to acquire increasingly complex knowledge and skills (Demetriou, Mouyi, & Spanoudis, 2011; Halford & Andrews, 2011; Siegler, 2009).

Behaviorism and its associative model of learning was a dominant force in psychology until the 1950s and 1960s, when many psychologists began to acknowledge that they could not explain children's learning without referring to mental processes such as memory and thinking. The term *cognitive psychology* became a label for approaches that sought to explain behavior by examining mental processes. Although a number of factors stimulated the growth of cognitive psychology, none was more important than the development of computers. The first modern computer, developed by John von Neumann in the late 1940s, showed that inanimate machines could perform logical operations. This suggested that some mental operations might be carried out by computers, possibly telling us something about the way human cognition works. Cognitive psychologists often draw analogies to computers to help explain the relation between cognition and the brain (Martinez, 2010). The physical brain is compared with the computer's hardware, cognition with its software. Although computers and software aren't perfect analogies for brains and cognitive activities, nonetheless the comparison contributed to our thinking about the child's mind as an active information-processing system.

What two characteristics of cognitive resources have an important influence on memory and problem solving?

COGNITIVE RESOURCES: CAPACITY AND SPEED OF PROCESSING INFORMATION

As children grow and mature, and as they experience the world, their information-processing abilities increase, influenced by concurrent increases in both capacity and speed of processing. These two characteristics of capacity and speed are often referred to as *cognitive resources* and are proposed to have an important influence on memory and problem solving.

Both biology and experience contribute to growth in cognitive resources (Bjorklund, 2011). Think about how much faster you can process information in your native language than in a second language. The changes in the brain we described in Chapter 10 provide a biological foundation for increased cognitive resources (Zelazo & Lee, 2011). As children grow and mature, important biological developments occur both in brain structures, such as changes in the frontal lobes, and at the level of neurons, such as the blooming and pruning of connections between neurons that produces fewer but stronger connections (Nelson, 2011). Also, as we discussed in Chapter 10, myelination (the process that covers the axon with a myelin sheath) increases the speed of electrical impulses in the brain. Myelination continues at least through adolescence (Paus, 2009).

Most information-processing psychologists argue that an increase in capacity as well as speed improves processing of information (Ashcraft & Radvansky, 2010; Siegler, 2009). For example, as children's information-processing capacity increases, they likely can hold in mind several dimensions of a topic or problem simultaneously, whereas younger children are more prone to focus on only one dimension. Adolescents can discuss how the varied experiences of the Founding Fathers influenced the Declaration of Independence and Constitution. Elementary-age children are more likely to focus on simple facts about the founders' lives.

What is the role of processing speed? How fast children process information often influences what they can do with that information. If an adolescent is trying to add up mentally the cost of items he is buying at the grocery store, he needs to be able to compute the sum before he has forgotten the price of the individual items. Children's speed in processing information is linked with their competence in thinking (Bjorklund, 2005, 2011). For example, how fast children can articulate a series of words affects how many words they can store and remember. Generally, fast processing is linked

Thinking Back/Thinking Forward

Nearly twice as many synaptic connections between neurons are made than ever will be used. Connections that are used become strengthened and survive; unused ones become replaced by other pathways or disappear. Chapter 10, p. 278

with good performance on cognitive tasks. However, some compensation for slower processing speed can be achieved through effective strategies.

Researchers have devised a number of ways for assessing processing speed (Bonafacci & others, 2010). For example, it can be assessed through a *reaction-time task* in which individuals are asked to push a button as soon as they see a stimulus such as a light. Or individuals might be asked to match letters or numbers with symbols on a computer screen.

There is abundant evidence that the speed with which such tasks are completed improves dramatically across the childhood years (Kuhn, 2009). For example, a recent study of 8- to 13-year-old children revealed that processing speed increased with age, and, further, that the developmental change in processing speed preceded an increase in working memory capacity (Kail, 2007).

Controversy exists as to whether the increase in processing speed is due to experience or biological maturation. Experience clearly plays an important role. Think how much faster you could process the answer to a simple arithmetic problem as an adolescent than as a child. Also think about how much faster you can process information in your native language than in a second language. The role of biological maturation likely involves myelination.

MECHANISMS OF CHANGE

According to Robert Siegler (1998), three mechanisms work together to create changes in children's cognitive skills: encoding, automaticity, and strategy construction.

Encoding is the process by which information gets stored in memory. Changes in children's cognitive skills depend on increased skill at encoding relevant information and ignoring irrelevant information. For example, to a 4-year-old an *s* in cursive writing is a shape very different from an *s* that is printed. But a 10-year-old has learned to encode the relevant fact that both are the letter *s* and to ignore the irrelevant differences in their shape.

Automaticity refers to the ability to process information with little or no effort. Practice allows children to encode increasing amounts of information automatically. For example, once children have learned to read well, they do not think about each letter in a word as a letter; instead, they encode whole words. Once a task is automatic, it does not require conscious effort. As a result, as information processing becomes more automatic, we can complete tasks more quickly and handle more than one task at a time (Mayer, 2008). Imagine how long it would take you to read this page if you did not encode words automatically but instead focused your attention on each letter in each word.

Strategy construction is the creation of new procedures for processing information. For example, children's reading benefits when they develop the strategy of stopping periodically to take stock of what they have read so far. Developing an effective repertoire of strategies and selecting the best one to use on a learning task is a critical aspect of becoming an effective learner (Bjorklund, 2011; Scanlan, Anderson, & Sweeney, 2010).

In addition to these mechanisms of change, children's information processing is characterized by *self-modification* (Siegler, 1998, 2007, 2009). That is, children learn to use what they have learned in previous circumstances to adapt their responses to a new situation. For example, a child who is familiar with dogs and cats goes to the zoo and sees lions and tigers for the first time. She then modifies her concept of "animal" to include her new knowledge. Part of this self-modification draws on **metacognition,** which means "knowing about knowing" (Hacker, Dunlofsky, & Grasser, 2009). One example of metacognition is what children know about the best ways to remember what they have read. Do they know that they will remember what they have read better if they can relate it to their own lives in some way? Thus, in Siegler's application of information processing to development, children play an active role in their cognitive development when they develop metacognitive strategies.

DEVELOPMENT

RESEARCH

Thinking Back/Thinking Forward

Teachers can help students to develop a number of effective strategies. Chapter 12, pp. 350 and 364

---

encoding The process by which information gets into memory.

automaticity The ability to process information with little or no effort.

strategy construction Creation of a new procedure for processing information.

metacognition Cognition about cognition, or "knowing about knowing."

Review, Reflect, and Practice

1 Describe the information-processing approach.

REVIEW

- What view does the information-processing approach take of children as learners?
- What are two important cognitive resources and how do they contribute to developmental changes in children's information processing?
- What are some key mechanisms of change in the information-processing approach?

REFLECT

- In terms of your ability to learn, are there ways that you wish you were more like a computer? Or are you better than any computer in all aspects of processing information? Explain.

PRAXIS™ PRACTICE

1. Information processing is most closely aligned with
   a. behaviorism.
   b. cognitive psychology.
   c. social cognitive theory.
   d. ecological theory.

2. According to the information-processing approach, a 15-year-old can compute faster than a 10-year-old because the
   a. 15-year-old's brain has had more time to develop, and the 15-year-old has had more experience working with numbers.
   b. 15-year-old has had more experiences of both positive and negative reinforcement.
   c. 15-year-old's brain has lost many of its original connections and undergone demyelinization.
   d. 15-year-old has had much more time to develop rote memory skills.

3. Ms. Parks wants her students to know their basic math facts without having to stop to think about them. Therefore, Ms. Parks plays many math games with her second-grade students, such as addition and subtraction bingo, math bees, and card games. What is Ms. Parks' goal in playing these games with her students?
   a. to help her students to develop automaticity in knowing their math facts
   b. to encourage strategy construction
   c. to foster encoding skills
   d. to improve metacognitive skills, such as self-awareness

Please see the answer key at the end of the book.

2 ATTENTION

What Is Attention?   Developmental Changes

The world holds a lot of information that we need to perceive. What is attention and what effect does it have? How does it change developmentally?

WHAT IS ATTENTION?

Attention is the focusing of mental resources. Attention improves cognitive processing for many tasks, from hitting a baseball, reading a book, or adding numbers

attention The focusing of mental resources.

What attentional demands does multitasking place on children and adolescents?

DEVELOPMENT

selective attention Focusing on a specific aspect of experience that is relevant while ignoring others that are irrelevant.

divided attention Concentrating on more than one activity at a time.

sustained attention Maintaining attention over an extended period of time; also called vigilance.

executive attention Involves action planning, allocating attention to goals, error detection and compensation, monitoring progress on tasks, and dealing with novel or difficult circumstances.

(Hanania & Smith, 2010; Tang & Posner, 2009). At any one time, though, children, like adults, can pay attention to only a limited amount of information. They allocate their attention in different ways (Rhodes, Gelman, & Brickman, 2010). Psychologists have labeled these types of allocation as selective attention, divided attention, sustained attention, and executive attention.

- **Selective attention** is focusing on a specific aspect of experience that is relevant while ignoring others that are irrelevant. Focusing on one voice among many in a crowded room or a noisy restaurant is an example of selective attention.

- **Divided attention** involves concentrating on more than one activity at the same time. If you are listening to music while you are reading this, you are engaging in divided attention.

- **Sustained attention** is the ability to maintain attention over an extended period of time. Sustained attention is also called *vigilance.* Staying focused on reading this chapter from start to finish without interruption is an example of sustained attention. Recall one study difficulties in sustaining attention were the most common type of attentional problem characterizing children with ADHD (Tsal, Shalev, & Mevorach, 2005).

- **Executive attention** involves action planning, allocating attention to goals, error detection and compensation, monitoring progress on tasks, and dealing with novel or difficult circumstances. An example of executive attention is effectively deploying attention to effectively engage in the aforementioned cognitive tasks while writing a 10-page paper for a history course.

One trend involving divided attention is children's and adolescents' *multitasking,* which in some cases involves not just dividing attention between two activities, but even three or more (Bauerlein, 2008). A major influence on the increase in multitasking is the availability of multiple electronic media. Many children and adolescents have a range of electronic media at their disposal. It is not unusual for adolescents to simultaneously divide their attention among homework, instant messaging, surfing the Web, and looking at an iTunes playlist.

Is this multitasking beneficial or distracting? Since it expands the information children and adolescents attend to and forces the brain to share processing resources, multitasking can distract attention from what might be most important at the moment (Begley & Interlandi, 2008).

Sustained and executive attention are very important aspects of cognitive development. As children and adolescents are required to engage in larger, increasingly complex tasks that require longer time frames to complete, their ability to sustain attention is critical for succeeding on the tasks. An increase in executive attention supports the rapid increase in effortful control required to effectively engage in these complex academic tasks (Tang & Posner, 2009).

DEVELOPMENTAL CHANGES

Some important changes in attention occur during childhood (Courage & Richards, 2008; Dixon, Zelazo, & De Rosa, 2010). Much of the research on attention has focused on selective attention. One study of 5- to 7-year-old children found that the older children and more socially advantaged children in a sample resisted the interference of competing demands and focused their attention better than the younger children and more socially disadvantaged children (Mezzacappa, 2004).

The length of time children can pay attention increases as they get older. The toddler wanders around, shifts attention from one activity to another, and seems to spend little time focused on any one object or event. In contrast, the preschool child might watch television for half an hour at a time. One study that observed 99 families in their homes for 4,672 hours found that visual attention to television dramatically increased in the preschool years (Anderson & others, 1985).

Preschool children's ability to control and sustain their attention is related to school readiness (Posner & Rothbart, 2007). For example, a study of more than 1,000 children revealed that their ability to sustain their attention at 54 months of age (4.5 years) was linked to their school readiness (which included achievement and language skills) (NICHD Early Child Care Research Network, 2005). In turn, children whose parents and teachers rated them higher on a scale of having attention problems at 54 months of age had a lower level of social skills in peer relations in the first and third grades than their counterparts who were rated lower on the attention problems scale at 54 months of age (NICHD Early Child Care Research Network, 2009). Sustained attention improves from 5 to 6 years to 11 to 12 years of age, and this increased attention is linked to better performance on cognitive tasks (Betts & others, 2006).

RESEARCH

Control over attention shows important changes during childhood (Posner & Rothbart, 2007). External stimuli are likely to determine the target of the preschooler's attention; what is salient, or obvious, grabs the preschooler's attention. For example, suppose a flashy, attractive clown presents the directions for solving a problem. Preschool children are likely to pay attention to the clown and ignore the directions, because they are influenced strongly by the salient features of the environment. After the age of 6 or 7, children pay more attention to features relevant to performing a task or solving a problem, such as the directions. Thus, instead of being controlled by the most striking stimuli in their environment, older children can direct their attention to more important stimuli. This change reflects a shift to *cognitive control* of attention, so that children act less impulsively and reflect more. Recall from Chapter 10 that the increase in cognitive control during the elementary school years is linked to changes in the brain, especially more focal activation in the prefrontal cortex (Durston & others, 2006).

DEVELOPMENT

Thinking Back/Thinking Forward

Researchers have found increased focal activation in the prefrontal cortex from 7 to 30 years of age. Chapter 8, p. 279

Attention to relevant information increases steadily through the elementary and secondary school years (Davidson, 1996). Processing of irrelevant information decreases in adolescence.

As children grow up, their abilities both to direct selective attention and to divide attention also improve. Older children and adolescents are better than younger children at tasks that require shifts of attention. For example, writing a good story requires shifting attention among many competing tasks—spelling the words, composing grammar, structuring paragraphs, and conveying the story as a whole. Children also improve in their ability to do two things at once. For example, in one investigation, 12-year-olds were markedly better than 8-year-olds and slightly worse than 20-year-olds at allocating their attention in a situation involving two tasks (divided attention) (Manis, Keating, & Morrison, 1980). These improvements in divided attention might be due to an increase in cognitive resources (through increased processing speed or capacity), automaticity, or increased skill at directing resources.

DEVELOPMENT

As we saw, individual variations also characterize children, with some children having such significant attention problems that they are classified as having attention deficit hyperactivity disorder (ADHD). One study revealed that such attention problems in childhood are linked to information-processing difficulties in late adolescence (Friedman & others, 2007). In the study, 7- to 14-year-old children with attention problems (including inattention, disorganization, impulsivity, and hyperactivity) had difficulty inhibiting responses and working memory difficulties at 17 years of age.

RESEARCH

TEACHING CONNECTIONS: Best Practices
Strategies for Helping Students Pay Attention

With so many classroom tasks to complete and so many children in a class, it is easy to overlook working with children to improve their information-processing skills, such as attention. Following are some effective strategies to adopt in improving children's attention.

1. *Encourage students to pay close attention and minimize distraction.* Talk with children about how important it is to pay attention when they need to remember something. Give them exercises with opportunities to give their undivided attention to something. For example, in countries such as Hungary, kindergarten children participate in exercises designed to improve their attention (Mills & Mills, 2000; Posner & Rothbart, 2007). In one such exercise, the teacher sits in the center of a circle of children, and each child is required to catch the teacher's eye before being permitted to leave the group. In other exercises, teachers have children participate in stop-go activities during which they have to listen for a specific signal, such as a drumbeat or an exact number of rhythmic beats, before stopping the activity.

2. *Use cues or gestures to signal that something is important.* This might involve raising your voice, repeating something with emphasis, and writing the concept on the board or on a transparency. Sometimes it is helpful to be very explicit, "pay attention to this; it is important."

3. *Help students generate their own cue or catch phrase for when they need to pay attention.* Possibly vary this from month to month. Give them a menu of options to select from, such as "Alert," "Focus," or "Zero in." Teach them to say their word or pet phrase quietly but firmly to themselves when they catch their minds wandering.

4. *Make learning interesting.* Boredom can set in quickly for students, and when it does, their attention wanes. Relating ideas to students' interests increases their attention; in other words, what we teach should be relevant to students' lives. Infuse the classroom with novel, unusual, or surprising exercises. Start off a biology exercise on heredity and aging with a question such as "Can you live to be 100?" or "Might someone be able to live to be even 400 some day?" Think of relevant questions such as these to introduce various topics, as students will be more likely to pay attention to material that they can relate to.

5. *Use media and technology effectively as part of your effort to vary the pace of the classroom.* Video and television programs have built-in attention-getting formats, such as zooming in on an image; flashing a vivid, colorful image on the screen; and switching from one setting to another. Look for relevant videos and television programs that can help you vary the classroom's pace and increase students' attention. Unfortunately, too many teachers show videos only to keep students quiet, which does not promote learning. However, if the curriculum is dull, it doesn't matter what kinds of "tricks" or "splashes" the teacher uses—students will not learn effectively. Make sure that the media and technology you use captures students' attention in meaningful ways that promote effective learning.

TECHNOLOGY

Computer exercises recently have been developed to improve children's attention (Jaeggi, Berman, & Jonides, 2009; Tang & Posner, 2009). For example, a recent study found that the attention exercises in Captain's Log (Braintrain), a commercially available program, were effective in reducing first-grade students' attention problems (Rabiner & others, 2009). Ten attention exercises that focus on training auditory and visual attention were used in the study. In one exercise, a student has to press the space bar on a computer each time that a symbol appears that matches one already on the screen. Other tasks require students to remember the locations of objects that have been recently presented. To advance through the program, students have to sustain their attention longer as tasks become more difficult.

RESEARCH

6. *Focus on active learning to make learning enjoyable.* A different exercise, a guest, a field trip, and many other activities can be used to make learning more enjoyable, reduce student boredom, and increase attention. In Through the Eyes of Teachers, middle school English and drama teacher Lynn Ayres describes how games can add interest at all grade levels.

THROUGH THE EYES OF TEACHERS
Turning Boring Exercises into Active Learning Games

I have found that the most boring exercises (such as the kind you find on worksheets and textbooks) can be turned into an active learning game. One favorite game in my seventh-grade English class was "sit-set, rise-raise." I'd put two students in chairs next to tables and place a book on each table. If I said "rise," they were to stand. If I said "raise," they were to raise the book. They were to seat themselves if I said "sit," and they were to place the book on the table if I said "set." If I said "rise," and one of them stood up and the other student lifted the book, the student with the book held up was out and was replaced by a teammate. Or if they both

TEACHING CONNECTIONS: Best Practices
Strategies for Helping Students Pay Attention

stood up, the one who stood up first stayed, and the other student was replaced by a teammate. The students loved that game, and they really learned the difference between those two commonly confused pairs of verbs in the process.

That game taught me the effectiveness of getting students physically involved. I developed dozens of other games involving bells and timers and teams that had students running around the room, ringing bells, trying to beat a member of the opposing team in telling me if a word was a noun or an adjective. Almost any workbook or textbook exercise can be turned into a physical activity game if you put some thought into it, and middle school students learn so much more from doing an exercise that is both physical and mental.

7. *Don't overload students with too much information.* We live in an "information overload" society. Students who are given too much information too fast often have difficulty focusing their attention (Cowan & others, 2010).

8. *Be aware of individual differences in students' attentional skills.* Some students have severe problems in paying attention. You will need to take this into account when presenting material. You might develop a prompt to bring back students whose attention has waned. You might also use their wandering attention as a cue to you that students either need a break or a change in activity.

9. *Consider developmental changes in attention.* As discussed above, the length of time students are capable of attending to something changes as they develop. Don't expect young children to sit and pay attention to a lesson for long periods of time. They need frequent changes in activity. As attention span develops, children can focus their attention for longer periods of time. However, even adolescents and adults benefit from frequent breaks. Be aware that young children have difficulty with selective attention.

10. *Minimize distractions.* Before you begin an exercise, look around the room for potential distractions, such as an open window to a playground where students are being noisy. Close the window and draw the shade to eliminate the distraction. This is particularly important for young children who have not yet developed selective attention.

11. *Occasionally accept the attentional hold of a distraction and incorporate it into your day.* Among children, the first snow of the school year is often a real attention-grabber. Construction going on outside the school is another. Rather than battling against their curiosity and excitement, it may be more prudent to stop what you are doing, acknowledge the distraction, and allow the students to spend a few minutes attending to it. Because their attention spans are not very long, young children in particular will not be likely to attend to the distraction very long either and you will be able to begin teaching again soon, with the distraction no longer a problem.

I recently asked teachers what they do to help students focus their attention in class. Following are their responses.

EARLY CHILDHOOD   Very young children are just developing their attention span. To help them along, we often use songs or instruments for transitions from

play time to work time. When material is introduced, we call out the children's names and ask questions, thus engaging them with the newly introduced item. During story time, we use exaggerated physical gestures and take on the voices of characters in the book to keep children motivated and listening.

—**VALARIE GORHAM**, *Kiddie Quarters, Inc.*

ELEMENTARY SCHOOL: GRADES K–5   One strategy I use to keep my fourth-grade students focused is to get into a role. For example, when I read *Bubba, the Cowboy Prince,* I put on a cowboy hat and create an accent. I also find that saying, "You will see this on your homework tonight," and, "This will be on your test," also grab their attention.

—**SHANE SCHWARZ**, *Clinton Elementary School*

MIDDLE SCHOOL: GRADES 6–8   My students especially stay focused when I let them teach each other—that is, I let them take turns playing the role of teacher.

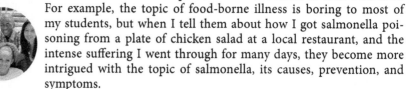

—CASEY MAASS, *Edison Middle School*

HIGH SCHOOL: GRADES 9–12   High school students stay more focused when they know how events and information presented in class relate to their own lives. For example, the topic of food-borne illness is boring to most of my students, but when I tell them about how I got salmonella poisoning from a plate of chicken salad at a local restaurant, and the intense suffering I went through for many days, they become more intrigued with the topic of salmonella, its causes, prevention, and symptoms.

—SANDY SWANSON, *Menomonee Falls High School*

Review, Reflect, and Practice

2 Characterize attention and summarize how it changes during development.

REVIEW
- What is attention? What are four ways attention can be allocated?
- How does attention develop in childhood and adolescence?

REFLECT
- Imagine that you are an elementary school teacher and a child is having difficulty sustaining attention on a learning task. What strategies would you use to help the child sustain attention?

PRAXIS™ PRACTICE

1. Ms. Samson teaches first grade. Often while she is working with one group of children, she must monitor the behavior of the rest of the class, occasionally intervening in some manner. Sometimes she has three or four students at her desk, each needing something different from her. This does not seem to faze her in the least. She can talk to one student while tying another's shoes and monitoring the behavior of the rest with no problem. What skill has Ms. Samson mastered?
   a. divided attention
   b. selective attention
   c. sustained attention
   d. personal attention

2. Mark shifts his attention very quickly from one thing to another. The more colorful and noisy the thing, the more likely it is to draw his attention. He rarely attends to any one thing for more than a few minutes. From this description, Mark is most likely to be a
   a. toddler.
   b. preschooler.
   c. elementary-school-age child.
   d. adolescent.

Please see the answer key at the end of the book.

| What Is Memory? | Encoding | Storage | Retrieval and Forgetting |

Twentieth-century playwright Tennessee Williams once commented that life is all memory except for that one present moment that goes by so quickly that you can hardly catch it going. But just what is memory?

WHAT IS MEMORY?

Memory is the retention of information over time. Educational psychologists study how information is initially placed or encoded into memory, how it is retained or stored after being encoded, and how it is found or retrieved for a certain purpose later. Memory anchors the self in continuity. Without memory you would not be able to connect what happened to you yesterday with what is going on in your life at present. Today educational psychologists emphasize that it is important to view memory not in terms of how children add something to their memory but rather how they actively construct their memory (Ornstein & Light, 2010; Ornstein & others, 2010).

The main body of our discussion of memory will focus on encoding, storage, and retrieval. Thinking about memory in terms of these processes should help you to understand it better (see Figure 12.1). For memory to work, children have to take information in, store it or represent it, and then retrieve it for some purpose later.

As you learned earlier, *encoding* is the process by which information gets into memory, *storage* is the retention of information over time, and *retrieval* means taking information out of storage. Let's now explore each of these three important memory activities in greater detail.

ENCODING

In everyday language, encoding has much in common with attention and learning (Reed, 2010). When a student is listening to a teacher, watching a movie, listening to music, or talking with a friend, he or she is encoding information into memory. Focusing attention—whether by visual inspection, physical manipulation, or using words—highlights features of an event or material being remembered and thus improves encoding (Ornstein, Coffman, & Grammer, 2009; Ornstein & Light, 2010). In addition to attention, which we just discussed, encoding consists of a number of processes: rehearsal, deep processing, elaboration, constructing images, and organization.

Rehearsal The process of **rehearsal** is the conscious repetition of information over time to increase the length of time it stays in memory. For example, when you make a date to meet your best friend for lunch, you are likely to repeat, or rehearse, the date and time: "OK—Wednesday at 1:30." Rehearsal works best when you need to encode and remember a list of items for a brief period of time. When you must retain information over long periods of time, as when you are studying for a test you won't

memory The retention of information over time, which involves encoding, storage, and retrieval.

rehearsal The conscious repetition of information over time to increase the length of time it stays in memory.

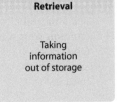

Encoding	**Storage**	**Retrieval**
Getting information into memory	Retaining information over time	Taking information out of storage

FIGURE **12.1** PROCESSING INFORMATION IN MEMORY

As you read about the many aspects of memory in this chapter, think about the organization of memory in terms of these three main activities: encoding, storage, and retrieval.

The Cobwebs of Memory

I think the point of having memories is to share them, especially with close friends or family. If you don't share them, they are just sitting inside your brain getting cobwebs. If you have a great memory of Christmas and no one to share it with, what's the point of memories?

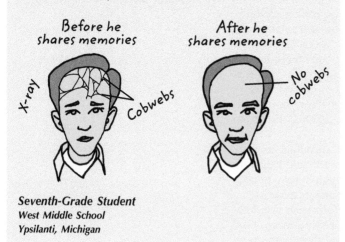

Seventh-Grade Student
West Middle School
Ypsilanti, Michigan

DEVELOPMENT

RESEARCH

levels of processing theory The theory that processing of memory occurs on a continuum from shallow to deep, with deeper processing producing better memory.

elaboration The extensiveness of information processing involved in encoding.

take until next week, other strategies usually work better than rehearsal. Rehearsal does not work well for retaining information over the long term because it often involves just rote repetition of information without imparting any meaning to it. When you construct your memory in meaningful ways, you remember better. As we will see next, you also remember better when you process material deeply and elaborate it.

Deep Processing Following the discovery that rehearsal is not an efficient way to encode information for long-term memory, Fergus Craik and Robert Lockhart (1972) proposed that we can process information at a variety of levels. Their **levels of processing theory** states that the processing of memory occurs on a continuum from shallow to deep, with deeper processing producing better memory. Shallow processing means analyzing a stimuli's sensory, or physical, features at a shallow level. This might involve detecting the lines, angles, and contours of a printed word's letters or a spoken word's frequency, duration, and loudness. At an intermediate level of processing, you recognize the stimulus and give it a label. For example, you identify a four-legged, barking object as a dog. Then, at the deepest level, you process information semantically, in terms of its meaning. For example, if a child sees the word *boat*, at the shallow level she might notice the shapes of the letters, at the intermediate level she might think of the characteristics of the word (for instance, that it rhymes with *coat*), and at the deepest level she might think about the last time she went fishing with her dad on a boat and the kind of boat it was. Researchers have found that individuals remember information better when they process it at a deep level (Otten, Henson, & Rugg, 2001).

Elaboration Cognitive psychologists soon recognized, however, that there is more to good encoding than just depth of processing. They discovered that memory benefits from the use of **elaboration,** which refers to extensiveness of information, in the process of encoding (Ashcraft & Radvansky, 2010). Thus, when you present the concept of democracy to students, they likely will remember it better if they come up with good examples of it. Examples based on self-reference are especially effective in elaborating information. If you are trying to get students to remember the concept of fairness, the more they can generate personal examples of inequities and equities they have personally experienced, the more likely they are to remember the concept.

The use of elaboration changes developmentally (Schneider, 2011). Adolescents are more likely to use elaboration spontaneously than children are. Elementary school children can be taught to use elaboration strategies on a learning task, but they are less likely than adolescents to use the strategies on other learning tasks in the future. Nonetheless, verbal elaboration can be an effective memory strategy even with young elementary school children. In one study, the experimenter told second- and fifth-grade children to construct a meaningful sentence for a keyword (such as "The postman carried a letter in his cart" for the keyword *cart*). As shown in Figure 12.2, both second- and fifth-grade children remembered the keywords better when they constructed a meaningful sentence containing the word than when just the keyword and its definition were told to the child (Pressley, Levin, & McCormick, 1980).

One reason elaboration works so well in encoding is that it adds to the distinctiveness of memory code (Hunt & Ellis, 2004). To remember a piece of information, such as a name, an experience, or a fact about geography, students need to search for the code that contains this information among the mass of codes in their long-term memory. The search process is easier if the memory code is unique (Hunt & Kelly, 1996). The situation is not unlike searching for a friend at a crowded airport—if your friend is 6 feet 3 inches tall and has flaming red hair, it will be easier to find him in the crowd than if he has more common features. Also, as a student elaborates information, more information is stored. And as more information is stored, it becomes easier to differentiate the memory from others. For example, if a student witnesses another student being hit by a car that speeds away, the student's memory of the car will be far better if she deliberately encodes her observations that the car is a red 2005 Pontiac with tinted windows and spinners on the wheels than if she observes only that it is a red car.

Constructing Images   When we construct an image of something, we are elaborating the information. For example, how many windows are there in the apartment or house where your family has lived for a substantial part of your life? Few of us ever memorize this information, but you probably can come up with a good answer, especially if you reconstruct a mental image of each room.

Allan Paivio (1971, 1986) argues that memories are stored in one of two ways: as verbal codes or as image codes. For example, you can remember a picture by a label (*The Last Supper,* a verbal code) or by a mental image. Paivio says that the more detailed and distinctive the image code, the better your memory of the information will be.

Researchers have found that encouraging children to use imagery to remember verbal information works better for older children than for younger children (Schneider, 2011). In one study, experimenters presented twenty sentences to first- through sixth-grade children to remember (such as "The angry bird shouted at the white dog" and "The policeman painted the circus tent on a windy day") (Pressley & others, 1987). Children were randomly assigned to an imagery condition (make a picture in your head for each sentence) and a control condition (children were told just to try hard). Figure 12.3 shows that the imagery instructions improved memory more for the older children (grades 4 through 6) than for the younger children (grades 1 through 3). Researchers have found that young elementary school children can use imagery to remember pictures better than they can verbal materials, such as sentences (Schneider & Pressley, 1997).

Organization   If students organize information when they are encoding it, their memory benefits. To understand the importance of organization in encoding, complete the following exercise: Recall the 12 months of the year as quickly as you can. How long did it take you? What was the order of your recall? Your answers are probably a few seconds and in natural order (January, February, March, and so on). Now try to remember the months in alphabetical order. Did you make any errors? How long did it take you? There is a clear distinction between recalling the months in natural order and recalling alphabetically. This exercise is a good one to use with your students to help them understand the importance of organizing their memories in meaningful ways.

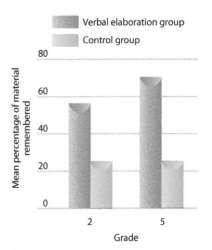

FIGURE **12.2** VERBAL ELABORATION AND MEMORY

Both second- and fifth-grade children remembered words better when they constructed a meaningful sentence for the word (verbal elaboration group) than when they merely heard the word and its definition (control group). The verbal elaboration worked better for the fifth-graders than for the second-graders.

RESEARCH

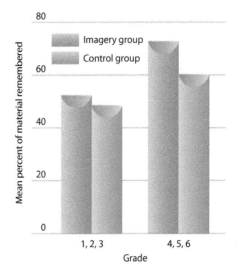

FIGURE **12.3** IMAGERY AND MEMORY OF VERBAL INFORMATION

Imagery improved older elementary school children's memory for sentences more than younger elementary school children's memory for sentences.

Frank and Ernest

FRANK & ERNEST © Thaves/Dist. by United Feature Syndicate, Inc.

The more you present information in an organized way, the easier your students will remember it. This is especially true if you organize information hierarchically or outline it. Also, if you simply encourage students to organize information, they often will remember it better than if you give them no instructions about organizing (Mandler, 1980).

Chunking is a beneficial organizational memory strategy that involves grouping, or "packing," information into "higher-order" units that can be remembered as single units. Chunking works by making large amounts of information more manageable and more meaningful. For example, consider this simple list of words: *hot, city, book, forget, tomorrow, smile.* Try to hold these in memory for a moment, then write them down. If you recalled all six words, you succeeded in holding 30 letters in your memory. But it would have been much more difficult to try to remember those 30 letters. Chunking them into words made them meaningful.

STORAGE

After children encode information, they need to retain, or store, the information. Children remember some information for less than a second, some for about half a minute, and other information for minutes, hours, years, even a lifetime. The three types of memory, which correspond to these different time frames, are *sensory memory* (which lasts a fraction of a second to several seconds); *short-term memory* (lasts about 30 seconds), and *long-term memory* (lasts up to a lifetime).

Sensory Memory **Sensory memory** holds information from the world in its original sensory form for only an instant, not much longer than the brief time a student is exposed to the visual, auditory, and other sensations.

Students have a sensory memory for sounds for up to several seconds, sort of like a brief echo. However, their sensory memory for visual images lasts only for about one-fourth of a second. Because sensory information lasts for only a fleeting moment, an important task for the student is to attend to the sensory information that is important for learning quickly, before it fades.

Short-Term Memory **Short-term memory** is a limited-capacity memory system in which information is retained at least 30 seconds unless it is rehearsed or otherwise processed further, in which case it can be retained longer. Compared with sensory memory, short-term memory is limited in capacity but relatively longer in duration. Its limited capacity intrigued George Miller (1956), who described this in a paper with a catchy title: "The Magical Number Seven, Plus or Minus Two." Miller pointed out that on many tasks, students are limited in how much information they can keep track of without external aids. Usually the limit is in the range of 7 +/− 2 items.

The most widely cited example of the 7 +/− 2 phenomenon involves **memory span**, the number of digits an individual can report back without error from a single presentation. How many digits individuals can report back depends on how old they are. In one study, memory span increased from two digits in 2-year-olds, to five digits in 7-year-olds, to six to seven digits in 12-year-olds (Dempster, 1981) (see Figure 12.4). Many college students can handle lists of eight or nine digits. Keep in mind that these are averages and that individuals differ. For example, many 7-year-olds have a memory span of fewer than six or seven digits; others have a memory span of eight or more digits.

Related to short-term memory, British psychologist Alan Baddeley (2000, 2007) proposed that **working memory** is a three-part system that temporarily holds information as people perform tasks. Working memory is a kind of mental "workbench" where information is manipulated and assembled to help us make decisions, solve problems, and comprehend written and spoken language. Notice that working memory is not like a passive storehouse with shelves to store information until it moves

"Can we hurry up and get to the test? My short-term memory is better than my long-term memory."

© 2006; reprinted courtesy of Bunny Hoest and *Parade.*

DEVELOPMENT

chunking Grouping, or "packing," information into "higher-order" units that can be remembered as single units.

sensory memory Memory that holds information from the world in its original form for only an instant.

short-term memory A limited-capacity memory system in which information is retained at least 30 seconds unless it is rehearsed, in which case it can be retained longer.

memory span The number of digits an individual can report back without error in a single presentation.

working memory A three-part system that holds information temporarily as a person performs a task. A kind of "mental workbench" that lets individuals manipulate, assemble, and construct information when they make decisions, solve problems, and comprehend written and spoken language.

to long-term memory. Rather, it is a very active memory system (Ang & Lee, 2010; Baddeley, Eysenck, & Anderson, 2009; Martinez, 2010).

Figure 12.5 shows Baddeley's view of working memory and its three components: phonological loop, visuospatial working memory, and central executive. Think of them as an executive (central executive) with two assistants (phonological loop and visuospatial working memory) to help do your work.

- The *phonological loop* is specialized to briefly store speech-based information about the sounds of language. The phonological loop contains two separate components: an acoustic code, which decays in a few seconds, and rehearsal, which allows individuals to repeat the words in the phonological store.

- *Visuospatial working memory* stores visual and spatial information, including visual imagery. Like the phonological loop, visuospatial working memory has a limited capacity. The phonological loop and visuospatial working memory function independently. You could rehearse numbers in the phonological loop while making spatial arrangements of letters in visuospatial working memory.

- The *central executive* integrates information not only from the phonological loop and visuospatial working memory but also from long-term memory. In Baddeley's view, the central executive plays important roles in attention, planning, and organizing behavior. The central executive acts much like a supervisor who monitors which information and issues deserve attention and which should be ignored. It also selects which strategies to use to process information and solve problems. As with the other two components of working memory—the phonological loop and visuospatial working memory—the central executive has a limited capacity.

Working memory is linked to many aspects of children's development (Cowan & Alloway, 2009; Cowan & others, 2010). For example, children who have better working memory are more advanced in attentional skills, reading comprehension, math skills, and problem solving than their counterparts with less effective working memory (Alloway, Gathercole, & Elliott, 2010; Carretti & others, 2009; Hoffman & Schraw, 2009).

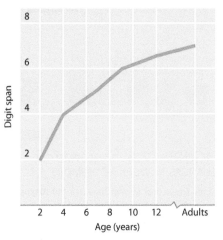

FIGURE 12.4 DEVELOPMENTAL CHANGES IN MEMORY SPAN

In one study, memory span increased about three digits from 2 years of age to five digits at 7 years of age (Dempster, 1981). By 12 years of age, memory span had increased on average another one and a half digits.

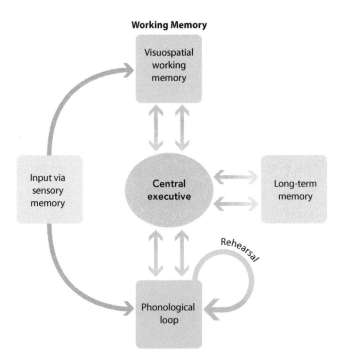

FIGURE 12.5 WORKING MEMORY

In Baddeley's working memory model, working memory consists of three main components: the phonological loop, visuospatial working memory, and the central executive. The phonological loop and visuospatial working memory serve as assistants, helping the central executive do its work. Input from sensory memory goes to the phonological loop, where information about speech is stored and rehearsal takes place, and to visuospatial working memory, where visual and spatial information, including imagery, is stored. Working memory is a limited-capacity system, and information is stored there for only a brief time. Working memory interacts with long-term memory, drawing information from long-term memory and transmitting information to long-term memory for longer storage.

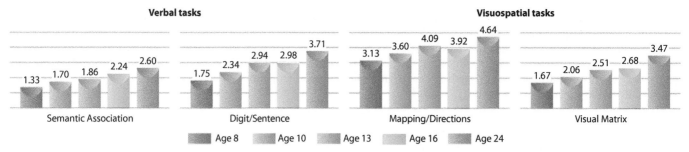

Verbal tasks

Semantic Association: 1.33, 1.70, 1.86, 2.24, 2.60

Digit/Sentence: 1.75, 2.34, 2.94, 2.98, 3.71

Visuospatial tasks

Mapping/Directions: 3.13, 3.60, 4.09, 3.92, 4.64

Visual Matrix: 1.67, 2.06, 2.51, 2.68, 3.47

Age 8 Age 10 Age 13 Age 16 Age 24

FIGURE **12.6** DEVELOPMENTAL CHANGES IN WORKING MEMORY

Note: The scores shown here are the means for each age group and the age also represents a mean age. Higher scores reflect superior working memory performance.

The following three recent studies illustrate how important working memory is in young children's cognitive development:

• Working memory and attention control predicted growth in emergent literacy and number skills in young children in low-income families (Welsh & others, 2010).

• Working memory capacity at 9 to 10 years of age predicted foreign language comprehension two years later at 11 to 12 years of age (Andersson, 2010).

• Working memory capacity predicted how many items on a to-be-remembered list that fourth-grade children forgot (Asian, Zellner, & Bauml, 2010).

Is the working memory of adolescents better than the working memory of children? One study found that it was (Swanson, 1999). Investigators examined the performances of children and adolescents on both verbal and visuospatial working memory tasks. As shown in Figure 12.6, working memory increased substantially from 8 through 24 years of age no matter what the task. Thus, the adolescent years are likely to be an important developmental period for improvement in working memory.

Long-Term Memory **Long-term memory** is a type of memory that holds enormous amounts of information for a long period of time in a relatively permanent fashion. A typical human's long-term memory capacity is staggering, and the efficiency with which individuals can retrieve information is impressive. It often takes only a moment to search through this vast storehouse to find the information we want. Think about your own long-term memory. Who wrote the Gettysburg Address? Who was your first-grade teacher? You can answer thousands of such questions instantly. Of course, not all information is retrieved so easily from long-term memory.

long-term memory A type of memory that holds enormous amounts of information for a long period of time in a relatively permanent fashion.

Atkinson-Shiffrin model A model of memory that involves a sequence of three stages: sensory memory, short-term memory, and long-term memory.

A Model of the Three Memory Stores This three-stage concept of memory we have been describing was developed by Richard Atkinson and Richard Shiffrin (1968). According to the **Atkinson-Shiffrin model,** memory involves a sequence of sensory memory, short-term memory, and long-term memory stages (see Figure 12.7). As we have seen, much information makes it no further than the sensory memories of sounds and sights. This information is retained only for a brief instant. However, some information, especially that to which we pay attention, is transferred to short-term

FIGURE **12.7** ATKINSON AND SHIFFRIN'S THEORY OF MEMORY

In this model, sensory input goes into sensory memory. Through the process of attention, information moves into short-term memory, where it remains for 30 seconds or less, unless it is rehearsed. When the information goes into long-term memory storage, it can be retrieved over the lifetime.

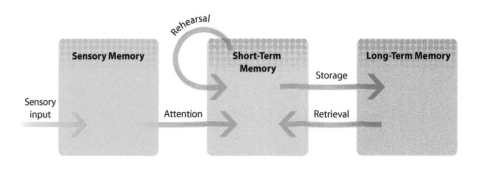

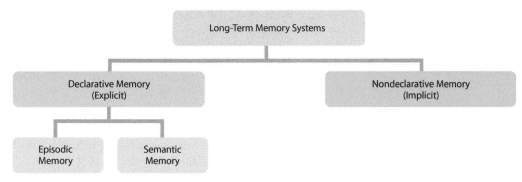

FIGURE **12.8** CLASSIFICATION OF LONG-TERM MEMORY'S CONTENTS

memory, where it can be retained for about 30 seconds (or longer with the aid of rehearsal). Atkinson and Shiffrin claimed that the longer information is retained in short-term memory through the use of rehearsal, the greater its chance is of getting into long-term memory. Notice in Figure 12.7 that information in long-term memory also can be retrieved back into short-term memory.

Some contemporary experts on memory believe that the Atkinson-Shiffrin model is too simple (Bartlett, 2010). They argue that memory doesn't always work in a neatly packaged three-stage sequence, as Atkinson and Shiffrin proposed. For example, these contemporary experts stress that working memory uses long-term memory's contents in more flexible ways than simply retrieving information from it. Despite these problems, the model is useful in providing an overview of some components of memory.

Long-Term Memory's Contents   Different types of memory can be distinguished not only by how long they last but also on the basis of content. For long-term memory, many contemporary psychologists accept the hierarchy of contents described in Figure 12.8 (Bartlett, 2010). Here long-term memory is divided into the subtypes of declarative and nondeclarative memory, and one of those subtypes, declarative memory, is divided into episodic memory and semantic memory.

Declarative and Nondeclarative Memory   The long-term memory subtype of **declarative memory** is the conscious recollection of information, such as specific facts or events that can be verbally communicated. Declarative memory has been called "knowing that" (versus "knowing how") and more recently has been labeled "explicit memory" (versus "implicit memory"). Demonstrations of students' declarative memory could include recounting an event they have witnessed or describing a basic principle of math. However, students do not need to be talking to be using declarative memory. If students simply sit and reflect on an experience, their declarative memory is involved.

The long-term memory subtype of **nondeclarative memory** is procedural knowledge in the form of skills and cognitive operations. Nondeclarative memory cannot be consciously recollected, at least not in the form of specific events or facts. This makes nondeclarative memory difficult, if not impossible, to communicate verbally. Nondeclarative memory is sometimes called "knowing how," and it also has been described as "implicit memory." When students apply their abilities to perform a dance, ride a bicycle, or type on a computer keyboard, their nondeclarative memory is at work. It also is at work when they speak grammatically correct sentences without having to think about how to do it.

Episodic and Semantic Memory   Cognitive psychologist Endel Tulving (2000) distinguishes between two subtypes of declarative memory: episodic and semantic.

declarative memory The conscious recollection of information, such as specific facts or events that can be verbally communicated.

nondeclarative memory Procedural knowledge in the form of skills and cognitive operations. Nondeclarative memory cannot be consciously recollected, at least not in the form of specific events or facts.

Characteristic	Episodic Memory	Semantic Memory
Units	Events, episodes	Facts, ideas, concepts
Organization	Time	Concepts
Emotion	More important	Less important
Retrieval process	Deliberate (effortful)	Automatic
Retrieval report	"I remember"	"I know"
Education	Irrelevant	Relevant
Intelligence	Irrelevant	Relevant
Legal testimony	Admissible in court	Inadmissible in court

FIGURE 12.9 SOME DIFFERENCES BETWEEN EPISODIC AND SEMANTIC MEMORY

These characteristics have been proposed as the main ways to differentiate episodic from semantic memory.

episodic memory The retention of information about the where and when of life's happenings.

semantic memory An individual's general knowledge about the world, independent of the individual's identity with the past.

network theories Theories that describe how information in memory is organized and connected; they emphasize nodes in the memory network.

schema theories Theories based on the premise that when we construct information, we fit it into information that already exists in our mind.

schema Information—concepts, knowledge, information about events—that already exists in a person's mind.

Episodic memory is the retention of information about the where and when of life's happenings. Students' memories of the first day of school, whom they had lunch with, or the guest who came to talk with their class last week are all episodic.

Semantic memory is a student's general knowledge about the world. It includes the following:

- Knowledge of the sort learned in school (such as knowledge of geometry)
- Knowledge in different fields of expertise (such as knowledge of chess, for a skilled 15-year-old chess player)
- "Everyday" knowledge about meanings of words, famous people, important places, and common things (such as what the word *pertinacious* means or who Nelson Mandela is)

Semantic memory is independent of the person's identity with the past. For example, students might access a fact—such as "Lima is the capital of Peru"—and not have the foggiest idea when and where they learned it. Figure 12.9 compares the characteristics of episodic and semantic memory.

Representing Information in Memory How do students represent information in their memory? Three main theories have addressed this question: network, schema, and fuzzy trace.

Network Theories The **network theories** describe how information in memory is organized and connected. They emphasize *nodes* in the memory network that stand for labels or concepts. Consider the concept "bird." One of the earliest network theories described memory representation as hierarchically arranged, with more-concrete concepts ("canary," for example) nestled under more abstract concepts (such as "bird"). However, it soon became clear that such hierarchical networks are too neat to accurately portray how memory representation really works. For example, students take longer to answer the question, "Is an ostrich a bird?" than to answer the question, "Is a canary a bird?" Thus, today memory researchers envision the memory network as more irregular and distorted (Ashcraft & Radvansky, 2010). A typical bird, such as a canary, is closer to the node, or center, of the category "bird" than is the atypical ostrich.

Schema Theories Long-term memory has been compared with a library of books. The idea is that our memory stores information just as a library stores books. In this analogy, the way students retrieve information is said to be similar to the process they use to locate and check out a book. The process of retrieving information from long-term memory, however, is not as precise as the library analogy suggests. When we search through our long-term memory storehouse, we don't always find the exact "book" we want, or we might find the "book" we want but discover that only "several pages" are intact—we have to reconstruct the rest.

Schema theories state that when we reconstruct information, we fit it into information that already exists in our mind. A **schema** is information—concepts, knowledge, information about events—that already exists in a person's mind. Unlike network theories, which assume that retrieval involves specific facts, schema theory claims that long-term memory searches are not very exact. We often don't find precisely what we want, and we have to reconstruct the rest. Thus, when asked to retrieve information, we may fill in the gaps between our fragmented memories with a variety of accuracies and inaccuracies.

We have schemas for all sorts of information (Martinez, 2010). If you tell virtually any story to your class and then ask the students to write down what the story was about, you likely will get many different versions. That is, your students won't remember every detail of the story you told and will reconstruct the story with their own particular stamp on it. Suppose you tell your class a story about two men and two women who were involved in a train crash in France. One student might reconstruct the story by saying the characters died in a plane crash, another might describe three men and three women, another might say the crash was in Germany, and so on. The reconstruction and distortion of memory is nowhere more apparent than in the memories given by courtroom witnesses. In criminal court trials such as that of O. J. Simpson, the variations in people's memories of what happened underscore how we reconstruct the past rather than take an exact photograph of it.

In sum, schema theory accurately predicts that people don't always store and retrieve bits of data in an accurate computer-like fashion. The mind can distort an event as it encodes and stores impressions of reality (Pipe & Salmon, 2009).

A **script** is a schema for an event. Scripts often contain information about physical features, people, and typical occurrences—the kind of information that is helpful when teachers and students need to figure out what is happening around them. In a script for an art activity, students likely will remember based on past experience that you will instruct them on what to draw, that they are supposed to put on smocks over their clothes, that they must get the art paper and paints from the cupboard, that they are to clean the brushes when they are finished, and so on. For example, a student who comes in late to the art activity likely knows much of what to do because he has an art activity script.

"Why? You cross the road because it's in the script—that's why!"
© Bernard Schoenbaum/The New Yorker Collection/www.cartoonbank.com

Fuzzy Trace Theory Another variation of how individuals reconstruct their memories is **fuzzy trace theory,** which states that when individuals encode information, it creates two types of memory representations: (1) a *verbatim memory trace,* which consists of precise details; and (2) a *fuzzy trace,* or gist, which is the central idea of the information (Brainerd & others, 2006; Reyna & Rivers, 2008). For example, consider a child who is presented with information about a pet store that has ten birds, six cats, eight dogs, and seven rabbits. Then the child is asked two different types of questions: (1) verbatim questions, such as "How many cats are in the pet store, six or eight?" and (2) gist questions, such as "Are there more cats or more dogs in the pet store?" Researchers have found that preschool children tend to remember verbatim information better than gist information, but elementary-school-age children are more likely to remember gist information (Brainerd & Gordon, 1994). So in fuzzy trace theory, the increased use of gist information by elementary-school-age children accounts for their improved memory, because fuzzy traces are less likely to be forgotten than verbatim traces.

RETRIEVAL AND FORGETTING

After students have encoded information and then represented it in memory, they might be able to retrieve some of it but might also forget some of it. What factors influence whether students can retrieve information?

Retrieval   When we retrieve something from our mental "data bank," we search our store of memory to find the relevant information. Just as with encoding, this search can be automatic or it can require effort. For example, if you ask your students what month it is, the answer will immediately spring to their lips. That is, the retrieval will be automatic. But if you ask your students to name the guest speaker who came to the class two months earlier, the retrieval process likely will require more effort.

An item's position on a list also affects how easy or difficult it will be to remember it. In the **serial position effect,** recall is better for items at the beginning and end

script A schema for an event.

fuzzy trace theory States that memory is best understood by considering two types of memory representations: (1) verbatim memory trace and (2) fuzzy trace, or gist. In this theory, older children's better memory is attributed to the fuzzy traces created by extracting the gist of information.

serial position effect The principle that recall is better for items at the beginning and the end of a list than for items in the middle.

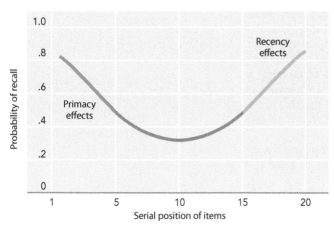

FIGURE 12.10 THE SERIAL POSITION EFFECT

When a person is asked to memorize a list of words, the words memorized last usually are recalled best, those at the beginning next best, and those in the middle least efficiently.

of a list than for items in the middle. Suppose that when you give a student directions about where to go to get tutoring help, you say, "Left on Mockingbird, right on Central, left on Balboa, left on Sandstone, and right on Parkside." The student likely will remember "Left on Mockingbird" and "Right on Parkside" better than "Left on Balboa." The *primacy effect* is that items at the beginning of a list tend to be remembered. The *recency effect* is that items at the end of the list also tend to be remembered, even better than those at the beginning.

Figure 12.10 shows a typical serial position effect with a slightly stronger recency effect than primacy effect. The serial position effect applies not only to lists but also to events. If you spread out a history lesson over a week and then ask students about it the following Monday, they likely will have the best memory for what you told them on Friday of last week and the worst memory for what you told them on Wednesday of last week.

Another factor that affects retrieval is the nature of the cues people use to prompt their memory (Homa, 2008). Students can learn to create effective cues. For example, if a student has a "block" about remembering the name of the guest who came to class two months ago, she might go through the alphabet, generating names with each letter. If she manages to stumble across the right name, she likely will recognize it.

Another consideration in understanding retrieval is the **encoding specificity principle:** that associations formed at the time of encoding or learning tend to be effective retrieval cues. For example, imagine that a 13-year-old child has encoded this information about Mother Teresa: She was born in Albania, lived most of her life in India, became a Roman Catholic nun, was saddened by seeing people sick and dying in Calcutta's streets, and won a Nobel Prize for her humanitarian efforts to help the poor and suffering. Later, when the child tries to remember details about Mother Teresa, she can use words such as *Nobel Prize, Calcutta,* and *humanitarian* as retrieval cues.

The concept of encoding specificity is compatible with our earlier discussion of elaboration: The more elaboration children use in encoding information, the better their memory of the information will be. Encoding specificity and elaboration reveal how interdependent encoding and retrieval are.

Yet another aspect of retrieval is the nature of the retrieval task itself. *Recall* is a memory task in which individuals must retrieve previously learned information, as students must do for fill-in-the-blank or essay questions. *Recognition* is a memory task in which individuals only have to identify ("recognize") learned information, as is often the case on multiple-choice tests. Many students prefer multiple-choice items because they provide good retrieval cues, which fill-in-the-blank and essay items don't do.

encoding specificity principle The principle that associations formed at the time of encoding or learning tend to be effective retrieval cues.

cue-dependent forgetting Retrieval failure caused by a lack of effective retrieval cues.

interference theory The theory that we forget not because we actually lose memories from storage but because other information gets in the way of what we are trying to remember.

Forgetting One form of forgetting involves the cues we just discussed. **Cue-dependent forgetting** is retrieval failure caused by a lack of effective retrieval cues. The notion of cue-dependent forgetting can explain why a student might fail to retrieve a needed fact for an exam even when he is sure he "knows" the information. For example, if you are studying for a test in this course and are asked a question about a distinction between recall and recognition in retrieval, you likely will remember the distinction better if you possess the cues "fill-in-the-blank" and "multiple-choice," respectively.

The principle of cue-dependent forgetting is consistent with **interference theory,** which states that we forget not because we actually lose memories from storage but rather because other information gets in the way of what we are trying to remember.

For a student who studies for a biology test, then studies for a history test, and then takes the biology test, the information about history will interfere with remembering the information about biology. Thus, interference theory implies that, if you have more than one test to study for, you should study last what you are going to be tested on next. That is, the student taking the biology test would have benefited from studying history first and studying biology afterward. This strategy also fits with the *recency effect* we described earlier.

Another source of forgetting is memory decay. According to **decay theory,** new learning involves the creation of a neurochemical *memory trace,* which will eventually disintegrate. Thus, decay theory suggests that the passage of time is responsible for forgetting. Leading memory researcher Daniel Schacter (2001) now refers to forgetting that occurs with the passage of time as *transience.*

Memories decay at different speeds. Some memories are vivid and last for long periods of time, especially when they have emotional ties. We can often remember these "flashbulb" memories with considerable accuracy and vivid imagery. For example, consider a car accident you were in or witnessed, the events of your high school graduation, an early romantic experience, and where you were when you heard about the destruction of the World Trade Center towers. Chances are you will be able to retrieve this information many years afterward.

I recently asked teachers how they help their students improve their memory skills. Following are their responses.

EARLY CHILDHOOD   Repetition often helps preschoolers remember. For example, as a weekly theme, we focus on a letter of the week. Children are asked to write the same letter throughout the week. They also hear stories related to just that one letter and are asked to bring in something for "show and tell" that starts with the letter being highlighted that week.

—**MISSY DANGLER,** *Suburban Hills School*

ELEMENTARY SCHOOL: GRADES K–5   One strategy that works well with my students is to play the game *Jeopardy!* and use categories like math, grammar, science, social studies, and famous stories. The game keeps them excited and focused on the topics. Students receive bonus points for correct answers, which they can trade in for certain classroom privileges.

—**CRAIG JENSEN,** *Cooper Mountain Elementary School*

MIDDLE SCHOOL: GRADES 6–8   I use self-tests to help my seventh-graders improve their memory. Based on notes taken in class, students create their own quizzes and tests. Questions are on one side of the paper, answers on the other. When they study, they are seeing the questions, not the answers. This approach not only helps them remember, but also helps eliminate test anxiety for many students because they know what the test looks like before they get to class.

—**MARK FODNESS,** *Bemidji Middle School*

HIGH SCHOOL: GRADES 9–12   I find that mnemonic devices, silly little rhymes, and dances work best when helping my students remember information. Amazingly, as goofy as this may sound, my high school students remember information using these techniques.

—**JENNIFER HEITER,** *Bremen High School*

decay theory The theory that new learning involves the creation of a neurochemical *memory trace,* which will eventually disintegrate. Thus, decay theory suggests that the passage of time is responsible for forgetting.

TEACHING CONNECTIONS: Best Practices
Strategies for Helping Students Improve Their Memory

As with attention, memory skills in students can improve when teachers use certain strategies.

1. *Motivate children to remember material by understanding it rather than merely memorizing it.* Children will remember information better over the long term if they understand the information rather than just rehearsing and memorizing it (Bjorklund, 2011). Rehearsal works well for encoding information into short-term memory, but when children need to retrieve the information from long-term memory, it is much less efficient. For most information, encourage children to understand it, give it meaning, elaborate on it, and personalize it. Give children concepts and ideas to remember and then ask them how they can relate the concepts and ideas to their own personal experiences and meanings. Give them practice on elaborating a concept so they will process the information more deeply. Follow this by not expecting verbatim textbook responses on assessments.

2. *Repeat with variation on the instructional information and link early and often.* Memory development research expert Patricia Bauer (2009) recommends improving children's consolidation and reconsolidation of the information they are learning by two methods: (a) providing variations on a lesson theme to increase the number of associations in memory storage and (b) linking to expand the network of associations in memory storage. Both strategies expand the routes for retrieving information from storage.

3. *Assist students in organizing what they put into their memory.* Children will remember information better if they organize it hierarchically. Give them some practice arranging and reworking material that requires some structuring.

4. *Teach mnemonic strategies.* Memory aids for remembering information, *mnemonics,* can involve imagery and words (Homa, 2008). Different types of mnemonics include

   - For young children:
      - *Rhymes.* Examples of mnemonic rhymes for young children include the jar top/water faucet rule, "righty tighty; lefty loosey and
      - the spelling rule *"i before e except after c,"* the month rule, "Thirty days hath September, April, June, and November," the bolt-turning rule "Right is tight, left is loose,"
      - *Songs:* Examples include the alphabet song and *Head, Shoulders, Knees and Toes.*
      - *Phrases:* To use this strategy, form a sentence with each word beginning with the letter of the items to

be remembered. For example, young children would be able to remember cardinal directions using the mnemonic phrase *"Never eat soggy waffles."*

   - For older children:
      - *Rhymes:* Examples of mnemonic rhymes for older children include the spelling rule, "I before e except after c and when sounded like a as in neighbor and weigh;" and "Thirty days hath September, April, June, and November."
      - *Acronyms.* This strategy involves creating a word from the first letters of items to be remembered. For example, *HOMES* can be used as a cue for remembering the five original Great Lakes: *Huron, Ontario, Michigan, Erie,* and *Superior* and *ROY G. BIV* can be used for remembering the colors of the rainbow, *red, orange, yellow, green, blue, indigo,* and *violet.*
      - *Phrases:* Appropriate mnemonic phrases for older children include *"My very educated mother just served us noodles"* as a cue to remembering the planets in the solar system in order from the sun, *Mercury, Venus, Earth, Mars, Jupiter, Saturn, Uranus,* and *Neptune.* This phrase excludes Pluto due to its demotion in 2006.

   - For adolescents:
      - *Acronyms:* Appropriate mnemonic acronyms for adolescents include *FOIL* for the rule for multiplying the individual terms in two binomial quantities, *first terms, outside, inside, last.*
      - *Phrases:* Appropriate mnemonic phrases for adolescents include, *"Please excuse my dear aunt Sally,"* for the order of operations in math—*parentheses, exponents, multiplication, division, addition,* and *subtraction.*
      - *Method of loci.* Here children develop images of items to be remembered and mentally store them in familiar locations. Rooms of a house and stores on a street are common locations used in this memory strategy.
      - *Rhymes.* Examples of mnemonic rhymes are the spelling rule, *"I before e except after c,"* the month rule, "Thirty days hath September, April, June, and November," the bolt-turning rule "Right is tight, left is loose," and the alphabet song.
      - *Acronyms.* This strategy involves creating a word from the first letters of items to be remembered. For example, *HOMES* can be used as a cue for remembering the five original Great Lakes: *Huron, Ontario, Michigan, Erie,* and *Superior.*

TEACHING CONNECTIONS: Best Practices
Strategies for Helping Students Improve Their Memory

○ *Keyword method.* Another mnemonic strategy that involves imagery is the *keyword method,* in which vivid imagery is attached to important words. This method has been used to practical advantage in teaching students how to rapidly master new information such as foreign vocabulary words, the states and capitals of the United States, and the names of U.S. presidents. For example, in teaching children that Annapolis is the capital of Maryland, you could ask them to connect vivid images of Annapolis and Maryland, such as two apples getting married (Levin, 1980) (see Figure 12.11).

Some educators argue against teaching children to use mnemonics because they involve rote memorization. Clearly, as we said earlier, remembering for understanding is preferred over rote memorization. However, if children need to learn lists of concepts, mnemonic devices can do the trick. Think of mnemonic devices as a way for children to learn some specific facts that they might need to know to solve problems.

FIGURE 12.11 THE KEYWORD METHOD

To help children remember the state capitals, the keyword method was used. A special component of the keyword method is the use of mental imagery. For example, to help children remember that Annapolis is the capital of Maryland, they were encouraged to envision two apples being married, thus associating *apple* with Annapolis and *marry* with Maryland.

5. *Embed memory-relevant language in your teaching.* Teachers vary considerably in how much they use memory-relevant language, such as strategies and metacognitive questions (questions related to students' knowledge of how memory works) that encourage students to remember information. In recent research that involved extensive observations of a number of first-grade teachers in the classroom, Peter Ornstein & his colleagues (Ornstein, Coffman, & Grammer, 2009; Ornstein & others, 2007, 2010) found that for the time segments observed, the teachers' use of strategy suggestions ranged from 1 to 14 percent, their use of metacognitive questions ranged from 1 to 10 percent, and their combined use of deliberate memory demands and cognitive structuring activities ranged from 10.0 to 35 percent. Further, when lower-achieving students were placed in classrooms in which teachers were categorized as "high-mnemonic teachers" who frequently embedded memory-relevant information in their teaching, their achievement increased (Ornstein & others, 2007).

RESEARCH

Review, Reflect, and Practice

③ Discuss memory in terms of encoding, storage, and retrieval.

REVIEW

• What is memory? What is necessary for it to work?
• How are these five processes—rehearsal, deep processing, elaboration, constructing images, and organization—involved in encoding?
• What are the three time frames of memory? How are long-term memory's contents described? What are three theories about how they might be represented in memory? What makes a memory easier or harder to retrieve? What are some theories about why we forget?

REFLECT

• Which principles and strategies in our discussion of memory are likely to be useful for the subjects and grade levels at which you plan to teach?

(continued)

Review, Reflect, and Practice

PRAXIS™ PRACTICE

1. Natalie is playing a game called "Memory" at a birthday party. A covered tray with 15 objects is brought into the room. The cover is removed, and the children have 30 seconds to memorize the objects. They will then write down the objects they remember. The child who correctly remembers the most objects wins the game. Natalie notices that five of the objects are hair-related items—a comb, a brush, shampoo, a barrette, and a ponytail holder. She notices that another five objects are school supplies—a pencil, a pen, a ruler, a marker, and a glue stick. The final five objects appear to be random. Natalie has no problem remembering the items that she was able to group by type. She only remembers two of the other items. What memory strategy is Natalie using?
   a. chunking
   b. constructing images
   c. elaboration
   d. rehearsal

2. To test his students' memory skills, Mr. Watkins reads lists of nonsense words to them and asks them to recall as many as they can. Veronica can recall five words. If she performs as is expected for age, how old is Veronica most likely to be?
   a. 4
   b. 7
   c. 12
   d. 17

3. When asked to describe in detail how to make a peanut-butter-and-jelly sandwich, Maria skips several steps. When asked to make the sandwich, Maria does so flawlessly. Why is it that although Maria knows how to make the sandwich, she is unable to describe the process in detail?
   a. It is difficult to translate procedural memory into words.
   b. Maria has not encoded the process into long-term memory.
   c. It is difficult to translate episodic memory into semantic memory.
   d. Maria's episodic memory is faulty.

4. Mr. Madison wants his students to know the names of all of the states in the United States. To help them, he teaches them a song in which each state name is sung in alphabetical order. Most of his students learn the song with relative ease. They even sing the song to themselves when he gives them a quiz that requires them to write down the name of each state. However, when he gives them blank U.S. maps to fill in with state names, his students cannot complete them successfully. Why were they able to remember the names of the states, but not their locations?
   a. Mnemonic devices, such as the song Mr. Madison taught his students, are not effective for memorizing material.
   b. Mnemonic devices, such as the song Mr. Madison taught his students, increase the likelihood of cue-dependent forgetting.
   c. Mnemonic devices, such as the song Mr. Madison taught his students, increase the serial position effect.
   d. Mnemonic devices, such as the song that Mr. Madison taught his students, involve rote memorization and do not generalize to other memory tasks.

Please see the answer key at the end of the book.

4 EXPERTISE

| Expertise and Learning | Acquiring Expertise | Expertise and Teaching |

In the last section, we considered various aspects of memory. Our ability to remember new information about a subject depends considerably on what we already know about it (Ericsson, Krampe, & Tesch-Romer, 2009). For example, a student's ability to recount what she saw when she was at the library is largely governed by what she already knows about libraries, such as where books on certain topics are likely to be and how to check books out. If she knew little about libraries, the student would have a much harder time recounting what was there.

The contribution of prior content knowledge to our ability to remember new material is especially evident when we compare the memories of experts and novices in a particular knowledge domain (Nippold, 2009). An expert is the opposite of a novice (someone who is just beginning to learn a content area). Experts demonstrate especially impressive memory in their areas of expertise. One reason that children remember less than adults is that they are far less expert in most areas.

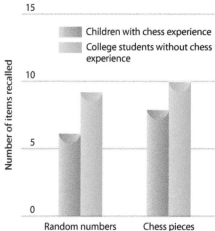

FIGURE **12.12** MEMORY FOR NUMBERS AND CHESS PIECES

EXPERTISE AND LEARNING

Studying the behavior and mental processes of experts can give us insights into how to guide students in becoming more effective learners (Ericsson, Krampe, & Tesch-Romer, 2009; Papageorgi & others, 2010). What is it, exactly, that experts do? According to the National Research Council (1999), they are better than novices at the following:

- Detecting features and meaningful patterns of information
- Accumulating more content knowledge and organizing it in a manner that shows an understanding of the topic
- Retrieving important aspects of knowledge with little effort
- Adapting an approach to new situations
- Using effective strategies

In this section, we will consider various ways that you can help your students learn and remember these skills that experts use so effortlessly.

Detecting Features and Meaningful Patterns of Organization Experts are better at noticing important features of problems and contexts that novices may ignore (Blair & Somerville, 2009; Bransford & others, 2006). Thus, the attentional advantage of experts starts them off at a more advantageous level than novices in a learning context. Experts also have superior recall of information in their area of expertise. The process of *chunking*, which we discussed earlier, is one way they accomplish this superior recall. For example, "Chess masters perceive chunks of meaningful information, which affects their memory of what they see. . . . Lacking a hierarchical, highly organized structure for the domain, novices cannot use this chunking strategy" (National Research Council, 1999, p. 21).

In areas where children are knowledgeable and competent, their memory is often extremely good. In fact, it often exceeds that of adults who are novices in that content area. This was documented in a study of 10-year-old chess experts (Chi, 1978). These children were excellent chess players but not especially brilliant in other ways. As with most 10-year-olds, their memory spans for digits were shorter than an adult's. However, they remembered the configurations of chess pieces on chessboards far better than did the adults who were novices at chess (see Figure 12.12).

Expert teachers recognize features and patterns that are not noticed by novice teachers (National Research Council, 1999, pp. 21, 25). For example, in one study,

RESEARCH

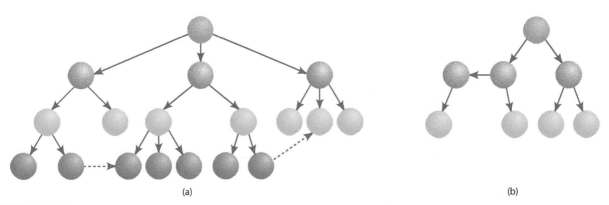

(a)

(b)

FIGURE **12.13** AN EXAMPLE OF HOW INFORMATION IS ORGANIZED IN THE MIND OF AN EXPERT AND A NOVICE

(*a*) An expert's knowledge is based on years of experience in which small bits of information have been linked with many other small pieces, which together are placed in a more general category. This category is in turn placed in an even more general category of knowledge. The dotted lines are used as pointers, associations between specific elements of knowledge that connect the lower branches and provide mental shortcuts in the expert's mind. (*b*) The novice's knowledge shows far fewer connections, shortcuts, and levels than an expert's knowledge.

expert and novice teachers had a very different understanding of the events in a videotaped classroom lesson in which three screens showed simultaneous events taking place throughout the classroom (left, center, and right areas) (Sabers, Cushing, & Berliner, 1991). One expert teacher said, "On the left monitor, the students' note taking indicates that they have seen sheets like this before; it's fairly efficient at this point because they're used to the format they are using." One novice teacher sparsely responded, "It's a lot to watch."

Organization and Depth of Knowledge Experts' knowledge is organized around important ideas or concepts more than novices' knowledge is (National Research Council, 1999). This provides experts with a much deeper understanding of knowledge than novices have (Bransford & others, 2006).

Experts in a particular area usually have far more elaborate networks of information about that area than novices do (see Figure 12.13). The information they represent in memory has more nodes, more interconnections, and better hierarchical organization.

The implications for teaching are that too often a curriculum is designed in a way that makes it difficult for students to organize knowledge in meaningful ways. This especially occurs when there is only superficial coverage of facts before moving on to the next topic. In this context, students have little time to explore the topic in depth in order to get a sense of what the important, organizing ideas are. This type of shallow presentation can occur in any subject area but is common in history and science texts that emphasize facts (National Research Council, 1999).

Fluent Retrieval The effort involved in retrieval of relevant information can vary greatly. Experts in a certain type of information can retrieve it almost effortlessly, or *fluently,* whereas novices must expend a great deal of effort in retrieving the same information (Posner & Rothbart, 2007).

The advantage of fluent retrieval is that it places fewer demands on conscious attention. Since the amount of information a student can attend to at one time is limited, ease of processing information in some aspects of a task frees up capacity to attend to other aspects of a task.

Consider expert and novice readers. Expert readers can quickly scan the words of a sentence and paragraph, which allows them to devote attention to understanding what they are reading. However, novice readers' ability to decode words is not yet fluent, so they have to allocate considerable attention and time to this task, which restricts the time they can give to understanding a passage. An important aspect of teaching is to help students develop the fluency they need to competently perform cognitive tasks (Beck & others, 1991).

Adaptive Expertise An important aspect of expertise "is whether some ways of organizing knowledge are better" than others for helping people to be "flexible and adaptive to new situations" (National Research Council, 1999, p. 33). *Adaptive experts* are able to approach new situations flexibly rather than always responding in a rigid, fixed routine (Gambrell, Malloy, & Anders-Mazzoni, 2007). An important theme in the book *Preparing Teachers for a Changing World* (Darling-Hammond & Bransford, 2005, p. 3) is to "help teachers become 'adaptive experts' who are prepared for effective lifelong learning that allows them to continually add to their knowledge and skills." In other words, teachers characterized by adaptive expertise are flexible and open to rethinking important ideas and practices to improve their students' learning (Hammerness & others, 2005).

Innovation and efficiency are the two main dimensions of one model of adaptive expertise (Bransford & others, 2006). Experts characterized by *efficiency* can quickly retrieve and apply information in skillful ways to explain something or solve a problem. Experts characterized by *innovation* are able to move away from efficiency, at least on a short-term basis, and unlearn previous routines. Innovation occurs when individuals "let go" and rethink their routine way of doing something.

In this model, adaptive experts possess a balance of efficiency and innovation (Bransford & others, 2006). For example, efficiency is at work when a teacher teaches students to speedily complete math computations, but this efficiency may limit the students' competence when they face new math problems. When this efficiency-oriented teacher adapts and adds teaching for understanding and application, innovation is taking place. The new skills she teaches are likely to increase the students' competence when they encounter new math problems.

Adaptive experts are motivated to learn from others (Hammerness & others, 2005). This may not be that difficult when the learning involves making a teacher's existing routines and practices more efficient. However, as we just indicated, adaptive expertise also includes innovation that requires sometimes replacing or transforming prior routines and practices, which is often not easy to do. Your teaching likely will benefit if you seek feedback from other competent teachers, even if their approaches are different than yours. This might occur when you watch a videotape of your teaching with other teachers who provide feedback about your teaching or invite a colleague to come to your classroom to observe your teaching.

In sum, adaptive expertise is a critical aspect of being an outstanding teacher. Teachers who are knowledgeable and adept at adapting different methods, practices, and strategies to meet the needs of different students are most likely to guide students to higher levels of learning and achievement (Gambrell, Malloy, & Anders-Mazzoni, 2007).

Strategies   Experts use effective strategies in understanding the information in their area of expertise and in advancing it (Ornstein, Coffman, & Grammer, 2009; Ornstein & Light, 2010). Earlier in the chapter we described a number of strategies that students can use to remember information, and later in the chapter we will further examine strategies in our discussion of metacognition.

Patricia Alexander (2003) uses the label *acclimation* to describe the initial stage of expertise in a particular domain (such as English, biology, or mathematics). At this stage, students have limited and fragmented knowledge that restricts their ability to detect the difference between accurate and inaccurate or between relevant and tangential information. To help students move beyond the acclimation stage, teachers need to guide students in determining what content is central and what is peripheral, as well as what is accurate and well supported and what is inaccurate and unsupported. In Alexander's (2003) view, students don't come to the classroom equipped with the strategies they need to move beyond the acclimation stage. Teachers must help students learn effective strategies and practice them in relevant situations before students can experience their value. Students also need to be encouraged to change and combine strategies to solve the problem at hand.

Spreading Out and Consolidating Learning   Students' learning benefits when teachers talk with them about the importance of regularly reviewing what they learn. Children who have to prepare for a test will benefit from distributing their learning over a longer period rather than cramming for the test at the last minute. Cramming tends to produce short-term memory that is processed in a shallow rather than deep

> **Thinking Back/Thinking Forward**
>
> Strategy construction refers to the creation of new procedures for processing information. Chapter 12, p. 346
>
> Learning how to use strategies usually takes time. Chapter 12, p. 378

What are some good study strategies?

manner. A final, concentrated tune-up before the test is better than trying to learn everything at the last minute.

Asking Themselves Questions When children ask themselves questions about what they have read or about an activity, they expand the number of associations with the information they need to retrieve. At least as early as the middle of elementary school, the self-questioning strategy can help children to remember. For example, as children read, they can be encouraged to stop periodically and ask themselves questions such as, "What is the meaning of what I just read?" "Why is this important?" and "What is an example of the concept I just read?" Students can use the same self-questioning strategy when they listen to you conduct a lesson, hear a guest give a talk, or watch a video. If you periodically remind children to generate questions about their experiences, they are more likely to remember the experiences.

Taking Good Notes Taking good notes from either a lecture or a text benefits learning (Santrock & Halonen, 2009). When children are left to take notes without being given any strategies, they tend to take notes that are brief and disorganized. When they do write something down, it often is a verbatim record of what they have just heard. Give children some practice in taking notes and then evaluate their note taking. Encourage children not to write down everything they hear when they take notes. It is impossible to do this, anyway, and it can prevent them from getting the big picture of what the speaker is saying. Here are some good note-taking strategies:

- *Summarizing.* Have the children listen for a few minutes and then write down the main idea that a speaker is trying to get across in that time frame. Then have the child listen for several more minutes and write down another idea, and so on.
- *Outlining.* Show the children how to outline what a speaker is saying, using first-level heads as the main topics, second-level heads as subtopics under the first-level heads, and third-level heads under the second-level heads.
- *Using concept maps.* Help the children practice drawing concept maps, which are similar to outlines but visually portray information in a more spiderlike format.

All three note-taking strategies described so far—summarizing, outlining, and using concept maps—help children evaluate which ideas are the most important to remember. Outlining and concept maps also help children arrange the material hierarchically, which underscores an important theme of learning: it works best when it is organized.

Using a Study System Various systems have been developed to help people to remember information that they are studying from a book. One of the earliest systems was called *SQ3R*, which stands for *Survey, Question, Read, Recite,* and *Review.* A more recently developed system is called *PQ4R*, which stands for *Preview, Question, Read, Reflect, Recite,* and *Review.* Thus, the PQ4R system adds an additional step, "Reflect," to the SQ3R system. From the later elementary school years on, students will benefit from practicing the PQ4R system. The system benefits students by getting them to meaningfully organize information, ask questions about it, reflect on it, and review it. Here are more details about the steps in the PQ4R system:

- *Preview.* Tell your students to briefly survey the material to get a sense of the overall organization of ideas—to look at the headings to see the main topics and subtopics that will be covered.
- *Question.* Encourage the children to ask themselves questions about the material as they read it.
- *Read.* Now tell the children to read the material. Encourage your students to be active readers—to immerse themselves in what they are reading and strive to understand what the author is saying. This helps students to avoid being

SELF-ASSESSMENT 12.1
How Effective Are My Memory and Study Strategies?

Teachers who themselves practice using good memory and study strategies are more likely to model and communicate these to their students than teachers who don't use such strategies. Candidly respond to these items about your own memory and study strategies. Rate yourself on this scale: 1 = never, 2 = some, 3 = moderate, 4 = almost, or 5 = always. Then total your points.

	1	2	3	4	5

1. I'm a good time manager and planner.

2. I'm good at focusing my attention and minimizing distractions.

3. I try to understand material rather than rotely memorizing it.

4. I ask myself questions about what I have read or about class activities.

5. I take good notes in class and from textbooks.

6. I regularly review my notes.

7. I use mnemonic strategies.

8. I'm very organized in the way I encode information.

9. I spread out my studying to consolidate my learning.

10. I use good retrieval cues.

11. I use the PQ4R method or a similar study method.

SCORING AND INTERPRETATION

If you scored 50–55 total points, you likely use good memory and study strategies. If you scored 45–49 points, you likely have some reasonably good memory and study strategies. If you scored below 45, spend some time working on improving your memory and study strategies.

If you would like to learn more about effective memory and study strategies, one resource is a book called *Your Guide to College Success* (Santrock & Halonen, 2009). Also, to gain more experience in developing good memory and study strategies, contact the study-skills center at your college or university; specialists there likely will be able to help you.

empty readers whose eyes just track the lines of text but whose minds fail to register anything important.

- *Reflect.* By occasionally stopping and reflecting on the material, students increase its meaningfulness. Encourage the children to be analytic at this point in studying. After they have read something, challenge them to break open the ideas and scratch beneath their surface. This is a good time for them to think out applications and interpretations of the information, as well as connecting it with other information already in their long-term memory.

- *Recite.* This involves children self-testing themselves to see if they can remember the material and reconstruct it. At this point, encourage the children to make up a series of questions about the material and then try to answer them.

- *Review.* Tell your students to go over the material and evaluate what they know and don't know. At this point, they should reread and study the material they don't remember or understand well.

To evaluate the extent to which you use good memory and study strategies, complete Self-Assessment 12.1.

ACQUIRING EXPERTISE

What determines whether or not someone becomes an expert? Can motivation and practice get someone to expert status? Or does expertise also require a great deal of talent (Sternberg & Ben-Zeev, 2001)?

Practice and Motivation   One perspective is that a particular kind of practice—*deliberate practice*—is required to become an expert (Rosenzweig & Bennett, 2009). Deliberate practice is at an appropriate level of difficulty for the individual, provides corrective feedback, and allows opportunities for repetition (Ericsson, Krampe, & Tesch-Romer, 2009).

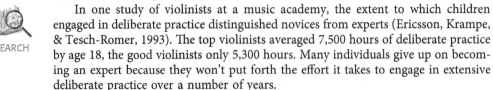

RESEARCH

In one study of violinists at a music academy, the extent to which children engaged in deliberate practice distinguished novices from experts (Ericsson, Krampe, & Tesch-Romer, 1993). The top violinists averaged 7,500 hours of deliberate practice by age 18, the good violinists only 5,300 hours. Many individuals give up on becoming an expert because they won't put forth the effort it takes to engage in extensive deliberate practice over a number of years.

Such extensive practice requires considerable motivation. Students who are not motivated to practice long hours are unlikely to become experts in a particular area. Thus, a student who complains about having too much work, doesn't persevere, and doesn't extensively practice solving math problems over a number of years is not going to become an expert in math.

Talent   A number of psychologists who study expertise stress that it requires not only deliberate practice and motivation but also talent (Hunt, 2006; Sternberg, 2009).

A number of abilities—music and athletic, for example—seem to have a heritable component (Plomin & others, 2009). For example, is it likely that Mozart could have become such an outstanding musical composer just because he practiced long hours? Is it likely that LeBron James became such a fantastic basketball player just because he was motivated to do so? Many talented individuals have attempted to become as great as Mozart or James but have given up trying after only mediocre performances. Clearly, heredity matters. Nonetheless, Mozart and James would not have developed expertise in their fields without being highly motivated and engaging in extensive deliberate practice. Talent alone does not make an expert.

EXPERTISE AND TEACHING

Being an expert in a particular domain—such as physics, history, or math—does not mean that the expert is good at helping others learn it (Bransford & others, 2006). Indeed, "expertise can sometimes hurt teaching because many experts forget what is easy and what is difficult for students" (National Research Council, 1999, p. 32).

Pedagogical Content Knowledge   Some educators have distinguished between the content knowledge required for expertise and the pedagogical content knowledge necessary to effectively teach it. *Pedagogical content knowledge* includes ideas about common difficulties that students have as they try to learn a content area, typical paths students must take to understand the area, and strategies for overcoming the difficulties they experience.

Expert teachers are good at monitoring students' learning and assessing students' progress. They also know what

An expert teacher monitoring students' learning. *What are some characteristics of expert teachers?*

types of difficulties students are likely to encounter, are aware of students' existing knowledge, and use this awareness to teach at the right level and to make new information meaningful. Some educational psychologists argue that in the absence of expert pedagogical awareness of their own students, inexpert teachers simply rely on textbook publishers' materials, which, of course, contain no information about the particular pedagogical needs of students in the teacher's classroom (Brophy, 2004).

Technology, Expertise, and Teaching   Richard Mayer (2008, 2009) has presented a number of ideas and conducted research on ways to incorporate expertise and technology in the classroom. In his cognitive theory of multimedia learning, Mayer (2009) highlights the following:

TECHNOLOGY

- There are two separate channels (auditory and visual) for processing information, which is sometimes referred to as *dual-coding theory.*
- Each channel has a limited (finite) capacity, similar to the concept of *cognitive load.*
- Learning is an active process of filtering, selecting, organizing, and integrating information based on prior knowledge.

Mayer's (2010) current interests in technology and expertise focus on (1) multimedia learning, such as discovering how illustrations influence the way students learn from scientific text and how students can learn to solve problems from videogames, and (2) human computer interaction, including how novices learn to interact with computers, strategies for designing e-learning environments that effectively promote learning, and how students learn from computer-based tutors.

Review, Reflect, and Practice

4 Draw some lessons about learning from the way experts think.

REVIEW

- What do experts do that novices often don't do in the process of learning?
- What does it take to become an expert?
- Is subject experience enough to make a good teacher? What else is needed?

REFLECT

- Choose an area in which you feel at least somewhat of an expert. Compare your ability to learn in that field with the ability of a novice.

PRAXIS™ PRACTICE

1. The case studies in this text are designed to help educational psychology students learn the material and begin to develop expertise. The first question of each case study asks students to identify the issues in the case. The author most likely included this question for each case because he understood that
   a. it is important for students to consolidate their learning.
   b. it is important for students to learn to determine what content is central and what is peripheral.
   c. in learning, it is important to strike a balance between efficiency and innovation.
   d. students need a great deal of help in developing fluent retrieval skills.

(continued)

Review, Reflect, and Practice

PRAXIS™ PRACTICE (CONTINUED)

2. Ryan is the best player on his soccer team. His coach thinks of him as a coach's dream player because he works so hard. It is rare for Ryan to perform a skill better than his teammates when it is initially introduced, but by the time the next practice comes, he will have mastered the skill. At one point, Ryan decided that he wanted to be able to score from a corner kick. He gathered up all the soccer balls he could find and kicked them one after another from the corner, trying to curl them into the goal. When he had finished, he gathered the balls and did it again. He continued this for an entire afternoon, and thereafter for at least an hour after school each day. His coach was very happily surprised when, in the next game, Ryan scored a goal from a corner kick. Why has Ryan developed expertise in soccer?
   a. He engages in extensive deliberative practice.
   b. He is relying on an inborn talent.
   c. He has an excellent teacher in his coach.
   d. He uses the PQ4R method 3.

3. Mr. Williams is a former college history professor who is now teaching high school American history. He discusses his research and writing with his students and tries to make history come alive by telling them about how historians find out about the past. After a month of teaching, he finds that his students seem confused during class discussions and perform poorly on tests of factual knowledge. The most likely explanation is that Mr. Williams lacks
   a. content expertise.
   b. pedagogical content knowledge.
   c. metacognition.
   d. cue-dependent knowledge.

Please see the answer key at the end of the book.

5 METACOGNITION

| Developmental Changes | The Good Information-Processing Model | Strategies and Metacognitive Regulation |

So far in this chapter, we have examined a number of ways that you help students improve their ability to process information as they learn, including how to improve their attention and memory, as well as strategies that can increase the likelihood that they will make the transition from being a novice to being an expert. Another way that you can help children process information more effectively is by encouraging them to examine what they know about how their mind processes information (Ghetti, Castelli, & Lyons, 2010). As you read at the beginning of this chapter, this involves *metacognition,* which involves cognition about cognition, or "knowing about knowing" (Flavell, 2004). A distinction can be made between metacognitive knowledge and metacognitive activity. *Metacognitive knowledge* involves monitoring and reflecting on one's current or recent thoughts. This includes both factual knowledge, such as knowledge about the task, one's goals, or oneself, and strategic knowledge, such as how and when to use specific procedures to solve problems. *Metacognitive activity* occurs when students consciously adapt and manage their thinking strategies during problem solving and purposeful thinking.

Metacognition helps children to perform many academic tasks more effectively (Williams & Atkins, 2009). Metacognitive skills also have been taught to students to help them solve problems (Serra & Metcalfe, 2009). In one study, in which each of 30 daily lessons involved math story problems, a teacher guided low-achieving students in learning to recognize when they did not know the meaning of a word, did not have all of the information necessary to solve a problem, did not know how to subdivide the problem into specific steps, or did not know how to carry out a computation (Cardelle-Elawar, 1992). After the 30 daily lessons, the students who were given this metacognitive training had better math achievement and better attitudes toward math.

One expert on children's thinking, Deanna Kuhn (2009), argues that metacognition should be a stronger focus of efforts to help children become better critical thinkers, especially at the middle school and high school levels. She distinguishes between first-order cognitive skills, which enable children to know about the world (and have been the main focus of critical-thinking programs), and second-order cognitive skills—meta-knowing skills—which involve knowing about one's own (and others') knowing.

DEVELOPMENTAL CHANGES

How does metacognition change in childhood? Are there further changes in metacognition during adolescence?

DEVELOPMENT

Childhood   Many studies have focused on children's *metamemory,* or knowledge of how memory works (Ghetti, Castelli, & Lyons, 2010). In the last several decades, there has been extensive interest in children's theories about how the human mind works.

Metamemory   By 5 or 6 years of age, children usually know that familiar items are easier to learn than unfamiliar ones, that short lists are easier than long ones, that recognition is easier than recall, and that forgetting becomes more likely over time (Lyon & Flavell, 1993). In other ways, however, young children's metamemory is limited. They don't understand that related items are easier to remember than unrelated ones or that remembering the gist of a story is easier than remembering information verbatim (Kreutzer & Flavell, 1975). By fifth grade, students understand that gist recall is easier than verbatim recall.

Preschool children also have an inflated opinion of their memory abilities. For example, in one study, a majority of preschool children predicted that they would be able to recall all ten items of a list of ten items. When tested, none of the young children managed this feat (Flavell, Friedrichs, & Hoyt, 1970). As they move through the elementary school years, children give more realistic evaluations of their memory skills (Schneider & Pressley, 1997).

RESEARCH

Preschool children also have little appreciation for the importance of memory cues, such as, "It helps when you can think of an example of it." By 7 or 8 years of age, children better appreciate the importance of cueing for memory. In general, children's understanding of their memory abilities and their skill in evaluating their performance on memory tasks is relatively poor at the beginning of the elementary school years but improves considerably by age 11 or 12 (Bjorklund & Rosenblum, 2000).

Theory of Mind   Even young children are curious about the nature of the human mind. They have a **theory of mind,** which refers to awareness of one's own mental processes and the mental processes of others. Studies of theory of mind view the child as "a thinker who is trying to explain, predict, and understand people's thoughts, feelings, and utterances" (Harris, 2006, p. 847). Researchers are increasingly discovering that children's theory of mind is linked to cognitive processes and disabilities (Doherty, 2008; Wellman, 2011). For example, theory of mind competence at age 3 is related to a higher level of metamemory at age 5 (Lockl & Schneider, 2007). Researchers also have found that autistic children have difficulty in developing a theory of mind, especially in understanding others' beliefs and emotions (Hall, 2009). Sometimes this has been referred to as *mindblindness* (Jurecic, 2006).

theory of mind Awareness of one's own mental processes and the mental processes of others.

DEVELOPMENT

Children's theory of mind changes as they develop through childhood (Gelman, 2009; Wellman, 2011). The main changes occur at 2 to 3 years of age, 4 to 5 years of age, middle and late childhood, and adolescence.

- *Two to Three Years of Age.* In this time frame, children begin to understand three mental states: (1) perceptions, (2) emotions, and (3) desires. *Perceptions:* The child realizes that another person sees what is in front of his or her own eyes and not necessarily what is in front of the child's eyes. *Emotions:* The child can distinguish between positive (for example, happy) and negative (sad, for example) emotions. A child might say, "Tommy feels bad." *Desires:* The child understands that if someone wants something, he or she will try to get it. A child might say, "I want my mommy." Children refer to desires earlier and more frequently than they refer to cognitive states such as thinking, knowing, and beliefs (Rakoczy, Warneken, & Tomasello, 2007). Two- to three-year-olds understand the way that desires are related to actions and to simple emotions (Harris, 2006). For example, they understand that people will search for what they want and that if they obtain it, they are likely to feel happy, but if they don't they will keep searching for it and are likely to feel sad or angry.

- *Four to Five Years of Age.* Children come to understand that the mind can represent objects and events accurately or inaccurately. The realization that people can have *false beliefs*—beliefs that are not true—develops in a majority of children by the time they are 5 years old (Wellman, Cross, & Watson, 2001) (see Figure 12.14). In one study of false beliefs, young children were shown a Band-Aids box and asked what was inside (Jenkins & Astington, 1996). To the children's surprise, the box actually contained pencils. When asked what a child who had never seen the box would think was inside, 3-year-olds typically responded "pencils." However, the 4- and 5-year-olds, grinning at the anticipation of the false beliefs of other children who had not seen what was inside the box, were more likely to say "Band-Aids."

  Children's understanding of thinking has some limitations in early childhood (Wellman, 2011). They often underestimate when mental activity is likely occurring. For example, they fail to attribute mental activity to someone who is sitting quietly, reading, or talking (Flavell, Green, & Flavell, 1995).

- *Middle and Late Childhood.* It is only beyond the early childhood years that children have a deepening appreciation of the mind itself rather than just an understanding of mental states (Wellman, 2011). Not until middle and late childhood do children see the mind as an active constructor of knowledge or processing center (Flavell, Green, & Flavell, 1998). In middle and late childhood, children move from understanding that beliefs can be false to an understanding of beliefs and mind as "interpretive," exemplified in an awareness that the same event can be open to multiple interpretations (Carpendale & Chandler, 1996).

- *Adolescence.* Important changes in metacognition also take place during adolescence (Kuhn, 2009, 2011). Compared with children, adolescents have an increased capacity to monitor and manage cognitive resources to effectively meet the demands of a learning task. This increased metacognitive ability results in more effective cognitive functioning and learning. A recent longitudinal study revealed that from 12 to 14 years of age, young adolescents increasingly used metacognitive skills, and used them more effectively, in math and history classes (van der Stel & Veenman, 2010). For example, 14-year-olds monitored their own text comprehension more frequently and did so more effectively than their younger counterparts.

  Adolescents have more resources available to them than children (through increased processing speed, capacity, and automaticity), and they are more skilled at directing the resources. Further, adolescents have a better meta-level understanding of strategies—that is, knowing the best strategy to use and when to use it in performing a learning task (Kuhn, 2009).

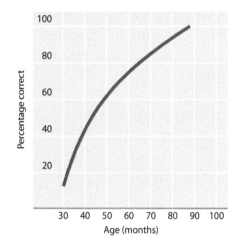

FIGURE **12.14** DEVELOPMENTAL CHANGES IN FALSE-BELIEF PERFORMANCE

False-belief performance dramatically increases from 2½ years of age through the middle of the elementary school years. In a summary of the results of many studies, 2½-years-olds gave incorrect responses about 80 percent of the time (Wellman, Cross, & Watson, 2001). At 3 years, 8 months, they were correct about 50 percent of the time, and after that, gave increasingly correct responses.

Keep in mind, though, that there is considerable individual variation in adolescents' metacognition. Indeed, some experts argue that individual variation in metacognition is much more pronounced in adolescence than in childhood (Kuhn, 2009). Thus, some adolescents are quite good at using metacognition to improve their learning, others far less effective.

THE GOOD INFORMATION-PROCESSING MODEL

Michael Pressley and his colleagues (Pressley, Borkowski, & Schneider, 1989; Schneider & Pressley, 1997) developed a metacognitive model called the *Good Information-Processing model*. It emphasizes that competent cognition results from a number of interacting factors. These include strategies, content knowledge, motivation, and metacognition. They argue that children become good at cognition in three main steps:

1. *Children are taught by parents or teachers to use a particular strategy.* With practice, they learn about its characteristics and advantages for learning *specific knowledge*. The more intellectually stimulating children's homes and schools are, the more specific strategies they will encounter and learn to use.

2. *Teachers may demonstrate similarities and differences in multiple strategies in a particular domain, such as math, which motivates students to see shared features of different strategies.* This leads to better *relational knowledge*.

3. *At this point, students recognize the general benefits of using strategies, which produces general strategy knowledge.* They learn to attribute successful learning outcomes to the efforts they make in evaluating, selecting, and monitoring strategy use *(metacognitive knowledge and activity)*.

STRATEGIES AND METACOGNITIVE REGULATION

In the view of Pressley and his colleagues (Pressley, 1983, 2007; Pressley & Harris, 2006; Pressley & Hilden, 2006), the key to education is helping students learn a rich repertoire of strategies that results in solutions of problems. Good thinkers routinely use strategies and effective planning to solve problems. Good thinkers also know when and where to use strategies (metacognitive knowledge about strategies). Understanding when and where to use strategies often results from the learner's monitoring of the learning situation.

Pressley and his colleagues argue that when students are given instruction about effective strategies, they often can apply strategies that they previously have not used on their own. They emphasize that students benefit when the teacher models the appropriate strategy and overtly verbalizes its steps. Then students should practice the strategy, guided and supported by the teacher's feedback until they can use it autonomously. When instructing students about employing a strategy, it also is a good idea to explain to them how using the strategy will benefit them. However, there are some developmental limitations to this approach. For instance, young children often cannot use mental imagery competently.

Just having students practice the new strategy is usually not enough for them to continue to use the strategy and transfer it to new situations. For effective maintenance and transfer, teachers should encourage students to monitor the effectiveness of the new strategy relative to their use of old strategies by comparing their performance on tests and other assessments (Harris & others, 2008). Pressley says that it is not enough to say, "Try it, you will like it"; you need to say, "Try it and compare."

An important aspect of metacognition is monitoring how well one is performing on a task (Graham & Olinghouse, 2009). This might involve becoming aware that one has not studied enough for a test or needs to reread a particular section of a chapter to understand it better. Mismonitoring is common. For example, elementary school students often think they are better prepared for a test than they actually are and think they understand text material better than they do. One

What are some strategies for improving metacognitive regulation?

TEACHING CONNECTIONS: Best Practices
Strategies for Helping Students Use Strategies

Following are some effective ways that teachers can guide students to develop strategies for helping students use strategies (Pressley, 1983, 2007; Pressley & McCormick, 2007):

1. *Recognize that strategies are a key aspect of solving problems.* Monitor students' knowledge and awareness of strategies for effective learning outcomes. Many students do not use good strategies and are unaware that strategies can help them learn. And after students learn a strategy, they tend to shorten and reduce it, in the process losing important components. Thus, be sure to monitor students who modify strategies in ways that make the strategies less effective.

2. *Model effective strategies for students.*

3. *Give students many opportunities to practice the strategies.* As students practice the strategies, provide guidance and support to the students. Give them feedback until they can use the strategies independently. As part of your feedback, inform them about where and when the strategies they used are most useful.

4. *Encourage students to monitor the effectiveness of their new strategy in comparison to the effectiveness of old strategies.* Students are much more likely to continue to use new strategies if they perceive them to be more effective than their old strategies. Help them to see the efficacy of their new strategies if they are unable to monitor the effectiveness themselves.

5. *Remember that it takes students a considerable amount of time to learn how to use an effective strategy.* Be patient and give students continued support during this tedious learning experience. Keep encouraging students to use the strategy over and over again until they can use it automatically.

6. *Understand that students need to be motivated to use the strategies.* Students are not always going to be motivated to use the strategies you want them to use.

Especially important to students' motivation is their expectations that the strategies will lead to successful learning outcomes. Explicitly point out their successes in relation to strategy use. It can also help if students set goals for learning effective strategies. And when students attribute their learning outcomes to the effort they put forth, their learning benefits.

7. *Encourage children to use multiple strategies.* Most children benefit from experimenting with multiple strategies, finding out what works well, when, and where.

8. *Read more about strategy instruction.* Two good resources are *Best Practices in Literacy Instruction* (Gambrell, Morrow, & Pressley, 2007) and a chapter by Michael Pressley and Karen Harris (2006) titled "Cognitive strategies instruction: From basic research to classroom instruction," both of which include numerous helpful ideas about how to improve children's use of strategies. Especially good online sources are (a) **http://shop.ascd.org/ProductDisplay .cfm?ProductID=402086** (strategy instruction is shown in a video focusing on teaching in elementary and middle school classrooms), (b) **http://iris/peabody .vanderbilt.edu/index.html** (a free online interactive tutorial on strategy instruction), and (c) **www.unl.edu/csi** (Robert Reid's excellent Web site that is devoted to strategy instruction).

9. *Ask questions that help to guide students' thinking in various content areas.* These might include, "How can proofreading help me in writing a paper?" "Why is it important periodically to stop when I'm reading and try to understand what is being said so far?" and, "What is the purpose of learning this formula?"

10. *Recognize that low-achieving students and students with disabilities often need more support and time to become effective in independently using strategies.*

strategy is to encourage students who mismonitor to create practice tests and questions to assess how complete their understanding is.

Learning how to use strategies effectively often takes time (Bjorklund, 2011). Initially, it takes time to learn to execute the strategies, and it requires guidance and support from the teacher. With practice, students learn to execute strategies faster and more competently. *Practice* means that students use the effective strategy over and over again until they perform it automatically. To execute the strategies effectively, they need to have the strategies in long-term memory, and extensive practice makes this possible. Learners also need to be motivated to use the strategies. Thus, an important implication for helping students develop strategies such as organization is that once a strategy is learned, students usually need more time before they can use it efficiently (Schneider, 2004). Further, it is important for teachers to be aware that students may drop an effective strategy or continue to use a strategy that does not help them (Miller, 2000).

Do children use one strategy or multiple strategies in memory and problem solving? They often use more than one strategy (Bjorklund, 2011). Most children benefit from generating a variety of alternative strategies and experimenting with different approaches to a problem and discovering what works well, when, and where (Schneider & Bjorklund, 1998). This is especially true for children from the middle elementary school grades on, although some cognitive psychologists argue that even young children should be encouraged to practice varying strategies (Siegler, 2009).

Pressley and his colleagues (Pressley & others, 2001, 2003, 2004) have spent considerable time in recent years observing the use of strategy instruction by teachers and strategy use by students in elementary and secondary school classrooms. They conclude that teachers' use of strategy instruction is far less complete and intense than what is needed for students to learn how to use strategies effectively. They argue that education needs to be restructured so that students are provided with more opportunities to become competent strategic learners. Recall from earlier in the chapter in our discussion of memory that teachers vary considerably in how frequently they make suggestions for strategy use as well as how often they use metacognitive questions (Ornstein, Coffman, & Grammer, 2009; Ornstein & others, 2007, 2010).

A final point about strategies is that many strategies depend on prior knowledge. For example, students can't apply organizational strategies to a list of items unless they know the correct categories into which the items fall. The point about the importance of prior knowledge in strategy use coincides with the emphasis in our discussion earlier in the chapter of how experts use more effective strategies than novices.

Review, Reflect, and Practice

⑤ Explain the concept of metacognition and identify some ways to improve children's metacognition.

REVIEW

- How do young children compare with older children in their metacognitive abilities? According to Pressley and colleagues' Good Information-Processing model, competent cognition results from what interacting factors?
- How can children be helped to learn metacognitive strategies and self-regulation?

REFLECT

- How might the three steps in the Good Information-Processing model be part of teaching a topic to children? Select a topic that you might teach one day and try working through it as an example.

PRAXIS™ PRACTICE

1. Sharmala's uncle has just played a trick on her. He presented her with a can that looked like a can of peanuts. However, when she opened the can, a cloth snake sprang out at her. Sharmala thought the trick was very funny and could hardly wait to play it on her brother. When her uncle asked her what she thought her brother would expect to be in the can, she giggled and responded, "Peanuts, but won't he be surprised." This is an example of Sharmala's development of
   a. the ability to allocate attention to different aspects of a problem.
   b. problem-solving expertise.

(continued)

Review, Reflect, and Practice

PRAXIS™ PRACTICE (CONTINUED)

   c. metamemory skills.
   d. theory of mind.

2. Marvel has learned to use strategies to solve math problems but does not use them to study for history exams or spelling quizzes. According to the Good Information-Processing model, the next step for Marvel's metacognitive development would most likely be to
   a. ask his teacher for specific strategies for studying history.
   b. ask his parents about the benefits of using strategies for math.
   c. understand shared features of many different strategies.
   d. learn to attribute successful learning to use of strategies.

3. Mr. Quinton has taught his students the PQ4R strategy for reading textbooks in hopes that it will help them on their next history test. The majority of his class improves their scores. Mr. Quinton is disappointed when in spite of improved performance, many of his students don't continue using the PQ4R strategy. What is the most plausible explanation for the students' behavior?
   a. They did not compare the results of using the PQ4R with their prior strategies.
   b. They don't have the requisite background knowledge to use the PQ4R strategy effectively.
   c. They have not had enough practice to use the strategy effectively.
   d. They have not yet developed expertise in using the strategy.

Please see the answer key at the end of the book.

Connecting with the Classroom: Crack the Case

The Test

George has a test next week in his eighth-grade history class. He is having considerable difficulty remembering terms, names, and facts. On his last test, he identified General Sherman as a Vietnam War hero and Saigon as the capital of Japan. Historical dates are so confusing to him that he does not even try to remember them. In addition, George has difficulty spelling.

The test will consist of 50 objective test items (multiple-choice, true/false, and fill-in-the-blank) and 2 essay items. In general, George does better on essay items. He purposely leaves out any names about which he is uncertain and always omits dates. Sometimes he mixes up his facts, though, and often loses points for misspelled words. On objective items he has real problems. Usually, more than one answer will appear to be correct to him. Often he is "sure" he is correct, only to discover later that he was mistaken.

Before the last test, George tried to design some mnemonic devices to help him understand. He used acronyms, such as *HOMES* (for *H*uron, *O*ntario, *M*ichigan, *E*rie, and *S*uperior).

Although he remembered his acronyms quite well, he could not recall what each letter stood for. The result was a test paper filled with acronyms. Another time a classmate suggested that George try using concept maps. This classmate lent George the concept maps she had designed for her own use. George looked at them and found them to be very busy and confusing—he couldn't figure out what they even meant. They were not at all useful to him.

George has decided he is in need of some serious help if he is to pass this class. He has sought you out for help.

1. What are the issues in this case?
2. With what type of learning is George having difficulty?
3. What type of learning is easier for George?
4. Design a study-skills program for George drawing on principles of the cognitive information-processing approach.

The Information-Processing Approach

1 THE NATURE OF THE INFORMATION-PROCESSING APPROACH: Describe the information-processing approach.

Information, Memory, and Thinking

The information-processing approach emphasizes that children manipulate information, monitor it, and strategize about it. Central to this approach are the processes of memory and thinking.

Cognitive Resources: Capacity and Speed of Processing Information

Capacity and speed of processing information, often referred to as cognitive resources, increase across childhood and adolescence. Changes in the brain serve as biological foundations for developmental changes in cognitive resources. In terms of capacity, the increase is reflected in older children being able to hold in mind several dimensions of a topic simultaneously. A reaction-time task is often used to assess speed of processing. Processing speed continues to improve in early adolescence.

Mechanisms of Change

According to Siegler, three important mechanisms of change are encoding (how information gets into memory), automaticity (ability to process information with little or no effort), and strategy construction (creation of new procedures for processing information). Children's information processing is characterized by self-modification, and an important aspect of this self-modification involves metacognition—that is, knowing about knowing.

2 ATTENTION: Characterize attention and summarize how it changes during development.

What Is Attention?

Attention is focusing mental resources. Four ways that children and adolescents can allocate their attention are selective attention (focusing on a specific aspect of experience that is relevant while ignoring others that are irrelevant), divided attention (concentrating on more than one activity at the same time), sustained attention (maintaining attention over an extended period of time), and executive attention (involves action planning, allocating attention to goals, error detection and compensation, monitoring progress on tasks, and dealing with novel or difficult circumstances). Multitasking is an example of divided attention, and it can have possible harmful effects on children's and adolescents' attention when they are engaging in a challenging task.

Developmental Changes

Salient stimuli tend to capture the attention of the preschooler. After 6 or 7 years of age, there is a shift to more cognitive control of attention. Selective attention improves through childhood and adolescence.

3 MEMORY: Discuss memory in terms of encoding, storage, and retrieval.

What Is Memory?

Memory is the retention of information over time and involves encoding, storage, and retrieval.

Encoding

In everyday language, encoding has much to do with attention and learning. Rehearsal, deep processing, elaboration, constructing images, and organization are processes involved in encoding, which is the mechanism by which information gets into memory. Rehearsal increases the length of time that information stays in memory. In deep processing, information is processed semantically, in terms of its meaning. Elaboration refers to the extensiveness of information processing. Constructing images helps to elaborate the information, and the more information is presented in an organized way, the easier it is to remember.

Storage

One way that memory varies involves its time frames: sensory memory, short-term memory, and long-term memory. There is increasing interest in working memory, a kind of mental workbench. The Atkinson-Shiffrin model states that memory involves a sequence of three stages: sensory, short-term, and long-term memory. Long-term memory includes different types of content. Many contemporary psychologists accept this hierarchy of long-term memory's contents: division into declarative and nondeclarative memory, with declarative memory divided into episodic and semantic memory. Declarative memory (explicit memory) is the conscious recollection of information, such as specific facts or events. Nondeclarative memory (implicit memory) is knowledge of skills and cognitive operations about how to do something; it is hard to communicate verbally. Episodic memory is the retention of information about the where and when of life's happenings; semantic memory is a general knowledge about the world.

Three major approaches to how information is represented are network theories (which focus on how information is organized and connected, with emphasis on nodes in the memory network); schema theories (which stress that students often reconstruct information and fit it into an existing schema); and fuzzy trace theory (which states that memory is best understood by considering two types of memory representation: (1) verbatim memory trace and (2) fuzzy trace, or gist. In this theory, older children's better memory is attributed to the fuzzy traces created by extracting the gist of information. A script is a schema for an event.

Retrieval and Forgetting

Retrieval is influenced by the serial position effect (memory is better for items at the beginning and end of a list than for items in the middle), the effectiveness of retrieval cues, encoding specificity, and the retrieval task (such as recall versus recognition). Forgetting can be explained in terms of cue-dependent forgetting (failure to use effective retrieval cues), interference theory (because information gets in the way of what we are trying to remember), and decay (losing information over time).

4 EXPERTISE: Draw some lessons about learning from the way experts think.

Expertise and Learning

Five important characteristics of experts are that they (1) notice features and meaningful patterns of information that novices don't, (2) have acquired a great deal of content knowledge that is organized in a manner that reflects deep understanding of the subject, (3) can retrieve important aspects of their knowledge with little effort, (4) are adaptive in their approach to new situations, and (5) use effective strategies.

Acquiring Expertise

Becoming an expert usually requires deliberate practice, motivation, and talent.

Expertise and Teaching

Being an expert in a particular area does not mean that the expert is good at helping others learn it. Pedagogical content knowledge is required to effectively teach a subject.

5 METACOGNITION: Explain the concept of metacognition and identify some ways to improve children's metacognition.

Developmental Changes

Children's metamemory improves considerably through the elementary school years. At 5 years of age, a majority of children understand that people can have false beliefs, and in middle and late childhood they understand that people actively construct knowledge. Adolescents have an increased capacity to monitor and manage resources to effectively meet the demands of a learning task, although there is considerable individual variation in metacognition during adolescence.

The Good Information-Processing Model

Developed by Michael Pressley and his colleagues, the Good Information-Processing model stresses that competent cognition results from several interacting factors including strategies, content knowledge, motivation, and metacognition.

In the view of Pressley and his colleagues, the key to education is helping students learn a rich repertoire of strategies that result in solutions to problems. Most children benefit from using multiple strategies and exploring which ones work well, when, and where. For example, teachers can model strategies for students and ask questions that help guide students' thinking in various content areas.

KEY TERMS

information-processing approach 344
encoding 346
automaticity 346
strategy construction 346
metacognition 346
attention 347
selective attention 348
divided attention 348
sustained attention 348

executive attention 348
memory 353
rehearsal 353
levels of processing theory 354
elaboration 354
chunking 356
sensory memory 356
short-term memory 356
memory span 356

working memory 356
long-term memory 358
Atkinson-Shiffrin model 358
declarative memory 359
nondeclarative memory 359
episodic memory 360
semantic memory 360
network theories 360
schema theories 360
schema 360

script 361
fuzzy trace theory 361
serial position effect 361
encoding specificity principle 362
cue-dependent forgetting 362
interference theory 362
decay theory 363
theory of mind 375

PORTFOLIO ACTIVITIES

Now that you have a good understanding of this chapter, complete this exercise to expand your thinking.

Independent Reflection Developing Expert Knowledge. Think about the experts you know. Are your parents or instructors considered experts in their fields? How do you think they came to become experts and how long did it take? Based on what you know about how experts process information, which strategies do you think these experts use to organize, remember, and utilize their knowledge and skills? (INTASC: Principles *2, 4, 9*)

Collaborative Work Strategies to Enhance Memory. Get together with three or four other students in the class and brainstorm about the best ways to guide students in developing better memory and study strategies. Discuss how you might do this differently for children and adolescents at different grade levels. For example, at what

age should students start learning effective note-taking strategies? For children too young to be taking elaborate notes, are there gamelike activities that might help them begin to learn the concept and value of taking notes or keeping running records of some event? Write your conclusions. (INTASC: Principles *2, 4*)

Research/Field Experience Capturing Students' Attention. Observe a kindergarten, elementary, middle school, and high school classroom and focus on how the teacher maintains students' attention. How effective are each teacher's strategies? Would you do things differently to capture the students' attention? (INTASC: Principles *2, 9*)

Go to the Online Learning Center for downloadable portfolio templates.

STUDY, PRACTICE, AND SUCCEED

Visit www.mhhe.com/santrockep5e to review the chapter with self-grading quizzes and self-assessments, to apply the chapter material to

two more Crack the Case studies, and for suggested activities to develop your teaching portfolio.

Module 5
Applying Learning and Cognition

CHAPTER **THIRTEEN**

Deciding to Know Yourself

Your personality affects your decisions. What aspect(s) of your personality contributed to your decision to enroll in college?

YOU DECIDE

To *wonder* means to think or have curiosity about. Things and ideas you wonder about often mask a need for a decision. Check the items below that apply to you.

In terms of my talents and skills, I've been wondering . . .

☐ 13.1 Which skills are among my best and which would I like to improve?

☐ 13.2 How do my values affect the choices I make?

☐ 13.3 How do my study surroundings affect the quantity or quality of what I learn?

☐ 13.4 What's the best way for me to learn?

☐ 13.5 What are my preferences for learning information?

☐ 13.6 What kinds of intelligences do I have?

☐ 13.7 How does my personality affect learning?

☐ 13.8 How does my instructor's teaching style affect my learning preferences?

Each of these decision points corresponds to the numbered modules that follow. Turn to the module for immediate help.

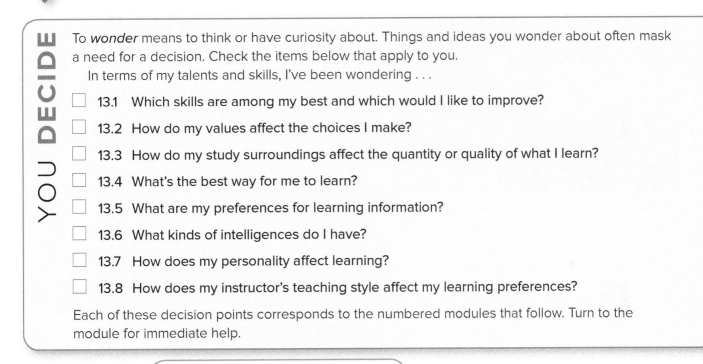

CHOOSING TO BE AN ACTIVE LEARNER

SURVEY

Before reading this chapter, prepare for learning. Purposefully skim the title, introduction, headings, and graphics. As you survey, decide what information you already know and what information is new to you.

QUESTION

Change each section's heading into a question. This forms your learning goal for reading.

READ

Read the section without marking. Reread and mark key information that answers your question.

RECITE

Stop after each section and make sure you understood the content. Organize or summarize content and make notes.

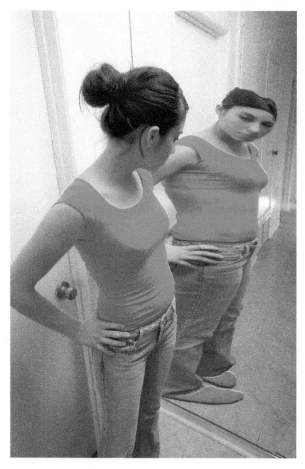

Studying yourself is sometimes not as clear as you'd like it to be.

Few people start a journey without knowing if they have what it takes to get there. Instead, they make sure their transportation is reliable. They look at a map or Mapquest for the best route. They make sure they have enough cash to take them where they want to go.

As a college student, you, too, are on a journey. You are on your way to a college education. You, too, must see if you have what you need to make the trip. The first step is to become aware of what you do and do not know. Your first subject is yourself. This chapter provides you with ways to learn more about yourself. It also includes tips for using the results to your advantage in learning situations.

Some college students spend years learning everything from accounting to zoology. But they often fail to study one of the most interesting and revealing subjects of all—themselves. As a result, they often find themselves puzzled by the choices they make and unhappy with the consequences of those choices on their lives. The 5C process (Define the **C**hallenge; Identify **C**hoices; Predict **C**onsequences; **C**hoose an option; **C**heck your outcome) helps you avoid this problem.

You are a key part of any decision that affects you. So you need to analyze yourself to understand clearly your role in the situations you face. You are the product of your personality and experience. The way you approach life, your attitude, comes from the interaction of your aptitudes, abilities, interests, values, and learning style.

For instance, are you more comfortable in structured or casual situations? Would you rather learn by seeing, hearing, or doing? Do you focus more on details or on the "big picture" of a task? You may know that you have particular talents, interests, and abilities. Maybe you also know you believe in certain things—your values. You probably also have preferences for your learning environment, the way you best acquire information, and the way you process information most effectively. These together make up your **learning style.**

learning style
The mix of attributes that describe the ways that you best acquire and use information.

While you can learn in ways and situations that do not match your style, knowing your style preferences helps you make informed decisions about the learning options. For instance, being aware of your style lets you decide if online classes are better for you than face-to-face classes. Your decision to include your learning style into your study process is not a shortcut to learning. It is an asset in maximizing how you think, learn, and remember. Finally, your learning style affects your responses to your instructor's teaching style.

Aptitudes and Abilities

Has someone ever said that you had a talent or knack for doing something? Such natural or inborn traits and talents are called **aptitudes.** They reflect your potential. Some aptitudes are evident from an early age. For instance, children who play music by ear, draw well, win at sports, or solve math problems easily often do so because of aptitude. Your aptitude for doing something well may correspond to your having an interest in doing it. Other aptitudes are hidden. While you have an interest in a subject, you do not realize that you have the talent for that subject. For example, you might be interested in how cars work but don't realize that you could easily become your own mechanic. Learning about new aptitudes and interests is an integral part of being in college. As you experience new people and new situations, both will develop naturally.

> **aptitudes**
> Inborn traits or talents.

Most likely, you have already recognized and developed noticeable aptitudes. That leaves the hidden ones for you to explore. Taking an aptitude test helps you do so. General aptitude tests estimate verbal, numerical, spatial, and some coordination skills. More specialized aptitudes, such as music and art, are not assessed by general aptitude tests. The advising, placement, or career center at your college (see Chapter 2) probably gives aptitude tests at little or no cost. Such tests help you find new possibilities for your consideration.

Abilities are what you can do. They are the results of aptitude combined with experience. Abilities are not constant. They increase with practice and decrease with disuse. And having ability does not equal success. Motivation and persistence also play a role (see Chapter 6).

> **abilities**
> Capabilities that result from aptitude combined with experience.

Unlike aptitude, which is an estimated quality, ability can be measured by performance on formal and informal evaluation tools. Formal tests measure generalized areas of ability such as analytical intelligence or verbal skills. In contrast, informal assessments often help you identify specific abilities and individual strengths and weaknesses. For instance, each test you take in a class is a kind of subject-specific assessment of your ability to understand and use the information in the course.

Both aptitudes and abilities factor into the decisions you make whether you are at home, at school, or on the job. One way to increase your specific abilities is to analyze your preparation strategies as well as your score after each test. Consider what went well and explore what went wrong. Note the new skills you developed and the ones that still need work.

What Are Your Aptitudes?

Read through the following aptitudes, definitions, and examples.

Aptitude	Definition	Examples
Verbal or Nonverbal Communications	Communicating ideas, emotions, or information through spoken or unspoken language	Public speaking Writing essays, poems, plays Performing before an audience Teaching others Using Facebook or Twitter
Verbal Comprehension	Understanding verbal or nonverbal communications	Emphatic or sympathetic listening Selling Competing in debate Using Facebook or Twitter
Logical Understanding	Applying reason or logic	Solving mysteries Completing word or jigsaw puzzles Conducting scientific experiments Writing a computer program
Artistic Talent	Using artistic, musical or dramatic talents	Drawing Writing poems or plays Playing a musical instrument Singing Taking photographs Arranging displays
Mechanical Skills	Understanding relationships between parts of machines and/or how things are made and work	Putting a computer back together Repairing an automobile Reading blueprints Building models
Numerical Skills	Working with numbers	Working math problems Bookkeeping/working with spreadsheets Reading number graphs
Clerical Skills	Completing basic office work	Word Processing Filing records Controlling inventory Sending and receiving e-mail
Spatial Understanding	Understanding how parts of things fit together or multidimensional understanding	Completing a jigsaw puzzle Putting together models Reading blueprints
Physical Dexterity	Moving with bodily strength, coordination, and agility	Lifting weights Moving furniture Dancing
Organizational Talents	Planning, implementing and evaluating actions for yourself or others	Planning a party Organizing a trip Creating and editing simple databases
Intellectual Abilities	Original thinking, seeking knowledge, thinking ahead, and developing concepts	Reading books Studying Creating a new recipe Developing a business plan

1. Write a paragraph each about four experiences in your life you particularly enjoyed.

2. Reread your descriptions of each experience, and decide which of the list of aptitudes shown in the chart above best represents each experience.

3. Create a three-column chart of your own. List the aptitudes you identified in question 2 in the first column. In the second column, list the interests and experiences you have had that support your choice of aptitudes. In the third column, list the aptitudes you'd like to develop or improve.

4. Use the 5C process to identify how your aptitudes and abilities can guide your decisions about coursework and college experiences. First, state one of your aptitudes or abilities you wish to improve as a *Challenge* that requires a choice. For instance your statement might be "I want to perform before an audience." Next, identify your *Choices*—the courses or activities at your institution that might provide you with that experience. This might include joining the campus choir, auditioning for a play, or taking a class in dance. Your interests, aptitudes, and abilities naturally affect the choices you make. Consider how you might develop a further interest or acquire a new skill before you make a choice. What are the *Consequences* for each option? That is, if you implement that option, what would be the benefits of it? Which option would you *Choose*? How might you *Check* the outcome of your choice?

How do my values affect the choices I make?

Values

values
Personal beliefs and standards expressed in the topics and activities that are important to you.

Values are personal beliefs and standards that are reflected in your experiences. Whether you are consciously aware of them or not, you have a core set of personal values. When you look at the lives of people, you see the values that guide them. Perhaps you know someone who volunteers at a hospital. You may know someone who spends free time at art museums. Perhaps you know someone who is active in their church, synagogue or mosque. What each of these people does is directly related to what they value—service to others, art, or religion. The same is true of you.

You get some of your values from your family and friends. Your thoughts and reactions to situations and people form other values. Events and people you learn about through television, literature, and other media also shape them. In Activity 2 that follows you will find a list of common values. The importance you place on each one determines its value to you. There may be other aspects of life you value more.

One way to identify your values is to explore why you sit where you do now—that is, why are you in college? Recognizing the real reason or reasons why you're in school forms the first step in understanding your values because it helps show how and why you made one very important choice—to enroll in college.

Research suggests that students attend college for different reasons. The reasons, however, can be divided into three groups. First, some people attend college to reach self-fulfillment. They expect college to help them become the best, most learned persons that they can be. Second, some people come to college to get the education they need for the career they hope to have someday. While often uncertain about the specifics of that career choice, they know that they want to work as a professional and they see college as the road to that destination. Third, some people are avoiders. They attend college not to accomplish self-fulfillment or career goals but to satisfy the wishes of parents or peers or to avoid or delay making other important life decisions. Each of these reasons reflects differences in values.

Whatever your values, be assured that knowing your values strengthens everything concerned with them. Knowing your values and committing to them is an important step in achieving success and well-being.

What's Important? What's Not?

What are your values? Circle the top 10 terms in the list below that describe your values. Rank the ones you circled in order from most important (#1) to least important (#10). Think carefully about these values. Then think of a personal challenge and use the 5C (Define the **C**hallenge; Identify the **C**hoices; Predict the **C**onsequences; **C**hoose an option; **C**heck your outcome) approach to make a decision regarding the challenge reflecting your values. You may use one of the following questions to help you identify a challenge:

- Do my activities/school/job/career plans reflect my most important values?

- Are my values being met?

- What can I do to meet my values?

- I just feel that now that I know my values, so what? What action steps should I take?

- How might my values affect career choice?

achievement	agreement	ambition
authority	beauty	belonging
career/professional success	comfort	communication
competition	courage	creativity/innovation
equality	excellence	excitement/challenge/adventure
fame/prestige	family	financial stability/wealth
freedom/independence	friendship/companionship	happiness/personal satisfaction
health	helping	honesty/truth/integrity
honor	knowledge	leisure activity/play/fun
logic/wisdom	love	mental/intellectual development
neatness/orderliness	passion	peace/conflict resolution/harmony
physical development	power	responsibility
security	self-esteem	self-control
self-respect	social life	social recognition/respect of others
spiritual development	tradition	trust
truth	wisdom	

Environmental Preferences

environmental preferences
Physical surroundings that are most comfortable for you.

Where you learn–your **environmental preferences**–can be just as important as what you learn and how you learn it. For instance, you might prefer to study seated at a desk or spread out on the floor. You might like the room to be cool or warm. You might prefer to read in a well-lit room or in a darker room with light focused only on the page.

Accommodating these preferences adds to your learning efficiency and effectiveness. You probably can't always control where your classes are located. But you often can control some aspects of your classroom environment and most aspects of your learning environment. For instance, you might choose to study in a quiet library instead of in a noisy coffee shop. You might decide to take an online course rather than a face-to-face class.

Some people have to study where they can hear themselves think. Others prefer sound to help them study.

Checking Environmental Preferences

PART 1A: Your Preferences

Directions: Check the conditions you prefer in each section.

LIGHTING

_____ **1.** I often turn on extra lamps for reading.

_____ **2.** People sometimes tell me I'm reading in the dark.

_____ **3.** I prefer to sit by windows at home, at work or in class.

_____ **4.** I prefer to sit in the back or corner of a classroom or work area.

_____ **5.** I often choose seats directly below overhead lights.

_____ **6.** I find I sometimes shade my eyes while reading or solving math problems.

_____ **7.** Low light makes me sleepy.

STRUCTURE

_____ **1.** I prefer to stand and move around when studying or working.

_____ **2.** I prefer to study seated on the floor rather than at a desk.

_____ **3.** I find it more difficult to concentrate in lectures than in lab courses.

_____ **4.** I find I fidget after sitting for a short length of time.

_____ **5.** I find myself tapping my foot or knee after sitting for a short length of time.

SOUND

_____ **1.** I prefer to study or work in silence.

_____ **2.** When I really concentrate, I don't hear a thing.

_____ **3.** I find myself easily distracted by noises in class, even when I am interested in the topic under discussion.

_____ **4.** Background noises—conversation, soft music, TV—don't affect my ability to work or study.

_____ **5.** Sometimes I wish I could tell my classmates or co-workers to be quiet.

_____ **6.** I often hum to myself or tap while working.

_____ **7.** I prefer podcasts and lectures to reading.

VISUAL

_____ **1.** I am often distracted by classroom movement, even when I'm interested in the topic under discussion.

_____ **2.** When I study, I have notes, papers, books, and other materials spread around me.

_____ **3.** I find busy environments—crowded stores, cluttered desks, messy rooms—confusing.

_____**4.** I prefer highly colored, bold, and busy patterns.

_____**5.** I am very organized; when I study, I only have the bare essentials of what I need at hand.

_____**6.** I enjoy courses in which the lecturer is theatrical and moves freely around the classroom.

PART 1B: *Scoring and Analysis*

LIGHTING

If you checked the odd-numbered items, you probably prefer to study or work in strong light. If you checked the even-numbered items, you probably prefer to learn or work in more subdued light. Look for ways to adjust the lighting in your environment.

STRUCTURE

If you checked any three of the five statements, you probably prefer less structure and more mobility in your learning or work environment. Although you probably can't change your classroom environments, you can structure your study environment so that you can move around and feel less confined.

SOUND

If you checked the odd-numbered statements, you probably prefer to learn or work in quiet or silent surroundings. If you checked the even-numbered statements, you learn better with some background noise.

VISUAL

You withstand a high degree of visual stimulation if you checked the even-numbered statements in this category. If you checked the odd-numbered statements, you may be more easily distracted by what you see.

PART 2: Really Preferences or Just Habits?

Review what you checked in each category. Consider if what you checked is truly a preference or just a habit. For instance, do you actually learn better when seated in the back of a classroom or is that just where you usually sit? For this 5C (Define the Challenge; Identify the Choices; Predict the Consequences; Choose an option; Check your outcome) application, use one of the environmental preference categories (stucture, sound, visual) as your challenge. For example, your challenge might be "In terms of structure, what kind of study environment is best for me?" Generate choices for both structured and unstructured environments (e.g., studying at a desk in the library versus standing/walking, seated on the floor, or in another less traditional environment). What do you think might be the consequences of each choice for you? What is the best evironment for you to choose? How can you check the outcome of this choice to determine if it is really the best or just a habit?

Sensory Preferences

Sensory preferences involve the way or ways in which you like to acquire information. If you are a visual learner, you like to aquire information through what you see. This includes pictures and written words. If you like to acquire information through what you hear, you are an auditory learner. This includes all kinds of sounds from spoken words to musical rhythms. If you are a tactile/kinesthetic learner, you learn through touch and physical experiences. This includes hands-on activities and other ways to learn by doing.

Once you know your sensory preferences, you can use them to maximize your performance. For example, suppose you have a list of items to remember. If auditory learning is your preference, you could create a song to help you recall the list. If visual learning is what you prefer, you might draw pictures of the items. If you are tactile/kinesthetic learner, you might make flash cards and then sort them into stacks, arranging the cards in order of importance to a particular topic or in order of how well you know the information. While you may show a preference for one type of learning or another, you may actually learn best if you combine two or more learning preferences. For example, you could use flash cards that have pictures you drew that you sort into stacks.

Some people find that bright colors and bold patterns help them think.

Making the Most of Your Sensory Preferences

Visual Learners . . .	Auditory Learners . . .	Tactile/Kinesthetic Learners . . .
Sit near the front of a class to minimize visual distractions	Listen to podcasts of lectures	Use hands-on activities such as labs and models
Create flash cards and games	Take part in class discussions and ask questions in class	Think of real-life applications
Use supplemental handouts and text illustrations	Restate what you learn in your own words	Role-play concepts
Take notes while listening	Sit in the front of the class to avoid distractions	Take notes as you listen or read
Underline information		Use computers
Use different colors to highlight ideas in text or online	Get ebooks or use software that reads information on your computer aloud	Make and use learning games
		Rewrite class notes
Create graphic or symbolic arrangements of information on paper or online	Read notes and text aloud	Practice writing responses to exam questions
	Participate in tutorials or tutor others	Teach others
Use pictures, diagrams and other visuals		

 **activity 4**

Identifying Your Sensory Preferences

Directions: Rate your preference for each item using the following scale:
Almost always = 4 points, Often = 3 points, Occasionally = 2 points, Rarely = 1 point

Visual Modality

_____ I remember information better if I see it.

_____ When someone asks me how to spell a word, I have to see it spelled several different ways to know which one is correct.

_____ Looking at a person helps keep me focused on what s/he says.

_____ I need a quiet place to get my work done.

_____ When I take a test, I can see the textbook page in my head.

_____ I need to read directions for myself, not just hear them verbally.

_____ Music or background noise distracts me.

_____ I don't always get the meaning of a joke.

_____ I doodle and draw pictures on the margins of my notebook pages.

_____ I have trouble following lectures.

_____ I react very strongly to colors.

_____ I remember faces more easily than names.

_____ I learn best by watching someone else before trying something myself.

_____ When preparing for a test, I often use flash cards and study guides.

_____ The one thing I need in life is TV and videos.

_____ **Total**

Auditory Modality

_____ My papers and notebooks always seem messy.

_____ When someone asks me how to spell a word, I can easily identify the correct auditory spelling or verbally say how the word is spelled.

_____ When I read, I use my index finger to track my place on the line.

_____ I do not follow written directions well.

_____ If I hear something, I will remember it.

_____ Writing has always been difficult for me.

_____ I often misread words from the text (i.e., *them* for *then*).

_____ When I do math, I say the numbers and steps to myself.

_____ I would rather listen and learn than read and learn.

_____ I'm not very good at interpreting an individual's body language.

_____ Pages with small print or poor quality copies are hard for me to read.

_____ My eyes tire quickly, even though my vision checkup is always fine.

_____ I remember names more easily than faces.

_____ I learn best from lectures and verbal directions.

_____ When studying for a test, I often use tapes or go to study groups.

_____ The one thing I need in life is music.

_____ Although I don't always contribute, I like in-class discussions.

_____ When I have to read, I read softly to myself.

_____ **Total**

Tactile/Kinesthetic Modality

_____ I start a project before reading the directions.

_____ When someone asks me how to spell a word, I have to see it spelled several different ways to know which one is correct.

_____ I hate to sit still for long periods of time.

_____ I prefer to learn by doing.

_____ I can handle multiple tasks.

_____ I use the trial-and-error approach to problem solving.

_____ I like to read my textbook while riding an exercise bike.

_____ I take frequent study breaks.

_____ I have a hard time giving step-by-step instructions to others.

_____ I enjoy sports and excel at several different types of sports.

_____ I use my hands when describing things.

_____ I have to rewrite or type my class notes to reinforce the material.

_____ I often "play" with small objects such as paper clips or pencils.

_____ When studying for a test, I often reorganize my notes or create maps.

_____ The one thing I need in life is sports.

_____ I like to make things to help me study.

_____ **Total**

Scoring: Total the score for each section. The highest of the three scores indicates the most efficient method of information intake. The second highest score indicates the modality that boosts the primary strength.

GROUP APPLICATION: Compare your results with those of other students in the class. What kinds of instructional and learning activities meet the need of visual learners? Auditory learners? Tactile/kinethetic learners? What kinds of study skills will meet the needs of each of these kinds of learners? What work situations would be best for each of these types of learners?

Processing Preferences

Once you get information, your brain processes it to incorporate it into your own thinking. Like all learners, you probably have a preference for either global or logical thinking. Global thinkers focus more on the "big picture" rather than details. They tend to be creative and visual. They are good at drawing conclusions and dealing with emotions. Logical thinkers are, by definition, more rational. They focus on details rather than main ideas. Logical thinkers approach information more systematically. They prefer to make decisions based on facts rather than emotion. The following table gives additional traits for logical and global processing.

What happens if you have an instructor whose thinking or teaching style differs from yours? For example, suppose you prefer structure such as outlines, intermediate deadlines, and detailed instructions, and your instructor likes to free-associate information? You will need to carefully note these free associations and then later create more organized notes for yourself either individually or in a study group, and by meeting with the instructor. Or, if you are a hands-on learner whose instructor provides only print information, you will need to create your own flash cards and look for activities on the Web to support the concepts you are learning.

Logical and Global Processing Traits

Logical	Global
Language (speech and writing)	Pattern recognition
Recall of names	Recall of faces
Recall of words in a song	Recall of a song's melody
Planned	Spontaneous
Math	Synthesis
Time	Holistic overview
Rhythm	Visual information
Systematic	Random
Sequencing	Spatial order
Analysis	Feelings
Linearity	Intuitiveness
Details	Creativity
Orderliness	Imagination
Abstraction	Multitasking
Factual or realistic applications	Nonverbal information
Objective test formats	Metaphoric thinking
	Improvisation
	Subjective test formats

Analyzing Your Preferences for Global or Logical Thinking

Directions: Circle the choice you prefer in each question.

1. How do you prefer making decisions? a. intuitively b. logically

2. Is it easier for you to remember people's names or faces? a. names b. faces

3. How do you schedule activities? a. plan activities in advance b. do things spontaneously

4. In social situations, which do you prefer to be? a. the listener b. the speaker

5. What do notice most when listening to a speaker? a. what the speaker says b. the speaker's body language

6. Do you consider yourself to be a goal-oriented person? a. yes b. no

7. How would you describe your main study area? a. messy b. neat and well organized

8. Are you usually aware of what time it is and how much time has passed? a. yes b. no

9. How would you describe your writing style? a. let ideas flow freely b. plan the sequence of ideas in advance

10. What do you remember about music? a. words b. tunes

11. Which do you prefer doing? a. watching a movie b. talking to others

12. Do you frequently move your furniture around in your home? a. yes b. no

13. Are you a good memorizer? a. yes b. no

14. When you doodle, what do you make? a. shapes b. words

15. Clasp your hands together. Which thumb is on top? a. left b. right

16. Which subject do you prefer? a. algebra b. geometry

17. How do you usually plan your day? a. list what you need to accomplish b. just let things happen

18. Are you good at expressing your feelings? a. yes b. no

19. What are you more likely to do in an argument with someone else? a. listen and consider the point of view of the other person b. insist that you are right

20. At the beginning of winter, are you likely to find change in last year's coat pocket? a. yes b. no

SCORING: Check or circle your answers below.

GLOBAL	1A	2B	3B	4A	5B	6B	7A	8B	9A	10B
LOGICAL	1B	2A	3A	4B	5A	6A	7B	8A	9B	10A

GLOBAL	11A	12B	13B	14A	15A	16B	17B	18A	19A	20A
LOGICAL	11B	12A	13A	14B	15B	16A	17A	18B	19B	20B

Total your answers: Total # Global _____ Total # Logical _____

GROUP APPLICATION: Share your totals for each type of processing with your group. What similarities and differences do you discover among your group's scores? Divide a piece of paper into four quadrants for recording your responses. In the top left quadrant, create a chart that describes how five of the logical processing traits in the list in Module 13.5 could be converted into strategies for learning. In the top right quadrant, identify how five of the global traits in that list could be converted into strategies for learning. In the bottom left quadrant, identify three ways in which a person who lacks skills in logical traits could develop those skills. In the right quadrant, identify three ways in which a person who lacks skills in global traits could develop those skills. Why is it important for a person to develop both logical and global traits in college? in the workplace?

Your Multiple Intelligences

Intelligence was once defined as the ability for thinking. People thought you were born with it. Standardized tests measured it. The result of this test was your IQ (intelligence quotient) score. Supposedly, the score determined if you were smart or not. But guess what? Like many standardized tests, the IQ tests were not always accurate.

Harvard researcher Howard Gardner defined intelligence differently. Intelligence, to him, was an ability to create a valuable product or offer an important service. Gardner said intelligence consisted of a set of skills that helped you solve different kinds of life problems, whether those were personal, social, work, or educational. And, he said, the intelligences could be developed and strengthened.

Gardner identified eight basic types of intelligences, which he called *multiple intelligences*. The table on the following page lists and defines these eight types. The table also shows preferences of and ways to develop each one.

The Eight Different Intelligences

Type	Definition	Preferences	Ways to Develop
Verbal-linguistic	Language and thoughts in terms of meaning and sound of words	Stories, jokes, arguments, poetry, reading, speaking	Listening to guest speakers, doing word puzzles, learning vocabulary, writing fiction and nonfiction
Logical-mathematical	Abstractions, numbers or reasoning	Solving math problems, sorting information, offering advice, computer programming, inventing	Finding patterns, using a calculator, finding examples, solving logic puzzles, classifying and organizing information
Spatial	Visualization and use of pictures and space	Seeing things in relationship to others things; parallel parking, design or decoration of personal spaces, packing items	Jigsaw puzzles, artwork, concept mapping, color coding, rearranging items in a room or space, examining similarities and differences
Bodily-kinesthetic	Control of physical movements and skill in handling objects	Acting, dancing, sports, hands-on activities	Stretching, charades, sign language, working with arts and crafts, individual and group sports
Musical	Use of rhythm, pitch, and timbre	Play or write music, create rhythm games or songs, dance	Playing instruments, having environmental music in the background, putting information to a rhythm, creating rhymes to remember information
Interpersonal	Understanding and responding appropriately to emotions, motivations, and goals of others	Small groups, peer learning, service learning	Cooperative groups, creating teams, sharing responses, clarifying emotions and motivations
Intrapersonal	Understanding and responding appropriately to one's own emotions, motivations, and goals	Individual work and achievement, journal writing, self-discovery	Provision of time for reflection, keeping a journal, reading published journals or diaries, self-assessments, identifies attitude, personality traits and learning styles
Naturalist	Recognition, categorization, and use of plants, animals and other objects in nature	Field trips, science experiments, observing how natural objects are similar and different	Lab courses, working in pairs on experiments, writing a journal about science experiments, reading about different scientists

Analyzing Your Intelligences

Directions: Circle the items you prefer in each box. Then rank your preferences with #1 being your strongest preference.

Box A Rank _____	Box B Rank _____	Box C Rank _____	Box D Rank _____
I like to read.	Math is one of my strengths.	I need to use visuals in order to learn new things.	I can tell when instruments play out of tune.
I like to write reports.	I like to solve logic problems and mysteries.	I have a good imagination.	I like to browse around music stores.
Names, places, dates, and details are easy to recall.	I like computers.	I like to look at videos.	I drum and tap on almost everything.
I prefer using a word processor to handwriting.	I can usually figure out how something works.	Mazes are fun.	I often listen to music while I study or work.
I use tape recorders to save/replay information.	I like to explore new things.	People say I am artistic.	I am highly aware of environmental sounds.
I can tell good stories or jokes.	I like to analyze things.	I can read maps and charts easily.	I listen to rhythm of a song more than the words.
I really like social studies subjects.	I enjoy puzzles and riddles.	I like to look at photographs.	I like to sing.
I like to browse in bookstores or libraries.	I like to sort and classify things.	I can design and give a media presentation.	Recalling melodies is easy for me.
I like to read books and magazines.	Science is interesting.	I like looking around at museums.	I can play one or more musical instruments.
Giving a speech isn't a problem for me.	I enjoy conducting experiments.	I like to daydream.	I enjoy live music.
I can write stories.	I like forms of instructional technology.	I can look at a 2-dimensional drawing and create it in 3-dimensions.	I can match pitches.

Box E Rank _____	Box F Rank _____	Box G Rank _____	Box H Rank _____
I like to touch things.	People say I'm a born leader.	People say I have confidence in myself.	I like being outdoors more than being indoors.
Sports personalities fascinate me.	I enjoy discussions.	I don't like group projects and study groups.	I do things to protect the environment.
People say I talk with my hands.	I like study groups.	I know what my strengths and abilities are.	People say I have a green thumb.
I have good fine motor coordination.	I am a good peacemaker.	I know how to get help to attain the goals I want to achieve.	I like animals.
I am good at sports.	I can organize other people.	I like cumulative writing projects.	I like to order things in hierarchies.
I enjoy watching sports events.	I am a "people person."	I like to sit quietly and think.	Ecological issues are important to me.

Box E Rank _____	Box F Rank _____	Box G Rank _____	Box H Rank _____
I can do arts and crafts.	I like to interview others.	I like pursuing my personal interests and hobbies.	I have plants in my house.
I like hands-on learning.	I can debate issues easily.	I prefer independent research projects.	I own at least one pet.
I have a difficult time keeping still.	I solve problems by talking though them.	I set goals for myself and achieve them.	Animal behavior interests me.
I like to communicate through movement or dance.	People think I am a good listener.		I like to camp and hike
I like to move around (sit, stand, walk, etc.).	I am a good communicator.		I know the names of different kinds of plants.

KEY

Box A = Verbal/Linguistic

Box B = Mathematical/Logical

Box C = Visual/Spatial

Box D = Musical/Rhythmic

Box E = Bodily/Kinesthetic

Box F = Interpersonal/Directed toward others

Box G = Intrapersonal/Directed toward self

Box H = Naturalist

List your intelligences in order from #1 to #8.

1. _____

2. _____

3. _____

4. _____

5. _____

6. _____

7. _____

8. _____

GROUP APPLICATION: Divide into groups based on your #1 rankings (e.g., everyone that ranked Verbal as #1 in a group, etc.). Give an example of something you do that exemplifies your strongest intelligence. Discuss how the results of this intelligence preference have more, or less, effect on success in college. If the effect is negative, discuss how you can minimize the effect. Compare your current majors and career interests. Discuss how specific intelligences might lead to decisions about majors and careers.

Your Personality Type

Personality-type preferences affect how you interact with people, objects, and situations. Many college advising-and-career centers administer the *Myers-Briggs Type Indicator* (*MBTI*) to students, and you would benefit from taking the entire scale. Until you do so, the following assessment provides you with a quick and informal estimate of personality type.

The results of this assessment form a starting point for identifying your learning preferences and the strengths of these preferences. Your results will consist of a four-letter type formed by your preferences in each of the following pairs: extraversion (*E*) or *introversion* (*I*), *sensing* (*S*) or *intuition* (*N*), *thinking* (*T*) or *feeling* (*F*), and *perceiving* (*P*) or *judging* (*J*).

Preferences for Each Dimension

The first letter in your type will be an *E* or *I*. This indicates whether you get your energy from people (*E* for *extraverted*) or ideas (*I* for *introverted*). If you are an extravert (*E*), you tend to like variety and activity. You prefer working with others in short bursts of energy rather than working alone for long periods. As a result, you may almost welcome interruptions and lose patience when you have to concentrate for extended periods. As an *E*, you often learn what the instructor expects, but you may act too quickly or lose interest rather than thinking things through or persevering. On the other hand, if you are an *introvert* (*I*), you can focus on single topics for long periods when working alone in quiet places where there are few interruptions. You prefer to set your own standards rather than figuring out "what the instructor wants." Although you tend to stick with a task until it's finished, you might work on a detail of it until you miss the deadline for completion.

The second set of letters—*S* or *N*—concerns the kind of information you tend to notice first and prefer to use. If you are an *S* (*sensing*), you focus on what you learn through your senses—tasting, touching, smelling, hearing, and feeling. Thus, you learn best from hands-on or multisensory experience. Because you are more oriented to the present, you often need to know the rationale for a task before beginning it. You probably prefer to work on realistic, goal-oriented activities with practical applications rather than on vague or theoretical assignments. You like to refine current skills instead of learning new ones. You probably tend to work patiently and steadily using a detailed, step-by-step approach. If you are an N (iNtuitive), you give more importance to gut feelings or conclusions. Your orientation to the future results in your interest in abstract concepts and theoretical or imaginative applications. You learn more from reflectively reading, thinking, or visualizing than from hands-on activities. You work in short bursts of energy and are ready to move on to new things once skills have been mastered. Details are not as important to you as they are to your S counterparts. As a result, your attentiveness to the "big picture" and belief that things will eventually "come together" allow you to feel comfortable with incomplete understanding of an idea or task.

The next set of letters (T and F) involves the criteria you use in making decisions. If T (thinking) is your preference, the words logical, fair, firm, objective, and unemotional probably describe the way you decide. You are task-oriented and motivated by a desire for achievement. You use standard criteria for evaluation whatever the circumstances. If F (feeling) is your dominant style, your decisions are swayed by how they affect you or others and are described by words such as subjective, flexible, and relevant. You are motivated by a desire to be appreciated, and you apply personal, rather than standard, criteria in your evaluations.

The last letter (P or J) concerns your decision-making process. If your preference is P (perceiving), you like to gather information and delay making decisions until you know everything. In fact, you'd probably choose not to decide at all. Although you tend to be a self-directed learner who likes flexibility in assignments, you like to know only what is needed to accomplish a task. You probably find process more important than product and enjoy thinking and adapting more than activity and completion. If you are a J (judging), you want to make a decision—any decision—and get on with life. Unlike perceivers, you tend to focus on one task at a time and limit commitment. You tend to be a rigid, persistent perfectionist who plays only after work is completed. Because you find the product more important than the process, you are goal-directed and prefer structured deadlines.

No single letter or combination of letters may accurately capture all your personality traits because your results probably show that you have degrees of preference for each attribute. Both life and stress alter your personality, so the personality type you show a partiality for today might change as your life does. Nonetheless, knowing your type can aid you in making all sorts of decisions, including those you make as a student.

The combination of individual dimensions creates 16 types which can be described by different characteristics. Rather than examining dimensions individually, analyzing the type provides a more global look at an individual's thoughts and actions.

Personality Types and Descriptions

Type	Description
ISTJ	Loyal, and responsible, ISTJs enjoy order, structure, organization, and traditions. Like all introverts, they need personal space and time to re-energize. They attend to details and can be counted on to follow through on tasks. Often preferring to work alone, they tend to work steadily and complete projects on time. For them, team projects must have clearly defined roles and responsible team members. In terms of applying the 5C approach, ISTJs are good at gathering facts, generating possibilities, and identifying logical consequences; however, they sometimes overlook long-range solutions in favor of more immediate solutions, lack diplomacy in
ISFJ	Like ISTJs, ISFJs are also loyal and responsible; however, they enjoy harmony as well as order. Because they are more feelers than thinkers, they are more considerate of the feelings of others. They make choices based on personal values, commitment to the task and others, and integrity. They dislike conflict and confrontation. In terms of the 5C approach, their problem-solving approach is much like that of the ISTJ in that they are good at gathering facts, generating possibilities, and identifying logical consequences. However, their feeling side sometimes leads them to catastrophize when generating outcomes and thus appear pessimistic. Their focus on the feelings of others may cause them to appear more inequitable than fair.
INFJ	Committed to meaning and relationships, INFJs have a gift for intuitively understanding people and situations. They have the capacity to organize, and motivate others to achieve their vision for the common good. Like all introverts, they need personal space and time to re-energize. In terms of the 5C approach, they are good at gathering the facts, taking the needs and feelings of others into consideration, generating possible options, and identifying logical consequences. Because they rely more on intuition than on sensing, they may not always get and consider all the facts, and because decisions are often based on feelings, others may perceive their choices as capricious rather than logical or fair. Once they commit to a vision, they may pursue it with determination, even if the vision is impractical or illogical.
INTJ	Mentally quick and efficient, INTJs expect the best from themselves and others. Like all introverts, they need personal space and time to re-energize. They are intolerant of inefficiency and confusion in either people or situations. They have both the capacity for broad global visioning and the capability to transform those visions into reality. They excel at problem solving that involves complex situations or abstract ideas and rely on their abilities to find patterns and form new insights. In terms of the 5C approach, INTJs sometimes rely on intuition and may not always gather all the facts they need. They are good at generating options and logical outcomes; however, since they are thinkers rather than feelers, their decisions are often viewed as logical, but not necessarily popular with others.
ISTP	Tolerant and flexible, ISTPs are quiet observers until a problem appears, then they act quickly to find workable solutions. They prefer realistic applications to abstract theories and excel at seeing how things work. Like all introverts, they need personal space and time to re-energize. In terms of the 5C approach, they excel at gathering information, generating options, and considering logical outcomes. With their focus on sensing and thinking, they solve problems in a computer-like fashion in taking in large amounts of data, organizing it and making logical decisions. However, their decisions, while expedient and efficent, do not always take the feelings or needs of others into account. And because they tend to trouble-shoot problems with speed, they may arrive at a good choice for the present situation, but not the best one in the long run.

ISFP	Harmonious and kind, ISFPs tend to be "doers" who enjoy the present moment and what's going on around them. Like all introverts, they need personal space and time to re-energize. They dislike routines and prefer the freedom to set their own goals and schedule; however, they are strongly committed to fulfilling their obligations. In terms of the 5C approach, ISFPs gather information but are sometimes unable to deal with the complexity of the information they get. They consider personal values and well as the needs and feelings of others in making decisions. However, they sometimes reject logical approaches and fail to see the larger implications of in-the-moment choices.
INFP	Idealistic and caring, INFPs like to think about patterns and possibilities, especially when they involve or affect people. The prefer flexibility and spontaneity, following new insights and possibilities as they arise. They have a desire to see self and others grow and develop. Their intuitive skills allow them to see and honor the feelings of others even if others have not recognized or expressed those feelings. Like all introverts, they need personal space and time to re-energize. In terms of the 5C approach, INFPs are less likely to gather all the facts. They take the feelings of others and themselves into account when identifying options and outcomes and often make decisions based on pleasing others rather than on logic. As perceivers, they often feel that they don't have enough information to see the pattern and will procrastinate in making a final decision until they do.
INTP	Analytical, yet flexible, INTPs are deep thinkers and independent problems solvers who search for the logical answers to life's "why" questions. They enjoy theoretical and abstract thinking rather than practical applications. Like all introverts, they need personal space and time to re-energize. In terms of the 5C approach they gather information and look for patterns or connections among them. They may appear to be insensitive to the needs of others in generating options and overzealous in pursuing a logical, if not practical, outcome.
ESTP	Analytical and resourceful, ESTPs have a zest for life and enjoy living in the moment. Like all extraverts, they are energized by being around others. ESTPs take a pragmatic whatever-it-takes approach toward problem solving that is focused more on immediate results than on following rules or procedures. They have a gift for making work fun and are good at resolving conflicts. In terms of the 5C approach, they are good at gathering facts; however, they may only collect data that is immediately available. They excel as take-charge trouble-shooters who take a direct, no-nonsense, pragmatic approach; however, they sometimes act impulsively without regard for how their actions affect others or for the broader implications of immediate decisions. They don't always follow through on commitments.
ESFP	Warm and tactful, ESFPs are often described as social and exuberant lovers of life, people, and material comforts. Like all extraverts, they are energized by being around others. As keen observers of human behavior, ESFPs like to work with others to handle problems and make things. Their approach is based on common sense, but with a disregard of rules that may hamper a direct solution. In terms of the 5C approach, they pay attention to details, but tend to take them at face value rather than examining information for deeper meaning. ESFPs make decisions based on their personal values and their perceptions of the feelings and needs of others. Because they tend to live in the moment, ESFPs sometimes are distracted or impulsive and don't always take the needed steps to meet future deadlines.
ENFP	Enthusiastic and imaginative, ENFPs tend to view life and people as full of possibilities both in the present and in the future Like all extraverts, they are energized by being around others. They excel at supporting and affirming others

	and value harmony and goodwill. In terms of the 5C approach, they easily and quickly connect events and information very quickly, and confidently act on the patterns they see. They prefer experimentation and working toward broad goals rather than following rules and attending to detail. They like starting things, but often fail to meet deadlines or follow through. They may generate options and outcomes, but their decisions are based more on expediency and feeling than on logic.
ENTP	Ingenious and outspoken, ENTPs are good at looking for opportunities or possibilities for both situations and people. Like all extraverts, they are energized by being around others and particularly skilled at reading people and situations. In terms of the 5C approach, ENTPs tend to focus more on insightful use of information than on the actual collection of information. They excel at generating options and logical conclusions; however, routine bores them and they rarely do the same thing in the same way twice. They don't always pay enough attention to the feelings and needs of others when making decisions. Because they are always trying out new ideas and innovative approaches, ENTPs may sometime be perceived as having a lack of focus and consistency,
ESTJ	Conscientious and dependable, ESTJs organize projects and people to accomplish tasks or achieve goals in a timely and efficient manner. Like all extraverts, they are energized by being around others but they prefer to know what is expected rather than what is possible. In terms of the 5C approach they are good at collecting detailed information and generating options and logical outcomes based on rules and procedures As a result, they tend to choose the tried-and-true approach rather than the innovative approach. They excel at creating and maintaining traditional management systems which allow them to meet deadlines with efficiency; however, their preference for making quick decisions often means that the decision they make is good and safe, but not necessarily the best or most innovative choice. And because they base decisions on logic rather than the feelings and needs of others, they may fail to consider the long-term outcomes on individuals affected by the decision.
ESFJ	Warm and conscientious, ESFJs deal with situations and people in a factual, yet personal basis to accomplish tasks efficiently and on time. Tradition and authority are important to ESFJs. Like all extraverts, they are energized by being around others and they especially value harmony and work to achieve it. They attend to the needs of the group or individual with kindness and tact and can always be counted on to follow through on commitments with diligence and accuracy. They like and need to be recognized for their contributions. In terms of the 5C approach, ESFJs are good at gathering information. Their ability to generate options and logical outcomes may be skewed by their overwhelming desire to please others and meet their needs. They tend to make choices that are traditional rather than innovative.
ENFJ	With empathy and enthusiasm, ENFJs are people persons who have the capacity to understand the needs, motivations, and concerns of others and the capability of supporting and encouraging the development of others. Like all extraverts, they are energized by being around others. Their intuitive strengths enable them to see possibilities in others. This enables them to facilitate and inspire personal change in others. In terms of the 5C approach, ENFJs may overlook information in their efforts to realize their ideas. They may be so attuned to the needs of others that they fail to think of all options and logical outcomes. Their decisions may result in favorable outcomes for individuals but not for the situation as a whole.

ENTJ	Decisive and impersonal, ENTJs have a take-charge, businesslike approach to people and situations. They are natural leaders and organizational problem solvers. Like all extraverts, being around others energizes them but they often prefer conflict over harmony in interactions and like to be in control of situations and sometimes people. In terms of the 5C approach, they are more adept at seeing patterns in information that in collecting information. They are strategic visionaries who excel at both seeing options and logical outcomes and then transforming those possibilities into plans to achieve short-term objectives as well as long-term goals. Their focus as thinkers and judgers often means that they set personal standards and apply them to others without considering how others might feel or think about them. They may make decisions just to get things settled and gain closure although they enjoy exploring and discussing new ideas.

Identifying Your Personality Type

activity 7

Print the assessment OR write the letter (A or B) of the phrase that you prefer. In some cases, both A and B may seem preferable, or neither will be preferable. Still, try to make a choice between the two. Work quickly—first impressions are most likely to be correct. Total your scores for each section and record your type in the blanks below.

I prefer . . .

1. A. loud parties   OR   B. quiet gatherings of friends
2. A. working on a project   OR   B. thinking about an idea
3. A. working with others   OR   B. working alone
4. A. managing many projects OR   B. focusing on one project
5. A. talking about an idea OR   B. writing about an idea
6. A. discussion classes   OR   B. lecture classes
7. A. outgoing people   OR   B. reflective people
8. A. being part of a crowd OR   B. being alone

Total A responses _____ = EXTRAVERT Total B responses ____ = INTROVERT

I prefer . . .

1. A. practical applications of ideas   OR   B. theoretical considerations of a topic
2. A. lab courses/hands-on projects   OR   B. reading and listening
3. A. factual descriptions   OR   B. metaphorical descriptions
4. A. proven solutions   OR   B. untried solutions
5. A. to go places that I've been to before OR B. to go to new places
6. A. to attend to details   OR   B. to focus on main ideas
7. A. tasks in which I achieve   OR   B. accomplishing goals over an extended
      goals quickly   period of time
8. A. information derived from logic   OR   B. information that results from conclusions

Total A responses ___ = SENSING   Total B responses ___ = INTUITIVE

I prefer . . .

1. A. self-satisfaction in a job well done OR B. appreciation of others for a job well done
2. A. multiple-choice tests OR B. essay tests
3. A. logical arguments OR B. emotional appeals
4. A. impartial people OR B. compassionate people
5. A. rules and standards OR B. negotiation and compromise
6. A. for people to follow the rules OR B. to allow for exceptions to rules
7. A. professional expertise OR B. helpful attitude
8. A. to make decisions based on logic OR B. to let my heart influence a decision

Total A responses ___ = THINKING   Total B responses ___ = FEELING

I prefer . . .

1. A. to be on time OR B. to get places when I get there
2. A. well-thought-out decisions OR B. spur-of-the-moment decisions
3. A. organization OR B. flexibility
4. A. expected activities OR B. improvised activities
5. A. structured assignments OR B. unstructured assignments
6. A. step-by-step approaches OR B. random approaches
7. A. planned parties OR B. surprise parties
8. A. serious people OR B. casual people

Total A responses ___ = JUDGING   Total B responses ___ =

PERCEIVING

Now, identify your composite type by circling the letter that reflects your preference in each set.

E I   S N   T F   J P

INTERPRETATION OF RESULTS: Your results can be interpreted in two ways. One way is to look at what preferences for each dimension involve for you. A second way is to look at your total combination of preferences.

GROUP APPLICATION: Divide into groups based on each pair of dimensions (E/I, N/S, T/F, P/J). Discuss how the dimension affects personality.

Your Instructor's Style

No matter what course you take, instructors vary in the ways in which they structure their classes. Even instructors of the same topic structure their courses differently. Some instructors rely on verbal information. They just talk or lead a discussion among class members. The information in such classes is given only in spoken form. Other instructors provide visual reinforcement of what they say (for example, outlines, written lecture guides, overhead transparencies, or electronic presentations). Still others give demonstrations or lab activities that supply virtual or actual experiences.

Online courses also reflect an instructor's style. Some online courses are very structured with consistent features in each week's units, regularly scheduled deadlines, and easily usable navigation. Others, like the thinking of the faculty that create them, are more free-flowing. Many online courses depend more on written information to transmit directions and content. Others include interesting graphics, links to videos and websites, interactive games and flash cards, PowerPoint presentations enhanced with audio, files that can be downloaded and played on iPods or MP3 players, or content that can be accessed via cell phones.

College faculty differ from high school teachers in several ways. High school teachers must have a minimum of a four-year undergraduate degree. The degree is generally in some area of education. Their coursework specifically prepared them to teach. College faculty must generally have an advanced degree—either a master's or doctorate—to teach. Their degrees focus on specific subjects (such as history, math, or psychology). Their coursework provided them with additional information about the subject rather than ways to teach it. Many college campuses provide faculty development workshops to help instructors learn new teaching techniques; but it is often up to each faculty member to attend these and put the content into effect in their own classrooms. As a result, many instructors teach as they were taught or as they feel comfortable.

As a result, you may find some course styles—both in face-to-face and online classes—meet your needs better than others. You will also find that you will be able to adapt to some styles better than others. Whatever the case, learning remains your responsibility. Luckily, you can rethink information and structure it in ways that suit you.

What's Your Instructor's Teaching Style?

Select an instructor you feel has a teaching style that is the most different from your learning style.

Use the following inventory to identify your instructor's teaching style in terms of modality and thinking preferences.

PART 1: Sensory Prefernces

Uses lecture or podcasts as primary means of delivering information	Uses text as primary means of delivering information	Uses labs, demonstrations, or activities as primary means of delivering information
Uses large group discussion	Provides outlines and written study guides	Includes service learning
Provides verbal instructions or podcasts for assignments	Provides written instructions and examples for assignments	Demonstrates how assignments should be completed or provides a video clip to show how the assignment should be completed
Uses guest speakers or tells stories	Shows videos as lecture launchers	Uses problem or case-based learning
Subjective, essay exams	Objective, multiple-choice exams	Performance exams

Total the number of boxes you checked in each row. The following key helps you identify an instructor's sensory preferences: Column 1, auditory; Column 2, visual; Column 3, tactile-kinesthetic.

PART 2: Thinking Preferences

Student-centered classrooms	Subject-centered classrooms
Grades on a curve or more subjectively	Set grading system (e.g., grading rubrics)
Invites creativity in completing assignments; assignments may seem unclear	Clear, structured assignments
Focus on broad issues and application of ideas	Focus on details and memorization of specific knowledge
Flexible schedules for information and completing of assignments	Specified schedules and firm deadlines for coverage of information and assignments
General syllabus with broad topics assigned to nonspecific time frames	Organized syllabus with content identified for specific dates
In face-to-face classes, moveable desks arranged loosely in rows, small groupings; in online classes, includes icebreakers, activities and discussions to foster group interactions	Moveable desks placed in straight rows and columns; provides little opportunity for peer-to-peer interactions
No attendance requirement as long as students complete the work	Attendance requirement with assigned seats
Students can sit where they wish	Assigned seating

Total the number of boxes you checked in each row. The following key helps you identify an instructor's preferred modality: Column 1, global; Column 2, logical.

GROUP APPLICATION: Divide into pairs—one logical- and one global-processing student to each pair. Once you have identified your instructor's style, discuss ways you can make allowances for the differences between your learning style and the instructor's teaching style.

chapter review

Respond to the following on a separate sheet of paper or in your notebook.

1. What is the difference between aptitudes and abilities?
2. Other than aptitude, what affects the development of abilities?
3. How can course exams help you identify strengths and weaknesses in ability?
4. Choose one of the values you circled in Activity 2. How do you use that value in making decisions about your home life? School? Work?
5. List and define the types of intelligences a person can have. Which of your intelligences were you aware of? Which surprised you? What will you do to develop your intelligences?
6. What differences have you noted between college faculty and high school teachers or bosses on the job? Do you prefer to learn from college faculty or high school teachers or bosses on the job? Why?
7. Who ultimately controls learning—the instructor or the student? Explain.
8. Consider your learning style and preferences. How do they affect (a) the small decisions you make (for example, to miss a class or not) and (b) the big decisions you make (that is, selecting a major, for example)? Be specific.
9. Compare intelligences and aptitudes. What are the commonalities? Why do they exist?
10. Consider your MBTI type as determined in Activity 7 and the description of attitudes and learning styles associated with it. Do you agree that it describes you? How or how not?

did you decide?

Did you accomplish what you wanted to in this chapter? Check the items below that apply to you.

Review the *You Decide* questions that you identified at the beginning of the chapter, but look at them from a new direction. If you didn't check an item below, review that module until you feel you can confidently apply the strategies to your own situation. However, the best ideas are worthless unless they are put into effect. Use the 5Cs to help you decide what information you found most helpful in the chapter and how you plan to use it. Record your comments after the statements below.

☐ **13.1.** I know which skills are among my best and which I would like to improve.

_____

_____

☐ **13.2.** I see how my values affect the choices I make.

_____

_____

☐ **13.3.** I can alter my study surroundings to improve the quantity and quality of what I learn.

_____

_____

☐ **13.4.** I recognize my own best way to learn.

_____

_____

☐ **13.5.** I can organize my study to best use my own preferences for learning information.

_____

_____

☐ **13.6.** I know what kinds of intelligences I have.

_____

_____

☐ **13.7.** I know how my personality affects learning style.

_____

_____

☐ **13.8.** I understand how my instructor's teaching style affects my learning preferences and can adapt to it.

_____

_____

perspectives

In the following article, "Olson Looks for Career in Education," journalist Morgan Muhlenbruch describes one student's interests and talents as well as his major.

Think about and answer these question:

1. Given Olson's experiences, how would you describe him? Why?
2. What do you think are Olson's interests?
3. Given Olson's background and interests, do you predict that he would enjoy being a teacher? Why or why not?
4. Describe how the 5C decision-making process applies to Olson.

   A. What was Olson's **C**hallenge in terms of choosing a major?

   B. What key **C**hoices do you think were open to him?

   C. What do you think are the major **C**onsequence(s) of each choice?

   D. What did Olson **C**hoose?

   E. How can he **C**heck the outcome of his decision?

Hit by a car.
Fell off a 30-foot waterfall.
Run over by a tractor.

Mychal Olson, an education major at NIACC, has done just that. Invincible? You tell me.

He has somehow survived several crazy stunts, giving him a status somewhere near Evil Knievel. Now he says he is settling down to become a teacher and survive in a classroom in the future.

Olson possesses many talents. In high school, he participated in football, basketball, track, band, dance team and drama/theater.

Olson said he debated about being a teacher while he was in high school, so he sat down and had a heart to heart conversation with one of his favorite teachers, Schlumbomb.

Olson said Schlumbomb told him that he should just go for it in the field of education. Olson is currently enrolled in classes to help him pursue his dream. He said Introduction to Teaching, taught by NIACC instructor Kacy Larson, is currently his favorite class. In the course, students learn about various factors that will affect them as teachers, such as the location of the school within the community or the organization and administration of schools. In Introduction to Teaching, many in-class group assignments are given, and many discussions are held.

"He is engaging [during discussions]," classmate Hannah Lupkes said. "When he speaks, you just want to hear more."

Another class that Olson said he is enrolled in is a field experience and seminar course. Olson said he will get to go into a classroom of his choice for 22 hours and observe a teacher. For this course, Olson goes to Waverly-Shell Rock High School to observe another favorite teacher, Mrs. Hanfelt. Olson said he is excited about becoming a teacher, which is why he enjoys these courses.

"It's the first step," Olson said. "I love it."

"Mychal has a great sense of humor that [future] students will really enjoy in the classroom," Larson said. "He also has the ability to think critically about topics being discussed."

Once Olson graduates from NIACC, he said he plans to transfer to UNI, so he can continue his education and further pursue his dreams. Eventually, Olson said he wants to be an English teacher at a small high school in Iowa. Despite the fact that he has traveled to all of the contiguous 48 states, he said his heart is stuck in Iowa.

"I feel best when I'm helping others feel at their best," Olson said. "The best way to do that is to teach."

reflecting on decisions

Now that you've gotten the big picture about your assets, what have you learned about your aptitudes, abilities, interests, values or preferences that can help you make decisions more effectively?

SERVICE LEARNING

Learn and Serve America's National Clearinghouse defines service learning as "combining service objectives with learning objectives with the intent that the activity changes both the recipient and the provider of the service. This is accomplished by combining service tasks with structured opportunities that link the task to self-reflection, self-discovery, and the acquisition and comprehension of values, skills, and knowledge content." Rather than an unrelated volunteer experience, service learning serves to extend thinking about the content of a course. For instance, students in a freshman composition course might volunteer at community agencies and then write descriptive papers about their experiences or a letter to someone at the agency to persuade them to change something at the site. Students also reflect on the meaning of their service in terms of how the service impacted the recipients and the community as a whole, affected themselves, and resulted in clearer understanding of course content. Check to see which courses on your campus include service learning and think about taking one. You'll gain new insights about yourself, others, your course, and the world. Use the 5Cs—Define the **C**hallenge; Identify the **C**hoices; Predict the **C**onsequences; **C**hoose an option; **C**heck your outcome—to determine if a course that has a service learning component is one you'd like to take.

‹ CHOOSING TO SERVE

REVIEW

Skim the notes you made throughout the chapter. How does the content fit together? What information is still unclear? Were your learning goals met? Can you answer the review questions and define terms?

‹ CHOOSING TO BE AN ACTIVE LEARNER

CHAPTER **FOURTEEN**

Choices for Succeeding in Class and Online Courses

One of the most important skills in life is listening, not simply hearing. Respond to the following: How do you decide what's important to listen for in lectures?

YOU DECIDE

To *wonder* means to think or have curiosity about. Things and ideas you wonder about often mask a need for a decision. Check the items below that apply to you.

In terms of my listening and notetaking, I've been wondering . . .

- ☐ **14.1** What can I do to be a better listener?
- ☐ **14.2** What should I listen for in different classes?
- ☐ **14.3** Am I a good notetaker?
- ☐ **14.4** What should I do with notes after I take them?
- ☐ **14.5** What digital technologies can be used for notetaking?

Each of these decision points corresponds to the numbered modules that follow. Turn to the module for immediate help.

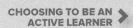
CHOOSING TO BE AN ACTIVE LEARNER

SURVEY

Before reading this chapter, prepare for learning. Purposefully skim the title, introduction, headings, and graphics. As you survey, decide what information you already know and what information is new to you.

QUESTION

Change each section's heading into a question. This forms your learning goal for reading.

READ

Read the section without marking. Reread and mark key information that answers your question.

RECITE

Stop after each section and make sure you understood the content. Organize or summarize content and make notes.

Have you ever sat in class and thought, "Boring! I'm never going to need to know this." When you feel this way, it's easy to lose interest and even easier to tune out. But what if someone paid you to sit in class and *really* listen and take notes with enthusiasm? What is the minimum amount you would take for the job? $100 an hour? $50 an hour? $25 an hour? $10 an hour? Minimum wage? For most students, there is a dollar amount that would guarantee their interest. Some students say they would take the job for $10 an hour or less.

Right now, college is at least one of your jobs. The classroom is one of your worksites. This job, like most others, is work—and by definition, work isn't always fun. In college, you work for yourself and your future. As an adult, you know that you are more motivated in situations in which you are in control. That works well in college because you control how you approach the job of being a student.

But, honestly, will you need the lecture information again? Yes . . . and no. In many courses you are, indeed, learning specific skills—how to write well, ways to use computers, what to do in a medical emergency—that you will apply directly on the job. Still, in these and many other college courses, *what* you learn is only part of the experience. Your college courses also teach you *how* to learn new information and think critically about it.

Learning, then, becomes *less* of a product that may or may not be useful and *more* of a process that can be applied to any situation. For instance, you might be in college to take courses for computer certification. However, once you complete the certification, the software company releases a new version of the software. You have new software to learn but you also have the skills for learning it. Or, perhaps your company adopts a different kind of software that performs similar functions. No problem. You now possess the ability to compare the versions, analyze the differences, and adapt to the new one.

Thus, while you may never use the exact content of a course lecture again, the processes you acquire—the ability to think and learn—will have practical value no matter what you do. They will be just as relevant to achieving your goals in the work world as they will to achieving your academic goals. This chapter provides you with four such processes: becoming an **active listener;** preparing for and participating in learning in class; developing a system for recording and reviewing information; and taking notes from online courses.

active listener
A student who consciously controls the listening process through preplanned strategies.

14.1 module

What can I do
to be a better
listener?

Choosing to Become an Active Listener in Class

Did you know that babies can hear before they're born? If it's something we've done since before birth, why aren't we better listeners? The answer is that hearing and listening are not the same. Hearing is passive. Listening is an active process you choose by what you do, and what you don't do, in class.

What to Do in Class

As you've probably noticed, not all instructors would win points on *American Idol*. Few radiate star power. They are just regular people who are experts in their fields. Their job is to communicate information to you, not to entertain you. Your job is to acquire the content no matter how it is presented.

Consider this. What if someone forced you to stand outside in the cold, rain, or heat for several hours? Would you do it? How would you feel? What if you were waiting in line to get tickets to a ballgame or a concert? Would this change how you feel? Why? Motivation is the difference. You do lots of things that you don't necessarily like if you choose to do so. Interest in course information is a choice you make as you prepare for class.

Being prepared is a good way to make sitting through a lecture a more positive experience. Look again at the survey and question steps of the SQ3R process at the start of this chapter. You can apply this process to prepare you for what the instructor will be covering. Phrase the lecture topic to yourself as a question. It makes what's said in class relevant.

What you do in class also helps you focus on lecture content. First, bring your course materials to class so that, should your instructor refer to them, you'll have them. This includes your textbook, notebook, handouts, and perhaps even information from your class's online site.

Second, arrive on time. If you are late, you might miss introductory statements that set the tone for the rest of the lecture. Also being late could contribute to your feeling disorganized or panicked. These feelings could lessen your ability to listen attentively.

Sometimes a favorite instructor becomes a mentor.

Third, choose your seat strategically. When possible, sit near the front of the classroom. This is especially important if you have an attention disorder. If you sit in the middle or back, you can get distracted by people sitting between you and the instructor. If window views, hall noise, or friends distract you, sit away from them. If you are a visual or auditory learner (see Chapter 13), you need to sit where you can see or hear best. Choose your seat based on what's best for your focus and concentration.

Fourth, when you get to class, spend the time before an instructor begins, briefly reviewing your previous class notes to refresh memory and provide continuity. Because notes are taken in a class-by-class fashion, many students tend to think of their subject in a piece-by-piece manner. This review helps you avoid that.

Fifth, you need to be aware of the impression you make. Talking to friends, texting, playing on your laptop, or looking bored makes a lasting impression on instructors. It also shifts your focus away from content.

Last, respond to lecture material with body language, mental comments, and written notes. Your body language tells the instructor how well you understand the lecture. Mental comments–the thoughts you have about the lecture–should question what is said as well as what and how you think about it. As you listen, ask yourself, "What?" "So what?" and "Now what?" These help you identify "*What* is this about?" "*So what* does that mean to me?" and "*Now what* is coming next?" Written notes are your summary of the answers to these mental questions.

mentors
Wise and trusted counselors or teachers who advise, instruct or train a student outside a regular classroom.

advisors
Persons who provide information and advice on a range of topics including college policies and course schedules.

Class preparation and participation have another important benefit. Sometimes the same faculty member teaches more than one course that you need to take. The favorable impression you create will pay dividends in your continued coursework. The instructors in your field of study may become your **mentors** or faculty **advisors.** During your college career, mentors and advisors provide valuable insights about fields of study and careers. You will need some to write letters of recommendation when you finish your degree. Mentors also provide tips and leads on job opportunities after you leave school. A mentor's help can be so valuable that many students maintain professional contacts with their mentors after they leave the institution.

⟩ What Not to Do in Class

Speakers talk at a rate of about 125–150 words per minute but most people can listen at a rate of about 400–500 words per minute. What happens during the rest of the time? You have plenty of time to think about other things while you appear to be listening. This often results in either day-dreaming or worry. To avoid this, you must make a decision to consciously avoid the two. After all, you can choose what you think. Most worries can't be resolved during class so you should put them aside until you can do something about them. One way to do so is to jot notes about the problems and put the notes away. This allows you to put them out of sight and out of mind until class ends.

A second way to get back on track is to ask yourself, "What is the best use of my time right now?" Chances are the things that distract you can't be resolved while you are in class. And you'll probably have to spend more time catching up on what you missed than the time you would be spending in class. So, in most cases, you will conclude that the best use of your time will be actively listening to the lecture.

Everything–from interesting window views to classroom noises–has the power to divert your attention. To refocus, you need to follow a couple of steps. First, be aware of what distracts you. If you can, move to another seat where the distractions are less evident. Second, sit as close to the speaker as possible. This helps you focus your attention.

Hunger, room temperature, fatigue and other physical concerns affect concentration. The best way to handle factors like these is to take care of these before class. Have a snack, take along a jacket, get rest, or go to the bathroom before you go to class.

Academic freedom in higher education means the freedom to teach or communicate ideas or facts even if unpopular or controversial, and this often may mean that instructors say things that contradict what you think and value. This might arouse such emotional responses in you that you stop listening as you mentally argue with the speaker. To resolve this situation is to become aware of your responses. Decide to continue listening and hear the person out. If necessary, jot down your arguments. This may release some pent-up feelings and energy. Keep in mind that sometimes an instructor says things just to create discussion or to make you think.

academic freedom
Freedom to teach or communicate even ideas or facts that are unpopular or controversial.

Tapping, doodling, clicking a pen, or other physical behaviors detract from your focus and can distract others. To avoid this, put your physical energies to work in notetaking and participating in class. Create drawings to help you recall lecture information.

Negative comments from your inner critic or child (see Chapter 6) such as "Who cares?" "I am never going to figure this out," "The instructor talks funny," "I should have never taken this class; it's too hard for me," "What shall I do after class?" and so forth affect concentration. To solve this problem, you decide to monitor and control your self-talk. Replace negative comments with more positive ones such as "I don't really care about this, but it must be important information so I'm going to be sure I understand it," "I don't get this, but I've figured out difficult things before," "The instructor has a different way of saying things, but what is said is more important than how it is said," "This is a hard class but I'll see the instructor to get help or join a study group," or "I'll think about what to do after class."

You, like many other students, might take your notebook computer with you to take notes. First, be sure that your instructor allows you to do so. Then be sure that you are using it to take notes rather than playing games, checking e-mail, surfing the net, and sending IMs. Not only is it a distraction to you, but most instructors can see what you're doing. Should you leave your computer at home? Not necessarily. Like many other distractions,

A computer taken to class is best used for notetaking only.

awareness is the first step. Once you get to class, open only your word processor. Choose to leave all other applications unopened or unavailable.

Unlike high school, no bells ring to signal the start and end of class. Some students watch the clock and pack up early so they can be ready to race out the door at the end of class. Not only is this rude and distracting–it's ineffective. Instructors often provide summaries of key points, reminders of impending assignments, and other important content in the last few minutes of class.

You attend class at your instructor's discretion. If your behavior is not appropriate (e.g. you engage in side conversations, make or answer cell phone calls, act rudely), your instructor can dismiss you from class and/or drop you from the course.

activity 1 Becoming an Active Listener

Access http://www.mhhe.com/business/management/buildyourmanagementskills/updated_flash/topic13b/quiz.html

Complete the inventory there and read the suggestions for active listening. Use the 5C approach to identify and make a decision about your active learning skills. Summarize what you decided in the space below.

Listening in Different Learning Situations

As a college student you'll listen to lectures, complete lab experiments, and work in groups to solve problems . . . all in the same day. Just as one size doesn't fit all bodies, one listening strategy doesn't fit all classes. Listening in traditional lecture classes differs from listening in classes that deliver content through discussion or hands-on activities

Traditional Classes

Your academic success often depends on your ability to listen for the heart—or pattern—of lectures. Many students think that lecture information can be arranged in an infinite number of ways. But there are really only a few main patterns. It's just that lectures often flow from one pattern to another. Once you know which words signal each pattern, you can start to organize information more easily. Your instructor gives signals that point to other important information as well.

During class, record everything you think is relevant to the topic. When your lecturer tells a story, write the topic of the story and a few key details. If possible, record how you think the story related to the lecture. If the relationship is not immediately clear, leave some space and keep taking notes.

After class, look for the connection. Why would the lecturer have included that story? What was the point, in terms of the course content? Record your conclusions in the space you left during the notetaking phase. If you're still not sure, talk to other classmates about their conclusions. You might also ask the lecturer to discuss your notes with you outside of class. You can tell how well you have taken notes when you get your first test. Its content should help you pinpoint how, if at all, a lecturer's stories relate to your understanding of course content.

Many students use laptop computers to take notes. That's both a good and bad idea for several reasons. First, your classroom might be wireless. This works well if you need to connect to course materials that the instructor has placed online. Another plus to using a computer is that printed notes are easier to study. You'll never waste time trying to read your handwriting. Digital notes are also easier to manipulate. That is, you can move notes around to make studying materials easier. But this can work against you because the writing by hand you normally do in making flash cards or other study materials contributes to **tactile/kinesthetic** memory.

tactile/kinesthetic
Sense of touch.

Of course, the disadvantages of the laptop are integral to it. You'll need to keep your battery charged and find space for it on your desk or table in the classroom. And sometimes computers crash. If you use a notebook computer, e-mail notes to yourself or save them on a flashdrive as soon as class is over. For this same reason, don't forget to print a hard copy to study as soon as you have access to a printer.

Nontraditional Class Formats

What if there isn't a lecture? Many instructors use discussions among students as their delivery format. Discussions generate ideas among class members. They help students debate pros and cons or explore solutions to problems.

Because a discussion seems like a kind of conversation, students often lay down their pencils/close their computers, sit back, and simply listen. But of course discussions are more like a business meeting. That means someone, namely you, needs to be taking minutes–a record of main points, lists of ideas, sequences of events, pros and cons and so on. Later, in a business meeting, the group as a whole reviews the notes for accuracy and completeness. They use the notes to remind themselves of meeting content and to look for trends or relationships that might not have been clear during the meeting. You need to review your notes for this same sort of information. You are both the notetaker who records ideas and the participant who reviews them.

Lab courses like nursing, computer-aided drafting, automotive technology, biology, or art provide you with hands-on activity. Practice, experimentation, observation, and practical application form the content. The first step in taking notes in a lab course is recording your starting point. This includes the materials you're using and your hypothesis or goals for the session. As you work, make occasional notes about your progress. When the class ends, record your final conclusions and thoughts. You can also revise your hypothesis or set goals for the next session while your work is fresh in your mind.

Table 14.1 Lecture Signals and Meanings

Signal	Meaning
Today's lecture covers . . . To sum up, in summary, as a review, in conclusion (located at either the beginning or end of a discussion).	**Introductory/summary pattern:** briefly previews topics to be covered or highlights main points of the lecture.
First, second, third . . . First, next, and, then . . . Finally . . . Most/least important . . .	**List/sequence pattern:** lists points in a topical list or steps in a sequence.
Comparisons: Similarly Both As well as In like manner Likewise *Contrasts:* However On the other hand On the contrary But Instead of Although Nevertheless Yet	**Comparison/contrast pattern:** shows likenesses and differences among concepts.
Therefore, thus, as a result, because, in turn, then, hence, for this reason, results in, cause(s), effect(s).	**Cause/effect or problem-solving pattern:** how or why things happen and their reasons; problems and solutions; premises and conclusions.
Instructor repeats information or speaks more slowly.	Such wait time is usually a cue for you to record information in your notes.
Instructor changes tone of voice, tempo of speech, or uses body language to emphasize information.	Variations of any kind in speech or body language generally mean that such information is important.
Instructor refers to information by page number or refers to information as a test item.	Generally means that the information is important to your understanding of course content and ability to perform well on a test.
Instructor writes on board, has notes on a Web page, or uses other visual aids.	The extra effort that goes into finding and using markers or using visual aids shows that the information they provide is important to your understanding and academic success.

Analyzing Instructors

Identify two of your instructors who lecture frequently. Use the list below to analyze what they do by marking either A—Always; U—Usually; S—Sometimes; or N—Never. Then write a paragraph in which you compare the two instructors. Consider your behavior in each class. In which class do you perform better? Why?

	Instructor #1	Instructor #2
Review previous lecture materials before beginning the new lecture?		
State main ideas in introduction and summary of lecture?		
Provide an outline of the lecture?		
Provide "wait time" for writing notes?		
Speak clearly with appropriate volume?		
Answer questions without sarcasm?		
Stay on topic?		
Refrain from reading directly from the text?		
Emphasize main points?		
Use transition words?		
Give examples to illustrate difficult ideas?		
Write important words, dates, and so forth on board?		
Define important terms?		
Use audiovisual aids to reinforce ideas?		

Scoring: The more *A*s and *U*s your instructor has, the less you have to do as a listener. Note the items that you rated *S* or *N*. You may need to do what your instructor doesn't provide you.

The following table provides suggestions for coping with an instructor's lecture style.

If your instructor fails to . . .	Then you . . .
1. Explain the goals of the lecture.	Use your text and syllabus to set objectives.
2. Review previous lecture material before beginning a new lecture.	Set aside time before each class to review notes.
3. State main ideas in an introduction and summary of a lecture.	Write short summaries of the day's lecture immediately after class.
4. Provide an outline of the lecture.	Preview assigned readings beforehand.
5. Provide "wait time" for writing notes.	Politely ask instructor to repeat information or speak more slowly.
6. Speak clearly with appropriate volume.	Politely ask instructor to repeat information or speak more loudly, or move closer to the instructor.
7. Answer questions without sarcasm.	Refrain from taking comments personally.
8. Stay on topic.	Discover how anecdotes relate to the content or use them as a memory cue.

If your instructor fails to . . .	Then you . . .
9. Refrain from reading from the text.	Mark passages in the text as instructor reads and/or summarize or outline these in the text margin.
10. Emphasize main points.	Supplement lectures through text previews and reading.
11. Use transition words.	Supplement lectures through text previews and reading.
12. Give examples to explain difficult ideas.	Politely ask instructor for an example, discuss idea with other students and/or create an example for yourself.
13. Write important names, dates, ideas, etc.	Supplement notes with terms listed in text and highlight information contained in lecture and/or text.
14. Define important terms.	Use text glossary or definition.
15. Use audiovisual aids to reinforce ideas.	Relate information to what you know about the topic or create an example for yourself.

Taking Good Lecture Notes

formal outline
Main points arranged
vertically first using Roman
numerals and indented
capital letters, and then
Arabic numerals and
lowercase letters to se-
quence supporting ideas.

informal outline
Same idea as formal
outline, but uses spacing
as you like and special
markings you choose
(e.g., all capital letters,
dashes, stars).

Notes differ from dictation. You can't and shouldn't record everything your instructor says. Lecture notes are just that–a way to help you note the major and minor points of a lecture. Ultimately, they will help you under-stand and remember new information.

You can take notes in many ways. Contrary to popular rumor, there is no one best form for notes. The format you prefer varies depending on the ways you learn best (see Chapter 13). It also depends on the subject and the instructor's lecture style.

Structured notes often suit learners whose brain dominance favors the logical side. In using a **formal outline** to take notes that arranges main points vertically using Roman numerals and indented capital letters, and then Arabic numerals and lowercase letters to sequence supporting ideas, the structure of your notes is highly organized. **Informal outlines** use the same structural format but in a more creative way, by using spacing as you like and special markings you choose (e.g., all capital letters, dashes, stars, etc.). But unless your instructor clearly cues new main points, you are responsible

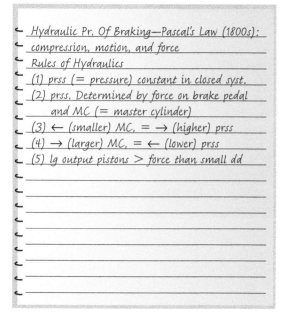

Figure 14.1 Automotive Technology Notes: Running Text Form with Abbreviations.

Figure 14.2 Automotive Technology Notes: Formal Outline.

Figure 14.3 Automotive Technology Notes: Informal Outline.

Hydraulic Principles of Braking
• Based on Pascal's Law (1800s)
• compression, motion, and force Rules
  of Hydraulics
• Pressure is constant in a closed system.
• Brake system pressure determined by
  force applied
  ~~ to brake pedal
  ~~ to cross-section of master cylinder
• The smaller the master cylinder (input)
  piston, the higher the system pressure
  with a given amount of pressure.
• The larger the master cylinder (input)
  piston, the lower the system pressure
  with a given amount of pressure.
• Large output pistons have greater force
  than small ones.

Figure 14.4 Automotive Technology Notes: Cornell Form.

RECALL NOTES

—3 factors of | Hydraulic Pr. of Braking—Pascal's Law
Pascal's Law | (1800s): compression, motion, and force
—What are the 5 | Rules of Hydraulics
Rules of Hydraulics? | (1) prss (= pressure) constant
| in closed syst.
| (2) prss. determined by force on
| brake pedal and MC (= master cylinder)
| (3) ← (smaller) MC, = → (higher) prss
| (4) ← (larger) MC, = → (lower) prss
| (5) lg output pistons. force than small

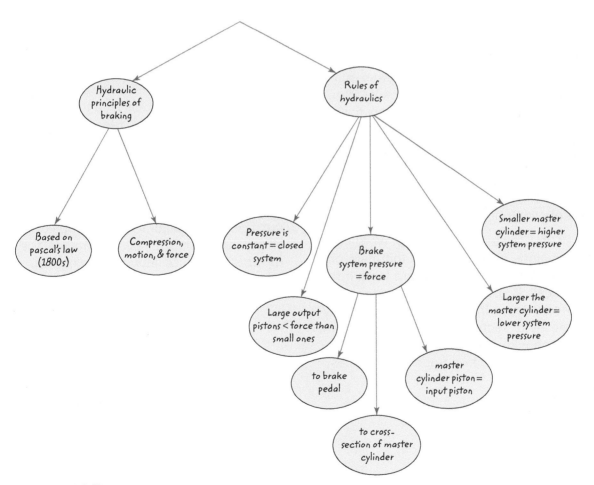

Figure 14.5 Automotive Technology Notes: Idea Map.

DATE IT. Date each day's notes. Writing the date helps if you need to compare notes with someone or identify missing notes.

GET ORGANIZED. If you handwrite notes, use the same legible notetaking system for each course (e.g., Cornell, outline, informal outline, paragraphs, idea map). As you take notes, use only one side of your paper and number pages as you go. You can use the back of pages to summarize, correct, or add information after class. It may sound like a given, but keep notes together. If you handwrite notes, use a single spiral notebook or ring binder for each subject, or two multisubject notebooks or loose-leaf binders, one for Monday-Wednesday-Friday classes and one for Tuesday-Thursday classes. Notebooks or binders with pockets are especially helpful for storing course handouts or other class materials. If you take notes on a computer, create folders for each class. Your notes can be in separate files by day or week or in a continuous file. Be sure to back up your files on a regular basis.

STICK TO IT. As you take notes, leave blank spaces to separate important groups of ideas. Abbreviate when possible. Develop a key for any symbols and abbreviations and record it in your notebook. Note words or references you don't understand. Do not try to figure them out at the time. Look them up later or ask about them in class. You need to be flexible. Adjust your listening and notetaking pace to the lecture.

GET THE POINT. Listen for transition words that signal main points. As you identify the main patterns of the lecture, try to group and label information for recall. If you can't do this as you take notes, you can do so in your after-class follow-through (see next section). Highlight important text information with a colored pen or marker or with the highlight feature on your word processing program.

for deciding how to organize your outline. Thus, to use these styles, you have to figure out which points are main ideas and which subpoints support main ideas. Previewing the chapter before class is one way to figure out which is which. Formal and informal outlines also work well with subjects that involve step-by-step processes such as math or science problem solving. Some instructors lecture in an outline fashion. They take the pressure off you by clearly identifying main ideas and giving details in an orderly way.

Cornell notes combine less structure and more structure. To take these notes, you divide a page into two sections by drawing a vertical line about one-third from the left side of the page. In the larger right section of the page, you take notes during class. Almost anything goes here as you get key ideas on the page in whatever way you wish. After class, you review what you wrote and write more organized notes in the smaller left column. This side will become your recall column for the details in the larger column. This combination makes it a good fit for different personal styles, subjects, and instructor approaches. It encourages you to analyze notes recorded in class so you can organize the left side of the page.

Global or visual learners tend to use more pictorial forms such as **idea mapping.** Maps help capture relationships among ideas. Thus, this style works well for topics such as literature, the arts, or social sciences. It can also be used when instructors provide common characteristics for each topic. For instance, an instructor lecturing on theories of psychology might always provide the theorist, key points, impact, and problems.

Cornell notes
Page divided vertically into two sections with right side about ⅔ of the page for class notes and left column for recall tips you create afterward.

idea mapping
Graphical picture you make of main ideas and details.

Notes reflect course information that will likely show up on course exams. So they are crucial for you to study for exams. Thus, your notes need to be the best that they can be for each course you take. Notetaking effectiveness varies according to the format and content of each class. Thus, you should assess your notes for each course you take so you can improve your notetaking. Use the following form to rate your notes in each class you take. Record your score next to each course you listed. Are your assessment scores similar? Why or why not? What can you do to make your notes more effective? Use the 5Cs to determine which notetaking format works best for you. Then begin using that format in all of your classes immediately. At first, it may feel strange. With time and with practice, it will become natural.

CHECKLIST FOR EVALUATING CLASSROOM NOTES

Assess your notes in each class you take. If your scores differ by class, what accounts for those differences? If your scores are not as high as you want, try using a different method. After a week, reassess and make a decision about your notetaking.

	Yes	Sometimes	No
PRE-CLASS PREPARATION			
1. I read or preview assigned chapters and readings before class.			
2. I do not review notes until I am studying for an exam			
3. I get to class early enough to sit close to the front of the room.			
4. My notes flow from one class to the next without a discernable beginning or end.			
IN-CLASS NOTE-TAKING			
1. I use a mobile device for taking notes			
2. I take a mobile device to class for notes, but spend more time checking email, texting, or other.			
3. I use pen and paper to take notes.			
4. My handwriting is so poor that I can't even read them.			
5. When I take notes on paper, I use only the front sides of looseleaf paper which I keep in a binder.			
6. When I take notes—either on a mobile device or paper, I cover the page and leave little, if any, room for editing or adding information.			
7. I use headings, symbols (e.g., !!, *), underlining or circles to indicate important information.			
8. As much as possible, I write exactly what the instructor says.			
AFTER-CLASS FOLLOW-THROUGH			
1. I review class notes as soon as possible after class and at least within 24 hours.			
2. I recopy my notes.			
3. I add examples, summaries in my own words, questions about content, and highlights.			

RESULTS: Odd-numbered items represent good note-taking strategies. Total the number of odd-numbered items that you answered YES and multiply by 2. Total the number of odd numbered items that you answered SOMETIMES and multiply by 1. Add these two scores.

Even numbered items are ineffective behaviors. Total the number of even-numbered items that you answered YES and multiply by 2. Total the number of even-numbered items that you answered SOMETIMES and multiply by 1. Add these two scores.

Subtract the even numbered score total from the odd-numbered score total.

13–16 You have great note-taking strategies!

9–12 You need to fine-tune your note-taking strategies 8 or less You need to improve your notetaking strategies.

Your Courses	Scores

module

144

What I should
do with notes
after I take
them?

After-Class Follow-Through

Lecture notes and study notes are not always the same. Lecture notes are often little more than words you write during class or brief bits of information you gather from a lecture. They may—or may not—be good enough for study. Your after-class follow-through transforms them into a more powerful learning tool: study notes.

You don't create study notes by just recopying lecture notes more neatly because you can copy information without thinking about it. Instead, you need to reorganize and summarize information to find connections, draw conclusions, and analyze information. The resulting study notes comprise a complete source of information that includes everything you need to learn the information you need. To create a good set of study notes, you may need to add textbook details and your own analysis or comments.

Completed by hand or on a computer, you can use the same kinds of formats that you use for lecture notes. For instance, you can organize information using formal or informal outlines or visually using idea maps. You can write summaries in paragraph form. If you use Cornell notes, you can write key words and questions in the recall column.

It's easy to forget the connecting information that you didn't have time to write in your notes. As a result, your notes might fail to make sense when you use them to study before an exam. So *when* you make study notes and *how often* you review them are just as important as *what* you include in them.

Because most people tend to forget about half of lecture content very quickly, the most effective review occurs within an hour of the time you took your notes. A brief first review of 5 to 10 minutes is all you need to read over your notes and add missing details while they are still fresh in your mind. Review your notes again during a weekly review of all course notes. This helps you reconnect ideas and build understanding.

Why do you need to review so often? Last-minute processing doesn't give you enough time to absorb information fully. As a result, you may not get the same insights that you will after thinking about information over time. It's practice that makes permanent. At the least, you should update your notes as soon as possible after class or at least within a few hours of taking them.

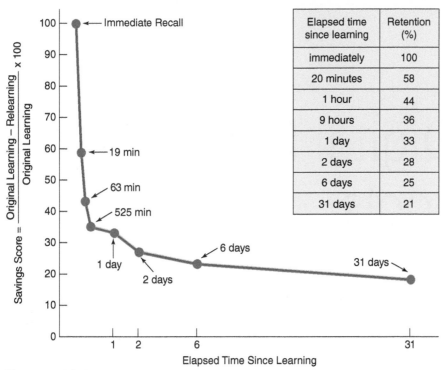

Elapsed time since learning	Retention (%)
immediately	100
20 minutes	58
1 hour	44
9 hours	36
1 day	33
2 days	28
6 days	25
31 days	21

Figure 14.6 The Curve of Forgetting.

Processing Your Notes

To complete this activity, you will need three days of lecture notes. Create a set of study notes using the format you prefer: formal or informal outline, idea map, paragraphs, or Cornell recall column. Write the information that came from your lecture notes in one color of ink or marker. Use a second color to show information that comes from the textbook or other course material. Use a third color for your own comments, reflections, and questions.

Digital Notetaking Tools

Whatever notetaking method you choose, you need to process the material actively as part of the after-class follow-through. If you use Microsoft Word, you can use the *track changes* tool to make notes and comments on the electronic copy. You can also write notes directly on your printed copies. Or, you can open Notepad, and use it to take notes. Additionally, you can use online notetaking tools such as *Google Notebook, MyNoteIT, Notefish, Yahoo* or *Notezz!* For instance, *A Note* is a free online notetaking program. When the program closes, it uploads and saves your notes. When you restart the program, the notes are downloaded. Because the notes are stored somewhere other than your computer, you can use your notes on different computers. If you wish to link written notes with lecture content, you might consider using a smartpen. Smartpens are high-tech tools for writing that come with special notetaking paper. As you write on the paper, the pen records the auditory lecture content. Then if you have questions about what was said, you tap any word on the page with the pen, and the pen replays that part of the lecture. Smartpens are sold by a variety of companies.

In a way, your notes in an online class are much like the notes you create in a discussion course. Rather than noting the contributions of each person, your notes document and summarize the information contributed by each online source: readings, assignments, discussion boards, chats, and so on. Organizing these notes into bulleted lists of key terms or an outline of key points helps you process information more deeply.

Or, if you prefer using graphics to structure information, you may need to acquire a program like *Inspiration*, a program for creating idea maps. *Thinkport.org* provides a variety of graphic organizers in various formats including WORD, and pdf while *Mindomo.com* allows you to create online mind maps. *MindNode* is for mind-mapping and brainstorming. Should you find information complicated or puzzling, open the discussion board and post questions or comments. Once your notes are organized, the review process is the same that you use for face-to-face classes.

Digital Sticky Notes

Wouldn't it be nice if you could put sticky notes on digital documents you find online? Actually, you can. Go online and search for *Web 2.0 digital sticky notes.* Choose one you find and try it out. Create a document with your name and the name of your college. Add a digital sticky note that provides three adjectives that describe your college.

GROUP APPLICATION: Compare the digital sticky note tool you used with others in your class in terms of ease of use and features. List the ones you like best.

chapter review

Respond to the following on a separate sheet of paper or in your notebook.

1. What is the difference between thinking of education as a product and thinking of it as a process?

2. List three ways to prepare for lectures. Which do you prefer and why?

3. This chapter listed ways to make a favorable impression through classroom behavior. List five ways to create an *unfavorable* impression that you've observed at your institution.

4. Based on your observations, what listening problem do you think is most common in your classes? Why?

5. Compare notetaking in lecture, discussion, online and lab courses. What do you see as the main differences? How do you accomodate those differences in your notes?

6. Reexamine the suggestions for taking notes. Put a check mark by the suggestions you already use. Put an exclamation point by the suggestions that were new to you.

7. Imagine that the person who used to sit next to you in class hasn't come to class for three weeks. She left a message on your answering machine asking to borrow your notes. In a brief paragraph, explain how effective you judge your notes to be and provide an argument for why she should or should not get a copy of your notes.

8. What is the difference between lecture notes and study notes? Draw a Venn Diagram to show the relationship between your lecture notes and your study notes for one class you currently take.

did you decide?

Did you accomplish what you wanted to in this chapter? Check the items below that apply to you.

Review the *You Decide* questions that you identified at the beginning of the chapter, but look at them from a new direction. If you didn't check an item below, review that module until you feel you can confidently apply the strategies to your own situations. However, the best ideas are worthless unless they are put into effect. Use the 5Cs to help you decide what information you found most helpful in the chapter and how you plan to use it. Record your comments after the statements below.

☐ **14.1** I know what I can do to be a better listener.

_____

☐ **14.2** I understand what I should listen for in different classes.

_____

☐ **14.3** I have some ideas for improving my notetaking.

_____

☐ **14.4** After I take them, I know how to use my notes for study purposes.

_____

☐ **14.5** I can use digital technologies for notetaking.

_____

perspectives

George Lucas, Academy Award–winning American film director, producer, screenwriter, chairman of Lucasfilm, and graduate of the University of Southern California—was named as a Distinguished Community College Alumnus in 2004. This article, "Changing Landscapes," by Evelyn L. Kent, discusses the role education has had and continues to play in his success.

Think about and answer the questions that follow:

1. In what way do you think Lucas has changed the landscape of what is possible?
2. In what ways does Lucas support education?
3. Identify three companies in the Lucas "empire."
4. What does the George Lucas Educational Foundation do?
5. What event caused Lucas to enroll in a junior college?
6. Lucas donates funds to many educational causes. Imagine that he is thinking about giving your college some money and wants your help in deciding specifically what he should fund. How could you use the 5C process to help make that decision?

    A. What is a group, service, department, or individual that needs financial assistance on your campus? This is your **C**hallenge.

    B. What other **C**hoices are available for funding?

    C. What would be the major **C**onsequence(s) of each choice?

    D. Should Lucas **C**hoose to contribute his funds to your idea?

    E. How can you help Lucas **C**heck the outcome of this decision?

George Lucas has something in common with community colleges—they both change the landscape of what is possible.

The movie producer, director, and writer hardly needs an introduction. Since 1973 when *American Graffiti* was an enormous success, America has been familiar with Lucas. *Star Wars* moved that familiarity to intimacy in 1977.

In 1997, the *San Francisco Chronicle* wrote: "So many years, so much exposure, so many spin-offs, special-effects trends and continuous warp-speed hype have made it nearly impossible to look at 'Star Wars' as just a movie anymore. It remains an icon on the ever-changing pop culture landscape . . ."

Lucas readily admits that school was not a priority for him. "Frankly, I was not very engaged in my classes; in fact, as a boy, I liked to daydream and write stories," he writes in the resource book *Edutopia: Success Stories for Learning in the Digital Age.*

Regardless, after a near-fatal car accident, he began his venture into higher education at Modesto Junior College in California, where he earned an associate of arts degree in history in 1964.

He earned a bachelor's from the University of Southern California in 1966 and began making movies. His empire includes the visual effects company Industrial Light & Magic (formed during the making of *Star Wars*), THX, and Lucasfilm.

In 1992, the Board of Governors of the Academy of Motion Pictures Arts and Sciences bestowed the Irving G. Thalberg Memorial Award, which honors "creative producers whose bodies of work reflect a consistently high quality of motion picture production," on Lucas.

In addition, in 1999 he received the DigiGlobe Award for his ongoing contribution to culture and entertainment through the use of information technology.

The father of three adopted children, Lucas also is the founder and chairman of the board of the

George Lucas Educational Foundation, which focuses on best practices and innovation in primary education. It focuses on project-based learning that stimulates children's passions and emphasizes well-prepared teachers to improve student learning.

On his website, www.glef.org, Lucas says, "Our Foundation documents and disseminates the most exciting classrooms where these innovations are taking place." The foundation does this through the creation and dissemination of media—from films, books, and newsletters, to CD-ROMs and DVDs.

He remains active in the Modesto-area community and nationally through his support of children's charities. In addition, Lucas and his sisters recently gave Modesto Junior College a cash gift to be used toward the construction of an arts center on campus.

reflecting on decisions

Now that you've learned about listening and notetaking, what decisions about these processes will help you achieve your academic or career goals?

CREATING A
RECORD OF SERVICE

Taking notes about the service you do may not seem all that important. But a record of service serves two purposes. One, while you are in school, you can track how your service relates to your classes. It also helps you keep track of new experiences and skills you gain. Two, this record of service can be documentation for future employers. You can keep a record of your community service online. **Networkforgood.org** provides you with an online space to note your service. The benefit here is that you can return to your notes as often as you like and can access them from wherever you need to. To create your Record of Service, go to **https://www.presidentialserviceawards .gov/tgact/ros/dspROSlogin.cfm.**

CHOOSING TO SERVE

R E V I E W

Skim the notes you made throughout the chapter. How does the content fit together? What information is still unclear? Were your learning goals met? Can you answer the review questions and define terms?

CHOOSING TO BE AN ACTIVE LEARNER

CHAPTER **FIFTEEN**

Decisions about Study and Test Taking

Tests often seem like obstacles to overcome. In reality, they are a measurement of what you know and how well you know it. They allow you to show or prove that you know and understand the material. How do you decide what to study?

YOU DECIDE

To *wonder* means to think or have curiosity about. Things and ideas you wonder about often mask a need for a decision. Check the items below that apply to you.

In terms of studying and test taking, I've been wondering . . .

☐ **15.1** What do I need to prepare to study?

☐ **15.2** How do I get my notes, text content, and other materials organized?

☐ **15.3** How do I remember what I need to know on a test?

☐ **15.4** What online tools can help me prepare for an exam?

☐ **15.5** How do I keep from getting stressed before and during tests?

☐ **15.6** What can I do to maximize my success on exams?

☐ **15.7** What can a returned test tell me?

Each of these decision points corresponds to the numbered modules that follow. Turn to the module for immediate help.

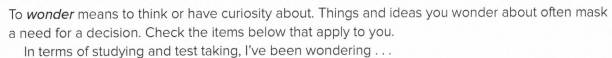

CHOOSING TO BE AN ACTIVE LEARNER ➤

SURVEY

Before reading this chapter, prepare for learning. Purposefully skim the title, introduction, headings, and graphics. As you survey, decide what information you already know and what information is new to you.

QUESTION

Change each section's heading into a question. This forms your learning goal for reading.

READ

Read the section without marking. Reread and mark key information that answers your question.

RECITE

Stop after each section and make sure you understood the content. Organize or summarize content and make notes.

Decisions about Study Preparation

studying
The purposeful acquisition of knowledge or understanding.

Although the goal of college is learning, you often show what you learned by how you do on tests. Such preparation is called **studying,** or, in terms of SQ3R, Review. Although you might think of review as passive repetition of content, it's actually much more. It is an active decision to learn. You start through your decisions about preparation. This includes knowing when, where, what, and how much to study as well as if you should study alone or with others.

Deciding When and Where to Study

Deciding when and where to study puts you in control of your learning. This control lets you make the most of your study sessions. You start by setting a regular time and place for study. This helps you focus attention through conditioning. It creates a "worksite" where you know your job is to study rather than relax or do other things. Just as distractions in the classroom cause you to lose focus, distractions and disorganization at your study site (e.g., noise from family or others; messy work areas) sabotage study time. Look for a secluded study site away from visual, auditory, and moving stimuli. If your study site is cluttered, you'll find your concentration split. Remove extra materials and keep out only what you need. If you use your computer to take notes while you study, close other applications.

Similarly, the same thoughts—worry, boredom, procrastination and so on—that distract your attention during class also affect study time. Setting learning goals and using time management strategies help. Analyzing and then organizing what you need to learn help you focus. For instance, when you can divide a large job (e.g., learning 10 chapters for a history exam) into smaller, more manageable tasks, it becomes easier to stay on task. Varying activities and using active study strategies keep you from getting bored. For instance, you might read for 20 minutes and then create a timeline that shows the time periods you covered. Studying using your learning style helps maximize memory as well. For example, if you are a visual learner, mapping content or drawing pictures may help you recall information more easily. If you are an auditory learner, create study tapes or digital audio files to listen to. If you are a kinesthetic learner, make learning hands-on by typing, drawing, or creating flash cards you can manipulate. Finally, pace yourself. Cramming produces panic and keeps you from concentrating fully.

Deciding How Much and What to Study

You decide how much you need to study. Like other decisions you make, you base your choices on your goals and values. There may be times when family, work, or other coursework comes before study. But such choices must be conscious ones you can live with. For instance, if you need to work, you may decide that making a B, C, or even a D grade is OK from time to time. The key is knowing your level of comfort. If you feel you need an A in every course, you must be prepared to make the decisions that will let you to do that. If your life requires you to balance other responsibilities with study, you may need to reconcile yourself to less than perfect grades sometimes.

Once you make your choices, answer the following questions to help you decide what to study. Your responses to these questions will help you create a study checklist of specific topics and chapters to address.

1. **What does the test cover?** The scope of the information often helps you decide how many details you need to know. The more information an exam covers (e.g., numerous lectures, several chapters, other materials) or the fewer the questions on the exam, the broader the questions will be. Tests over fewer chapters or that have more questions may be more detailed.

   For instance, if a test over six short stories consists of only three essay questions, your responses should fit several concepts into each answer. You may have to find broad relationships among several stories in each essay. On the other hand, a multiple-choice test of 50 questions over the same information often requires you to isolate and analyze information more specifically.

2. **Is the test comprehensive?** Comprehensive exams include all information from the beginning of the course. Tests that are not comprehensive cover all information discussed since the last exam.

3. **What is the format of the test: objective (e.g., matching, multiple choice, true-false) or subjective (essay or short answer)?** Objective tests require you to recall and use information to solve problems and choose answers from given choices. Subjective exams require you to produce written responses—usually in paragraph or essay form—to questions.

4. **What levels of thinking will I be expected to use?** In general, you will be asked few, if any, questions requiring simple recall of memorized information. Most questions require you to interpret, analyze, and apply what you've learned.

5. **How much does the test count in my final grade?** This helps you decide how much time and effort to devote to test preparation. For instance, perhaps you have the same average in two courses. The final for one course counts for 10 percent of your grade. The final for

TIPS FOR STUDYING FOR AN EXAM

1. Have a regular place to study that is free from distraction. Keep all your study materials there.

2. Synthesize (combine) lecture, textbook, and other notes.

3. Make a test review that includes the following:

   - Points emphasized in the textbook

   - Points stressed during class lecture or other content

   - Questions in study guides, old quizzes and tests

   - Review questions from the end of textbook chapters

   - Lists of terms and their definitions

4. Once you know what you need to study, separate it into tasks. Divide the tasks into the number of days you have before the exam. Set and stick to deadlines. Schedule specific times to study and identify learning goals for each of your study sessions.

5. Plan each study session to include breaks.

6. Create a practice test several days before your exam is scheduled. Take the practice test on the day before your exam. Review only the information you miss.

the other course counts for 25 percent of your grade. If you must make decisions about what to study, you would be better served by studying for the second exam.

6. **What special materials will I need for the test?** Some materials (e.g., calculator) may be permitted for an exam (check with your instructor). Other materials (e.g., #2 pencils, blue book, standardized answer form) are essential to your ability to take the test. Don't wait until the morning of the exam to ask what supplies you should bring.

7. **What time constraints affect my study time?** Compare how much study time you think you need to get the grade you want with the amount of time you have to prepare. If needed, find ways to shift priorities to reallocate to time study time. Schedule specific times to study and identify learning goals for each of your study sessions.

Deciding Whom to Study With: Alone or in Groups

Studying on your own has advantages. Finding mutually beneficial times to meet is not a problem in that case. Missing a study session affects no one but yourself. You don't have to worry about the possibility of group members letting you down by not doing their share of the work. Studying on your own can also have disadvantages. You have no one to depend on but yourself. If you miss a study session, you miss out. You don't have anyone to help share the load. In truth, studying with others has many other benefits as well.

A **study group** is a valuable way for you to meet others and get involved in campus life. But the highest value of a study group is what study groups actually do: actively discuss and share information and study. Therefore, members of a study group need to have good communication skills, a common purpose, the ability to set goals, and the skills to achieve those goals. Creating and maintaining such groups are often easier said than done.

Research suggests that study groups provide optimum learning opportunities. For instance, small-group learning works better than studying in large groups, independent study, or in some cases one-to-one tutoring from a faculty member. Why?

Study groups let you see, hear, and practice your problem-solving, communication, and learning skills. They ensure active learning through

study group

Two or more students who work together to learn information.

participation. They allow you to observe the way other people think and to hear what they think about course content. Being in a study group also focuses your attention. You are less likely to let your mind wander when engaged in a discussion. Study groups force you to keep regularly scheduled study times. You will experience less stress because study group members encourage and support each other.

Getting the Most from Your Study Group

1. **Select group members who have similar academic interests and dedication to the success of the group.** Friends do not always make the best study partners. Study group members need to be prepared to discuss the topic at hand, not what happened at last night's party. If you aren't sure which class members want to form a study group, ask your instructor to make an announcement, place a sign-up sheet on a nearby bulletin board, or e-mail the class through your course management system.

2. **Seek group members with similar skills and motivation.** The group functions best when each member adds to the overall learning of the group and no one uses the group as a substitute for personally learning information. Dismiss members who fail to live up to their time, preparation, or participation commitments.

3. **Limit group size to five or fewer students.** You need to feel comfortable with and actively participate in a study group. Too many people limit participation. In addition, scheduling meeting times for a large number of members tends to be an impossible task.

4. **State the purpose and lifetime of the group.** Some groups tend to drag on without a real focus or end. Instead, the group should begin by answering some key questions: What do we want to do and how long will it take? Will we meet until the next test, the completion of a project, or the end of the course? Will we focus on problem solving, conceptual development, or a class project? Group goals require measurable outcomes and deadlines. Each session needs a purpose. Feelings of achievement and closure at the end of each study session and at the end of the group's life span add to your academic success.

5. **Schedule regular group meetings at the same time and place.** Meetings should start and end on time. Although needless interruptions should be discouraged, you should schedule breaks in study sessions as long as the group agrees to return to the task.

6. **Get acquainted.** As a group member, you invest a lot of time and effort with the members of your group. Although you don't need to know their life histories, it does help to know something about each member's level of ability in a course (Are they majoring in history or is this their first course?), their current commitments (Do they have jobs, family, social, or other activities that affect the time at which they can and cannot meet?), and their expectations for the group (Do they want to prepare for the next exam, work on problems, or share reading assignments?). At the very least, exchange names and contact information (phone numbers; e-mail addresses) so that you can reach members in case of an emergency.

5Cs and Test Taking

Use the 5C approach—Define the **C**hallenge; Identify **C**hoices; Predict **C**onsequences; **C**hoose an option; **C**heck your outcome—to determine your biggest test-taking problem and find a solution for it.

15.2 module

Organizing Study Materials

How do I get my notes, text content, and other materials organized?

Now that you are prepared to study, it's time to get organized. Organizing with **charts** and **maps** helps you actively divide and conquer the materials you need to learn through association. Charts and maps show how you mentally think about and structure information. Much of your learning occurs as you think about and create your charts and maps.

chart
Information presented in columns and rows.

map
A graphic representation of main ideas and details.

Charts

Charts summarize and categorize information. They help you identify and compare or contrast the same factors across differing elements. Making these comparisons lets you find trends. Charts also condense and simplify information. They arrange information by order or time. They emphasize important points. Figure 15.1 shows an example of a chart. The following are the main steps in charting information:

1. Make a vertical list of the concepts you want to compare.
2. List horizontally the factors you want to use in comparing each concept.
3. Draw a grid by sketching lines between each concept and each factor.
4. Locate and record the information that fills each box of the grid.

Explorers and Discoveries

Who?	From Where?	Discovered What?	When?
John Cabot	Italian	Newfoundland	1497
Vasco da Gama	Portugal	Sea route to India	1498
Francisco Fernández de Córdoba	Spain	Yucatan peninsula of Mexico	1517

Figure 15.1 Sample Chart.

Concept Maps

Concept maps organize ideas graphically by showing relationships among them. They show how you organize and think about information. These maps help you integrate notes with text information, gaining greater depth and understanding. This forms your synthesis, or understanding, of the topic as a whole. Concept maps can be created in different ways and show many kinds of information. For instance, they can show rankings of details by branching out from the central topic. Or, maps can show how details relate to a topic by showing a progression of steps or chronological order of events or historical periods. Processing information with maps helps you prepare for all sorts of test questions. Figure 15.2 shows some different mapping structures you might use. The following are the steps in creating a map:

1. Choose a word or phrase that represents your subject or topic (might be a chapter title, purpose-setting question, heading, objective, main term, etc.).

2. Write that word or phrase at the top or center of a page.

Type	Example of Elements	Content Area Applications	Visual Structure
Introductory/ Summary	main ideas supporting details	applicable to any content area	
Subject Development/ Definition	definitions supporting details examples characteristics types or kinds	scientific concepts psychological, medical educational, or other case studies genres of literature styles of music political philosophy	
Enumeration/ Sequence	main points details steps elements procedures	mathematical process historical chronology literary plot scientific method computer science programs	
Comparison/ Contrast	similarities pros cons opinions time periods	authors composers case studies political philosophies psychological treatments educational principles scientific theories	
Cause/Effect	problems solutions	historical events scientific discovery mathematical principles scientific principles health and nutrition sociological conditions psychological problems	

Figure 15.2 Mapping Structures.

3. On a separate sheet of paper, list information about the topic (details, components, steps, functions, reasons, etc.). If you feel unsure about how information connects, complete step 3 on separate cards or sticky notes and arrange and rearrange to discover relationships.

4. Examine the elements. How do they relate to each other?

5. Choose the type of idea map that best represents the relationships you identify. (See Figure 15.2.)

6. Lay out the information.

7. Draw lines or arrows to indicate relationships.

Charting and Mapping

activity 2

1. Create a chart that compares charting and mapping in terms of purpose and format.

2. Using what you read and learned in Module 15.1 in this chapter, create a concept map that shows how to prepare to study in terms of *when, where, what, how much,* and with *whom.*

3. Which process do you like better, charting or mapping, and why? Do you think that charting and mapping would work better for different subjects? Why?

GROUP APPLICATION: In groups, identify your learning style preferences and your mapping or charting preferences. Are there any surprises? Why might this be so?

Choices for Practicing and Remembering Content

Memory is a skill, like playing baseball or playing the piano. No team or band waits until the night before the big game or concert to prepare. Why? They know practice over time is more effective than cramming at the last minute. Although people think practice makes perfect, that's only true if what you practice is correct. What practice does is make permanent. Thus, memory also needs frequent practice.

What's the best way to use practice to improve memory? First, practice needs to be an active process. Say and/or write what you need to learn. Creating and using flash cards, revising concept maps, discussing information and taking self-tests are part of the active process you need to learn. Second, practice in the form you expect to face during your exam. For instance, if a classroom test includes essay questions, make sure your practice includes actually writing a response by hand in standard essay format. If your test will be timed, practice answering questions with time limitations. Third, be realistic about the amount of time that you can concentrate. No matter what you think, the reality is that you can concentrate for about an hour at a time. Trying to do so for longer results in your attention wandering.

What exactly can you accomplish in an hour of study? Plenty. First, spend the first few minutes of the hour setting a learning goal(s). You should be able to identify what you intend to do during the given time. For instance, you might want to review note cards, create a concept map or outline an essay response. Second, practice actively for approximately 40 minutes. Write, talk, or physically manipulate (e.g., flash cards, mapping, writing, word processing) what you want to remember. Next spend five minutes reviewing what you practiced. Finally, take a break. The break gives your brain time to assimilate information, provides closure and feelings of accomplishment, and gives you a fresh start on your next practice session.

Mnemonics
Set of techniques for improving your memory skills.

Need an extra boost to recall that formula or term that you always seem to forget? **Mnemonics** are memory tricks that cue your recall. Have a look at Table 15.1. Try several mnemonics until you find the one(s) that work best for you for the content you need to remember.

Table 15.1 Common Mnemonics

Acronyms	Create a "word" from the first letter of the concepts you're trying to recall.	*FACE* (spaces on the treble clef in music), *ROY G. BIV* (colors of the rainbow), and *HOMES* (names of the Great Lakes: Huron, Ontario, Michigan, Erie, and Superior.)
Acrostics	Create a "sentence" from the first letter of the concepts you're trying to recall.	*Every Good Boy Does Fine* (lines of the treble clef in music: E, G, B, D, F), *Please Excuse My Dear Aunt Sally* (order of operations in math: parentheses, exponents, multiplication, division, addition, subtraction).
Association	Link what you need to know with a cue. Think of a humorous or extreme cue.	Green notebook (GO on a traffic light) is notebook for first class on Monday. Yellow notebook (color of the sun) is notebook for astronomy. Black notebook (sum of all colors; night) is planner.
Location	Think of a route you commonly take (e.g., from home to school). As you visualize the route, mentally "place" information you need to know at landmarks along the route. You can also use location by visualizing "where" information is in a book or notes. Adding other visual cues (e.g., exclamation points, highlights in colors, sketches, etc.) makes it more memorable.	You need to recall chemical symbols. You think about the route you take on campus from Building 1 to Building 5. You assign one of the symbols (e.g., Iron = Fe) to each of the buildings.

Patterns	Create an image or record your mental image in written form; this is also called a mnemonigraph (e.g., exclamation points, highlights in colors, sketches, etc.).
	
	Look for ways that concepts are alike or different (e.g., all concepts start with the same letter, end in *ing*, or have similar meanings).
		For example, to remember that similes use *like* or *as*:
		A
		S I M I L E
		     I
		     K
		     E

Word Games	Think of a rhyme, song, limerick, jingle, or saying.	"*I* before *E* except after *C* or when sounded like *A* as in *neighbor* or *weigh*."

Creating Your Own Mnemonics

Identify three concepts you need to learn for your next exam in this course. Develop a mnemonic to recall each one.

GROUP APPLICATION: Compare the mnemonics you created with others in your group. Which do you like best? The mnemonics you create for yourself are generally more memorable than those you learn from others. Do you think that is true for you? Why or why not?

What online
tools can help
me prepare for
an exam?

Using Online Tools for Test Preparation

Get a headstart on concept mapping. If you like to create your own, search for concept mapping software on the Web. If you prefer to fill in standard concept mapping templates, search for graphic organizer maker or graphic organizer templates. These allow you to print ready-to-go maps that you can complete. The text website provides links to online concept mapping and graphic organizers sites.

Flash cards no longer have to be written by hand on 3 × 5 note cards. Search for online flash card generators. These allow you to make, use, store, print and even share flash cards. Some also let you practice content in test question formats and as games. Virtual flash cards can also be developed for your iPod and cell phone that allow you to create, organize, and practice content. See the text website for links to flash card generators.

Some cell phones have applications that help you study. More are being developed every day. Visit the website of your cell phone provider and search for study applications. You may be surprised by what you find.

Mobile Learning Apps

Use Google, another search engine, or your cell phone to identify three iPod or cell phone apps that you could use for learning. List each, the cost, and the pros and cons of their use.

GROUP APPLICATION: Compare the mobile learning tools you found with others in your group.

Overcoming Test Anxiety

Remember the first day of school? Not college . . . but your first day in kindergarten or first grade. Children are excited to be "big kids" and get to go to school. Generally, most are excited and eager to learn. That soon changes as some children realize that they don't measure up. They don't get the stars on their papers. They get red F's and a note to take home. The pressure to perform—and the anxiety that goes with it—starts early and often continues through elementary and high school years. Or, perhaps you were one of those students that got the stars and the A's on your paper. But you've found the demands in college to be greater. At times, you don't do as well as you'd hoped and the fear sets in.

For some reason, humans most often remember and believe the worst rather than the best about themselves and others. You, too, might find yourself dwelling on past embarrassments, problems, and failures. In similar situations, you think that the same disasters will recur. Your anxiety mounts, you lose confidence, and the cycle repeats itself.

Anxiety about coursework is one of these cyclical processes. When prompted, you feel pressure from within and without. You lack the confidence to succeed. Voices echo in your mind. Examples of this self-talk include statements like, "If I fail this test, I know I'll fail the course." "What if I freeze up?" "I must, I must, I must but I can't, I can't, I can't."

The secret to combating anxiety is twofold. First, figure out what stresses you and why. Is the voice you hear your own? Is it a ghost from your past? Can you believe what is being said? Is it true? Have you *never* performed well under pressure? Have you *never* been able to recall information? What is reality? What is not?

Second, replace negative messages with positive ones (see Chapter 6 for information about self-talk). Consider the coach of a team sport. The coach doesn't say, "Well, our opponent is tough. I don't see any way we can win." Instead, the coach acknowledges the opponent's worth. Then he or she says, "Well, our opponent is tough. But we've practiced hard all week, and I know we're prepared. We can beat them." The coach's talk before a game motivates players to excel even in stressful situations. You can take steps to fight a negative mindset. Success messages help you motivate yourself to succeed.

Remember, however, that the best messages are those you create for yourself. They are personal and meaningful. They help you prepare for success. To be effective, you need to practice them. For example, during a

TIPS FOR OVERCOMING MATH ANXIETY

Students who have math anxiety often try to memorize rules and formulas rather than understand the process of math. Once that happens, anxiety takes the places of numbers and letters. Math is a linear process, and understanding that process is absolutely essential. Once you realize you know the process, it's easy to overcome math anxiety.

- Be positive. Use self-talk.

- Be brave. There's no such thing as a dumb question. Ask questions. Make sure you understand the process. Ask for sample problems, illustrations and/or demonstrations.

- Practice. Practice. Practice. Work sample problems until you can do them without looking at the solutions. Then immediately work them again. If you can't immediately rework the problem correctly, you didn't understand it.

- Don't be shy. Go to your instructor's office, visit the learning center, get a tutor or work with a study partner or group.

test, make sure your self-talk focuses on the task rather than on yourself: *What is the question I have to answer? What do I need to do? I know information about it. I know worry won't help. This is not a life and death situation. One task at a time. I can do this.* Once the test is over, reinforce your coping mechanisms and successes. Your self-talk might be one of the following statements: *I did it! I answered every question. The test wasn't as bad as I thought it would be.*

Visualization takes positive self-talk one step further. Instead of imagining the worst and seeing yourself fail, you imagine success. Visualization is a powerful process that can produce results through practice. Start your visualization by closing your eyes. Imagine yourself in class. Picture yourself as a confident student who understands lectures and participates actively in class. Watch yourself study for the course. See yourself actively reading and understanding text information. Imagine yourself preparing for a test. You do not feel anxious or tired. Feel yourself learning and feeling good about what you learn. After all, you've done your homework. You can expect to do well.

The feeling grows stronger. You feel prepared. Imagine yourself closing your books and gathering your notes. Picture yourself falling asleep. Feel yourself waking up refreshed and ready. Watch yourself review the information. You are calm and prepared. See yourself going to the class in which you have an exam. See yourself walking into the class and sitting down. Visualize yourself being calm and collected. Watch your instructor give you your test. Imagine yourself carefully listening to the verbal instructions and estimating the time needed to complete each section. Watch yourself take the test. You are calm and confident. You think logically. You remember accurately. Watch yourself complete the test and turn it in. Visualize yourself leaving the room. You feel pleased with yourself and your performance. Yes, you *can* do it.

"Relax, you won't feel a thing," say many nurses right before they give you an injection. And, while you're sure to feel the needle going in, it really does hurt less if you can ease the tension in your body. Similarly, **relaxation** eases nervousness and stress. Even in the middle of an exam, you can relax.

You relax your muscles by doing a physical body check. Whenever you feel tense, stop and see if any muscles are involved that really don't need to be. For example, suppose you feel your shoulders tense as you take or prepare for a test. Since shoulder muscles play little part in test taking, make a conscious effort to relax them. Finally, conscious, deep breathing also relaxes the body.

Suppose you fail to control your anxiety, and you "block" information while taking the test. Everyone experiences **memory blocks.** The trick is to prepare for them. When you get hit by a memory block, take a few deep breaths to regain your composure, make your best guess, and

relaxation
A positive feeling created through the loosening of muscles.

memory blocks
Sudden losses of memory for a specific piece of information.

continue with the test. Maintain appropriate self-talk so that you stay confident and focused. "Of course I know that, I'll think of it in a minute," relieves stress better than, "What is the matter with me? I must be an idiot! If I can't remember this, I won't be able to remember anything else."

As you continue the test, your brain generally continues processing and looking for the information. If you've ever wracked your brain to think of a name and given up only to recall it later, you've experienced such processing. In addition, as you continue the test, information in other questions may cue your recall. When you return to the question, take a deep breath, think logically, and review everything you know about the topic. Associations of various kinds—recall of when or where you heard or read information, recall from different points of view and so on—often serve to trigger the memory. Sometimes saying the alphabet slowly will unlock the memory of a specific fact. Ask yourself, does it start with *A? B?* and so on.

Measuring Your Test Anxiety

How much test anxiety do you have? Answer the following questions with "True" or "False."

_____ **1.** While taking an important exam, I find myself thinking of how much brighter the other students are than I am.

_____ **2.** If I were to take an intelligence test, I would worry a great deal before taking it.

_____ **3.** If I knew I was going to take an intelligence test, I would feel confident and relaxed.

_____ **4.** While taking an important exam, I perspire a great deal.

_____ **5.** During class examinations, I find myself thinking of things unrelated to the actual course material.

_____ **6.** I get to feeling very panicky when I have to take a surprise exam.

_____ **7.** During a test, I find myself thinking of the consequences of failing.

_____ **8.** After important tests, I am frequently so tense my stomach gets upset.

_____ **9.** I freeze up on things like intelligence tests and final exams.

_____ **10.** Getting good grades on one test doesn't seem to increase my confidence on the second.

_____ **11.** I sometimes feel my heart beating very fast during important exams.

_____ **12.** After taking a test, I always feel I could have done better than I actually did.

_____ **13.** I usually get depressed after taking a test.

_____ **14.** I have an uneasy, upset feeling before taking a final examination.

_____ **15.** When I'm taking a test, my emotional feelings do not interfere with my performance.

_____ **16.** During a course examination, I frequently get so nervous that I forget facts I really know.

_____ **17.** I seem to defeat myself while working on important tests.

_____ **18.** The harder I work at taking a test or studying for one, the more confused I get.

_____ **19.** As soon as an exam is over, I try to stop worrying about it, but I just can't.

_____ **20.** During exams, I sometimes wonder if I'll ever get through school.

_____ **21.** I would rather write a paper than take an examination for my grade in a course.

_____ **22.** I wish examinations did not bother me so much.

_____ **23.** I think I could do much better on tests if I could take them alone and not feel pressured by time limits.

_____ **24.** Thinking about the grade I may get in a course interferes with my studying and performance on tests.

_____ **25.** If examinations could be done away with, I think I would actually learn more.

_____ **26.** On exams I take the attitude, "If I don't know it now, there's no point in worrying about it."

_____ **27.** I really don't see why some people get so upset about tests.

_____ **28.** Thoughts of doing poorly interfere with my performance on tests.

_____ **29.** I don't study any harder for final exams than for the rest of my coursework.

_____ **30.** Even when I'm well prepared for a test, I feel very anxious about it.

_____ **31.** I don't enjoy eating before an important test.

_____ **32.** Before an important examination, I find my hands or arms trembling.

_____ **33.** I seldom feel the need for "cramming" before an exam.

_____ **34.** The university should recognize that some students are more nervous than others about tests and that this affects their performance.

_____ **35.** It seems to me that examination periods should not be made such intense situations.

_____ **36.** I started feeling very uneasy just before getting a test paper back.

_____ **37.** I dread courses where the instructor has the habit of giving "pop" quizzes.

Scoring with the Test Anxiety Scale is very easy. The total number of TRUE answers is your test anxiety score. A score of 12 or below ranks in the low test anxiety range. A score of 12 to 20 ranks in the medium range. Any score above 20 signifies high test anxiety. Scoring 15 or greater is a good indication you experience considerable discomfort about taking tests.

activity 6

Anxiety and Performance

Identify one course in which stress affects your test performance. Specify the aspect of the course that causes the most anxiety. This is your challenge. Now use the remainder of the 5C process (Define the **C**hallenge; Identify **C**hoices; Predict **C**onsequences; **C**hoose an option; **C**heck your outcome) to find a solution you can use to combat this stress.

GROUP APPLICATION: Share individual answers with your group. What similarities and differences do you discover among your group's answers? What factors might contribute to these similarities and differences?

Choices for Exam Success

You've done the work. You're prepared for the test. Now all you have to do is take it, right? It's not always as easy as it sounds, but there are choices you can make to maximize your performance and your grade. Some test formats (e.g., multiple choice, essay) require special strategies. Other strategies work for all kinds of tests.

First, make sure you are mentally prepared. Be sure you have the materials you need for the test (e.g., #2 pencils, calculator, test forms, etc.). Otherwise, you'll feel panicked. Avoid personal conflicts prior to the test. Getting upset destroys your focus. Get a good night's sleep and eat something nourishing before the exam. Getting physically ready helps you be more mentally ready.

Second, get to the exam on time. If you arrive early, avoid talking to others. Their fears tend to be contagious. If you arrive late, you may miss important verbal directions or you may feel rushed and anxious.

Third, read the exam directions carefully. Although it might seem like a given, many students are so focused on answering the questions that they skip over the directions. However, directions often provide key information you need. Thus, once you get your exam, read the directions. Underline key terms and steps in the directions to ensure that you read them carefully.

Fourth, preview the test. Note total number of questions and variations, if any, in point values. Estimate the amount of time you plan to spend on each item and plan to spend the most time on questions receiving the most credit.

Fifth, answer the easiest questions first. This builds your confidence and triggers your memory for other information. Also, if you run out of time, you will have answered the questions you know. Mark difficult questions, but skip them and go on. Return to them when you have more time to consider them. If there is no penalty for guessing, attempt to answer every question. Make your responses as neat and legible as possible.

Sixth, work at your own pace. Don't worry if some students finish and leave before you do.

Seventh, if time permits, review your questions and answers. Be sure you understood the question

Answers come to all who wait . . . whether they're correct or not depends on preparation.

and have marked the answer you intended. Some students think it's better to stick with their first response. Actually, that depends on your past performances on tests. Some students find their initial nervousness resulted in their misreading directions or questions. If there's time, this sort of review helps you determine if your decisions were correct.

Taking Objective Exams

One of the two types of exams given most often in college is the **objective test,** a test in which you select an answer from several choices provided by an instructor. Objective tests require that you recognize or reason out information from the options you are given. There are some ways you can maximize your performance on an objective test.

You need to begin by looking at the stem (the question part) and trying to create an answer before reading the distractors (choices you select from). This helps you focus your thoughts and keeps you from being led astray by **attractive distracters,** that is, incorrect choices that seem plausible. For instance, which of the following presidents left office before impeachment? A. Bill Clinton; B. John F. Kennedy; C. Richard M. Nixon. While you may recall that Clinton's and Kennedy's reputations with the ladies were questionable, and that Clinton faced impeachment, it was Richard Nixon who left office before he was impeached for the Watergate incident.

Even if you don't know the answer to the question, take a guess and go on to the next question. If the question is one you can answer with a little work, take your best guess, mark it, and go on. Return to the question when you have more time.

Often all of the responses are correct in some way. You may be looking for the best choice of the group–check your instructions. It's easy to confuse the first correct answer you see with the *best* choice of correct answers.

The wording of the question affects responses. Look for small words like *not* or *except* that completely change the meaning of the question. Double negatives cancel each other. For example, *not unlucky* means *lucky.* Words that set limits (e.g., *few, sometimes, often*) are more likely to be correct than those that are all-inclusive (e.g., *all, none, always, never*).

You should also watch for responses that are essentially the same. Usually this means that neither answer is correct. For example, in the following question answers B and C are synonymous; therefore, neither can be correct.

The _____ branch is the part of the government responsible for interpreting laws.

A. executive

B. legislative

C. congressional

D. judicial

A final suggestion, should you find yourself confused, is to make your exam a true-false exam. To do this, you use the stem (the question part) and each possible choice as a true-false question when you feel confused by similar choices. This helps you isolate answers in a logical manner.

Answering Essay Questions

Although instructors may give objective tests, they may also ask you to respond to **subjective questions.** Some specialized tips help maximize your performance.

First, you should consider choosing a title for your essay or response. Even though you don't actually entitle an answer, a title helps you focus your thoughts and narrow your subject. It will help if you know what information your instructor is asking for. The list in Table 15.2 describes common

> **subjective questions**
> Prompts which require you to write answers in essay or paragraph form.

Table 15.2 Answering Essay Questions

If You Are Told . . .	As in This Example . . .	Take This Action . . .
Explain, discuss, describe, delineate	Explain how to set up and run a business.	Write as much detail as possible about the topic in a clear, concise, complete manner.
Compare, find the similarities	Compare businesses in the U.S. to businesses in another country.	Discuss the ways in which the two topics are alike.
Contrast, find the differences	Contrast businesses in the U.S. to businesses in another country.	Discuss the ways in which the two topics are not alike.
Criticize, critique, evaluate, review	Criticize current U.S. economic policy toward small business owners.	Discuss the positive and negative aspects of the topic, and conclude with a summary that makes a judgment based on the pros and cons cited.
Justify, support, give a rationale	Justify the need for government aid to minority businesses.	Give facts and figures to defend the topic.
List, enumerate, name, outline	List the three laws that pertain to business.	Give a detailed, numbered list of the items requested.
Summarize	Summarize the major principles that support the North American Free Trade Agreement.	Construct a clear, concise statement that includes all main ideas.
Paraphrase	Paraphrase the following ad copy for a business.	Reword a selection expressing the main ideas in synonymous terms.
Define, clarify, interpret	Define the following terms: entrepreneur, collective bargaining, Consumer Price Index.	Explain the meaning.
Elaborate	Elaborate on the following statement: "U.S. import tariffs should be abolished."	Explain in great detail.
Classify	Classify businesses according to sector of the economy.	Organize in categories.
Trace	Trace the development of accounting ethics in a specific company.	Explain the sequential development of the topic.
Illustrate, diagram, chart	Illustrate the relationship between earnings and taxes.	Draw a graphic representation.
Label	Label the categories of entrepreneurs in the following figure.	Name each part.
Calculate or compute	Using a company's financial statements, calculate its total assets and current liabilities.	Solve a problem.

question/instruction words in essay tests, examples of how they might be used in a question or instruction, and strategies for responding to them. In addition, the key words help you identify the transitions you need for clarity.

Next, take a few minutes to outline your response or list a few main points before you begin. An outline keeps you from omitting important details. Write this outline somewhere on your bluebook or paper. Even if you run out of time, your instructor will be able to see where the essay was going. You might receive partial credit.

Standard essay format matters. Using it makes you seem like a more prepared student and a better writer. Introduce your subject, develop the topic, and summarize.

Finally, you need to do a final reading to make sure that your response answers the question that was asked. You need to check organization, coherence, and clarity. It's also important to proof your work. You should check spelling, grammar, and punctuation.

Taking Math and Applied Science Exams

Math and applied science exam preparation begins with your class notes and textbook. To be sure you understand completely, first you need to re-examine the notes you took while your instructor was demonstrating how to solve each problem and the homework problems you have completed. Look for similarities and differences among problems, especially those with which you are having difficulty. Sometimes your understanding of one problem helps you see how to solve another one.

Second, your textbook provides example problems for your practice. You need to study these just as you studied class work and homework examples. In addition, as you work through the examples, you need to identify the concepts, formulas, methods, steps, and rules each example uses. Consider defining these using a list of concepts, and so forth, possibly on index cards. You need to write definitions in your own words, accompanied by a sample problem.

Finally, you need to find additional problems and create for yourself a test similar to the one you think your instructor will give. Then, take it a step further and test yourself under realistic conditions. Give yourself the same amount of time you will have for the real test. It might even help reduce test anxiety if you take your practice exam in the math or applied science classroom.

On the math or science exam itself, you need to solve problems. That's what most math and science instructors want to see. Following are steps in taking math and applied science exams:

1. Quickly examine the exam to locate difficult problems and estimate how much time problems will take.

2. Work in this order: easiest and highest point value; second easiest and highest point value; difficult and highest point value; and difficult and lowest point value.

3. Read each phrase of the problem and underline or write all pertinent information.

4. In your own words, identify what the problem wants you to do.

5. Ask yourself "What do I need to do to solve this problem?" Note relationships among data and relevant formulas.

6. If you get stuck, try one or all of these:

   - Recall an example problem similar to the one you are working, and write the sample problem on paper so you can better study it.

   - Break the problem into parts and work the parts you can. Look for a relationship between what you understand and what you don't.

   - If you cannot work the problem, skip it and go on.

7. Check your solution. Make sure you have the answer in the proper form, and use any checking method you like to double-check your work.

8. Show all your work. Some instructors give partial credit. Even if an instructor doesn't, he or she might indicate where your thinking went astray. This is valuable information for the next exam.

Taking Online Exams

In many ways, taking an online exam is the same as taking a paper and pencil one. The same tips you use for objective, subjective, math, and science questions apply. However, there are a few differences.

If the exam is part of your course management system, be sure you know how to access and find your way around it. There may be special instructions for submitting responses that, if not followed, mean that your exam is never submitted. You may be able to see all the questions at once or you may only get one question at a time. Check and double-check the availability of the exam. Most have specific times at which they open and close. Check to see if the exam is timed. This helps you manage your time.

If you are taking the exam in a testing center, the same rules of conduct apply. You will probably not be allowed to use your text or other materials. But if the exam is one that you can take on your own time at home or in a computer lab, it may be an open-book exam in which you can use course materials. Such exams might seem easy since you can look up the answers. However, instructors often ask more complex questions on open-book tests which require you to find related information, understand it, and apply it to a new situation. Although you don't necessarily need to memorize and practice what you learn, you do need to understand and know where to find it prior to the test.

Taking Final Exams

What do you think of when you hear the word *finals?* Often college finals have a bad reputation. But there's really nothing to fear. Perhaps you've been doing all the right things to make a good grade in the course. You've gone to class regularly. You've kept up with your assignments. All you have to do now is take the final.

To begin preparing for the final, review the suggestions for taking other kinds of exams. The same rules apply. Use them. In addition, find out when and where the exam will be. Final exam schedules do not always follow regular class times. You will really panic if you get to your class and nobody is there.

Many finals are more long than hard. They are almost like tests of endurance. They are usually no harder than other tests, just longer. Because they are longer, finals are often fair tests of your knowledge. They cover more information. You have a better chance because they focus on many topics.

Here are some other tips for taking finals.

1. Know where you need to spend your time. Some exams will be more difficult than others. Some may be easier in content. Some may be worth more points than others. Make a list of all your exams, their point value in terms of your overall grade, and then evaluate what you need to do.

2. Schedule several study group meetings at least 2 weeks before the exam. For all the reasons a study groups excel, there is no better time than now to work with others. Know what your group will cover each time and be prepared.

3. With your study group, create a comprehensive study guide. You can outline or map information. The creation of the study guide is in fact studying so when you use it to study, your work counts double.

4. With your study guide in place, look for omissions and areas where you need further information. Ask questions among your group members.

5. As a group, go to any review sessions offered *in addition to your scheduled group meetings.* Your instructor is an available and important source of information in terms of course materials and the exam itself. What questions your group cannot answer, he/she can.

6. In addition to your study guide, use the *Survey* step of SQ3R to review textbook chapters.

7. Do your best to stay rested and not get stressed. You cannot master all the information for a final at once. You need to take breaks, eat well, exercise, and sleep during this time. Cramming is *not* an option.

Ethical Academic Behavior

ethics
Standards of behavior that tell us how human beings ought to act in certain situations.

You know when you are acting ethically or are being your best self. **Ethics** are standards of behavior that tell us how human beings ought to act in certain situations. One type of ethics is called *virtue ethics.* Honesty, integrity, fairness, and self-control are all examples of virtues. Virtue ethics asks of any action, "What kind of person will I become if I do this?" or "Is this action consistent with my acting at my best?"

In all classrooms, and particularly in testing situations, instructors trust you to decide to act according to virtue ethics. They count on you to value your honesty or moral integrity more than your course grade. Instructors also assume that you realize at least two other consequences of cheating. First, getting caught means a failing grade. Failing grades lower your GPA. Second, it's embarrassing and troubling for both you and your instructor. In some cases, cheating can lead to expulsion.

Cheating takes many forms. It includes using cheat sheets (in print or technological form), getting answers from others during tests, and stealing copies of exams. Using your cell phone to get information during an exam (even if it's only the dictionary to check spelling) is cheating. You want to avoid any appearance of cheating. When in doubt, ask yourself, "What would my instructor say?" If you think an instructor would disapprove, it's probably cheating.

Each college has a written code of conduct. It clearly states what it expects of you in terms of ethical behavior. Your college's code of conduct is on the campus website and in the college catalog.

Test-Taking Strategies

1. Reflect on the information contained in this module. Rewrite the "no" answers you gave on the text anxiety scale as positive statements.

2. Use the 5C approach (Define the **C**hallenge; Identify **C**hoices; Predict **C**onsequences; **C**hoose an option; **C**heck your outcome) to determine your biggest test-taking obstacle and develop a plan for overcoming it.

What can a returned test tell me?

After-Exam Analysis

You finished the exam, turned it in, and got a grade. What can you possibly learn from that exam? A lot, depending on what you do when a test is returned to you.

Reviewing your test helps you decide which of your study and test-taking strategies work and which do not. You can use this information to improve future test preparation and performance. Figure 15.3 shows a form

Test Item Missed	Insufficient Information						Test Anxiety						Lack of Test Wisdom					Test Skills						Other	
	I did not read the text thoroughly.	The information was not in my notes.	I studied the information but could not remember it.	I knew main ideas but needed details.	I knew the information but could not apply it.	I studied the wrong information.	I experienced mental block.	I spent too much time daydreaming.	I was so tired I could not concentrate.	I was so hungry I could not concentrate.	I panicked.	I carelessly marked a wrong choice.	I did not eliminate grammatically incorrect choices.	I did not choose the *best* choice.	I did not notice limiting words.	I did not notice a double negative.	I changed a correct answer to a wrong one.	I misread the directions.	I misread the question.	I made poor use of the time provided.	I wrote poorly organized responses.	I wrote incomplete responses.		
Number of Items Missed																								

Figure 15.3 Worksheet for Examining Returned Tests.

for examining your test paper. To use it, list the number of each item you missed in the first column. Then mark an X under the description that best explains why you missed a question. Sometimes you will mark more than one reason for a question. Next, add the number of X's under each reason. These numbers indicate the areas of study and test-taking strategies that need more attention.

After you use the form to analyze your study and test-taking habits, look for information about how your instructor constructs exams. Look for patterns in the types of questions asked. See if your instructor emphasized text or lecture information. This information helps you prepare for the next exam.

Strategic planning, a buzzword in the corporate world, is important in college as well. Strategic planning is a decision-making process that involves setting goals, devising a plan for achieving them, evaluating the results, and then rethinking your plan to be sure it's the most effective, efficient way to reach your goals. You are in the process of strategically planning your college career. You've made decisions about the goals you want to achieve and how you plan to accomplish them. Course exams help you determine where you stand in your attainment of your goals; however, it's your after-exam evaluation that helps you assess the effectiveness of the plan you've selected.

strategic planning
A design that gathers, analyzes, and uses information to make decisions.

Your After-Exam Follow-Through

activity 8

1. Photocopy the after-exam worksheet contained in Figure 15.3. Use this worksheet with a recent exam from one of your courses.

2. On a separate sheet of paper or in your notebook, answer each of the following:

   a. How much time did you study for this exam?

   b. Specifically, what did you do to prepare for the exam?

   c. Were you satisfied with your score? Why or why not?

   d. What have you learned about the way your instructor creates exams?

   e. What have you learned about yourself in terms of test preparation and/or test-taking skills?

   f. What problems have you identified in terms of test preparation and/or test taking?

   g. How can you use the 5C approach (Define the **C**hallenge; Identify **C**hoices; Predict **C**onsequences; **C**hoose an option; **C**heck your outcome) to confront this problem?

chapter review

Respond to the following on a separate sheet of paper or in your notebook.

1. What aspect of planning to study causes the most difficulty for you? Why? How can you solve this problem?

2. What kinds of negative self-talk affect your study and test performance? Why? What is your plan for changing this?

3. What is the difference between charting and mapping? Which do you prefer? Why?

4. Which mnemonic do you use most often? Why?

5. Do you tend to get better scores on objective or subjective exams? Why?

6. Which method for controlling anxiety have you used before? Never used? Which one are you most likely to try? Why?

7. How do personality and learning style affect how you study?

8. What did you learn from returned exams? What suprised you?

did you decide?

Did you accomplish what you wanted to in this chapter? Check the items below that apply to you.

Review the *You Decide* questions that you identified at the beginning of the chapter, but look at them from a new direction. If you didn't check an item below, review that module until you feel you can confidently apply the strategies to your own situation. However, the best ideas are worthless unless they are put into effect. Use the 5Cs to help you decide what information you found most helpful in the chapter and how you plan to use it. Record your comments after the statements below.

☐ 15.1 I know what I need to prepare to study.

_____

☐ 15.2 I understand how to get my notes, text content, and other materials organized.

_____

☐ 15.3 I have some ideas to help me remember what I need to know on a test.

_____

☐ 15.4 I am aware of some online tools that can help me prepare for an exam.

_____

☐ 15.5 I have a plan to keep from getting stressed before and during tests.

_____

☐ 15.6 I know how to maximize my success on exams.

_____

☐ 15.7 I understand the things a returned test can tell me.

_____

perspectives

Some students think study is more important than sleep during exam periods. They don't realize that everything you do . . . including sleep or not sleep . . . is a decision. The following article from a college newspaper, "Lack of Sleep May Lead to Lack of Future," by Mary Allen, describes how your choices might affect your academic success.

Think about and answer the questions that follow.

1. What are some of the effects of sleep deprivation?
2. What did you think was the most important tip for combating sleep deprivation?
3. According to the article, what is a negative effect of caffeine?
4. According to the article, what percentage of students do not get enough sleep?
5. What is R.E.M. sleep?
6. You can use the 5C decision-making process to make decisions about sleep.
   A. What sleep **C**hallenge do you have?
   B. What key **C**hoices are open to you?
   C. What would be the major **C**onsequence(s) of each choice?
   D. What will you **C**hoose to do?
   E. How might you **C**heck the outcome of your decision?

They can be seen wandering zombie-like, bleary-eyed, sleep hair sticking up on their heads, or slumped over their keyboards. What are we talking about here, hangovers? No, they are sleep-deprived Glendale Community College students, and missing too much sleep can affect one intellectually, physically and emotionally.

Sixty-three percent of college students do not get enough sleep, according to a recent study by the National Sleep Foundation. "Studies have shown that chronically sleep-deprived people believe that they have adapted to their lack of sleep while actually their test performances continue to deteriorate," said Michael H. Silber, president of the American Academy of Sleep Medicine. "We can't keep as many things online at any one time when we're sleep deprived. Sleep deprivation significantly impairs attention, working memory performance, our ability to drive. It has the same effect as alcohol does," said Dr. Sean Drummond, who works with the University of California at San Diego.

To keep themselves alert, students have increased their caffeine intake. Caffeine is starting to come in many different forms; Jolt, the highly caffeinated soda, now has a gum. Its big selling point is that the caffeine gets into your blood stream quicker because it is absorbed through the tongue. You can also buy Umph tablets. They are described as effervescent caffeine tablets that you can pop into any of your favorite beverages. Milk that can get you wired?

Caffeine may do the trick for a little while, but there is no substitute for sleep. "We have done lab studies on healthy people who are sleep-restricted and find they are memory-impaired. We know the more they sleep the better. Eight hours are good; 10 hours are better," says Dr. David Hudgel, of Henry Ford Hospital's Sleep Disorder Clinic in Detroit. Researchers have found that interruption of sleeping patterns can lead to depression. In addition, "The body needs to adjust and recuperate from sleep deprivation, which takes more than just a few days. It can take up to a month to see a real change; sleep resets emotions," according to Dr. Peter L. Franzen, a researcher at Western Psychiatric Institute and Clinic.

To combat sleep deprivation: Avoid stimulants; avoid caffeine after 2 p.m. (coffee, tea, colas); the stimulant effect of caffeine can last up to 12 hours. Alcohol might help onset of sleep, but later withdrawal effects can lead to sleep disruption. Avoid all-nighters: Remember that memory is very dependent on adequate sleep. Studying late into the night can be detrimental to learning if sleep is reduced. The best preparation for an exam is a good night's sleep. Light: Bright light in the morning helps you to be "awake"; darkness at night helps you to sleep.

GCC photography students Nate Harris and Daniela Behm both value sleep before play; but they do not always get their 8–10 hours every night. Nate Harris say he tries to get 6–7 hours sleep a night. His priorities are school, work, sleep, and play. Though he sometimes feels drowsy, he rarely falls asleep. He uses energy drinks to stay awake. Daniela Behm says, "Tuesday and Thursday I only get about five to six hours, and the rest of the week less than eight hours a night." As far as priorities go, she says, "Sleep is number one, even though I do not get as much as I should! If I do not get enough sleep, I feel in a fog for the rest of the day. School takes up a lot of time. I also just moved here from Michigan so I am still trying to get used to the new lifestyle. I always have times during the day where I feel like I need a nap!"

Students that are unable to get 8–10 hours of sleep at night should think about taking a nap. Sleep specialist Dr. Maas maintains, "Brief naps taken daily are far healthier than sleeping in or taking very long naps on the weekend." They are also far better than caffeine as a pick-me-up. "Consumption of caffeine will be followed by feelings of lethargy and reduced R.E.M. (or dream) sleep that night," Dr. Maas writes. "A debt in your sleep bank account is not reduced by artificial stimulants."

reflecting on decisions

Now that you've learned about studying for and taking tests, how will that affect decisions about the tests you take?

END WORLD HUNGER ONE
ANSWER AT A TIME

What if you could learn and help end world hunger at the same time? With Free Rice, **http://www.freerice.com/,** you can! The goals of this site are (1) free education for all and (2) free rice for hungry people. This site provides multiple-choice questions for learning vocabulary and other subjects (e.g., foreign languages, chemistry, English). Each answer you get right generates ten grains of rice which are paid for by the site's sponsors. Ten grains per response isn't much until you multiply it by the thousands of people who might be using the site at one time. The site provides totals of how much rice is generated by year, month, and day. You can help feed hungry people . . . one right answer at a time!

◀ CHOOSING TO SERVE

R E V I E W

Skim the notes you made throughout the chapter. How does the content fit together? What information is still unclear? Were your learning goals met? Can you answer the review questions and define terms?

◀ CHOOSING TO BE AN ACTIVE LEARNER

CHAPTER **SIXTEEN**

Exploring Career Options and Opportunities

What do you want to be when you "grow up"? You've probably heard that question many times. Think as far back as you can remember into your earliest years of childhood. What did you want to be then when you grew up? Why? How has that changed?

YOU DECIDE

To *wonder* means to think or have curiosity about. Things and ideas you wonder about often mask a need for a decision. Check the items below that apply to you.

In terms of my education and career, I've been wondering . . .

☐ 16.1 How do I decide on a major?

☐ 16.2 What's the difference between a Certificate and an Associate's and a Bachelor's degree?

☐ 16.3 How do I choose courses for each semester?

☐ 16.4 What career skills might I need?

Each of these decision points corresponds to the numbered modules that follow. Turn to the module for immediate help.

CHOOSING TO BE AN ACTIVE LEARNER

SURVEY

Before reading this chapter, prepare for learning. Purposefully skim the title, introduction, headings, and graphics. As you survey, decide what information you already know and what information is new to you.

QUESTION

Change each section's heading into a question. This forms your learning goal for reading.

READ

Read the section without marking. Reread and mark key information that answers your question.

RECITE

Stop after each section and make sure you understood the content. Organize or summarize content and make notes.

The drive to choose a career starts early. Even before you were born, your family may have been planning your future. As you grew, adults asked, "What do you want to be when you grow up?" As you played, you may have pretended to be a police officer, a doctor, or a teacher. When you started to work, you probably had a variety of jobs—which may or may not have reflected what you wanted to be.

What's the difference between a job and a career? A job is work you do for a set amount of money. A career is a lifetime journey of making choices about your knowledge, skills, and experiences in the context of the opportunities available to you.

The U.S. Department of Labor reported that the average person holds approximately 11 jobs by the age of 42. Whether or not your collection of jobs becomes a career—or just a lot of disconnected jobs—depends on you and the decisions you make along the way. Your career comes from a series of related jobs in the same field. Thus, a career is not just a goal you attain in the future. Your career is a lifelong learning trip as you develop your knowledge, refine your expertise, and choose experiences that reflect your interests, values, and goals.

Students come to college with diverse job and career experiences. Students who have been out of high school for a while may already have had a career, or at least a job. They may be back in school to train for a new career, one that will be better in terms of interest, pay, or stability. Other students are recent graduates. Most of these students will have had "jobs"—flipping burgers or selling clothes at the mall—but not careers. A few students will have worked throughout high school and beyond with a clear and focused career direction. Perhaps they volunteered or have already worked in a job that matches their career goals. Such students are ahead of the game. Some students know that they want to

pursue their educations but are not sure what they want their majors to be. They may be undecided about what fields they will ultimately work in. Some students may feel completely undecided without a clear idea of what major is right for them. None of these situations is unique, and none is ultimately correct or better, as long as you know where you stand and are ready to take positive action to move forward—to whatever that might be.

Whatever your situation, this chapter will help you clarify your goals for college and career and discover resources that will help you achieve them.

Choosing a Major

Today's workers often change careers–not just jobs–many times in their lives. So how important is the major you choose? Well, that depends on whom you ask and what your goals are. If you plan to become a nurse or a paramedic, you should major in nursing or allied health sciences. If your goal is to become a general building contractor, majoring in construction management would be a good idea. In other words, if your career goals directly translate into a specific major and career, then you should probably major in that subject. But if your goal is to transfer to a four-year college to get a degree that will open doors for you in any number of careers, your degree options are likewise wide open. Here are some other suggestions to help you choose a major that's right for you.

❯ Guidelines for Choosing a Major

Think about yourself. Consider your aptitudes, abilities, interests, needs, and values (see Chapter 2) in terms of career choices. For instance, what are (or could be) your strengths? Some careers require extensive time or lifestyle commitments. How would that fit into your personal, family, and other values? What personal traits do you have that make you suitable (or unsuitable) for a particular career?

Picture your ideal working environment. Do you want to work inside or outside? Do you prefer urban or rural areas? Do you like to work with people, information, or things? If you want to work with people, what age group would you prefer? Look for majors that reflect your choices.

Pay attention to what you enjoy. What are you passionate about? What courses, activities, topics, and people interest you now or have in the past? Why? What majors and careers offer those same kinds of interests?

Don't confuse your hobbies with your career. Maybe you do love music, but you don't sing well enough to be a professional and you don't want to teach. You can always sing in community groups and other places without making a career of it. You might enjoy cooking or reading, but you can't imagine wanting to do either professionally as a chef or an editor.

Research the career you want. Check out the government website for the *Occupational Outlook Handbook* (OOH) (http://www.bls.gov/OCO/). The website describes itself as "a nationally recognized source of career information, designed to provide valuable assistance to individuals making decisions about their future work lives." Revised every two years, the OOH identifies educational/training requirements, what a worker does on the job, and typical working conditions for the job. It also projects expected demand for the job and salaries by state. Search for other Web resources. For example, search using *What can I do with a degree in XXX?* (Substitute the degree you are considering for the XXX.) Look online for professional organizations related to your career choice. The content of their websites will generally describe what professionals do, required job skills, standards or certification requirements, and current trends. Try to research as many resources as possible. You are researching your future.

Weed out what you don't want to do. Get your college catalog and look through the majors and curricula. There will be many majors that don't fit your interests. For instance, perhaps you have no interest or skill in art. That leaves out many choices and majors from art history to graphic design. Or, maybe you faint at the sight of blood or find medical environments stressful. If so, a health care major may not be a good choice.

Avoid stereotypical thinking. Some careers (e.g., horticulture, industrial management, or funeral services) may not be as familiar to you as others (e.g., nursing, education, business). As a result, you might discount some careers that, upon further thought, would be good ones for you. Thus, as you look through your catalog's course options, take a second look at those majors that you don't know much about.

Look at the big picture. Some students find the right major in their last term. They think twice about it because a different major will take another semester or two in college. So if you graduate at the age of 25 and work until the age of 64, you have 40 years to work at a career you don't like. If you spend an extra year in college, you could work in a career you love for 39 years. How do you want to spend your life?

Read job descriptions. Check job descriptions in your local paper if you plan to stay in the area. Check job descriptions on Internet sites (e.g., Careerbuilder.com, Monster.com, Yahoo!, HotJobs.com) if you can be more flexible. Look for those jobs that make you think, "I'd like to do that." As you read, take note of what they require in terms of degrees and experience. This helps you make more informed choices about majors, internships, and other career options.

Talk to others. Many college faculty have had work experiences prior to teaching. Your campus career center is another resource you shouldn't forget. Both faculty and career center counselors can give you insider insights based on their career experiences. They may also be able to refer you to people who are currently working in the career you are considering. They can answer your questions and also serve as contacts for future job opportunities. Finally, you can always talk to other students about their career interests and work.

Finish your degree. Many employers hire workers with degrees, not necessarily a degree in specific areas. Employers often want to see that you had the perseverance to complete something. They'll often train you to do what they need. Just because you have an associate's degree in nursing doesn't mean that you wouldn't be good in business.

Build a career out of something you enjoy.

Don't be afraid to change your mind. Some people stay in majors because that's what they said they were going to do. Sometimes they worry more about what they'll tell others than what they really want to do. Don't be one of them. When people ask, simply reply, "I thought I knew what I wanted to do, but I changed my mind."

Keep your eyes open. Your first, or even second, job may not be your dream job. But, they may give you skills and information that qualify you for jobs you never even imagined. Unless you're psychic, there's no way to know what the future holds. You can prepare for the future by taking advantage of as many opportunities as are available to you to learn.

Considering Majors

activity 1

Using your institution's college catalog, your Challenge is to find two majors that you would consider. If you are planning to pursue a Bachelor's degree, you may use a catalog from a school you have under consideration. Use the 5C approach to identify Choices and determine Consequences for each major. Discuss these with an advisor before you complete the final two Cs.

Degree Options

Career decision making often involves finding the degree or program at your college that will take you where you want to go. On most campuses, you can choose between an Associate of Arts (AA), an Associate of Science (AS), and an Associate in Applied Science (AAS) degree, all of which are two-year degree programs, or a certification program which may have varying time periods for completion.

Community colleges often provide the greatest range of options for associate degrees. Such degrees usually can be completed within a couple of years. Associate degrees vary by institution. You may find anything from animal health technology to travel and tourism. An Associate of Arts (AA) degree allows you to transfer to a four-year degree program. An Associate of Science (AS) degree generally leads to a work career rather than to completion of a Bachelor's degree. AS degrees do require general education courses such as English, math, science, and social science but emphasize practical applications in career-specific areas. An Associate of Applied Science (AAS) degree focuses on the knowledge a student needs to succeed in a particular job. A Bachelor's degree is a four-year degree from a college or university.

Certificate programs are not degree programs, but they ensure that someone has met qualification standards in terms of knowledge or skill. Although many certification programs may require basic academic skills or other coursework prior to enrollment, they focus more on career-specific content. Some certification programs have corporate (e.g., Novell Network Engineer) or national (e.g., American Sign Language Interpreter) certification. Other programs–such as child care or business–provide institutional certification for program completion. Four-year colleges as well as community colleges offer certification programs.

Four-year degrees involve more coursework and higher degrees often result in higher paying, higher status jobs and careers. Of course, not all satisfying careers come with high salaries. For instance, neither social workers nor teachers make a lot of money even though many of them have graduate degrees. Still, both are important professions that add to the quality of people's lives. You have to balance the extra time and cost of a four-year degree with how much you will earn and–most importantly–how much you will enjoy the career you choose.

There may be times when you want to move from one college to another. For example, you may decide that there is another program at a different school that better meets your needs. First, where will you go? Before you transfer, obviously you need to know that the major you seek is offered at the school you choose. But, just as important, you need to know that the major comes from a division in the school which is **accredited,** or recognized

accredited
Institution recognized as maintaining standards requisite for its graduates to achieve credentials for professional practice.

as maintaining standards requisite for its graduates to achieve credentials for professional practice. If you cannot find this information on the school's website, you need to ask.

Second, plan ahead to be sure that your high school or college credits will transfer and apply to the major you want. If you are already a college student, find out if your college has an **articulation agreement,** which is an agreement between two institutions to accept credits of equivalent courses for transfer, with the four-year college you want to attend. If your college does not have an articulation agreement, it is up to you to contact the registrar of the degree-granting institution to learn what you need to do to make sure that your credits will transfer.

Third, it's also important to know if there are any other requirements you need to have to be accepted at the new institution. This could include a minimum GPA or standardized test score, completion of specific coursework, audition, development of a portfolio, personal interview, or other criteria. Identify these criteria as soon as you decide which institution you hope to attend. Otherwise, you may find that you've taken courses that do not transfer or that your GPA is not high enough for admission. Keep in mind that minimum qualifications for entry may be just that: minimum. Some programs do have minimum qualifications, but choose the best. So while the minimum GPA might be 3.2, those students that are getting accepted might have a 3.5. Thus, you need to determine if the program you want limits enrollment to only the best.

If you plan to transfer credit, you will need to have a copy of your **transcript** sent to the school you are transferring to. Get a copy sent to yourself as well. When it arrives, don't open it. An unopened copy keeps it "an official copy." When you visit your new school, take your copy of the transcript (just in case the school's copy failed to arrive) and a copy of your current school's catalog. This will help advisors at your new school make informed assessments about what you've done and what you still need to do.

It's not too early to think about graduate school, especially if you're thinking about a career like medicine or law. The academic record you're building now will, in part, determine your future acceptance to such programs. You want your grades to be an asset, not a liability. Graduate schools are most interested in the grades you receive within your major, because those courses will be most relevant to graduate school coursework; however, your total GPA is also important to maintain.

> **articulation agreement**
> An agreement between two institutions to accept credits of equivalent courses for transfer.

> **transcript**
> List of courses taken, grades and credit received, and quality points given.

Examining Courses

Using your catalog, compare the kinds of programs and degrees (e.g., AA, AS, AAS, Certificate programs) offered at your college. What coursework, if any, do they share? Why do you think those courses have commonalities? Is there coursework that you think you'd particularly enjoy? Are there courses you'd like to avoid? Now use the 5C process to create a short list of possible majors.

Scheduling Coursework

OK. You're thinking about different careers. You're comparing different degrees. You haven't decided what you really want to do, but you need to schedule classes for the next term. What do you do now? Luckily, college faculty and other academic staff provide a wealth of information that can help you make major choices and career decisions.

❯ Seeing Advisors and Career Counselors

At some colleges faculty advisors help students with scheduling and career questions. Special staff advisors may be available for students who are undecided about their majors. Other colleges have departmental advisors as well as advisors for undecided majors. Career counselors serve many of the same functions as advisors. But while their expertise may provide all sorts of information about school and also work concerns, remember that it is ultimately you who are responsible for the courses you take and the grades you make.

If you don't have an assigned advisor, get one by going to enrollment services or the admissions office and asking for one. If you have one, consider that person to be your ally and mentor. Take the opportunity to get to know your advisor and familiarize him or her with your goals. Check in often.

Because of their past experience and knowledge with college policies, programs, and courses, advisors are experts on what you should take. But they can't help you unless you are ready for their help. When you go to see them, come prepared with ideas and questions about the majors and degrees you are considering. Then you can ask advice about choosing courses that overlap several different majors while still gaining insight into career-specific courses.

For instance, you might be interested in computers as a career but don't want to take the math needed for computer science majors. In that case you may want to pursue coursework and a major that will build your computer skills while preparing you in a more general way for the work world. In this case, you could list the careers (e.g., business, digital media) or settings (law firm, hospital, school) you think you would enjoy and bring this to your advising appointment. Faculty members or advisors can provide the names of faculty in each academic discipline you are considering. By meeting with those instructors, you learn more about potential majors before you enroll in the courses.

Colleges also have career counseling services. They, too, can tell you about your college's courses, degrees, and programs. They know how those might transfer to four-year colleges or translate into career opportunities. They also keep track of labor demands and salary trends. This means that they know what careers will be in demand in the future. They can tell you how much you can expect to be paid.

Career counselors often network with local and other employers. They can help you connect with the people you need to know in order to take the next step in the career you want. As a result, many career offices also help you get internships while you're in school. Internships let you try out career interests as well as gain knowledge and experience. Internships can provide valuable work experience while you are still in school and they always look good on a résumé. Most important, career counselors provide you with the tools and resources you need for making career choices in the future.

Semester Scheduling for Undecided Majors

If you are unsure of your major, you can often choose courses that fit several different majors. Depending on the majors that interest you, you may be able to do this for the first term or two. For instance, you might be looking at first-year requirements in majors as diverse as business administration, dental hygiene, or criminal justice (a four-year degree).

After analyzing each one (see Table 16.1), you realize:

- English is needed in all curricula. Taking English 101 or 102 would be a good choice.

- College Math is required in Dental Hygiene. It is also one of the choices for math in Criminal Justice. College Math is the prerequisite course for the Algebra required course in Business Administration. Taking Math 121 and 122 meets the needs of all three majors.

- Biology is required for Dental Hygiene. By choosing it, you also meet the science elective for the other two majors.

Table 16.1 Sample First-Year Curricula

Business Administration		Dental Hygiene		Criminal Justice	
Business 101	3	Intro to Allied Health	3	Criminal Justice 107	3
Econ 121	3	English 101, 102	6	English 101, 102	6
English 101, 102	6	College Math 121, 122[4]	6	College Math 115, 116[4] or	
Algebra 155, 156[3,4]	6	Biology 101, 102, 121	8	College Math 121, 122[4]	6
Science Electives[1]	6	Speech for Non-Majors 161	3	Science Electives[1]	6
Speech for Non-Majors 161	3	Intro to Psychology 100	3	Intro to Psychology 100	3
General Ed. Electives[2]	9	General Ed. Electives[2]	3	Sociology 101	3
				General Ed. Electives[2]	6
TOTAL	**33**	**TOTAL**	**32**	**TOTAL**	**33**

[1] Choose from Biology, Physics, Botany, Zoology, Chemistry, Geology, Astronomy.
[2] Choose from Art, Foreign Language, Psychology, Sociology, Music, Economics, History, Geography, Speech.
[3] Prerequisite courses are College Math 121, 122.
[4] Math 090 or a passing score on the Math Placement Test is a prerequisite of all math courses.

- Speech for non-majors is required in Business Administration and Dental Hygiene and satisfies the general education elective for Criminal Justice.

- Taking Introduction to Psychology fulfills the Dental Hygiene and Criminal Justice requirement and serves as a general education elective in business.

You could also decide to take one of the introductory courses (Business 101, Introduction to Allied Health, or Criminal Justice 107) in place of one of the elective courses. Although the course you choose might not apply toward all of the degrees, it would help you decide what major you want to pursue.

Studying Away

You may consider the opportunity of studying away. For example, you might want to take courses on another campus in the United States. Visit the National Student Exchange (http://www.nse.org/) for more information. You might even want to study in another country. While most foreign students who study in the United States are pursuing a full degree, most American students study abroad for only one or two academic terms. The majority of U.S. students now choose short-term study abroad programs that are available through their schools.

What are the advantages of studying away? Whether you study in the United States or elsewhere, going to a new place helps you understand and analyze information from a new perspective. You learn about new people and cultures which broadens your worldview. This, in turn, improves your resume as it shows you that you are independent and ready to confront new challenges and experiences.

Located in Spain, IE University is one of the top-ranked universities in Europe, and Dr. Rolf Strom-Olsen of IE University suggests that there are several factors you should consider when selecting a school away. With the exception of the last one, these considerations are important to consider when studying away in the United States as well. First, you need to anticipate the type of social and career network you want in your life. A new school will have a more diverse student body, and you will make myriad friends and colleagues from many different places. A second consideration is the faculty of the school. Just as the student body is different, so too will be your instructors. If you are particularly interested in a topic, look for a school whose faculty is renowned in it. The classroom environment is a third factor to consider. Size and duration of classes as well as pedagogy will change form one school to another. Fourth, campus life needs to be considered. Depending on the size of the institution, you have more opportunities to mix and learn from other students. Another factor you should think about is your career plans. If you want to be a doctor or a schoolteacher, for example, you are probably much better served by pursuing your studies in the United States. However, if you want an international career, then studying outside the United States is a choice.

If possible, you should visit the universities you are thinking about attending to sit in on a lecture or two and get a feel for campus life. Where you pursue your university education will be one of the most important decisions of your life, so it is worth investing the time and energy to make sure you choose the right place. That is not always feasible of course, particularly if you are thinking of institutions that are far away from home. What you can do, however, is talk to students who are already there. No one can tell you more about the institution, its culture, the professors, the curriculum, even the quality of the cafeteria food, than the students.

Every university should make available someone with whom you can have an honest discussion about the pros and cons of attending. You should take advantage of the opportunity to speak with such a spokesperson. At one institution there is a program that pairs student volunteers with prospective freshmen. And while the students who volunteer are generally enthusiastic, they are not there to shill for the university but will give you honest and straightforward answers about the academic and social life on and off campus.

All things considered, no matter your motivation, if you are given the opportunity to study away, it may be too valuable an experience not to consider it.

Creating an Educational Plan

At some point, you will choose a major. Then you need a plan for completing it. Degree programs—for both two- and four-year degrees—list courses by term. Colleges that use a **semester system** generally list courses for fall and spring semesters. Colleges using a **quarter system** list courses for three quarters. Summer schedules are generally quite different varying from intensive one-week classes to classes that meet throughout the summer and everything in between. Courses can also be taken online or by correspondence. The educational plan you create will contain all of the courses for your degree, but not necessarily in the neatly listed curriculum found in your catalog.

For instance, due to work, family or other commitments, you may need to take fewer than 15 hours a semester. Thus, you might decide to take nine hours in regular semesters and not take any coursework in summers. At that rate, a 60-hour program would require about seven semesters. Or, perhaps your degree requires four math courses starting with calculus as the first credit math course; but you're not ready for calculus. You may need to take a preparatory math course first. Although some students think prep courses delay their graduation, the truth is that prep courses help to ensure graduation by creating a more solid foundation for future coursework. Other prerequisite courses (typically college algebra and trigonometry) will need to be scheduled first. Because the courses must be taken in sequence, you might need additional semesters to complete the math requirements. The plan you create should fit your needs.

A plan is just that—a plan. It helps you determine what you need to do, but it is not set in stone. Changes in your life or a lack of course availability can alter the details. That's one reason that meeting your general education requirements first is a good idea. Still, having a plan helps you see what you need to do to stay on course to reach your goal.

semester system
Typically a 15- or 16-week term.

quarter system
Typically a 10- or 12-week term.

Creating a Tentative Schedule and Educational Plan

PART 1:   Tentative Schedule

Using the majors that you thought of considering in Activity 2, list the courses that you could take next semester. Make a tentative schedule with a rationale of how the courses that you chose fit into each curriculum.

PART 2:   Educational Plan

Choose the degree program that you think is your top choice. Using your college catalog and the form below, create an educational plan for the courses by term. Provide a written rationale for the number of courses you plan to take each semester (e.g., prerequisite courses, other commitments).

FALL 20____	
Course	Credits
TOTAL CREDITS:	

SPRING 20____	
Course	Credits
TOTAL CREDITS:	

FALL 20____	
Course	Credits
TOTAL CREDITS:	

SPRING 20____	
Course	Credits
TOTAL CREDITS:	

GROUP APPLICATION: Compare your semester schedules and educational plans. What can you learn from looking at other students' schedules and educational plans?

Planning for a Career

Sometimes even a college degree doesn't seem to be enough today. How can you lay the groundwork for the world of work while you're still getting used to college? This may seem an overwhelming task when you first think about it. It's really not, however.

Start by assessing your strengths. Once you know what these are, you can build on them. For instance, you can tap on-campus resources to develop your career skills. In today's competitive job market, you need to have every advantage you can. When you apply for a job, everyone will have some degree and varying levels of experience. You need to make the experiences you have stand out in ways that appeal to future employers. Making conscious decisions about the job skills you want is not only smart. It pays off in future job searches.

Workplace Skills

Over 20 years ago, the U.S. Department of Labor authorized the Secretary's Commission on Achieving Necessary Skills (SCANS)—a list of foundation skills and workplace competencies that are still valuable in today's workplace. SCANS divides foundation skills into three groups. These are *basic literacy skills* in language and math; *thinking skills* such as creativity, problem solving, and decision making; and *personal qualities* such as responsibility and self-management. It divides workplace competencies into five groups: resource management (e.g., time, money, people, things); interpersonal skills (e.g., teamwork, tolerance of diversity, leadership); information management skills; organizational management; and technology (computer) skills.

Lists like SCANS are available on the Internet. You might look at the Job Skills Checklist at the Purdue Online Writing Lab (http://owl.english.purdue.edu/owl/resource/626/01/); or Job Skills Inventory at the University of Minnesota-Duluth (http://careers.d.umn.edu/inventories/skills_test_intro.html). You can use these in several ways. First, look at the list and check off the skills you already possess. Second, think about how your coursework helps you refine and develop skills. For instance, which courses provide ways for you to increase writing skills? Which ones help you develop creativity or problem-solving skills? Which ones require group projects that foster interpersonal skills? Which ones involve computer or other technology use? Rather than taking these skills for granted, collect specific examples of ways in which you demonstrate such skills in a portfolio. You can use these later to market yourself when you apply for jobs.

If you find your expertise lacking in any area, look for specific ways to develop that skill or competency. For instance, if you want to develop speaking skills, take a speech course or audition for a campus play. If you aren't satisfied with the quantity and quality of your leadership experiences, start a study group or run for an office in a campus organization. Or, if you want to increase your tolerance for diversity, join clubs or organizations that involve diverse people or attend campus programs and functions that focus on diversity. Again, document what you learned for future reference in job applications.

Opportunities in Campus Organizations

Have you ever heard, "Lead, follow, or get out of the way!" Colonial American patriot Thomas Paine wrote these immortal words to the New England citizenry about the fight for independence. They are equally true for you as you struggle to find your future. Whether as a leader or follower, joining a campus organization provides ways for you to add to your career skills.

The first step in any organization is membership. Joining campus organizations (e.g., Culinary Student Association, Future Teachers, Criminal Justice Organization, Peace Initiative, Chess Club) often gives you a chance to talk to students, meet faculty advisors, and learn more about the careers they reflect. Regularly attending meetings and other organization events lets you know what the group's mission is, who the officers are, and what their responsibilities and duties involve. You hear issues discussed. You gain an education that is outside the classroom. Once you've gotten a good idea of what the organization is about, you can then think about taking a leadership role.

So, how do you become a leader? One way is to start small. You could chair a committee or lead a group project. Or, you can ask officers what you can do to help. Most officers appreciate members who are willing to arrive early and arrange chairs, distribute materials at the meeting, or clean up after the meeting ends. So, volunteer!

At the same time, participate in meetings and look for ways to contribute. For instance, if you are good with computers, offer to develop the organization's website. If you like graphic design, offer to create fliers for advertising group meetings or projects. Or, suggest a fund-raiser or service activity and offer to organize it.

Many students think there are few chances for leadership roles on a college campus. After all, each organization only has a limited number of officers. And if you're new to a school, how would you ever get enough people to vote for you? The truth is that few people run for office in an organization, because everyone assumes that getting elected is impossible to achieve. All organizations need people who can take charge and be responsible. So, identify two or three offices that you would like to hold or that you think might contribute to your personal skills and competencies. Talk to the officers that currently hold those positions, or ask the group sponsor or advisor for more information. By learning firsthand about their experiences, you can decide if you want to follow in their footsteps.

Service Learning and Volunteerism

Do you ever wonder what your college courses have to do with real life? Have you ever felt like what you're learning is too abstract and theoretical? Would you like to help others but wonder what one person can really do? Perhaps you should look into the options for service learning or volunteerism at your college. Many campus organizations provide service to your campus or local community. While the goal is to provide assistance to others, these volunteer experiences can supply a valuable service to you as well.

Volunteer experiences build the skills you want to develop. For instance, you may learn teamwork by being part of a group that builds a house for Habitat for Humanity. Or, you might chair a fund-raiser and learn how to manage time, money, materials, facilities, and people.

Volunteer experiences also provide ways for you to sample careers before investing an entire degree in them. For instance, you might be thinking about a career in teaching. Volunteering as a tutor for a campus Big Brother/Big Sister organization can help you decide if you have the right stuff.

Volunteer experience may open an avenue of interest you've never even considered. For instance, perhaps a campus religious organization sponsors conversational English sessions for international students. Although you've never traveled out of the country, your participation may lead you to consider careers in international business, travel, communications, or teaching.

In addition, some colleges also offer service learning courses that apply course information to volunteer opportunities. For instance, students in a freshman composition course might volunteer to work with senior citizens and then write essays about their experiences. Students in a nursing course might volunteer to provide educational programs on healthy choices to high school students. Students in a horticulture program might help a neighborhood start a community garden.

The opportunities for service—and learning—are endless. What good can one person do? Actor Whoopi Goldberg once said that if every American donated just five hours a week, it would equal the labor of 20 million full-time volunteers. Even if you contribute an hour a week or a few hours a semester, it all adds up and makes our world a better place.

Networking

You've probably heard the phrase, "It's not what you know, it's who you know." To some degree, that has merit. While you may still have to have a degree or certification to get into the career you want, it may be the people you know that help you get a job in that career. A first step is to network with faculty and advisors. Tell them about your goals and interests. Ask about internships—both paid and unpaid—as well as opportunities to shadow someone on the job. These allow you to meet and work with career professionals. Such contacts may be worth more than any amount you might be paid. Joining campus organizations that are affiliated with your fields of interest is another way you can learn about professionals and meet people who will be your colleagues. You might also consider joining some professional online communities. For example, LinkedIn (www.LinkedIn.com) is a professional network of members in over 150 industries and 200 countries. Joining this network allows you to find, meet, and interact with professionals in the careers you want to pursue. You can find, be introduced to, and collaborate with qualified professionals that you need to work with to accomplish your goals.

Finally, remember that networking is not just simply getting people to know you. It's about developing mutually beneficial relationships and finding ways in which both you and the people in your networks can help one another. It's a two-way, not one-way, street.

❯ Continuing Education

Learning doesn't end when you get your degree or certification. It may not seem like it now, but in practically no time, you'll complete your education at your college and then . . . keep learning. Your college education prepares you for whatever you encounter. That doesn't always mean that you'll know all that you need. It does mean that you'll know what you need to know. You'll recognize your need for additional information, training, and experience. Continuing education may come from conferences, on-the-job training, online workshops, professional organizations, or keeping up with the latest trends in the news or on the Web. In a perfect world, your employer might pay for such education. But in today's world, employer funding is less common than it used to be. Keep in mind that your professional development benefits you and your future goals. A lack of funds doesn't have to keep you from continuing your education. For instance, you might not be able to afford an expensive conference; but you might find free online workshops that meet your needs. Lifelong learning is part of every career. You can decide now that it will be part of yours.

So, whether you keep up on the latest research in industry publications and journals, attend seminars and conferences, or take additional coursework in a classroom or online, your journey will continue. You now have the tools you need—personal desire, the ability to identify what you know and what you don't know, and a decision-making process.

Use the 5Cs—Define the **C**hallenge; Identify the **C**hoices; Predict the **C**onsequences; **C**hoose an option; **C**heck your outcome—to plan your career.

1. Use your responses to Activity 1 of this chapter to identify the Choices you are considering.

2. Research the Consequences for each option by using the *Occupational Outlook Handbook* (http://www.bls.gov/OCO/). Determine type of degree, salary trends, working conditions, and demands for each option. Find information about the career using any three of the following: identification of relevant job skills, specific service learning opportunities at your college, internships at your college, professional organizations, networking opportunities, volunteering possibilities, LinkedIn, interview with faculty or professional in the field.

3. Next, given the information you have, explain which option you would now Choose. How will you apply this information to your career planning?

4. Describe how you would Check the outcome of your choice.

GROUP APPLICATION: Share your findings with others in your group. What can you learn from their research strategies and results? What can you learn from the way they made decisions about their careers?

chapter review

Respond to the following on a separate sheet of paper or in your notebook.

1. Which tips for choosing a major did you find most valuable? Why?

2. What are the differences among associate's degrees, bachelor's degrees, and certificate programs? What kinds of degrees and programs are offered at your college?

3. In terms of the majors you are considering, what kinds of workplace skills do you think are most important to develop while you are in college? In what areas of SCANS do you find them?

4. How can service activities or volunteer projects affect your career goals?

5. According to a survey at George Mason University, lifelong learning is part of every career. What does this mean? Does that finding encourage or discourage you? Why?

6. What studying away opportunities does your institution offer? Are there any ones you might enjoy?

did you decide?

Did you accomplish what you wanted to in this chapter? Check the items below that apply to you.

Review the *You Decide* questions that you identified at the beginning of the chapter, but look at them from a new direction. If you didn't check an item below, review that module until you feel you can confidently apply the strategies to your own situation. However, the best ideas are worthless unless they are put into effect. Use the 5Cs to help you decide what information you found most helpful in the chapter and how you plan to use it. Record your comments after the statements below.

☐ 16.1. I understand the process of deciding on a major.

_____

_____

☐ 16.2. I know the difference between a Certificate and an Associate's and a Bachelor's degree.

_____

_____

☐ 16.3. I can knowledgeably choose courses for each semester.

_____

_____

☐ 16.4. I know what career skills I might need.

_____

_____

perspectives

Below you will read excerpts from a high school commencement speech made by Pulitzer Prize–winning cartoonist and author Doug Marlette.

After reading the article, answer the questions which follow:

1. Marlette says that he was not one of the smart or popular students in high school. How do you think this affected him as an adult?

2. List the components Marlette sees as the keys to success. Which do you think you possess? How do you know?

3. What do you see as the main idea of the speech?

4. What effect does this speech have on you?

5. Examine the advice Marlette gives graduates. Using the 5C approach, identify one of them that could result in a decision about your future.

    A. What is your **C**hallenge?

    B. What **C**hoices do you have?

    C. What is the major **C**onsequence(s) of each choice?

    D. What would be the best **C**hoice?

    E. How could the outcome of the decision be **C**hecked?

Now there's something about the commencement address that brings out the pompous and pretentious in all who deliver them. . . . For all I know, by the time I'm done I'll be speaking with a British accent.

But don't worry, this is not a self-help commencement talk. For one thing, selves are not that easy to help. Selves, as you will discover, take time and hard work. I should know. I was a loser in high school. With grades, with girls, with sports. I did not excel. I stayed home and drew. *Mad Magazine* was my inspiration. I once concocted a parody of the popular Batman TV show called "Ratman," which featured several of my teachers at school. My friends laughed at "Ratman" but one said scornfully, "You spent your weekend doing this?" Yes, I was a geek, a dweeb, a dork, a tool. I still am, but for a cartoonist that's a job description. . . .

And I'm here to tell all my fellow dweebs and losers that your day will come. . . . Things change. You change. Baby fat melts away. Faces clear up. There is hope. And today is the beginning, Square One, for all of you. Commencement. Today the graduating class of 2005 says "Dude, whassup, yo?" to the real world. . . .

Plato and Aristotle asked: "How ought one to live?" Kierkegaard put it another way: "What must I do to be saved?" Today higher education asks: "How did you do on your SATs?" I'm not going to tell you what I made on my SATs but let me put it this way: none of your places at Princeton would have been threatened. I know it's hard to believe but in real life nobody cares what you made on your SATs. I'm not saying it doesn't matter how you scored—those fat and skinny envelopes from the spring attest—but I want to help put SATs and tests in general in perspective.

A few years ago I was at a dinner in New York with a bunch of people who were getting something called the Golden Plate, an achievement award for doing well in their fields. Some were celebrities—Barbara Walters, Calvin Klein, Colin Powell—others were less well-known, but had done things like discover the planet Pluto. Oprah emceed. I was the least famous person there. The idea was to get a bunch of "achievers" together and bring in four hundred high school National Merit Finalists from around the country for three days of schmoozing with the accomplished. The idea, I suppose, was that achievement was contagious, like pink eye. . . .

At a black-tie dinner where we collected our Golden Plates the final night I was seated between the soap star Susan Lucci and the Pulitzer Prize–

winning poet James Merrill. The next morning at breakfast I was discussing the event with a Nobel Prize–winning physicist from Stanford who had discovered the subatomic particles called quarks. What would a cartoonist and a physicist have to say to each other? The Nobel Laureate asked me, "Would you have been invited to something like this when you were in high school?" I laughed and said, "No, I wasn't a very good student." He shook his head and said, "I didn't even finish high school." I was stunned. "You're kidding." "I had to get my high school equivalency later," he confessed. Then, looking around us, he said, "I wonder how many of the others invited here were National Merit Scholars in high school." What he was hinting at was the puzzle of human personality, the mystery of success, late-blooming talent and confidence, the ineffable qualities of character, drive and ambition, qualities that are often key components of achievement and are sometimes even galvanized by those early high school humiliations.

Since I seem to have fallen into the trap of all commencement speakers and started to give you the advice I promised I wouldn't, what-the-hey, let me finish before the British accent kicks in. Here's my advice:

- Don't get caught downloading music.

- Don't e-mail anything you wouldn't want forwarded.

- Practice, practice, practice. It's hard to get worse at something if you practice. But talent is not enough. Talent is not creativity, just as a seed is not a crop. You have to till the soil, plant the seed, work it, water it, harvest it. Creativity is hard work.

- Don't worship celebrities. With the fall of communism the only ism left to worry about is showbizm.

- Read. Reading is active. TV, movies and video are passive. Reading engages your imagination. Video substitutes for your imagination. Reading takes you into life, while television distracts you from life.

- Recognize political correctness for what it is: a bureaucratic substitute for thinking. It evolved out of a righteous impulse to rectify historic wrongs—racism, sexism, various forms of bigotry—but it has morphed into a Stalinist means of suppressing free speech. It thrives on campuses and in the human resources departments of large corporations. It's a way for businesses to pretend to have consciences. It's cheaper to install handicapped parking spaces and make employees watch films on sexual harassment and attend sensitivity training sessions than to pay them decent wages. . . . Repent of labels, the sophisticated name-calling we dispatch so easily—manic-depressive, bipolar, OCD, ADD—to summarize and pigeonhole and reduce the complexity of human beings to a sound-bite. Such labels dehumanize people and enslave us to stereotypes and limit us with reduced expectations, all defined by the word "can't."

- Be suspicious of experts. Especially those promiscuous dispensers of labels and meds. Question authority, including your own. But always trust your own experience and instincts over the experts. . . . Strive for excellence. But don't condemn yourself when you fall short. High expectation without condemnation. . . .

- Be competitive, but remember, envy is not competition. The word "competition" derives from the Latin *con,* which means "with" and *petere,* which means "to strive." Competition: to strive together. Competitors are in secret alliance, not to do each other in, but to bring out the best in each other.

- Don't do drugs. I know I sound like the mom in "Almost Famous," but she was right. Anybody can do drugs. It takes no special talent to get drunk or get high. I worry especially about children of privilege like you, and the secret guilt you may feel about your advantages. You may drug yourselves to level the playing field, to dumb yourselves down. Don't. Life's a gift. Don't anaesthetize yourself to it. Feel life in all its pain and mystery. If you can't feel pain, you won't feel joy, either. There's plenty of time to be comatose, like for the rest of eternity.

- Above all, remember: You are not your résumé. External measures won't repair you. Money won't fix you. Applause, celebrity, no number of victories will do it. The only honor that counts is that which you earn and that which you bestow. Honor yourself. And despite all I've said about the authorities, honor your parents. You will eventually realize that there are no grownups. . . . But you will learn in time that this is a good thing. If we didn't insist that you do as we say, not as we do, civilization would crumble. . . . In fact, a pretty good definition of maturity is knowing how immature you are. A pretty good definition of sanity is knowing how crazy you are. A pretty good definition of wisdom is knowing how foolish you are.

reflecting
on decisions

Now that you've read this chapter, how does what you learned affect your decisions about your major and future career?

INTERNSHIPS
MOVING FROM
THEORY TO PRACTICE

Unpaid or paid internships are one way you can serve while getting practical career experience. They are a valuable component on any resume because they indicate that you were a worker who learned things you learn in the field that you do not learn in a classroom. Internships may be for credit and vary over time and duties. Getting an internship is practice for getting a job. You generally have to find an internship, apply, interview, and have it awarded. Then you must work at it just as you would a job. Go to **internships. com** or **internshipfinder.com** to find internships that meet your needs.

◀ CHOOSING TO SERVE

R E V I E W

Skim the notes you made throughout the chapter. How does the content fit together? What information is still unclear? Were your learning goals met? Can you answer the review questions and define terms?

◀ CHOOSING TO BE AN ACTIVE LEARNER

glossary

A

abilities Capabilities that result from aptitude combined with experience

academic calendar Calendar of the school year starting in August or September rather than in January; shows information such as registration and drop dates or exam periods

academic freedom Freedom to teach or communicate even ideas or facts that are unpopular or controversial

accommodation Piagetian concept of adjusting schemas to fit new information and experiences

accredited Institution recognized as maintaining standards requisite for its graduates to achieve credentials for professional practice

active listener A student who consciously controls the listening process through preplanned strategies

adjunct Part-time faculty

adult One of the three inner dialogue voices, the part of you that thinks analytically and solves problems rationally

advisors Persons who provide information and advice on a range of topics including college policies and course schedules

amygdala The seat of emotions in the brain

analogical premise A premise containing an analogy or comparison between similar events or things

anecdotal evidence Evidence based on personal testimonies

anthropocentrism The belief that humans are the central or most significant entities of the universe

applied behavior analysis Application of the principles of operant conditioning to change human behavior

aptitudes Inborn traits or talents

argument Reasoning that is made up of two or more propositions, one of which is supported by the others

articulation agreement An agreement between two institutions to accept credits of equivalent courses for transfer

assimilation Piagetian concept of the incorporation of new information into existing knowledge (schemas)

associative learning Learning that two events are connected (associated)

asynchronously Hybrid course content delivered not at the same time

Atkinson-Shiffrin model A model of memory that involves a sequence of three stages: sensory memory, short-term memory, and long-term memory

attention The focusing of mental resources

attractive distracters Incorrect choices on objective tests that seem plausible

automaticity The ability to process information with little or no effort

B

backward planning Setting goals by starting with an end goal and working backward

behaviorism The view that behavior should be explained by observable experiences, not by mental processes

body language Nonverbal communication

bookmark To mark a document or a specific address (URL) of a Web page so that you can easily revisit the page at a later time

browse Follow links in a Web page, or explore without specific direction, as the spirit moves you, until you find what you want

burnout Physical or emotional exhaustion

C

centration Focusing, or centering, attention on one characteristic to the exclusion of all others; characteristic of preoperational thinking

character Attributes or features that make up and distinguish an individual and are considered constant and relatively noncontroversial by most people

chart Information presented in columns and rows

cheating Using or providing unauthorized help

child The part of you that wants to have *fun* and have it *now*.

chunking Grouping, or "packing," information into "higher-order" units that can be remembered as single units

citing Telling the source of information

civility Interacting with others with respect, kindness, and good manners

classical conditioning A form of associative learning in which a neutral stimulus becomes associated with a meaningful stimulus and acquires the capacity to elicit a similar response

closure The positive feeling that occurs when you complete a task

cognitive behavior approaches Changing behavior by getting individuals to monitor, manage, and regulate their own behavior rather than letting it be controlled by external factors

cognitive development The process by which one becomes an intelligent person

cognitive dissonance A sense of disorientation that occurs in situations where new ideas directly conflict with a person's worldview

college catalog Book describing services, curricula, courses, faculty, and other information pertaining to a postsecondary institution.

conclusion The proposition in an argument that is supported on the basis of other propositions

concrete operational stage Piaget's third cognitive developmental stage, occurring between about 7 to 11 years of age. At this stage, the child thinks operationally, and logical reasoning replaces intuitive thought but only in concrete situations; classification skills are present, but abstract problems present difficulties

conditional statement An "If . . . then . . ." statement

confirmation bias The tendency to look only for evidence that supports our assumptions; at the dualistic stage of research, seeking out only evidence that supports your view and dismissing evidence that contradicts it

conservation The idea that some characteristic of an object stays the same even though the object might change in appearance; a cognitive ability that develops in the concrete operational stage, according to Piaget

contracting Putting reinforcement contingencies into writing

Cornell notes Page divided vertically into two sections with right side about 2/3 of the page for class notes and left column for recall tips you create afterward

corpus callosum Where fibers connect the brain's left and right hemispheres

course management system An electronic message center that serves groups with similar interests; software used by faculty and students to deliver online learning (e.g., Angel, moodle, Blackboard)

critic Role that suggests that you are unworthy or incapable

critical thinking A collection of skills we use every day that are necessary for our full intellectual and personal development

5Cs Five-point decision-making process

cue-dependent forgetting Retrieval failure caused by a lack of effective retrieval cues

D

decay theory The theory that new learning involves the creation of a neurochemical *memory trace*, which will eventually disintegrate. Thus, decay theory suggests that the passage of time is responsible for forgetting

declarative memory The conscious recollection of information, such as specific facts or events that can be verbally communicated

deductive argument An argument that claims its conclusion necessarily follows from the premises

definitional premise A premise containing the definition of a key term

democracy A form of government in which the highest power in the state is invested in the people and exercised directly by them or, as is generally the case in modern democracies, by their elected officials

dependent premise A premise that supports a conclusion only when it is used together with another premise

descriptive premise A premise that is based on empirical facts

diffusion of responsibility The tendency, when in a large group, to regard a problem as belonging to someone else

diversity Variety in the academic environment as the result of individual differences

divided attention Concentrating on more than one activity at a time

doublethink Holding two contradictory views at the same time and believing both to be true

download To copy data (usually an entire file) from their main source to your own computer or disk

E

egocentrism The belief that the self or individual is the center of all things

elaboration The extensiveness of information processing involved in encoding

emotional intelligence The ability to understand and manage oneself and relate effectively to others

empathy Understanding and having compassion for others

empirical fact A fact based on scientific observation and the evidence of our five senses

empiricist One who believes that we discover truth primarily through our physical senses

encoding The process by which information gets into memory

encoding specificity principle The principle that associations formed at the time of encoding or learning tend to be effective retrieval cues

environmental preferences Physical surroundings that are most comfortable for you

episodic memory The retention of information about the where and when of life's happenings

equilibration A mechanism that Piaget proposed to explain how children shift from one stage of thought to the next. The shift occurs as children experience cognitive conflict, or disequilibrium, in trying to understand the world. Eventually, they resolve the conflict and reach a balance, or equilibrium, of thought

ethics The principles of conduct that govern a group or society standards of behavior that tell us how human beings ought to act in certain situations

ethnocentrism The belief in the inherent superiority of one's own group and culture

evidence Reasons for believing that a statement or claim is true or probably true

executive attention Involves action planning, allocating attention to goals, error detection and compensation, monitoring progress on tasks, and dealing with novel or difficult circumstances

explanation A statement about why or how something is the case

external locus of control The belief that success or failure is due to outside influences, such as fate, luck, or other people

F

false memory syndrome The recalling of events that never happened

formal operational stage Piaget's fourth cognitive developmental stage, which emerges between about 11 and 15 years of age; thought is more abstract, idealistic, and logical in this stage

formal outline Main points arranged vertically first using Roman numerals and indented capital letters, and then Arabic numerals and lowercase letters to sequence supporting ideas

fuzzy trace theory States that memory is best understood by considering two types of memory representations: (1) verbatim memory trace and (2) fuzzy trace, or gist. In this theory, older children's better memory is attributed to the fuzzy traces created by extracting the gist of information

G

gambler's error The belief that a previous event affects the probability in a random event

GPA Grade point average

H

hardiness A personal characteristic that combines commitment, control, and challenge, giving one the courage and motivation to turn rough patches into opportunities for personal growth

hearsay Evidence that is heard by one person and then repeated to another

hybrid courses Blend of distance learning and face-to-face formats

hybrids Courses that are a combination of face-toface and online content

hyperlink A piece of text or a graphic that serves as a cross-reference between parts of a document or between files or websites

hypothetical-deductive reasoning Piaget's formal operational concept that adolescents can develop hypotheses to solve problems and systematically reach (deduce) a conclusion

I

idea mapping Graphical picture you make of main ideas and details

independent premise A premise that can support a conclusion on its own

inductive argument An argument that only claims that its conclusion probably follows from the premise

informal outline Same idea as formal outline, but uses spacing as you like and special markings you choose (e.g., all capital letters, dashes, stars)

information-processing approach A cognitive approach in which people manipulate information, monitor it, and strategize about it. Central to this approach are the cognitive processes of memory and thinking

integrity Firm adherence to a code of moral values

interference theory The theory that we forget not because we actually lose memories from storage but because other information gets in the way of what we are trying to remember

internal locus of control The belief that control over life is due to behavior choices, character, and effort

intranet Internal network

intuitive thought substage The second substage of preoperational thought, lasting from about 4 to 7 years of age. Children begin to use primitive reasoning and want to know the answer to all sorts of questions. They seem so sure about their knowledge in this substage but are unaware of how they in this substage but are unaware of how they know

issue An ill-defined complex of problems involving a controversy or uncertainty

K

knowledge Information which we believe to be true and for which we have justification or evidence

L

lateralization The specialization of functions in each hemisphere of the brain

learning A relatively permanent influence on behavior, knowledge, and thinking skills that comes about through experience

learning style The mix of attributes that describe the ways that you best acquire and use information

levels of processing theory The theory that processing of memory occurs on a continuum from shallow to deep, with deeper processing producing better memory

locus of control A person's expectations about who or what causes events to occur

logic The study of the methods and principles used to distinguish correct or good arguments from poor arguments

long-range goals Goals that take a long time, even a lifetime, to accomplish

long-term memory A type of memory that holds enormous amounts of information for a long period of time in a relatively permanent fashion

M

map A graphic representation of main ideas and details

maturity The ability to control impulses, to think beyond the moment, and to consider how words and actions affect others

memorable-events error A cognitive error that involves our ability to vividly remember outstanding events

memory The retention of information over time, which involves encoding, storage, and retrieval

memory blocks Sudden losses of memory for a specific piece of information

memory span The number of digits an individual can report back without error in a single presentation

mental processes Thoughts, feelings, and motives that cannot be observed by others

mentors Wise and trusted counselors or teachers who advise, instruct or train a student outside a regular classroom

metacognition Cognition about cognition, or "knowing about knowing."

method of belief A method of critical analysis in which we suspend our doubts and biases and remain genuinely open to what people with opposing views are saying

method of doubt A method of critical analysis in which we put aside our preconceived ideas and beliefs and begin from a position of skepticism

mid-range goals Goals that serve as a checkpoint on the way to achieving long-term goals

Mnemonics Set of techniques for improving your memory skills

motivation An inner drive that moves a person to action

myelination The process of encasing many cells in the brain with a myelin sheath that increases the speed at which information travels through the nervous system

N

negative reinforcement Reinforcement based on the principle that the frequency of a response increases because an aversive (unpleasant) stimulus is removed

neo-Piagetians Developmental psychologists who believe that Piaget got some things right but that his theory needs considerable revision; emphasize how to process information through attention, memory, and strategies

netiquette Abbreviation for Internet etiquette

network theories Theories that describe how information in memory is organized and connected; they emphasize nodes in the memory network

nondeclarative memory Procedural knowledge in the form of skills and cognitive operations. Nondeclarative memory cannot be consciously recollected, at least not in the form of specific events or facts

O

objective test A test in which you select an answer from several choices provided by an instructor

observational learning Learning that involves acquiring skills, strategies, and beliefs by observing others

operant conditioning Also called *instrumental conditioning*, this is a form of learning in which the consequences of behavior produce changes in the probability that the behavior will occur

opinion A belief based solely on personal feelings rather than on reason or facts

organization Piaget's concept of grouping isolated behaviors into a higher-order, more smoothly functioning cognitive system; the grouping or arranging of items into categories

P

plagiarism To steal and pass off the ideas or words of another as one's own stealing another person's work and presenting it as your own

positive reinforcement Reinforcement based on the principle that the frequency of a response increases because it is followed by a rewarding stimulus

prefrontal cortex The highest level in the frontal lobes; involved in reasoning, decision making, and self-control

Premack principle The principle that a high probability activity can serve as a reinforcer for a low-probability activity

premise A proposition in an argument that supports the conclusion

preoperational stage The second Piagetian stage, lasting from about 2 to 7 years of age, symbolic thought increases, but operational thought is not yet present

prescriptive premise A premise in an argument containing a value statement

preview Reading a chapter's introduction, headings, subheadings, boldfaced terms, and summary before a full reading of the content

priorities The people or items that you feel are most important to you

probability error Misunderstanding the probability or chances of an event by a huge margin

procrastination Delaying or putting off assignments or other activities

prompt An added stimulus or cue that is given just before a response, thus increasing the likelihood the response will recur

proposition A statement that expresses a complete thought and can be either true or false

punishment A consequence that decreases the probability that a behavior will occur

Q

quality points Numerical value assigned to each letter grade from A to F when given as the final grade in a course; used to calculate grade point average

quarter system Typically a 10- or 12-week term

R

rationalist One who claims that most human knowledge comes through reason

reframing Choosing to see a situation in a new way

rehearsal The conscious repetition of information over time to increase the length of time it stays in memory

reinforcement (reward) A consequence that increases the probability that a behavior will occur

relaxation A positive feeling created through the loosening of muscles

relevance Importance to your topic

response cost Taking a positive reinforcer away from an individual

resilient Able to recover from or adjust easily to misfortune or change

retention Keeping students in school until they meet their goals or finish a degree or program

rhetoric The defense of a particular position usually without adequate consideration of opposing evidence in order to win people over to one's position

S

scaffolding A technique that involves changing the level of support for learning. A teacher or more-advanced peer adjusts the amount of guidance to fit the student's current performance

schedules of reinforcement Partial reinforcement timetables that determine when a response will be reinforced

schema Information–concepts, knowledge, information about events–that already exists in a person's mind

schemas In Piaget's theory, actions or mental representations that organize knowledge

schema theories Theories based on the premise that when we construct information, we fit it into information that already exists in our mind

script A schema for an event

search engine An Internet program that searches documents for specified keywords and returns a list of the documents where the keywords were found

selective attention Focusing on a specific aspect of experience that is relevant while ignoring others that are irrelevant

self-efficacy The belief that one can master a situation and produce positive outcomes

self-esteem How you feel about yourself; sense of self worth

self-instructional methods Cognitive behavior techniques aimed at teaching individuals to modify their own behavior

self-regulatory learning The self-generation and self-monitoring of thoughts, feelings, and behaviors in order to reach a goal

self-talk The internal communication that you have with yourself; can be positive or negative; affects time management and self-confidence

semantic memory An individual's general knowledge about the world, independent of the individual's identity with the past

semester system Typically a 15- or 16-week term

sensorimotor stage The first Piagetian stage, lasting from birth to about 2 years of age, in which infants construct an understanding of the world by coordinating sensory experiences with motor actions

sensory memory Memory that holds information from the world in its original form for only an instant

serial position effect The principle that recall is better for items at the beginning and the end of a list than for items in the middle

seriation A concrete operation that involves ordering stimuli along some quantitative dimension

shaping Teaching new behaviors by reinforcing successive approximations to a specified target behavior

short-term goals Goals that can be achieved in a relatively short amount of time

short-term memory A limited-capacity memory system in which information is retained at least 30 seconds unless it is rehearsed, in which case it can be retained longer

skim Read quickly for key ideas

S.M.A.R.T.E.R. Acronym for the necessary parts of a goal: Specific, Measurable, Achievable, Relevant, Time-Sensitive, Evident, and Recorded

social cognitive theory Bandura's theory that social and cognitive factors, as well as behavior, play important roles in learning

social constructivist approach Emphasizes the social contexts of learning and that knowledge is mutually built and constructed; Vygotsky's theory exemplifies this approach

social dissonance A sense of disorientation that occurs when the social behavior and norms of others conflict with a person's worldview

SQ3R An active reading strategy developed by Francis Robinson consisting of five steps: Survey, Question, Read, Recite and Review

strategic planning A design that gathers, analyzes, and uses information to make decisions

strategy construction Creation of a new procedure for processing information

study group Two or more students who work together to learn information

studying The purposeful acquisition of knowledge or understanding

subconclusion A proposition that acts as a conclusion for initial premises and as a premise for the final conclusion

subject directory A set of topical terms that can be browsed or searched by using keywords

subjective questions Prompts which require you to write answers in essay or paragraph form

suspension Prohibition from enrolling in coursework

sustained attention Maintaining attention over an extended period of time; also called vigilance

syllabus Outline of course content for a term

symbolic function substage The first substage of preoperational thought, occurring between about 2 to 4 years of age; the ability to represent an object not present develops and symbolic thinking increases; egocentrism is present

synchronously Hybrid course content delivered at the same time

systematic desensitization A method based on classical conditioning that reduces anxiety by getting the individual to associate deep relaxation with successive visualizations of increasingly anxiety-provoking situations

T

tactile/kinesthetic Sense of touch

technology Computers and the digital resources accessed by them

theory of mind Awareness of one's own mental processes and the mental processes of others

time-out Removing an individual from positive reinforcement

transcript List of courses taken, grades and credit received, and quality points given

transitivity The ability to reason and logically combine relationships

V

values Personal beliefs and standards expressed in the topics and activities that are important to you.

visualization Creating mental visual images of achieving a goal

W

web pages Specially formatted documents that support links to other documents, as well as graphics, audio, and video files

websites Sites (locations) on the Web owned by a person, company, or organization that have a home page, the first document users *see* when they enter the site, and often additional documents and files

working memory A three-part system that holds information temporarily as a person performs a task. A kind of "mental workbench" that lets individuals manipulate, assemble, and construct information when they make decisions, solve problems, and comprehend written and spoken language

Z

zone of proximal development (ZPD) Vygotsky's term for the range of tasks that are too difficult for children to master alone but that can be mastered with guidance and assistance from adults or moreskilled children

index

movies
  fact *vs.* fiction in, 216
Moyers, Bill, 194
Muhlenbruch, Morgan, 419
Multiple intelligence
  analyzing, 406-407
  explanation of, 404
  types of, 405 (*See also* specific types)
Musical intelligence, 405
Muslims, stereotypes of, 196
myelination, 278
Myers-Briggs Type Indicator (MBTI), 408
MyNoteIT, 440

narrow-mindedness, 194-197
nationalism, uncritical, 196
natural disasters, responding to, 181, 198
Naturalist intelligence, 405
Nazis, 173, 179
Needs and desires, 94
Needs, hierarchy of, 130
Negative attitude, 93
Negative comments, 427
negative reinforcement, 312-313, 317
neo-Piagetians, 294
Netiquette, 69-70
NETS (search strategy), 61
network theories of memory, 360
Networkforgood.org, 444
Networking, 7, 491-492
Nigeria, 230
Nixon, Richard, 202
Noncredit classes, 38
Nonverbal communication
  body language as, 41
  inappropriate use of technology as, 41
Norcross, John C., 125
Note (online notetaking program), 440
note taking, 370
Note-taking, 7
  during lectures, 428-429, 434-436
  in lab courses, 430
  with computers, 427, 428-429, 440-441
Notefish, 440
Notes
  Cornell, 435, 436
  effectiveness, assessment of, 437
  idea mapping, 435, 436
  lecture, 438
  processing, 439
  study, 438
  tips for effective, 436
Notezz!, 440
Numerical skills, 390

Obama, Barack, 204
  and USA Patriot Act, 196
  in 2008 presidential election, 190
obedience, Milgram study of, 173-174,
    177, 179-180, 186, 194
Objective test, 464

observational learning, 326-331
  defined, 326
  models in the classroom, 327-328
  models in the media, 330
  processes in, 326-327
  self-assessment of, 329
  teaching strategies using, 328, 330, 331
Occupational Outlook Handbook (OOH),
    479-480
Okagbue, Richard, 78-79
"Olsen Looks for Career in Education"
    (Muhlenbruch), 419
"one of us/one of them" error, 230-231,
    232, 233
Online classes
  and distance learning, 71
  guidelines for, 43-44
  instructor's teaching style in, 415
Online discussion groups, 107
Online newsletters, 6
Online tests, 467
Open communication, 47
open-minded skepticism, 180-181
open-mindedness, critical thinking and,
    244
operant conditioning, 312-314
  associative learning in, 308
  defined, 312
  evaluating, 322-323
  generalization, discrimination, and
    extinction in, 313-314
  in applied behavior analysis, 315-324
  reinforcement and punishment in,
    312-313
opinions, definition of, 176
optical illusion, 220, 222
optimism, power of, 195, 226
organization
  depth of knowledge and, 368
  detecting patterns of, 367-368
  in Piaget's theory, 284
  memory and, 355-356
Organizational talents, 390
Outlines, notes, 434
Overcoming obstacles, learning style/
    instructor's teaching style
  discouragement, 101-104
  positive mind shifts, 104-105

Patterns, mnemonics, 457
Payne, Calvin, 96
Paynter, Royston, 238-239
Peak performer, 103
Peak performer profile
  Amanpour, Christiane, 109
pedagogical content knowledge, 372-373
Penn State volleyball team, 167-168
Perceiving, personality type preference,
    409
perceptual errors, 219-222
Perfectionism, 154